UNDERSTANDING
HUMAN RIGHTS

Understanding Human Rights

Edited by
CONOR GEARTY AND ADAM TOMKINS

GRIFFITH COLLEGE CORK
Cove Street,
Sullivan's Quay, Cork.
Tel. +353 - 21 - 450 7027
Fax. +353 - 21 - 4507659
www.gcc.ie

PINTER

LONDON AND NEW YORK

First published 1996 by
Mansell Publishing Limited, *A Cassell imprint*
Wellington House, 125 Strand, London WC2R 0BB, England
370 Lexington Avenue, New York, NY 10017-6550, USA

© Institute of Advanced Legal Studies 1996

Reprinted in paperback in 1999 by Pinter, *A Cassell imprint*

British Library Cataloguing-in-Publication Data
Understanding Human Rights
  I. Gearty, C.A. II. Tomkins, Adam
  323
  ISBN 0-7201-2295-3 (hardback)
      1-85567-609-5 (paperback)

Library of Congress Cataloging-in-Publication Data
Understanding human rights/edited by Conor Gearty and Adam
Tomkins
     p. cm.
  Includes bibliographical references (p.) and index.
  ISBN 0-7201-2295-3 (hardback) 1-85567-609-5 (paperback)
    1. Human rights. 2. Human rights—Great Britain. 3. Human
  rights—Canada. I. Gearty, C.A. II. Tomkins, Adam.
  K3240.6.U53 1996
  323—dc20   95–34235
                                                         CIP

Printed and bound in Great Britain by Biddles Limited, Guildford and
King's Lynn

Contents

The Contributors

Gavin W. Anderson, Lecturer in Law, University of Warwick
Nicholas Bamforth, Lecturer in Law, University College London
Elizabeth Chadwick, Senior Lecturer in Law, Manchester
   Metropolitan University
C. M. Chinkin, Professor of Law, University of Southampton
Simon Deakin, Lecturer in Law and Assistant Director, ESRC
   Centre for Business Research, University of Cambridge
G. E. Devenish, Professor of Law and Head of the Department of
   Public Law, University of Natal
Sionaidh Douglas-Scott, Lecturer in Law, King's College London
Costas Douzinas, Senior Lecturer in Law, Birkbeck College, London
K. D. Ewing, Professor of Public Law, King's College London
Sandra Fredman, Fellow and Lecturer in Law, Exeter College,
   Oxford
Conor Gearty, Reader in Law and Director of the Civil Liberties
   Research Unit, King's College London
Timothy H. Jones, Lecturer in Law, University of Manchester
Clíona J. M. Kimber, Lecturer in Law, University of Aberdeen
James Kingston, Research Officer, British Institute of International
   and Comparative Law
Beverley McLachlin, Justice of the Supreme Court of Canada
Sheena N. McMurtrie, Lecturer in Law, University of Buckingham
Maleiha Malik, Lecturer in Law, King's College London
Leslie J. Moran, Lecturer in Law, Lancaster University
Siobhán Mullally, Lecturer in Law, University College, Cork
R. Jayakumar Nayar, Lecturer in Law, University of Warwick
Donal Nolan, Lecturer in Law, King's College London
Gwyneth Pitt, Professor of Law, University of Huddersfield
Mike Radford, Lecturer in Law, University of East Anglia
Anne Scully, Lecturer in Law, Brunel University
Carl F. Stychin, Lecturer in Law, Keele University
Adam Tomkins, Lecturer in Law, King's College London
Mark Tushnet, Professor of Law, Georgetown University Law Center

Geraldine Van Bueren, Senior Lecturer in Law and Director of the
Programme on International Rights of the Child, Queen Mary
and Westfield College, London
Clive Walker, Professor of Law and Director of the Centre for
Criminal Justice Studies, University of Leeds

Acknowledgements

This book began life as a workshop, and the process first of planning and putting on the workshop, and then of turning a list of workshop papers into (we hope) a coherent collection of essays, has been an enjoyable if challenging one, from which we as editors have learnt a great deal. It is a process which has been made considerably easier through the help and encouragement we have received from a number of people who have at various times been involved with our project.

First, we would like to thank all those at the Institute of Advanced Legal Studies who worked so hard to make the workshop run smoothly and efficiently, especially Belinda Crothers, Terence Daintith and David Phillips as well as the attendants and all the Institute's staff who generated such a feeling of warmth and hospitality during the three days of the workshop. We would also like to acknowledge our debt to all the participants at the workshop. We are particularly grateful to those who gave papers and to Andrew Puddephatt, Kristina Stern, Aileen McColgan, Maleiha Malik, Leo Flynn, Peter Oliver and Robert McCorquodale, who chaired the various workshop sessions.

But a successful workshop needs more than simply good papers and intellectual stimulation, and we are also extremely grateful to everybody who made the three days of the workshop such great fun. Both the Institute and the School of Law at King's College London hosted receptions and provided refreshments which contributed significantly to the success of the workshop.

Finally, in terms of the book itself, we owe a great debt to our publishers, and especially to Veronica Higgs and Sarah Roberts at Mansell, both of whom have been always patient and have shown great support and enthusiasm for the whole project throughout.

Preface to Paperback Edition

Since this book was published in hardback in 1996, there have been many remarkable developments in the law relating to human rights. Membership of the Council of Europe has continued to grow at a fast pace. The treaty of Amsterdam, which came into force on 1 May 1999, has specifically referred to human rights as a principle underpinning the Union. In the United Kingdom, the election of the new Labour Government in May 1997 quickly led to enactment of the Human Rights Act 1998 and the measure is expected to come fully into force sometime during 2000. The effect of the Act is to incorporate into UK domestic law the bulk of the substantive provisions of the European Convention on Human Rights, albeit in a way which will not allow Acts of the Westminster Parliament to be directly struck down. The Human Rights Act is already in force in those parts of the United Kingdom – Scotland and Wales at the time of writing – to which power has been devolved under another part of the Labour Government's constitutional agenda.

It is clear from all these dramatic developments that human rights is about to become a fully legal subject in both the European Union and in the domestic law of the United Kingdom. As such, it will attract far more study than in the past, and produce a far greater number of textbooks and articles of legal scholarship. As the case-law continues to emanate from the restructured European Court of Human Rights in Strasbourg, and begins also to emerge from both the European Court of Justice and the UK courts, the subject is likely to develop a very particular and highly specialized legal form. Human rights law can be expected to take on a very different and more technical complexion than the phrase 'human rights' has previously suggested.

The roles played by the ECHR on both British and pan-European stages will inevitably grow in prominence as a result of these recent developments, but the narrowness of the rights and of the legal jargon which pervades the ECHR should not be allowed to eclipse the potential radicalism and the rich diversity of both subject-matter and approach which a broader understanding of human rights can still generate. The constitutionalization of Europe and the jurisdiction of the British constitutional order – in respect of both of which the law of rights plays a central role – make the broad, ethically founded essays in this volume ever more pertinent to today's changing politico-legal landscape. These essays demonstrate that rights talk does not end with incorporation, and that the power of human rights cannot be reduced to the technicalities of the ECHR and the Human Rights Act.

Conor Gearty and Adam Tomkins
May 1999

Introduction

This book is the result of the W. G. Hart Legal Workshop that was held at the Institute of Advanced Legal Studies in London in July 1994. The title of the workshop was 'Understanding Human Rights' and all the chapters in this volume are revised versions of papers that were delivered during its three days of plenary and workshop sessions. Despite the breadth of the title, this book is primarily a collection of legal essays. Its contributors are all lawyers, just as were the vast majority of the participants in the workshop itself. In various ways the essays all seek an understanding of human rights law or, perhaps more accurately, an understanding of the relationship between the law and human rights.

The narrowness implicit in this legal focus is more apparent than real. There can be few fields of study more interdisciplinary than human rights. To pick just the most obvious examples, the subject can also be viewed from philosophical, anthropological, political, historical and even rhetorical perspectives. While aspects of the law relating to human rights have clearly been our primary concern, these other perspectives are neither ignored nor sidelined. In our organization of the workshop and in the subsequent editing of this book, we have endeavoured to connect human rights both to these many interdisciplinary contexts and also to the subject's historical roots in subversion and in the instinctive suspicion of authority that was so evident in many of the early advocates of human rights. The book represents something of a departure from the norm in terms of traditional human rights legal scholarship. It seeks neither to be authoritative nor descriptive. It advocates no single 'line' either as to the supposed content of human rights or as to how best they are to be protected. As the title suggests, the book is not so much about 'defending', 'vindicating' or 'guaranteeing' human rights as it is about understanding what this deceptively simple phrase means. The essays in our collection

Introduction

lift the celebratory veil that has sometimes stifled the intellectual growth of human rights law and inquires critically both as to the limitations of the subject and as to what it has the potential to achieve. This is not to say that the tone of the book is either hostile to or negative about the idea of human rights law; indeed the overwhelming feeling at the end of the workshop was one of great promise and (cautious) hope as to its potential in the future.

Optimism is at its most cautious in the field of international human rights law, and there are valuable chapters here on deconstructing the mythologies surrounding the subject, by Geraldine Van Bueren; on international humanitarian law by Elizabeth Chadwick; and on international human rights law relating to women by Christine Chinkin. In their different ways, these authors demonstrate the difficulties that lie in the way of making international human rights standards work in practice. But the volume's remit is wider than would be found in a standard international law collection. An example of this broader approach can be seen in our three chapters on theoretical foundations of rights. Each has a recognizably philosophical dimension, while dealing at the same time with issues of great contemporary and legal significance. Costas Douzinas considers the extent to which many of our most straightforward assumptions about what rights are can survive critical scrutiny in the light of the recent surge of new thinking across a range of disciplines. Maleiha Malik assesses the impact of communitarian writing on the traditional rights analyses of scholars such as John Rawls and Ronald Dworkin. Her willingness to search for a fresh synthesis between such authors and communitarian scholars displays an originality of mind that is also to be found in Jayakumar Nayar's ambitious effort to restructure human rights discourse along the lines of our 'basic human needs' rather than civil and political freedoms.

While the commitment that our authors show to 'human rights' might be more critical than adulatory, they are intuitive believers in the kind of society that the phrase seems to signify. That this does not prevent them from exploring critically the ways in which it is applied in practice is nowhere clearer than in the work of two leading scholars in this field, intellectual iconoclasts whose criticisms of the whole legal edifice that has been constructed around 'human rights' have been motivated by an unquestioned and deep commitment to civil liberties. Mark Tushnet has perhaps done more than any other writer to make US scholars think afresh about the nature of their commitment to human rights and about the extent to which the US Bill of Rights contains costs as well as benefits for US society. Tushnet's chapter provides a valuable overview of his own position and draws attention to a line of US cases on the topical issue of campaign funding which graphically demonstrates one of the less well-known risks in too slavish an adherence to free speech. Keith Ewing is equally well known in the UK as a trenchant critic of the proposal to incorporate the European Convention on Human Rights into UK law and in his chapter he examines the extent to which the concept of human rights is compatible with the political agenda that would be followed by a government committed to social democracy rather than to liberalism. In a not dissimilar intellectual vein, three other contributors explore the way in which supposedly equal rights can conflict with each other: James Kingston appraises the role of rights talk in the abortion debate; Siobhán Mullally contrasts the right to freedom of religion with the right to non-discrimination on the basis of sex; and Sheena McMurtrie looks at the theory behind the legal control of pornography in a way which inevitably leads her to tackle difficult issues of free speech. Like the three contributors from the international law perspective, each of these three writers is concerned to show that the application of 'human rights' law is more complex in practice than it might seem in theory, and in this way all six echo Clive Walker's important but depressing essay about the limitations of the language of human rights in the context of anti-terrorism law, a field in which it might be thought that it should have a special importance.

Other essays seek to understand human rights by offering comparative perspectives. Timothy Jones considers certain recent judicial developments in Australia which are already becoming a major factor in the rights debate in the UK. The Canadian Charter has been enormously influential for over a decade now and in her chapter, Beverley McLachlin (a justice in the Canadian Supreme Court) offers not only a helpful analysis of the operation of the Charter since its enactment in 1982, but also a well-informed response to those who say that the power reposed in the judges under such a constitutional arrangement is incompatible with the requirements of the democratic process. Gavin Anderson's theme is also drawn from recent Canadian jurisprudence, and his exposition of the case law on the public–private divide under the Charter contains points of general relevance to any constitutional arrangement rooted in a traditional liberal approach to rights, particularly in so far as such an approach is based on the assumption that the only power that needs to be counteracted by such a document is the power of the state. George Devenish's explanation of the way in which a commitment to human rights has been vital to the success of recent constitutional changes in South Africa is the essay in the book that comes closest in tone to the purely celebratory. This is hardly surprising, given the pragmatic as well as the principled arguments marshalled by Devenish in favour of the value of human rights as a way of reconciling opposites in an otherwise divided society. His chapter is a reminder of the moral force and rhetorical value of the subject matter of our volume.

In addition to these critical and comparative contributions, other chapters display the extent of the potential for creative reasoning which exists under this loose umbrella, 'human rights law'. This is true of all the essays gathered under our three substantive headings: 'equality revisited', 'rights and personal liberty' and 'new frontiers'. Each of the authors in these sections is concerned with the ways in which the language of human rights can be used as a means of shaping the development of the law along progressive lines. Most of our contributors are protagonists for such creativity. Both Gwyneth Pitt and Simon Deakin demonstrate how much potential there is in the language of rights even in such a traditionally collectivist world as that of employment law. Anne Scully deals with the impact of the language of rights on individuals who are HIV-positive or who have AIDS. In a more historical vein, Leslie Moran traces how the debate on homosexual freedom in the UK eventually came to be seen in human rights terms, while Nicholas Bamforth considers the role of law reform in the same area. The traditional human rights interest in equality is the focus of four chapters, each of which deals with the topic in a fresh and invigorating way. Both Carl Stychin and Sandra Fredman critically appraise the limitations of equality law in the areas of sexual orientation and women's rights respectively, with the two essays combining to undermine simple assumptions about the value of an unreflective commitment to 'equality'. In his imaginative and powerful contribution, Donal Nolan argues the case for a right to meritorious treatment as 'an embraceable interpretation of the law of anti-discrimination and unfair dismissal'. In a similar vein, Clíona Kimber considers that the concept of equality 'contains central flaws' which diminish its effectiveness, and then lays out how the international law idea of 'self-determination' could be deployed in this area to refreshing effect. Pushing the frontiers out even further, Mike Radford sets out the case for another set of rights of enormous contemporary importance, those capable of belonging to animals. But that there are frontiers eventually is demonstrated by Sionaidh Douglas-Scott's powerful and uncompromising rejection of the whole concept of environmental rights.

What unites all the essays in this volume is a pride in the potential for justice and fairness in the language of human rights. The eclipse of Marxist and broadly socialist political ideology may or may not be permanent. It is clear, however, that the undoubted decline of these essentially idealistic philosophies has given human rights thinking a new opportunity to rediscover its radical roots. The simple notions of individual human dignity and of equal rights for all were revolutionary when they first gained common currency in eighteenth-century Europe. They continued to terrify the wealthy and powerful until they were submerged by the misleading spell cast by universal enfranchisement and by the supposed danger posed by Marx-inspired thought. The door is now open for the idea of human rights to break free of establishment opinion and to rediscover itself as the agent of change on behalf of the poor, the marginalized and the dispossessed; on behalf, in other words, of those many people whose human rights are continuously mocked by their inhuman daily predicaments.

PART ONE:

CONSTITUTIONAL RIGHTS

1

Living with a Bill of Rights

Mark Tushnet

Although the recent spate of constitution-making has brought the question of adopting an entrenched and judicially enforceable bill of rights to the fore around the world, the debate on that question in the UK has extended over the past few decades. To some extent it has been affected by a sense of inevitability. The European Convention on Human Rights already binds the UK to international human rights norms, and can be enforced through the European Court of Human Rights. Those who support adopting a bill of rights for the UK argue, in part, that it would be better to 'domesticate' human rights norms. Not only would the UK then be in a better position to defend itself against international challenges, but it could also develop a bill of rights adapted to the particular circumstances of the UK.

As others have observed, however, a nation with an entrenched and judicially enforceable bill of rights is not necessarily better off than a nation without one. By definition, entrenched bills of rights impede legislatures as they attempt to respond to changing social, economic and political circumstances. And, by definition, judicially enforceable bills of rights are enforced by an institution staffed by people with legal training whose specifically legal culture inevitably affects the way in which the bill of rights is interpreted.

Often, those who advocate and those who oppose adopting a bill of rights for the UK describe potentialities and possibilities: a bill of rights *might* do some good, advocates say; the judges who interpret the bill of rights *might* construe it to impose an undesirable rigidity and conservatism on legislation.[1] Cast in such forms, the arguments are essentially unanswerable. What one would like to know are the relative chances of one or the other outcome.

I doubt that there is any assured method of determining those chances. Still, examining the experience in the USA with an entrenched and judicially enforceable bill of rights may be illuminating. That experience is probably the world's most extensive, and the reputation of the US Bill of Rights is quite high. In addition, the legal cultures of the USA and the UK are both based on the common law.[2] That makes it more likely that a bill of rights in the UK would be enforced through the ordinary courts, as in the USA, rather than through the more political institutions like the French Constitutional Council that provides the main alternative model for enforcement of constitutional rights.

In this Chapter I offer a *political* evaluation of the institution of an entrenched bill of rights, based on the US experience.[3] By *political* I mean that I will offer some comments on what I believe to be the likely effects of an entrenched bill of rights on political outcomes, using standard political terminology: is a bill of rights likely to have a relatively *progressive* effect, or a relatively *conservative* one? And, again in the nature of a definition, when I refer to an entrenched bill of rights, I mean one whose provisions will be enforced by a judiciary relatively insulated from the pressures of day-to-day politics, because of the judges' training, professional orientation and tenure.

My general thesis, stated broadly, is that, if adopted today, an entrenched bill of rights enforced by a judiciary like that in the UK is likely to have a *relatively conservative* effect on political outcomes. I have inserted temporal and geographical qualifications in this formulation deliberately, because I do not want to be taken as arguing that there is something inherent in the concept of an entrenched bill of rights that makes it conservative. I do believe, however, that in the modern era those bills of rights that are likely to be adopted and enforced by the judiciaries in place at the time the bills are adopted will have a particular conservative form.[4]

Progressives might be disappointed with the effects of an entrenched bill of rights in two ways. The less important, I believe, is this: progressives may hope that by adopting a bill of rights they will encourage courts to intervene against repressive forces more readily than the courts would in the absence of a bill of rights. So, for example, if a bill of rights contains express guarantees of procedural protections against certain forms of police investigation that were common before the bill of rights was adopted, progressives might hope that courts would enforce those guarantees and thereby limit the activities of the police.

That hope might be realized, of course, but it also might be defeated. Deferring to the asserted expertise of the police and the perceived requirements of law and order, judges might interpret the new guarantees so that they do not restrict police activities. So, for example, in the USA the Fourth Amendment to the Constitution bars police from conducting 'unreasonable' searches, but the Supreme Court has been willing to stamp nearly every troublesome form of police activity as either not a search or not unreasonable. Oddly enough, the Court has made the law in this area nearly unintelligible because – apparently out of concern that it has to take the Constitution seriously at least occasionally – it sometimes invalidates police practices that hardly seem bothersome. For example, the Supreme Court found a constitutional violation when police officers, lawfully present in a suspect's apartment, moved his stereo equipment slightly to check its serial number; it would have been all right if the police had been able to see the number without touching the stereo, but moving it shifted their inspection over the line.[5]

And yet, when more troublesome activities are involved, the Court has approved. The most notable example recently is *Florida* v. *Bostick*, in which the Supreme Court held that the Fourth Amendment was not violated by a police practice of 'asking permission' of everyone on a bus to allow a search of their possessions.[6] Anyone who objected, the Court said, could readily refuse the 'request' and get off the bus. Because they could avoid being searched – or even answering the request for permission to search – by leaving the bus, they were not seized within the meaning of the Fourth Amendment: this notwithstanding the facts, obvious to everyone, that getting off the bus meant not taking the trip, that bus transportation is a preferred means of transit for the relatively poor, and that these so-called consent searches were targeted at racial minorities.

As troubling as this sort of decision is – and the examples could be multiplied, drawing from experience not only in the USA but also with the European Court of Human Rights – it is not what I want to focus on. For, in one sense, this sort of political outcome cannot be *attributed* to the bill of rights. Arguably, progressives are no worse off with a bill of rights than they were without one: in both situations the police are allowed to search – *without* a bill of rights because there are no judicially enforced limits on what they can do, and *with* a bill of rights because what they have done is found to be consistent with the bill of rights' guarantees.[7] Yet it is at least *possible* that, as a practical political matter, there is a difference between a decision saying that the police can do whatever they want because we do not have a bill of rights, and one saying that the police activity was consistent with the bill of rights we have. The latter decision might send a signal to the public – or to informed observers – not merely that the police activity was not prohibited, but that it was quite all right.[8]

Conceptually, the world of political activities in a system regulated by a bill of rights consists of three categories: actions that are unconstitutional, actions that are merely permissible under the bill of rights, and actions that are affirmatively desirable (and constitutionally permitted). A decision finding no violation of the bill of rights merely says, again on the conceptual level, that the activity does not fall in the first category. But the bill of rights may come to have such an exalted status in the public mind that the distinction between the two other categories may become blurred. A court decision that an action is merely 'not unconstitutional'

may be understood by the public as a decision determining that the
action is affirmatively desirable. In the USA at least, that confusion sometimes arises. When it does, the existence of the Bill of Rights has
affirmatively contributed to a progressive defeat; it has not merely failed
to alter the situation as it existed before the Bill of Rights was adopted.[9]

Thus far I have discussed the possibility that progressives might not
get what they hope for from a bill of rights. More important, I think, is
that progressives will get *more than* they hope for. That is, progressives
may find that courts enforce the bill of rights to *restrict* what progressives
might be able to accomplish through ordinary political means.

A signal of the difficulty is that, under current US constitutional law,
at least some of the restrictions on racist speech in UK and European
Union law might well be violations of our free speech provision as interpreted by the Supreme Court – or, at least, they would be subject to
serious constitutional challenges that would take a long time, and much
expense, to resolve.[10] Many progressives in the USA and elsewhere
regard such restrictions as good public policy. Other progressives disagree, citing concerns about whether such restrictions actually reduce the
amount of racist expression in a society. In the USA, the decentralized
political system means that a huge number of public officials would be
empowered to enforce such restrictions, and among that number there
are surely those who would abuse the power. Whether adopting such
restrictions would in fact advance progressive political interests is a quite
complex matter. Whether framing the discussion of their wisdom as a
matter of fundamental rights is a good thing is, for me, a simpler one. I
would far prefer to have the discussion about these proposals conducted
purely on the ground of policy: would they actually advance their proponents' goals, for example, or are they likely to entrench rather than
displace existing power centres? The difficulty a bill of rights creates is
that discussion can too easily get diverted from these basic policy questions into unproductive and contentious controversies about 'what the
First Amendment means'.

But I must again emphasize that the examples that follow do not rest
on anything *inherent* in the very idea of having a bill of rights. Much of
the story is historically and institutionally contingent. So, for example,
early in this century, and through most of the 1930s, the US Supreme
Court interpreted the Constitution to limit what it called 'labor laws pure
and simple'.[11] These included general minimum wage and maximum
hours laws, which the Court understood to be the result of a pure political struggle by organized labour to capture from employers some of the
employers' profits. I do not believe that any country adopting a bill of
rights today will find its constitutional court making precisely the same
rulings. More recently, the US Supreme Court has begun to place limits

on regulations that governments adopt to protect the environment, find-ing the regulations to be 'takings' of private property for which compensation must be paid.[12] I do not believe that any country adopting a bill of rights today, even one with a requirement that takings of prop-erty be compensated, would find its constitutional court following precisely the same course. I am concerned here with overall tendencies, and I do believe that under present circumstances there will in fact be a tendency in systems that adopt bills of rights in the near future to enforce them in ways that obstruct progressive political changes.

My main example involves what many constitutional scholars believe to be the most important question in contemporary constitutional law in the USA. Political campaigns in the USA are 'private', in the sense that the money used to finance political campaigns comes from contributions from individuals, organized political lobbies, and what are known as 'political action committees' or PACs, which collect money from many individuals and coordinate their contributions. Over the past decades many people in the USA have become disenchanted with their system of campaign financing, believing that it leads elected representatives to be more concerned about satisfying the demands of the people who give them the most money than they are about doing what the people elected them to do. The need to raise money to finance a campaign, in addition, diverts legislators from the task of legislating.[13]

Private financing of political campaigns is embedded in the US politi-cal system for many reasons. The diffuse party structure, for example, makes it difficult for any political party to develop secure and permanent financing sources. Perhaps more important, the right to contribute money to political campaigns is, under current interpretations of the Constitution, protected by the right of free expression.

In response to concerns about abuses in the campaign finance system, the US Congress enacted a series of campaign finance reforms in the 1970s, which are now widely regarded as having failed. Campaign finance regulations fall into several categories. First, legislatures might provide money for campaigning. Second, they might limit campaign *con-tributions*. Third, they might limit campaign *expenditures*. And, finally, they might combine a system of public campaign financing with the other kinds of limits, saying that candidates can receive public money for their campaigns only if they agree to limit their expenditures or the contribu-tions they accept. For my purposes, the details of campaign finance regulations do not matter, which is fortunate, because the field has gen-erated an increasingly elaborate body of detailed constitutional rules.

Why do some people think that the system of campaign finance should be changed? Typically, they offer three reasons: corruption, alienation, and equality. The concern with corruption is straightforward. Historical

experience shows that individuals or corporations that make large contributions to a legislator's campaign can sometimes persuade that
legislator to vote for the contributors' position – even if that position is
contrary to the public interest or, less pejoratively, contrary to what the
legislator would have done if he or she had taken a detached view of the
public policy issues at stake. And, even if the public cannot be confident
that a legislator voted under a contributor's influence, we might be concerned that votes would *seem* to be driven by contributions rather than by
consideration of the public policy issues. The Supreme Court has agreed
with this line of thinking, and has upheld the constitutionality of limits
on campaign contributions.[14]

The problem of alienation is more difficult. It occurs because
'ordinary' people, seeing how expensive it is to mount a serious campaign for office, begin to think that politics is a game for the well-to-do
and well-organized. They lose interest in politics, and fail to communicate their views to their representatives. What results is not only
disaffection but distortions of public policy, as legislators respond to the
wishes of the small group that remains interested in politics even if the
whole community – if its views were known – would prefer some other
policy. Eventually, as public policy gets more remote from the concerns
of ordinary people, government becomes the preserve of an elite.

The equality concern also arises from the amount it costs to conduct a
campaign. It has two facets. First, when campaigns are very expensive,
some potential candidates are simply priced out of the market. They
know that they will be unable to raise enough money to mount a credible
campaign, and will refrain from entering the field. Second, even if an
under-financed candidate does decide to run, he or she may be drowned
out by the political advertising that better-financed rivals can distribute.

The alienation and equality concerns are both connected to the huge
amounts needed to run a decent campaign. They could be alleviated if
legislatures limited campaign expenditures. The Supreme Court *has*
allowed legislatures to combine limits on expenditures with public
financing; it upheld the federal system dealing with presidential campaigns, which allows candidates to accept public financing but limits what
such candidates can spend. It has *not* allowed legislatures to limit campaign expenditures directly, though, and it even barred Congress from
limiting expenditures supporting candidates who accepted public financing, if those expenditures were made independently of the candidates'
campaigns.[15]

In *Buckley* v. *Valeo* the Court relied on free speech principles to explain
why legislatures may not restrict campaign expenditures.[16] First, it said,
'virtually every means of communicating ideas in today's mass society
requires the expenditure of money'.[17] It followed that a spending limit

'necessarily reduces the quantity of expression by restricting the number of ideas discussed, the depth of their exploration, and the size of the audience reached'.[18] Finally, addressing the equality concern directly, the Court said, 'the concept that government may restrict the speech of some [in] order to enhance the relative voice of others is wholly foreign to the First Amendment'.[19] Proponents of spending limits disagree with the second and third of these propositions. If some views are 'drowned out' by massive expenditures, limiting spending might actually *increase* 'the number of ideas discussed' and 'the depth of their exploration'. Further, proponents question the claim that restricting the speech of some 'to enhance the relative voice of others is wholly foreign to the First Amendment'.

The problem with the Court's position on campaign finance is captured in the rhetoric at the conclusion of its most important campaign finance decision. 'In the free society ordained by our Constitution,' the Court said, 'it is not the government, but the people – individually as citizens and collectively as associations and political committees – who must retain control over the quantity and range of debate on public issues in a political campaign.'[20] What, though, is the *government* but *the people organized collectively*? And why does the Constitution ordain a free society in which the people organized collectively as associations must necessarily be preferred to the people organized collectively as a government?

All these are standard criticisms of the Supreme Court's campaign finance decision. Two points are worth noting here. First, campaign finance reform is an important part of the progressive political agenda in the USA, and progressives believe that the Supreme Court's interpretation of the Constitution stands in the way of an effective system of such reform. Second, progressives might think that allowing private wealth to dominate the campaign finance process is particularly pernicious because, roughly speaking, if only those who cater to the wealthy are able to raise enough money to campaign effectively, it is quite unlikely that, once elected, those same people will do anything that would significantly reduce the disparities of wealth that progressives typically are concerned about.

Here, then, is an example of a constitutional provision that obstructs progressive change. And, notably, I have not been dealing with some minor aspect of a bill of rights. The US Supreme Court has interpreted the free speech provision to bar important aspects of campaign finance reforms.

Another set of decisions about free speech may not seem to be closely related to the campaign finance decision, but it is. These decisions involve the free speech protection given to what US constitutional doctrine calls commercial speech. The Supreme Court entered this arena in

some apparently innocuous cases. It held, for example, that free speech
principles barred states from prohibiting the advertising of abortion services that were legal in one state even at a time when abortions were
illegal in the state banning the advertising.[21] And it struck down state
laws barring pharmacists from advertising the prices of the drugs they
sold.[22]

These decisions were relatively uncontroversial, at least in part
because it was hard for many to see the point of the regulations. But
through these decisions the Supreme Court put in place a doctrine
under which commercial activities can claim constitutional protection for
their speech. As technology has developed, those claims have become
more significant. Everyone agrees that publishers in the classical sense –
those who own and operate the print media – are protected by free
speech principles. What, though, of those who own and operate the modern media? In particular, when, as in the USA, the television and cable
mass media are held in private hands, why should their owners not be
able to claim the same protection that the owners of newspapers claim?

For a couple of decades the Supreme Court has held the line, allowing
substantially more regulation of the broadcast media than of the print
media. I have little doubt, though, that the line is soon to crumble,
because the Court's distinctions – which rely primarily on the notion that
the broadcast media use a scarce resource while the print media do not
– cannot be sustained for much longer. Already, substantial free speech
challenges have been mounted to proposed regulation of the mass
broadcast media. In 1994, the Supreme Court addressed a challenge
brought by the operators of cable systems against a statutory requirement
that cable systems carry certain programmes, such as those originated by
our public television stations.[23] Although the Court did not resolve the
controversy on the merits, it did hold that this restriction had to satisfy a
rather stringent standard of review. Four justices would have held the
statute to be an unconstitutional restriction on free speech. Recently
there have been moves in Congress to regulate the amount of violent
programming directed at children. Those efforts have been challenged
on the ground, again, that imposing such restrictions would violate free
speech principles.

These proposals are typically part of the progressive political agenda.
Perhaps these proposals are unwise and ought not be adopted. I think it
is clear, however, that it is profoundly unhelpful to debate them in constitutional terms. It is much more important for people to think through
whether they believe restricting violence on television would be a good
thing or not, given how regulators are likely to define 'violence', than it
is for them to puzzle over whether restricting violence on television is
somehow incompatible with a national commitment to free speech.

Of course one might respond to these examples by suggesting that, whatever was the case in the USA, *here* (or wherever) we can count on the courts to interpret a bill of rights more sensibly. It is not a bill of rights that is a bad idea for progressives; it is a badly interpreted bill of rights. How, though, can progressives ensure that the bill of rights will be interpreted well rather than badly?

We might deal with the kinds of examples I have given in a number of ways. The bill of rights might itself provide a guide to interpretation, encouraging judges to interpret it in a direction consistent with progressive political wishes. Whether judges protected against political control would consistently do that over the long term is, as discussed below, a complex question.

A second method would be to make provisions in a bill of rights that the constitutional protections it affords simply do not apply in certain situations. This is the common strategy, I believe, to deal with questions of affirmative action. Many people believe that affirmative action programmes violate basic principles of equality. Modern constitutions all contain equality provisions, and proponents of affirmative action understand that those provisions might be used to obstruct the programme they favour. Therefore, they have written into modern constitutions express provisions specifying that the general equality provisions do not bar governments from adopting affirmative action programmes.[24] Similar strategies might be used to protect against anti-progressive interpretations of the free speech provisions of a bill of rights: simply list the programmes – e.g. campaign finance, regulation of the mass media – that you are worried about, and say that the provisions do not apply. This strategy has the obvious flaw that people today cannot anticipate the kinds of programmes they might favour in the future, and therefore cannot write a comprehensive list of those programmes. But there is a deeper problem, which arises from the conception of a bill of rights as limiting government power.

Both of my central examples – campaign finance and television regulation – involve situations in which free speech principles are said to *limit* the power of government to regulate private property. And, I believe, conceiving of bill of rights restrictions in that way is almost natural. The point of having a bill of rights, many people think, is precisely to ensure that those who have the concentrated power of a government in their hands do not abuse the rest of us: bills of rights, that is, are designed exactly to limit *government* power. In one standard terminology, bills of rights are negative guarantees, barring governments from doing things.

Those who favour campaign finance regulation and regulation of the mass media believe that concentrated government power is not the only thing we need to worry about. They are concerned that those who have the concentrated power of wealth in their hands might abuse the rest of us at least as much as the government can. If bills of rights are directed only at the possibilities of abusing government power, they might not only *allow* private abuses of power to continue, but, as my examples suggest, they might affirmatively *protect* the holders of private power against efforts to regulate them.

The situation in Italy is illustrative: a person controlling important media outlets, which are conceptualized as that person's property, is able to use those outlets to support a political agenda. The problem is broader than the Italian illustration, though, where we might think that the problem arises because of near-monopolization. Yet, wherever the mass media are privately owned, it is nearly certain that what they offer the public will be 'tilted' in a specific political and cultural direction – in support of the *status quo* that, after all, put the media's owners in the positions they already hold. As Professor Steven Shiffrin has recently put it, 'the news media tend to cover those arguments that divide corporate interests, but not those arguments directed against that which unites them'.[25]

As Shiffrin points out, this is hardly a conclusive argument against a constitutionalized free speech principle. Detailed political analysis of specific societies would be needed to determine whether progressives would be better or worse off with such a principle. Without it, they are vulnerable to direct repression by governments influenced by those who benefit from the *status quo*. With it, they can resist such repression, but may find themselves limited in what they can achieve in conditions of 'freedom' where those who benefit from the *status quo* have their own constitutional protections. Perhaps my scepticism about a bill of rights rests in the end on my sense that, in the contemporary USA, there would be somewhat greater space for progressive political activity without a free speech principle than there is with one.[26]

The key to understanding the views of bills of rights solely as restrictions on government power is that they take the background distributions of power and wealth as settled, not attributable to exercises of government power, and therefore unchallengeable through constitutional litigation. When people use their wealth and power to speak, by making contributions to political campaigns or by investing in the mass media, they are not, on this view, exercising public power and therefore are not subject to the controls that a bill of rights places on government power.

There are two obvious – and, in my view, equivalent – strategies to deal with the problem posed by bills of rights that are conceptualized solely as restrictions on the exercise of government power. One strategy is represented in the various efforts, spread throughout the world, to ensure that 'social charter' provisions are written into the constitution as well: guarantees of a minimum standard of subsistence, of housing and jobs, and the like. The other is addressed in the USA under the heading of the 'state action' doctrine. According to one controversial analysis of that doctrine, we can re-characterize the exercise of private power as the exercise of a power *delegated* to individuals and corporations by the government but always ultimately attributable to the government. Under this strategy, if a private person does something that looks like an abuse of power, it is regulated by the bill of rights because the action is in the end the government's.

I have serious doubts about whether modern constitutions are likely to adopt either social charter provisions – which I will also refer to as affirmative rights – or a sensible solution to the state action problem. Yet, unless one or the other course is followed, the risk that a bill of rights will obstruct progressive political change is substantial.

There is a standard argument against constitutionalizing affirmative rights. Consider a constitutional provision guaranteeing each able-bodied person a right to a job. Many critics of such provisions, and some supporters, argue that no government can actually implement such a right, considering the fiscal constraints that governments are under. So, the argument goes, no court can realistically enforce that guarantee. Then, however, consider what might happen. Suppose the court says that the affirmative right is merely an exhortation, stating a policy that elected legislatures should do their best to carry out but not creating an entitlement that courts will enforce as they enforce other legal entitlements. This creates two sets of constitutional rights, the 'real' ones the courts enforce, and the 'fake' ones they do not.

Having two sets of constitutional rights is a problem, for a number of reasons. First, if people believe that the affirmative rights are really important, and observe that they are not being enforced, they may conclude that the bill of rights as a whole really is not worth much. As I understand it, this was a widespread popular reaction to the constitutions of eastern Europe and the former Soviet Union. Second, those who would like to abuse government power will say, 'Well, why should we treat the negative restrictions on our power differently from the affirmative rights? All we have to do to comply with the bill of affirmative rights is to do our best, so all we ought to have to do to comply with the bill of negative rights is to do our best as well – and that is what the challenged practice is.' That is, treating affirmative rights as exhortations opens the way to treating negative guarantees as mere exhortations as well. All this leads people, including those who find the idea of affirmative rights attractive, to conclude that bills of rights ought not to include affirmative rights.[27]

If the state action problem were solved, specific protection for affirmative rights would be unnecessary. I need to elaborate on the state action problem to make my points here. The state action problem arises from the fundamental distinction made in a negative rights theory between the *government,* which the bill of rights restricts, and *private* people, who are free to do what they want – free, that is, precisely because the government's power to regulate them is limited by the bill of rights.

To return to the issue of campaign finance regulation, the problem arises because people who have made money through their investments decide to spend it, not on fancy cars or houses, but on political candidates. If a legislature wanted to limit their spending on fancy houses, it could, because, at least under modern US law, nothing stops a legislature from regulating the economy. But if the legislature wanted to limit spending on political candidates, it could not, because that, according to the Supreme Court, raises free speech questions. Free speech simply means, in the negative conception, that the government cannot tell people what to say, and people these days say things with money.

The state action solution to this problem is to push the inquiry back. Where, it asks, did these people get their money from in the first place? From some economic activity, of course, and they were able to do so just because the government had made a decision that allowed them to invest in that activity, which it need not have done. Now, consider the conceptualization of a bill of rights as a restriction only on government action. The free speech objection to campaign finance regulation is that the government is acting in limiting what people can do with their money. Yet the government acted just as much in setting up the rules of property law that allowed these people to accumulate enough money to invest in political candidates. If the accumulated money is spent in ways that we find bothersome, we ought to be able to say that the property rules violate free speech principles.

Now, I confess immediately that working out a set of constitutional doctrines that would subject to free speech regulation only those property rules that lead to problematic outcomes is not going to be easy.[28] My present point, though, is conceptual, not practical. By attributing private power to the background rules of property law (which are, everyone concedes, government action), we can subject private power to the restrictions embedded in a bill of rights that seems to protect only negative liberties.

The general difficulty that I have been addressing is that progressives typically want to use government power to restrict private power, and that a bill of rights conceived of as a restriction on government power alone may obstruct progressive programmes. Either the affirmative rights approach or the approach attributing private power to the government would avoid this difficulty. Why, then, am I sceptical about the utility of a bill of rights from a progressive point of view?

One source of my scepticism is a blend of historical and conceptual points. Both the affirmative rights approach and an expansive vision of government action raise a serious problem in a political tradition that – often for good reason – seeks to distinguish between the public and private domains. We all, I think, have some notion that there is a core of private activity into which a well-constituted government simply cannot intrude (although we may well differ over defining that core). But the expansive vision of government action makes it quite difficult to identify that core in any coherent way.

I will take an example from parallel discussions in the USA. Most progressives believe that an individual woman has a right to choose whether or not to bear a child. The right to choose, that is, is located within the private domain into which the government cannot intrude. But, as many feminists have argued, women's choices are not 'their own' in some abstract sense; they are highly structured by a dense network of social relations, some of which arise from the government and its legal rules. One cannot even begin to say whether a woman's choice to bear a child or have an abortion is 'hers' without knowing what sorts of social provision for medical care and child-rearing assistance the society in which she lives offers, for example.

If the government is everywhere, in this sense, the idea of a private domain collapses. That, however, is unacceptable to virtually everyone. The only way to stave off the collapse is to deny the expansive vision of government action. That, however, reintroduces the problem for progressives of insulating some of the important social consequences of nominally private action from government regulation.

Another set of reasons for my scepticism about bills of rights arises from a certain parochialism, but one that I think is likely to have some influence on the adoption of bills of rights in the modern era. I have little doubt but that the US experience with enforcing a bill of rights is widely regarded as the most successful example of bill of rights enforcement in the world. Nations that have recently adopted bills of rights typically emulate at least some aspects of US constitutional jurisprudence.[29]

Now, if courts enforcing bills of rights elsewhere look to the US for guidance, they will find all the problems I have identified: a scepticism about the capacity of courts to enforce affirmative rights, coupled with a relatively vigorous sense that courts can and should enforce negative rights. That, however, is a formula for the frustration of progressive efforts to modify, through government action, the effects of existing distributions of wealth and power. This problem might be exacerbated by some aspects of what I call the legal-judicial culture. Here I have in mind the general cast of mind that a judge brings to the task of enforcing a

written bill of rights. I want to distinguish between two ways of interpreting a bill of rights, which I call formalist and instrumentalist.

Formalists treat a bill of rights as ordinary, though supreme, law. They
interpret it just as they would interpret any other legal document: primarily with an eye to its text, its structure, and the background against
which it was adopted. They are relatively inattentive to the evils at which
it was directed, although they do not disregard them. Instrumentalists,
in contrast, pay most attention to those evils; in resolving a question of
constitutional interpretation, instrumentalists will ask which of the competing interpretive alternatives is more likely to advance the purposes
that the provision at issue is supposed to promote.

Instrumentalism and formalism pose different problems for bills of
rights. Roughly speaking, the risk of instrumentalism is that it will fall to
the pressures of the moment: precisely the same reasons that led legislatures to adopt constitutionally questionable acts – which seemed like
good reasons for the legislature – will seem good enough reasons to
believe that the purposes of the bill of rights are best served by interpreting the bill of rights to allow the legislature to do what seems sensible
enough.[30] And the risk of formalism is that it will degenerate into an
apparently purposeless enforcement of restrictions on government
power to no apparent good end – or, even worse, that it will become the
vehicle that obstructionist judges use to impede the enforcement of programmes that they simply disagree with.

These difficulties are more likely to appear over an extended period
than they are in the immediate aftermath of the adoption of a bill of
rights. I have little doubt that, immediately after a bill of rights is
adopted, people will get pretty much what they expected from it: some
restrictions on government action they had not had before, some
impetus to government action that had been lacking earlier. That, however, should not lead us to conclude that these effects are attributable to
the bill of rights itself.

After all, a bill of rights is always adopted as part of – and as the result
of – a political mobilization. The people who advocate its adoption do so
because they expect it to yield some results. And, ordinarily, it will. The
results may occur because they are clearly written into the bill of rights.
Or they may occur when judges take interpretative instructions written
into the bill of rights seriously. Or, finally, they may occur when judges,
interpreting ambiguous provisions, recall the political struggles that led
to their adoption and, acting either as formalists or instrumentalists but
in any event being prudent about these things, enforce the outcome of
those political struggles.

The question, though, has to be: do these results occur because there
is a bill of rights in place, or because there was a political mobilization that

led to the adoption of the bill of rights? To put the point starkly, if you can pass a bill of rights that places substantial restrictions on police activity, why could you not have passed a statute that placed exactly those same restrictions on police activity?

Bruce Ackerman has recently suggested an answer, although I think that it is unsatisfactory.[31] Again roughly, Ackerman's response to my sceptical question is something like this: 'Well, if you actually were able to mobilize people into political action, you might be able to get statutes that are effectively equivalent to the bill of rights that others are proposing. But, as a matter of sheer historical fact, it just turns out that you cannot get people to act politically in this way all that often. And it turns out that one way of getting people to mobilize – getting them to act politically – is to present their political choices to them in such fundamental packages as are represented by modern bills of rights.'

The idea here, then, is that there may not be a significant conceptual difference between passing a bill of rights and passing a statute, but there is a real political difference. The claim is that mobilizing around a platform of 'We Need a Bill of Rights' is more likely to energize the people in a progressive direction than mobilizing around a platform of 'Get the Police Under Control'. In the USA, Shiffrin points out, campus radicals got things going at least in part by mobilizing what they called the Free Speech Movement, rather than the 'Fight the Multiversity Movement'.

Sometimes, I am sure, that is true, and Ackerman himself is careful to describe his project as an attempt to capture the experience of constitutionalism in the USA, not as an effort to describe constitutionalism *per se*.[32] Rather, I would suggest that the political case for using 'Enact a Bill of Rights' as a platform may be crucially dependent on the weak party structure that exists in the USA. If political parties had more coherent substantive platforms, perhaps 'Elect Us' would do just as well in getting reforms adopted.

There is, however, a second question. Even if a political movement focused on entrenching a bill of rights is the only method of securing the rights presently available, what are the long-term effects of entrenching a bill of rights? Of course, precisely because the questions ask for speculation about effects over decades or even longer, they cannot be answered definitively. The US experience suggests, however, that the risks of both formalist and instrumentalist degeneration are not trivial.

Perhaps whatever enthusiasm there is for adopting a bill of rights in the UK results from the perception that the party system is not as coherent as it has been. If so, the 'Enact a Bill of Rights' platform may be a decent substitute. It is not, however, a platform to lead progressives into the promised land.

NOTES

1. The comprehensive survey of the arguments offered in M. Zander, *A Bill of Rights?* (3rd edn, London, 1985) demonstrates how pervasive the conditional form is.

2. The contemporary legal culture in the UK appears to me more formalist, less affected by legal realist jurisprudence, than the US legal culture, however.

3. This essay is a development of arguments earlier made in M. Tushnet, An essay on rights, (1984) 62 *Texas Law Review* 1364; M. Tushnet, Rights: an essay in informal political theory (1989) 17 *Politics and Society* 403; and M. Tushnet, The critique of rights (1993) 47 *SMU Law Review* 23. It also incorporates material to be included in L. M. Seidman and M. Tushnet, *Remnants of Belief: Contemporary Constitutional Issues* (forthcoming, Oxford University Press). I remain unsure whether I have provided either too much detail about US law, or not enough detail to make my argument intelligible to an audience not steeped in US constitutional law.

4. Things might be different if, in the sort of regime transformation we have recently seen elsewhere in Europe, there were a wholesale replacement of judges, but even in those countries that has proved hard to accomplish. The experience over the next decade in South Africa may prove quite instructive on these matters.

5. *Arizona* v. *Hicks*, 480 US 321 (1987).

6. 501 US 429 (1991).

7. Of course, there may be limits on what the police can do that result from deeply embedded cultural assumptions not embodied in law. A bill of rights is unnecessary to ensure that such limitations are respected.

8. In addition, the protections afforded by the bill of rights, such as they are, may displace other protections. Having found that a practice does not violate the bill of rights, judges may find it easier to say that it is authorized by statute, or consistent with the common law. Without a bill of rights, the judges might give more thought to the possibility that the common law bars the practice, or that it is not authorized by statute.

9. This argument depends on the proposition that, without a bill of rights, a court decision allowing the challenged police activity would *not* be taken as an endorsement of the activity. I am inclined to accept that proposition, because in a world where everything is permitted, it is unclear to me how a specific decision to uphold a particular activity could be understood to endorse it; on this view it is only the possibility that *some* activities might not be permitted – a possibility that arises only in the presence of a bill of rights – that makes it possible for people to interpret a holding of 'not unconstitutional' as a determination of affirmative desirability. I would not want to push this too hard, though, because I know that in no non-totalitarian regime is it really the case that 'everything is permitted' to the government. Statutes and administrative regulations limit what police and other authorities can do, and it may be that judicial holdings that a police activity did not violate some statute or regulation would be interpreted by the public as an endorsement of the activity.

10. For a discussion, see M. Matsuda, Public response to racist speech: considering the victim's story (1989) 87 *Michigan Law Review* 2320.

11. *Lochner* v. *New York*, 198 US 45 (1905).

12. *Lucas* v. *South Carolina Coastal Commission*, 112 SCt 2886 (1992); *Dolan* v. *City of Tigard*, 114 SCt 2309 (1994).

13. As it appears from a distance, some of these problems seem to have migrated across the Atlantic, particularly to Italy.

14. *Buckley* v. *Valeo*, 424 US 1 (1976).

15. Most observers are sceptical about claims that such expenditures are truly 'independent', though.

16. 424 US 1 (1976).

17. *Ibid.*, p. 19.

18. *Ibid.*

19. *Ibid.*, pp. 48–9.

20. *Ibid.* p. 57.

21. *Bigelow* v. *Virginia*, 421 US 809 (1971). One thinks here of the recent controversies in Ireland.

22. *Virginia Board of Pharmacy* v. *Virginia Citizens Consumer Council*, 425 US 748 (1976).

23. *Turner Broadcasting System, Inc.* v. *FCC*, 114 SCt 2445 (1994).

24. See, for example, Canadian Charter of Rights and Freedoms, Article 15(1) ('Every individual is equal before and under the law and has the right to equal protection and equal benefit of the law without discrimination'), Article 15(2) ('Subsection 1 does not preclude any law, program or activity that has as its object the amelioration of conditions of disadvantaged individuals or groups'); Constitution of India, Article 15(1) ('The State shall not discriminate against any citizen on grounds only of religion, race, caste, sex, place of birth or any of them'), Article 15(4) ('Nothing in this article. . . shall prevent the State from making any special provision for the advancement of any socially and educationally backward classes of citizens or for the Scheduled Castes and Scheduled Tribes').

25. S. Shiffrin, The politics of the mass media and the free speech principle (1994) 69 *Indiana Law Journal* 689, p. 712.

26. Shiffrin, I should say, disagrees with this political evaluation.

27. For my scepticism about the argument I have just sketched, see M. Tushnet, Civil rights and social rights: the future of the reconstruction amendments (1992) 25 *Loyola of Los Angeles Law Review* 1207. I believe that it is just as much within the capacity of judges to enforce affirmative rights as negative liberties. I find it interesting, for example, that some who object to constitutional guarantees of minimum subsistence or of jobs or housing are much less troubled by constitutional guarantees of environmental protection, which seem to me to raise the same problems of enforceability.

28. I am inclined to think that a neat way to do so would be to impress all economic activity with what we might call a 'public interest easement', under which the public would be entitled to override an owner's desires to use property in one way, in the service of some general public interest.

29. My favourite example here comes from the state action doctrine itself. In the USA, that doctrine has come under intense scholarly attack, largely because people see it as incoherent. The testing cases are two: the Supreme Court held that it *was* state action for a court to enforce a covenant on property restricting its resale to white persons only; virtually everyone agrees that it would *not* be state action for a court to enforce a ban on trespass, when asked to do so by a homeowner who objected to a racial minority walking across the property. Figuring out why one form of government action falls under the constitutional ban on race discrimination while the other does not is extremely difficult. The Canadian Supreme Court, though, in its first major confrontation with the state action problem, decided that actions by judges enforcing common law rules were not subject to constitutional restrictions, (*Retail, Wholesale & Department Store Union, Local 580* v. *Dolphin Delivery Ltd*, [1986] 2 SCR 573). This avoids some of the problems associated with the US state action doctrine, but creates a raft of new ones.

30. As I noted earlier, the instrumentalist degeneration may not make society worse off than it would have been without a bill of rights. The instrumentalist degeneration means that courts approve what legislatures have done, just as they would in the absence of a bill of rights.

31. B. Ackerman, *We The People* (Cambridge, MA, 1991).

32. I am sceptical about Ackerman's account of US constitutional history too, but that is not something to be taken up here.

2

The Canadian Charter and the Democratic Process

Beverley McLachlin

INTRODUCTION

This conference has put me in mind of the first 'bill of rights' paper I ever wrote. The year was 1967; I was a law student. Canada, in the process of celebrating her 100th birthday, was beginning to discuss a constitutional bill of human rights. The thesis of my paper, which I contended was supported by a historical survey of the experience of the USA, was that an entrenched bill of rights is no guarantee of progress on human rights and may even harm such progress. At the time, my view was unpopular. Now, I discover, it has gained academic legitimacy. And now, I also discover, I no longer adhere to it. Whether behind my time or ahead, it seems that I am definitely out of step.

My change of view has more to do with pragmatism than with theory. It is based on reflection on the values that currently drive democratic societies and on the Canadian experience, admittedly brief, with a constitutional bill of rights. As we approach the twenty-first century, human rights are emerging as the dominant ethic. All over the world, even where they are observed more in the breach than in practice, they are accepted as the fundamental norm upon which liberal democracy is founded. This is true, whether countries possess entrenched bills of rights or not. So we cannot avoid the rights issue. The only question is how we deal with it. In my view, an entrenched bill of rights offers certain advantages over the alternatives of legislation or judicially created rights. First, it has in our experience been the most effective means of achieving human rights gains. Canada has tried different methods of advancing human rights. It had a long experience with legislated codes of human rights. For over a decade, it had a quasi-constitutional bill of rights. These documents achieved modest progress on the human rights front. But it was not until 1982, when Canada adopted a constitutional Charter of Rights and Freedoms,[1] that consistent, serious progress on human rights issues was achieved. Second, an entrenched bill of rights offers the opportunity to strike a balance between excessive individualism on the one hand and majoritarian rule on the other – something which may be difficult to do with a series of legislated or judicial *ad hoc* measures. As such, it provides a firm foundation for judicial decisions and the development of practical norms in this most difficult of areas. Finally, it is my belief that an entrenched bill of rights accords a stature to human rights that other alternatives may not.

WHAT DOES THE CANADIAN CHARTER DO?

Against this background, I approach my assignment – to offer certain reflections on the Canadian Charter of Rights and Freedoms a dozen years after its entrenchment. At the heart of every democracy lies an inherent tension between individual and minority rights on the one hand, and the will of the majority on the other. This tension is itself reflected in a tension between the judicial and the legislative branches of government. As Mr Justice Megarry has remarked, the traditional role of the judge is as protector of minority interests against the tyranny of the majority, which tends to be represented by the elected parliamentarians.[2] As his comments attest, this is so even in states lacking formal guarantees of rights. But in such states, protection of individual and minority interests may be haphazard and somewhat uncertain. The effect of a constitutional bill of rights is to provide an incontestable foundation for the assertion of individual and minority rights, thus strengthening their position in relation to the majority. Parliament's right to legislate is limited; it cannot override guaranteed rights except as permitted by the constitution, which is in turn interpreted by judges.

Thus a charter of rights strikes a balance between the will of the majority as expressed through the legislatures and the rights of the individual as defined by law and the courts; a balance between the concepts of legislative supremacy and guaranteed fundamental rights. The Canadian Charter, which has been referred to as the 'quintessential Canadian compromise',[3] effects this balance in a unique, inelegant but arguably practical way. It does not follow the US model, which casts individual rights in absolute terms and posits them negatively against the alien state. Rather, it sees individual rights as complementary to state rights and responsibilities. The individual has rights, but they are necessarily limited by each other and by the greater public good.

The Canadian compromise consists, on the one hand, of strong

assertions of the fundamental human rights which are guaranteed to
every Canadian. Many of these are the sort of classic guarantees that are
familiar to Western political thought and tradition. Guarantees of freedom of expression, religion, peaceful assembly and association are among
the fundamental provisions of the Charter. Canadians are also guaranteed
democratic rights and mobility rights. And there are rights which can be
asserted against the state in its exercise of the criminal law power. Rights
against unreasonable search and seizure, rights to a fair trial within a reasonable time and the right not to be subject to cruel and unusual
punishment are also contained in the Charter. Finally, there is a guarantee of equality – in s. 15 of the Charter – which the Court has interpreted
as conferring not merely the sterile legal equality of treating likes alike,
but a substantive, ameliorative equality aimed at rectifying the legal disadvantages which members of certain groups suffer in our society.

However, the Charter does not end with a recitation of rights. It contains
three provisions which allow for the potentially uneasy fit of the individual
Charter guarantees with traditional notions of parliamentary supremacy –
s. 33, s. 1 and s. 24(2). Perhaps the most controversial of these provisions is
s. 33, known as the legislative override or the 'notwithstanding clause'.
Section 33 permits a legislature, provincial or federal, to declare expressly
that particular legislation will operate notwithstanding the guarantees of
certain fundamental freedoms. Thus, by a simple legislative declaration –
which must be renewed every five years – a law may be enacted which legislators know is in violation of, for example, the guarantee of freedom of
expression or of equality. The effect of s. 33 is to suspend the operation of
the Charter in respect of that provision for 5 years.

Yet despite the presence of the provision, it has been used infrequently.[4] It can be an unpopular move by a government to invoke s. 33,
signalling as it does conscious legislative intention to act in contravention
of the fundamental guarantees of the people. Its recent invocation by the
province of Quebec to shield a language law from the dictates of the
Charter provoked considerable anger from Canadians both inside and
outside the province, and has led some to call for an amendment to the
Charter which would repeal this 'notwithstanding clause'. Others, however, continue to see it as the ultimate safeguard for parliamentary
supremacy over rule by appointed judges.

Much more important as an expression of the Canadian 'compromise'
in the Charter is the provision that is uniformly referred to in Canadian
legal circles as 'section 1'. Section 1 states that the Charter 'guarantees the
rights and freedoms set out in it subject only to such reasonable limits
prescribed by law as can be demonstrably justified in a free and democratic society'. Section 1 expressly recognizes that sometimes it is right
and just that individual freedoms should give way to the greater good as

expressed by Parliament or the legislators. As such, it provides a mechanism for balancing individual rights and freedoms against the considered majoritarian view as expressed by the legislators. It may be noted that s. 1 operates only where there is a 'law' and hence cannot 'save' administrative acts which violate individual rights.

Unlike the 'notwithstanding' clause contained in s. 33, s. 1 figures prominently in the Canadian constitutional picture. Courts frequently find a legislative provision to violate particular guarantees of the Charter, but find that it is 'saved' or 'justified' under s. 1. This means that although a law is found to offend a Charter guarantee, the court is prepared to excuse the violation on the ground that it is demonstrably justified in a free and democratic society. For example, the Supreme Court of Canada in 1990 concluded that a law making it a criminal offence wilfully to promote hatred violated the Charter guarantee of freedom of thought, belief, opinion and expression.[5] The law was 'saved', however, under s. 1. The majority of the Court held that the hate law, while offending the guarantee of free expression, was 'saved' as a reasonable limit on the freedom of expression, a different result from that which has been obtained under the more absolute guarantees of the US Constitution. In other words, a progressive enactment aimed at improving Canadian society was upheld under s. 1 notwithstanding a violation of personal freedoms; the public good was deemed to outweigh the individual interest at stake. Let me mention another example. Parliament criminalized the creation and distribution of pornography. It was argued that the provision impinged on the Charter guarantee of free expression. But it was counter-argued that if it did, the limitation was justified in a free and democratic society. The Court agreed with respect to pornography which involved violence or was degrading and dehumanizing.[6]

The Charter contains yet a third mechanism by which the impact of breaches of fundamental rights may be attenuated, of particular importance to the criminal process. Section 24(2) permits a court to receive evidence obtained in violation of the Charter. The test is whether its reception would bring the administration of justice into disrepute. This permits the courts to weigh the seriousness of the infringement of the right against the majoritarian concern with obtaining a proper verdict.

The inclusion in the Canadian Charter of Rights and Freedoms of these three mechanisms for effecting case by case compromises between individual rights and majoritarian concerns constitutes a fundamental and most important distinction between the Canadian Charter and the US Bill of Rights. In the USA such compromises, if they are made at all, must be made under the guise of 'reading down' the citizen's constitutional rights. Viewed in this way, the Charter is much less extreme and much more flexible than its US counterpart.

HAS THE CHARTER CHANGED THINGS
AND, IF SO, WHY?

Against this background, I turn to the question posed – has the Charter changed the Canadian political and legal scene? The answer is 'yes'. As to why this is so, I think that the answer lies in the balance which the Charter attempts to strike and the process by which it has been introduced and enforced. I believe most observers would agree that the Charter has changed things in Canada, although they might differ on whether the changes have been good or bad or both. The changes have occurred in the way we view and use our democratic institutions; and on the legal and judicial scene, in an increased voice for minorities and disadvantaged groups. I will consider each of these in greater detail.

Much of the change stems from the mere existence of new constitutional constraints on those exercising power. But, as the US record demonstrates, even the strongest bill of rights can be used as an agent of repression rather than liberation. What is all-important is how the people and the judiciary use and view a bill of rights. When the Charter was adopted in Canada in 1982, many expected that it would be narrowly interpreted and applied and consequently would have a minor effect upon the Canadian scene. In fact, this did not occur. The question is why? Why did Canadian courts, with a long record of judicial conservatism behind them, adopt a different approach to the Charter? Equally important, why did so many individuals and groups bring actions and interventions under the new document? The answer, in large part, may lie with the process which preceded the adoption of the Charter. The Charter was preceded by years of debate. Parliamentarians and interested individuals and groups devoted countless hours to debating what clauses should be included and how they should be worked. This was reflected in public debate. Then, too, the Charter was part of a package that symbolized to Canadians the bringing home from Westminster of their country's constitution, as a final step in political and legal emancipation. As such, it was bathed in a positive ambience. Canadians were, in law as well as fact, 'doing it their way'. All this meant that when the Charter came to be used and interpreted, people took it seriously. It would have been unthinkable, after all the time and effort and excitement, not to take it seriously. So it was that from the beginning, people took it up and the courts gave it real substance – substance in some cases beyond that foreseen by those who had been involved in its drafting.

The Political Scene

I use 'political' in the widest sense, to encompass the participation of various individuals and groups in society in the governance and organization of that society. The primary means for people to participate in the governance of a democratic society is through the election of representatives to legislative bodies. Those bodies then enact laws. This, in essence, is parliamentary supremacy. Because the representatives can be voted out of office at the next election, the system is also called responsible government. Parliamentary supremacy is never absolute. Second chambers have the power to modify and sometimes block the will of parliament. In a federal state, additional limitations are imposed; the will of parliament is subject to court rulings on whether a particular law is within the competence of parliament or the legislature in question. A constitutional charter of rights further intrudes on the supremacy of parliament by permitting judicial review on the basis that the law in question violates the guaranteed rights and freedoms. The Charter thus effects an additional transfer of power from elected representatives to judges who are not elected but appointed, usually for life or until retirement. In this sense the Canadian Charter has altered the political landscape.

Does this mean that the Charter has weakened Canadian democracy? Some argue that it has:

> Just as the 1960s are remembered by Canadian historians as the decade of the Quiet Revolution, so the 1980s will be remembered as the decade of the Charter Revolution. The adoption of the Charter of Rights and Freedoms in 1982 has transformed both the practice and theory of Canadian politics. It has replaced a century-old tradition of parliamentary supremacy with a new regime of constitutional supremacy that verges on judicial supremacy. Judges have abandoned the deference and self-restraint that characterized their pre-Charter jurisprudence and become active players in the political process. Encouraged by the judiciary's about-face, interest groups – many funded by the very governments whose laws they are challenging – have increasingly turned to the courts to advance their policy objectives. The Charter has made the courtroom a new arena for the pursuit of politics. Charter litigation – or its threat – also casts its shadow over the more traditional arenas of electoral, legislative, and administrative politics.[7]

In short, a measure of the legislatures' once supreme power has been passed to the judges, who are neither elected by the people nor removable by the people. And these unelected judges are conferring rights and remedies upon minorities which the popular will would not otherwise give them. As a former premier of Ontario put it: 'If you had told the people what the Charter was going to mean in 1982 – with respect to things like abortion and the Lord's Prayer – you never would have gotten it.'[8] The argument that the Charter has transferred some measure of power from elected to unelected persons is irrefutable. What is less certain is the inference that this has weakened Canadian democracy. Critics often facilely conclude that the latter follows upon the former. But that is so only if one equates excellence in democracy with absolute populism. If one accepts that democracy at its best reflects a tension between majoritarian will and individual rights, as did Mr Justice Megarry, then it is far from evident that the transfer of a measure of power from the legislatures to the courts has weakened Canadian democracy. Indeed, a case can be made that it has strengthened democracy by guaranteeing the fundamental values on which democracy rests and by enabling individuals and minorities to participate more fully in the democratic institutions of our society. In my view, the Canadian experience bears out the latter view.

The notion that liberal democracy is at its best when it strikes a balance between majoritarian and individual concerns is hardly radical. As one scholar put it:

> [L]iberal democracy is a broad and flexible concept. It is capable of embracing various roles for government and the individual. At its outer edges, liberal democracy is threatened by totalitarianism and nihilism. Totalitarianism, the tyranny of the majority, imposes absolute governmental control upon the citizenry; nihilism and gross individualism lead to the total rejection of community institutions and values. Both extremes are to be feared.[9]

Viewed from this perspective, the question whether the Charter has weakened or strengthened democracy in Canada is not answered by the assertion that the Charter transfers a measure of power from the legislatures to the courts. In fact, this question misdirects the inquiry. We ought rather to be asking whether the Charter strikes the right balance between the power of the majority and the rights of the individual.

In adopting a charter of rights such as that found in Canada, which seeks to marry individual rights to parliamentary sovereignty, the people may be taken to have expressed their settled view in favour of a democracy which balances majoritarian and individual interests, and to have entrusted to the courts the delicate task of maintaining the proper balance between majoritarian and individual rights. The courts are not merely the protectors of individual rights – they are the protectors of the will of the majority as well. This is reflected in the Canadian Charter, which guarantees values essential to the proper functioning of democracy. At this point it is necessary to challenge a second assumption often made by Charter critics – the assumption that individual rights and majoritarian rights are inevitably in conflict. It cannot be denied that minority interests are often different from majority interests. But on a broader plane, the preservation of individual liberties may be viewed as the precondition of a functioning democracy. The Charter arguably strengthens democracy by sustaining individual rights and enhancing values which are essential to the proper working of democracy. The right to free expression and a free press are essential underpinnings of a strong and effective democracy. The same may be said for the guarantee of the right to vote, and the entrenched requirement that national elections be held at least once every five years. The guarantee of equality before and under the law is another example of the Charter's commitment to the essential components of democratic government. If it may be said that the deep conditions of democratic government include 'political participation, equality, autonomy and personal liberty', then a vigorous and committed judicial approach which underscores these conditions of democracy is one of the strongest arguments in favour of the Charter.[10]

From this perspective the Charter and judicial review emerge as supportive of democracy, not opposed to it.[11] This is a view that has found its way into the Supreme Court's jurisprudence on the Charter. The Court has held that the scope of freedom of expression must be based on a recognition of its fundamental value to a free and democratic society. Former Chief Justice Dickson stated that freedom of expression was constitutionally entrenched 'to ensure that everyone can manifest their thoughts, opinions, beliefs, indeed all expressions of the heart and mind, however unpopular, distasteful or contrary to the mainstream'. A free and democratic society, he continued, prizes 'a diversity of ideas and opinions for their inherent value both to the community and to the individual'.[12] The underlying value of the guarantee, deserving vigilant protection, includes the seeking of truth and the participation in social and political decision-making.[13] The Charter, by enhancing the values and freedoms on which democracy rests, ensures a climate of freedom within which democracy can thrive. But the Charter functions as more than a backdrop. A second way in which it supports democracy is by enhancing the participation of individuals and groups within democracy, effectively enfranchising people who in the past may have been excluded from the process of governance and societal change.

Traditionally, the political process in Canada at the national and provincial levels has been (and continues to be) driven by the large, mainstream political parties. Participation in this process, apart from voting, was largely confined to lobbying – an activity which requires a great deal of organization and money channelled through the large political parties. In this structure, the political agenda tends to be set by the party in power, supplemented, depending on their clout, by the opposition parties. The usual result is that individuals and unempowered groups – women, racial minorities and the poor – have little influence in initiating a particular political issue unless they are well connected or members of the mainstream parties; it is the majoritarian concerns and the agendas of the rich and powerful which capture the attention of the government. The Charter does not destroy this political power equation, but it alters it. Through its inclusive language it creates new 'insiders' in the Canadian political and constitutional order. Two groups in particular, women and aboriginal people, are explicitly recognized and have their place in society affirmed in the Charter. Similarly, the multicultural nature of the country is *constitutionally* recognized, as are equality rights regardless of race, national or ethnic origin, colour, religion, sex, age or mental or physical disability. The provisions of the Charter, 'by giving rights to citizens and by handing out particular constitutional niches to particular categories of Canadians, such as women, aboriginals, etc., implicitly suggests some citizen role in constitutional change,'[14] and, indeed, the entire sphere of political activity. Not only does the Charter give new status to particular groups – it gives formal and visible expression to interests, e.g. liberty, security of the person and equality. The recognition that such interests are of constitutional importance is of great symbolic and practical significance. It empowers individuals; it tells them that they have worth and that they can make a difference. It encourages individuals to identify themselves more strongly with certain groups and to focus on particular goals – for example gender equality. The result is increased and broader-based participation in debate on public issues.

The third way in which the Charter arguably enhances democratic participation is by providing a new tool by which real participation in public affairs can be realized. Prior to the Charter, the courts in Canada did not function significantly as a means of initiating and participating in political change and action. The Charter facilitates the ability of members of the public to challenge the validity of legislation. This draws judicial and, eventually, legislative attention to areas of the law which may be out of step with the values and aspirations of the country, as expressed by the constitution, thus opening up the law reform process.[15] Individuals and groups can influence the agenda of law reform by challenging laws in the courts. Government action may similarly be challenged, and such review may even extend to cabinet deliberations on security.[16] The participation of disadvantaged groups in Charter litigation was abetted by a government funding programme, suspended for a time but now about to be reinstated.

Fourth, recourse to the courts on the basis of the Charter is perceived as a means of obtaining redress for difficult issues which are left unaddressed by the legislative process. It has frequently been noted that the US Supreme Court has tended to step in when the legislative process has proved incapable of dealing with a difficult issue. For example, the desegregation movement of the 1960s was immeasurably aided by prior decisions of that Court.[17] The same phenomenon has been observed in Canada. After Parliament refused to reconsider the difficult issue of doctor-assisted suicide for the terminally ill, the courts were asked to rule.[18] Currently, court decisions are provoking a legislative review of taxation of child support payments in the hands of the custodial parent.[19]

Finally, the Charter may serve as the vehicle by which substantive inequalities may be redressed and a progressive agenda furthered. One of the most important decisions of the Supreme Court of Canada under the Charter was *Andrews* v. *Law Society of British Columbia*.[20] The Court there laid down the foundation of the s. 15 equality doctrine. Section 15, it held, was not to be interpreted in a legalistic 'treat likes alike' fashion. Rather, its purpose was to reduce distinctions and conduct which adversely impacted upon groups which had traditionally been disadvantaged. Thus defined, s. 15 holds the promise of ameliorating the economic condition of women, racial minorities and the aged, among others. A similar equalizing effect may flow from other provisions of the Charter. Consider the issue of the right of a person detained by the police 'to retain and instruct counsel without delay and to be informed of that right': s. 10(b). The Supreme Court recently ruled that this requires the police to tell the detainee about existing legal aid and duty counsel schemes.[21] At least to this extent, the right to counsel is not dependent on the possession of funds.

The Supreme Court, alive to the individual–public balance which the Charter aims to strike, has on the whole manifested great concern not to intrude any more than necessary into the proper domain of Parliament and the legislatures. While adopting a broad and purposive interpretation of the rights guaranteed by the Charter, the courts have been concerned to leave the last word to elected representatives wherever possible. The doctrine under s. 1 and s. 24 developed early in the life of the Charter attests to this. Section 1, which permits the Court to uphold laws which breach the fundamental rights guaranteed by the Charter, was read so as to require the courts to defer to the legislature's policy choices.[22] Similarly, s. 24 has been interpreted so as to permit evidence obtained in breach of the Charter to be received against an accused person in a wide spectrum of cases.[23] Even in the context of s. 52, which

declares legislation which violates the Charter to be invalid, the courts
have been respectful of the legislative process and reluctant to permit
laws to fall without giving the legislators a chance to amend or replace.
On the theory that policy questions are for the elected members not the
courts, they have temporarily upheld laws which violate the Charter.[24]
And the option of striking out offending portions of a law, thereby changing its import from what the legislator intended, has been approached
cautiously; the courts will 'read up' or 'read down' legislation only where
it is apparent that the legislature would have endorsed the proposed
change.[25] All this suggests that whether the courts actually strike the right
balance between majoritarian and individual concerns case by case – there
is great debate concerning whether they do or do not – the courts are
keenly aware that their task is to attempt to strike that balance, and that
deference to the expressed intention of the legislatures is as great a concern as is upholding the rights of individuals in the overall perspective.

One fear expressed by the opponents of an entrenched bill of rights is
that it may be used to strike down progressive legislation. Apart from the
criminal law, the number of cases in which progressive legislation has
been struck down under the Charter are few, and generally confined to
laws which are overbroad – that is, which are more invasive of rights than
is necessary to achieve their goal. In the criminal field, a number of procedural and substantive provisions have been struck down or read down.
For example, a blanket rape shield provision was struck down.[26] But the
Court affirmed that even without the law, unlimited cross-examination of
complainants would not be tolerated. In due course, Parliament
responded with a new bill. It seems to me that this process – legislation,
corrective judicial opinion, re-legislation – is not one antithetical to progressive social change. Rather, it confirms social change without
permitting it to invade individual rights unduly. The debate about election funding, an important issue in the USA whenever the role of a bill
of rights in democratic functioning is discussed, has not yet been litigated
in Canada, and I cannot comment on it. However, an argument can be
made that the different approach to free expression in Canada might
lead to a different result on the issues of limiting and funding electoral
debate.

The Judicial Scene

The Charter has altered not only the role of Parliament and the legislators, but also that of the courts. This has impacted upon the courts in
various ways, not all of them pleasant. Judges are more noticed and more
criticized. The advent of the Charter in Canada has elevated judges from

a position where they once toiled in relative obscurity, to the level of media figures. Now, more than ever before, the contributions made by the courts are seen to have such a direct and profound impact on the everyday life of the country that judgments of the Supreme Court receive regular and extensive attention from the news media. And that focus is not restricted merely to a concern with the substance of the courts' output. There is an accompanying increase in public interest in the judges themselves, not only as judicial figures but also as people. To take a recent example which I cannot help but remember strongly, I was recently engaged to be married. I was rather surprised to discover that this event would warrant a story in one of Canada's largest newspapers![27] The personal lives of Supreme Court judges would certainly not have garnered much press prior to the Charter.

The Canadian public in the post-Charter era takes the view that it is entitled to know who its judges are. As one columnist recently put it:

> In Ottawa, the nine judges on the Supreme Court of Canada are more consequential than all but a handful of politicians at the top of the political process. Yet outside the legal fraternity they remain largely unknown.[28]

Judges at the Supreme Court level are increasingly scrutinized for their personal views on certain issues. As a result, there is a concern that the courts be representative of the public which they are required to serve; the appointment of women and racial minorities to the Bench is seen as essential. And the increased level of scrutiny has brought calls for a re-examination of the manner in which judges are appointed in Canada. Judges in Canadian superior courts are presently appointed by the federal government after private consultation with various groups, including the Canadian Bar Association. Traditionally the process of selecting Canada's judges, particularly for appointment to the Supreme Court, has been one which has eschewed partisanship and ideology. It stands in stark contrast to the US process, where the selection of Supreme Court justices has become a highly politicized and complex ideological contest between the President, elected representatives and various national interest groups that sometimes seems to have little to do with getting the best judge for the job.[29]

As the US experience demonstrates, there are no easy solutions to the problem of developing a workable, yet public, judicial appointment process. Yet, given the prominent role which judges play under the Charter, calls for a more open judicial appointment process in Canada will doubtless continue. They tend to surface in Canada in the wake of cases which force the courts to balance clear statements of legislative policy against the fundamental freedoms enshrined by the Charter. A recent decision from a judge in the Province of Quebec declared federal legislation banning tobacco advertising an unjustified infringement of freedom of expression. As one national journalist wrote:

> The more we push parliamentary supremacy into the shadow of the judiciary, and encourage the courts to resolve essentially political (in a non partisan sense) issues, the more necessary it becomes that political debates about the suitability of judges occur before their nominations.[30]

But to reduce the debate about entrenchment of human rights to the convenience or popularity of judges or the means by which they are appointed is to trivialize it. The more important question is how the Charter has affected the functioning of the judicial system.

One concern is that entrenchment of rights gives rise to a flood of frivolous litigation – Charter mania, as it is dubbed. In Canada there was a surge, but not a flood, of litigation after adopting the Charter. Such actions as were clearly frivolous were generally disposed of in the usual way at early stages through motions to strike. What remained tended to be serious questions. Twelve years after the adoption of the Charter, I am informed by trial justices that Charter work comprises only a small portion of their docket. In short, the evidence simply does not support the allegation that the Charter has opened the gates to floods of frivolous litigation, although it may have increased it somewhat. However, it *is* fair to say that the Charter tends to lengthen criminal trials. There are more hearings to determine whether evidence was taken in a way that breached the Charter, and, if so, whether it should be received under s. 24(2). Some say that the reason for this lies in part not in the Charter itself, but in the fact that court decisions have imposed strictures that go beyond the spirit of the Charter, which adopts the repute of the administration of justice as its ultimate criterion for the admissibility of violative evidence. On the other hand, the Charter's guarantees of a prompt trial have reduced the time taken to bring accused persons to trial from years in some jurisdictions to a matter of months – not, however, without a price: the dismissal of many cases for violative delays.

Another way in which the Charter impinges on the litigation process is by expanding the ambit of inquiry in a particular lawsuit. In an article in the *Law Quarterly Review*,[31] I discussed the fact that judges are often required to consider not only what is right between the parties, but also the wider impact of their decisions on persons not party to the litigation. A Charter tends to transform the debate from an adversarial debate between two parties to a polycentric inquiry, where effects on persons not before the court become relevant. This poses new challenges for the litigation process. How do we hear from the unrepresented parties? One answer, which the Canadian Supreme Court has adopted, is to receive the submissions of intervenors, who in some cases have changed the course of the law. And there are other problems. How does the court assess the social impact of going one way or another on a controversial policy issue when called upon to determine whether an infringement of individual rights is justified by the aim of the legislation? How does it get evidence on such questions? Are appellate courts confined to the record before the court on such matters, or can they receive additional information, apply common sense or take judicial notice of facts? Such questions increasingly bedevil courts even in countries possessing no entrenched charter of rights. But there can be no doubt that a charter magnifies these problems.

In addition, the Charter may be changing the way in which judges go about judging. Donovan Waters, referring to the willingness of Canadian courts to reassess legal doctrine from the standpoint of first principles, has written:

> In Canada also the Charter of Rights and Freedoms, which came into force in 1982, has put the courts into the front line of what in my opinion can only be described as policy-making. I cannot over-emphasize the impact this constitutional change has increasingly had on judicial attitudes throughout the country, and at all levels of courts. So far as private law is concerned, the fresh winds of a novel kind that were generated by Lord Denning's period of judicial office were received with particular welcome in Canada, and they are welcome still. As one might expect, then, there is an open attitude towards generalised principle that to all appearances was not in existence a quarter of a century ago.[32]

Finally, it may be noted that not only has the Charter changed the role of legislators and courts, but it may also be changing the way in which they work together to improve the law. Canada's former abortion law provides an example. The Supreme Court struck it down in 1988,[33] leading the way to new draft legislation and a political debate which has yet to be resolved.[34] In other areas, however, the judicial–legislative partnership has proved more productive. One example is the introduction of a revised rape-shield law.[35] In other cases, when the courts have struck down legislation, the legislators have moved to rectify the deficiency, even where the rectification was arguably against the government's immediate political interests. An example is the *Dixon* case, on which I sat as a trial judge.[36] I found the electoral boundaries in the province of

British Columbia to violate the Charter guarantee of the right to vote. Rather than declare the electoral law immediately invalid – which would have left the province without the means to hold an election should one become necessary – I stipulated a time period during which the government could introduce the necessary reforms. The government did so without undue delay.

I like to think that Canada is developing a new constitutional tradition predicated on recognition that the courts and legislators each have a role to play in governance. The courts, for their part, must respect the proper legislative role and must be careful not to trench too much upon it. The legislators, for their part, must discharge that role by responding appropriately when legislation is declared unconstitutional. As former British Columbia Chief Justice Nemetz said:

> If any law is inconsistent with the provisions of the Charter, it is the court's duty, to the extent of such inconsistency, to declare it to be of no force or effect (s. 52(1)).

> Before the Charter, the courts could and did declare legislation invalid on the division of powers grounds. When they did so, we know of no recent occasion when the legislative branch of government did not faithfully attempt to correct the impugned legislation. Likewise, when this court declares a statute or portion thereof to be 'of no force and effect' where it is inconsistent with the Charter, it is for the legislature to decide what remedial steps should be taken in view of that declaration. Section 24(1) of the Charter empowers the courts to grant citizens remedies where their guaranteed rights are infringed or denied . . . .

> It would be anomalous, indeed, if such powers were reserved only for cases where limitations are expressly enacted and not for cases where an unconstitutional limitation results because of omission in a statute.[37]

As a result of the changes that the Charter has brought to the Canadian legal system, Canadian judges and lawyers are beginning to seek ways to revise their processes to cope with the new demands imposed by the Charter and other recent developments such as the increasing use of social impact expert evidence. The Supreme Court of Canada, in the years after the enactment of the Charter, conducted a thorough reorganization of its procedures. The result is that the Court, while hearing more cases and rendering more important decisions than ever before, is up to date and efficient. I am convinced that similar changes can be made in other areas.

The Charter and the Individual

I have left for last the most difficult effect of the Charter to gauge, and perhaps the most troubling. I refer to the relationship between a constitutional bill of rights and the values which a society espouses. At the outset of this chapter and during its course, I have been drawn to comment on the tension between the state and the individual, between the majority and the minority. I have suggested that the Charter may serve as a device for maintaining an optimal balance between the extremes that lie at the edges of liberal democracy – totalitarian majoritarianism at the one extreme and excessive individualism at the other extreme. But lurking behind the neat equation is a suspicion that a Charter may complicate it in ways we cannot fathom – a suspicion that perhaps a charter of rights and freedoms possesses its own unique dynamic which presses the democracy which embraces it towards the extreme of excessive individualism, regardless of the efforts of well-meaning and deferential judges to maintain an even balance between individual rights and the broader social interest; the suspicion – and I cannot put it higher than that – that the emphasis on individual rights that a charter effects may lead to an excessive concentration on the broader social plane on the rights of the individual. This fear, I sometimes suspect, lies at the heart of most of the criticisms the Charter has engendered among those who have paused to reflect upon it.

US scholars have noted a correlation between the growing ethic of self (the 'me generation') and a preoccupation with individual rights and litigiousness. One writer says:

> Americans' obsession with individual rights and their demands for compensation when they believe that those rights have been compromised ignore the reality that individuals do not live in a vacuum, but in a polity, or society, the largest of social institutions. In a polity, rights are often in conflict. Given limited resources, citizens often cannot exercise their rights without trampling upon the rights of others. Because rights often are incapable of being fully exercised, it is improper to 'fully' compensate an individual for the trampling of those rights. As such, '[r]ights are neither natural nor equal, they are not even equivalent or like.' They are reciprocal.[38]

A charter of rights, insofar as it emphasizes and gives public recognition to the ethic of individual rights, may be argued to abet the individualistic ethic at the expense of broader social responsibility. But it is perhaps more accurate to see a charter of rights as the full and inevitable consequence of a philosophical preoccupation with the individual that began with Rousseau, flowered with Freud, and has come to full maturity with the narcissism of the latter half of the twentieth century. Hence the pre-occupation throughout the world with charters of rights. Charters of rights are the natural and proper expression of the individualism which is the hallmark of our society. The question in such a society is not so much whether it should adopt a constitutional bill of rights, but of how and when the drive for recognition of individual rights should occur. Even in societies which have not formally adopted a charter of rights, rights are an issue. Thus in Australia, the High Court has been criticized for judicially 'creating' a charter of rights as a consequence of two recent decisions recognizing an implied right of free political expression.[39] The Chief Justice, Sir Anthony Mason, noting the imperative of individual rights in a modern democratic society, has suggested that a formally adopted bill of rights may in fact leave less scope for judicial creativity. The people are considered to have spoken through such a charter and the courts are not seen as creating rights but defining them.[40] The courts, in the absence of a charter of rights, are caught in the squeeze between the populist majoritarian view which would deny all individual rights when they conflict with the majority's will, and the twentieth-century ethic of individual rights. The Australian experience thus suggests that the absence of a charter of rights may not be the solution to the rights question in a modern democratic society.

If we accept that the rights debate is with us, charter or no charter, the question becomes one of how a modern democracy can best reflect the individualist ethic of society, while fulfilling its responsibilities towards the collective morality. It seems to me that the best way to do this is through a carefully drafted charter of rights, which guarantees individual rights in the context of society as a whole. This, as I see it, is what the Canadian Charter of Rights and Freedoms seeks to do. It is not merely a compendium of absolute guarantees of individual rights, on the model of the US Bill of Rights. Rather, it acknowledges through sections 1, 24 and 33 that rights must sometimes yield to each other and to the superior interest of the collectivity. These provisions, buttressed by an emerging jurisprudence that sees rights as qualified and limited by each other,[41] give promise of the capacity to provide the balance between individual rights and the collective good which our society so desperately needs.

CONCLUSION

It is true that the Charter is far from perfect. Having worked with it for the past 12 years, I cannot help but be aware of its shortcomings and, indeed, of my own shortcomings as a judge. Yet for all its imperfections and for all the criticisms, I remain firmly convinced that Canadians feel that their charter is working, that it is viable, and that it would be wrong to give it up. One of the strongest indicators of this feeling is that during recurrent episodes of constitution-making that have marked the decade following the adoption of the Charter, the one thing which no one seriously suggested was that it should be repealed. In this imperfect world, where strife, indignity and marginalization pose the greatest threat, I believe that the Canadian Charter of Rights and Freedoms offers us hope and a means to combat that threat.

NOTES

1. Part I of Schedule B to the Canada Act, 1982 (UK) (31 Eliz. 2, c. 11); also cited as the Constitution Act, SC 1982, Pt. 1.
2. Rt. Hon. Sir R. Megarry, The Judge (1983) 13 *Manitoba Law Journal* 189, at p. 190.
3. P. H. Russell, The effect of a charter of rights on the policy-making role of Canadian courts (1982) 25 *Canadian Public Administration* 1, at p. 32.
4. In an act of protest against the Charter, Quebec's Parti Québécois government passed Bill 62, entitled An Act Respecting the Constitution Act, 1982, SQ 1982, c. 21, which added a standard-form notwithstanding clause to every statute in force in Quebec on 16 April 1982 and every statute passed thereafter. This practice was discontinued in 1985 with the election of a Liberal government, and the blanket override was allowed to lapse in 1987. Nevertheless, a notwithstanding clause has been inserted in five subsequent statutes in Quebec to preclude Charter challenges. While four of these appear to have occasioned little if any comment, the fifth has been the subject of much controversy. Bill C-178, An Act to Amend the Charter of the French Language, SQ 1988, c. 54, prohibited the use of languages other than French on outside commercial signs. At the expiration of the five-year override period, the Language Bill was allowed to die, and a new bill which complied with the Charter was adopted.

Outside Quebec, the section has been used only once. The province of Saskatchewan inserted a notwithstanding clause to protect back-to-work legislation (the SGEU Dispute Settlement Act, SS 1984–85–86, c. 111) which had been held to be unconstitutional by the Saskatchewan Court of Appeal: *RWDSU* v. *Government of Saskatchewan*, [1985] 5 WWR 97. The Supreme Court of Canada later allowed the government's appeal: [1987] 1 SCR 460. This latter decision indicated that the use of s. 33 had been unnecessary. Neither the federal Parliament nor any other province has invoked s. 33. See P. Hogg, *Constitutional Law of Canada*, 3rd edn (Toronto: Carswell, 1992), pp. 891 *et seq.*
5. *R.* v. *Keegstra* [1990] 3 SCR 697.
6. *R.* v. *Butler* [1992] 1 SCR 452.
7. F. L. Morton, The charter revolution and the court party (1992) 30 *Osgoode Hall Law Journal* 627.
8. *Ibid.*, p. 627. Statement attributed to the Honourable David Peterson, former Premier of Ontario.
9. P. S. Stamatakos, The bar in America: the role of elitism in a liberal democracy (1992–3) 26 *University of Michigan Journal of Law Reform* 853, at pp. 873–4.
10. J. D. Whyte, On not standing for notwithstanding (1990) 28 *Alberta Law Review* 347, at p. 352. Whyte acknowledges that not all interests in the Charter can be justified on the basis that they enhance the democratic process. He also looks to legalism and federalism as

two other concepts which justify the role of the Charter and judicial review.

11. Other similar views may be found in J. H. Ely, *Democracy and Distrust* (Cambridge, Mass.: Harvard University Press, 1980), and Chapter 6 of P. Monahan, *The Charter, Federalism and the Supreme Court of Canada* (Toronto: Carswell, 1987). The opposing view is presented, among other places, in A. Petter and A. C. Hutchinson, Rights in conflict: the dilemma of charter legitimacy (1989) 23 *UBC Law Review* 531.

12. *Irwin Toy Ltd* v. *Quebec* (AG) [1989] 1 SCR 927, at p. 968.

13. *Ibid.*, p. 976.

14. A. Cairns, Ritual, taboo and bias in constitutional controversies in Canada, or constitutional talk Canadian style (1990) 54 *Saskatchewan Law Review* 121, at p. 127. Professor Cairns, a University of British Columbia political scientist, has developed this theme in several lectures and papers.

15. P. H. Russell, Political purposes of the Canadian Charter of Rights and Freedoms (1983) 61 *Canadian Bar Review* 30, at pp. 48–50.

16. The susceptibility of executive action to review was discussed in *Operation Dismantle* v. *The Queen*, [1985] 1 SCR 441.

17. The most famous of these decisions is that in *Brown* v. *Board of Education* 347 US 483 (1954), where the Court refused to follow *Plessy* v. *Ferguson* 163 US 537 (1896), which had established the 'separate but equal' doctrine authorizing racial segregation in public facilities.

18. *Rodriguez* v. *British Columbia (Attorney General)* [1993] 3 SCR 519.

19. *Thibaudeau* v. *Canada* [1994] 2 F.C. 189 (CA), rev'd [1995] 2 SCR 627.

20. [1989] 1 SCR 143.

21. *R.* v. *Brydges* [1990] 1 SCR 190.

22. *R.* v. *Edwards Books and Art* [1986] 2 SCR 713; *R.* v. *Chaulk* [1990] 3 SCR 1303.

23. See, for example, *R.* v. *Collins* [1987] 1 SCR 265; *R.* v. *Duarte* [1990] 1 SCR 30; *R.* v. *Thompson* [1990] 2 SCR 1111; *R.* v. *Grant* [1993] 3 SCR 223; *R.* v. *Plant* [1993] 3 SCR 281; *R.* v. *Wiley* [1993] 3 SCR 263.

24. In *Reference re Manitoba Language Rights* [1985] 1 SCR 721, the Court declared that the unilingual enactments of the Manitoba Legislature were inconsistent with the requirements of the Manitoba Act, 1870, RSC 1970, App. II, and were invalid and of no force and effect because the constitutionally required manner and form for their enactment had not been followed. However, in order to avoid the creation of a legal vacuum in the province, the Court delayed the effect of its declaration for the minimum time required for translation into both official languages, re-enactment, printing and publishing.

The Court has also delayed declarations of invalidity in *R.* v. *Brydges op. cit.* (right to be informed of duty counsel when detained), *R.* v. *Swain* [1991] 1 SCR 933 (automatic detention of an accused found not guilty by reasons of insanity contrary to ss. 7 and 9 of the Charter) and in *R.* v. *Bain* [1992] 1 SCR 91 (right of the prosecution to peremptorily challenge four jurors and ask up to 48 jurors to stand by violative of s. 11(d) of the Charter). See also *Dixon* v. *A.G.B.C.* (1989) 35 BCLR (2d) 273 (S.C.).

25. *Slaight Communications Inc.* v. *Davidson* [1989] 1 SCR 1038.

26. *R.* v. *Seaboyer*; *R.* v. *Gayme* [1991] 2 SCR 577.

27. *Toronto Star*, 7 July 1991.

28. J. Simpson, The Charter intrudes on yet another essentially political question, *The Globe and Mail*, 7 August 1991.

29. At least one respected observer suggests that this exists as a possibility in Canada, particularly if the ideologies of the major political parties in Canada become more polarized on issues which may arise in Charter litigation: P. H. Russell, *The Judiciary in Canada: The Third Branch of Government* (Toronto: McGraw-Hill Ryerson, 1987), p. 117.

30. J. Simpson, *op. cit.*

31. B. McLachlin, The role of judges in modern commonwealth society (1994) 110 *Law Quarterly Review* 260.

32. 'The Remedial Constructive Trust', presented at the Oxford Symposium on Unjust Enrichment, Summer 1993.

33. *R.* v. *Morgentaler* [1988] 1 SCR 30.

34. Draft legislation was defeated in the Senate and there has been no subsequent attempt to introduce another bill.

35. Bill C-49, An Act to Amend the Criminal Code (Sexual Assault), SC 1992, c. 38, was enacted following the decision of the Supreme Court in *R.* v. *Seaboyer*; *R.* v. *Gayme, op. cit.*

36. *Dixon* v. *A.G.B.C.* (1989), 35 *op. cit.*

37. *Hoogbruin* v. *Attorney General of British Columbia* [1986] 2 WWR 700 (BCCA), at pp. 704–5.

38. P. S. Stamatakos, *op. cit.*, at p. 884 (footnote omitted).

39. *Australian Capital Television Pty Ltd* v. *Commonwealth* (1992), 108 ALR 577 and *Nationwide News Pty Ltd* v. *Wills* (1992), 108 ALR 681. See H. P. Lee, The Australian High Court and implied fundamental guarantees [1993] *Public Law* 606.

40. In private conversation.

41. This approach was first enunciated by Wilson, J in *Edmonton Journal* v. *Alberta (Attorney General)* [1989] 2 SCR 1326. It has since been reaffirmed in a number of cases, including *Rocket* v. *Royal College of Dental Surgeons of Ontario* [1990] 2 SCR 232; *R.* v. *Keegstra, op. cit.*; *Committee for the Commonwealth of Canada* v. *Canada* [1991] 1 SCR 139; *R.* v. *Seaboyer*; *R.* v. *Gayme, op. cit.*; and *Young* v. *Young* [1993] 4 SCR 3.

3

Human Rights, Social Democracy and Constitutional Reform

K. D. Ewing

INTRODUCTION

In this chapter I propose to address a central question relating to the current debate in the UK concerning constitutional reform, including in particular the better protection of human rights. Many commentators have considered this question before, though they have not always revealed the complexity or more significantly the ideological significance of the issues raised. My concern is not to argue against human rights, but rather to consider the extent to which their constitutional entrenchment on the North American model can really be justified in a society which still accepts the legitimacy of the principles of social democracy.

CONSTITUTIONAL REFORM

Constitutional reform has become one of the few industries to have grown in recent years, born largely of the excesses and abuses of life under the Thatcher governments and their progeny. Foremost among the demands of the reformers is the adoption of a bill of rights or the incorporation into domestic law of the European Convention on Human Rights (ECHR), though there are other items on the menu. The case for a bill of rights or for the incorporation of the ECHR is supported by such distinguished bodies as the IPPR[1] and Liberty,[2] as well as by Charter 88. It is also supported by the Liberal Democrats[3] and by the Labour Party, which is in favour of incorporating the ECHR as the first step towards the introduction of a UK bill of rights. Distinguished judges have jumped on board, the initiative having the support of the Lord Chief Justice[4] and the Master of the Rolls.[5] In the view of the latter, there is no task more central to the purpose of modern democracy, or more central to the judicial function, than that of seeking to protect, within the law, the basic human rights of the citizen, against invasion by other citizens or by the state itself.[6] Yet the ability of English judges to protect human rights and reconcile conflicting rights is said to be inhibited by the failure of successive governments over many years to incorporate into UK law the ECHR.

The case for constitutional reform is strong and its proponents influential. Given the galaxy of stars in favour of the entrenchment of rights in particular, it is with some hesitation that I venture to dissent. This is all the more so when I read that the case for entrenchment is so powerful that the burden lies 'on the opponents to make good their grounds of opposition'.[7] It is perhaps this casual shifting of the burden of proof which makes some of us so nervous of the venture and cautious of those who want more power. But opposition to the entrenchment of rights cannot be based solely on our concern that there are those who wish to exercise power over us, particularly as in this case it is done with the noblest of intentions and for our own good. Opposition to these changes must have a more rational basis, which I would suggest is rooted in our perceptions of what our vision of democracy involves and the contribution which entrenched rights would have in promoting or obstructing that vision. The essence of my case is that before we ask whether we want constitutional reform, we must have a clear view of the type of society in which we want to live and draft accordingly. We must tailor our constitution to the goals of that society so that it will sustain rather than subvert these goals.

The case for reform reflects a view of government based on the notion of limited popular sovereignty subordinated to certain liberal values.[8] Limited sovereignty in the sense that what the reformers have in mind is the transfer of power from a sovereign parliament to the courts. This unelected, unrepresentative and (largely) unaccountable body of public officials will be empowered to tell a popularly elected parliament what it may or may not do,[9] in terms of a document which its supporters concede is open-ended and the meaning of which will 'change as social and political attitudes develop'.[7] It is a view of government subordinated to certain liberal values in the sense that neither a bill of rights nor the ECHR could possibly be regarded as in any sense ideologically neutral. So much was recognized by the so-called bourgeois (non-socialist) parties, in Sweden, where the ECHR was incorporated into domestic law only last year. It was done at the initiative of the political right, which saw the ECHR as a restraint on social democracy – perhaps they exaggerate its practical significance. But they did see it as an important symbol for the better protection of certain liberal icons (such as private property) and to restrain certain social democratic institutions (such as strong trade unions).

But apart from this liberal democratic agenda, there is a different democratic agenda in terms of the role of the individual as a participant in the life of the community and in terms of the role and function of the state and its institutions. This may be referred to as a social democratic or democratic socialist agenda, still a legitimate form of government despite events in Berlin in November 1989. The concept of social democracy is admittedly rather elusive, with one valuable study pointing out that the debate about its content is long and usually circuitous.[10] It is also a dynamic concept and perhaps also culturally sensitive in many of its aspects. But so far as the constitutional lawyer is concerned, social democracy is about the power of representative institutions on the one hand and the way in which that power is exercised on the other. The constitutional structure ought to be one which gives the fullest expression to the right of political equality and one which facilitates rather than impedes measures designed to promote either social and economic equality or social and economic equity. I am not denying that the classical civil liberties have a role to play in this.[11] But I would contend that there is no role for entrenched rights if their effect is to subvert what may be the legitimate aims of constitutional government. It is my view that it is not possible to entrench civil and political rights on the north American model consistently with the goals of social democratic constitutionalism which I have identified.

THE PRINCIPLE OF PARLIAMENTARY SOVEREIGNTY

The first principle of social democratic constitutionalism relates to the power of representative institutions. It is the principle of parliamentary sovereignty. I appreciate that it may seem strange to many radicals that this highly contentious principle should be defended and even celebrated rather than traduced, for there is perhaps no easier target to unite all constitutional reformers. Sir Thomas Bingham has referred to the 'weakening of parliamentary influence on the conduct of government'[12] while Lord Hailsham has condemned the elective dictatorship[13] and Tony Benn has criticized the 'absolute premiership'.[14] Even Paul Hirst has joined the debate, asserting that 'Parliament is a pre-democratic institution' and that 'the core of Britain's constitution . . . pre-dates ideas about constitutional limitation of the powers of the legislature that one finds in the American constitution and all constitutions derived from it'.[15] It would be hard to deny that the power of Parliament has diminished or indeed that democracy was added slowly after 1832. But in a sense that is not the point. You cannot reduce a democratic deficit by doubling it, any more than you can do the same with a financial deficit. Nor does it follow from the origins of a principle that it cannot metamorphise to serve a contemporary imperative.

So although it cannot be denied that there are problems concerning the weakness of Parliament in the British constitution, it is important that in our criticisms we should maintain a sense of balance and perspective. The doctrine of parliamentary sovereignty does not exist as an end in itself. Nor does it exist to enable the government (them) to do things to the people (us). Rather, as an instrument of social democratic constitutionalism, it would be simply the constitutional and legal expression of the first principle of any social democratic society, which is the right of the people of the community to political equality – a right which may be regarded as one of the most fundamental of all human rights. As is recognized by the Swedish Instrument of Government of 1974, a social democratic society is one which above all is based on the notion of political equality, that is to say 'equality of influence over decision-making'. That right of equality of influence applies equally to everyone (subject to a number of contested qualifications relating to age and capacity) and it applies regardless of sex, race or social status. As Jack Lively has written, 'To allow or encourage universal entry into the political community is to recognise all people as sources of values and to accept in consequence that each has a right to be consulted and play a part in the social allocation of values'.[16]

Despite its pre-democratic origins, the doctrine of parliamentary sovereignty is a necessary feature of social democracy as the legal and constitutional expression of the popular sovereignty of the people, all participating as equals in the election of representatives who in turn are popularly accountable on a regular basis. I understand that there are problems about the efficiency of Parliament. I understand also that there may be a strong case for its reform. But I cannot understand how we can remain faithful and loyal to this first principle – the right of equality in decision-making – by transferring power from Parliament to the courts. The effect of such a move would be to transfer sovereign power and the right to participate in the supreme political decision-making body of the state to a small group of public officials over whom we have no control and to a process from which we are effectively excluded. Unlike rule-making through a sovereign Parliament in the election of which everyone potentially plays an equal part, and in which everyone is entitled to equal respect, rule-making by constitutional adjudication is reserved for appointed judges, and self-selecting and highly trained advocates, with community participation being confined to the role of lit-igant, a process of participation available to those with the financial resources required. The people have no say in making the most funda-mental of all the rules by which they are all to be governed.[17]

It is here that the onus of proof is firmly back in the court of those who propose the entrenchment of human rights. By virtue of the doctrine of the legal sovereignty of Parliament, political sovereignty is vested in sev-eral million electors. Under an entrenched bill of rights or the ECHR, both legal and political sovereignty would be vested in 13 people, nor-mally sitting in little groups of five at a time. But quite apart from the existence of this juristocratic veto on the democratic decisions of the com-munity, surely the other subversive feature of entrenched rights is the fact that the veto may be initiated by groups who have no standing what-soever in the democratic process of the state. The entrenchment of rights is a way of undermining the power of the people still further by effec-tively enfranchising the corporation, for so far as I can tell, constitutional rights may have been intended for real people, but in practice they apply equally to multinational corporations, with all their resources, as they do to individuals. As Ralph Nader and Carl Mayer have pointed out, 'cor-porations enjoy virtually the same umbrella of constitutional protections as individuals do'.[18] We thus have the spectacle of an unelected and un-accountable body of people acting at the suit of a multinational corporation to determine in the name of human rights what it is that the elected and accountable representatives of the people can or cannot do on their behalf. That is not only contrary to principle – it is also grotesque.

Without wishing to exhume decently buried arguments about the nature of the corporation, the debate between the Realists and others (the debate involving Maitland, Geldart and Dicey[19]), it does seem rather bizarre that the corporation – the creature of the state – should be em-powered to dictate to the community how the people may or may not govern themselves.[20] Yet this is precisely what will happen, with Nader and Mayer pointing out that in the USA the legal system is 'creating unaccountable Frankensteins that have human powers but are constitu-tionally shielded from much actual and potential law enforcement'.[18] But it is not only in the USA that we find a 'corporate drive for constitutional parity with real people'.[18] Recent decisions of the Supreme Court of Canada have recognized the right of the corporation to rely on constitu-tional guarantees of freedom of religion,[21] freedom of expression,[22] and freedom from arbitrary search and seizure,[23] while in Australia the new implied bill of rights has been used by television companies complaining about restrictions on election broadcasts introduced to promote fair elections.[24] The ECHR also applies to corporations, as a number of recent cases have shown, the most important of these being *Autronic AG v. Switzerland*,[25] in which it was held by 16 votes to 2 that neither the applicant's legal status as a limited company nor the fact that its activities were commercial could deprive it of the protection of Article 10. The right to freedom of expression applies to everyone, whether natural or legal persons, and it is applicable to profit-making corporate bodies in the business sphere. The ECHR thus properly becomes a subject for study in the commercial law class.

POLITICAL EQUALITY AND THE ROLE OF CIVIL LIBERTIES

So, it is suggested that the entrenchment of human rights would not serve a social democratic agenda, but would rather frustrate it: first, because it would undermine the principle of political equality (in terms of giving some citizens a greater entrenched role than others), and second, because it would facilitate the political exercise of economic power (that is to say the enfranchisement of corporations which have no claim to be represented in government in the first place). This is not to say, however, that the classical civil liberties or human rights should not be protected by law. No-one is denying their importance, which is clear and compelling, and well described by Eduard Bernstein, who wrote that

> the idea of the oppression of the minority by the majority ... is absolutely repugnant to the modern mind. Nowadays we find the oppression of the minority by the majority 'undemocratic', although it was originally held to be quite consistent with government by the people. As we understand it today, the concept of democracy includes an idea of justice, that is, equality of rights for all members of the community, and this sets limits to the rule of the majority – which is what government by the people amounts to, in any concrete case.[26]

But although there may be little room for argument about the need to protect these rights, there may be scope for debate about their purpose and the most appropriate method for their protection. So far as purpose is concerned, it is possible to argue that these rights and freedoms are desirable ends in themselves. But it is also possible to argue that, although important, they are nevertheless secondary in the sense that they are designed to facilitate and reinforce one of the most fundamental of all rights and freedoms, which is the right to political equality. Questions about purpose lead directly to considerations of the method by which political rights and freedoms are to be recognized or protected by law. Essentially, there are at least three ways by which this could be done. The first is by the common law, as is currently the position in Britain. Second, it could be done in a rather stronger manner by legislation, subject always to the power of Parliament to amend and adjust. We have some experience of this technique in this country, most notably in the Representation of the People Act 1983 in so far as it deals with the right to vote. Third, it could be by some constitutional device, which at its strongest would withdraw power from Parliament, unless certain conditions were said to exist, such as a threat to national security or public order.[27]

So even if we can satisfactorily answer the questions raised earlier about the integrity of a *process* which is subversive of our principle of political equality, we must now ask a further question. To what extent would the *operation in practice* of the constitutional entrenchment of civil and political liberties tend to reinforce or subvert the democratic goals which they are designed to serve? The clear answer would appear to be that it is not only the *process* of constitutional entrenchment, but also its *likely results*, which are subversive of the goal of political equality. As a result, our desire to give legal recognition to the classical civil and political liberties can rationally only be by a form which is weaker than constitutional entrenchment on the North American model. The evidence from a number of common law jurisdictions, starting with the landmark decision of the US Supreme Court in *Buckley* v. *Valeo*,[28] shows clearly and conclusively that the entrenchment of civil and political rights serves to entrench political inequalities of a different sort: not this time by excluding the people from the sovereign decision-making process, but in the sense of permitting money and economic power disproportionate access to the decision-making process and a disproportionate influence in determining the outcome of that process. The entrenchment of rights thus brings those who wield economic power the freedom disproportionately to influence political outcomes and, if unsuccessful, to challenge in the courts the political decisions of which they disapprove. And to recap, the wealth in question may not even be the wealth of a citizen, but of a foreign-based but domestically trading multinational corporation.

The concern about the malignant influence of money in the political process has led in a number of countries to the introduction of sometimes detailed legislation designed to control the political influence of economic resources. In the UK there is legislation which serves the same end, such as the Broadcasting Act 1990, which forbids the broadcast of advertisements for a political purpose.[29] But perhaps the most notable, detailed and comprehensive legislation of this kind is that which was passed in the USA just before and just after Watergate in the early 1970s,[30] though similarly intentioned measures have been introduced in Australia and Canada, restricting speech in the interests of free and fair elections.[31] The US legislation addressed a number of issues, requiring: the mandatory reporting and disclosure of donations to political parties and candidates; a restriction on the amount which could be donated to any candidate or political party by an individual or political action committee; a restriction on the total permitted expenditure by political parties, candidates and so-called third parties; and a system of public funding for presidential elections. Both the publicity requirements and the contribution limits were upheld by the Supreme Court but the spending limits ran into the buffers of the First Amendment, despite having been supported by the Court of Appeals. Although it was accepted there that the main concern was with large contributions to candidates, it was also accepted by the lower court that corrupt and pernicious practices are likely to occur when there are no effective limits on campaign expenditures.

In reversing the lower court the Supreme Court struck down the spending limits as they applied to candidates and third parties. It was not simply that the limits were too low, though they were low. The reasons appear to go deeper and are perhaps best reflected in the immortal line that 'the concept that government may restrict the speech of some elements of our society in order to enhance the relative voice of others is wholly foreign to the First Amendment, which was designed to secure the widest possible dissemination of information from diverse and antagonistic sources'.[32] The Court continued by asserting in even more memorable terms that 'The First Amendment's protection against governmental abridgement of free expression cannot properly be made to depend on a person's financial ability to engage in public discussion'.[33] This explicit entrenchment of political inequality has been described by one recent commentator as the 'modern analogue' of *Lockner* v. *New York*,[34] 'offering an adventurous interpretation of the Constitution so as to invalidate a redistributive measure having and deserving broad democratic support'.[35] But for all that, and despite being the most important Supreme Court decision since *Brown* v. *Board of Education*,[36] *Buckley* v. *Valeo* is barely known in this country and rarely mentioned in the literature. Yet it can hardly be dismissed as the eccentric decision of an eccentric court, for apart from the fact that only Justice White dissented on the point, the decision has been adopted by courts in Canada (twice)[37] and Australia, with McHugh J in the latter jurisdiction reading *Buckley* v. *Valeo* with approval as a decision which held unconstitutional 'laws im-

posing restrictions on campaign expenditures by various people notwithstanding that the object of the laws was to prevent the rich from
corrupting the political process'.[38]

THE POLITICAL PURPOSE OF SOCIAL DEMOCRACY

The first objection to the entrenchment of rights is thus that it would present serious problems on a number of levels for what ought to be our most
cherished principle, the principle of political equality. The problems with
entrenchment relate to questions of access to decision-making and also to
the power to influence the outcome of the democratic process. A second
question for consideration is how would such a device relate to the social
and economic goals of a social democratic society? As suggested above,
social democracy is about the power of representative institutions, but also
about the way in which that power is exercised. The essence of a social
democratic state, as John Griffith hinted in *Socialist Register*, is strong
government to harness public power for the public good.[39] The state is
thus a means of empowering people, rather than something of which they
ought to be suspicious. The purpose of a social democratic constitution
should be to lubricate rather than constrain this function of the state, as a
force which can do things for us as well as to us. The question we must
now consider is whether or not the entrenchment of civil and political
rights would present any difficulty for the constitutional objectives of a
social democratic state. But before we can answer that question, there are
a number of others which we must consider.

The first is to identify the objectives of a social democratic state. They
are not easy to articulate, but a possible starting point is Article 2 of the
Swedish Instrument of Government of 1974. This provides that

> The personal, economic, and cultural welfare of the individual shall
> be the fundamental aims of the activities of the community. In par-
> ticular it shall be incumbent upon the community to secure the
> right to work, to housing, and to education and to promote social
> care and security as well as a favourable living environment.

But this is only part of the story. As is reflected in the Council of Europe's
Social Charter of 1961[40] and in various ILO Conventions (but particularly Convention 87 on freedom of association and Convention 98 on the

right to organize and collective bargaining),[41] the development of a social democratic agenda does not just mean the exercise of state power directly to promote the social, economic and cultural welfare of the community. It also anticipates the development of strong autonomous institutions as a means through which people may assert control over their own lives and as a means of defending and promoting their interests. What is anticipated then is the use of the power of the state to confer benefits, in the shape of rights, freedoms and immunities on individuals and their organizations. This may also require the imposition of controls on those who exercise great private power, to ensure that that power is not exercised in a manner which is inconsistent with the needs of the community as a whole.

But just as the entrenchment of civil and political rights is subversive of the right to political equality, so the entrenchment of civil and political rights is potentially subversive of a social democratic political agenda. Again there are two reasons for this, one being based on questions of principle, while the other relates to the impact in practice of an entrenched code of civil and political liberties. So far as the former is concerned, the primary difficulty concerns the subordinate status which would thereby be accorded to social and economic rights. Although it is true that the social democratic agenda is one which both respects and seeks to protect civil liberties and political freedom, it does not follow that the protection of those rights should enjoy an elevated or preferred constitutional status. If the goal is to promote the social and economic welfare of the people consistently with civil liberties and political freedom, this does not mean the pursuit of these goals subordinated to other concerns, but at best in a symbiotic relationship with these concerns. What this means in turn is that at the very best civil liberties and political freedoms should as a matter of principle enjoy constitutional parity with social and economic rights, both in terms of the manner of their protection and in terms also of the manner of their enforcement. So if the ECHR is to be entrenched as a higher form of law, then so too should the Council of Europe's Social Charter of 1961, and it should be entrenched in the same way and have the same effect.

Under the UK's current 'political constitution'[42] it has been largely unnecessary to confront matters of this kind. It has been possible to accommodate the development of social democratic principles and the election of social democratic governments without the need for formal constitutional change.[43] Social and economic rights have been developed in conjunction with and have not been subordinated to a veto exercised in the name of civil liberties and political freedom. If, however, the ECHR is formally incorporated into domestic law that will, of course, change, inviting some consideration of the parallel incorporation of the Social

Charter of 1961 (and the incorporation of both in a manner which is consistent with the principle of political equality discussed above). Yet
although there has been much debate about the incorporation of the
ECHR, little attention has been paid to the Social Charter, even by those
on the left. Indeed, those who have considered the matter appear to have
rejected the idea. Thus, in the introduction to an interesting collection of
essays published on behalf of the IPPR, Anna Coote argues that 'in a
democracy civil liberties deserve a different constitutional status from
social rights' in the sense that

> if all individuals in a society were comfortably housed and enjoyed
> reasonable standards of health care, education and social insurance,
> but had no civil rights, that society would offer them no constitu-
> tional means of winning the rights they lacked. By contrast, a
> society in which individuals enjoyed the right to vote, and freedoms
> of speech, assembly, movement and so forth, would hold out the
> possibility of winning social rights through the democratic process.
> Civil rights can thus be seen as a means of achieving social rights.[44]

There are a number of problems with this approach, not the least of
which is that we already have the civil rights and political freedoms to
which Coote refers. What is not clear, however, is how their constitutional
entrenchment would better enable the homeless to be housed, the sick to
be cured, or the jobless to find work. But that is not all. A second problem is that such analysis diminishes the importance of the social
democratic vision by creating a veto on the introduction of social and
economic initiatives – a veto of indeterminate scope exercised in the
name of civil liberties and political freedom. What this approach also
elides is the fact that this veto is a source of power in the hands of those
with a record of frustrating social democratic initiatives. Admittedly, it is
unclear how the courts would respond to those challenging the social
democratic agenda in the courts, just as it is equally unclear how the formal incorporation of social and economic rights would be a safeguard
against unwelcome judicial decisions. But before examining how social
democratic institutions have fared under constitutional adjudication, it is
worthy of recall that the liberal values embraced by the common law[45]
have been unable easily to cope with the institutions of social democracy
or their activities. We need only look at the cases which almost destroyed
the early Labour Party,[46] undermined the power of the trade unions,[47]
and restricted the power of Labour local authorities seeking to implement equal pay for women and fair wages for all their staff.[48]

SOCIAL DEMOCRACY AND JUDICIAL REVIEW

How then is an entrenched bill of rights or an incorporated ECHR likely to affect the operation of social and economic rights? It is impossible to say for sure, but we can learn some lessons from the jurisprudence of the European Court of Human Rights, as well as from the experience of other jurisdictions, while we should always be mindful of our own experiences with the common law. It has to be said that concern about the operation of entrenched rights is not new. It is now well known that the UK played a key, if sometimes reluctant, part in drafting the ECHR. But, as Geoffrey Marston has shown, by no means all the members of the Cabinet were untroubled by the initiative. The sceptics included the Chancellor of the Exchequer, Sir Stafford Cripps, who reportedly claimed that 'a Government committed to the policy of a planned economy could not ratify this Convention', drawing attention to various draft articles 'which were inconsistent with the powers of economic control which were essential to the operation of a planned economy'. He is reported to have gone on to say that 'The draft Convention would be acceptable only to those who believed in a free economy and a minimum amount of State intervention in economic affairs.'[49]

It is far from clear whether these fears are well founded. But it is clear that social democratic institutions have not fared very well under the ECHR. The problem should not be overstated, but equally we are bound to learn from the lessons of the past. The point is illustrated by the jurisprudence under Article 11 of the ECHR, which provides a right to freedom of association, including the right to form and join trade unions. This is subject to the normal exceptions in paragraph 2. A number of cases have now tested the meaning of this guarantee, but none has succeeded where the complainant was seeking to enrich the content of the protection. Thus, the GCHQ unions failed to establish that their right to organize had been violated by the ban in 1985,[50] despite repeated findings to this effect by the ILO supervisory agencies.[51] Although it might be argued that the language of Article 11(2) was a major obstacle to the complaint, the same excuse is not available to explain the failure of the Court in a number of other cases to develop the meaning of Article 11(1) to include a right to bargain and a right to strike.[52] Taking a very minimalist view of the meaning of freedom of association, the Court concluded that Article 11 does not guarantee any particular treatment of trade unions or their members by the state but leaves to each state a free choice of the means to be used to allow unions to promote and protect their interests.

This policy of restraint contrasts sharply with the approach of the Court to the negative right of association, looked at so fondly by the Swedish bourgeois or non-socialist parties in their campaign for incorporation. There is in fact no negative right in the ECHR but it has been created by a less than subtle process of judicial activism. The leading case is the *British Rail* case, which challenged the practice of the closed shop as it then operated under the authority of what was then the Trade Union and Labour Relations Act 1974, as amended in 1976.[53] Although the Court was unwilling to imply a full right not to join a trade union as part of the guarantee in Article 11,[54] it expressed concern: first, about the fact that existing non-union employees could be required to join a trade union after a closed shop agreement was signed; second, about the fact that workers were not given a choice as to which unions to join; and third, because no provision was made to exempt people who had conscientious (as opposed to religious) objections to trade union membership. This exercise of judicial power (since extended to include a full right of non-association), to create a right which the *travaux préparatoires* show to have been deliberately excluded from the ECHR precisely because of the operation of the closed shop in some jurisdictions, which included the UK, contrasts sharply with the restraint of the Court when asked to take the technically easier step of adopting a less minimalist approach to the positive right.[55] When all is said and done, the Court has refused to intervene to protect trade unions but has been seen, rightly or wrongly, to undermine their collective strength in the name of individual liberty. Without wishing to intrude too far into the debates about the merits or otherwise of the closed shop, it remains, for all the problems it creates, not only a device for exercising power over people, but more importantly a device for exercising power on behalf of people.

This tension between judicial restraint and judicial activism in the social field is not confined to the European Court of Human Rights. The constitutional jurisprudence of a number of common law jurisdictions tells much the same story, the starting point perhaps being the landmark decision of the Privy Council in *Collymore* v. *Attorney General of Trinidad and Tobago*.[56] An attempt was made in that case to challenge legislation of 1956 which it was alleged had effectively removed the right to bargain and the right to strike. But in dismissing claims that the legislation had thereby contravened freedom of association guarantees in the Trinidad and Tobago constitution, the Privy Council held that freedom of association does not include the right to engage in collective bargaining or the right to strike, despite the surely correct assertion of counsel that without such protection the right to freedom of association would be empty of any worthwhile content. We find the same approach adopted by the Supreme Court of Canada in the famous trilogy of cases in 1987 on the right to strike.[57] There it was held that the constitutional guarantee of freedom of association merely includes the freedom to work for the establishment of an association, to belong to an association, to maintain it and to participate in its lawful activities. But it does not include the constitutional protection of the right to bargain or the right to strike. According to McIntyre J, freedom of association does not include the right to strike, because it cannot be said that it has become so much a part of our social and historical traditions that it has acquired the status of an immutable, fundamental right, firmly embedded in our traditions, our political and our social philosophy. This was a matter for the legislature and not the courts.

Yet while trade unions have gained very little at the trough of constitutional adjudication, as with the experience of the ECHR entrenched civil and political rights have been a source of irritation. The possibility then is of a measure of incompatibility between the entrenchment of civil and political rights on the one hand and the active promotion of a social democratic agenda on the other. Thus, in the Republic of Ireland the right to freedom of association was used to challenge trade union recognition legislation which created a system giving one union the status of exclusive bargaining agent.[58] In the same country 14 years later the same constitutional provision was used to restrict the right to take industrial action to enforce the closed shop,[59] and later still to protect individuals from dismissal because of their non-membership of a trade union.[60] Again, there is no express right not to associate: it is a matter purely of judicial invention.[61] A similar though not identical story can be told of the USA, where union shop and agency shop arrangements have been upheld, though at a high price. Legislation permitting union shop arrangements withstood First Amendment challenge, partly, it seems, because people could not be expelled from the union for any reason other than the non-payment of dues.[62] But in authorizing this very weak form of trade union security, the Supreme Court also said in 1977 that workers in a union or agency shop can be required to pay dues only for the purpose of defraying the cost of collective bargaining.[63] The contributions of dissenting members cannot be used to finance the union's political or ideological activities which are not germane to collective bargaining, even though, as was later recognized by the Supreme Court of Canada, it is necessary for unions 'to play a role in shaping the political, economic and social context within which particular collective agreements and labour relations disputes will be negotiated or resolved'.[64]

SOCIAL DEMOCRACY, HUMAN RIGHTS AND CONSTITUTIONAL REFORM

The essence of my argument so far is that before we ask whether we want constitutional reform, we must have a clear idea of the type of society we want to live in. We must tailor our constitution to the goals of that society so that the constitution will promote rather than subvert these goals. What I have also argued, though perhaps more explicitly, is that if we still see social democracy as a legitimate goal of government, then we need to think hard about the entrenchment of civil and political liberties on the North American model: first, because the operation of such a regime would tend to undermine the principle of political equality; second, because it would tend to extend the political opportunities of corporate power; and third, because it would tend to irritate the operation of social and economic reform and the institutions of social democracy. This is not to say, however, that there is no place for the better institutional protection of civil and political liberties. But it must be achieved in such a way as to support rather than subvert the principles which I have tried to outline, and it must be done in a manner which accords equal constitutional status to social and economic rights.

There is, I think, a way forward, though it is a form of protection by political rather than legal means. There is no reason in principle why civil and political rights should be entrenched on the North American model. There are other methods, as the experience of Sweden demonstrates. The Swedish Instrument of Government sets out in chapter 2 a list of fundamental freedoms. Some of these are absolute, such as the prohibition of capital punishment, and could be revoked or qualified only by a constitutional amendment. Others, however, may be qualified, including freedom of expression, freedom of assembly, and freedom of association. As originally drafted, the Constitution provided that these latter measures 'could be restricted by law', apparently without the need to satisfy any substantive conditions. So although set out in the Constitution, the civil and political liberties of the people of Sweden were not a great deal different from those of the people of the UK, to the extent that these are founded in the common law and may thus be restricted or qualified by legislation. In 1979, however, the Instrument of Government was amended in a number of ways.[65] First, there had now to be some 'purpose which is acceptable in a democratic society' before a restriction could be imposed on a constitutionally recognized right. The amendment also provided, however, that it would be the responsibility of the Constitutional Committee of the Riksdag to determine whether any bill affected one of the freedoms concerned.[66]

Under the Swedish system, the primary responsibility for the review of legislation is thus that of the legislature. This is not to deny that the courts also have a role. First, there is a system of what has been referred to as 'judicial preview' of legislation by a body called the Law Council, a body of three senior judges who are seconded full time to scrutinize legislation to ensure that it is consistent with the Constitution and, from the end of 1993, the ECHR, following its incorporation. Its views are clearly influential but not necessarily conclusive, and Parliament may ignore its advice. Second, it should not be suggested that there is no scope for judicial review under the Swedish Instrument of Government. But it would be true to say that it is quite limited. Thus the courts have the power under the Constitution to refuse to apply a statute only if the 'fault is manifest'.[67] This is taken to mean that there is little room for judicial scrutiny, with the courts observing the literal words of the Constitution in a manner which would not be recognized by their common law brothers and sisters. So far as I am aware, only a few statutes have been set aside by the courts, the grounds being that they were retrospective in their operation. It is regarded as one of the great achievements of the current social democratic opposition in Sweden that although the ECHR was incorporated in 1994,[68] they were able to resist any extension of the judicial power either to enforce the ECHR or to enforce the Constitution itself.[69] To the extent that it has been incorporated, it has been done principally by incorporating it into the procedure of scrutiny of legislation with only the same limited opportunity for the judicial review of legislation as in the case of alleged breaches of the Constitution.

What is particularly interesting for present purposes about the Swedish system is the principle and practice of parliamentary scrutiny. There is much, I think, to be said for adopting and adapting a procedure of this kind. It is more sympathetic than is judicial review to the notion of political equality in the sense that the final decision remains vested in the elected representatives of the people. In a social democratic system it would presumably also operate in a manner faithful to the social democratic goals of the Constitution. It could, however, be given a helping hand in this direction in the sense that an adapted arrangement of this kind could have a wider jurisdiction than its Swedish counterpart. Thus in order to ensure that social and economic rights enjoyed at least the same formal status as civil and political rights, such an arrangement could provide the basis for the incorporation into domestic law not only of the ECHR, but also of the Council of Europe's Social Charter, as well as key ILO Conventions, in particular Conventions 87 and 98, which are said to be fundamental to the ILO's existence,[70] but which the UK government has been found to have violated repeatedly in relation to the deregulatory free market labour law introduced since 1979. Indeed, if we

are concerned about the protection of rights, the sorry tale of the violation of ILO Conventions suggests that there is a more urgent case for the
constitutional protection of social and economic rights in this country
than there is for civil and political rights. We still have the right to vote
and the right to freedom of expression if we can afford it. But many
people no longer have a right to organize, a right to bargain, or a right
to strike.

Apart from these questions of jurisdiction, difficult questions are also
bound to arise with regard to the composition and powers of any such
scrutiny committee. One of the criticisms of the Swedish Committee, on
which the government has a majority, is that its members tend to divide
along party lines in what is a very strong party system of government. It
has also been suggested as a result, in a study by a retired justice of the
Supreme Court, that the Committee reaches conclusions that would not
be reached by a court and that it is no substitute for a stronger system of
judicial review. It is also said, however, that the risk of scrutiny by the
Committee and the danger of delay to legislation means that bills are
more carefully considered before they are introduced and that the views
of party members on the Committee will properly be taken into account.
The other question about such a committee, apart from its jurisdiction
and composition, relates to its powers. In Sweden, if the Constitutional
Committee concludes, at the request of not less than 10 members of the
Riksdag, that a bill does affect constitutional rights, the bill can be
delayed for a year, though the objections can be overridden by a special
majority of the House, which in this case is at least five-sixths, a possibly
impossible figure in a highly disciplined party system of government.
Any number of possibilities would be open for consideration were such a
method of scrutiny to be adopted in the UK. The committee could be
empowered simply to draw questions to the attention of the House; it
could have the stronger power to require the delay of legislation; or it
could go further still and provide that an elected second chamber could
veto legislation which had been called into question by the committee
(which conceivably could be a joint committee of both Houses).[71]

CONCLUSION

I have argued that, despite recent political developments throughout the
world, the promotion of social democratic ideals is still a legitimate objective for any community. If we are prepared to accept meaningful social
democracy as a legitimate goal, it may mean the rejection of that instru-

ment of liberal fundamentalism, the bill of rights. In effect a form of censorship on the power of a community, such a device undermines the first principle of social democratic forms of government (though not apparently liberal democratic forms of government), namely the right of political equality. It does this by transferring sovereign power to a small Platonic group, to whom access is denied except for a privileged few. As I have also argued, the evidence tends to suggest that the operation of such a device would tend to frustrate the effective operation and implementation of social and economic policy initiatives. I have also argued that, although they are undoubtedly important, civil and political liberties ought properly to service rather than subvert the goals of a social democratic society. These relate to the method and purposes of government.

The difficulty of this for lawyers is that it tends to deny them a role. I am bound to say, however, that I do not see this exclusion as a source of difficulty. If there are lawyers who wish to engage in making the rules by which the community is to be governed, they should stand for office, get elected and exercise power in an accountable manner. No one is suggesting that political scrutiny of the type proposed here will be perfect in its operation. But I would suggest that the same is true of judicial review. Anthony Lester tells us in his 1969 Fabian Society pamphlet that a sufficient bulwark against the tyranny of the majority is 'most needed during these periods of crisis in which popular prejudice or mass hysteria threaten a minority'.[72] If this is the reason for a bill of rights, then we are likely to be disappointed. The existence of a bill of rights did nothing to protect the Japanese Americans during World War II, or Communists from the most evil persecution during the Cold War.[73] As Lester himself concedes in a piece supportive of a bill of rights, the fact that such a device exists in the USA 'has not prevented alarming epidemics of populist intolerance from sweeping across that country'.[74] It is difficult to see why a bill of rights would not be of equally limited value in the UK, where the courts have colluded in many acts of intolerance, with one senior judge expressing the view recently that 'National security and civil liberties are on the same side'.[75] But the ineffectiveness of judicial review is another story for another day.[76]

NOTES

1. IPPR, *The Constitution of the United Kingdom* (London, 1991).
2. Liberty, *A People's Charter: Liberty's Bill of Rights* (London, 1991).
3. Liberal Democrats, *We, The People*, Federal Green Paper No. 13 (1990).

4. See 560 HL Debs 1142–3 (25 January 1995) (Lord Taylor).

5. T. H. Bingham, The European Convention on Human Rights: time to incorporate (1993) 109 *Law Quarterly Review* 390.

6. *Ibid.*, p. 390.

7. *Ibid.*, p. 399.

8. For a good account of this dilemma of liberalism, see J. Lively, *Democracy* (London, 1975).

9. See K. D. Ewing and C. A. Gearty, *Democracy or a Bill of Rights* (London, 1991).

10. W. E. Paterson and A. H. Thomas (eds), *Social Democratic Parties in Western Europe* (London, 1977), p. 11.

11. For a vigorous defence of civil liberties in the literature of democratic socialism/social democracy, see E. Bernstein, *The Preconditions of Socialism* (Cambridge, 1993).

12. Lord Hailsham, *The Dilemma of Democracy* (London, 1978).

13. T. Benn, The case for a constitutional premiership (1980) 33 *Parliamentary Affairs* 7.

14. Bingham, *op. cit.*, p. 391.

15. P. Hirst, *After Thatcher* (London, 1989), Chapter 2.

16. J. Lively, *op. cit.*, p. 134.

17. For a fuller account of this issue see J. Waldron, A right-based critique of constitutional rights (1993) 13 *Oxford Journal of Legal Studies* 18.

18. R. Nader and C. J. Mayer, Corporations are not persons, *New York Times*, 9 April 1988.

19. See F. W. Maitland, Introduction to O. F. von Gierke, *Political Theories of the Middle Ages* (Cambridge, 1900); W. M. Geldart, Legal personality (1911) 27 *Law Quarterly Review* 90; A. V. Dicey, The combination laws (1904) 17 *Harvard Law Review* 404.

20. See especially *First National Bank of Boston v. Bellotti*, 435 US 765 (1978).

21. *The Queen v. Big M Drug Mart Ltd* [1985] 1 SCR 295.

22. *Irwin Toy Ltd v. Quebec* (1989) 58 DLR (4th) 577 (Commercial speech case; action failed as a result of s. 1 of the Charter).

23. *Hunter v. Southam Inc.*[1984] 2 SCR 145.

24. *Australian Capital Television Pty Ltd v. Commonwealth of Australia* (1992) 66 ALJR 695.

25. [1990] 12 EHRR 485.

26. E. Bernstein, *op. cit.*, p. 141.

27. See generally E. C. S. Wade and A. W. Bradley, *Constitutional and Administrative Law* (11th edn by A. W. Bradley and K. D. Ewing, London, 1993), Chapter 19.

28. 424 US 1 (1976). See Chapter 1, above, p. 8.

29. See G. Robertson and A. Nicol, *Media Law* (3rd edn, Harmondsworth, 1992), p. 640.

30. See K. D. Ewing, *Money, Law and Politics. A Study of Electoral Campaign Finance Reform in Canada* (Oxford, 1992), Chapter 7.

31. On Australia, see K. D. Ewing, The legal regulation of electoral campaign financing in Australia: A preliminary analysis (1992) 22 *University of Western Australia Law Review* 239. On Canada, see K. D. Ewing, *op. cit.*

32. 424 US 1 (1976).

33. *Ibid.*, pp. 48–9.

34. 198 US 45 (1905).

35. See C. Sunstein, Political equality and unintended consequences (1994) 94 *Columbia Law Review* 1390, at p. 1397.

36. *Brown v. Board of Education*, 347 US 483 (1954).

37. *National Citizens' Coalition Inc. v. Attorney General for Canada* (1985) 11 DLR (4th) 481; *Sommerville v. Attorney General for Canada*, 30 June 1993.

38. *Australian Capital Television Pty Ltd v. Commonwealth of Australia* (1992) 66 ALJR 695. See [1993] *Public Law* 256 and (1993) 109 *Law Quarterly Review* 168.

39. J. Griffith, The rights stuff (1993) *Socialist Register* 106.

40. On the Social Charter, see D. Harris, *The European Social Charter* (Charlottesville, 1984).

41. On ILO Conventions, see K. D. Ewing, *Britain and the ILO* (London, 2nd edn, 1994).

42. See J. A. G. Griffith, The political constitution (1979) 42 *Modern Law Review* 1.

43. See A. Wright, British socialists and the British constitution (1990) 43 *Parliamentary Affairs* 322.

44. A. Coote (ed.), *The Welfare of Citizens* (London, 1992).

45. On which see T. R. S. Allan, *Law, Liberty and Justice. The Legal Foundations of the British Constitution* (Oxford, 1993), especially Chapter 6.

46. *Amalgamated Society of Railway Servants* v. *Osborne* [1910] AC 87.

47. See for example, *Taff Vale Railway Company Ltd.* v. *Amalgamated Society of Railway Servants* [1901] AC 426.

48. *Roberts* v. *Hopwood* [1925] AC 578. See P. Fennell, Roberts v Hopwood: the rule against socialism (1986) 13 *Journal of Law and Society* 401.

49. G. Marston, The United Kingdom's part in the preparation of the European Convention on Human Rights (1993) 42 *International and Comparative Law Quarterly* 796.

50. *Council of Civil Service Unions* v. *United Kingdom* [1988] EHRR 269.

51. See, generally, K. D. Ewing, *op. cit.*, pp. 23–30.

52. For a discussion of the cases, see M. Forde, The European Convention on human rights and labor law (1983) 31 *American Journal of Comparative Law* 301.

53. *Young, James and Webster* v. *United Kingdom* [1982] 4 EHRR 28. See M. Forde, The closed shop case (1982) 11 *Industrial Law Journal* 1.

54. Though now see *Sigurjonsson* v. *Iceland* [1993] 16 EHRR 462.

55. See especially *Schmidt and Dahlstrom* v. *Sweden* [1975] 1 EHRR 617.

56. [1970] AC 538.

57. See especially *Reference re Public Service Employee Relations Act and Police Officers' Collective Bargaining Act* (1987) 38 DLR (4th) 161.

58. *NUR* v. *Sullivan* [1947] IR 77.

59. *Educational Company of Ireland Ltd* v. *Fitzpatrick (No. 2)* [1961] IR 345.

60. *Meskell* v. *Córas Iompair Eireann* [1973] IR 121.

61. For an account of judicial review of social measures, see C. A. Gearty, Democracy and a bill of rights: some lessons from Ireland. In K. D. Ewing, C. A. Gearty and B. A. Hepple (eds), *Human Rights and Labour Law* (London, 1994).

62. *Railway Employees Department* v. *Hanson*, 351 US 225 (1956).

63. *Abood* v. *Detroit School Board*, 431 US 209 (1977).

64. *Lavigne* v. *Ontario Public Services Union* (1991) 81 DLR (4th) 545.

65. E. Holmberg and N. Stjernquist, Introduction, *The Constitution of Sweden* (Stockholm, 1989), p. 17.

66. *The Constitution of Sweden, Instrument of Government*, Chapter 2: 12.

67. *The Constitution of Sweden, Instrument of Government*, Chapter 11: 14.

68. For the background to incorporation, see *Fri-och rättighets – frågor, Del A, Regeringsformen*; and *Fri-och rättighets – Frågor, Del B, Inkorporering av Europakonventionen*, SOU 1993: 40. See also *Regeringens proposition 1993/94*: 117.

69. Konvention blir svensk lag, *Svenska Dagbladet*, 22 August 1993.

70. The point is made also in K. D. Ewing, Challenging the power to violate standards (1993) 1(4) *International Union Rights* 21.

71. See K. D. Ewing and C. A. Gearty, *op. cit.* See also D. Kinley, *The European Convention on Human Rights* (Aldershot, 1993).

72. A. Lester, *Democracy and Individual Rights* (London, 1969), p. 3.

73. See *Korematsu* v. *United States*, 323 US 214 (1944) and *Dennis* v. *United States*, 341 US 494 (1951). See generally S. Walker, *In Defense of American Liberties. A History of the ACLU* (New York, 1990).

74. A. Lester, *op. cit.*, p. 13.

75. *R* v. *Home Secretary, ex parte Cheblak* [1991] 1 WLR 890.

76. Today I should like to record my thanks to the judges, parliamentarians, civil servants, and academics in Sweden who made themselves available for interview during a visit to Stockholm in June 1994. I should especially like to thank Dr Iain Cameron of Uppsala University, though he bears no responsibility for any errors and must not be taken to agree with any of the views expressed.

4

Human Rights in a Divided Society

G. E. Devenish

INTRODUCTION

South Africa is a deeply divided society. It has been a country of inordinate human suffering, trauma and the gross violation of human rights. Its recent transformation from a racial oligarchy to a democracy with a rigid Constitution and a justiciable Bill of Rights creates the prospect of a new era of justice, peace and prosperity after centuries of white domination. In this regard the Bill of Rights in the Interim Constitution[1] will play a seminal role in promoting human rights in one of the most divided societies in the world.

Chapter 3 of the Republic of South Africa's Constitution Act[2] contains a justiciable Bill of Rights which is of profound importance for all the people of South Africa. It is South Africa's first Bill of Rights and constitutes a powerful jurisprudential manifestation of universally acknowledged moral and ethical norms[3] clearly set out to constrain the legal behaviour of political and administrative office bearers in all branches of government and administration, and even the conduct of individual citizens in relation to one another in certain circumstances.[4]

Most of the rights set out in Chapter 3 of the Constitution are contained in broad and inclusive language, usually without qualification. The style of the drafting of the Bill of Rights is such that the rights are encapsulated in 'broad entitlements'[5] expressed in simple language that is accessible to lay persons. Broadly phrased principles, using a continental style of drafting, lend themselves to 'evolutionary interpretation and constitutional growth'.[6]

Like other parts of the Constitution, the Bill of Rights reflects the political and legal compromises that were necessary to obtain a political and constitutional settlement in a culturally and racially divided country. These compromises invariably resulted in rendering problematic the interpretation of the Bill of Rights. This position is compounded by the fact that Chapter 3 does not provide in general for a hierarchy of rights or values.[7] It will be the arduous task of the Supreme and Constitutional

Courts to determine how conflicts between fundamental rights should be resolved and whether the limitations satisfy the conditions set out in s. 33. It is obviously not possible to discuss the Bill of Rights in its entirety and analyse its complete impact on all human rights. Those aspects of the Bill of Rights that are germane to human rights in a divided society are discussed, analysed and commented on in this chapter.

The Vertical and Horizontal Application of the Bill of Rights

Section 7(1) stipulates that Chapter 3 on fundamental rights 'shall bind all legislative and executive organs of state at all levels of government'.[8] By implication this section authorizes the judiciary to strike down any legislation, including parliamentary statutes, and to overturn any executive action that is in conflict with the provisions of the Bill of Rights. This means that the Constitutional Court can exercise a testing right, by which is meant that it can invalidate an Act of Parliament if such Act is in conflict with the Constitution. This is always an acutely controversial political and constitutional issue. It is for this reason that the Interim Constitution provides for a less drastic alternative in s. 98(5), which states:

> In the event of the Constitutional Court finding that any law or any provision thereof is inconsistent with this constitution, it shall declare such law or provision invalid to the extent of such inconsistency: Provided that the Constitutional Court may in the interests of justice and good government, require Parliament or any other competent authority, within a specified period of time by the Court, to correct the defect in law or provision, which shall then remain in force pending correction or expiry in the period so specified.

This is certainly an interesting innovation and appropriate for a politically divided society where the exercise of the testing right could result in a constitutional and political crisis.

The drafters retreated from their earlier intention to make the Bill of Rights binding, where appropriate, on the courts, and, where just and equitable, on non-governmental bodies and private persons.[9] It can be argued that since the judiciary is not mentioned, it does not have to enforce the Bill of Rights between citizens *per se*. However, it is clear that Chapter 3 applies to all law in force, which must of necessity include the common law, such as the law of property, the law of succession, the law of contract and customary or indigenous law. Furthermore, the phrasing of many specific provisions of the Bill of Rights indicates clearly that they have a horizontal application.[10]

Provision is therefore manifestly made for verticality, by which is meant the regulation of legal relations between the state and the subject[11] and to a lesser extent either expressly or by implication for horizontality (i.e. the relationship between citizens *per se*) in the operation of certain fundamental rights. These fundamental rights will be able to be enforced in relation to 'all laws in force and all administrative decisions taken and acts performed during the period of operation of this Constitution'.[12] Provisions in this chapter must be read in the light of the Constitution as a whole and taking into account all the other provisions of the chapter. A holistic and value-coherent method of interpretation is necessary.[13]

The conventional approach is to perceive the Constitution as a document that restricts governmental activity and subjects such conduct to judicial review. However, a more contemporary view is that it is not the state but the exercise of private power that poses the greatest threat to the exercise of fundamental rights.[14] For this reason it is necessary to have a horizontal application of fundamental rights, i.e. what the Germans call *Drittwirkung*. Obviously this is necessary in a deeply divided society in which racial prejudice is ingrained and in which economic power is very much still in the hands of the white minority.

SUBSTANTIVE RIGHTS

Equality

Taking into account the tragic and traumatic history and consequences of apartheid that resulted in the emasculation of human rights in South Africa, the equality provision in the Constitution is of seminal importance and is appropriately the first right enumerated in Chapter 3. In any deeply divided society that is in the process of transformation from racial oligarchy to democracy, equality is the cornerstone on which the entire democratization process and rehabilitation must rest. Section 8 states:

(1) Every person shall have the right to equality before the law and equal protection of laws.

(2) No person shall be unfairly discriminated against, directly or indirectly, and, without derogating from the generality of this provision, on one or more of the following grounds in particular: race, gender, sex, ethnic or social origin, colour, sexual orientation, age, disability, religion, conscience, belief, culture or language.

(3) (a) This section shall not preclude measures designed to

achieve the adequate protection and advancement of persons or groups or categories of persons disadvantaged by unfair discrimination, in order to enable their full and equal enjoyment of all rights and freedoms.

(b) Every person or community dispossessed of rights in land before the commencement of this constitution under any law which would have been inconsistent with subsection (2) had that section been in operation at the time of dispossession, shall be entitled to claim restitution of such rights subject to and in accordance with sections 121, 122 and 123.

(4) *Prima facie* proof of discrimination on any grounds specified in subsection (2) shall be presumed to be sufficient proof of unfair discrimination as contemplated in that subsection, until the contrary is proved.

Equality before the law, required by s. 8(1), is inherent in the concept and practice of the rule of law and requires every legal subject of whatever status to be subordinate to the law of the land. Regrettably, equality before the law is a myth and even in democratic countries, affluence, race and political power do inevitably to a greater or lesser extent influence the administration of justice. For this reason socio-economic upliftment as envisaged by the ANC's Reconstruction and Development plan is indispensable for the rehabilitation of economically deprived communities.

The right to equality before the law does not require that all persons must be treated in exactly the same way. What is required is that the justification for differentiation must be legitimate. The celebrated Aristotelian formulation that equals must be treated equally and those who are not equal must to the extent of their inequality be treated unequally is a good starting point, but it certainly does not resolve all the complex issues that arise.

Unfair discrimination, whether direct or indirect, is prohibited. Indirect discrimination occurs by means of actions or policies designed to achieve an apparently neutral objective. This occurs if a practice has the effect of placing a group at a disadvantage because of past discrimination or present circumstances. Thus an ostensibly neutral test, for instance a linguistic, numeracy or literacy test, could have the effect of disadvantaging African people, whose poor schooling system ill equips them to cope with these tests.[15]

The use of the phrase 'equal protection of the law', adopted from the celebrated Fourteenth Amendment to the US Constitution, which has precipitated one of the most contentious and penetrating constitutional and jurisprudential debates in that country, creates the possibility that it could introduce into South African constitutional law and litigation the vast and complicated US jurisprudence relating to the prohibition of discrimination. However fascinating this may be from a comparative and jurisprudential viewpoint,[16] it must be treated with a measure of circumspection by our courts, since in many cases the political and legal context is unique to the USA. Nevertheless, the Americans have, in a traumatic human rights experience, pioneered the jurisprudence of constitutional equality in a divided society which has a history of desegregation, from which South Africa could learn. This debate and controversy in the USA is exacerbated by the fact that the US Constitution does not explicitly authorize affirmative action.[17] In contrast to the US Constitution, s. 8(3)(a) of the Interim Constitution expressly authorizes affirmative action.

The US courts have accepted that there can be a legitimate differentiation between men and women on a rational and just basis. Thus a law allowing females pregnancy benefits should not be set aside because there are no comparative benefits for males. Sexual discrimination in taxes against married women in South African tax law and practice is unconstitutional since the implementation of the Interim Constitution.[18]

The equality provision is by virtue of s. 8(3)(a), however, qualified to permit affirmative action in order to enable persons disadvantaged by unfair discrimination to obtain 'their full and equal enjoyment of all rights and freedoms'. Affirmative action is likely to be a contentious matter and the Constitutional Court will be involved in the interpretation and application of this provision. The Bill of Rights therefore sanctions affirmative action by shielding from challenge 'measures designed to achieve the adequate protection and advancement of persons or groups or categories of persons disadvantaged by unfair discrimination'. The term 'adequate protection and advancement' is obviously qualitative and vague and will have to be interpreted by the Constitutional Court.

The earlier versions of this section used the word 'aimed' and not 'designed'. The latter is undoubtedly preferable because not every programme 'aimed' at, will in fact, achieve its aim. On the other hand, the word 'designed' does, as Mureinik[19] observes, invite a court to review both aims and means, i.e. the intention of the programme and its effect. This will allow the courts to weigh up the cost-effectiveness of affirmative action programmes and to disallow those that are indeed counterproductive, since they would not be designed to achieve their goal.

However, the Interim Constitution is premised according to its preamble on the 'need to create a new order in which there is equality between men and women and people of all races so that the citizens shall be able to enjoy and exercise their fundamental rights and freedoms'. Section 8(3) constitutionalizes preferential treatment in favour of victims of previous discrimination in order to eliminate its detrimental consequences. It is inevitable that certain innocent persons will have to bear the burden of the constitutional remedy. In this regard, permissible affirmative action will constitute fair discrimination.

The Constitutional Court will have to develop consistent and legitimate criteria to effect a judicious balance between the competing interests of the victims of past discrimination, the victims of preferential treatment and the socio-economic needs of the community as a whole. This will require a balance between social justice and economic growth. It must therefore be borne in mind that large-scale affirmative action programmes that would seriously harm the economy would be counter-productive and would kill the goose that lays the proverbial golden egg. Some of the problems that the Constitutional Court is likely to encounter in dealing with affirmative action matters are, according to Ngcobo,[20] whether the Constitution as a whole read with s. 8(3) imposes a duty on the state and the administration, in particular to adopt affirmative action measures, the vexed question of quotas and how to establish unfair discrimination.

There is uncertainty whether the courts will adopt a horizontal interpretation of the equality clause. This seems likely,[17] taking into account s. 33(3) discussed below; however, if they do not, the equal protection clause would be limited to public institutions, and would not apply to private bodies and individuals. Parliament, however, in all probability will adopt, regardless of the interpretation of the courts, legislation to regulate the matter that is comparable with US civil rights legislation, thereby extending the application of fundamental rights to private institutions and individuals.[21]

Section 181 provides for the recognition of traditional leaders and indigenous law. However, the sex equality provision set out in s. 8(2) most certainly does not inhibit challenges to indigenous law based on sex discrimination. The indigenous leaders were thus unsuccessful in their endeavour to insulate customary law from the guarantee of sex equality. In an illuminating article, Professor Mureinik explains[9] that this was really a Pyrrhic victory for the feminists. He comments *inter alia* that as the Bill of Rights is expressed to bind only the legislative and executive organs of government,[22] indigenous law is only reviewable under the Bill of Rights when it has been translated into legislation or is being applied by government. This means that where the unwritten customary law is being applied by a court to a dispute between private individuals, the Bill of Rights itself seems to put it beyond challenge for a violation of a right guaranteed in the Bill.[23] However, it must be borne in mind that according to s. 35(3), in the interpretation of any law and the development of the common law and customary law, the court shall have due regard to the spirit, purport and objects of Chapter 3. Exactly how the

Constitutional Court will deal with such customary matters is not entirely clear. The latter approach would obviously be preferable, since the preservation of sex inequality through the application of customary law would be a glaring anomaly and an anachronism.

The significance of the prohibition of discrimination on the grounds of 'sexual orientation' means that homosexuals and lesbians will also benefit from the equality provision. This will obviously apply to the conduct of the state, but it will, it is submitted, also apply in the workplace as a result of the right to fair labour practices set out in s. 27. Whether discrimination against homosexuals by private institutions such as insurance companies will be unconstitutional is not clear. This would involve the horizontal application of the Bill of Rights, a matter concerning which there is as we have seen no complete clarity. If the insurance company refused to insure homosexual persons, the action of a court of law forcing the company to accept such a contract would constitute a violation of freedom of contract, which is enshrined in s. 26.

The equality provision in s. 8 has an important socio-economic dimension, since it will require an equal distribution of all available resources on a geographical, racial and cultural basis. This applies *inter alia* to health and education. Obviously, this equitable distribution of resources will take great organizational effort and planning on the part of government.

The Right to Life

Section 9 stipulates that every person shall have the right to life. This broad constitutional protection of life spawns certain contentious moral and social issues such as capital punishment, euthanasia and abortion. The Constitutional Court will have to decide whether indeed this right involves a complete bar on capital punishment[24] and the extent to which abortion is affected. In regard to capital punishment, s. 11(2), which reads as follows, is pertinent: 'No person shall be subject to torture of any kind, whether physical, mental or emotional, nor shall any person be subject to cruel, inhuman or degrading treatment or punishment.' The Constitutional Court will have to decide whether capital punishment is a violation of this particular provision.[25] Constitutional courts around the world have reached different decisions on the compatibility of capital punishment with a bill of rights, particularly in regard to a provision proscribing cruel and unusual punishment.[26]

The contentious moral issue of euthanasia,[27] or mercy killing of a person who is suffering acutely, will have to be resolved by the Constitutional Court by weighing up the competing interests and values protected respectively by the right to life on the one hand and the right to and respect for the dignity and privacy of a person on the other hand.

As far as abortion is concerned, the Constitutional Court will in the application of the 'right to life' provision have to take into account s. 13, which deals with the right to privacy and states: 'Every person shall have a right to his or her privacy, which shall include the right not to be subject to searches of his or her person, home or property, the seizure of private possessions or the violations of private communications. This vexed question involves a conflict between, on the one hand, freedom of conscience and the right to privacy, and, on the other hand, the right to life if the fetus is considered a 'life'. The Constitutional Court will have to decide whether a restriction on the right to life is sanctioned. This may indeed by the case, because in the view of Leyshon[28] 'it is beyond dispute that many liberal democracies regard abortion as a reasonable and justifiable option for women'.[29] According to the Race Relations Survey for 1993/1994,[30] a survey conducted by the Society of Psychiatrists of South Africa in 1992, 89 per cent of the psychiatrists surveyed believed that legislation governing abortion was unacceptable and needed revision. Seventy-eight per cent supported abortion on request for girls under 14 years of age and 87 per cent for girls under 16 years of age. The Constitutional Court will have to take a decision on abortion, taking all the conflicting interests and scientific evidence into account.

Freedom and Security of Person

This important right is embodied in s. 11, which reads:

>   (1) Every person shall have the right to freedom and security of the person which shall include the right not to be detained without trial.
>   (2) No person shall be subject to torture of any kind, whether physical, mental or emotional, nor shall any person be subject to cruel, inhuman or degrading treatment or punishment.

Torture, which regrettably is still widely used in many parts of the world and was used extensively under the old apartheid regime in South Africa, is prohibited in terms of s. 11(2). Nevertheless, its express proscription in international law and international law instruments is binding on all states. Internationally, therefore, this right is absolute. As far as the Interim Constitution is concerned, this right is also unqualified and absolute.[31] Under no circumstances can this right be limited or eroded. Its limitation can never be reasonable or justifiable in an open and democratic society based on freedom and equality as required by the limitation provision in the Bill of Rights.[32]

An examination of the definitions contained in various international instruments and the decisions of courts and commissions furnishes a clear indication of the kinds of treatment that fall within the ambit of torture. Furthermore, the use of the adjective 'emotional' in s. 11(2) increases the ambit of the definition of torture in comparison with the international definitions. Conduct incorporating third-degree methods clearly falls within the parameters of the definition. Section 11(2) is stated in broad general language. In addition to torture of any description, which is proscribed, conduct which could fall short of torture and be described as cruel, inhuman or degrading treatment is also prohibited. Chapter 3 protects all persons, and therefore non-citizens and even illegal aliens can rely on the fundamental rights contained in it.

Freedom of Religion, Belief and Opinion

South Africa abounds with religious and political heterogeneity of belief and opinion. Whites, and in particular Afrikaner nationalists, were in the past highly intolerant of beliefs other than their own.

Section 14 states:

> (1) Every person shall have the right to freedom of conscience, religion, thought, belief and opinion, which shall include academic freedom in institutions of higher learning.
>
> (2) Without derogating from the generality of subsection (1) religious observances may be conducted at state and state-aided institutions under rules established by appropriate authority for that purpose, provided that such religious observances are conducted on an equitable basis and attendance at them is free and voluntary.
>
> (3) Nothing in this chapter shall preclude legislation recognising –
>
> > (a) a system of personal and family law adhered to by persons professing a particular religion; and
> >
> > (b) the validity of marriages concluded under a system of religious law subject to specified procedures.

As with the other substantive rights, the rights referred to above can be limited in terms of s. 33, which will result in the Constitutional Court developing a jurisprudence on the scope and application of the above freedoms.[33] As far as the free exercise of religion is concerned, the US case of *Cantwell* v. *Connecticut*[34] provides some guidance. In this case the

Supreme Court held that while the freedom to believe is absolute, freedom to act pursuant to one's religion cannot be. 'Conduct remains subject to regulation for the protection of society.'[35]

Section 14(2) deals with the question of prayers and religious practices at state or state-aided schools which has been so controversial in the USA, where virtual neutrality towards religion prevails. The controversial case of *Engel* v. *Vitale*,[36] in which the Supreme Court struck down a prayer composed by the Board of the Regents on the basis of the principle that 'it is no part of the business of government to compose official prayers for any group of American people to recite as part of a religious program carried on by government', reflects this neutrality.[37] In *Wallace* v. *Jaffree*[38] the Supreme Court held that a one-minute period of silence 'for meditation or voluntary prayer' violated the principle that government must follow a course of 'complete neutrality towards religion'.[39]

The term 'an equitable basis' will have to be interpreted. It could conceivably involve an element of 'coerced ecumenism'[40] for state-aided, religiously based schools. The legal significance of this is that there will not be a complete separation between state and church. Failure to comply with the requirement of ecumenism would cause the operation of state-aided schools to be in violation of the Bill of Rights. Existing religious schools, such as the Anglican, Methodist, Roman Catholic and Jewish schools, will therefore have to move towards ecumenism if they wish to retain their state subsidies. If they wish to retain a distinctly denominational and essentially sectional religious character, they will have to, it is submitted, forfeit all state aid. This is, however, an issue that the Constitutional Court will have to consider.

The Interim Constitution does most certainly not provide for religious neutrality, as is the position in the USA, but, as Mureinik[41] explains, it favours believers over non-believers. It is therefore a manifestation of 'religious freedom' that does not amount to religious equality. The latter requires the state to favour 'neither Christian over Muslim nor devout over faithless'.[41] The Constitution itself is not a religiously neutral document, since, *inter alia*, in the preamble it opens with the words 'In humble submission to Almighty God'. South Africans as a people are deeply religious, and the Constitution as a whole reflects a bias in favour of religion as opposed to apostasy.

Freedom of Expression

Freedom of expression is fundamental to a liberal democracy. The contentious issue is the extent to which it should be permitted and the way in which the courts balance it against equally fundamental rights and considerations applying in a democratic society. In the divided society that South Africa is, it is unlikely that freedom of expression will be given the exceptionally wide interpretation it has received through the application of the US doctrine of prior restraint.[42] According to this doctrine, prior restraints are highly suspect and are as a result subject to a rebuttable presumption of unconstitutionality. In endeavouring to justify use of such restraints, the executive carries a heavy burden of proof. The Supreme Court has intimated that it uses the clear and present danger criterion in reviewing such restraint.[43]

For decades South Africans have lived with a myriad of laws designed to restrict freedom of speech and expression. The interests of a virtually totalitarian government were protected at the expense of the public's right to know. This was part of a notorious policy which nurtured profound suspicion and bred corruption on an unprecedented and exponential scale in the political administration of South Africa.

Section 15 states:

> (1) Every person shall have the right to freedom of speech and expression, which shall include freedom of the press and other media, and freedom of artistic creativity and scientific research.
>
> (2) All media financed by or under the control of the state shall be regulated in a manner which ensures impartiality and the expression of a diversity of opinion.

It is important to note that most of the fundamental rights found in Chapter 3 are not absolute. This is abundantly clear from s. 33(3), which stipulates that:

> The entrenchment of rights in terms of this chapter shall not be construed as denying the existence of any other rights and freedoms recognised and conferred by the common law, customary law or legislation to the extent that they are not inconsistent with the provisions of this Chapter.

Furthermore, as indicated above, there is in general no hierarchy of rights provided for.[7] The courts will therefore have to weigh up conflicting rights. Rights involving freedom of expression will have to be balanced against other rights, such as the rights to equality, dignity, privacy, political campaigning, fair trial, economic activity and property. Therefore, freedom of expression and of the press do not, for example, sanction sedition, defamation, or obscenities or pornography.

Although freedom of expression is not absolute, it is a fundamental right that is indispensable for an authentic democratic order because other fundamental freedoms depend on it.[44] Therefore, freedom of speech, of necessity, must enjoy a considerable measure of protection. The extent of the protection will depend on the context. In a political context, meaningful freedom of expression is essential to allow persons to make informed political decisions. Freedom of expression in regard to pornography, obscenity and sexual intimacy is a different matter, and other considerations prevail in the balancing of interests and rights in this regard. There are two categories of speech, so-called political speech, and speech relating to artistic and scientific endeavour. This categorization is inherent in the functioning of s. 33,[32] which 'by providing for a hierarchy of permissible limitations clearly affords more protection to speech in so far as it relates to free and fair political activity'.[45] It is therefore apparent that the Constitution gives a higher priority to political as opposed to non-political speech.

To determine the scope of free speech, it is necessary now to consider the limitations clause found in s. 33 of the Constitution. The limitations clause allows curtailment of freedom of speech if it is reasonable and justifiable in an open and democratic society and does not negate the essential content of the right. Should the speech, however, relate to political activity, then there is an additional requirement that the curtailment must also be deemed to be necessary in a democratic society. Therefore in regard to the kinds of expression, there is a hierarchy of rights.[45] Infringements of political speech are subject to a stricter scrutiny than infringements of non-political speech. In the USA the courts have developed a strict scrutiny test. This involves two key elements:[46]

> (1) The executive will be required to satisfy the court that it is pursuing a compelling or overriding interest which justifies the limitation upon constitutional rights; and
> (2) If the executive succeeds in regard to the above it must demonstrate that the law in question which infringes the right is necessary to attain the compelling or overriding interest.[47]

In the Canadian case of *R* v. *Butler*[48] the Canadian Supreme Court had to decide if a section of the criminal code of Canada violated the guarantee of free expression in the Canadian Charter. It held that the prohibition on pornography did indeed violate the guarantee of freedom of expression but this was justified as 'being a reasonable limit prescribed by law'. One of the arguments accepted by the court was that a failure to proscribe pornography was a negation of equal protection, since pornography is essentially degrading to women. In contrast, the equal rights reasoning has not been used in the USA[49] as a basis for upholding a prohibition on pornography. Despite the fact that pornography has been found 'central in creating and maintaining sex as a basis of discrimination',[50] it has generally been held that 'the very fact that it harms women proves "the power of pornography as speech" and consequently justifies its protection under the. . . Free Speech Clause'.[51]

Freedom of Association, Movement and Residence

Freedom of association is intrinsic to a democratic society and obviously is of inordinate importance for a deeply divided society. In contemporary society, freedom of association is 'a vital means for competing in the marketplace of ideas and controlling government'.[52] Political organizations and interest groups vie for public attention and support and, in the process, they promote to a greater or lesser extent ideals and values of the democratic process. Controversy relates to the means that are used to attain the objects of the association. The vital question for South Africa is whether the Constitution will be interpreted to allow associations to promote anti-democratic and racist ideas and practices. A horizontal application of the Bill of Rights could prevent such a phenomenon. This would indeed be desirable, taking into account the deeply divided nature of our society and the negative legacy of apartheid. As indicated in the discussion on verticality and horizontality, it is private power that poses the greatest potential threat to fundamental rights and thus necessitates a horizontal application of the Bill of Rights.

Sections 17, 18 and 19 respectively state:

> Every person shall have the right to freedom of association;
> Every person shall have the right to freedom of movement anywhere within South Africa; and
> Every person shall have the right to choose his or her place of residence anywhere in South Africa.

The rights are subject to limitation and obviously must operate in a way that does not make fundamental inroads into other core rights such as equality. Freedom of association cannot, therefore, be construed in such a way as to validate 'private apartheid'.[53] The reason for this is that s. 33(4) stipulates that measures may be activated to prohibit unfair discrimination by private individuals, societies, organizations and companies. This is a further example of horizontality in the operation of the Bill of Rights. This means that s. 17 read with s. 33(4) stops short of outlawing private discrimination, but it expressly empowers the new national legislature, i.e. Parliament, to outlaw private discrimination.[54] US courts have not sanctioned private discrimination 'where entry qualifications turned on an open relationship between the clubs and the public'.[55]

These rights, like most other rights in the chapter, are not absolute rights, and where appropriate can be limited by a law of a general application according to s. 33(1). This means, for instance, that police warrants for the searching of individuals and their property would be permissible despite the privacy and procedural guarantees.

Since the inception of European colonization in South Africa, the indigenous people have been subject to restrictions on their freedom of movement. The Constitutional Court will have to determine whether this right is applicable to private as well as public property. The Trespass Act[56] and common law relating to trespass provide the owner of private property with a measure of protection. These conflicting rights will have to be weighed up against one another in order to determine the ambit of the right of freedom of movement.

In the past under the apartheid laws, race determined where a person could live. It is probably for this reason that the Interim Constitution enumerates the right to residence as a separate right.[57] This provision refers to natural and not juristic persons. The word 'person' is used and not the word 'citizen', thereby implying that this right extends to non-citizens. It is conceivable that the immigration laws will be permitted to impose reasonable limitations. Provincial constitutions and laws will have to be compatible with this right, which allows persons to choose any place in any of the nine provinces constituting the national territory.

Political Rights

Successive South African governments eroded and denied black people political rights. The heroic struggle waged by the ANC and other liberation movements and liberal organizations and parties was essentially motivated by the legitimate desire to obtain these coveted rights for all South Africans.

These rights are dealt with in s. 21, which stipulates that:

(1) Every citizen shall have the right –
(a) to form, to participate in the activities of and to recruit members for a political party;
(b) to campaign for a political party or cause; and
(c) freely to make political choices.
(2) Every citizen shall have the right to vote, to do so in secret and to stand for election to public office.

Section 21 provides for universal adult franchise. This is the most fundamental of all political rights. The great challenge to South African statesmen and women is to make democracy work in a deeply divided society with inordinate socio-economic problems. The Government of National Unity is a manifestation of consociational democracy[58] designed to provide stability and security for a transitional period. Consociational democracy is a means of protecting minorities using *inter alia* the 'grand coalition' mechanism which in South Africa has taken on the form of a Government of National Unity.[59] The constitutional principles[60] of the Interim Constitution make provision for the establishment of a Volkstaat Council, to be established for the purpose of determining the viability of a Volkstaat. This was done in order to bring the right-wing parties into the election process and to allay their fears.

The right 'freely to make political choices' and the secret ballot are both of fundamental importance for the establishing of a genuine democratic system of government and culture. Intimidation is a very serious threat to the conducting of free and fair elections, particularly where there are millions of illiterate and semi-literate people who in the recent past have been subjected to an oppressive government in response to which a liberation struggle was waged. A democratic system of government therefore does not depend merely on the existence of adult universal franchise but on basic political tolerance within the multicultural community that makes up South Africa, something that was patently lacking in many parts of the country in the run-up to the election.

A Bill of Rights is not a panacea for all the maladies of a deeply divided society with great socio-economic problems. There has to be a genuine commitment on the part of the political leaders to a culture of human rights and political tolerance. The Constitution creates both Human Rights and Gender Commissions and a Public Protector (Ombudsman) to facilitate and promote a culture of human rights as well as to help secure the actual materialization of such rights.

Economic Activity

There has been great contention about the most appropriate economic model for South Africa. In the early years of National Party rule, a quasi Afrikaner–socialist economic policy was followed coupled with Afrikaner affirmative action in order to benefit the economically disadvantaged Afrikaner community. In the years in which the liberation movements were in exile and were banned, they were favourably disposed to socialism. The unbanning of the ANC and the politics of reconciliation have brought about a confluence of thinking in regard to economic philosophy, resulting in a broad acceptance of the merit of a mixed economy and the principles of social democracy.

Section 26(1) states that every person shall have the right to freely engage in economic activity and to pursue a livelihood anywhere in the national territory. Section 26(2) qualifies s. 26(1) by stipulating that

> subsection (1) shall not preclude measures designed to promote the protection and improvement of the quality of life, economic growth, human development, social justice, basic conditions of employment, fair labour practices or equal opportunity for all, provided that such measures are justifiable in an open and democratic society based on freedom and equality.

Economic freedom has important legal consequences. Statutory and common law regulation of the economy, found in a plethora of manifestations in South African law, inhibits this freedom. It is for this reason that there is a wide qualification in regard to the principle set out in s. 26(2), the purpose of which is to validate the laws and regulations crafted to fulfil the objects enumerated.

In the Interim Constitution an endeavour is made to effect a balance between economic growth[61] and social justice. What emerges is a social market and mixed economy. Of necessity, the Constitution will therefore require the Government of National Unity to be involved in policies of social democracy. This will require economic growth so that the state is able to obtain the large sums of revenue necessary to pursue policies of social upliftment and rehabilitation. South Africa is characterized by the economic disparity between an affluent white community that benefited from apartheid and the unbridled capitalist policies of the past, and impoverished black communities that constitute the have-nots. Socio-economic rehabilitation is essential for the transformation of South Africa. If the vast majority of the black people of South Africa continue to live in abject poverty, the political human rights such as freedom of expression or religion or association enumerated in the Bill of Rights will have very little meaning, and such a situation could contribute to or precipitate a populist revolt[62] that could overthrow the democratic order, with disastrous consequences for human rights. Fortunately, the Bill of Rights contains certain second-generation or socio-economic rights that will contribute to and facilitate the economic rehabilitation of the impoverished black communities of South Africa.

Property

As far as the economic system is concerned, the fundamental right relating to property is of seminal importance. In this regard, s. 28 is very significant and stipulates:

> (1) Every person shall have the right to acquire and hold rights in property and to the extent that the nature of the right permits, to dispose of such rights.
> (2) No deprivation of any rights in property shall be permitted otherwise than in accordance with a law.
> (3) Where any rights in property are expropriated pursuant to a law referred to in subsection (2) such expropriation shall be permissible for public purposes only and shall be subject to payment of agreed compensation and within such period as may be determined by a court of law as just and equitable, taking into account all relevant factors, including in the case of determination of compensation, the use to which the property is being put, the history of its acquisition, its market value, the value of the investments in it by those affected and the interests of those affected.

The issue of compensation for expropriated property and nationalization is one of the most vexed and problematic constitutional and political conundrums in the South African body politic. The above provision represents the compromise reached by the parties through the multi-party negotation process. It is therefore clear that expropriation or nationalization will have to be accompanied by 'just and equitable compensation' as set out in s. 28(3) above. What is, however, categorically clear is that nationalization without compensation as found in socialist economic systems is prohibited.

The above provision, which, as indicated, was a product of political compromise, is based on the present South African concept of property rights, could serve merely to entrench white privilege and the present unequal distribution in regard to land. It is likely that the Government of National Unity and the Constitutional Assembly when it drafts the final Constitution will revisit this provision in order to formulate a different legal framework and policy premised on 'shared values with respect to land; which places basic human rights such as the right to security and family life at the heart of the concept of property.'[63]

The Environment

Section 29 deals with the environment and stipulates that every person shall have the right to an environment which is not detrimental to his or her health or well-being.

This provision deals with third-generation or green rights. These kinds of rights have come to the fore as a result of an increasing aware-ness of the vulnerability of the environment and the need for balanced economic development. Their importance is reflected in the African Charter on Human and People's Rights, which provides in s. 24 that 'people shall have the right to a general satisfactory environment favourable to their development'.

The courts, and in particular the Constitutional Court, will have to determine the extent to which this provision is justiciable. What is required is a careful and judicious balance between economic develop-ment and environmental protection. It is not entirely clear whether in the application of this right, horizontality of application is implied, and the extent to which it would impose obligations on private individuals and juristic persons, or whether the rights in accordance with s. 7 only apply vertically. This will be a matter to be decided by the Constitutional Court. Cachalia *et al.* are of the opinion that these rights cannot be enforced against 'private concerns such as factories, which for example, emit a harmful effluent'.[64] However, they point out that the section would permit the invalidation of a statute permitting such conduct. It is, however, not inconceivable that the Constitutional Court could adopt an assertive approach to environmental rights, resulting in horizontal enforcement.

The effective preservation of the environment is likely to become a matter of increasing national and global importance. South Africa is pro-foundly involved in international environmental protection; indeed, it is a dynamic participant in no less than 23 international conventions on the preservation of the environment.[65] Public international law is also increasingly reflecting environmental concerns.

In South Africa, environmental protection is regulated by the Environmental Protection Act.[66] South African common law also pro-vides remedies in respect of hazards to health and well-being. The Constitutional Court will, however, be confronted with a dilemma because vast economic development is needed to provide employment for millions of people in South Africa. Such development may have a detrimental influence on the environment. Some kind of *via media* will have to be worked out to reconcile conflicting interests.

Children's Rights

Section 30 deals with children's rights. This provision is in accordance with the Universal Declaration of Rights and the Declaration of the Rights of the Child. Children need very special protection because of their acute vulnerability to violations of human rights arising out of socio-economic malaise, civil commotion and war. This is also obviously acutely the position in South Africa, where there is so much poverty and where the legacy of apartheid has created so many socio-economic maladies in a deeply divided society. The fact that the Constitution contains a 'Children's Charter' reflects a profound concern in our community for the plight of children and the abuse that they are subject to and have been subjected to in the past. In contrast, although gender issues are addressed in the Constitution, there is not a 'charter of women's rights'.

This provision makes directly enforceable certain socio-economic rights or second-generation rights as far as children are concerned. It also places an obligation on parents and persons *in loco parentis* and people in general and is therefore a manifestation of horizontality in the application of fundamental rights, which is complementary to the general tendency of the chapter, which expressly provides for verticality in the application of fundamental rights. This provision reads as follows:

> (1) Every child shall have the right –
>   (a) to a name and nationality as from birth;
>   (b) to parental care;
>   (c) to security, basic nutrition and basic health and social services;
>   (d) not to be subject to neglect or abuse;
>   (e) not to be subject to exploitative labour practices nor to be required to or permitted to perform work which is hazardous or harmful to his or her education, health or well-being.
> (2) Every child who is in detention shall, in addition to the rights which he or she has in terms of section 25, have the right to be detained under conditions and to be treated in a manner that takes account of his or her age.
> (3) For the purpose of this section a child shall mean a person under the age of 18 years and in all matters concerning such child his or her best interest shall be paramount.

This provision, which constituted a compromise on the controversial issue of the guarantee of socio-economic rights in a Bill of Rights, means that certain basic services required to sustain life are guaranteed to children alone and not to the population at large. Every child is therefore guaranteed the right to security, to basic nutrition and basic health services.[67] These terms are, however, not clear and the Constitutional Court will at some stage have to give them greater definition. Also, the compromise itself can be impugned because, as Mureinik observes, there are thousands of adults in South Africa who, because of the way our society is structured and the legacy of apartheid and deprivation, cannot satisfy their basic needs without the assistance of the state. Also, he explains that it is not clear how a court invited to enforce these rights could possibly make the necessary choices among the multiple ways of realizing them.[67]

Language and Culture

These are matters of inestimable importance to South Africans. Afrikaners waged a heroic struggle for the recognition of their language and culture against British imperial hegemony after the Anglo-Boer war which ignited the flames of Afrikaner nationalism. Under the aegis of the policy of separate development or grand apartheid, nascent black ethnic nationalism was exacerbated as part of a divide and rule strategy pursued to ensure white Afrikaner hegemony. Differences in African languages and culture were exploited to the disadvantage of the intrinsic merit of these cultures.

According to s. 31, 'Every person shall have the right to use the language and participate in the cultural life of his or her choice.' This is not an absolute right and it is subject to qualifications. It must be read in conjunction with s. 3, which creates 11 official languages. Provision is also made for the promotion of respect for certain other languages set out in s. 3(9)(c). In particular, s. 3(3), s. 3(4), s. 3(5) and s. 3(6) set out below need to be considered:

> (3) Wherever practicable, a person shall have the right to use and to be addressed in his or her dealings with the public administration at the national level of government in any official language of his or her choice.
>
> (4) Regional differentiation in relation to language policy and practice shall be permissible.
>
> (5) A provincial legislature may, by a resolution adopted by a majority of at least two-thirds of all its members, declare any language referred to in subsection (1) to be an official language for the whole or any part of the province and for any or all powers and functions within the competence of that legislature, save that neither the rights relating to language nor the status of an official language as existing in any area or in relation to any function at the time of the commencement of this Constitution, shall be diminished.
>
> (6) Wherever practicable, a person shall have the right to use and

to be addressed in his or her dealings with any public administration at the provincial level of government in any one of the official languages of his or her choice as contemplated in subsection (5).

It would place an intolerable financial burden on the state actually to provide effective services for the people of South Africa in 11 official languages. This is indeed a veritable tower of Babel. Indigenous languages like Zulu and Xhosa are more likely to enjoy practical recognition at a provincial rather than national level. English is likely to emerge as the lingua franca in South Africa as a whole, regardless of the official position.

The use and importance of Afrikaans as a national official language is, however, likely to diminish considerably, in contrast to the indigenous languages, which are likely to increase in use and importance. It is of very great importance that the use and development of the indigenous languages be encouraged in the interest of nation building and the individual self-esteem of black people in South Africa.

Education

Section 32 also deals with a provision that involves second-generation or socio-economic rights. Education is of fundamental importance as far as human rights are concerned, since education liberates people from the bondage of ignorance, superstition and fear. It gives to them dignity and self-confidence and is a seminal right on which the materialization of other rights depends. Apartheid education wrought havoc in South Africa. It created a lost generation of unskilled and angry black people in the townships of South Africa. Section 32 provides that:

Every person shall have the right –

(a) to basic education and to equal access to educational institutions;
(b) to instruction in language of his or her choice where this is reasonably practicable; and
(c) to establish, where practicable educational institutions based on a common culture, language or religion, provided that there shall be no discrimination on the grounds of race.

Although s. 32(a) does not require that all education be free and compulsory, it does provide rights for indigent children, but does not 'preclude a sliding scale of fees'.[68] This provision will place a very great economic burden on the state. Considered in conjunction with the equality provision set out in s. 8, it would require an equal distribution of educational resources throughout the country and amongst the different racial and cultural communities of South Africa. It will take time for this to be achieved. Furthermore, the right to education is not restricted to children, since s. 32 states that 'Every person shall have the right (a) to basic education'. Thus illiterate adults could also claim this right. This provision clearly involves a socio-economic or second-generation right.

OTHER PROVISIONS

The Limitation Provision

It is widely accepted in most states, in international law and affairs, and in international and other human rights documents, that only a limited number of rights and freedoms are absolute. These include freedom from torture, and freedom of conscience, belief, thought and opinion. The overwhelming majority of human rights and liberties are of necessity restricted by the inherent duty, which should be perceived as the inextricable counterpart of a corresponding right, to respect the rights of others.[69] The limitation clause plays a seminal role in the interpretation and application of the Bill of Rights and is fundamental to the kind of constitutional review involving the principle of proportionality, set out in the Canadian case of *R* v. *Oakes*,[70] involving a two-stage process. To determine whether indeed there has been a violation of a provision of the Bill of Rights, the relevant section setting out the right in question and s. 33 must be considered together. The first stage involves asking the question, has there been an infringement of a right protected by the Bill of Rights? The second involves asking whether the policy underlying the act or omission which caused the infringement is democratically justifiable in a free and open democracy, and whether an acceptable method has been used for its implementation.[71] The model of constitutional review inherent in *R* v. *Oakes* involves a judicious weighing up of competing jurisprudential and other relevant issues using the principle of proportionality. The principle of proportionality, conceived and developed in administrative law, is based on the idea that law must be 'geared to the objective it seeks to achieve, and must consequently form part of the quantifiable causal relationship between means and end aimed at achieving a desired result'.[72] This requires that the extent of the limitation or erosion of a fundamental right must be necessary to advance a politically legitimate policy.

According to s. 33(1), the limitation:

     (a) shall be permissible only to the extent that it is –
       (i) reasonable; and
       (ii) justifiable in an open and democratic society based on free-
       dom and equality; and
     (b) shall not negate the essential content of the right in question,
     and provided further that any limitation to –
       (aa) a right entrenched in sections 10, 11, 12 and 14(1), 21, 25
       or 30(1) (d) or (e) or (2); or
       (bb) a right entrenched in sections 15, 16, 17, 18, 23, or 24 in
       so far as such right relates to free and fair political activity,
       shall in addition to being reasonable as required in paragraph
       (a) (i) also be necessary.
(2) Save as provided in subsection (1) or any other provision of this
constitution, no law, whether a rule of common law, customary law,
or legislation, shall limit any right entrenched in this Chapter.
(3) The entrenchment of rights in this Chapter shall not be construed as denying the existence of any other rights or freedoms
recognised or conferred by common law, customary law or legislation to the extent that they are not inconsistent with this Chapter.
(4) This Chapter shall not preclude measures designed to prohibit
unfair discrimination by bodies and persons other than those
bound in terms of section 7(1).

Chapter 3 rights may be limited by a law of general application under the
conditions set out in s. 33(1). However, such limitation must never
'negate the essential content' of the right in question.[73]

The following rights also attract the additional requirement of necessity in their limitation, in so far as they relate to free and fair political
activity:
     (a) freedom of expression;
     (b) the right to assemble and demonstrate and petition;
     (c) the right to freedom of association;
     (d) the right to freedom of movement;
     (e) the right to access to information; and
     (f) the right to administrative justice.

    The use of a general circumspection provision facilitates the process of
interpretation of the provisions of a Bill of Rights. The alternative to this
is, as Corder points out,[74] 'specific (and often different) limitation of each
right, which can render tortuous the task of interpretation and the rank-
ing of rights'.

The Suspension of the Provisions of this Chapter and the Declaration of a State of Emergency

Even in democratic states it is necessary to make provision for the threat to the existence of the democratic order by serious civil commotion and threat of armed invasion, especially in deeply divided states, like South Africa, where the threat of civil commotion and even civil war are more likely. The awful legacy of apartheid has bequeathed to the new democratic South Africa many serious problems of a political and socio-economic nature. Frightening expectations have been created for the Government of National Unity to deal with. There is still the potential for serious and endemic violence in KwaZulu/Natal. A populist revolt is also a possibility. Security, which must be a priority for the new government, poses a dilemma, since the Government of National Unity is committed to a democratic constitution and ethos, which precludes the methods used by totalitarian regimes which can ride roughshod over human rights, as successive South African governments did when confronted with popular uprisings such as those in Sharpeville and Soweto.

In general, the constitutional limits set out in s. 34 on the exercise of emergency powers 'follow international human rights law in regard to procedural requirements for the exercise of emergency powers, necessary checks and balances against the abuse of emergency powers, and the enumeration of rights which may not be abridged even in an emergency'.[75]

Section 34 permits the use of emergency powers after a procedurally correct declaration to that effect has been made. There must be an authentic threat to the existence of the state. It provides for political control through parliamentary supervision, in that the executive would have to justify the continuation of the emergency by means of political argument and debate in the democratically and directly elected lower house and in the Senate. In addition, provision is made for judicial supervision in terms of s. 34(3). It is also clear that, by implication, detention in solitary confinement, which has serious psychological consequences for detainees, is prohibited by s. 25(1)(b).

The state of emergency does not give the executive *carte blanche*, since it is in terms of s. 34(5) prohibited from creating retrospective crimes and the indemnification of the state or persons acting under its authority for unlawful actions during the state of emergency. Although, in general, rights may be suspended, certain specified rights and corresponding procedures are declared to be inviolable.[76]

Section 34(6) sets out certain conditions that must be complied with when persons are detained pursuant to an emergency declaration. A court of law is empowered to test the legality of a detainee's detention, and if it comes to the conclusion that it is unjustified it may order the person's release, and 'such a person shall not be detained again on the same grounds unless the state shows good cause to a court of law prior to such re-detention'. Detention without trial remains constitutionally permissible during a state of emergency. Such detention remains an odious phenomenon but unfortunately 'old habits die hard'[77] and its retention must be viewed with grave suspicion by civil libertarians even if, in the circumstances of an emergency, it may be a necessary evil.

The Interpretation of the Bill of Rights

Section 35 is the last provision of Chapter 3. It deals with the seminal issue of interpretation and provides guidance to the judiciary on this matter. It reads as follows:

> (1) In interpreting the provisions of this Chapter a court of law shall promote the values which underlie an open and democratic society based on freedom and equality and shall, where applicable, have regard to public international law applicable to the protection of the rights entrenched in this Chapter, and may have regard to comparable foreign case law.
> (2) No law which limits any of the rights entrenched in this Chapter, shall be constitutionally invalid solely by reason of the fact that the wording used prima facie exceeds the limits imposed in this Chapter, provided such a law is reasonably capable of a more restricted interpretation which does not exceed such limits, in which event such law shall be construed as having a meaning in accordance with the said norm restricted interpretation.

The ambit of s. 35 is, however, not restricted to merely the interpretation of this Chapter. This is manifestly clear from s. 35(3), which states: 'In the interpretation of any law and the application and development of the common law and customary law, a court shall have due regard to the spirit, purport and objects of this Chapter.' This provision has important consequences for the interpretation of all South African statute law, common law and customary law. In effect, it authorizes a value-coherent or teleological[78] methodology of interpretation and the supplanting of the jurisprudence of positivism with a new jurisprudence that will have inherent in it a cogent element of natural law. Section 35(3) must inexorably effect a complete transformation of South African jurisprudence, since the common law and African customary law are to be infused with a culture of fundamental rights and liberal democratic values, more especially the values of race and gender equality,[79] which find such cogent expression in the Bill of Rights. The technical committee on fundamental rights explained why it added s. 35(3) as follows:

> This subclause has been added in order to facilitate the incorporation of the values embodied in this chapter throughout the legal system. It allows for judicially controlled 'seepage' of the provisions of this chapter to relationships other than those contemplated in clause 7(1).[80]

It is important to note that what s. 3 authorizes is a departure from literalism in interpretation and regard to the 'spirit, purport and objects' of the Bill of Rights in the process of interpretation of any law. This *par excellence* includes the Constitution. What is required is a value-based interpretation.

CONCLUSION

The provisions of the Bill of Rights are stated in general and broad terms in a way which allows 'for the evolutionary interpretation and the growth of the instrument which entrenches fundamental rights and freedoms'.[81] Most of them are not absolute and they may, to a greater or lesser extent, be limited by legislation which accords with the Constitution. The Constitutional Court is given, in regard to general and vague terms, considerable latitude and opportunity for innovative jurisprudence. Certain crucial moral and jurisprudential issues are not explicitly addressed. Thus the Bill of Rights does not provide an answer to the legal status of abortion and capital punishment.[82] The exact compensation for the expropriation of property is not apparent and nor is the fate of certain aspects of customary law that reflect gender inequality. How the Constitutional Court will determine the compensation according to the basket of considerations set out in s. 28(3) remains to be seen. It is not entirely clear whether religious prayers will be permissible in government schools. It is also not clear whether detention without trial, outside of a state of emergency, is permissible or whether guarantees of free speech in the Bill of Rights are compatible with traditional remedies for defamation.[83] The Constitutional Court will have to give final decisions on all these and many other vexed moral and jurisprudential questions.

The Constitutional Court is the lynchpin of the whole Constitution. It will be a powerful watchdog for the fundamental rights enshrined in the Constitution. The political profile of the courts must of necessity increase very greatly in a legal system involving the supremacy of the Constitution and a justiciable Bill of Rights.[84] With the Interim Constitution, South Africa has inexorably moved away from the doctrine of parliamentary supremacy to judicial supremacy and judicial review. The practice of judicial review involving justiciable fundamental rights is foreign to South Africa's legal and constitutional history and tradition. Most South African judges, practitioners and legal academics will have to undergo a demanding learning experience to operate within the new juris-prudential paradigm. An educational programme is required for the population as a whole to inculcate a human rights culture.

The next phase in the liberation of black people in South Africa relates to their emancipation from poverty, disease, illiteracy and unemployment. This requires the social and economic transformation of South Africa, giving rise to a more equitable distribution of the resources in the country. Without it, blacks will remain impoverished and their human rights inchoate. This is the challenge facing the ANC-led Government of National Unity, which has responded with its Reconstruction and Development Plan. It is difficult to argue with the programme's goals. The vital question is whether they are achievable. The goals must be pursued in a way that strengthens the South African economy rather than in a way that emasculates it. The proverbial goose that lays the golden egg must not be destroyed. This is indeed what Mr Mandela announced in his historic address to the first session of the new democratic Parliament on 24 May 1994, when he committed his administration to fiscal restraint and an incremental or phased reconstruction programme.[85]

Human rights are not merely a legal and political issue; they have moral and sociological dimensions. It is not only the obligation of the state to secure human rights for people; the community and its institutions must be involved. The religious institutions, the universities, the press and the great private financial institutions, i.e. the mining houses, the banks and insurance companies, have an important contributory role to play in the process of the economic, sociological and political transformation of South Africa.

For the Bill of Rights to be effectively implemented, a rights culture will have to be carefully nurtured by, among others, the Government of National Unity, the media, the churches and the legal profession. This requires foresight, sensitivity and compassion from professional bodies that have in the past been legalistic and indifferent to the fundamental issues of justice in our society. The Interim Constitution and the Bill of Rights have involved a 'paradigm shift'[86] that will require a jurisprudential adjustment from both the judiciary and the legal profession. The judiciary and different branches of the legal profession and the influential organizations that represent them, which have in the past been perceived by oppressed black people to be manifestly elitist and essentially mercenary, must become more representative of the whole South African community in regard to both race and gender and by their conduct gain the confidence and trust of the South African nation.

The endemic and serious violence that plagued South Africa in the period before the election on 27 April remains the most serious threat to human rights in the country. The violence has its roots in a variety of factors, such as the intense rivalry between the ANC and Inkatha, right-wing political radicalism and fear, and appalling socio-economic conditions that give rise to criminal conduct on the part of gangs and individuals. These problems will not go away and must be tackled by the leaders of the Government of National Unity, who, with Mr Mandela and Mr de Klerk at the helm, have committed themselves to both reconciliation and reconstruction. Failure to do this will mean that the Bill of Rights with its lofty principles will constitute a dead letter and could give rise to a populist revolt.[87] South Africa requires a process of healing and rehabilitation. It has the human and material resources to bring this about. Whether this materializes will depend on the quality of the statesmanship that prevails in the Government of National Unity. Mr Mandela has demonstrated that he is a person of profound compassion, political tolerance and steely determination. In the 'beloved country', (to use the words of the distinguished South Africa liberal author Alan Paton in his celebrated novel[88]), whose history has been marred by poignant and profound suffering and tragedy, there is at last cause for great hope and guarded optimism.

NOTES

1. The Republic of South Africa Constitution Act 200 of 1994.
2. Act 200 of 1994.
3. See D. J. Leyshon, Justice and Peace Commission: a new Constitution for South Africa, unpublished article, 18 February 1994, p. 7.
4. Discussed under the application of the provisions of Chapter 3.
5. H. Corder, S. Kahanovitz, J. Murphy, C. Murray, K. O'Regan, J. Sarkin, H. Smith and N. Steyther *A Charter for Social Justice* (Cape Town, 1992), p. 17.
6. *Ibid.*, p. 18.
7. A. Cachalia, H. Cheadle, D. Davis, N. Haysom, P. Maduna, and G. Marcus *Fundamental Rights in the New Constitution* (Cape Town, 1994), p. 53.
8. This provision conflicts with s. 4(2), which reads: 'This Constitution shall bind all legislative, executive and judicial organs of state at all levels of government. The former refers to the chapter of the Constitution dealing with the Bill of Rights and the latter refers to the

Constitution as a whole.

9. E. Mureinik, Customary law is faring well, *The Star*, 15 October 1993.

10. A. Harber, Get to know your rights, *Mail & Guardian*, 22 to 28 April 1994, p. 2.

11. E. Mureinik, Time to read your rights, NP, *Bench Marks*, 7 May 1993.

12. Section 7(2).

13. See s. 35, discussed below.

14. Cachalia *et al.*, *op. cit.*, p. 20.

15. See A. Rycroft, Equal protection, 3, unpublished paper presented at the course on constitutional litigation at the University of Natal on 30 April 1994.

16. See s. 35(1), which authorizes that where applicable regard may be had to comparable foreign case law.

17. See S. Ngcobo, Equal protection and affirmative action, unpublished paper presented at the course on constitutional litigation at Natal University on 23 April 1994.

18. Income Tax Act sexism now illegal, *Natal Mercury*, 6 June 1994.

19. Advancement must be real, *The Star*, 14 September 1994.

20. S. Ngcobo, Equal protection and affirmative action 28. Paper presented at the course on constitutional litigation at the University of Natal on 13 April 1994. It appears inconceivable that the courts would sanction private discrimination in the new South Africa.

21. The approach adopted by US courts in this regard is well illustrated by the judgment in *Shelley* v. *Kraemar* 334 US 1 (1948), where the court denied judicial enforcement to restrictive racial covenants, holding that although such private voluntary agreements do not violate the equal protection clause, their enforcement by the state courts does.

22. Section 7(1).

23. See further E. Mureinik, Don't close door to openness, *The Star*, 29 October 1993.

24. Capital punishment has been hotly debated in South Africa recently. The ANC advocated abolition in its Bill of Rights, whereas the SALC vacillated. See H. Corder *et al.* *A Charter for Social Justice* p. 34.

25. W. B. Lohart, Y. Kamisar, J. H. Chopper and S. Shiffen, *Constitutional Law* (St Paul, Minnesota, 1986), p. 559.

26. See *Furman* v. *Georgia* 408 US 238 (1972).

27. The right to die also arises under the rubric of a person's right to privacy. This is the position in the USA. See *Cruzan* v. *Director, Missouri Department of Health* 110 SCt 2841 (1990).

28. See D. J. Leyshon, *op. cit.*, p. 14.

29. Note that the ANC's draft health policy, released in January 1994, proposed the legislation of abortion on demand, but hedged its bets by saying there should be further consultation and discussion on the issue. See A. Harber and B. Ludman, *A–Z of South African Politics* (London, 1994), p. 253.

30. SA Institute of Race Relations, *1993/1994* at p. 130.

31. See *Ex Parte Attorney General, Namibia; In re Corporal Punishment by Organs of State* 1991 (3) SA 76.

32. See above, p. 82.

33. H. Corder, *op. cit.*, p. 37.

34. 310 US 296 (1940).

35. J. A. Barron and C. T. Dienes, *Constitutional Law* (St Paul, Minnesota, 1991), p. 425.

36. 370 US 421 (1962).

37. The case of *Abington School Dist.* v. *Schempp* 374 US 203 (1963) extended *Engel* v. *Vitale* 370 US 421 (1962) beyond officially composed prayers to prohibit Bible reading and recitation of the Lord's Prayer. On the other hand, it was held that the Establishment clause does not embody 'a philosophy of hostility to religion' in *Zorach* v. *Clauson* 343 US 306 (1952).

38. 472 US 38 (1985).

39. J. A. Barron and C. T. Dienes, *op. cit.*, p. 416.

40. See D. J. Leyshon, *op. cit.*, p. 8.

41. E. Mureinik, They're playing with words in the Interim, *The Star*, 1 September 1993.

42. J. A. Barron and C. T. Dienes, *op. cit.*, p. 287.

43. *Nebraska Press Association* v. *Stuart* 427 US 539, 562–3, 96 SCt 2791, 2804–5, 49 LEd 2d 683 (1976).

44. See *United States* v. *Schwimmer* (1929), 279 US 644.

45. See K. Govender, Freedom of expression and opinion. Unpublished paper presented at the course on constitutional litigation at the University of Natal, 1 June 1994.

46. See *Boos* v. *Barry* 485 US 312, at p. 321.

47. See Gunther, Foreword: In search of evolving doctrine on a changing Court: a model for a newer equal protection (1972) 86 Harvard Law Review 46. See also the case of *Texas* v. *Gregory Lee Johnson* 491 US 109 SCt 2533 (1989).

48. 89 DLR (4th) 1992.

49. *Millers* v. *California* 413 US 15 (1973).

50. *American Booksellers Association Inc.* v. *Hudnut* 771 F 2d 323 (7th Cir 1985) affr'd without opinion, 475 US 1001 (1986) as quoted by A. Rycroft, *op. cit.*, pp. 10 and 11.

51. Pornography, equality, and a discrimination–free workplace: a comparative perspective (1993) 106 *Harvard Law Review* 1075, at p. 1083.

52. J. A. Barron and C. T. Dienes, *op. cit.*, p. 302.

53. See D. J. Leyshon, *op. cit.*, p. 9.

54. See E. Mureinik, NP conspicuous by its failures, *The Star*, 23 November 1993.

55. A. Cachalia *et al.*, *op. cit.*, p. 61.

56. Act 6 of 1959.

57. A. Cachalia *et al.*, *op. cit.*, p. 65.

58. L. J. Boulle, *South Africa and the Consociational Option* (Cape Town, 1984), p. 45 *et seq.*

59. The four general principles of consociationalism are: (a) grand coalition; (b) mutual veto; (c) proportionality; and (d) segmental authority. See L. J. Boulle, *op. cit.*

60. Principle 34.

61. Section 196, which deals with the primary objectives of the SA Reserve Bank, constitutionalizes a 'balanced and sustainable economic growth in the Republic'.

62. See F. van Zyl Slabbert, Plea to make RDP work, *Daily News*, 23 May 1994.

63. Rev. S. Luckett, Restitution: a precondition for a new nation, *The Natal Mercury*, 25 May 1994.

64. A. Cachalia *et al.*, *op. cit.*, p. 98.

65. See the South African Law Commission Report on Group and Human Rights, p. 541.

66. Act 73 of 1989.

67. E. Mureinik, What now for a Bill of Rights, *The Star*, 31 October 1993.

68. A. Cachalia *et al.*, *op. cit.*, p. 104.

69. See *Fundamental Rights*, Third Report, 28 May 1993, at p. 8(27).

70. (1986) 26 DLR (4th) 200.

71. H. Corder *et al.*, *op. cit.*, pp. 14–15.

72. J. Schwarze, *European Administrative Law* (London, 1992), p. 679.

73. The rights which attract the additional requirement of having to be necessary are: (a) the right to human dignity; (b) the right to freedom and security of person; (c) the right not to be subject to servitude and forced labour; (d) the right to freedom of religion, belief and opinion; (e) the right to political rights; (f) the rights of accused persons upon arrest or detention; (g) the right of a child not to be subject to neglect or abuse and the right not to be subject to exploitative labour practices.

74. H. Corder *et al.*, *op. cit.*, p. 29.

75. A. Cachalia *et al.*, *op. cit.*, p. 117.

76. These are set out in s. 34(5).

77. See D. J. Leyshon, *op. cit.*, p. 15.

78. See G. E. Devenish, *Interpretation of Statute* (Cape Town, 1992), p. 39.

79. See D. J. Leyshon, *op. cit.*, p. 13.

80. See collection of documents entitled *Technical Committee on Fundamental Rights during the Transition*, Tenth Report, 5 October 1993, at p. 31 (141).

81. *Fundamental Rights*, Fifth Report, 11th June 1993, at p. 3(49).

82. See Death penalty moratorium, *Daily News*, 6 June 1994.

83. See A. Cachalia *et al.*, *op. cit.*, p. 55.

84. *Fundamental Rights*, Third Report, 28 May 1993, at p. 12(31).

85. See *The Natal Mercury*, 25 May 1994.

86. E. Price, Legal fraternity unprepared, *The Star*, 23 June 1994.

G.E. Devenish

87. F. van Zyl Slabbert, *op. cit.* See also the United Nations Human Development Report for 1994 as reported in the *Daily News*, 6 June 1994.

88. Paton received international acclaim for his novel *Cry, the Beloved Country*, first published in 1948, the year in which the National Party came to power and began to implement its iniquitous policy of apartheid.

5

Fundamental Rights in Australia and Britain: Domestic and International Aspects

Timothy H. Jones

INTRODUCTION

The adequacy of the legal protection given to fundamental rights and freedoms is a topic of concern in both Australia and Britain, two juris-dictions which share a common legal heritage.[1] Both have witnessed extensive debates in recent times about the desirability or otherwise of a bill of rights designed to protect human rights.[2] The issue has been brought to the fore in Britain largely as a result of the unimpressive record of the UK before the European Court of Human Rights. British laws have been found to be inadequate in the protection given to funda-mental rights and have had to be changed to reflect the requirements of the European Convention on Human Rights (ECHR). The UK's membership of the European Union (EU) has also had a considerable impact both on the content of the law and on traditional legal attitudes. As the previous Australian Chief Justice, Sir Anthony Mason, has com-mented, these European advances 'will affect the traditional affinity between Australian law and English law and serve to emphasise our legal isolation'.[3] The further significance of these developments for Australia is that the areas of the law which have been found to contradict funda-mental rights are 'all but identical with Australian common law'[4] and '[t]here is little reason to assume that legal protection of individual rights in Australia would measure up any better'.[5] Judges in both Australia and Britain are coming to recognize the inadequacy of their traditional, com-mon law conceptual framework where fundamental rights are concerned. This essay examines the nature of current Anglo-Australian academic and judicial debates, identifying common themes and drawing parallels where appropriate.

THE COMMON LEGAL INHERITANCE

Australia and Britain have remarkably few constitutional guarantees of fundamental rights. This is not to say, of course, that the two countries are without any such protections. The Magna Carta of 1215 ('that great confirmatory instrument ... which is the ground work of all our Constitutions'[6]) and the Bill of Rights of 1689 ('the product of an alliance between parliamentarians and common lawyers'[7]) remain, but they have a limited field of operation[8] and are inadequate as modern statements of fundamental rights.[9] And as subsequent discussion will demonstrate, the Australian Constitution does have something to say on the subject. It is nevertheless the case that the Anglo-Australian tradition has been to place faith in the common law, supplemented by legislation in specific areas, together with responsible and representative parliamentary government, as the best means by which fundamental rights can be protected. As Sir Anthony Mason has noted: 'the founders accepted, in conformity with prevailing English legal thinking, that the citizen's rights are best left to the protection of the common law'.[10] The preference has been not to set those rights out in a fundamental, constitutional statement of rights and freedoms. In modern times this reliance upon the common law has come under increasing strain in both Australia and Britain. Common law rights have been seen to possess two inherent weaknesses. First, they are always vulnerable to abrogation or removal by statutory law. Second, common law rights are seldom declaratory, but are merely the balance remaining after prohibited conduct has been dealt with. The traditional view has been that freedom of expression, for example, is a residual right which exists only to the extent that it is not restricted by the law relating to defamation, contempt of court, obscenity, blasphemy, trade descriptions, and so forth.[11] As Sir John Donaldson MR explained in *Attorney-General* v. *Guardian Newspapers Ltd (No. 2)*: 'The starting point of our domestic law is that every citizen has a right to do what he likes, unless restrained by the common law ... or by statute.'[12] The Constitutional Commission reached the following conclusion:

> While we agree ... that Australians owe many of the freedoms they currently enjoy to the common law, we think that the faith which many people appear to have in the common law as a safeguard of their freedoms is misplaced. The common law affords some freedoms, but much of it is inhibitory.[13]

A further impetus to the revision of traditional attitudes in Britain has come from the fact that in recent times the European Court of Human

Rights has concluded that a number of areas of the common law fail to provide the necessary protection for fundamental rights and freedoms. In *Malone* v. *Commissioner of Police for the Metropolis (No. 2)*[14] an English judge (Megarry V-C) reluctantly chose to apply the traditional common law theory that restriction of a fundamental right is legal unless forbidden by law, and decided that secret surveillance of telephone conversations was legal: 'it can lawfully be done simply because there is nothing to make it unlawful'.[15] This approach did not find favour with the European Court.[16] The *Malone* case highlights the inadequacy of the traditional approach to the protection of fundamental rights. The common law will often fail to provide the necessary safeguard: it does not create or formulate positive rights. English judges increasingly appear to be aware of these flaws. The High Court judge Sir John Laws has commented that

> the citizen should enjoy the assurance that where the subject-matter [of a governmental decision] engages fundamental rights such as freedom of speech and person, or access to the courts, any decision adverse to him will only survive judicial scrutiny if it is found to rest on a distinct and positive justification in the public interest.[17]

The second major aspect of the shared legal inheritance is the principle of responsible and representative parliamentary government, and the faith placed in Parliament to protect the rights of citizens. Within the context of a federal system (which itself places certain limitations upon the organs of governance), the Australian Constitution was designed to establish the principle of responsible and representative government as practised in the Westminster system.[18] Australia adopted the British tradition that it is Parliament, together with the courts, which provides an effective means protecting fundamental rights and that no general bill of rights is required. It was Sir Robert Menzies who claimed:

> In short, responsible government in a democracy is regarded by us as the ultimate guarantee of justice and individual rights. Except for our inheritance of British institutions and the principles of the Common Law, we have not felt the need of formality and definition.[19]

Few would today express such a complacent view. The point hardly needs making that the domination of Parliament by the executive in modern times, together with the commanding role of the political party, undercuts this approach to the protection of fundamental rights. The rapid growth in the field of judicial review of administrative action in both Australia and Britain is eloquent testimony to the fact that Parliament cannot be relied upon to ensure the accountability of the executive to the law. One curious feature of this eager acceptance of British attitudes is that the Australian Constitution does contain a number of 'rights provisions', albeit aimed at limiting the powers of the Commonwealth Parliament rather than the executive. Any such limits are, nevertheless, contrary to the approach epitomized by Dicey, which would maintain that Parliament is 'an absolutely sovereign legislature'.[20]

THE EUROPEAN DIMENSION

Superimposed on British law there is now the ECHR. The impact of the ECHR has been considerable. It seems unlikely, however, that when the UK signed the ECHR in 1950, or accepted the right of individual petition in 1966, there was any real appreciation of the profound legal change which would be brought about. It was believed that the general principles enshrined in the ECHR were already well protected under existing laws. This is why there was thought to be no need to incorporate the ECHR into domestic law.[21] For some time, this analysis seemed to be correct. But in a series of cases over the last 20 years British law has been called into question by decisions of the European Commission, judgements of the Court of Human Rights, and decisions of the Committee of Ministers.[22] As a distinguished British judge has commented: 'It is a most singular feature that the law of this country, which has for so long prided itself on protecting individual freedom, has been found to be in breach of the ECHR on more occasions than any other signatory'.[23] There has been an obligation on the government to rectify the situation and to bring the law into line with the ECHR.

The fact that the ECHR has not been incorporated into British law does mean, however, that effective judicial remedies for breaches of the ECHR are lacking. Nevertheless, the ECHR is still capable of having a considerable impact on the decisions of the courts. The ECHR and the decisions of the European Court are treated as persuasive where there is an ambiguity in a statute and 'as a legitimate aid to establish what the policy of the common law should be'.[24] As regards statutory interpretation, the courts apply a proposition that Parliament intends its legislation to comply with the existing treaty obligations of the UK, including the ECHR.[25] For this principle to be applied, however, there must be a real ambiguity. The words in the statute must be capable of bearing more than one interpretation. In *Ex Parte Brind*[26] the House of Lords held that the presumption that legislation complies with international treaty obligations did not apply so as to limit the meaning of clear general words. Their Lordships expressed the view that the judges would be usurping their role if they were to incorporate by the back door a convention which Parliament had not incorporated into domestic law. But the House of Lords did recognize that stricter judicial scrutiny of administrative decisions is appropriate where fundamental rights and freedoms are affected. This is an example of what might be termed the 'indirect effect' of the ECHR upon British law. As Lord Browne-Wilkinson has said:

> If the E.C.H.R. fulfils no other purpose, it has already... and will continue to... [bring] home to the judicial mind that there are wider principles, more fundamental than the merits of the particular case, and that ultimately our freedom depends on defending those principles, come what may.[27]

In the common law field, judges are coming to recognize increasingly 'that the ECHR jurisprudence is a body of legal material to which the common law may legitimately have regard in arriving at the right result when faced with a difficult issue involving a conflict of rights'.[28] The most striking examples to date are provided by the decisions of the Court of Appeal and House of Lords in *Derbyshire County Council* v. *Times Newspapers Ltd*.[29] Both courts made reference to Article 10 of the ECHR (and its attendant case law), which protects freedom of expression, in determining that a government body cannot sue in libel to protect its governing reputation. Were a government body to possess that right, it would have the effect of stifling legitimate criticism of its activities. It would have imposed an undesirable fetter on freedom of expression which was unnecessary in a democratic society.

There is a difference in approach between the Court of Appeal and the House of Lords. The Court of Appeal utilized Article 10 when, in determining the scope of the common law of libel, it declared in the words of Butler-Sloss, L J that it had

> to balance the competing interests of the freedom of the press to provide information, to comment, criticise, offend, shock or disturb, against the right of a governmental corporation to be protected against the false, or seriously inaccurate, or unjust accounts of its activities.[30]

The court overruled a previous precedent,[31] the application of which would have permitted the council's action to proceed. A preference was expressed for the reasoning of the Supreme Court of the USA in *New York*

Times v. *Sullivan*[32] as to the undesirability of a common law rule which compelled the critic of government activity to guarantee the truth of his or her statements, on pain of unlimited damages. Such a rule would lead to self-censorship.

In the House of Lords the emphasis was on the development of the common law, rather than the application of the ECHR. As the Court of Appeal had done, Lord Keith (with whom all the other judges agreed) made reference to US authorities, saying that the public interest considerations which underlay them were no less valid in Britain. His Lordship went on to hold that, as a matter of principle, government bodies should not be allowed to maintain a cause of action in libel: 'It is contrary to the public interest because to admit such actions would place an undesirable fetter on freedom of speech.'[33] In the conclusion to his speech Lord Keith made the following remark:

> The conclusion must be, in my opinion, that under the common law of England a local authority does not have the right to maintain an action of damages for defamation. This was the conclusion reached by the Court of Appeal, which did so principally by reference to Article 10 of the European Convention on Human Rights... I have reached my conclusion upon the common law of England without finding any need to rely upon the European Convention.[34]

Despite Lord Keith's evident lack of enthusiasm for applying the ECHR, this case is of considerable significance as a precedent for 'the development of the common law's substantive principles with the aid of the Convention'.[35] It was only by having regard to the European human rights jurisprudence that his Lordship was able to reach the conclusion he did.

The unincorporated ECHR also has a considerable potential for impact on domestic law by virtue of the UK's membership of the EU.[36] EU law is directly applicable within the UK and may, depending on the type of measure, be of 'direct effect'.[37] The jurisdiction of the European Court of Justice extends to holding British legislation incompatible with EU law. In such circumstances, the Act concerned is overridden.[38] British courts are under an obligation to decide any issues of EU law arising before them 'in accordance with the principles laid down by and any relevant decision of the European Court'.[39] The European Court of Justice has a long-established jurisprudence that international treaties for the protection of fundamental rights, most notably the ECHR, provide guidelines and indications for the standards which should be adopted in EU law.[40] The Court has demonstrated its preparedness to take the provisions of the ECHR into account when determining the legality of acts of the EU.[41] Indeed, it has gone one stage further and has declared British legislation to be incompatible with EU legislation, having read into the EU legislation the condition of compliance with fundamental rights.[42]

Thus, within the limits imposed by the UK government's continuing refusal to incorporate the ECHR, one can still be optimistic that the British courts will continue to explore the opportunities open to them to make use of the ECHR and of the case law of the European Court(s). The impact of the series of cases where British law was found lacking in the protection afforded to fundamental rights should not be underestimated. This was an experience 'which concentrated the mind wonderfully on the relevance of international human rights standards to the judicial process'.[43]

FUNDAMENTAL RIGHTS IN AUSTRALIA

Sir Owen Dixon is numbered amongst those who have taken the view that the 'founding fathers' believed that the establishment of a representative democracy with responsible government would provide all the necessary protections for fundamental rights.[44] Indeed, Australian nationhood was not borne out of a violent struggle with Britain. It was, rather, the result of negotiation and of a gradual progression. It is not too surprising, therefore, that 'guarantees of individual right are conspicuously absent'[45] from the Australian Constitution. Bailey has suggested: 'The political rights included in the Constitution reflected the primary concern of the founders in ensuring continuance of the democratic Parliamentary tradition and continued effective operation of the States.'[46] There is also a less charitable – if equally accurate – explanation which can be put forward to explain the lack of a rights focus in the Constitution: that the 'founding fathers' saw dangers in provisions which would promote equality and prevent racial discrimination.[47]

It has become a commonplace view that the Constitution contains only a handful of rights provisions: trial by jury – s. 80; freedom of religion – s. 116; acquisition of property on just terms – s. 51(31); rights of electors – ss. 24 and 41; prohibition against discrimination towards interstate residents – s. 117; and freedom of movement among the states – s. 92.[48] As Bailey has commented:

> [T]he rights provisions in the Constitution have been built into its interstices in typical British tradition. They tend to be specific and ad hoc rather than general statements of broad principle. They do not contain ringing phrases, with the possible exception of s. 92, but are specifically detailed to address particular issues. Further,

following the British . . . tradition, the provisions rarely refer to rights as such. Rather, they address a particular issue. The fact that a right is being created is a matter of interpretation rather than of explicit statement.[49]

The fact is that the few rights provisions contained in the Constitution have in the past been interpreted narrowly, thereby limiting their significance for the protection of fundamental rights.[50] More recently, however, the signs are that the High Court is not averse to a more expansive interpretation of the individual rights intrinsic to the Constitution.[51] This challenge to past orthodoxy is most clearly shown in the rejuvenation of the doctrine of implied fundamental rights in the Australian Constitution: the notion that some basic rights are so fundamental to Australian democracy that they should be recognized as implicit in the Constitution.[52] These freedoms, it has been argued, are 'so elementary that it was not necessary to mention them in the Constitution'.[53] It was the late Justice Murphy who made a number of unsuccessful attempts to have a doctrine of implied constitutional rights accepted by fellow members of the High Court.[54] In particular, in a series of chimerical judgments handed down in the 1970s and 1980s he expressed the view that the provisions of the Constitution providing for the election of Parliament required freedom of movement, speech and other communication between the States and in and between every part of the Commonwealth. He maintained that a representative system of government required these same freedoms between elections, describing them as 'not absolute, but nearly so'.[55]

The recent decision of the High Court in *Australian Capital Television Pty. Ltd and Ors.* v. *Commonwealth of Australia [No. 2]*[56] suggests that perhaps Justice Murphy's attempt to read rights into the Constitution should no longer be regarded as quite so heterodox.[57] In this case the High Court held invalid most of Part IIID of the Broadcasting Act 1942, as introduced by the Political Broadcasts and Political Disclosures Act 1991, which purported to regulate the broadcasting of political advertisements.[58] Six members of the High Court held that the Constitution contains an implied guarantee of freedom of communication as to public and political discussion. Chief Justice Mason and Justices Deane, Toohey and Gaudron held the regime in Part IIID to be wholly invalid.[59] Chief Justice Mason found that the legislative powers of the Commonwealth Parliament were subject to an implied limitation which precluded it making a valid law 'trenching upon that freedom of discussion of political and economic matters which is essential to sustain the system of representative government prescribed by the Constitution'.[60] In their joint judgment, Justices Deane and Toohey were clear that the Constitution does contain implications of freedom of communication which extend to all matters apt for an ordered and democratic society: 'Freedom of political communication is implicit in, and of fundamental importance to, the effective working of the doctrine of representative government which is embodied in our Constitution.[61] Justice Dawson powerfully dissented, making the old argument that the Constitution put its faith in Parliament and that implied constitutional guarantees which fettered its powers were undemocratic. He observed that[62]

> those responsible for the drafting of the Constitution saw constitutional guarantees of freedoms as exhibiting a distrust of the democratic process. They preferred to place their trust in Parliament to preserve the nature of our society and regarded as undemocratic guarantees which fettered its powers. Their model in this respect was, not the United States Constitution, but the British Parliament.

Justice Dawson was adamant in his view that, 'there is no warrant in the Constitution for the implication of any guarantee of freedom of communication which operates to confer rights upon individuals or to limit the legislative power of the Commonwealth'.[63]

A second strongly 'pro-rights' decision of the High Court is that in *Nationwide News Pty. Ltd* v. *Wills*.[64] At issue in this case was the validity of a contempt provision of the Industrial Relations Act 1988[65] under which the publication of a vitriolic attack on the Industrial Relations Commission had been prosecuted. The High Court was unanimous in declaring unconstitutional the provision which made it an offence to write or say anything which was likely to bring the Commission or its members into disrepute, with Justices Brennan, Deane, Toohey and Gaudron all invoking an implied constitutional guarantee of freedom of political expression. Justice Brennan pointed out that: 'Freedom of public discussion of government (including the institutions and agencies of government) is not merely a desirable political privilege: it is inherent in the idea of a representative democracy.'[66] Justices Deane and Toohey noted that the total ban would operate even if the criticism were 'justified and true'.[67]

The *Australian Capital Television* case in particular demonstrates the potential volatility of the interpretation of the Constitution. It is indicative of a preparedness to expand the constitutional protection afforded to fundamental rights. It is too early to say how, or whether, the doctrine of implied fundamental rights will develop in the future. If the High Court were fully to endorse a version of the doctrine, this would have profound implications for expansion of coverage of those rights which can be found in (or 'read into') the Constitution. It is arguable that 'an implied "bill of rights" might be constructed'.[68] One limit to the approach may be that personal rights are not created directly,[69] as they would be in an 'explicit' bill of rights. Limits are set on legislative and executive power, which establishes an area of freedom secure from governmental interference. Justice Brennan argued in the *Australian Capital Television* case that the constitutional guarantee of freedom of political communication 'cannot be understood as a personal right the scope of which must be ascertained in order to discover what is left for legislative regulation; rather, it is . . . an immunity consequent on a limitation of legislative power'.[70] It also merits pointing out that the decision indicates the degree to which the meaning to be given to an implied right can be dependent upon the membership of the High Court.[71] Although Justice Brennan agreed with the majority of his colleagues in the *Australian Capital Television* case as to the existence of the implied right in question, both there and in the *Nationwide News* case he propounded a rather different view as to the role of the judiciary *vis-à-vis* that of the legislature in its protection:

> The role of the court in judicially reviewing a law that is said to curtail the freedom unduly and thereby exceed legislative power is essentially supervisory. It declares whether a balance struck by the Parliament is within or without the range of legitimate legislative choice. In a society vigilant of its democratic rights and privileges, it might be expected that the occasions when Parliament deliberately steps outside the range of legitimate choice would be few.[72]

With his recognition of the existence of a 'margin of appreciation' to be granted to Parliament, Justice Brennan's philosophy is reminiscent of the approach of the European Court of Human Rights. Those judges in the majority in the *Australian Capital Television* case took a more uncompromising approach to restrictions on the freedom of political communication.

The most likely criticism of the doctrine of implied rights is that the judges are seizing 'a blank cheque'.[73] Writing before the most recent High Court decisions, Zines described the then emerging trend as 'highly dangerous and certainly undesirable':[74]

> [L]egislative restrictions, which are not based on any specific provisions, provide no guidance or check to judicial aggrandisement or personal predilections . . . . To accept only . . . 'a free and democratic society' (as Murphy J. did) . . . as the starting point in reasoning is to invite a judge to discover in the constitution his or her own broad political philosophy.

It would be a mistake to think that the High Court is unaware of these difficulties. (Indeed, there is an explicit reference to the views of Professor Zines in Justice Brennan's judgment in the *Nationwide News* case.[75]) The High Court has not indicated that it is prepared to go as far as Justice Murphy in implying fundamental rights in the Constitution.[76] The implied right to political speech identified in the *Australian Capital Television* and *Nationwide News* cases is based firmly on those provisions in the Constitution which appear to encapsulate a representative democracy.[77]

A related criticism may be that the doctrine of implied rights is in some sense 'undemocratic'. One version of this critique would hold that the courts should rule on fundamental rights only with proper authority derived from a bill of rights. As Winterton had earlier observed:

> In view of the current . . . controversy over the introduction of a *statutory* Bill of Rights in Australia . . . and the United Kingdom, the introduction of an open-ended *constitutional* Bill of Rights by judicial fiat appears both surreptitious and, indeed, undemocratic – which is particularly ironic in view of its justification in community values, including democracy.[78]

A second argument would be the familiar one that the protection of rights ought to be the preserve of the democratically elected legislature, rather than that of the judiciary relying upon constitutional implications (or common law presumptions).[79] The sentiment would appear to be that expressed by a past Chief Justice, Sir John Latham: 'The remedy for alleged abuse of power or for the use of power to promote what are thought to be improper objects is to be found in the political arena and not in the Courts.'[80]

Neither of these contentions is particularly attractive or convincing. As Lee has pointed out:

> Just as the Court has no mandate to imply all manner of rights, the Parliament cannot claim, by the mere fact of election, a mandate to abrogate without any reasonable basis fundamental rights . . . The mere fact that parliamentarians are elected does not enable them to arrogate to themselves the legislative power to traverse necessary implications which accord with a constitution embodying values of a representative democracy.[81]

The effect of a doctrine of implied constitutional guarantees may be to limit the sovereignty of Parliament, but the democratic rights of the electorate are not diminished. Judicial employment of the doctrine shifts the onus on to those who wish to restrict a fundamental right to utilize the (deliberately difficult) mechanism for constitutional amendment. It should be seen as a development of the recognized judicial technique of interpreting legislation so as not to impinge upon common law free-doms[82] (or that, 'where possible, statutes will be interpreted so as not to conflict with the established rules of international law'[83]). As Justice Toohey has explained,

> it might be contended that the courts should . . . conclude . . . that where the people of Australia, in adopting a constitution conferred power to legislate with respect to various subject matters upon a Commonwealth Parliament, it is to be presumed that they did not intend that those grants of power extend to invasion of fundamen-tal common law civil liberties – a presumption only rebuttable by express authorisation in the constitutional document. *Just as Parliament must make unambiguous the expression of its legislative will to permit executive infringement of fundamental liberties before the courts will hold that it has done so, it might be considered that the people must make unambiguous the expression of their constitutional will to permit Parliament to enact such laws before the courts will hold that those laws are valid.*[84]

The reality is that there is a growing judicial recognition that the legal protection afforded to fundamental rights by the bare text of the Constitution (and by statutory and common law) is inadequate. In the continuing absence of a bill of rights, it is to be hoped that the High Court will continue to engage in providing the best such protection it can.[85] For, as Justice Kirby has observed,

> judges, considering what to do in a particular case before the court, may often have little confidence that restraint on their part will be rewarded with a finely tuned, sensitive and energetic protection of rights by the vigilant executive and legislative branches of govern-ment.[86]

AUSTRALIA AND THE INTERNATIONAL ENVIRONMENT

Australia ratified the International Covenant on Civil and Political Rights (ICCPR) in 1980 and it became applicable the same year.[87] It was the ICCPR which acted as the catalyst for the attempts made in the 1970s and 1980s to enact a bill of rights.[88] Although unincorporated into domestic law, the ICCPR has the potential to have a considerable impact on the decisions of the courts. It appears to be coming to occupy a role similar to that of the ECHR in Britain in the development of the common law and in the interpretation of statutes. There are considerable similarities between the Articles of the ECHR and the ICCPR, and the European case law will be of persuasive value. (The decisions of the Human Rights Committee on the ICCPR are much less developed as a source of case law than those under the European system.) In relation to the commion law, as Justice Brennan observed in *Mabo* v. *Queensland [No. 2]*,

> it does not necessarily conform with the international law, but international law is a legitimate and important influence on the development of the common law, especially when international law declares the existence of universal human rights. A common law doctrine founded on unjust discrimination in the enjoyment of civil and political rights demands reconsideration.[89]

And as the Chief Justice has said in relation to statutory law,

> there is a prima facie presumption that the legislature does not intend to act in breach of international law. Accordingly, domestic statutes will be construed, where the language permits, so that the statute conforms to the State's obligations under international law. The favourable rule of statutory interpretation goes some distance towards ensuring that the rules of domestic law are consistent with those of international law.[90]

Australia acceded to the Optional Protocol in 1991.[91] This event has caused considerable interest[92] and appears to have heightened awareness amongst the judiciary. In *Mabo* v. *Queensland [No. 2]* Justice Brennan remarked that accession to the Optional Protocol would bring 'to bear on the common law the powerful influence of the Covenant and the international standards it imports'.[93] But accession to the Optional Protocol has not affected the legal status of the ICCPR in domestic law.[94] The potential for judges to make use of the ICCPR in their decisions was already there,[95] although accession may encourage judges to make greater use of international human rights norms and to have regard to the jurisprudence of the Human Rights Committee.[96] What accession to the Optional Protocol signifies is a commitment by Australia to international human rights scrutiny and brings it into line with other major Western countries.

There are dangers, however, in attaching too much significance to assession to the Optional Protocol. The Committee is not a judicial body; it is not a Supreme Court of Human Rights.[97] Nor are the views expressed by the Committee legally binding. Nor are there any 'means of enforcement, apart from the Committee's moral authority and the potential pressure of public opinion'.[98] There is no equivalent to the follow-up procedure in the European system from the report of the Commission to the binding decisions by other competent organs, namely the European Committee of Ministers or the Court of Human Rights.

The problem of enforcement may give rise to acute difficulties in Australia's federal system of government. The first Australian complaint lodged with the Human Rights Committee under the Optional Protocol concerned the operation of Tasmanian criminal law in relation to homo-sexuals.[99] The applicant complained that Tasmanian law criminalizing homosexual acts between consenting adults in private[100] breached Article 17 of the ICCPR, which guarantees a right to privacy, and Article 26, which guarantees a right to equality before, and equal protection of, the law. The fact that the Committee reached the welcome conclusion that the Tasmanian law was in violation of Article 17 of the ICCPR[101] did not resolve the constitutionally controversial issue of how the law should be reformed. Short of Tasmanian capitulation, the only resolution would be for the Commonwealth Parliament to exercise the external affairs power in the Constitution to ensure compliance with the Committee's view.[102] This would signify a change of policy on the part of the Commonwealth government to reflect a greater willingness to intervene in cases of human rights violations by the States than it has shown to date.[103] In and of itself, therefore, accession to the Optional Protocol must be of limited direct significance for Australian law. Its importance lies in the fact that it may have an indirect influence as an encouragement to the courts to have greater regard to the ICCPR as a source of fundamental rights norms. It may also lead to a renewal of the debate concerning the neces-sity of a bill of rights. But if there is a need for a (constitutionally entrenched) bill of rights, this has not been met by accession to the Optional Protocol.

The international procedure under the ICCPR is less effective than the regional procedure under the ECHR. The latter 'offers several advantages in the area of logistics, local trust and homogeneity'.[104] There is a considerable commonality of economic, political and legal interests in Europe. This appears 'to facilitate debate over the substance of the rights to be protected, to assist in the development of . . . familiar systems of redress and, consequently, to enhance actual promotion and protection of human rights'.[105] There is also a degree of interdependence among European countries which results in 'a reciprocal tolerance and mutual forbearance . . . that can secure the cooperative transformation of universal proclamations of human rights into more-or-less concrete realities'.[105] This conclusion as to the preferability of a regional human rights regime, in terms of competence in defence of fundamental rights,[106] is an uncomfortable one for Australia. It is difficult to see Australia becoming part of a regional regime for the protection of fundamental rights.[107] As Yamane has noted:

> Unlike the European Convention on Human Rights which was made possible by a relative homogeneity of political institutions, a common conception of the respect of human rights and the will for European integration by the Member States, Asian countries have fewer common denominators for establishing a regional mechanism for the protection of human rights.[108]

And while Australia and Asia may be in relative geographic proximity and economically interdependent, there is only limited cultural or juridical affinity.[109] Australia itself must be prepared to take responsibility for the protection of fundamental rights.

CONCLUSION

This is not the place to rehearse fully the arguments for and against a bill of rights.[110] A bill of rights would set out the parameters of fundamental rights and freedoms, thereby limiting the scope for governmental or legislative encroachment.[111] It is no coincidence that it is the most senior members of the judiciary in both Australia[112] and Britain[113] who are prominent amongst those voicing their support for a bill of rights. They have come to know better than most the inadequacy of their traditional common law approach to the protection of fundamental rights. As Sir Ninian Stephen has commented: 'There appears to be growing support for such a Bill of Rights in Australia, even amongst those once inclined to defend the adequacy of the common law.'[114] Short of incorporation of the ICCPR into Australian law or the ECHR into British law, there are limits to what even the most enlightened judge can do to assimilate (international) rights norms into his or her reasoning. There is scope in the development of the common law and in the interpretation of legislation, but a

> court cannot deny the validity of an exercise of a legislative power expressly granted merely on the ground that the law abrogates

human rights and fundamental freedoms or trenches upon political rights which, in the court's opinion, should be preserved.[115]

The particular problem which arises is with unambiguous legislation[116]
which either advertently or inadvertently conflicts with the ICCPR or
ECHR. In Britain there is no domestic remedy in the courts.[117] The
European remedy can be effective in securing an eventual change in the
law, even if it is expensive both in financial terms and in time. In
Australia the scope would not appear to be very much greater, although
the High Court can strike down legislation which conflicts with the
Constitution and there is the embryonic notion of implied rights. As
Justice Brennan stated in the *Nationwide News* case,[118]

> where a representative democracy is constitutionally entrenched, it
> carries with it those legal incidents which are essential to the effec-
> tive maintenance of that form of government. Once it is recognised
> that a representative democracy is constitutionally prescribed, the
> freedom of discussion which is essential to sustain it is as firmly
> entrenched in the Constitution as the system of government which
> the Constitution expressly ordains.

It is a question of the extent to which the High Court is prepared to
incorporate rights requirements into the text of the Constitution.

It has been suggested that the international remedy available under
the Optional Protocol to the ICCPR will prove to be of limited value in
the provision of legal protection for fundamental rights in Australia. In
apparent contrast to this sentiment, Justice Kirby has observed:

> Having just begun the process of escaping the unquestioning
> capture by the ideas of the English legal system, Australian lawyers,
> on the brink of a new century, must now face the prospect of inter-
> national scrutiny of their system of laws.[119]

For the reasons explained earlier, this faith in international supervision
strikes one as overoptimistic.[120] As the Constitutional Commission recognized in 1988, what is required is greater domestic scrutiny.[121] (And as
Justice Kirby himself has advocated on numerous occasions, norms derived
from international human rights agreements can have an important role to
play.[122]) The Constitutional Commission recommended the addition of a
new Chapter VIA, 'Rights and Freedoms', in the Constitution, together
with some expansion of the existing rights provisions.[123]

The Australian and British legal systems are both contending with the
same issues when they seek to update their approach to the protection of

fundamental rights and freedoms. Both are in the course of 'escaping' from the past. In relation to freedom of expression, for example, the Australian and British courts (within their different legal and political contexts) are grappling with similar arguments concerning a fundamental right. In neither country would traditional constitutional analysis seem to recognize the existence of a positive right to freedom of expression. The freedom would be regarded as a residual right only, with its reach dependent upon the extent of common law or statutory restrictions. Both countries are bound by Article 19 of the ICCPR not to impose any unnecessary restrictions on freedom of expression, and Britain is similarly bound by Article 10 of the ECHR. It will be interesting to see whether Article 19 of the ICCPR has the same effect on the common law and constitutional law of Australia as Article 10 of the ECHR continues to have in Britain.[124] Australia and Britain will continue to derive mutual enlightenment from the attempts of their respective judiciaries to update their common theoretical framework, with its traditional reliance upon common law nostrums.

NOTES

1. See G. Sawer, Government and Law. In J. D. B. Mitchell (ed.), *Australians and British: Social and Political Connections* (1987), Chapter 2; G. Barwick, Law and Courts. In A. F. Madden and W. H. Morris-Jones (eds), *Australia and Britain* (1980), pp. 145–61.

2. See, for example, M. R. Wilcox, *An Australian Charter of Rights?* (1993); R. Brazier, *Constitutional Reform: Re-shaping the British Political System* (1991), Chapter 7; C. Spender (ed.), *Human Rights – The Australian Debate* (1987); M. Zander, *A Bill of Rights?* (3rd edn, 1985); C. Campbell (ed.), *Do We Need a Bill of Rights?* (1980). See also the works cited within note 110.

3. Sir Anthony Mason, A Bill of Rights for Australia? (1989) 5 *Australian Bar Journal* 79, at p. 80.

4. N. K. F. O'Neill, A never ending journey? A history of human rights in Australia. In C. Spender, *op. cit.*, pp. 7--23, at p. 15.

5. B. Gaze and M. Jones, *Law, Liberty and Australian Democracy* (1990), p. 32.

6. *Ex parte Walsh and Johnson: Re Yeats* (1925) 37 CLR 36, 79, *per* Isaacs J.

7. S. A. de Smith and R. Brazier, *Constitutional and Administrative Law* (7th edn, 1994), p. 76.

8. J. G. Starke, Durability of the Bill of Rights of 1688 as part of Australian Law (1991) 65 *Australian Law Journal* 695.

9. The Queensland Electoral and Administrative Review Commission's Issues Paper No. 20, *Review of the Preservation and Enhancement of Individuals' Rights and Freedoms* (1992), p. 45, makes the point that they can be seen as 'antithetical to equality and freedom because of their discriminatory preoccupation with . . . enshrining the Protestant faith and the rights of feudal land owners'.

10. Sir Anthony Mason, The role of a constitutional court in a federation: a comparison of the Australian and United States Experience (1986) 16 *Federal Law Review* 1, at p. 80.

11. See E. Barendt, *Freedom of Speech* (1985), p. 29. The traditional approach has been challenged increasingly of late. See E. Barendt, Libel and freedom of speech in English law

[1993] *Public Law* 449, at p. 459 *et seq.*; T. R. S. Allan, Constitutional rights and common law (1991) 11 *Oxford Journal of Legal Studies* 453, at pp. 453–4.

12. [1990] 1 AC 109, 178.

13. *Final Report of the Constitutional Commission*, Vol. 1 (1988), p. 468.

14. [1979] Ch. 344. The relevant law is now contained in the Interception of Communications Act 1985.

15. [1979] Ch. at 381.

16. *Malone* v. *United Kingdom* (1985) 7 EHRR 14.

17. Sir John Laws, Is the High Court the guardian of fundamental constitutional rights? [1993] *Public Law* 59, at p. 71. See also *R* v. *Advertising Standards Authority, ex parte Vernons Ltd* [1992] 1 WLR 1289, 1293, *per* Laws J.

18. See generally J. A. La Nauze, *The Making of the Australian Constitution* (1972).

19. Sir Robert Menzies, *Central Power in the Australian Commonwealth* (1967), p. 54.

20. A. V. Dicey, *The Law of the Constitution* (2nd edn, 1886), p. 35.

21. See A. Lester, Fundamental rights: the United Kingdom isolated [1984] *Public Law* 46.

22. See generally A. W. Bradley, The United Kingdom before the Strasbourg Court 1975–1990. In W. Finnie, C. M. G. Himsworth and N. Walker (eds), *Edinburgh Essays in Public Law* (1991), pp. 185–214; F. J. Hampson, The United Kingdom before the European Court of Human Rights (1990) 9 *Yearbook of European Law* 121.

23. Lord Browne-Wilkinson, The infiltration of a Bill of Rights [1992] *Public Law* 397, at p. 398.

24. Sir John Laws, *op. cit.*, p. 67. See generally N. Bratza, The treatment and interpretation of the European Convention on Human Rights by the English courts. In J. P. Gardner (ed.), *Aspects of Incorporation of the European Convention of Human Rights into Domestic Law* (1993), Chapter 6.

25. *Garland* v. *British Rail* [1983] AC 751; *Attorney-General* v. *B.B.C.* [1981] AC. 303; *R* v. *Miah* [1974] 1 WLR 683.

26. *R* v. *Secretary of State for the Home Department, ex parte Brind* [1991] 1 AC 696. See D. Kinley, Legislation, discretionary authority and the European Convention on Human Rights (1992) 13 *Statute Law Review* 63.

27. Lord Browne-Wilkinson, *op. cit.*, p. 410.

28. Sir John Laws, *op. cit.*, pp. 64–5.

29. [1992] 3 WLR 28 (CA); [1993] AC 534 (HL). (The judgment of Morland J at first instance is reported at [1991] 4 All ER 795.) For discussion, see I. Loveland, Defamation of 'government': taking lessons from America? (1994) 14 *Legal Studies* 206; E. Barendt, *op. cit.*; B. Bix and A. Tomkins, Local authorities and libel again (1993) 56 *Modern Law Review* 738; B. Bix and A. Tomkins, Unconventional use of the Convention? (1992) 55 *Modern Law Review* 721.

30. [1992] 3 WLR at 64. See also *ibid.*, at 45, *per* Balcombe LJ: 'article 10 requires a balancing exercise to be conducted: the balance to be struck in this case is between the right to freedom of expression and such restrictions as are necessary in a democratic country for the protection of the reputation of a non-trading corporation which is also a public authority'.

31. *Bognor Regis U.D.C.* v. *Campion* [1972] 2 QB 169.

32. 376 US 254 (1964).

33. [1993] AC at 549.

34. *Ibid.*, p. 551.

35. Sir John Laws, *op. cit.*, p. 67.

36. See N. Grief, The domestic impact of the European Convention on Human Rights as mediated through Community Law [1991] *Public Law* 555; M. Waelbroeck, La Convention Européenne des Droits de l'Homme Lie-t-elle les Communautés Européennes (1965) *Semaine de Bruges* 305.

37. European Communities Act 1972, s. 2(1).

38. See, for example, *R* v. *Secretary of State for Transport, ex parte Factortame (No. 2)* [1991] AC 603.

39. European Communities Act 1972, s. 3.

40. *Hauer* v. *Land Rheinland-Pfalz* [1979] ECR 3727; *Rutili* v. *Minister for the Interior* [1975] ECR 1219; *Nold* v. *Commission* [1974] ECR 491.

41. See, for example, *R* v. *Ministry of Agriculture, Fisheries and Food ex parte Fédération Européenne de la Santé Animale* [1991] 1 CMLR 507; *Orkem* v. *Commission* [1989] ECR 3283.

42. See *R* v. *Kirk* [1984] ECR 2689; and also *Johnston* v. *Chief Constable of the Royal Ulster Constabulary* [1986] ECR 1651.

43. A. Lester, The impact of Europe on the British Constitution [1992] *Public Law Review* 228, at p. 237.

44. Sir Owen Dixon, *Jesting Pilate, and other Papers and Addresses* (1965), pp. 101–2. Similarly, *Attorney-General (Cth.), ex rel. McKinlay* v. *Commonwealth* (1975) 135 CLR 1, 24, *per* Barwick CJ: 'unlike the case of the American constitution, the Australian Constitution is built upon confidence in a system of parliamentary Government with ministerial responsibility'.

45. W. H. Moore, *The Constitution of the Commonwealth of Australia* (2nd edn, 1910), p. 615.

46. P. H. Bailey, *Human Rights: Australia in an International Context* (1990), p. 84. See also E. Campbell, Civil rights and the Australian constitutional tradition. In C. Beck, *Law and Justice: Essays in Honor of Robert S. Rankin* (1970), pp. 295–322, at p. 303.

47. J. Goldsworthy, The constitutional protection of rights in Australia. In G. J. D. Craven (ed.), *Australian Federation: Towards the Second Century* (1992), pp. 151–76, at p. 154.

48. See generally P. Hanks, Constitutional guarantees. In H. P. Lee and G. Winterton (eds), *Australian Constitutional Perspectives* (1992), Chapter 4; D. Solomon, *The Political Impact of the High Court* (1992), Chapter 5; L. Zines, *The High Court and the Constitution* (3rd edn, 1992), pp. 325–30; P. H. Bailey, *op. cit.*, Chapter 4; N. K. F. O'Neill, Constitutional human rights in Australia (1987) 17 *Federal Law Review* 85.

49. P. H. Bailey, *op. cit.*, p. 84.

50. See, for example, *Adelaide Company of Jehovah's Witnesses Inc.* v. *Commonwealth* (1943) 67 CLR 116, and *Krygger* v. *Williams* (1912) 15 CLR 116 – s. 116; *R* v. *Federal Court of Bankruptcy, ex parte Lowerstein* (1938) 59 CLR 556, and *R* v. *Archdall and Roskruge, ex parte Carrigan and Brown* (1928) 41 CLR 128 – s. 80. For general discussion, see M. Coper, *Encounters with the Australian Constitution* (1988), pp. 292–324.

51. See, for example, *Street* v. *Queensland Bar Association* (1989) 168 CLR 461, overruling *Henry* v. *Boehm* (1973) 128 CLR 482. See G. Ebbeck, The future for Section 117 as a constitutional guarantee (1993) 4 *Public Law Review* 89.

52. *Theophanous* v. *The Herald and Weekly Times Ltd* (1994) 68 ALJR 713; *Australian Capital Television Pty. Ltd* v. *Commonwealth [No. 2]* (1992) 66 ALJR 695; *Nationwide News Pty. Ltd* v. *Wills* (1992) 66 ALJR 658. See G. Kennett, Individual rights, the High Court and the Constitution (1994) 19 *Melbourne University Law Review* 581; L. McDonald, The denizens of democracy: the High Court and the 'Free Speech' cases (1994) 5 *Public Law Review* 160; G. Williams, Civil liberties and the Constitution – a question of interpretation (1994) 5 *Public Law Review* 82; H. P. Lee, The Australian High Court and implied fundamental guarantees [1993] *Public Law* 606. A similar approach had been indicated in a number of pre-Charter cases in Canada. See *Retail, Wholesale & Department Store Union, Local 580 et al.* v. *Dolphin Delivery Ltd* (1986) 33 DLR (4th) 174, at 184–5, *per* McIntyre J.

53. *Ansett Transport Industries (Operations) Pty. Ltd* v. *Commonwealth* (1979) 139 CLR 54, at 88, *per* Murphy J.

54. Most recently in *Miller* v. *T.C.N. Channel Nine Pty. Ltd* (1986) 161 CLR 556, 581–3.

55. *Ansett Transport Industries (Operations) Pty. Ltd* v. *Commonwealth* (1979) 139 CLR 54, 88.

56. (1992) 66 ALJR 695. For a critical discussion of this decision, see the Symposium, Constitutional rights for Australia (1994) 16 *Sydney Law Review* 145; and also D. Z. Cass, Through the looking glass: the High Court and the right to speech (1993) 4 *Public Law Review* 229.

57. See R. Snell, Come back Lionel (1992) 17 *Alternative Law Journal* 206; M. Kirby, Lionel Murphy and the power of ideas (1993) 18 *Alternative Law Journal* 253.

58. The legislation professed to prohibit the broadcasting on television or radio during an election period of advertisements containing political matter. It also required the provision of free time for the use of certain political parties and candidates.

59. McHugh J thought that the regulation enforced in the Territories was valid.

60. (1992) 66 ALJR 695, at 708.

61. *Ibid.*, p. 718. See also their joint judgment in *Nationwide News Pty. Ltd* v. *Wills* (1992) 66 ALJR 658 at 681: 'Inherent in the Constitution's doctrine of representative government is an implication of the freedom of the people of the Commonwealth to communicate information, opinions and ideas about all aspects of the government of the Commonwealth.'

62. *Australian Capital Television*, at 723. Dawson J placed considerable emphasis upon *Amalgamated Society of Engineers* v. *Adelaide Steamship Co. Ltd* (1920) 38 CLR 129, which he regarded as having laid the ghost of the heresy that implied limitations having their origin outside the Constitution could be imported into it. For discussion of the significance of the *Engineers'*case, see L. Zines, *op. cit.*, pp. 7–15.

63. *Australian Capital Television*, at 722.

64. (1992) 66 ALJR 658.

65. s. 229(1)(d)(ii).

66. (1992) 66 ALJR, at 669.

67. *Ibid.*, at 678.

68. Justice J. Toohey, A government of laws, and not of men? (1993) 4 *Public Law Review* 158, at p. 170.

69. See D. Speagle, Case Notes: *Australian Capital Television Pty. Ltd* v. *Commonwealth* (1992) 18 *Melbourne University Law Review* 938, at p. 947. But see now *Cunliffe* v. *Commonwealth* (1994) 68 ALJR 791, at 799 *per* Mason CJ.

70. (1992) 66 ALJR 695, at 708.

71. This realist observation is not a novel one. It accords with the view expressed some sixty-five years ago by the minority in the *Report of the Royal Commission on the Constitution* (1929), p. 245: 'The present position is such that the Commonwealth Constitution is broad or narrow according to the way it is construed by the High Court, and the Constitution depends upon the trend of thought of the individuals who for the time being form that body.'

72. (1992) 66 ALJR 658, at 671.

73. L. Zines, *Constitutional Change in the Commonwealth* (1991), p. 52.

74. *Ibid.*, pp. 51–2.

75. (1992) 66 ALJR 658, at 668.

76. Some members of the High Court (apart from Murphy J) have indicated their pre-paredness to go further and to identify rights (for example equality) implied by the Constitution as a whole and not derived from specific provisions. In their joint judgment in *Leeth* v. *Commonwealth* (1992) 66 ALJR 529, at 542, Deane and Toohey JJ observed: 'Implicit in that free agreement [that is, the Constitution] was the notion of the inherent equality of the people as the parties to the compact.' Brennan J also appeared sympathetic to this notion. In *Street* v. *Queensland Bar Association* (1989) 168 CLR 461, at 554, Toohey J made reference to 'the principle that Australia was to be a commonwealth in which the law was to apply equally to all its citizens' (citation omitted). And in *Queensland Electricity Commission* v. *Commonwealth* (1985) 159 CLR 192, at 247, Deane J identified an 'implication of the underlying equality of the people of the Commonwealth under the law of the Constitution'.

77. ss. 7, 24. See H. P. Lee, *op. cit.*

78. G. Winterton, Extra-constitutional notions in Australian constitutional law (1986) 16 *Federal Law Review* 223, at p. 234.

79. This is but a variant of 'the political arguments against a Bill of Rights... that it is dan-gerous in that it transfers power to the unelected... judiciary', S. Lee, Bicentennial Bork, Tercentennial *Spycatcher*: do the British need a bill of rights? (1988) 49 *University of Pittsburgh Law Review* 777, at p. 787.

80. *South Australia* v. *Commonwealth* (1942) 65 CLR 373, at 429.

81. H. P. Lee, *op. cit.*, pp. 627–8.

82. See Justice M. Kirby, Human rights: the role of the judge, in J. Chan and Y. Ghai, (eds) *The Hong Kong Bill of Rights: a Comparative Approach* (1993), Chapter 10, p. 234: 'there is a kind of compact between the courts and the "political" branches of government that the courts will declare the meaning and effect of laws made by the other branches and the oth-

ers will accept that declaration. In doing so, the courts will presume that those other branches did not (unless they made their intention absolutely clear) intend to derogate from "basic rights", as the courts in turn declare them.'

83. *Koowarta* v. *Bjelke-Petersen* (1982) 153 CLR 168, at 204, *per* Gibbs CJ (citation omitted).

84. Justice J. Toohey, *op. cit.*, p. 170 (emphasis added). See also *Seamen's Union of Australia* v. *Utah Development Co.* (1978) 144 CLR 120, at 157, *per* Murphy J: 'The Constitution is a framework for a free society.'

85. The defence of the notion of implied constitutional rights outlined in the preceding paragraphs could be applied to the broad view of the concept, associated particularly with Murphy J, as well as to the narrow approach taken in the *Australian Capital Television* and *Nationwide News* cases. The argument in the text focuses upon the latter, since that approach has the support of a majority of the High Court.

86. Justice M. D. Kirby, The role of the judge in advancing human rights by reference to international human rights norms (1988) 62 *Australian Law Journal* 514, at p. 528.

87. See G. Triggs, Australia's ratification of the International Covenant on Civil and Political Rights: endorsement or repudiation? (1981) 31 *International and Comparative Law Quarterly* 278. The UK ratified the Covenant in 1976.

88. This history is recounted in P. H. Bailey, *op. cit.*, and also in B. Galligan, Australia's rejection of a Bill of Rights (1990) *Journal of Commonwealth and Comparative Politics* 344, at pp. 357–65.

89. (1992) 175 CLR 1, at 42 (Mason CJ and McHugh J concurring). See to the same effect *Dietrich* v. *The Queen* (1993) 67 ALJR 1, at 15, *per* Brennan J.

90. Sir Anthony Mason, The Relationship between international law and national law, and its application in national courts. Paper presented to the 64th Conference of the International Law Association, Broadbeach, 20 August 1990, p. 7. See also *Dietrich* v. *The Queen* (1993) 67 ALJR 1, at 30–1, *per* Dawson J.

91. The UK has not yet done so. Article 2 of the Optional Protocol provides that 'individuals who claim any of their rights enumerated in the Covenant have been violated and who have exhausted all available domestic remedies may submit a written communication to the [Human Rights] Committee for consideration'.

92. See C. Caleo, Implications of Australia's accession to the First Optional Protocol to the International Covenant on Civil and Political Rights (1993) 4 *Public Law Review* 175.

93. (1992) 175 CLR 1, at 42 (Mason CJ and McHugh J concurring). On the impact of recognition of the individual application on judicial attitudes, see R. Higgins, The relationship between international and regional human rights norms and domestic law. Paper presented at the Judicial Colloqium, Balliol College, Oxford, 21–23 September 1990, at pp. 3–6 and 14–15.

94. This elementary point has been reiterated in *Dietrich* v. *The Queen* (1993) 67 ALJR 1, at 6, *per* Mason CJ and McHugh J, at 36–7, *per* Toohey J.

95. See, for example, *Jago* v. *District Court of N.S.W.* (1988) 12 NSWLR 558, at 569, *per* Kirby P; *Daemar* v. *The Industrial Commission of N.S.W. and Ors.* (1988) 12 NSWLR 45, at 53, *per* Kirby P; *McInnis* v. *The Queen* (1979) 143 CLR 575, at 588, *per* Murphy J; *Dowal* v. *Murray* (1978) 143 CLR 410, at 430, *per* Murphy J; *Dugan* v. *Mirror Group Newspapers* (1978) 142 CLR 583, at 607–8, *per* Murphy J.

96. See, for example, *Dietrich* v. *The Queen* (1993) 67 ALJR 1, at 7, *per* Mason CJ and McHugh J, at 30 *per* Dawson J. See also *Director of Public Prosecutions for the Commonwealth* v. *Saxon* (1992) 28 NSWLR 263; *R* v. *Astill* (1992) 63 A. Crim. R. 148; *R* v. *Greer* (1992) 62 A. Crim. R. 442.

97. A. H. Robertson and J. G. Merrills, *Human Rights in the World* (3rd edn, 1989), p. 69.

98. T. Opsahl, The Human Rights Committee. In P. Alston (ed.), *The United Nations and Human Rights: A Critical Appraisal* (1992), pp. 369–443, at p. 431.

99. *Toonen* v. *Australia*, Comm. No. 488/1992. See W. Morgan, Sexuality and human rights: the first communication by an Australian to the Human Rights Committee under the Optional Protocol to the International Covenant on Civil and Political Rights (1993) 14 *Australian Yearbook of International Law* 277.

100. Criminal Code, ss. 122–3.

101. UN Doc. CCPR/C/50/D/488/1992 (31 March 1994). See W. Morgan, Identifying evil

for what it is: Tasmania, sexual perversity and the United Nations (1994) 19 *Melbourne University Law Review* 740.

102. s. 51(29). See *Richardson* v. *Forestry Commission* (1988) 77 ALR 237; *Commonwealth* v. *Tasmania* (1983) 158 CLR 1.

103. On which see the Joint Committee on Foreign Affairs, Defence and Trade, *A Review of Australia's Efforts to Promote and Protect Human Rights* (1992), pp. xxvii, 27–30.

104. T. Opsahl, *op. cit.*, p. 440.

105. B. H. Weston, R. A. Lukes and K. H. Hnatt, Regional human rights regimes: a comparison and appraisal (1987) 20 *Vanderbilt Journal of Transnational Law* 585, at p. 589 (footnote omitted).

106. Similarly, C. M. Tucker, Regional human rights models in Europe and Africa: a comparison (1983) 10 *Syracuse Journal of International Law and Commerce* 135, at pp. 139–40, 168; T. Buergenthal, The American and European Conventions on Human Rights: similarities and differences (1981) 30 *American University Law Review* 155, at pp. 155–6.

107. *Cf.* Joint Committee on Foreign Affairs, Defence and Trade, *op. cit.*, pp. 57–8.

108. H. Yamane, Asia and human rights. In K. Vasak and P. Alston (eds), *The International Dimensions of Human Rights*, Vol. 2 (1982), pp. 651–70, at p. 663 (endnote omitted).

109. See R. Little and W. Reed, *The Confucian Renaissance* (1989), especially pp. 83–4, 88–9. See also the Bangkok Declaration issued by a number of Asian states in April 1993, reported at (1993) 2(2) *Bills of Rights Bulletin* 78. Australia was not a party to this statement of 'the aspirations and commitments of the Asian region'.

110. Compare, for example, R. Dworkin, *A Bill of Rights for Britain* (1990) with J. Waldron, A right-based critique of constitutional rights (1993) 13 *Oxford Journal of Legal Studies* 18. See also J. Goldsworthy, *op. cit.*, pp. 160–76; R. Blackburn, Legal and Political arguments for a United Kingdom Bill of Rights. In R. Blackburn and J. Taylor (eds), *Human Rights for the 1990s* (1991), pp. 108–20; J. Finnis, A Bill of Rights for Britain? The moral of contemporary jurisprudence (1985) LXXI *Proceedings of the British Academy* 303.

111. This observation is based on the assumption that the rights will be enforced satisfactorily.

112. Including the previous Chief Justice (see Sir Anthony Mason, *op. cit.*), even if not 'enthusiastically' (*ibid.*, p. 79).

113. Including the Lord Chief Justice (see Lord Taylor, *The Judiciary in the Nineties* (1992), pp. 13–14) and the Master of the Rolls (see Sir Thomas Bingham, The European Convention on Human Rights: time to incorporate (1993) 109 *Law Quarterly Review* 390, at p. 398).

114. Stephen, *op. cit.*, p. 26.

115. *Nationwide News Pty. Ltd* v. *Wills* (1992) 66 ALJR 658, at 667, *per* Brennan J.

116. Or a settled common law rule which is a binding authority upon the court concerned, subject to the willingness of a higher court to allow an appeal and overrule the obstructive precedent.

117. Unless the measure is contrary to EU law.

118. (1992) 66 ALJR 658, at 669–70.

119. Justice M. Kirby, The New World Order and human rights (1991) 18 *Melbourne University Law Review* 209, at p. 213.

120. The point can be put more strongly. Sir Thomas Bingham, *op. cit.*, p. 19, has spoken in relation to Britain of 'the insidious and damaging belief that it is necessary to go abroad to obtain justice'.

121. See the Constitutional Commission, *op. cit.*, pp. 20–4 and Chapter 9.

122. See Justice M. D. Kirby, *op. cit.*

123. The 1988 attempt to effect amendments to the Constitution to implement some of these latter proposals was notably unsuccessful. See H. P. Lee, Reforming the Australian Constitution: the frozen continent refuses to thaw [1988] *Public Law* 535.

124. As evidenced, for example, by the judgments of Neill LJ in *Middlebrook Mushrooms* v. *T.G.W.U.* [1993] IRLR 232 and *Rantzen* v. *Mirror Group Newspapers* [1993] 3 WLR 953.

PART TWO:

THEORETICAL FOUNDATIONS OF RIGHTS

6

Justice and Human Rights in Postmodernity

Costas Douzinas

Are human rights the principle of our age in the sense that Heidegger claimed that reason was the epochal principle of modernity? The Heideggerian principle is not the anthropologist's collection of mores, customs, morals and institutions, nor the historian's conglomeration of guiding values and ideas. For Heidegger, 'humanity defines an epoch of its historical and spiritual existence by the natural energy at its disposal and the pressure such energy brings to bear'.[1] But are human rights the force behind the energy of our societies? Do they motivate the pressure that humanity applies? Of course, we may all be sceptical, if not cynical, about the attitude of governments to human rights, about the ringing declarations of international organizations, or the repeated public expression of grave concern in Whitehall, Washington, the Quay d'Orsay or Bonn about the killing streets of Sarajevo, Somalia, Rwanda, Grozny or whatever latest catastrophe attracts some fleeting attention on our television screens.

Human rights appear to have won the large ideological battles of modernity. The last two principles and movements to challenge liberal democracy, those of total state organization of society and of racial supremacy, are on the way out with the end of communism and the elimination of apartheid. Both left- and right-wing totalitarianisms, which routinely violated basic human rights, are thankfully abandoning the world scene. Respect for human rights seems to be the only regulative principle of state organization which unites every country, race and creed in the world. Human rights are the ideology after the end, the defeat of ideologies, or, to adopt a voguish term, the ideology at the 'end of history'.[2]

In Marxist theory, the working class had the unique position of being both a particular class with its own interests and concerns and the representative of the universal, the agent of the common good of the whole society; as one part of the capitalist system it was its creation but, at the same time, as the universal class it would lead to the overcoming of the very system that had created it. In a similar vein, human rights can be seen as a partial ideology which has now become universal and has eclipsed or made partial and suspect all other world-views. Human rights were initially linked with specific class interests and were the ideological and political weapons in the fight of the rising bourgeoisie against the claims of despotic political power and static social organization. But to the extent that their ontological presuppositions, the principles of human equality and freedom, and their political corollary, the claim that political power must be subjected to the demands of reason and law, have become part of the staple ideology of most contemporary regimes, the partiality of their position has been transcended. In this perspective their universal application and full triumph is a matter of time and of a final adjustment between the spirit of the age and a few recalcitrant regimes in the outer reaches of the world or a question of overcoming the hypocrisy of power and holding governments to their ideological declarations. But the spirit itself has won through and its victory is none other than the completion of the promise of the Enlightenment, of emancipation through reason.

And yet many doubts persist.[3] The record of human rights violations since their ringing declarations at the end of the eighteenth century is quite appalling. But can we doubt the principle of human rights and question the promise of emancipation through reason and law when it seems close to its final victory? Is there something in the nature of human rights discourse which has led to this gap between theory and practice? What is the contemporary meaning of the principle of human rights and how does it relate to their classical formulation? Let us signpost our route. We will examine first the metaphysical presuppositions of classical human rights discourse. Their ideology is based on certain constitutive exclusions and restrictions and on a totally contentless conception of human nature. These problems arguably are not unrelated to the difficulties in their application. Other underemphasized aspects of human rights then come into focus. Human rights introduce the logic of indeterminacy and the principle of negativity in society, law and identity. At the same time, they express an ethical attitude of respect for the concrete other person which points to their link with justice.

The classical conception of justice linked the ethical and the political realms through a teleology of the good (life). Modernity, on the other hand, by secularizing the foundations of authority and meaning, opened the independent normative realms of morality and legality.[4] Both are deprived, however, of overarching points of exteriority or transcendence and base their claims on the universalizing faculty of reason. Postmodernity recognizes the exhaustion of the exalted attempts to ground action upon cognition, reason or some *a priori* conception of the good and marks the beginnings of a new ethical awareness. But the re-linking of the two realms must pass through another conception of the good, in a situation where classical teleology is historically exhausted and religious transcendence is unable to command widespread or uniform acceptance. The argument of this chapter is that in their paradoxical linkage of symbolic openness and ethical determinacy, human rights can become the postmodern formulation of the principle of justice.[5]

THE METAPHYSICAL PRESUPPOSITIONS OF HUMAN RIGHTS

What type of political system does the declaration and recognition of human rights by the great revolutions of the eighteenth century usher in? The early modern statements and declarations present human rights as a series of individual entitlements and claims which belong to human beings on account of their basic humanity rather than as a result of grants by public power. But who is the 'man' of the rights of man, what humanity is promised and which nature is proclaimed in the classical declarations of human rights?

The modern conception of the human essence, of 'man's' nature, came into existence after the collapse of the orderly, purposeful and meaningful medieval universe which assigned people to determined and specified positions. The ordered world of political hierarchies, cognitive certainty and social stasis, underwritten by theological dogma, collapsed and was overtaken by an experience of dispersal and fragmentation. The earliest and most radical philosophical shift is the invention or creation of the modern subject which becomes the self-defining foundation of modernity. The subject, the origin and the basis of modern society, is no longer conceived as a mirror of some superior, external reality but as a lamp, as the source and centre of light illuminating the world.[6]

The clearest and most symbolic expression of this idea in politics and law is the triumph of the discourse of rights in the great revolutions of the eighteenth century. The institution of rights is a creation of Roman law. Classical natural law then introduced ideas of equality and liberty into pre-revolutionary enlightened opinion. Private law rights were recognized in civilian France, while the American colonists enjoyed many of the common law remedies and protections of the 'free-born Englishman'. What distinguished these revolutionaries from protagonists of earlier conceptions of rights was the foundation of a new type of state power grounded on and legitimized by the recognition and protection of rights.

The differences between the aims of the French social revolution and

the American Revolution and War of Independence have been extensively discussed. For the French, philosophy offers an insight into the
rational scheme of the new state based on the protection of rights. The
role of the revolution is to take philosophy to the barricades and make it
the legislator. When a gap exists between philosophical insight and public opinion, 'the practical task falls to the *philosophe* to secure political
recognition for reason itself by means of his influence on the power of
public opinion. The philosophers must propagate the truth, must propagate their unabridged insights publicly.'[7] The Americans, on the other
hand, in a more pragmatic fashion, believe that their Bill of Rights is a
restatement and clarification of the legal position of the English and that
it expresses the 'common sense' view on these matters. While the
American Revolution changed the ground of legitimation of state power,
the revolutionaries believed that the substance of rights remained unal-
tered. What unites the two revolutions, however, and makes them key
historical moments in early modernity, is their rhetorical commitment to
a political system, which has been arrived at freely by citizens, guided
either by the dictates of reason or by their experience of life, and which
guarantees the rights of freedom and equality. The task of modern political philosophy is to combine freedom, reason and morality against the
background of a polyphony of values. It is a Sisyphean task that finds its
first and most perfect – too perfect – philosophical solution in the work
of Kant.

After the destruction of the premodern communities of virtue, morality must be grounded solely on the isolated subject. But rationalism
abhors personal morality because it smacks of subjectivism and
relativism. In the absence of a substantive theory of the good, the morality of the Kantian autonomous subject becomes exclusively obedience to
the law. Respect for the other person is not based on the moral worth of
that person, but on the fact that his or her actions and moral disposition
are an instance and proof of law's existence. Moreover the (moral) law, in
the form of the categorical imperative, needs for its operation and
appeals to a universal community; the ethical substance becomes transferred and must be discovered in the universal form of the law. But as no
historical universal community exists, the moral law becomes a regulative
principle, a rationalizing and legitimizing device for a state law depleted
of any substantive ethical idea. Thus, in modernity universality becomes
the true meaning of normative generality. The only place where the universal makes a royal appearance is in the discourse of human rights.

International human rights discourse is such an instance of a universal law which addresses all states and all human persons *qua* human.
Article 1 of the Universal Declaration of Human Rights, which only
repeats the universalistic claims of the *Declaration des droits de l'homme et de*

Citoyen, states that all 'men are born equal in rights and in dignity'. The Declaration claims that human nature is abstract and universal and that it is being parcelled out in equal shares to everyone, to all people in all eternity. Formally, the UN document repeats the claims of the French and American declarations, but there is a crucial gap between the subjects of concrete legal proclamations, national or international, which are necessarily bound to a historical legislator and a national territory and citizenry, and the claims of universal human nature, the rights of 'man' of human rights discourse. The 'we' of the human rights legislator is perforce narrower than the subject of humanity. This gap, between the universal subject assumed in the declarations issuing in the name of 'we people' and the empirical legislator, is disguised and acquires its full historical force through another rhetorical operation. Declarations of rights appear to 'declare', to announce obvious historical facts that need only to be stated to be recognized for what they always were, the self-evident truth. But while they adopt the constative modality, in reality they are performative. They create what they declare; they give historical substance to that which they assert simply to recognize and state. It would not be inaccurate to suggest that political modernity is founded in the crucial space opened when the historical legislator claims to speak for the universal. Its legal history unravels according to the possibilities created in the paradoxical statement of an obvious law which creates in that statement what it claims merely to represent.[8]

Human rights are first and foremost the claims of universal reason, the assertion of the rights of a common humanity. Human rights are therefore based on their alleged universal validity upheld by the operations of reason; but their application is paradoxically supposed to respect the dignity of difference, to protect the uniqueness of each separate individual, and to defy the logic of necessity and the interests of the state for the claims of singularity and contingency. The problem of the relationship between the universal and the particular cannot be wished away or easily resolved through the subsumption of individuals to laws and principles or a purely inductive process of reasoning.

This is the reason why, when we move from the abstract subject of Kantianism and human rights declarations to the concrete human being in the world, human rights often turn into a discourse of legitimation or rebellion with little descriptive value. The community of human rights is universal but imaginary; it does not exist empirically and has limited value as a transcendental principle. In the universal community of reason, which acts as the horizon for the realization of the law, the other, the alien, the third and unrepresentable is easily turned into the same, the critical distance between self and other is reduced and the experience of moral conscience becomes grounded solely on the representation of the other by the knowing and willing ego. The alternative is the other's total exclusion, banning or forgetting. But the other who approaches me is singular and unique; he or she cannot be reduced to being solely an instance of the universal concept of the ego, and nor can he or she be subsumed as a case or example under a general rule or norm. The law of modernity based on self's right and the subject's empire is strangely immoral as it tries to assimilate or exclude the other. The assumed community of reason is based on an original violence and exclusion.[9]

In classical liberal constitutionalism, the necessary synthesis of will and reason passes through the creation of a polity that respects human rights by placing constitutional and legal restrictions upon the public power for the benefit of individual freedom. Law is asked to enforce this – self-imposed – restriction upon power, but that leads to a second paradox: law, the exclusive language and the privileged action of state power, is asked to restrict its own progenitor, power. When 'man' becomes the ground of meaning and action, the protection of the rights of man against state power becomes the essence of democracy and links human rights with law and justice. But the early philosophical answers to the problem, whose influence is still felt strongly in political and legal theory, soon ran out of steam and this led partly to the widely felt cynicism that human rights attract. The 'triumph' of human rights cannot be attributed exclusively either to universalism or to contractarianism, particularly after their – originally revolutionary – claims to equality before the law and freedom became a standard element of dominant Western ideology. The contemporary significance of human rights must be sought elsewhere.

HUMAN NATURE AND THE PROCLAMATION OF RIGHTS

The human nature assumed by the philosophy of modernity is pre-moral and its essence is to express itself in actions and work. The Kantian transcendental self exists prior to its earthly attributes, as ground of action and centre of meaning. This assumption is shared by most legal and moral philosophy, even though later versions of Kantianism turned the postulate of the autonomous self from a transcendental presupposition to either a heuristic device (Rawls) or a constructive assumption that appears to offer the best description of legal practice (Dworkin). The central theme of modernity, as Gaete puts it, is the 'notion of the human subject as a sovereign agent of choice, a creature whose ends are chosen rather than given, who comes by his aims and purposes by acts of will, as opposed, say, to acts of cognition'.[10] This attempt to found the good on law, to make morality a question of rule-following, is fully recognized by the morally neutral attitude of the human rights mentality. Human rights open morally indifferent areas of action within which free individuals can pursue their aims and conduct their activities without concern for any substantive value or principle. Conversely, any duties that might exist are not the outcome of membership in a community or of the operation of virtue, but the recognition of the limitations that the rights of others impose upon my freedom. Modern man's essence is a non-essence when compared with Aristotle's 'political animal'. This abstractness of human essence, which underpins human rights discourse, is the main ground of some of their most telling critiques, including Marxism and communitarianism.[11]

This abstract subject meets the modern need for universalization, when the function of commonality, of the shared attributes of humanity, can no longer be performed by objective essences or divine impositions. Human nature is both pre-moral and pre-individual, the common substratum out of which personal attributes, idiosyncracies and capacities will develop in their sovereign and unpredictable ways. The subject, as site of philosophical introspection, as outcome of genealogical development and as vehicle of legal rights, is the mediator between abstract human nature, parcelled out equally to all human beings at birth, and the concrete human being who travels life creating her own unique narratives and acting them out on the world. The (legal) subject is what gives the person solidity and stability, what makes her present to herself and links her to consciousness and history. Above all the subject, as the link between human nature and self, is what subjects self to the law, particularly to the law that the subject herself has legislated. The recognition of legal personhood is our accession to a public sphere of rights, legal limitations and duties, all based on the assumption of a shared, abstract and equal essence and of a calculating, antagonistic and fearful existence.

Legal rules ensure equality before the law and guarantee the freedom of the parties. But this equality is only formal: it necessarily ignores the specific history, motive and need that the litigant brings to the law in order to administer the calculation of the rule and the application of the measure. Similarly, legal freedom is the freedom to accede to the available repertoire of legal forms and rights, the freedom to be what the law has ordained, accompanied by the threat that opting out is not permitted, that disobedience to a legal norm is disobedience to the rule of law *tout court* and that life outside the legal form ceases. Legal rules and their mentality are strangely amoral; they promise to replace ethical responsibility with the mechanical application of predetermined and morally neutral rules, and justice with the administration of justice. The law, sharing the tendency to abstract and universalize, turns concrete people into generalized legal subjects. But the legal subject is a fiction and the natural (legal) subject is infinitely more fictitious than the corporate. The legal subject is a *persona*, a mask, veil or blindfold put on real people who, unlike the abstractions of moral philosophy, suffer pain.

This is a well-known and valid critique of great historical significance. It has contributed to the creation of a jurisprudence of economic and social rights and has led to the reformulation of classical liberal conceptions of rights so as to take account of the material conditions necessary for the realization of the promise of freedom and equality. The abstract 'man' of philosophy was too empty, devoid of empirical traits and characteristics and could scarcely become the ground of the political constitution. The function of human 'nature' or of the 'man' of the rights of man must be sought elsewhere.

The classical declarations claim that human rights belong to 'man'; they therefore presuppose logically a substratum, 'man' or human nature, to whom they are given. But the only ontological assumption of modern philosophy is that of the equally shared freedom of will which exists in its pristine nature before any predicate or determination. 'Man' in the abstract, legal personhood at large, is the being that proclaims rights; in other words, 'man's' essence lies in the act of *proclaiming*, of linguistically asserting without any ground other than himself. The act of proclamation recognizes the radical world-making character of language and establishes a political system based on linguistic possibilities and on the self-referential, groundless freedom of modernity. It is in the nature of human rights to be proclaimed, because there is no-one outside historical humanity to guarantee them and in the act of proclamation 'man' both recognizes and asserts his nature as free will. The central revolutionary element of the declarations is to be found in this act of self-foundation, in which specific rights are created in one and the same act, which establishes also the bearer of right ('man') and the power of the legislator to create all human rights *ex nihilo*.

The legitimacy of declarations should not be sought exclusively, therefore, in a fictitious original pact or in the equally mythical institutional rights of the self-governing and self-taxing English. Human rights declarations create their own legitimacy in their act of enunciation. Indeed, not only is it in the nature of human rights to be declared, but their declaration exhausts their claim to legitimacy. There is no need for any further argument, justification or reason for human rights other than the proclamatory act which confers upon the legislators the right to legislate and to claim that they belong to all. We should add here that while 'man' in the abstract or human nature is the bearer of the rights of the declarations, no human right in the abstract, no right to right, has been created. Human rights involve specific claims to free speech, security of the person etc. This specificity implicates them in concrete legal and institutional settings and national and local histories and traditions.

While the declaration of human rights turns the radical contingency of linguistic proclamation into a main constitutional principle of modernity, their character as *rights* returns us to the discipline of law and the principle of reason. Human rights open morally neutral areas in which willed action is free to follow its aims and purposes. Rights are sanctioned by the law according to established criteria and fall within the accepted repertoire of legal claims. If the proclamation symbolizes the freedom and groundlessness of modernity, the claim of right returns to the demand for practical reason and justification, for order and coherence. Rights presuppose and are consistent with the equal rights of others and take account in their operation of public interests. Rights claims refer to the action of right reason, to *logos* not as language but as an order of argumentation and justification which turns liberty into freedom under the law. There is a difference, therefore, between the bearer of rights, the 'man' of declarations, and the historical legislator or the individual subjects who claim the protection of legal rights. The birth and history of modernity must be traced in this crucial gap between self-founding humanity and historical acts of foundation which create their own foundation.

ON THE FLOATING SUBJECT OF RIGHTS

Human rights come into existence through their proclamation. To have human rights, which in modernity is synonymous with being human, you must claim them. The proclamatory nature links human rights claims with the 'man' of human rights, an empty vessel, an ever-present but undifferentiated and indeterminate attribute of human identity which awaits to be assigned predication, characteristics, a time and a place. The 'man' of rights functions as a floating signifier. As a *signifier*, it is a discursive element that is not automatically or necessarily linked with any particular meaning; on the contrary, it has the characteristics of a signifier, which is both empty of all meaning and can therefore be attached to a large number of signifieds, *and* has a surplus of symbolic value, which does not allow it to be fully and finally pinned down to any particular signified.[12]

A new right is recognized if it succeeds in fixing a – temporary or partial – signified upon the floating signifier. This process takes place in various political, ideological and institutional battles. Groups, campaigns and subjects fight in a number of different arenas and through divergent and interlocking practices for the recognition of a new human right. These occasionally disparate efforts are linked with each other through the symbolic and linguistic nature of the claim to human rights. The creative potential of language and rhetoric allows the original rights of man to break up and proliferate into the rights of various types of subject, e.g. the rights of workers, women, children or refugees, or the rights of a people to self-determination.

The mechanism of extension of rights involves the assertion of similarity and difference. The rhetorically asserted similarity between human nature and the nature of various limited subjects of rights grounds their claim to equal treatment. On the other hand, the difference between human nature *tout court* and the more restricted nature of the subjects of these rights grounds their claims to a differential treatment that respects their specific identity. Once a new group has established in law and fact its claims to equality (based on its similarity with human nature) and difference (based on its distinct identity and difference from other groups admitted to the status and dignity of human nature) it then becomes the 'ground' group for a further proliferation of right claims, in other words for new claims to similarity and difference. After the recognition of a general right to equality of gay people, for example, more concrete rights will be claimed, like the right to equal age of consent to sexual intercourse, or the right of gays to marry. Throughout this process of extension, the key operation is that of establishing similarity and difference, in other words the imaginative use of rhetorical and specifically of metaphorical transfers of meaning. The postmodern condition is characterized by an acceleration of the break-up of the common human nature, by a proliferation of claiming subjects and by the increasing use of metonymic mechanisms to establish right claims. The rhetorical operation of metonymy allows the transfer of the presumed dignity of human nature to entities that are by no means similar or analogous to 'man' or to human subjects but which are contiguous with them, like the unborn, the environment or animals. Within the Western philosophical tradition, animality is the other of human nature and the claim to animal liberation or animal rights cannot be based on an ontological similarity. But the rhetorical character of human rights discourse allows the crossing of one of the greatest metaphysical divides and permits what is 'proper' to humans to be claimed for animals.

But the 'nature' of human rights is not just an empty signifier; it is also full of symbolism, and carries surplus meaning which turns it into a *floating* signifier. 'Man' circulates through a large number of religious, legal, political, ideological and philosophical discourses and practices.

Often, contradictory or antagonistic conceptions of human nature are canvassed within each of those. But the aim behind all is to link the signifier to a particular signified and therefore to arrest its constitutive indeterminacy of meaning. Every successful bonding fixes human nature to a regional or partial conception and bestows upon it the symbolic surplus of meaning and dignity that the core concept carries. The fight for women's or gay rights succeeds when it manages to present women, gays etc. as valid instances of human nature. In doing so the characteristics and privileges of human nature are transferred and bestowed upon the subjects who pass the threshold. But at the same time, this partial linking gives content to the empty signifier and makes concrete the abstract and formal claims to equality and freedom implied by the concept of human nature. Every successful fixing of a partial signified to the floating signifier works, therefore, in two ways: it endows the new claim or claimant with the symbolic dignity of right and it arrests temporarily the flight of meaning by filling abstract right with an empirical determination or an historical predicate.

These battles over meaning are not devoid of ontological significance. The successful mobilization of the concept of human nature for the claims of women, gays or children or its metonymic extension to animals or the unborn plays an important role in the constitution of the identity of woman, child or foetus. The subjects of rights have no essential identities outside of those constructed within symbolic discourses and practices. A key aim of politics and of law is to fix meanings and to close identities by making the contingent, historical linkings between signifiers and signifieds permanent and necessary. But such efforts can succeed only partially, because identities are always open to new symbolic appropriations and articulations within different discourses and practices and every – partially – fixed identity is always overdetermined by the excess of meaning of the floating signifier. Let us examine this point further in relation to the operation of law.

Law plays an important part in the articulation and concretization of the floating signifier into specific and protected identities. The law uses the technical categories of legal subject and legal right to mediate between the most abstract and indeterminate concepts of human nature and right and the concrete human beings claiming protection. But if the essence of 'man' is to declare his rights and in this declaration modern self is born, then a radical absence is launched both in the heart of man and of law. Legal rights are the recognition of freedom under the law; their legislation and regulation aims to allow equal rights for others and to protect the common good. In a society of human rights, I am supposedly free to do that which allows the other an equal amount of freedom and I am also free to do what the law does not forbid. But if this is the case, the rights of others and the concerns of the polity are an integral part of what is recognized as 'me' and mine; my own right stops when the right of the other begins and my personhood depends on the absence of what is other and in principle antagonistic to my free will. Rights exist only in relation to other rights; a claim of right involves the recognition of others and their rights and of trans-social networks of mutual recognition and arrangement. There can be no free-standing, absolute right, because such a right would violate the freedom of everyone except its bearer and would be established on a ground different from that of universal human freedom. Rights are always relational – they involve their subjects in relations of dependence on others and responsibility to the law; they are a formal recognition of the fact that before my (legal) subjectivity always already has come another.

It is not just the trace of the (right of the) other that determines my own right. To the extent that right is defined, regulated and restricted by positive law, the law is launched in me alongside my own right; more accurately, it is the law's regulatory presence or constitutive absence that gives my own right its shape and my own (legal) person its identity. But if no right is ever absolute, no freedom is ever total and no identity closed. Identity is marked by negativity, by the constitutive absence of the other and of the law. Right and identity are thus contingent; my right depends on the exclusion of (the right of) the other and the interdiction of the law. All identity based on rights is therefore relational and is based on the exclusion and absence of what denies my right. Identity relies on two types of external conditions: first, some which are clearly contingent (the various claims of others); and second, some that may appear fixed at first instance (the determinations of the legal system) but which also will be revealed to be partly contingent. In both cases, rights introduce an element of unfixity at the heart of the subject and make identity a function of relational and contingent factors which do not allow any final completion of the project of subjectivization. Two absences, two types of negativity, are launched at the centre of modern (legal) identity; otherness, what is not self, and the law.[13] Subjection to the law, the key element of modern morality according to Kant, contributes to the non-essential character of human identity and gives the social its open character.

But at the same time, law is the main institution which attempts to stabilize society and identity. The 'legal subject' mediates between abstract human nature and concrete selves and, through this mediation, the law assigns attributes and predicates and fixes identities. The legal recognition of a particular category of rights, say women's rights, is at the same time the partial recognition of a particular type of identity linked with these rights. Conversely, an individual recognized as a legal subject in relation to women's rights is accepted as the bearer of certain attributes and the beneficiary of certain activities and, at the same time, as a person of a particular identity which partakes amongst others of the dignity of human nature. The identity of a particular woman is not exhausted, of course, in her identification as a subject of women's rights or in her recognition as the beneficiary of the equality and freedom of human nature (although this was the main aim behind the first phase of the legal struggles for women's rights or of every other social movement). Any real person will also have rights that emanate from her position in the economy (worker and social rights) or as a citizen of a particular state (political rights) or as the inhabitant of a particular environment etc. What is crucial, however, is that for law all these rights which are the symbolic extensions of the basic attribute of human nature will be arranged and organized according to the protocols of *legal* subjectivity and the technical specifications of legal rights. In other words, the legal subject and legal rights act as unified conceptions of 'human nature' through which the law assigns categories and fixes identities and tries to stabilize the proliferation of social meaning. An individual is therefore a human being, a citizen, a woman, a worker etc. to the extent that she is recognized as the legal subject of the respective rights; an individual becomes part of human nature to the extent that the law recognizes her as legal subject. And although we should insist that these determinations by no means exhaust the existence of any concrete person, the typically legal operation is to link publicly recognized characteristics through the concept of the legal subject and, to that extent, we all are legal subjects besides or through all our other determinations.

For the discourse of rights, the concrete person, the real man or woman in the street, is the end point, the site of recognized claims and the variable construct of acknowledged duties. She shares with others the abstract ability to act and the dignity that freedom gives; she differs from others to the extent that she carries a different bunch of claims, asserted and realized within the confines of positive law. 'Man' in general opens the experience of freedom and the countervailing discipline of reason. Concrete legal persons, on the other hand, are empirical expressions of regulated freedom, historical creatures of the law. Legal categories have a history and tradition from well before the coming of modernity. The legal subject, the *persona*, pre-dates the modern conception of 'man'. The specificities of legal history and tradition therefore will influence the application of legal rights. Reason and right may claim to be universal and diachronic but they are immersed in the impurities of genealogy and tradition.

We can conclude that legal personality is a key strategy of individuation. People in modernity are no longer the material vessels of the soul, the external form of a universal *psyche*. They acquire their public *persona*

exactly through their recognized legal attributes which allow them to
carry out acts that are significant to others. Legal subjectivity thus paradoxically represents both the principle of universalism and the process
through which individuation is carried out in modernity. In this sense
rights do not just belong to 'man'; rights make man by both recognizing
his legislative, right-making ability and free will and by endowing him
with the concrete powers and capacities through which he can realize his
free will.

   Rights are symbolic entities that develop relationally within social and
legal networks; this is what makes their full definition impossible and
opens them to continuous expansion and proliferation. Human rights
never reach a state of definite acceptance or final triumph because the
logic of rights cannot be constrained to any particular field or type of subject. The law of human rights is caught in yet another paradox: as law, it
acts as an agent of stabilization of identity and of rationalization of state
power; as human rights, it introduces into the state and into (legal) personality the openness of indeterminacy. The abstract concept of human
nature which underpinned the revolutionary declarations has been
replaced in postmodern societies by the proliferating claims to new and
specialist rights. As a result, right itself replaces human nature as the
ground concept and becomes the empty and floating signifier which can
be attached either to the logic of power and the state or to the logic of
justice and openness. There is nothing strange, therefore, about the way
in which human rights have been used for legitimatory purposes by the
ideologues of some of the most oppressive regimes; human rights were
always caught in the aporia between the universalistic potential of state
and law and the particularistic attempts of concrete persons to resist
power. Their development in one or the other direction does not depend
on their internal logic but on their articulation within political, institutional and ideological struggles.

HUMAN RIGHTS AND THE OPENNESS
OF LAW

Law is intrinsically implicated in the organization and arrangement of
human rights. As argued above, law and human rights intersect in two
main ways. The revolutionary declarations take the form of legal prohibitions upon state power, of constraints placed upon future legislators.
Legal forms and the institutional, professional and doctrinal autonomy
of law impose respect for human rights upon the state. Thus, the law, as

a principle of self-limitation and as a legitimizing device, introduces the negativity, contingency and indeterminacy that accompany all claims to personhood and right into the centre of political power. In this capacity, the law operates as a principle of unity and determination, of calculation, closure and order.

We can now offer a first explanation of the paradox at the heart of human rights discourse. On the one hand, modern law is removed from its previous natural state and emerges as the key institution whose function is to replace the lost unity and determinacy of the medieval order, to refill the empty place of power with substance,[14] to prevent the disintegration of the body politic and the dissemination of the signifier. The severity of the policing of legal validity and meaning and the near sacralization of the legal institution are the clearest signs of the fear of social indeterminacy. The law serves this purpose by trying to present its empire as coextensive with society. Legal discourse, according to much orthodox jurisprudence, follows the protocols of reason and is internally coherent, autarkic and orderly. If the social can become coeval with law, its boundaries will be fixed and its principle given. In this sense, the task of the law is to halt indeterminacy by setting the boundaries of society and stabilizing individual identities. Modern law is an attempt to establish society out of the openness of the social. But this task is opposed to the logic of human rights and can succeed only partially. When the law imposes order and authority and asserts the determinate power of rules and abstract principles, in other words when the law polices social indeterminacy and fixes social identity, it denies its main condition of existence, the negativity and unfixity of society and person that human rights express and the law carries as the cause and effect of its own action. *Human* rights express the openness of the symbolic organization of the social, while *rights* represent the restriction of the symbolic through the logic of reason.

But what is the specifically legal contribution to the proliferating claims of right? It is the operation of reason, the belief in a rational order of principle and argument which can determine the application of right, distinguish between justified and unacceptable restrictions and consistently control the extension of right from known to unknown instances. The domain of reason is where the legal person resides and the concept is sovereign. The expansion from the given to the new will follow the protocols of pure calculation, of equivalence and addition, of negation and contradiction. There is no need to engage in an extensive critique of this position here. The deconstruction of the claims of legal reason to control its own operation has been carried out in great detail in the last 20 years. It will suffice to say, with American critical legal studies, that the legal principles of human rights adjudication are beset by squatting parasitical counter-principles (for example, free speech against national security or the protection of privacy).[15] The inherent reversibility of the opposed pairs undermines the hopes of their rational reconciliation in the absence of any meta-principle to guide rational choice.[16] Reason cannot create the common framework for arbitrating between conflicting claims and interpretations, because legal principle and reason itself are caught in the polysemies of the written archive as much as the substantive texts of law and are constructs of the legal history, tradition and practice as much as the claims that come before the law. This is why the law cannot discover some clear and unambiguous principle of interpretation in cases of conflict of rights. As Gaete argues, the key hermeneutical principle, the interpretative value that permeates human rights, is that of 'man'.

> Man provides the Archimedean point, the decisive principle of reason that can check the excesses of rhetoric and can correct practices, grounding the distinctions and differences made within the human rights discourse. Man is the 'unwritten Constitution' which takes misreadings and renders determinate the indeterminacy of the Bills of Rights.[17]

But 'man' cannot act as the principle of interpretation, exactly because the aim of human rights discourse and practice is to partially fix the meaning of the signifier 'man' by assigning to it some controlled signified.

The texts of human rights are supposed to control their interpretations but the ever-expanding right claims lead to an unstoppable will to interpret in response. The quest for a hermeneutical grail internal to legal discourse is a duplication within the law of the attempt to use law to discipline social openness and cannot succeed. The protection of human rights, the most important element of modern law and of modernity, inscribes their symbolic and rhetorical character in the law and opens the law to its own continuous transcendence. The limited power of reason is supplemented by the infinite possibilities of rhetoric.[18] Practical reason is only a limited and regional part of what Fish calls law's 'rational rhetoricism', the practice of 'allowing an apparently rational discourse to unfold with no acknowledgment . . . of the "non-rational" determinations that reside at its heart'.[19] If human rights always expand to new areas and construct new identities, their action subjects the law of reason to the operations of language and the symbolic. When human rights become law, the law can no longer claim to be the exclusive domain of reason or to follow unperturbed the protocols of logic. *Logos* as reason is accompanied by *logos* as language and their linkage brings together the necessity of the concept and the contingency of freedom.

HUMAN RIGHTS AS THE PRINCIPLE OF JUSTICE

Human rights have the ability to create new worlds, by continuously pushing and expanding the boundaries of society and of law. Human rights transfer their claims to ever-expanding domains and to new types of (legal) subjectivity, they construct ceaselessly new meanings and values, and they bestow dignity and protection to novel subjects, situations and people. This ability is not a local or exceptional characteristic of human rights but their essence, what human rights are. The universal acceptance and declaration of human rights – the discourse of modernity *par excellence* – and their – rhetorical at least – triumph, marks the end of a type or period of history and coincides with the celebration of a certain 'postmodernity'. Their triumph is not just rhetorical, of course; it is the recognition of the law-making power of rhetoric and the symbolic. But if the protection of human rights is a main justification of legislation, and if their proclamation, awareness and defence a key element of postmodern identity, can there be a theory of justice and a just law after the triumph of groundlessness? Let us return for the last time to the ontology of human rights.

When the protesters against the Criminal Justice and Public Order Act proclaimed the 'right to party' or the 'right to the night' or when an abandoned lover demands his 'right to love', they are acting strictly within the human rights tradition, even though no such legal rights currently exist or are likely to be accepted by the legislator. The melancholic lover, the raver or the New Age traveller belong to a long and honourable lineage: the eighteenth-century revolutionaries, the nineteenth-century political reformers and this century's economic, social and cultural protesters share a common determination to declare the existence of, and thus create new types of, entitlements against received wisdom and the law. Human rights as the ontological and institutional experience of groundlessness are self-conferred. The absence of a legislator and even of opposition to new claims is their structural characteristic. Human rights have therefore a certain independence in relation to the context in which they appear and are proclaimed and which will eventually become part of their constitution by positive law. Indeed, their rhetorical nature, proclamatory enunciation and regular defiance of state law are the outcome of their ability to transcend the political, legal or social context of their appearance and to redefine their boundaries. Legal and social contexts are part of the definition of concrete rights; but it is in the essence of right to suspend any reference to the vagaries of time and the exigencies of place. Human rights accompany human nature both in democratic and in totalitarian regimes, both in sleepy First World states and in revolutionary or reactionary Second and Third World ones. Social contracts, universal and local declarations, legislation and case law, institutions, commissions, courts and inquiries are expressions of the positivity of human rights and of their historical character. But at the same time, the force of the claim of right does not depend on some natural or supernatural, national or international legislator and is not weakened in its scope or altered in its direction by historical or geographical contingencies. Right refers to what is proper to human beings on account of their humanity. Rights, the most historical and timely of human inventions, paradoxically partake of a strange timelessness and placeness.

The various references to 'human nature' in classical liberal theory occluded the divisions and exclusions that the constitution of modernity introduced. The deconstruction of the essentialist claims attached to the 'subject' of human rights has shown the historical and particular character of this most powerful discourse of the universal. And yet the continuous flight of meaning which creates ever-new rights appears anchored on a solid ethical residue, and the groundlessness of freedom seems to draw its world-making power from a moral foundation. If my right has meaning only in relation to another, whose action or entitlement are presupposed in the recognition or exercise of my right, the right of the other always and already precedes mine. The (right of the) other comes first; before my right and before my identity as organized by rights, comes my obligation, my radical turn towards the claim to respect and dignity of the other. The non-essential essence of human rights, the fleeting universal that all particular claims to rights involve, is this recognition of the priority of the other person whose existence before mine makes me ethically bound and opens to me the domain of language, intersubjectivity and right. This other cannot be, of course, the universal 'man' of liberalism or the abstract and formalistic 'subject' of rights. The other is always a unique, singular person who has a place and time, gender and history, needs and desires. If there is something truly 'universal' in the discourse of human rights, it is the recognition of the absolute uniqueness of the other person and of my moral duty to save and protect him or her.[20]

But if this is the case, human rights recognize two types of intersubjectivity and community. The first is the community of antagonistic subjects; rights organize a conflictual economy of need and desire and make personality dependent on the absence of the other. In this sense, the expanding claims of right express the human ability to transcend the contextual – natural or social – limits placed upon the exercise of rights and the ability of language and reason to transfer meaning and redefine its concepts and boundaries. But at the same time, rights express and presuppose a community of duties to others in their absolute singularity. Embedded within the community of external relations between egos, of limits and boundaries, prohibitions and restrictions placed around subjects, there is another community: a community of love and proximity, where I am turned towards the other, I am for the other, and my own self, uniqueness and freedom are the result of my answering the demand of the other which is only addressed to me. Levinas calls it the community of hostages to the other. For Levinas there is

> a goodness in peace, which is also the exercise of freedom, and in which the *I* frees itself from its 'return to self', from its auto-affirmation, from its egotism . . . *to answer for the other*, precisely to defend the rights of the other man . . . . My freedom and my rights, before manifesting themselves in my opposition to the freedom and rights of the other person, will manifest themselves in the form of responsibility, in human fraternity.[21]

This 'goodness', unlike the classical tradition, does not depend on and indeed rejects all ideas of a shared horizon of *teloi* and virtues; unlike the modern tradition, it does not just follow the law and it does not turn the other into an instance of generalized human nature or personhood. It is a goodness that does not exclude any other and does not try to impose the preferences of self upon the stranger and make her into an *alter ego*. Perhaps this radical moral sensitivity and responsibility towards the other can be seen as the postmodern moral substance – a non-substantial substance, always on the move, as it follows the shifting boundaries of the social and answers the singular demands of the suffering other.

Thus, the phenomenology of human rights indicates a paradoxical link between freedom and ethics. Human rights are a double discourse; they allow the experience of freedom and the openness of language to become a political strategy and operate on the social. But at the same time, they institutionalize the ethics of alterity and the duty to respect the singular and unique existence of the other. Human rights are the contemporary version of the aporia of justice. The element of groundlessness and freedom makes it impossible to define or describe a human rights society. Such a society always looks to redefinitions and reconceptualizations, to new possibilities and subjectivities. The time of such societies is the future because their principle is always still to be declared and met; they are societies of deferral, and deferral is their ontological condition. But a society of human rights operates also a – non-essential – theory of the good, and becomes a community of obligation to the singular, unique other and her concrete needs. Postmodern justice cannot be defined;[22] it is always on the move, caught between the claims to human dignity and to the continuous redefinition of what dignity should involve. But like its classical predecessor, postmodern justice denounces injustice: the injustice of reducing concrete people to instances of a rule or principle or of subsuming their unique needs and identities to examples of a concept.

Let us return, finally, to the problem of legal interpretation. The undecidability between the strict requirements of legal *logos* and the indeterminacy of the action of human rights is not only a structural characteristic of legal discourse; it is also the moral element in the operation of the legal system. Human rights are the modern element of justice; but as with all conceptions of justice they cannot find a positive definition, be reduced to a definite categorization and classification. Human rights represent modernity's denunciation of injustice and they remain necessarily and radically negative both in their essence and in their action. For a polity that protects human rights, injustice would be the attempt to crystallize and fix individual and group identities, to establish and police the boundaries of the social, to make it coextensive with itself and close it around some figure of authority or law. For a law that protects human rights, injustice would be to forget that humanity exists in the face of each person, in her uniqueness and unrepeated singularity, and that human nature (the universal) is constituted in and through its transcendence by the most particular.

Human rights find an uncomfortable place in the text of the law, national or international. To the extent that human rights become positivized legal discourse and join law's calculation, thematization and synchronization, they share the quest for subjecting society to a unique and dominant logic and necessarily violate the demand of justice. But at the same time, they are the promise of a justice always still to come: they are the symbol and image of the negative and the indeterminate in the person and in the state, and of the proximity of the community of peace with the concrete other upon which the claims of the universal and the abstract rise. Human rights denounce the injustice of every attempt to impose a fixed identity upon a person and the injustice of all organization of power and of law that does not turn the indeterminacy of social identity into its regulative principle. Like the early denunciations of injustice, the justice of human rights does not offer a definition and description of the just society or a prescription of its conditions of existence. This lack of definition, which is also the definition of lack, is logically necessary and ethically unavoidable. A society of human rights accepts that person and rights are radically contingent and that this contingency founds a strong ethical obligation; that the subject of rights is internal to rights discourse and has no external determination or ground; and finally that a defence of rights must be based on the concrete needs of he or she who comes before the law. Human rights have no proper place, time or ideology; they cannot be assigned to any particular epoch or party. They are open to application to new areas and fields, now following the logic of continuity and principled development and now the operations of rhetorical play which allows their unstoppable extension to contiguous fields. This is the dynamism of *logos*; but rights express also a primordial passivity towards the demand of the other and the proximity of the one for the other.

If the law is the attempt to halt the openness of the social and to fix identity, human rights are the denunciation of this injustice. When human rights are established as the – indeterminate – principle of the social, the law is open to questioning as much as society and identity. And this is not just in the sense that human rights are critical of totalitarian or dictatorial attempts to deny them; even more important is their challenge and overtaking of the limits of the social and of law. Their symbolic importance is that they infuse law and identity with the 'logic' of the symbolic, a logic open to its re-inscription in new chains of meaning, new partial fixings and unpickings of identity; in other words, that they inscribe futurity in law. Their ethical importance is the demand that each person be treated as sole incarnation of humanity and every need as the responsibility of law. Caught between the symbolic and the ethical, paradoxically ensnared in the indeterminacy of the future and the concreteness of the present, lies the postmodern principle of justice. Human rights can suffer and even be destroyed but they cannot triumph. Their victory and their justice will always lie in an open future and in a fleeting, but pressing, present. It is in this sense that human rights are our epochal principle: a negative principle which places the huge energy of freedom in the service of our ethical responsibility to the other.

NOTES

1. M. Heidegger, *The Principle of Reason* (Bloomington: Indiana University Press, 1991), p. 124. For a concise presentation of the tradition of reason in modernity see V. Descombes, *The Barometer of Modern Reason* (New York: Oxford University Press, 1993).

2. There are two versions of the 'end of history' story. The optimistic version declares that history has ended in the elimination of the great ideological and political battlefields of modernity, of left versus right, capital versus labour, black versus white. No conflict of dialectical dimensions is left, and as a consequence liberal capitalism and the principles of human rights cannot be transcended. This complacent view has been associated with the writings of Fukuyama. See F. Fukuyama, *The End of History and the Last Man* (London:

Hamish Hamilton, 1992) and see J. Derrida's critical comments in *Spectres de Marx* (Paris: Galilee, 1993). The pessimistic version is caught in a state of acute melancholia and claims that the world has been finally dominated by the logic of technocratic capitalism and there is no escape from the maniacal interventions of the all-powerful state. See L. Niethammer, *Posthistoire. Has History Come to an End?* (London: Verso, 1992).

3. R. Gaete, *Human Rights and the Limits of Critical Reason* (Aldershot: Dartmouth 1993). This is a powerful expression of the doubts about human rights demogogery and about the limitations of reason's ability in the face of state power.

4. G. Rose, *The Broken Middle* (Oxford: Blackwell, 1992), p. xiii. More generally, see G. Rose, *Dialectics of Nihilism. Post-structuralism and Law* (Oxford: Blackwell, 1984). For a detailed discussion of this separation between law and ethics and for possible ways for creating a postmodern principle of justice see C. Douzinas and R. Warrington, *Justice Miscarried: Ethics, Aesthetics and the Law* (London: Harvester, 1994).

5. See A. Heller, *Beyond Justice* (Oxford: Blackwell, 1987), Chapters 1 and 2, and C. Douzinas and R. Warrington, *op cit.*, Chapter 4.

6. See M. Heidegger, *Being and Time* (New York: Harper and Row, 1962); R. Kearne, *The Wake of Imagination* (London: Hutchinson, 1988); C. Douzinas and R. Warrington with S. McVeigh, *Postmodern Jurisprudence: The Law of Text in the Texts of Law* (London: Routledge, 1993), Chapter 1.

7. J. Habermas, *Theory and Practice* (London: Heinemann, 1974), p. 88.

8. For an analysis of the co-implication of constative and performative aspects in the revolutionary declarations, see J. Derrida, Declarations of Independence (1986) 15/7 *New Political Science* 7–15 and, more generally, Force of law: the 'Mythical Foundation of Authority' (1990), 11/5–6 *Cardozo Law Review*, 919–1047.

9. J. Derrida, *Margins of Philosophy* (translated by A. Bass) (Brighton: Harvester Press, 1982); R. Young, *White Mythologies* (London: Routledge, 1990).

10. R. Gaete, *op. cit.*, p. 124, quoting Sandel.

11. For a recent statement of the Marxist critique through a reading of Marx's classic statement in 'On the Jewish Question', see J. Berstein, Right, revolution and community. In P. Osborne (ed.), *Socialism and the Limits of Citizenship* (London: Verso, 1993). For a communitarian critique from a feminist perspective, see S. Benhabib, *Situating the Self. Gender, Community and Postmodernism in Contemporary Ethics* (London: Polity, 1992).

12. For a use of the psychoanalytical concept of 'overdetermination' in political theory, see E. Laclau and C. Mouffe, *Hegemony and Socialist Strategy* (London: Verso, 1985).

13. Although the approach in this chapter is not directly influenced by Lacanian psychoanalysis, there are similarities between its position and the work of the Ljubljana school. Renata Salecl's *The Spoils of Freedom* (London: Routledge, 1994) includes a very interesting essay on human rights from a Lacanian perspective. Salecl follows Lefort in highlighting the importance of the empty form of right and interprets it as a substitute for the fundamental prohibition of the symbolic order which functions in the same way as the *petit objet a*. While this analysis opens important new ways for understanding the operation of human rights, it remains highly formalistic; it underemphasizes the historical and institutional aspects of the legal arrangements of human rights and does not consider the ethical dimension of the lack and desire for the other.

14. See C. Lefort, *The Political Forms of Modern Society* (J. Thompson, ed.) (Oxford: Polity, 1986).

15. For a statement of the critical legal position, see Kairys, D. (ed.), *The Politics of Law* (New York: Pantheon, 1990).

16. S. Fish, *There is no such thing as Free Speech and it's a good thing too* (Oxford: Oxford University Press, 1994).

17. R. Gaete, *op. cit.*, p. 107.

18. For the relationship between law and rhetoric, see P. Goodrich, *Legal Discourse* (London: Macmillan, 1988); Sarat, A. and Kearns, T. (eds), *The Rhetoric of Law* (Ann Arbor: University of Michigan Press 1994). Goodrich's *Oedipus Lex* (Berkeley: University of California Press, 1995) presents the rhetorical construction and analysis of the legal text in terms of a symptomatology of the institutional unconscious. See also C. Douzinas and R. Warrington with S. McVeigh, *op. cit.*, Chapter 4.

19. S. Fish, Dennis Martinez and the uses of theory (1987) 96 *Yale Law Review* 1773–1800, at p. 1784.

20. This argument is pursued further both in its critical and constructive aspects in C. Douzinas and R. Warrington, *op. cit.*, Chapter 4.

21. E. Levinas, *Outside the Subject* (London: Athlone Press, 1993), pp. 124–5.

22. See C. Douzinas and R. Warrington, Antigone's Law. In C. Douzinas, P. Goodrich and Y. Hachamovitch (eds) *Politics, Postmodernity and Cortical Legal Studies: The Legality of the Contingent* (London: Routledge, 1994).

7

Communal Goods as Human Rights

Maleiha Malik

INTRODUCTION

It is increasingly being claimed that the 'collective rights' of peoples are fundamental human rights. This claim finds a variety of forms in the contemporary human rights debate, but it is usually expressed as the demand for 'people's rights' and third-generation rights. The concern with collective rights is not new. After World War I, the League of Nations introduced an International Protection of Minorities System which included some specific guarantees by introducing special minorities clauses in peace treaties, complete minority treaties and declarations. These mechanisms for protection focused on particular ethnic groups, and ensured protection for them by extending specific rights in such areas as religious, social and educational autonomy.[1] The focus on group rights as the appropriate mechanism for the guarantee of human rights did not survive into the post World War II period. The League of Nations' model of minority treaties and specific minority rights was regarded with suspicion by the new United Nations. Individual rights were considered to be a sufficient guarantee of the rights of minorities, without the need for specific group rights.[2]

Collective Identities in Search of a Right

A survey of current human rights policy documents, and to a lesser extent legal provisions, suggests that the issue of collective rights is once again on the human rights agenda. At the international level, UN human rights machinery is increasingly concerned with accommodating the rights of indigenous peoples.[3] The General Assembly has approved a Declaration on the Rights of Persons Belonging to National or Ethnic, Religious and Linguistic Minorities which includes an obligation that states should 'protect the existence and the national or ethnic, cultural, religious and linguistic identity of minorities within their respective territories, and shall encourage conditions for the promotion of that identity'.[4]

At the regional level in Europe, the recent ethnic conflict in the Balkans has given urgency to the issue of minority rights. Within the Council of Europe, whose most recent members are drawn from central and eastern European states, there have been a number of policy documents which seek to develop ways of protecting the rights of groups and minorities. The Parliamentary Assembly has adopted several recommendations in this area. For example, the rights of national minorities to develop their culture has been recognized[5] and there is now support for distinct political rights for national minorities: 'In the region where they are a majority the persons belonging to a national minority shall have the right to have at their disposal appropriate local or autonomous authorities or to have a special status.'[6] The European Charter for Regional or Minority Languages, which states in its Preamble that the use of a regional or minority right is an 'inalienable right', has been adopted by the member states of the Council of Europe.[7] The Conference on Security and Co-operation in Europe (CSCE), which is expected to take a more prominent role in promoting a new security order for Europe,[8] has taken a strong lead on the rights of groups and communities and has appointed a special High Commissioner for Minorities, with a mandate to provide mediation in ethnic disputes.

The African Charter on Human and Peoples' Rights, which entered into force in 1986 (also known as the Banjul Charter), deals specifically with peoples' (collective) rights, whilst also guaranteeing individual rights. It includes the right of peoples to development (Article 22); peace and security (Article 23) and, most significantly, a wide-ranging right in Article 20 stating: 'all peoples shall have a right to existence. They shall have the unquestionable and inalienable right to self-determination'.[9] A topical and contemporary example of this concern with the protection of collective rights can be found in the recent South African constitution, which was preceded by a careful study of the constitutional structures and provisions in existing constitutional democracies. The Constitution of the Republic of South Africa Act 1993 adopted 34 constitutional principles which form the foundations for the drafting of the permanent constitution of the Republic of South Africa.[10] These 34 principles essentially reflect the usual human rights norms guaranteeing individual rights. However, as well as the commitment to traditional individual rights, these principles include certain provisions which are an attempt to accommodate the special needs of certain groups within the new South African democracy. These principles, which include encouraging the diversity of language and culture (principle XI), and the recognition and protection of the collective rights of self-determination in forming, joining and maintaining organs of civil society, including linguistic, cultural and religious associations (principle XII), will be translated into constitutional rights in the final constitution. Most notable is principle XXXIV, which states that the right of South African people as a whole to self-determination does not preclude the constitutional provision for a notion of self-determination by any community sharing a common cultural and language heritage, whether in a territorial entity within the Republic or in any other recognized way, provided there is substantial proven support.[11] This last principle was included as a concession to the Freedom Alliance to encourage their participation in the South African elections in 1994.[12]

A Matter of Principle

The response of human rights organizations to the demand for collective, group rights has been *ad hoc* and reactive. Very often these issues are forced on to the human rights agenda after fierce political lobbying by pressure groups,[13] or as a response to an urgent political problem.[14] The resulting fragmentation of the collective rights issue has at times been encouraged by the collective rights lobby. For example, at the World Conference on Human Rights held in Vienna in June 1993, activists for the indigenous groups successfully lobbied for their interests to be dealt with in a declaration separate from that covering minorities generally. This trend towards fragmentation has also been exacerbated by the decision of the United Nations Commission on Human Rights to deal with the diverse claims which can be classified as collective rights as discrete, rather than related, matters.[15]

For the human rights lawyer, there is a significant connection, in form and substance, between these diverse types of collective rights claims. This suggests that all these issues could be incorporated within a single, coherent framework for analysis. The present fragmentation of these issues is not only unnecessary, but is often a very real barrier to a coherent and reasoned discussion. One particularly detrimental consequence of this fragmentation is that solutions and measures are proposed and adopted in an *ad hoc* fashion. It remains unclear whether the grant of collective rights claims is a matter of political expediency and a way of handling specific disputes, or whether such concessions are justified by reference to a theory of justice and rights. This reactive approach makes it difficult to formulate a principled discussion of these related areas of concern.

An important, albeit optimistic, bonus of using a coherent normative framework for the discussion of these issues, as matters of principle rather than political accommodation, may be that this approach facilitates the development of preventative strategies. In this way the political claims of certain groups and communities could be managed, and conflict minimized, before there is the type of chaotic breakdown of civil society which has characterized contemporary ethnic disputes.[16] The catastrophes in the former Yugoslavia and Rwanda are the two most obvious examples of this process of disintegration. Ethnic conflict is likely to continue in the Balkans, the Russian federation as well as many other states ranging from China, Indonesia and Turkey through to many parts of the Horn of Africa and South Africa. The wide-ranging violations of individual rights which characterize these disputes, as well as the socio-economic and humanitarian repercussions of the consequent refugee problems, make this an urgent issue for human rights law. The optimistic hope is that a principled approach is more likely to facilitate the development and use of preventative strategies and the accommodation of genuine collective rights claims within human rights law, thereby defusing tension before it degenerates into ethnic conflict on a large scale. The possibility of such high dividends justifies another tentative foray into an analysis of collective rights.

What is the justification for treating collective rights as human rights? This is the main question considered in this chapter. Whilst the search for a foundational justification for collective rights is treated as a matter of principle for a theory of justice and rights, empirical examples from human rights documents are used as a basis for discussion. Ultimately, this exercise may also assist in the questioning, clarification and reaffirmation of the existing commitment to human rights. Before moving on to the main discussion, it is important to identify the nature of the interests at stake in collective rights claims.

Communal Goods

It is sometimes claimed that the present human rights framework, with its concern for safeguarding individual civil and political rights, is hostile to all non-individualistic interests. These first-generation rights are, it is argued, atomistic and individualistic. However, these accusations are misleading and the charge of individualism and atomism is very often an unfair exaggeration. The meaningful protection of individual rights requires some collective action, in the sense that the individuals who constitute the political community, at the national and international level, act jointly in an effort to secure and protect these rights. These rights are protected, upheld and vindicated through positive collective action, which utilizes scarce collective resources and involves action by the state and society. Moreover, existing human rights documents recognize that these first-generation rights have to operate within a specific social context. Article 27 of the International Covenant on Civil and Political Rights (ICCPR) is one notable example. Article 14 of the European Convention on Human Rights (ECHR) is the analogous provision at the European level, although unlike Article 27 of the ICCPR, it is not a free-standing provision.[17]

Similarly, the rights to social and economic goods, as exemplified in Article 25(1) of the Universal Declaration of Human Rights 1948 and more recently in the new South African Constitution,[18] cannot be said to be atomistic and wholly individualistic. These second-generation rights typically include rights to social security, work and leisure, education and health care. Although some are individual claims, others require and facilitate participation in the social, cultural and economic life of the community. As with first-generation rights, they are claims which require some collective action on the part of the community.

What distinguishes first- and second-generation rights from the collective, third-generation category of rights is the type of interest which they are protecting. Ultimately, first- and second-generation rights can be understood as the expression of individual interests. Whether this is the private interest of the individual (expressed as rights to personal integrity or property) or the right of the individual to participate in the community (expressed in the form of the right to association or religion), it is still expressed as an individual interest. These rights may require collective action and help to make communal life possible, and their full protection may require collective action, but they can sensibly be understood as the interests of the individual.

The recent calls for collective rights which concern us seek to move the debate beyond these first- and second-generation rights. The distinguishing characteristic of the new third generation of rights is that they protect certain interests which cannot easily be broken down into the aggregate of their worth to individuals. These communal goods share with public goods the characteristics of joint production and non-excludability of individuals. The value of certain third-generation rights cannot be understood merely in terms of their aggregate value to all the individuals in the group, because this type of good can only be realized and enjoyed together by a group as collective entity. At an evaluative level, the value of the individual experiences is intrinsically linked to that of the group. An understanding of the value to the individual inherently requires a reference to the value beyond him or her and to the wider group.[19]

Accepting that certain communal goods such as community, culture, language and tradition are important for a developed and flourishing human society may lead to the conclusion that these are important goals which the state should promote. This provides a strong reason to provide, develop and facilitate these communal goods, which can in turn be weighed with competing reasons and interests, including utilitarian concerns. However, contemporary debates concerning this issue go beyond this modest claim. Proponents of collective rights claim that these interests are human rights. They are not merely one of a number of interests which the state should recognize and promote. Rather, like civil and political rights they are fundamentally important moral interests and, therefore, certain communal goods are a matter of entitlement which justify their entrenchment as enforceable human rights. Our present concern is with whether there is anything to justify this stronger claim that equates communal goods with fundamental human rights. The most natural starting point in the search for a justification can be found in contemporary liberal theories of justice.

LIBERALISM AND ITS LIMITATIONS

Procedural Liberalism

The theoretical foundations of current human rights standards can be attributed to liberal theories of justice which have dominated Anglo-American jurisprudence in the period following World War II. These theories are a product of eighteenth-century enlightenment, but owe much of their contemporary form to the influence of nineteenth-century German individualism. The writing of Immanuel Kant provides the usual and favoured basis for a constitutional and legal framework which protects individual liberty. A central feature of this philosophy is the premise that individuals should have the autonomy to determine their own ends, and pursue their own conception of the good life. Human dignity is not associated with any particular conception of what constitutes the common good or with individual participation in the realization of this collective goal; rather, individual human dignity is secured by having the power to consider, adopt or reject any goal. Autonomy, free choice and control are central features of this liberalism.

In its contemporary form, this philosophy is expressed in the work of theorists such as John Rawls and Ronald Dworkin. Contemporary liberalism's distinguishing characteristic is encapsulated in the slogan 'the priority of right over the good'. In his summary of liberalism,[20] Dworkin distinguishes between two kinds of moral commitments: on the one hand, there are concepts about what constitutes a good life (substantive principles); and on the other, there are ideas of what it is to treat others fairly, justly and in a way so as to respect their dignity as human agents (procedural principles). Dworkin argues that the distinguishing characteristic of a liberal theory of justice is that it takes no position as to the substantive views about the ends of life, but remains strongly committed to safeguarding the procedural principle of treating people with equal respect. Neutrality as to the substantive goals of individuals is essential, in Dworkin's terms, for showing each person equal respect and thereby respecting their dignity as human agents. Given the diversity of notions of the good, failure to remain neutral in relation to substantive principles would be tantamount to saying to those who do not share this preferred notion of the good that their views are not as worthy as those of other citizens. This in turn would be an infringement of their free choice and autonomy. It would be a failure to accord them dignity and individual liberty.[21]

The contemporary liberal concern is with neutrality as a principle of political morality. The requirement is not that all individuals should be neutral in their lives as to their conception of the good, but rather that laws, legislation and government should remain neutral between individual citizens' preferences as to what constitutes the good. Why does liberalism require the exercise of neutrality in these terms? The justification for this requirement lies in a specifically liberal conception of the self and the conditions under which freedom is realized. The priority of right is based on a conception of the person as capable of defining his or her own identity through the exercise of choice. Thus, the emphasis in contemporary liberal writing is on the value of personal autonomy, which is the belief that there is a particular value in the idea of a person organizing his or her own life, and making a deliberate effort to shape his or her own life. Kymlicka expresses this as the requirement to live a life chosen from within through free choice, rather than a life where choices have been made as a result of coercion and according to someone else's conception of the good. According to Kymlicka,[22] a life lived externally is not as valuable as a life lived from within.

The argument in support of neutrality in relation to the good, and the value of personal autonomy, is not necessarily an appeal to moral scepticism or the relativism of values. According to Dworkin, neutrality is required 'not because there is no right and wrong of the matter, but because that is what is right'.[23] Therefore, political community should be arranged according to principles that do not presuppose any conception of the good. The individual has a plan of the good life which is a strategy providing the basis of important decisions. It need not be a coherent plan, but it does involve the ability to stand back and review his or her life so far and exercise choice.

How does this theory of justice relate to a theory of rights? As Waldron notes, these theories take certain claims about the rights of individuals as their *input* which provides the initial frame for the problem of justice. Dworkin starts from the proposition that all individuals have the right to 'equal respect and concern'. Rawls in a *Theory of Justice* and more recently in *Political Liberalism* is committed to an initial starting point based on the idea that all citizens are free and equal.[24] In addition to these rights and principles as inputs, these theories produce certain rights as their *outputs*. For Dworkin these are the fundamental individual liberties which act as trumps over the collective goals and policies which would impose a certain notion of the common good on all citizens, thereby violating the requirement for neutrality as to substantive principles. In Rawls' terms, they are the two principles of justice: the first principle requires an equal right to the basic liberties, and has lexical priority over the second principle, which requires the equal distribution of opportunities and resources unless the difference principle applies. The first principle generates a strict priority for individual rights, which guarantee, for example, the integrity of the person and freedom of expression and association. These rights enjoy a strict priority over collective goals, socio-economic interests and utilitarian considerations.

Liberal Human Rights

The substance and form of the rights, which is the final product of these theories, is immediately familiar. In terms of content, these rights essentially protect two types of interests: first, the interests of the individual in liberty (e.g. freedom of speech, association, personal integrity and the values of the rule of law); and second, equal treatment on various grounds (e.g. race, religion, sex and sometimes sexual preference). The preferred form which protection of these rights takes is the provision of an individual right to judicial review of the acts of the state.

This is the preferred model for international and regional human rights documents and western domestic constitutional documents, although there is some variation in substance and form. For example, the Preamble to the Universal Declaration of Human Rights states: 'Whereas the peoples of the United Nations have in the Charter reaffirmed their faith in fundamental human rights, in the dignity and worth of the human person and in the equal rights of men and women . . .' The ICCPR guarantees individual rights, with a strong guarantee of equality before the law via Article 26 of the ICCPR.[25] The focus is on individual rights, and although Article 27 gives some protection to minorities, this is expressed as the rights of the individuals who constitute a minority.

The ECHR is another example of the debt owed to procedural liberalism by contemporary human rights documents. It is mainly concerned with securing human rights by safeguarding certain key individual rights without pursuing any substantive principle or goal. These individual rights are said to provide a procedural framework of protection: they safeguard individual choice in important spheres of human activity such as expression, religion, family life and association, and thereby leave individuals free to direct their own lives.[26] The jurisprudence of the European Court of Human Rights supports this analysis of the ECHR as a procedural human rights regime. An analysis of the case law supports the view that the court is not concerned with the task of evaluating the substantive quality of individual choice. Instead, the Court focuses on ensuring that there is a framework within which choice is available.[27] Moreover, the Commission and the Court have focused on the protection of individuals rather than groups. Although there is a non-discrimination provision in Article 14, as in Article 27 of the ICCPR this is an individual rather than collective right. Even in the case of the protection of minorities, procedural guarantees for the individual have been at the centre of the European Court's reasoning,[28] and at no stage are these minorities referred to as a group, either in the ECHR or in the jurisprudence of the European Court.[29]

At the domestic level there are a number of variations of this basic model. The US Constitution can be understood as being part of this tradition, which has in turn provided a precedent for a number of other domestic human rights documents such as the Canadian Charter. More recently, the South African Constitution has adopted this model in a constitutional settlement which includes, *inter alia*, a bill of rights which entrenches certain basic rights and a judiciary (a Constitutional Court is to be established) with the power of constitutional review. The Constitutional Court will have the jurisdiction to enforce the rights protected in the Constitution, to test the constitutionality of laws and administrative action, to settle disputes between organs of the state at all levels of government, to certify that any new constitutional text complies with the constitutional principles and to advise on the constitutionality of a bill.[30]

Much of the appeal of this human rights model lies in its apparent coherence. It brings together a number of different ideas. First, there is the conception of a person as an autonomous free chooser and the idea of the intrinsic worth of each person. The dignity and freedom of the individual resides in the power to control, and trump actions of the state and other individuals which interfere with these conditions for personal autonomy. A set of individual rights provides the framework within which individuals can be sure that their autonomy and choice will be respected. Remedial and enforcement issues are relatively unproblematic, as the right is vested in an individual who has the power to veto the acts of other citizens and the state where they infringe his or her fundamental interests. In turn, the state is the guarantor of these rights with the duty to safeguard them for all their citizens. In this paradigmatic and theoretical form, all these component parts hang together to form an impressively coherent structure.

Accommodating Communal Goods

But how does this model safeguard and promote communal goods? The assumption of procedural liberalism is that the guarantee of fundamental individual rights will be a sufficient condition to safeguard communal goods and the interests of groups. For example, the individual right to freedom of religion will adequately guarantee the rights of religious minorities, and freedom of association for individual citizens will ensure that they are able to form and support viable community and cultural associations in conjunction with others. These rights, which are vested in and for the benefit of individual citizens, ensure that should these individuals wish to secure the communal goods of community, culture or language, they will be free to do so. For Rawls, individual rights do not necessarily require that individualistic choices will be preferred. Communal goods form one of a range of values which an individual is free to choose once fundamental rights have been guaranteed. He states:

> There is no reason why a well-ordered society should encourage primarily individualistic values if this means ways of life that lead individuals to pursue their own way and to have no concern for the interests of others (although respecting their rights and liberties) . . . The basic liberties are not intended to keep persons in isolation from one another, or to persuade them to live private lives . . . but to secure the right of free movement between associations.[31]

In Dworkin's analysis, the primary function of individual rights is to safeguard the freedom of the individual, and to protect them against the coercive effects of enforced community standards. Rights are a trump over communal values and utilitarian considerations, and individuals are free to accept or reject communal goods. What is crucial, according to this view, is that as well as having the freedom to choose to benefit from access to a communal good, the individual should have the choice to reject a communal good and reject a community or cultural attachment which he or she currently has. Membership of a collective group, and access to communal goods, is ultimately a matter of individual choice, which is guaranteed by the availability of individual rights to all citizens.

Although in many cases this will be sufficient to guarantee that individuals have access to important communal goods, such as communities and associations, in certain cases meaningful access to a communal good will require positive action. In these cases, guaranteeing certain individual rights to all citizens will be insufficient to secure the communal interests of certain sections of society, particularly where the claim is by a member of a minority group with a distinct language, culture or tradition. In these cases, uniform treatment is inadequate, and there may be a need for differential treatment to recognize the special needs of the particular group, which may in turn require positive action to ensure the continued provision of the communal good.

The *Belgian Linguistics* case,[32] decided by the European Court of Human Rights, highlights this point. Belgium has two main linguistic and cultural groups, the Dutch-speaking Flemish and the French-speaking Walloons, as well as a small German-speaking minority within its national boundaries. Legislation passed in Belgium in 1963 divided the country into four linguistic regions: Flemish, French, German and a special conurbation around Brussels. Under this Act, each of these regions had a stable boundary and was constituted so as to have one dominant language within it. This legislation had a number of consequences: first, the language of education was to be that of the region in the areas designated as unilingual; second, the maternal language was to be determinative as the language of education in bilingual areas; and finally, there were special arrangements for the bilingual communes outside Brussels. In the unilingual areas, the Belgian state refused to establish any state schools or to subsidize private schools which would have delivered education in a language other than that of the region. It also refused to subsidize schools which would give instruction in non-subsidized classes in a language other than that of the region. In effect, for example, where a French language school operated in a Dutch unilingual region, there would be no public support or official recognition of that school.

The applicants were French-speaking Belgians who lived in a unilingual, Dutch-speaking area. They claimed that these legislative measures violated a number of their rights under the ECHR. The applicants argued that there had been a breach of Article 2 of the First Protocol to the ECHR, which guarantees a right to education and in the exercise of this right obliges the state to 'respect the right of parents to ensure such education and teaching in conformity with their religious and philo-sophical convictions'.[33] In particular, they urged the court to accept that the term 'religious and philosophical convictions' includes a linguistic requirement. In this way it was argued that in securing the right to edu-cation under Article 2 of the First Protocol to the ECHR, the contracting state is required to accommodate the linguistic and cultural preferences of the parents.

The applicants also argued that there had been a breach of Article 8 of the ECHR, the right to respect for private and family life, because one consequence of the existing legislation was that French-speaking parents in Dutch unilingual areas would be forced to send their children to French language schools, which were far from their homes, which would result in interference with private and family life. Finally, they argued that the actions of the Belgian state constituted discriminatory treatment under Article 14 of the ECHR.

The European Court of Human Rights held by a majority that the Belgian government was entitled to withdraw public support and official recognition from French language schools in unilingual areas which failed to comply with the 1963 legislation, because the right to education guaranteed a right of access to education without any specific linguistic requirement. The majority found that Article 2 of the First Protocol to the ECHR contained no linguistic requirement, but was merely the guar-antee of a right of access to an educational establishment. In relation to Article 8, it was held that any resulting separation of parent and child was not imposed by the state but was the consequence of the individual choice of the parents.

In relation to special status communes where legislation permitted nursery and primary schooling in French but which required in-depth study of Dutch, the Court found that there had been no interference under Article 8 and that to require a child to study a language in depth which was not his or her own could not be characterized as depersonal-ization. Finally, the Court found that the acts of the Belgian government did not constitute a breach of Article 14 (except on a few minor points relating to the measures which precluded certain children solely on the basis of the residence of their parents from having access to the French language schools in the 'special status' communes).

One way of understanding the claims of the applicants in this case is as a demand to have access to the communal good of a distinct linguistic and cultural identity. From this perspective, the approach of the Court was inadequate. Analysing the issue in terms of individual choice ignores the need for the provision of specific measures to preserve the distinct cultural and linguistic identity of a group, particularly where this group is a vulnerable minority. The particular problem of ensuring the communal good of language cannot be analysed merely in terms of individual rights. Here, there was no specific right which protected the communal interest in question: linguistic and cultural identity. In constructing and interpreting the individual rights under Article 2 of the First Protocol and Article 8, the court was not able adequately to safeguard these particular communal goods. Individual choice in these cases meant that in the Dutch unilingual areas, the French-speaking minority was subject to an assimilationist policy relating to language. The individuals who sought access to the communal good of French language and culture could not have their interest in this good protected by merely having the individual choice to speak this language, attend relevant schools or form French cultural associations. The full protection of these communal goods required the flourishing of a French community, which could not be realized merely by the exercise of individual choice.

The inadequacy of an approach which seeks to protect communal goods by relying solely on the provision of individual rights and uniform treatment becomes clear on comparing *Belgian Linguistics* with *Re Albania Schools*,[34] which was a case decided by the International Court under the League of Nations' International Protection of Minorities System. Pursuant to an amendment to its constitution in 1933, the Albanian state closed all private schools in the country. The Greek minority argued that this measure was in contravention of the Albanian Declaration of 1921, which ensured the protection of the minorities in that region. Article 5 of the 1921 Albanian Declaration stated:

> Albanian nationals who belong to racial, religious or linguistic minorities will enjoy the same treatment and security in law and in fact as other Albanian nationals. In particular, they shall have an equal right to maintain, manage and control at their own expense or to establish in the future, charitable, religious and social institutions, schools and other educational establishments, with the right to use their own language and to exercise their religion freely therein.

The Albanian government argued that inasmuch as all private schools (of the majority and the minority) were closed, no minority right was violated. The Council of the League of Nations requested an advisory opinion from the Hague Court. The Court held that there had been a breach of the 1921 Declaration. In the course of their reasoning the Court stated that the essence of the International Protection of Minorities System was that the minority group should have the 'possibility of living peaceably alongside that population and co-operating amicably with it, while at the same time preserving the characteristics which distinguish them from the majority, and satisfying the ensuing needs'. True equality between the majority and minority required equality between all the individual nationals of the state, the majority and the minority. In addition to this uniform treatment, meaningful protection required that there should be suitable means for the preservation of the minorities' special characteristics of race, tradition and other national characteristics. Although the extreme measure of the Albanian government in shutting down all private schools is not directly analogous to the less coercive effect of the legislation in *Belgian Linguistics*, the difference in approach in the two cases does serve to highlight the inadequacy of individual rights as a means of securing communal goods. Although procedural liberalism respects the identity of individuals as citizens by extending to all identical civil and political rights, it fails to give sufficient weight to, and respect for, the identity of individuals as members of a particular group with an interest in securing access to communal goods.

The claim to differential treatment, and the accommodation of this difference, raised by the minority groups in these cases is similar to other communal goods claims. For example, the claims of indigenous peoples are often based on the belief that there is a special connection between a group of peoples and the land of a particular region which cannot easily be broken down into a claim about individual ownership. These groups assert that there is a claim to the land by them as a collective entity, which is a claim in addition to any existing individual rights which each member of that group might have. Issues of self-determination raise similar problems at the political level. The liberal theories of Rawls and Dworkin appear to be comfortable with the idea that all citizens have identical and equal political rights; indeed, this notion is often said to be the centrepiece of liberal democracy. The call for self-determination by a minority group appears to challenge this principle. Minority groups claim different and distinct political rights which flow from the fact of their membership of a particular group, and are separate and distinct from the existing political rights they have as individual citizens.

Both at the theoretical and empirical level, the protection of communal goods in this context will very often require special rights. Traditional liberalism, with its emphasis on individual rights as a necessary and sufficient condition for the guarantee of communal goods, may be an inadequate starting point for safeguarding communal goods and justifying collective rights.[35]

THE UNFULFILLED PROMISE OF COMMUNITARIANISM

Situating Freedom – the limits of choice

By leaving the provision of communal goods to the vagaries of individual choice, procedural liberalism cannot fully accommodate communal goods claims. Communitarianism challenges the emphasis on individual choice as the central way of securing freedom. Traditional liberalism owes a significant debt to the Enlightenment project and to Kantian individualism. The work of Taylor and Sandel by contrast draws on the reaction against these ideas. In particular, they draw on Hegel's insight, which is critical of the overly individualistic nature of Kantianism and its neglect of the crucial fact that individuals operate within a wider community, which in turn provides the essential context within which morality and freedom can be realized. Hegel and contemporary communitarian writing emphasizes values and obligations which are contingent on our membership of a community, rather than the universalism of certain values and ideas of the right. Taylor draws from these sources certain conclusions about the nature of freedom and identity. In *Hegel and Modern Society*,[36] Taylor discusses the need to situate freedom: the full realization of freedom, he argues, cannot be achieved by any one individual on his or her own, but instead requires a certain social context. He explicitly acknowledges the debt which this modern attempt to situate freedom owes to Hegel. For Taylor, these ideas also have important implications for any meaningful understanding of the way in which personal identity is formed, and the necessary social preconditions for its realization.

Initially, communitarianism with its emphasis on community values and communal goods would seem to be the most obvious alternative justification for the protection of communal interests. The label is used indiscriminately, which renders problematic the task of identifying the distinguishing characteristics of communitarianism. Despite these difficulties, it is possible to isolate a number of themes which run through the main texts, and which recur in the work of political theorists such as Charles Taylor and Michael Sandel who are associated with communitarianism. There are two themes in particular which serve to illustrate the central ideas of these writers: the 'sources of the self' thesis and the idea of a 'constitutive community'.

Sources of the Self

The thesis that the identity of the self is not formed independently by an individual but is in part influenced by membership of a community is most fully set out by Taylor,[37] but also informs Michael Sandel's critique of Rawls' liberalism.[38] The underlying theme of Taylor's argument is that an individual's identity is not formed in isolation or as a monologue. Rather, identity is formed through interaction with significant others with whom we have social contact, and with whom we have been and are in a continuing dialogue. Consequently, the abstraction of the individual from his or her social situation which informs traditional liberal theories is inaccurate because it misconstrues the way in which individuals are influenced by, and are embedded in, their social roles. Sandel makes a similar point when he claims that the theories of contemporary liberals such as Dworkin and Rawls are based on the fallacy of the 'unencumbered self'. According to Sandel, the liberal conception of the person, as exemplified by Rawls, is based on the fallacy that at any particular point in time it is possible to detach the self from its ends: its aims, attachments, interests. According to Sandel, this traditional liberal conception assumes that individuals are capable of standing back from these important sources of value and can make a choice about whether to adopt, revise or abandon them. Sandel questions what he identifies as the liberal presumption that the self is prior to, rather than partly constituted by, its ends. He argues that this 'thin' and 'unencumbered' conception of the person contradicts our self-perception that our identity is defined and determined by these ends. He states:

> To imagine a person incapable of constitutive attachments such as these is not to conceive an ideally free and rational agent, but to imagine a person wholly without character, without moral depth... As a self-interpreting being, I am able to reflect on my history and in this sense to distance myself from it, but the distance is always precarious and provisional.[39]

In this way, like Alisdair MacIntyre,[40] Sandel adopts a view of practical reasoning which is based on self-discovery rather than judgment.

Constitutive Community

Although his conclusions are more modest than those of Sandel, Taylor's thesis about the way in which identity is formed has important implications for understanding freedom and for the importance of community.

Fundamentally valued communal goods, such as community, culture and language, are not merely a neutral context for the exercise of individual judgment and choice. These factors have a central causal role in the formation and realization of individual identity. The availability of a social context within which these communal goods are available is therefore a vital precondition for the exercise of meaningful freedom and choice. These are the social preconditions of situated freedom which atomistic liberal theories neglect. Sandel goes even further by making the bold claim that community is constitutive of identity. He argues that theories of justice can adopt different views of the community, which he categorizes as either individualistic, instrumental or constitutive. Sandel argues that Rawls' theory is not strictly individualistic because it does presume that citizens share certain final ends in common. However, Rawls' view of the community suffers from the fallacy of the priority of the self: he assumes that the individual can stand back and reconsider his or her communal ends as a matter of choice. For Sandel, this ignores the fact that the self is in fact constituted by these communal ends and that the separation of the individual from these ends is not feasible. Sandel proposes that his view, constitutive community, penetrates the self more profoundly. In this way the community is a mode of self-understanding which is partly constitutive of the identity of the individual. The individual members are bound by a sense of community and define their identity by reference to the community of which they are members. In his descriptions of constitutive community, Sandel suggests that this collective identity cannot be translated into an aggregate of individual attachments and associations without considerable loss.[41]

From Communal Goods to Collective Rights

Constitutive community is the virtual personification of the community. The interests of the community are not merely a matter for individual choice or an aggregation of individual interests. Communitarianism makes these interests critical and, for Sandel, independent values. Therefore, this should be a more comfortable starting point for those who claim that communal goods are of great importance and that they should be recognized as human rights. However, because these theories characteristically challenge the liberal focus on rights over other forms of political action, such as participating in institutional and community structures, and the devolution of power, communitarianism does not provide a detailed agenda for the translation of these interests into enforceable rights. Nevertheless, it is possible to consider some of the implications of extracting collective rights out of the communitarian project.

The language of rights has come to be reserved to express interests and values which are of sufficient importance to be matters of entitlement and which therefore deserve special priority in the event of a conflict with competing economic, social and political interests. The communitarian analysis suggests that certain communal goods are crucial and necessary to the exercise of meaningful freedom as civil and political rights. Prima facie, this provides a powerful argument for recognizing these interests as rights.

However, a number of conflicts and problems arise when communal goods are translated into collective rights. *Sandra Lovelace* v. *Canada*,[42] considered by the UN Human Rights Committee, serves to illustrate these difficulties. The case came before the Committee, which has supervisory powers in relation to the ICCPR in accordance with the Optional Protocol to that Covenant, as a result of a communication from Sandra Lovelace. Her complaint was against Canada, a party to the Optional Protocol. Lovelace was born in Canada, and by birth and registration she was a 'Maliseet Indian'. Therefore she had the status of an Indian pursuant to Canada's Indian Act. She subsequently married a non-Indian man and consequently lost her status as an Indian in accordance with s. 12(1)(b) of the Indian Act. An Indian man who had married a non-Indian woman would not have lost his status in this way. Before her marriage Lovelace had been living on an Indian reserve. Since her marriage, and following her divorce, she wished to return and live permanently on the reserve as a matter of right. Housing on the reserve was, according to the local band council, only granted to registered Indians. Lovelace argued that the Indian Act was discriminatory on the grounds of sex and that it was contrary to Articles 2, paragraphs (1) and (3), 23, paragraphs (1) and (4), as well as Articles 26 and 27 of the ICCPR. The Committee concluded that Lovelace had been denied the legal right to reside on the reserve and that this constituted a breach by Canada of Article 27 of the ICCPR. The Committee concluded that pursuant to Article 27 of the ICCPR, Lovelace, as a member of an ethnic minority, was entitled to associate with the relevant ethnic group on its reserved land.

The facts of *Lovelace* raise a number of issues which are relevant to an analysis of collective rights. The most intractable problems arise as a result of investing rights in a group, rather than in a human agent. In the case of first- and second-generation rights, the interests at stake can be understood as individual interests and the right is therefore appropriately vested in the individual. Investing rights in individuals will not raise agency problems, except in those exceptional cases where human agency is insufficient to allow effective decision-making capacity, such as, for example, in the case of the fetus or individuals who are in a permanent vegetative state. Where there is the grant of individual rights it is usually possible to resolve difficulties concerning the substantive nature of the interests, its interpretation and enforcement by reference to the interest of the individual, who has a recognized and independent capacity for decision-making and agency.

Groups and the Problem of the Russian Doll

The difficulty with groups is that it is not clear how they can exercise decision-making capacity and agency in a relevant manner. It is therefore not easy to understand how a group will reach decisions on issues such as interests, membership and enforcement of rights. The problems associated with formulating a definition of a group, people or community will also need to be resolved if the group is to be invested with rights. Despite the obvious problem that the criteria for selection will vary in each case, it may be possible to formulate some objective factors for the definition of a group, and therefore arrive at the criteria for determining whether an individual is a member of a group. An analogy with the definition of race suggests that factors such as a common territory, ethnic origin, historical experience, religion and culture will all be relevant. However, unless it can be said that an individual can be forced to be a member of a group, or conversely that an individual can gatecrash a group without consent, the definition of a group must have a subjective element. The individual member and the other members of the group share a state of mind which supports the view that they are parts of a larger collectivity.[43] The most significant difficulties arise when subjective criteria are introduced. If the collective group is left to define the criteria for its own existence and for resolving conflicts over membership, a number of questions arise. As in *Lovelace*, there is the danger that the individual will assert that he or she identifies with the particular community and wishes to be a member of that group, but the group, using recognized criteria which the individual has failed to meet, may refuse to admit him or her as a member of the group. Can an individual force himself or herself on a group and compel that group to admit him or her as a member? This problem becomes particularly acute where the group claims that the criterion which it is applying to deny an individual membership of the group is essential to preserve the identity of that community. In *Lovelace*, the Committee found that to deny Lovelace the right to reside on the reserve was not reasonable and necessary to preserve the identity of the tribe. However, there remains the possibility of claims where it can reasonably be argued that the exclusion of an individual from a group of which he or she wishes to be a part is essential to preserve the character of the group. Should this conflict be resolved by reference to the wishes of the collective group or the individual member?

Once it is recognized that the group is itself composed of smaller relevant units, a number of related problems become clear. There is the prospect of a conflict between different groups. Moreover, where rights are vested in the group which, like a Russian doll,[44] can be broken into smaller and smaller units there will be a potential for conflict between these component parts over issues such as membership criteria and the definition of the interests of the group. Human rights analysis is familiar with the idea of such conflicts and the resulting need for balancing interests. However, there is little precedent on how group conflict should be resolved.

The Russian doll problem becomes most acute once the doll is broken down to its smallest unit: the human agent who is the individual member of the group. At this stage it is possible to isolate two sources of human rights: first, there is the group which has certain collective rights in order to safeguard communal interests; second, this collective entity is in turn composed of individuals who are themselves vested with important civil and political rights by existing human rights law. Where the interests of the individual members are not the same as those of the group, as in *Lovelace*, the group right will not necessarily lead to a relevant benefit trickling down to the individual members. There will be a dichotomy between the individual and the group interest. In *Lovelace*, the Committee was not required to consider the possibility that s. 12 of the Indian Act constituted a violation of Articles 2 and 26 of the ICCPR, which protect the individual rights to equal protection and treatment. The rights of a community and culture (which provisions such as the Indian Act, and wide interpretations of Article 27 attempt to safeguard) may well require the violation of individual rights.

In reality there are a number of existing communities and cultures with illiberal practices and consequently there is a high likelihood of potential conflict between individual and group rights, if communal goods are translated into collective rights. This conflict is of particular concern if the justification for collective rights is to be found in a communitarian theory with tendencies towards relativism. Particular traditions of a society and the attachments developed within it introduce standards which are based on the specific, unique characteristics of that society. Accommodating these standards into a universalist human rights agenda means that collective rights need to be open-ended, both in terms of the substance of the right and in relation to the manner of its performance. This is illustrated by the existing collective rights guarantees in the African Charter and the new South African Constitution, which call for rights to culture and tradition without any greater specificity. This is no overwhelming reason to deny communal goods the status of human rights, as many existing individual human rights are also guilty of the charge of vagueness and indeterminacy in the content of their obligations. There is no reason to require a higher standard from the new generation of collective rights. However, as a practical matter, there exists the danger that the gap between the definition of these types of rights, their subsequent content and the manner of their performance will be filled by diverse communal practices, many of which may be illiberal.

Individual versus Community

How should a conflict between a group right and an individual right be resolved? The Committee in *Lovelace* confirmed that the Article 27 right must be consistent with the other rights in the Covenant, and they confirmed that the relevant interest in this provision is to secure *for the individual* the benefit of certain communal goods. Traditional liberal theories would prioritize the individual's interest, and provide no reason for preferring a group interest where this entails the violation of an individual's civil and political right.

However, if the justification for securing certain communal goods as human rights draws on communitarian theory, there is no overwhelming reason for prioritizing an individual right over a collective right. Although the lack of a coherent communitarian rights agenda hinders any attempt to predict how communitarianism will respond to this conflict, Charles Taylor's recent Princeton Lectures serve to clarify how a conflict between individual and communal rights may be resolved.[45] Taylor suggests that Liberalism I, Dworkin's and Rawls' procedural versions of liberalism, cannot sufficiently secure communal goods because they require the uniform application of fundamental individual rights and do not recognize important and relevant differences. He also argues that these versions of liberalism are intrinsically suspicious of collective goals. Taylor's alternative is Liberalism II, which secures important individual rights to all citizens, which are applied in a uniform way irrespective of group or cultural difference (he cites habeas corpus as an example of such a right). However, he goes on to argue that there are certain less fundamental rights which do not justify such a priority. In certain circumstances, a society committed to Liberalism II could justifiably prefer to secure a communal good which it values over an individual right. Although some rights such as habeas corpus can never be traded against a communal good, there are other rights which do not deserve such priority. In some cases, in an equation between two competing factors, the uniform application of these lower-level individual rights for all citizens on the one hand, and the realization of a communal good on the other, a society may justifiably opt in favour of the communal good.

Applied to human rights, this model provides a strong argument for collective rights by assigning them the same, and in some circumstances a higher, moral priority than individual human rights. Taylor recognizes that the argument that certain communal interests should have priority over individual rights is founded on the view that a community can justifiably pursue its own version of the common good. He states that models based on Liberalism II are 'in the end not procedural models of liberalism, but are grounded very much on judgements about what makes a good life – judgements in which the integrity of cultures has an important part'.[46] Redefining the interests of the community as an independent human right and allowing this, albeit under limited circumstances, priority over an individual civil and political right has serious implications. This undermines a central requirement of procedural liberalism that the state must remain neutral as to ideas of the common good. In Dworkin's terms, the whole point of having civil and political rights is to ensure that the individual's interests can trump the collective interests of the community, thereby limiting the sacrifice which an individual is required to make in the interests of a community. Liberalism II is not just another version of liberalism; it is a fundamentally different and competing model.

Thus, a communitarian foundation for translating communal goods into collective rights is likely to conflict with a central feature of procedural liberalism, which underpins the existing human rights framework. This possibility, when considered in conjunction with the other difficulties in ascribing rights to groups, suggests that the project of translating communal goods into collective rights should be approached with caution. Arguably, one of the strengths of the present system of human rights is its unity and coherence. The introduction of new rights which are based on a profoundly different theoretical basis raises the spectre of contradiction, conflict and confusion which may serve to undermine the concept of human rights.[47]

The initial view that communitarianism may provide a coherent and attractive justification for collective rights claims seems premature. The difficulties with the communitarian analysis and the ascription of rights to groups are significant. However, the urgent reasons motivating a search for a justification for collective rights remain. Groups continue to claim certain communal goods as human rights and increasingly their demands are met. Moreover, although there are considerable difficulties with communitarianism at a number of levels, liberalism does need to defend itself from the damaging claims that it is too individualistic, that it ignores important preconditions for meaningful freedom and that it is intrinsically hostile to communal goods and the collective interests which they represent. Communitarianism's richer and more complex analysis of the formation of identity, and the conditions under which individual freedom can be realized, deserves reflection, consideration and ultimately a coherent response by a liberal theorist. The most persuasive and coherent response to date has been provided by Will Kymlicka, although the solutions and modifications he proposes are not wholly free of the problems associated with collective rights claims.

LIBERALISM REVISITED

Reaffirming Choice – the importance of context

In *Liberalism, Community and Culture*,[48] Kymlicka presents a full and detailed critique of communitarian writing, which includes an analysis of the arguments of Taylor and Sandel. In addition, he defends liberalism against the charge that it is overly individualistic and hostile to communal goods. Although Kymlicka concentrates on communities and cultural groups, his analysis also applies to claims of linguistic, cultural, indigenous and minority rights. Many of Kymlicka's arguments relate to his specific aim of restating the Rawlsian principles which are the basis of liberal equality. However, it is possible to identify a number of more general points. Kymlicka suggests that it is possible to formulate an argument in favour of the protection of certain communal goods from within liberalism. The central liberal claim that individuals should be autonomous and free to choose their essential ends is reaffirmed. Kymlicka is committed to the belief that individuals should be able to stand back from their present ends and re-examine them, with a view to affirmation, modification or rejection. However, this does not mean that human beings are atomistic or that communal goods and values are unimportant. Rather, Kymlicka argues that the good of cultural membership, e.g. language, community and culture, provides the *context* within which individual choice operates. The argument for safeguarding these goods is not that they are interests of distinct and independent value, but that they are the essential prerequisites which give meaning to individual choice. Kymlicka states:

> Liberals should be concerned with the fate of cultural structures, not because they have some moral status of their own, but because it is only through having a rich and secure cultural structure that people can become aware, in a vivid way, of the options available to

them, and intelligently examine their value.[49]

The Right to Cultural Membership

Kymlicka remains committed to the liberal project of promoting the autonomy and dignity of the person, but combines this with the recognition that individuals need strong communities and associations to nurture this freedom. The liberal guarantee of individual rights shows respect for the individual by recognizing each of them as members of a political community. However, the guarantee of individual rights may be insufficient to secure important communal goods because it fails to accommodate the special needs of certain communities and their genuine call for positive action. The presumption that all individuals are equal citizens fails to accord sufficient weight to their interests in securing communal goods, and this problem becomes particularly acute in culturally plural societies. Kymlicka's argument suggests that there is an additional way in which individuals are respected, namely when the importance of their language and culture is recognized. This second way of showing respect means that we have to move beyond the traditional civil and political rights and recognize that there is an important *right to cultural membership* which requires that important communal goods should be available to citizens.

Kymlicka brings together two sources of showing respect for an individual: first, as citizens of a political community with civil and political rights, and second, as members of a cultural community, with a right to communal goods such as language and culture. A complete liberal theory must remain sensitive to both these sources of individual freedom and equal respect. In culturally homogeneous societies there will be a convergence between these two ways of showing respect, so that the guarantee of civil and political rights will usually be sufficient to secure both the rights of individuals as citizens and as part of their cultural community. However, in culturally plural societies where there are a number of different cultural communities within a larger political community, there will be a divergence between these two requirements. In these cases there may be a pressing need for specific mechanisms, such as differential treatment and special minority rights, in order to recognize the right to cultural membership of minority groups.

In this way, the accommodation of communal goods is realized without relinquishing the liberal concern with individual freedom, autonomy and choice. Kymlicka's arguments advocating the recognition of a right to cultural membership are quite different from communitarian justifications of collective rights and their associated embarrassments.

Kymlicka makes it quite clear that his theory is opposed to the vesting of rights in a collectivity or group. He states that there is

> no room in the moral ontology of liberalism for the idea of collective rights ... the community, unlike the individual, is not a self-originating source of valid claims ... the community has no moral existence or claims of its own. It is not that the community is unimportant to the liberal, but simply that it is important for what it contributes to the lives of individuals, and so cannot ultimately conflict with the claims of individuals.[50]

Unlike the communitarian project of recognizing the independent value of communal goods and its consequent willingness to, in certain cases, prioritize communal goods over individual rights, Kymlicka's concern with the community is instrumental. He provides a defence of communal goods which does not contradict the traditional liberal concern with the individual. Kymlicka's approach will not justify the personification of the community as an independent interest or the recognition of group rights in a strong sense. Nor does it provide overwhelming reasons for prioritizing collective over individual rights. However, it does have the potential for fulfilling two important objectives. First, it provides a useful starting point for a discussion of the way in which communal goods can be comfortably accommodated as a protected interest by contemporary human rights theories. Second, this object is achieved without the danger of inherent and acute conflicts, in theory and practice, which are a product of communitarian justifications of collective rights.

Illiberal Cultures – perplexing questions

Despite its attractions Kymlicka's arguments are not free of some of the perplexities which arise out of collective rights claims. Although his arguments support the view that conflicts between the individual and the group should be resolved in favour of the individual, he fails adequately to tackle the problems raised by the existence of illiberal cultures. To what extent should a liberal human rights regime be obliged to guarantee the continued existence and survival of illiberal cultures, where individuals claim that this culture is an important context for their individual choices? Does the right to cultural membership provide support for norms which are coercive and repressive? Kymlicka responds to this vexed question by distinguishing two different ways of interpreting culture.[51] In the first instance, it is defined in terms of the norms currently characterizing it, so that any significant change in the affiliations of its members destroys the old culture (culture I). However, there is a second way of defining culture which Kymlicka prefers: namely, as the existence of a cultural community of individuals with a shared heritage (culture II). Kymlicka asserts that it is implausible that allowing members of a community certain individual freedoms, such as freedom of religion or sexual freedom, would lead to a destruction of culture in this second sense. Although there will be a change in the culture according to the first definition, there will continue to be a pool of individuals who share sufficient common characteristics to constitute a community within which individuals can operate. Kymlicka makes a valiant attempt to deal with the problem of how cultures change and with the possibility of liberalizing cultures. However, it is likely that many existing cultures are less able to absorb liberalization and this degree of social change. Where there are inherently illiberal cultures, whose fundamental practices necessitate the restriction of certain individual freedoms and whose intrinsic criterion for membership is by references to illiberal practices, Kymlicka's distinction will be difficult to apply. In these cases it is likely that a major change in the coercive, but fundamentally important, norms of that culture (culture I) will impact on the availability of a community of like-minded individuals (culture II) in the long term and so threaten the continued survival of that culture, thereby undermining the possibility of securing for the individual a right to cultural membership. Kymlicka also argues that in rare cases the restriction of individual choice can be justified where the survival of a community is at stake. He states that this must be a temporary measure, to enable a culture to move towards a fully liberal society. However, as Kymlicka himself recognizes, we need to know more about the circumstances when a community's survival is at stake and when it is undergoing social change, as well as about the disintegration and liberalization of cultures. In the face of such indeterminacy, a wide-ranging qualification to the liberal commitment to individual freedom in order to secure cultural survival would seem to be a dangerous route.

These issues raise a more general question concerning the appropriateness of introducing 'culture' into a human rights analysis. In his 1993 Reith Lectures[52] Edward Said set out the difficulties faced by academics who theorize about cultures and who attempt to define objective criteria for such study. Although Charles Taylor has made some progress in this field by developing a method for evaluating cultures which avoids the twin evils of claims to scientific objectivity on the one hand, and the collapse into patronizing subjectivism on the other,[53] this does not help in the resolution of the most significant conflicts. Despite these theoretical concerns, there are persuasive reasons for paying closer attention to the issue of cultural membership. The view that cultural diversity and its importance would decline under modernizing conditions has now been

Maleiha Malik

modified.[54] An increasing number of societies are culturally plural, and parametric changes in economic organization and rapid technological change, which are often referred to under the label 'globalization', will contribute to the trend of increasing contact between different cultures. If the ideology of human rights is to be presented as a universal, viable and objective standard, then there are good reasons to face the challenges posed by cultural diversity.

SOME CONCLUSIONS

Kymlicka's approach is adopted, despite significant reservations, as an appropriate foundation for the accommodation of important communal goods within the human rights agenda. It provides the starting point from which to launch a number of further inquiries. Further detailed work needs to be undertaken using this analysis, particularly into the ways in which these new rights will interact with existing human rights provisions. A number of techniques for accommodating communal goods into the existing framework of human rights need to be developed.

One option is the reinterpretation of existing human rights provisions as a basis for securing access to communal goods. For example, in *Lovelace* a recognition of the importance of cultural membership as a right provides the justification for the special rights which the Indian Act extends to Canadian Indians as a cultural group, and for an expansive interpretation of Article 27 of the ICCPR to include the right to live on specially reserved land. Many of the resulting difficulties can be resolved by attending to the fact that in Kymlicka's terms access to communal goods is motivated by providing a *context* for individual choice. Consequently, in the case of a conflict between a group and individual right, the group right should be constructed and applied, as far as possible, so that it is in conformity with the individual right. Ultimately, where there is a conflict between a group right and an individual right, this must be resolved in favour of the individual, who should remain free to renounce his or her right under Article 27. In the *Belgian Linguistics* case, the recognition of a general right to cultural membership would strongly support the arguments of the applicants: that interpretations of the rights in Article 2 of the First Protocol should remain sensitive to the linguistic needs of the minority group, and that the minority group should not be placed at a disadvantage in exercising its fundamental rights under Article 8 of the ECHR which safeguards the right to respect for private and family life.

This approach also provides support for the Committee's decision in *Lovelace* to recognize the applicant as an Indian in the face of a contrary classification by the group. Further work needs to be undertaken on what it means to be a member of a particular group or community. The attempts to define nationality and citizenship within the European Union and in international law will provide useful analogies.[55] In addition, more radical proposals may also be a creative source of ideas.[56] These definitions need to attend to the historical and factual context within which the claim to the right arises in order to avoid arbitrary results. Therefore criteria need to be applied in a flexible way. A detailed and context-dependent analysis can also be used to formulate definitions of the group. What constitutes a collective group for the purposes of one right (such as language rights) need not necessarily determine a definition for another (such as special rights to land).[57]

There will be some cases where the recognition of a right to cultural membership requires the identification of those important communal goods which are not adequately protected by existing legislation, and the grant of a new right. In these cases a narrow, context-dependent response is essential. Recalling the dangers inherent in the translation of communal goods into collective rights, especially if the vacuum left by indeterminacy and open-endedness is filled by illiberal practices, these new rights should be formulated using an 'incremental approach'. Such an approach identifies the communal good to be provided with a high degree of specificity, and the right is formulated in a narrow and detailed manner. The adoption of the European Charter for Regional or Minority Languages is a good example of an 'incremental' response to the failure of the ECHR and the European Court to safeguard language rights. The Charter attempts to fill this specific gap in the existing European human rights framework by focusing on the 'inalienable right' to use a regional and minority language. It contains detailed proposals which include: a Preamble which refers specifically to the historical context which justifies the protection of language rights in Europe; a narrow definition of what constitutes a regional language (Article 1); a statement of the underlying objectives of the Charter (Article 7); the specific undertakings of the contracting state, e.g. in education; judicial activity and the media, (Articles 8–15); the relationship with existing individual rights (Article 4) and, finally, the methods of supervision and enforcement (Articles 15–18). This incremental approach is more likely to accommodate communal goods so that the new right granted coheres with the existing principles justifying human rights standards and is attentive to the need to overcome the embarrassing conflicts associated with collective rights.

There are also strategic reasons for preferring an incremental approach. One real difficulty in this area is that these rights are usually claimed against a state. Minority rights claims are often viewed as a prelude to secession, which is invariably perceived as a fundamental threat to the peace, security and, ultimately, the existence of the state. Modest demands are more likely to be seen as legitimate and acceptable than are calls for the recognition of a general human right guaranteeing 'the existence of a people' or a widely formulated 'right to culture and language'.

Activists and proponents of collective rights may consider this an unduly modest response to what are fundamentally important, but often neglected, interests. They may argue that the claims to justice for groups necessitates a more radical solution. However, if the solution is to be sought within the human rights framework, then considerations of principle and policy should encourage the adoption of an incremental approach, which recognizes the importance of communal goods as a context of individual choice. In this way, urgent and legitimate demands for communal goods can be accommodated without the danger of eroding the existing commitment to human rights.

NOTES

1. See, for example, Treaty on the Protection of Minorities in Greece, signed at Sevres, 10 August 1920, and the Declaration on the Protection of Minorities in Lithuania, signed at Geneva, 12 May 1922, Articles 3–5. M. O. Hudson (ed.), *International Legislation* (Washington: Carnegie Endowment for International Peace, 1931).

2. There is some protection for groups via Article 27 of the ICCPR, which extends general protection to the rights of the individuals who constitute a minority (see note 17 below).

3. The United Nations is considering proposals for a draft document setting out the rights of indigenous persons. The UN Sub-Commission on the Prevention of Discrimination and Protection of Minorities is the body directly involved in the drafting process on behalf of the Inter-governmental Commission on Human Rights. For recent developments see the text of the Sub-Commission's Working Party on Indigenous Populations, UN doc. E/CN. 4/Sub. 2/1993/29, and the Resolution of the Inter-governmental Commission, Report of the Forty-ninth Session, UN doc. E/CN. 4/Sub. 2/1993/122.

4. Article 1 of the Declaration, approved by the Commission on Human Rights at the Forty-eighth Session (Resolution 1992/16 of 21 February 1992).

5. Parliamentary Assembly of the Council of Europe, Recommendation 1134 (1990), which is supplemented by the Parliamentary Order No. 46 (1990), instructs the Committee on Legal Affairs and Human Rights to organize a parliamentary conference or symposium, with one of its main objects being the further elaboration and definition of the principles of the rights of minorities *with a view to the inclusion of these rights in an additional protocol to the ECHR or in a special Council of Europe convention*. See 33 *Yearbook of the European Convention on Human Rights*, pp. 295 and 298 (The Hague: Martin Nijhoff, 1990).

6. Parliamentary Assembly of the Council of Europe, Recommendation 1201 (1993), Article 11.

7. Strasbourg, 5.XI.1992, European Treaty Series, 148.

8. The CSCE is a body which groups together members of NATO, the former Warsaw Pact countries and several neutral and non-aligned states. It is now referred to as the

Organization for Security and Co-operation in Europe, OSCE. At a meeting in Budapest on 5 December 1994, the USA, Germany and Russia emerged as the leading proponents of a stronger CSCE: Leaders aim to upgrade CSCE role, *Financial Times*, 5 December 1994.

9. Official source: African Charter on Human and Peoples' Rights, Nairobi, June 1981; Doc. CAB/LEG/67/3/Rev. 5 (1981). For the text see: (1981) 21 *International Legal Materials* 58.

10. For references to the Constitution and generally see H. Corder, Towards a South African Constitution (1994) 57 *Modern Law Review* 491 and Chapter 4 above.

11. Principle XXXIV states, *inter alia*: '1. This Schedule and the recognition therein of the right of the South African people as a whole to self-determination shall not be construed as precluding, within the framework of the said right, constitutional provision for a notion of the right to self-determination by any community sharing a common cultural and language heritage, whether in a territorial entity within the Republic or in any other recognised way. 2. The Constitution may give expression to any particular form of self-determination provided there is substantial proven support within the community concerned for such a form of self-determination.'

12. See G. Bindman, The New South Africa – a revolution in the making (1994) 144 *New Law Journal* 647, and Corder *op. cit.* Principle XXXIV was added by the Constitution of the Republic of South Africa Act, No. 2 of 1994, s. 13(b).

13. For example, at the World Conference on Human Rights held in Vienna in 1993 the sustained lobbying of pressure groups was a crucial motivating factor behind the recent UN initiative to produce a draft indigenous people's treaty.

14. A good example of this is the recent initiative concerning minority rights issues by the Council of Europe and the CSCE which has followed the ethnic conflict in the former Yugoslavia.

15. The Commission has established separate policy studies headed by different special rapporteurs to consider the following areas: the rights of persons belonging to ethnic, religious and linguistic minorities (Rapporteur Capotorti); discrimination against indigenous populations (Rapporteurs Cobo and Eide); the implementation of UN resolutions relating to the rights of peoples under colonial and alien domination to self-determination (Rapporteur Espiell); and the right of self-determination (Rapporteur Cristescu).

16. Eastern Europe and the war in the former Yugoslavia are good examples. The extension of the membership of the Council of Europe to eastern European states will influence the human rights agenda in Europe. Misha Glenny in the epilogue to his analysis of the ethnic conflict in that region makes the point that the democratization of eastern Europe will bring to the fore long-standing ethnic conflicts and will ensure that minority rights remain an important concern. This lends some urgency to the need to develop coherent policies and strategies at the European level. See M. Glenny, *The Fall of Yugoslavia* (London: Penguin, 1992).

17. Article 27 states: 'In those States in which ethnic, religious or linguistic minorities exist, persons belonging to such minorities shall not be denied the right, in community with other members of their group to enjoy their culture, to profess and practice their own religion, or to use their own language.' Article 14 ECHR states: 'The enjoyment of the rights and freedoms set forth in this Convention shall be secured without discrimination on any ground such as sex, race, colour, language, religion, political or other opinion, national or social origin, association with a national minority, property, birth or other status.'

18. Article 25(1) of the Universal Declaration of Human Rights states *inter alia*: '1. Everyone has the right to a standard of living adequate for the health and well-being of himself and of his family, including food, clothing, housing and medical care and necessary social services, and the right to security in the event of unemployment, sickness, disability, widowhood, old age or other lack of livelihood in circumstances beyond his control.' For the socio-economic rights in the new South African constitutional structure see Corder, *op. cit.*, p. 512 and Chapter 4 above. Although the ECHR includes civil and political rights only, the European Social Charter of 1961, which was negotiated as part of the framework of the Council of Europe, deals with second-generation rights. For the text of the Charter see *European Treaty Series* No. 35, 18 October 1961.

19. For a full discussion of this special characteristic of third-generation claims to com-

munal goods see J. Waldron, *Liberal Rights, Collected Papers 1981–1991* (New York: Cambridge University Press, 1993), Chapter 14.

20. R. Dworkin, *A Matter of Principle* (Oxford: Oxford University Press, 1985), Chapter 8.

21. In Dworkin's terms this would be a failure to treat each individual with 'equal respect and concern'. Despite some changes in his theory of justice as fairness, John Rawls remains committed to the idea of neutrality between conceptions of the good and reaffirms the priority of the right over the good. See J. Rawls, *Political Liberalism*. Lecture V (New York: Columbia University Press, 1993).

22. W. Kymlicka, *Liberalism, Community and Culture* (Oxford: Clarendon Press, 1989), Chapters 2 and 3.

23. R. Dworkin, *op. cit.*, in particular pp. 191 and 203.

24. J. Rawls, Kantian constructivism in moral theory (1980) 77 *Journal of Philosophy* 515. Although in his most recent work, *Political Liberalism*, Rawls moves away from the position that the idea that individuals are free and equal provides a moral foundation for his theory of justice, he remains committed to the idea that all citizens are free and equal as a foundational principle of political liberalism. See J. Rawls, *Political Liberalism, op. cit.*, pp. 15–22.

25. See the International Covenant on Civil and Political Rights 1966, Part III; Article 26 of the ICCPR states: 'All persons are equal before the law and are entitled without any discrimination to the equal protection of the law. In this respect, the law shall prohibit any discrimination and guarantee to all persons equal and effective protection against discrimination on any ground such as race, colour, sex, language, religion, political or other opinion, national or social origin, property, birth or other status.'

26. ECHR Articles 2–12.

27. C. A. Gearty, The European Court of Human Rights and the protection of civil liberties: an overview (1993) 52 *Cambridge Law Journal* 89.

28. *Ibid.*, pp. 108–15.

29. In *East African Asians* v. *United Kingdom (No. 2)* (1973) 3 EHRR 76, there is a suggestion that differential treatment of individuals on the basis of their membership of a racial group could constitute 'degrading treatment', but at no stage is there any reference to the group being the focus of protection.

30. See ss. 71(2), 98(2) and 98(5) of the Constitution of the Republic of South Africa, Act 200 of 1993. See also H. Corder, *op. cit.*, pp. 511–21 and Chapter 4 above.

31. J. Rawls, Fairness to goodness (1975) *Philosophical Review* 84. This basic idea is reaffirmed in *Political Liberalism*, see Lecture I, parts 6 and 7, (note 21).

32. *Belgian Linguistics Case (No. 2)* (1968) 1 EHRR 252.

33. Article 2 of the first Protocol to the European Convention on Human Rights states: 'No person shall be denied the right to education. In the exercise of any functions which it assumes in relation to education and to teaching, the State shall respect the right of parents to ensure such education and teaching in conformity with their own religious and philosophical convictions.' See I. Brownlie, *Basic Documents on Human Rights*, 3rd edn (Oxford: Oxford University Press, 1992).

34. Minority Schools in Albania; Permanent Court of International Justice; Thirty-Fourth (Ordinary) Session; 6 April 1935 – *Permanent Court of International Justice* (1935) Series A/B, Volume 64.

35. There is increasing recognition that the meaningful accommodation of communal goods requires adopting measures which require the violation of accepted notions of formal equality. See Triggs, People's rights and individual rights, in J. Crawford (ed.), *The Rights of People* (Oxford: Clarendon Press, 1988).

36. C. Taylor, *Hegel and Modern Society* (Cambridge: Cambridge University Press, 1979).

37. C. Taylor, *Sources of the Self: the Making of Modern Identity*, Part 1 (Cambridge: Cambridge University Press, 1989). For the 'social thesis', see C. Taylor, Atomism, in C. Taylor, *Philosophical Papers II* (Cambridge: Cambridge University Press, 1989).

38. M. Sandel, *Liberalism and the Limits of Justice* (Cambridge: Cambridge University Press, 1982).

39. *Ibid.*, p. 179.

40. A. MacIntyre, *After Virtue* (London: Notre Dame, 1981). For his recent writing see A. MacIntyre, *Whose Justice? Which Rationality?* (London: Duckworth, 1988).

41. M. Sandel, *op. cit.*, pp. 147–55.

42. *Sandra Lovelace* v. *Canada*; Communication No. 24/1977; *Yearbook of the Human Rights Committee, 1981–82*, Volume II.

43. Contemporary difficulties in defining peoples and groups are analogous to the debate concerning the subjective and objective theories of minority identity under the League of Nations Minority Treaties system. See, for example, J. Stone, *Regional Guarantees of Minority Rights* (New York: Macmillan, 1933), p. 36.

44. Anthony de Jasay first used this phrase to refer to the problem of the rights of groups at *Individual and Collective Rights in National Context*, a conference held at the University of London, May 1991.

45. C. Taylor, *Multiculturalism and the Politics of Recognition* (Princeton: Princeton University Press, 1992).

46. *Ibid.*, p. 61.

47. Professor Ian Brownlie suggests that there are good reasons for some 'proposal for quality control' in human rights, in the context of the proliferation of third-generation human rights claims. See Brownlie, *The Rights of People in Modern International Law*, in J. Crawford (ed.), *The Rights of People* (Oxford: Clarendon Press, 1988).

48. W. Kymlicka, *Liberalism, Community and Culture* (Oxford: Clarendon Press, 1989).

49. *Ibid.*, p. 165.

50. *Ibid.*, p. 140.

51. *Ibid.*, pp. 168-70.

52. The text of the Reith Lectures is published by, and available from, *The Independent*.

53. See C. Taylor, *Multiculturalism and the Politics of Recognition*, *op. cit.*, pp. 61-73. See also C. Taylor, Understanding and ethnocentricity, in C. Taylor, *Philosophical Papers II* (Cambridge: Cambridge University Press, 1989).

54. E. Gellner, *Nations and Nationalism* (Oxford: Blackwell, 1983).

55. For recent discussions of citizenship within the European Union, see D. O'Keefe and P. Twomey, *Legal Issues and the Maastricht Treaty* (Chancery, 1994), especially Chapter 6 (Union Citizenship) and Chapter 7 (Citizenship of the Union and Nationality of Member States). See also A. Evans, Nationality Law and European Integration [1991] *European Law Review* 190. There are a number of relevant discussions of the issues of nationality and citizenship in International Law. See, for example, the decision of the Permanent Court of International Justice in the *Tunis and Morocco Nationality Decrees* case, PCIJ, Series B, No. 4. See also the *Nottebohm* case, [1955] 4 ICJ Reports, 20.

56. See, for example, G. Gottlieb, *Nation against State* (New York: Council on Foreign Relations, 1994).

57. See J. Crawford (ed.) *The Rights of People, op. cit.*, pp. 169–71.

8

Not Another Theory of Human Rights!

R. Jayakumar Nayar

This chapter is concerned with human welfare, and in particular with the potential for its protection and promotion through the application of an international legal concept of 'human rights'. The enquiry into human welfare, from an international legal perspective, has become synonymous with the study of modern concepts such as 'development' and 'human rights'. Continuous usage in international political and legal discourse has, however, not led to any clear consensus as to the meaning and implications of these concepts. The student/activist of development/human rights today is faced with a multitude of theories, philosophies, legal opinions and operational strategies on how best to confront and advance the cause of human welfare, not to mention the outright pessimism of many who regard the whole exercise as inherently futile. The problem is that often there is little by way of a coordinated response to the common aim which must inform international human rights discourse, namely the protection and enhancement of human welfare universally. Lack of a concerted approach in this respect can be attributed to the deficiencies which bedevil international human rights discourse.

In putting forward the case for the 'right to development' as a 'new' human right, Alston suggests that existing institutional and academic approaches to international human rights law suffer from the following weaknesses: the lack of depth in much human rights scholarship; the separation of international human rights law from other aspects of international law; the lack of an interdisciplinary approach to human rights issues; and the separation of the UN's human rights activities from its development activities.[1] Of these, it is the first two which will be the focus of this chapter; it is considered that an interdisciplinary approach is encompassed within what is required for a proper understanding of human rights, and the coordination of the UN's activities in both these areas of concern is necessarily contingent on a proper understanding of human rights.

The aim of this chapter is to provide a conceptually coherent and viable concept of human rights that is relevant to the real life experiences and struggles that constitute much of human life. In light of the above, it is worth stressing the point that what is intended here is not a 'theory' of human rights but rather a rationalization of the concept. The difference is a crucial one. Rather than putting forward a theory that attempts to provide a justification for the existence of human rights,[2] a rationalization of the concept is directed towards establishing a conceptual basis upon which human rights, as an international legal concept, can be built.

The criteria which have underpinned my attempt to reconceptualize human rights can be outlined as follows. First, I have based my arguments on the proposition that all human life is equal in value and that human rights are therefore possessed equally by all individuals simply by virtue of being human; the concept of human rights must be based on entitlements which are universally applicable for a life of dignity and self-respect. Second, in accepting the rich diversity of humanity, I recognize that the universal objectivity of human rights must not preclude cultural sensitivity – the meaningful application of the concept within diverse and culturally specific contexts. Third, I submit that human rights must be 'rights' capable of being possessed by the individual as legal rights, as opposed to benefits granted, thus conferring legal empowerment; the latter approach, although important in the context of enhancing the human condition (through the process of 'development'), must first be informed through a minimum standard of 'human dignity'. Last, the concept of human rights, although adopting individual human welfare as its final focus, must, I stress, avoid the danger of abstracting the individual from the social context of human life.

What follows is a conceptualization of human rights that is derived from a foundational concept of basic human needs (providing substance to the 'inherent dignity'[3] of the human individual) that, I believe, is contextually relevant, conceptually coherent and operationally viable as a legal concept. The first stop in our journey is the concept of basic human needs.

BASIC HUMAN NEEDS

Basic human needs are those components, qualitatively articulated, which are identified as the universally relevant constituents of what is understood as 'human life', irrespective of the rich diversity of humanity, which when satisfied within specific societal contexts give meaning to a distinctly human life.

The study of the concept of human needs is not a recent intellectual endeavour. The semantic of 'basic human needs' is, therefore, adopted with some caution. Despite the historical 'baggage' which attaches itself to a discussion of needs, the concept of basic human needs is employed here to serve as a reference point from which the human condition can be assessed. Admittedly this is done more for the sake of linguistic convenience than through allegiance to any particular conceptualization of the term 'needs'. It is not my aim in this section to carry out a philosophical review or a critical examination of past conceptualizations of human needs. This has been done elsewhere.[4] Rather, my aim is to provide a consistent theoretical foundation from which, I believe, we can build a concept of human rights.

I base my approach in explaining the concept of basic human needs (hereinafter BHN) on a simple schematic framework, expressed at this juncture as follows:

$$X \rightarrow needs \rightarrow Y \rightarrow for \rightarrow Z$$

Three interrelated questions, therefore, present themselves:

1. Who is the subject (X) of BHN;
2. What is the object (Z) of those needs; and therefore,
3. What are those BHN (Y)?

In dealing with these questions, I will in turn introduce a number of other concepts which I feel are necessary to give meaning to a theoretical foundation for the concept of BHN which satisfies both the requirements for universality and for sensitivity to diverse cultural traditions. I argue that the subject of BHN is the 'whole human individual', whose 'humanness' comprises the interplay and interrelationship of the 'human being', the 'self' and the 'person'. The object of articulating needs, it will be argued, is, therefore, to express the universal 'ends' towards which all human action is directed, derived from what will be called basic human propensities, namely to survive, to self-realize and to participate socially. Following from this proposition, BHN are those preconditions which, when satisfied within specific socio-cultural contexts, enable the whole individual to satisfy the universal human propensities for survival, self-realization and social participation.

The Subject of Needs: The Whole Individual

The concept of needs necessitates the identification of the subject whose specific characteristics provide the basis for enquiry. In the context of

BHN, therefore, it is necessary to identify the distinct entity which is referred to when we speak of a 'human individual'. Before we can attempt to articulate the contents or the proposed list of BHN, it is useful first to ascertain the distinctive characteristics of the 'human' subject of those needs. This entity will be referred to as the whole individual.[5] The following discussion will seek to provide a concept of the whole individual, as the subject of BHN, which will enable us in turn to appreciate the basic elements of the object of those needs.

The whole individual refers to the single ontological human entity. This concept tells us little about the specific characteristics of this entity; about the humanness of the whole individual. In order to do this, it is helpful to consider three modes of conceptualizing the whole individual: the human being, the self and the person. It ought to be emphasized that the concepts of human being, self and person do not function as distinct and separable components of the whole individual, but rather as three distinct ways in which the whole individual can be conceptualized and perceived.[6] McCall uses the analogy of the relationship of individual organs to the human body to explain the purpose of distinguishing the human being, self and person as modes of perceiving the single entity – the whole individual:

> The enterprise of analysing different ways of conceiving individuals is analogous to the dissection of a body . . . . Just as different organs and their related functions can be conceived of as being in some senses independent and in some senses dependent upon each other, and at the same time being dependent upon their integrated function within the organism as a whole, so the concepts of *person*, *self* and *human being* have distinct functions, whilst remaining interdependent . . . . Whilst investigation of organs independently from the whole organism may reveal some specific aspects of each organ, the functioning organs could not be understood without an understanding of their interrelationship, and their relationship to the organism as a whole.[7]

The purpose of making the distinction between the human being, self and person as different ways of understanding the integral whole individual is therefore to appreciate the core properties of the whole individual which emerge as a result of the interrelationship between these different perceptions of the individual. In the context of our discussion, this exercise is useful in order to help us understand that the concept of BHN can only be informed and defined through an appreciation of the various modes of perceiving what it is to be 'human'; of what core properties interplay to constitute the whole individual. What follows is a brief description of the core properties of the whole individual when conceived of through the interrelationship between the concepts of the human being, self and person.

THE HUMAN BEING

The human being is one way in which the whole individual is perceived, revealing its own distinctive characteristics. This concept is used to refer to the individual as a biological entity; an individual of the species *Homo sapiens*.[8] As a biological entity, and being a member of a specific species, certain characteristics and propensities of the individual can be identified. Determined by the physiological constitution and functioning of the human body, the human being can be observed to progress through the life cycle of birth, maturation and death. Governed by the biological laws that determine the survival of living organisms, the individual as a human being requires such sustenance and life conditions which are necessary for the preservation of life.

THE SELF

The concept of self pertains to those aspects of the whole individual which constitute the introspective perception of the individual. This is often referred to as self-consciousness. As McCall explains:

> The concept of self represents the experimental nature of the individual: the individual does not merely react to the environment, but experiences himself or herself so doing. The self is thus the location of experience, the aspect of an individual which can reflect upon experience, which 'has' those experiences, but which is not identified with the experience.[9]

The significance of self as the 'location of experience' is considerable. In the context of our earlier discussion on the concept of human being, the self represents the individual's capacity to experience, articulate and subsequently act (or also, importantly, to refrain from acting) upon the perceived necessities for survival. Herein also lies the source of such (much discussed) concepts as reason and rationality, self-respect and dignity, agency, choice, autonomy and creativity, the higher cognitive capacities associated with being human. The self, therefore, I would suggest, is the aspect of the individual which enables the convergence of the concept of the human being with that of the person to constitute the whole individual.

THE PERSON

The individual, perceived as a person, is a social entity. The concept of person therefore avoids the atomization and abstraction of the human individual from society. Recognizing the human individual as a person brings to prominence humankind's humanity; the human individual as a member of a particular community, identified and recognized as having specific characteristics and attributes. Personhood therefore, as McCall points out, is a 'public construction'.[10] A person exists only in society, and is defined and judged by society. It is through this aspect of the individual that the individual acquires an identity and knowledge of his or her social environment, therefore being capable of establishing relationships in the process of social participation. Simply put, the concept of person relates to the social recognition and participation of the individual.

THE WHOLE INDIVIDUAL

As suggested earlier, the whole individual which is the subject of needs is the holistic entity which is to be understood by the fusing of the concepts of human being, self and person. The interplay between the various ways by which perception of the individual occurs therefore defines the 'humanness' of the individual; in other words, the specific characteristics of the subject of needs. An example might be useful to illustrate the inter-relationship of the concepts discussed above.

Let us first consider the concept of human being. Based on the discussion above, the human being represents the perception of the individual purely from a biological perspective; that the particular individual concerned is a member of the species *Homo sapiens*. Described in this way, there is little to separate the individual from any other animal save in the fact that they are members of different species. The humanness of the individual is absent in this description, which merely refers to those qualities of the human individual which are shared to a greater or lesser degree with animals of other species. In the context of the needs of the individual, when perceived as a human being, what is identified are those physiological and environmental requirements which the biology of the individual needs in order to maintain life. Humanity does, however, begin to reveal itself when the concept of self is considered. Here the individual is more than a mere conglomeration of cells which are driven by biological motivations, but is also capable of self-conception: that is to say, perception of the individual by the individual. The self, however, does not perceive itself outside the social environment in which it exists, but, on the contrary, is defined by it; hence the interrelationship of the concept of person and self. It is the individual, perceived of and recognized as a person by society, which is then capable of perceiving itself and of evaluating experience. The resultant fusion of the concepts of human being, self and person in the whole individual therefore is the quality of humanness which enables the individual to, for example, feel hungry, articulate this experience and reflect and act on the means by which hunger can be relieved within his or her social environment.

Understanding that there exist various means by which the individual can be perceived provides insights into what constitutes the whole individual. This is significant for two reasons: first, because this avoids the false distinction being made as to objectively ascertainable hierarchies of needs; and second, because this demonstrates the importance of recognizing that the individual, and therefore his or her needs, cannot be abstracted from the social realities within which he or she is perceived.

Having discussed the subject of needs, it is now appropriate to consider what it is that directs the search for BHN; in other words, the object of needs.

The Object of BHN: Basic Human Propensities

Going back to the scheme outlined earlier:

$$X \rightarrow \text{needs} \rightarrow Y \rightarrow \text{for} \rightarrow Z$$

the question of what is Z represents the central issue which enables the identification of Y as needs. In the context of BHN, this question relates to the universal human ends for which BHN are needed.

A survey of human needs literature reveals two such ends which are most commonly used to provide the basis for human needs: the avoidance of serious harm,[11] and human well-being (sometimes referred to as worthwhile lives).[12] Miller defines harm as follows:

> Harm, for any individual, is whatever interferes directly or indirectly with the activities essential to his plan of life: and correspondingly, his needs must be understood to comprise whatever is necessary to allow these activities to be carried out.[13]

The main problem with this basis for human needs is that the identification of needs becomes a subjective exercise, depending on the particular life plan of the individual concerned. No universal assertion of human needs can therefore be maintained. Thompson overcomes this problem of relativism by linking his conception of serious harm, not to individual life plans, but rather to a universal notion of 'interest':

[T]he notion of an interest is relevant to the task of explaining the concept of a fundamental need in the following way. The primary goods we are deprived of when we are harmed (by lacking what we need) are good and worthwhile because they answer our interests, and not because they are desired. The notion of an interest defines the range and type of activities and experiences that partly constitute a meaningful, worthwhile life, and it defines the nature of their worth. These types of activities are primary goods and because they are good something which deprives us of them is bad, and harmful.[14]

Although Thompson neither specifies what these interests might be nor defines the primary goods that are essential to answer these interests, he puts forward the case for universality by distinguishing interests from desires: that interests, unlike desires, are not dependent on judgments and beliefs.[15] This assertion can be contested. The most obvious judgment or belief upon which Thompson's account of universal interest is based is the basic assumption that preservation of life is always in the individual's interest. Although this judgment might be true in most cases, failure to make explicit the fundamental assumptions upon which interests, and therefore the avoidance of harm, rest weakens the argument for universality. In this respect, Fitzgerald's critique that all conceptions of universal human needs are based on normative models of human excellence, on the meaning of worthwhile lives, must be addressed.[16] Universality of BHN is not necessarily refuted by this critique. What it does necessitate, however, is that the assumptions and criteria upon which universality is claimed must be explicitly clarified and demonstrated. It is submitted that the account of the avoidance of harm or interests as the basis upon which BHN are identified is insufficient for our purposes. If a case is to be made for a universally applicable concept of BHN, then such vague notions as interests and harm must be expanded upon. I propose the concept of 'basic human propensities' to serve this purpose.

Basic human propensities are the lowest common denominators which unite human existence, being the basic inclinations or tendencies[17] of human individuals. They represent the broad areas of concern and action which all human individuals have to make decisions about. Thus defined, the concept of basic human propensities might appear to be a restatement of the concept of interest mentioned above. The concept of basic human propensities differs from notions of 'our most basic human interests',[18] however, in that it is derived not from harm to life, based on the implicit acceptance that preserving life is necessarily a most basic human interest, but rather from an explicit account of what directs life, if the preservation of life is in fact pursued.[19] Being the basic inclinations or tendencies of the human individual, they do not definitely prescribe human action, but rather indicate the basic causes which direct such action. In order to determine what basic human propensities are, reference will now be made to the core characteristics of the whole human individual discussed above.

First, the human being; when perceived in this way, the individual is understood as a biological entity. The basic propensity which can be identified in this respect is the propensity for the individual to pursue such things that will ensure the preservation of life: the *propensity for survival*.[20] Second, the self; the concept of self relates to the introspective nature of the individual, to his or her capacity to evaluate and articulate experience. In this sense, the individual self part creates his or her own world.[21] Herein originates the propensity of human individuals to seek to give meaning to their own existence; to reflect on experiences and to articulate individual perceptions against the background of the self's social environment. I call this the *propensity for self-realization*. Third, the person is the individual when perceived by society. It denotes the participation of the individual within his or her social environment, recognition of the individual as a person thus referring to the socio-cultural perception of the individual. Personhood, therefore, is the source from which the propensity of individuals to live in a social environment is derived. This I call the *propensity for social participation*.

As stated above, the basic human propensities just outlined – for survival, for self-realization and for social participation – point towards broad and generalized areas of concern which direct the actions of all individuals, universally. Several points ought now to be made regarding both the concept of basic human propensities and the claim of universality.

First, the assertion that these propensities are universally true for all individuals does not prescribe that uniformity of action can be predicted, that all individuals would act in a certain determinable way in response to these propensities. That is too ambitious and arrogant an assertion. What the claim does mean, however, is that all human action can be explained by reference to any one, or a combination, of these basic human propensities. The validity of this assertion therefore lies not in empirically verifying that certain behaviours are prevalent crossculturally, but rather in its cross-cultural relevance in explaining behavioural patterns. This being so, I believe it is fair to place the burden on those who might seek to disprove the validity of this assertion, to show that any one of the three basic human propensities does not hold true in explaining human action within a specific context.

The second point that must be emphasized is that survival, selfrealization and social participation are not mutually exclusive human propensities. The extent to which action is undertaken in response to these human propensities is largely the result of the interplay between them, each mutually reinforcing the others. It is therefore consistent that differences exist in socio-cultural perceptions on the importance to be attached to actions pertaining to the various propensities. To use Dearden's example, the refusal of someone engaged in religious exercise to attach any importance to food, and thus to presupposed norms of health,[22] can be seen simply as a particular socio-cultural perspective influencing the actions of the individual with regard to the perceived comparative importance of self-realization over the propensity for survival.

Finally, the point ought to be made that the basic human propensities for survival, self-realization and social participation are not arranged in any hierarchy of prepotency.[23] No assertion is being made here that human individuals would necessarily prioritize action pertaining to one basic human propensity (e.g. survival) over another (e.g. social participation). Closely related to the point made earlier regarding the interconnectedness of basic human propensities, the prioritization of action relating to these propensities, it is suggested, is also dependent on the specific socio-cultural perceptions which are held by the individual. What is hoped to be conveyed by this account of basic human propensities as the source from which a needs enquiry can be based, is that what constitutes the whole individual, and therefore the basic human propensities which direct human action, must be understood from a holistic perspective. In turn, the BHN, which are derived from our conception of the whole individual, must also be seen, not as a hierarchical list of requirements to be ticked off as satisfaction occurs, but rather as a holistic interrelationship of those needs which are essential for survival, self-realization and social participation.

This discussion on basic human propensities was intended to provide us with an objective and universally applicable basis upon which to identify BHN. Going back to our schematic framework,

$$X \rightarrow needs \rightarrow Y \rightarrow for \rightarrow Z$$

we can now label the variables X and Z: X = the whole human individual, and Z = basic human propensities – survival, self-realization and social participation. The next section will consider the specific 'needs' that can be derived from the previous discussions on the subject (X) and the object (Z) of needs; in other words, we will now identify Y.

Basic Human Needs

The first question that has to be addressed in a discussion on BHN is what is 'basic' about the concept. As noted above, most commentators derive the concept of needs from a negative perspective; needs being such things that are required in order to avoid serious harm, however defined. The concept of BHN proposed here, however, is derived from the preceding concept of basic human propensities, which is in turn derived from the concept of the whole individual. What is basic about BHN is therefore that they intimately and directly pertain to the basic human propensities of the whole individual; they are those essential ingredients which fulfil the basic human propensities for survival, self-realization and social participation.

The concept of BHN is employed here as a qualitative rather than a quantitative expression of human requirements. What is attempted here is not a generalization of 'human nature' based on a quantitative measure of needs, but rather an expression of essential need areas which are universally experienced by all human individuals. The precise quantification of these requirements, as well as the priority that might be given to certain need areas over others by an individual in a given situation may, it is conceded, vary greatly depending on environmental and socio-cultural factors as well as personal individual preferences. This scope for potential diversity does not, however, detract from the concept of BHN as it is understood and applied in this chapter; the reason for this will be demonstrated below.

The following discussion will elaborate on the BHN which are derived from the basic human propensities for survival, self-realization and social participation.

SURVIVAL NEEDS

The basic human propensity for survival provides the basis for survival needs; those things which are required by the human organism for the preservation of its life-supporting systems. These needs are determined therefore by the physiological constitution of the human body and by the biological laws that govern the survival of living organisms. In this respect, survival needs represent the threshold requirements for the preservation of life.[24] The proposed list of needs which are derived from the propensity for survival are these: sustenance (food and water), shelter and physical and mental integrity.

Sustenance

Sustenance (the essential components of which are food and water) is the basic prerequisite for preservation of the physiological functioning of the human body. It comprises the essential fuel and nourishment upon which the human body as a living organism depends. At the most basic level, therefore, food can be seen to play a purely nutritional role. Studies to estimate nutritional requirements have been conducted, although disparities in quantitative requirements are acknowledged as inevitable.[25]

Shelter
The term shelter is used here to refer to both a place of dwelling and materials of clothing; those things which protect the human body from the natural elements. Although perceptions about what is regarded as dwellings or clothing vary greatly across cultural boundaries, largely influenced by climatic and cultural conditions, there is little dispute that they are basic needs. With regard to dwellings, a core set of principles can be outlined, to constitute the basis upon which a universal concept of the need for shelter can be founded: first, security – reasonable protection from exposure to extreme climatic conditions (this principle is also applicable for clothing) as well as from other life-threatening agents such as disease-carrying vectors and pests; second, adequate means for sanitation and waste disposal; and last, it should be appropriate to the social perception of private and public life, not being subject to extreme overpopulation.[26] It is quite obvious that the scope for diversity is great in the form and perception of what is considered to be adequate dwelling and clothing. This scope for diversity, however, does not affect the universality of the need.

Physical and Mental Integrity
Physical and mental integrity as basic needs comprise an elaboration of the general propensity for survival. They constitute both the need to preserve as intact the physical and mental faculties, and the need to protect and nurture the functioning of those faculties. Combined, they relate to the health of the individual. Definitions of health are often presented in two forms – negative and positive health. Negative definitions of health focus on the impairment of the biological functioning of the human body; health therefore being defined in terms of being free from disease.[27] Positive health is a more abstract concept, open to different cultural perceptions of what it is to be healthy, or unhealthy.[28] The distinction between the two can best be explained by the different conceptions of the human body which they adopt; the negative health approach adopting what is known as the biomedical model, whilst the positive health approach taking the holistic model of the human body.[29] For the purposes of our discussion, it is submitted that both conceptions of health should be adopted; the significance of physical and mental health as a BHN lies in both the physiological impact of ill-health as well as in the contribution of health to the functioning of the human individual in society. Put another way, the concept of health relates to all three

dimensions of the whole individual – the human being, self and person. In this respect, health as a BHN should not be viewed simply from the perspective of the biological functioning of the human body, but also from the perspective of its contributory role in social participation.[30]

The basic need for physical and mental health, therefore, must be understood as encompassing the preventative as well as the curative dimensions of health care; the need for such things which prevent the debilitating impact of disease on the one hand, and for curative treatment on the other.

SELF-REALIZATION NEEDS

It was set out earlier that the self represents the mode of perceiving the individual as an introspective and experimental entity; hence the proposition that the concept of self defines the universal propensity of an individual to part create his or her world through individual experience. Self-realization needs, it is suggested, are the prerequisites which determine the ability of the individual to, first, appreciate and evaluate experience, and, subsequently, to articulate this individual perception of experience against the background of his or her social environment.

Before proceeding with the discussion of cultural identity and expression as the two specific BHN derived from the propensity for self-realization, it is worth elaborating on the meaning that is attached to the concept of self-realization. A survey of human needs literature reveals a variety of concepts which are relevant to the notion of self-realization put forward here. Essentially, the various relevant concepts can be categorized under three general headings. The first is self-respect. Self-respect has been classified as a primary good[31] which includes the elements of a person's sense of his or her own value and the value of the plan of life pursued, as well as confidence in the ability to achieve this perception of the good.[32] The second is freedom of agency. The capacity of the individual to make informed choices has been identified as the minimal requirement for autonomy.[33] It is through the exercise of this capacity that individuals define their nature, give meaning to their lives and understand their role in society.[34] The third is the realization of human capacities/potentialities. Self-realization in this sense is defined as development to the fullest possible extent of all the capacities possessed by a person,[35] as an inherent evolutionary constructive force which pushes humans to realize individual potentialities.[36]

Self-realization, as put forward in this discussion, encompasses all the three aspects of individual introspection (to experience, to evaluate and to actualize) outlined above. The concept of the universal human propensity for self-realization is intended to express all aspects of the individual's perceptions and evaluations of his or her life; in other words, to include all things that are 'self-oriented'. The emphasis of self-realization is quite obviously on the individual's perception of his or her reality. This does not, however, mean that self-realization can be conceived of from the perspective of asocial individualism, the self abstracted from the social environment within which it exists. The point has been made that there exists no 'private language' of experience.[37] Instead, the process of self-realization arises from a 'social construct of reflection', being informed and influenced by a collective ideal of individuality.[38] The BHN which are derived from the propensity for self-realization, therefore, are those prerequisites which enable the individual to experience, to evaluate and to actualize, given the essentially social character of action and reflection, the need for cultural identity and expression.

Cultural Identity
The need for cultural identity expresses the basic need for the self to possess a qualitative reference point of identification in relation to the social environment within which the individual exists. Cultural identity provides the self with the knowledge and the values which inform self-conceptualization. It provides the public language which identifies experience, the standards by which experiences can be evaluated, and the values which influence self-actualization. Simply put, cultural identity answers the questions, who am I? what am I? and where am I going? Two universal facts of human life can be observed to demonstrate the need for cultural identity: the prevalence of institutionalized religion as a manifestation of spiritual belief, and the strong adhesive powers of ethnicity which can be so devastatingly demonstrated when cultural identity is threatened.

Expression
Expression, as a BHN, is little discussed in needs literature despite there being little dispute that such a need, despite distinctions in its forms, exists. The need for expression that is put forward here is the need for the self to manifest introspective perceptions in the form of intrapersonal language (examples would include the expressions of joy, sadness and depression) as well as to translate them into communicable interpersonal language (these could range from a simple smile to what is regarded as higher art forms). Often, the concept of expression is confined to mean the higher cognitive capacities of the human individual, the need for which is felt once the basic survival requirements of the individual are satisfied;[39] the 'higher' needs of free speech and artistic experience are examples of this. Such a limited meaning of the need for expression is not adopted here. Rather, it is suggested that the universal need for

expression is dynamic in its manifestation, its precise form being within a continuum of human expression, including both its aspects of intra-personal and interpersonal language.

SOCIAL PARTICIPATION NEEDS

The concept of person, discussed earlier, is a recognition of the social characteristics of the human individual as a 'social animal'. In the words of McCall:

> The concept of person represents an understanding of individuals as intentional beings who are granted rights and have obligations, who display psychological characteristics, are capable of second-order reflection and volition, and so forth. Because these properties are attributed to the individual by others and occasionally denied by others, the understanding of individuals as persons is a public understanding. The individual is a person as long as others conceive of the individual through this mode of understanding.[40]

Social participation needs are those needs which, when satisfied, facilitate the emergence of the individual as a person, identified and recognized as a member of society. The significance of social participation to the full realization of the capacities of the whole individual is well expressed by Naroll:

> To gain and hold esteem, a man or woman must perform skilfully and conscientiously the social roles assigned to him or her by the culture. A person who knows these roles and performs them well – who understands and assumes the full social responsibilities called for in the moral code of his or her people . . . gains respect in the eyes of family, friends and neighbours. And so gains his or her own self-respect.[41]

To deny social participation is to deny the essentially social nature of the human individual; it is to deny a person his or her humanity.[42] Education, association and work are put forward as the BHN which equip the human individual to fulfil that aspect of being human which arises from the human propensity for social participation.

Education
In the earlier discussion on self-realization needs, it was stated that the process of self-realization cannot be divorced from the 'social construct of reflection'. Education as a basic need provides the human individual with

the tools with which both the intrapersonal and the interpersonal processes of reflection and action can be initiated. 'Basic education' has been outlined by Abdun Noor[43] as including the following components: communication skills and general knowledge, which at the basic level include literacy (if possible), numeracy, and general civic, scientific, and cultural knowledge, values, and attitudes; life skills and knowledge, which embrace hygienic practices, sanitation, nutrition, family planning, the environment, management of the family economy, and creating and maintaining the home; and production skills, which embrace all forms of activity directed towards making a living or the production of goods and services, at whatever level of sophistication.

The concept of education that is put forward here refers to the process of learning and understanding, being either self-initiated or externally initiated, which informs the individual of his or her identity, teaches the individual the social skills necessary for effective social participation and provides the individual with the necessary skills in order to preserve and enhance his or her life. Often, the discussion on education as a basic need, despite the concept of education being recognized as involving both formal and informal education, is confined to such matters as literacy rates, enrolment in educational institutions and technical and vocational training, i.e. dimensions of formal institutionalized education discussed from a developmental perspective.[44] Education is given a broader meaning here. It involves the informal processes of acquiring knowledge, as well as the formal processes of teaching and learning which focus on training the individual to function effectively within specific societal contexts. Both are relevant to the understanding of education as a BHN, the latter being more significant when understood as a response to what are deemed to be requirements for social participation in the context of specific societal conditions.

Association

The concept of person arises as a result of human interaction through the existence of relationships between individuals which define mutual roles within a social environment. At the most basic level, the need for association is reflected in the child-parent relationship, extending forward to formal family units, kinships, tribes, village communities and further sophisticated social entities such as nations and states. The basic component of association as a human need is the perception of belongingness of the individual as a member of a social entity, the precise manifestation of that entity being irrelevant to the basic need for association which motivates the perceived allegiance. Love, friendship, ethnic identity and nationalism and ultimately, humanity itself are reflections of the need for association. Simply understood, the human need for association is the need for individuals to fulfil the inherent capacity to interact with other individuals; to understand their identities as participants and participators in society.

Work

Work has been recognized as essential for both material survival and for psychological fulfilment.[45] It is the dimension of human life that incorporates the individual into society through direct social participation in the productive endeavours necessary for societal development, and through the socio-cultural practices which define the nature of inter-relationships (the division of labour)[46] among individuals. Work, undoubtedly, represents different types and levels of activity in different social contexts. Often, the concept is used synonymously with formal employment; this may or may not reflect the reality of social participation in a given social context. However, what is important to appreciate is the range of possible activity that is performed by the human individual as a participant and participator in society, varying from simple manual labour for direct subsistence production and distribution, to social and cultural duties within society, and even achievement-based activities to enhance social recognition.

To conclude our discussion of BHN, it might be useful to present the full schematic form of the whole individual–needs relationship: X (as a human individual) → needs sustenance, shelter, physical and mental integrity, cultural identity, expression, education, association and work → for survival, self-realization and social participation which together constitute the propensities of the whole individual.

HUMAN RIGHTS

The concept of rights is a social construct, conceived by the human mind to reflect a certain desired social reality based on prescribed standards of human interaction in society. The rationale for asserting the conception of human rights is the recognition of the inherent dignity and worth of all human individuals. The concept of BHN provides a basis from which the inherent dignity and worth of the human individual can be derived. Thus, the minimum content of human rights can be expressed by saying that every individual has the human right not to be deprived of access to BHN.

As was stated above, the aim of the exercise undertaken in this chapter is to provide a conceptualization of human rights that is viable for the purposes of international law. What is attempted is a 'minimum' concept of human rights (what, if anything, human rights must mean). The process of rationalization, therefore, involves the building of the concept from first principles which form the minimum conceptual requirements for human rights, whilst at the same time being grounded in the realities of the human condition.

Based on the discussion of BHN, presented below is the proposed minimum concept of human rights, expressed as 'rights' with corresponding 'obligations'.[47]

Everyone has the human right not to be deprived of, and the human duty not to deprive others of: their means of sustenance; their physical and mental integrity; their means of shelter; their means of cultural identity; their means of self-expression; their means of education; their means of association; and their means of work. The functioning of 'human rights', when conceived of in this way, will now be demonstrated by considering briefly some of the main issues of contention, and of uncertainty, that have plagued international human rights discourse. Three main arguments will be addressed: first, that the minimalistic articulation of rights ignores the reality of underdevelopment; second, that the very concept of rights is a culturally specific expression of social order which is insensitive to the diversity of human value systems;[48] and third, that it is impossible to provide a universally applicable list of human rights.

The main thrust of the first of these is that the concept of human rights, having been articulated in minimalist terms, ignores the condition of 'underdevelopment' that is the prevailing reality and is, therefore, irrelevant to the demands of the world's majority. This can be termed the 'development thesis' of human rights. To respond, attention needs to be drawn to what I shall call the 'development myth'. The development thesis of human rights was a response to the recognized non-sense of the apparent early prioritization of civil and political rights (CPR) over economic, social and cultural rights (ESCR).[49] The first stage in the formulation of this thesis involved the constant reiteration of the interdependence, and, therefore, of the equal importance of both sets of rights leading up to the 'structural approach' to human rights.[50] Through a process of conceptual innovation, this approach has manifested itself as the 'right to development'.[51] The assumption that underpins the right to development, and the development thesis, is simply that development is good; that the true realization of human rights (ESCR and CPR) can only be achieved through the process of development. Although it would be false to say that the approach has been blind to the potential dangers that might be inherent in 'development', the thrust for development, defined and analysed with increasing care, has nevertheless been retained.[52]

Despite the impressive rhetoric of international institutions, states and sympathetic commentators alike, the reality of development is often far more sobering. Notwithstanding the 'era of development' since World War II,[53] the categorization of 'poverty' and the planning for its alleviation,[54] disparities between rich and poor still persist. Whilst development theory grapples with the many complexities of human existence,[55] and whilst development planners attempt to operationalize strategies for the enhancement of human welfare, it might be useful to provide some framework of reference. Adopting again the language of BHN, the following are suggested as the preliminary parameters of analysis. *Underdevelopment* is the human condition in which individuals within society are incapable of meeting their basic human needs and which does not provide the means or the resources whereby those needs can be met. It is a state of disempowerment. *Development* is a process which in fact enables the individuals within a community to meet their basic human needs and which further creates the conditions of enhanced human welfare. It is a process of empowerment. *Maldevelopment* is a process which, converse to development, interferes with the ability of individuals within society to meet their basic human needs, and which causes the deterioration of the necessary conditions for development. It is a process of disempowerment.

In recognition that there exists the possibility of a conflict in development, depending on the focus of analysis as macro or micro, societal or individual, the concept of human rights is expressed in the negative; the right not to be subjected to maldevelopment. Thus the concept of human rights serves its most critical function, namely to involve and protect the individual dimension of needs within the broader societal discourse on development.

The second argument goes to the very heart of any attempt to justify human rights. It is an argument that can be dismissed, by adopting the 'soft' option, which is to assert that all that is relevant is the international endorsement of the concept (e.g. the UN Charter, the Universal Declaration of Human Rights, the International Covenants on Human Rights). This is, however, highly unsatisfactory if the concept of human rights is to be seen as possessing more than merely formal relevance. In order for it also to be given substantive relevance as a concept which truly advances the cause of human welfare universally, it is necessary to confront the argument head on and to convince sceptics of the universal applicability of the concept. An attempt to do so will now be made.

When one speaks of cultural relativism, it is necessary to identify the comparative basis of the analysis. Various analyses have been conducted, from African, Chinese, Muslim and Indian perspectives, with substantial disagreements as to whether or not these cultures demonstrate the existence of a human rights concept.[56] The general accusation levied against the dominant discourse on human rights, however, can be condensed to the following: that the concept is a historically defined Western, liberal construct, based on individualistic assumptions of society which envisage the resolution of the distribution of power through conflicting claims as opposed to through reconciliation based on the mutuality of obligations.

The concept of human rights proposed above does indeed assume cultural uniformity. However, the uniform culture that is the basis of human rights, it is submitted, is the culture of statism. Thus, the function of human rights as envisaged is the protection of human welfare from excessive intervention arising from the structural conditions that are consequences of this dominant (in the politico-legal sense) social unit. The reason for this is the universalization of the impersonal state as the regulating centre of human activity. An examination of egalitarian traditional obligation-based societies reveals one crucial factor contributing to human welfare, namely the intimate connection and interdependence of individuals to the material and socio-cultural resources necessary for human welfare; they demonstrate the priority of the 'commons'. Thus

> the key to success of commons regimes lies in the limits that its culture of shared responsibilities place upon the power of any one group or individual. The equality which generally prevails in the commons, for example, does not grow out of any ideal or romantic preconceived notion of *communitas* any more than out of allegiance to the modern notion that people have 'equal rights'. Rather, it emerges as a by-product of the inability of a small community's elite to eliminate entirely the bargaining power of any one of its members, the limited amount of goods any one group can make away with under the others' gaze, and the calculated jockeying for position of many individuals who know each other and share an interest in minimizing their own risks and in not letting any one of their number become too powerful.[57]

The contrast with the modern state could not be greater. Rather than encourage individualism based on so-called Western liberal lines, the concept of human rights, as proposed above, provides the check against the destruction of local communitarianism by the impersonal state, as a precaution against enclosure.[57] The proposed concept of human rights, therefore, is primarily aimed at performing the function of facilitator in the protection and enhancement of human welfare.

Turning now to the third possible objection, given that the quest for a concept of human rights is a worthwhile one, the challenge is then to

establish the universal applicability of the 'list' of rights. The dominant
discourse on human rights approaches this task through the reinterpretation and reaffirmation of the historically derived articulation of
human rights as CPR and ESCR. That the conceptualization of CPR and
ESCR arose in the context of specific struggles, legitimized through the
prevailing moral and political philosophies, is not an issue of contention.
Neither might it be seen as relevant, particularly with the adoption,[58] and
subsequent coming into force,[59] of the International Covenants on
Human Rights; the point being that both sets of rights now form part of
positive international law. The matter, it is submitted, is not a closed one,
however. Reference here to the contextual specificity under which concepts of human rights emerged is not intended to revitalize the
philosophical and ideological disputes of the past to highlight the difference in nature between the two sets of rights. On the contrary, an
appreciation of the historical context of human rights documents proclaiming the existence and recognition of CPR and ESCR provides an
understanding of the essentially statist preoccupations of both. In this
context, several observations can be made. First, both traditions have as
their primary concern the regulation of the relationship between the
state and the individual. Second, they express the entitlements which
define the expectations, be they negative or positive, of the role to be
played by the state, and as such are claims made against the state as
opposed to all humankind. Third, they both derive from the vision of an
ideal socio-political order which is perceived to be conducive to the realization of a better life.

So much, it might seem, is obvious. Not so obvious, however, is the
question of how human rights are to be conceptualized from a universalist perspective. Much of the confusion relating to the cultural specificity
of human rights is the result of the failure to see human rights as a universal concept; the result of the historical 'baggage' that is still carried in
the name of 'international human rights'. The discussion on BHN above
was intended to overcome the ideological and cultural biases that run
through human rights as articulated in international instruments; the
aim being to put forward a universally viable conceptualization of human
rights as opposed to the existing, disguised statist conceptions of rights.
Of significance in this respect is the conscious emphasis on retaining the
universality of needs as an articulation of areas of concern which direct
human action, and the potential for diversity in relation to the action
undertaken in pursuance of those needs. This duality is retained without
detracting from the concept of human rights. Of crucial importance is
that the right is recognized as being universally relevant. Whether an
assertion is within the ambit of any particular right is subsequently capable of being determined.

Central to the approach adopted in this chapter is the conviction that the function of the conception of human rights is to serve the cause of human welfare, and not political dogma. The concept of human rights proposed here has sought to return human rights to the social human individual, with the choice being left open as to whether or not recourse to the language of rights is ultimately necessary for protection from injustice and violence in any given circumstance.

NOTES

1. P. Alston, Making space for new human rights: the case of the right to development (1983) *Harvard Human Rights Yearbook* Vol. 1, p. 3. It might appear surprising, however, that the approach adopted by Alston in response was to suggest the 'new' right to development rather than to attempt to rectify the identified deficiencies in the old approach. If, on the other hand, the right to development was intended as a possible solution to those problems, it was not demonstrated how this would be achieved in practice.

2. For examples, see D. T. Meyers, *Inalienable Rights: A Defense* (New York: Columbia University Press, 1985); J. M. Finnis, *Natural Law and Natural Rights* (Oxford: Clarendon Press, 1980).

3. See Preamble, Universal Declaration of Human Rights, UNGA res. 217 A(III), 1948.

4. See generally R. Fitzgerald (ed.), *Human Needs and Politics* (Oxford: Pergamon Press, 1977); G. Thompson, *Needs* (London: Routledge & Kegan Paul, 1987); and L. Doyal and I. Gough, *A Theory of Human Need* (Basingstoke: Macmillan, 1991).

5. It is appropriate at the onset to state that this account of the whole individual and of its constituent elements – the human being, the self and the person – is largely influenced by the work of Catherine McCall; see C. McCall, *Concepts of Person: An Analysis of Concepts of Person, Self and Human Being* (Aldershot: Avebury, 1990).

6. *Ibid.*, p. 7.

7. *Ibid.*, p. 9.

8. *Ibid.*, p. 15.

9. *Ibid.*, p. 14.

10. *Ibid.*

11. See, for example, G. Thompson, *op. cit.;* L. Doyal and I. Gough, *op. cit.*; and D. Miller, *Social Justice* (Oxford: Clarendon Press, 1976).

12. See, for example, R. Attfield, *A Theory of Value and Obligation* (London: Croom Helm, 1987), especially Chapter 4; and J. Raz, *The Morality of Freedom* (Oxford: Oxford University Press, 1986), Chapter 12.

13. D. Miller, *op. cit.*, p. 134.

14. G. Thompson, *op. cit.*, p. 76.

15. *Ibid.*, p. 70.

16. See R. Fitzgerald, Abraham Maslow's Hierarchy of Needs – an exposition and evaluation. In R. Fitzgerald, *op. cit.*; and R. Fitzgerald, The ambiguity and rhetoric of 'Need'. In R. Fitzgerald, *op. cit.*

17. See J. M. Hawkins and R. Allen (eds), *The Oxford Encyclopedic English Dictionary* (Oxford: Clarendon Press, 1991).

18. See L. Doyal and I. Gough, *op. cit.*, p. 55.

19. The semantics of it does not really matter here. My aim is not to refute the concept of interest as the basis for needs but merely to provide a satisfactory basis for BHN which thus far the conceptualization of interest has failed, in my view, to provide.

20. See G. G. Simpson, The history of life. In S. Tax (ed.), *The Evolution of Life: Evolution After Darwin* (Chicago, IL: University of Chicago Press, 1960).

21. See J. Raz, *op. cit.*, pp. 154–5. Here Raz discusses the characteristics of an autonomous agent. Although not specifically addressing the concept of self, the description of autonomy is consistent with the introspective perception of the self. Similar is the discussion by Doyal and Harris on freedom of agency: see L. Doyal and R. Harris, *Empiricism, Explanation and Rationality: An Introduction to the Philosophy of the Social Sciences* (London: Routledge & Kegan Paul, 1986), Chapter 5.

22. See R. F. Dearden, 'Needs' in education. In R. F. Dearden, P. H. Hirst and R. S. Peters (eds), *Education and the Development of Reason* (London: Routledge & Kegan Paul, 1973), p. 55. Although Dearden was using this example to illustrate the value-laden judgment of what constitutes a worthwhile life that lies behind much needs-based discourse, it is felt that this critique is worth bearing in mind in our current discussion in order to avoid the confusion between the universality of human propensities and the specific socio-cultural responses to them.

23. Contrast with the *propotency* of needs put forward in the famous work by Abraham Maslow: A. Maslow, A theory of human motivation (1943) 50 *Psychological Review* 370.

24. See J. McHale and M. C. McHale, *Basic Human Needs: A Framework for Action* (New Brunswick, NJ: Transaction Books, 1977), p. 30.

25. See, for example, FAO/WHO Expert Committee, *Energy and Protein Requirements* (Rome: FAO, 1973).

26. These principles are largely derived from Doyal and Gough's discussion on housing; see L. Doyal and I. Gough, *op. cit.*, p. 196.

27. See M. Stacey, *The Sociology of Health and Healing* (London: Unwin Hyman, 1988), p. 169.

28. This point has been made particularly forcefully by some authors with regard to perceptions on mental health; see, generally, A. Kleinman and B. Good (eds), *Culture and Depression* (Berkeley: University of California Press, 1985).

29. For a comparative analysis, see A. Caplan, H. T. Engelhardt jr, and J. J. McCartney, *Concepts of Health and Disease* (Reading, MA: Addison-Wesley, 1981).

30. See J. McHale and M. C. McHale, *op. cit.*, p. 76: 'In pursuing more positive health measures, as well as the reduction of disease, we should really seek for indicators that include variations in perceptions of health, and the attitudes and aspirations of those peoples under consideration. Like many of our needs, health is a moving target. Its definition, therefore, rather than being conceived in absolute terms may be better accommodated by considering changes in its perception and by transitions in health status brought about by indirect means.'

31. See, for example, J. Rawls, *A Theory of Justice* (London: Oxford University Press, 1972), p. 440.

32. See also Maslow's category of 'esteem needs' which added to self-respect is the desire for reputation or prestige, i.e. respect from others; A. Maslow, *op. cit.*

33. See L. Doyal and I. Gough, *op. cit.*, p. 53. The concept of autonomy, however, has been argued to involve more than freedom of agency. For the exercise of 'human rational autonomy', not only is freedom of agency, i.e. the capacity to choose, required, but also necessary is the existence of the appropriate opportunities to enable the realization of those choices; see L. Doyal and R. Harris, *op. cit.*, Chapter 5. This aspect of the exercise of autonomy relates to the social dimension of human action and will be considered during the discussion on social participation needs.

34. See, for example, G. Dworkin, *The Theory and Practice of Autonomy* (Cambridge: Cambridge University Press, 1988), p. 20.

35. See Raz, *op. cit.*, p. 375.

36. See discussion in S. I. Benn, *A Theory of Freedom* (Cambridge: Cambridge University Press, 1988), p. 207.

37. See L. Wittgenstein, *Philosophical Investigations* (Oxford: Blackwell, 1973), paras 200–72.

38. See L. Doyal and R. Harris, *op. cit.*, Chapter 4.

39. See, for example, C. Bay, *The Structure of Freedom* (Stanford: Stanford University Press, 1970), p. 372.

40. C. McCall, *op. cit.*, p. 178.

41. R. Naroll, *The Moral Order: an Introduction to the Human Situation* (London: Sage,

1983), p. 136, quoted in L. Doyal and I. Gough, *op. cit.*, p. 184.

42. 'Social life is an essential characteristic of individual humans, unlike the situation of an individual tree which just happens to be in a forest. Grown from a seed in isolation, a tree is still a tree; but humanity is the gift of society to the individual.' L. Doyal and R. Harris, *op. cit.*, p. 80. See also L. Doyal and I. Gough, *op. cit.*, pp. 184–5.

43. A. Noor, *Education and Basic Human Needs* World Bank Staff Working Paper No. 450 (Washington DC: World Bank, 1981), pp. 9–10, cited in V. B. Weigel, *A Unified Theory of Global Development* (London: Praeger Press, 1989), pp. 45–6.

44. The McHale Report provides a good example of this approach; J. McHale and M. C. McHale, *op. cit.*, pp. 84–94.

45. *Ibid.*, p. 232; J. Barington Moore, *Injustice*, (Basingstoke: Macmillan, 1978), Chapter 1; and P. Warr, *Work, Unemployment and Mental Health* (Oxford: Clarendon Press, 1987), Chapter 11.

46. See J. Barrington Moore, *op. cit.*

47. As Galtung correctly points out, 'the phrase "human rights" is actually a misnomer for the more complete, but awkward, "human rights/duties"'; see J. Galtung, The universality of human rights revisited: some less applaudable consequences of the human rights tradition. In A. Eide and B. Hagtvet, *Human Rights in Perspective: A Global Assessment* (Oxford: Blackwell, 1992), p. 159.

48. For the many permutations of the cultural relativism challenge to human rights, see, generally, J. Donnelly, Cultural relativism and universal human rights *(1984)* 6 *Human Rights Quarterly* 400; J. Donnelly, *Universal Human Rights in Theory and Practice* (London: Cornell University Press, 1989), Chapter 6; J. Berting, F. Geyer and R. Jurkovich, (eds.), *Human Rights in a Pluralist World: Individuals and Collectivities* (London: Meckler, 1990); A. Renteln, The unanswered challenge of relativism and the consequences for human rights (1985) 7 *Human Rights Quarterly* 514; and R. J. Vincent, *Human Rights and International Relations* (Cambridge: Cambridge University Press (For the Royal Institute of International Affairs), 1986), Chapter 3.

49. See, for example: 'Human rights, in their economic and social aspects, can only be achieved by a combination of high production and fair distribution. In theory at least, you could even have a society juridically so constituted that everybody enjoys civil rights and everybody is poor. In actual practice, however, aspirations are so high in all modern countries that you cannot maintain political stability in the unrest provoked by the lack of fulfilment of human wants.' J. Figueres, Some economic foundations of human rights, UN Doc. A/CONF. 32/L. 2, 8 February 1968, paras 35 and 36.

50. See P. Alston, Development and the rule of law: prevention versus cure as a human rights strategy. In *Development, Human Rights and the Rule of Law*, Report of a Conference held in The Hague on 27 April –1 May 1981, convened by the International Commission of Jurists (Oxford: Pergamon Press, 1981), p. 31.

51. See UNGA res. 41/128, 4 December 1986. The literature on the right to development is abundant. For a general flavour, see R-J. Dupuy (ed.), *The Right to Development at the International Level* (The Hague: Sijthoff and Noordhoff, 1980); R. Rich, The right to development: a right of peoples. In J. Crawford (ed.), *The Rights of Peoples* (Oxford: Clarendon Press, 1988), p. 39; P. Alston, *op. cit.*

52. Note, for example, the well-rounded definition of development in the Preamble to the UN Declaration on the Right to Development: '. . . development is a comprehensive economic, social, cultural and political process, which aims at the constant improvement of the well-being of the entire population and of all individuals on the basis of their active, free and meaningful participation in development and in the fair distribution of benefits resulting therefrom.' See also, P. Alston, Revitalising United Nations work on human rights and development (1991) 18 *Melbourne University Law Review*, p. 216.

53. See G. Esteva, Development. In W. Sachs (ed.), *The Development Dictionary: A Guide to Knowledge as Power* (London: Zed Books, 1992), p. 6.

54. See A. Escobar, Planning. In W. Sachs, *op. cit.*, p. 136.

55. For an excellent discussion of the history and political economy of development theory, see B. Hettne, *Development Theory and the Three Worlds* (Harlow: Longman, 1990).

56. See, generally, J. Berting, F. Geyer and R. Jurkovich (eds), *op. cit.*

57. The Commons: where the community has authority, in *The Ecologist* (1992) Vol. 22, No. 4 (Whose Common Future), July/August, 123, at p. 129.

58. International Covenant on Civil and Political Rights (ICCPR) and International Covenant on Economic, Social and Cultural Rights (ICESCR), simultaneously adopted by the UN General Assembly; UNGA Res. 2200 A(XXI) of 16 December 1966.

59. ICCPR on 3 January 1976; ICESCR on 23 March 1976.

PART THREE:

EQUALITY REVISITED

9

Less Equal Than Others – Equality and Women's Rights

Sandra Fredman

INTRODUCTION

Human rights for women, both internationally and domestically, have come to be based predominantly on the principle of equality. Equality is the central element of anti-discrimination law in the UK[1] and the key theme of European[2] and international law[3] on women's rights. Yet women's disadvantage in society has persisted. This prompts a re-evaluation of the notion of equality utilized in statutes, conventions and case law. It will be argued here that, although equality has led to some important gains for women, it is inherently limited in its ability to achieve substantial progress, and indeed can at times be counterproductive. This chapter aims to illuminate the limitations of the principle of equality by critically analysing the statutes and case law in the UK. Although the focus is on the UK, a similar analysis could be applied to European or international law.[4] The chapter begins with a brief description of the nature and causes of women's continuing disadvantage. The second part develops a critical analysis of the principle of equality, focusing on six problematic aspects. In the third part, the statutes and case law are critically assessed in the light of the analysis developed in the second part.

WOMEN'S CONTINUING DISADVANTAGE

Although women have achieved formal equality before the law in the course of the twentieth century, they remain in a position of substantial social and economic disadvantage. This is most evident by considering their position in the paid workforce. In 1994, gross hourly earnings of full-time women were still only 79.5 per cent of those of men (excluding overtime),[5] and figures since 1988 show that the pace at which the gap is narrowing is excruciatingly slow. Of even greater concern is the fact that aggregate figures mask larger disparities among specific groups of workers. Thus gross hourly earnings of full-time women manual workers were only 72.5 per cent of those of male manual workers, and those of women non-manual workers were a mere 67.9 per cent of the earnings of their male colleagues. Moreover, women's gross weekly earnings were only 72.25 per cent of those of men, reflecting women's limited access to additional elements such as overtime, shift premia and incentive pay. Women's disadvantage in the workforce is not merely relative: women also cluster at the bottom of the earnings distribution. Thus as many as 46.6 per cent of women in 1994 earned less than £210 per week, compared with 21.4 per cent of men. Women are particularly scarce among top earners: whereas one in five men earned £470 or more per week, they were joined by only one in 20 women.

In order to tackle this problem, it is important to understand its causes. The persistence of severe pay differentials despite the eradication of separate pay scales for men and women suggests that the causes are more complex than mere prejudicial behaviour directed against women. A more detailed analysis of the statistics reveals at least four central contributing factors. The first is extensive job segregation: women are clustered in predominantly female jobs, which tend to be low-paid and of low status. Women also congregate on the lower levels within mixed occupations. The second main contributing factor concerns the difference between the patterns of work of men and women. Whereas men tend to work continuously and full-time, many women work part-time and their participation in the paid workforce is often interrupted or sporadic. Women form the vast majority of part-time workers, who are in a particularly poor position so far as terms and conditions of work are concerned. Third, women have traditionally been less able to use their industrial muscle to improve their position than men. Although there have always been militant women inside and outside the unions, women have frequently worked in non-unionized sectors, or, where there are unions, have found themselves less well supported by unions than are their male colleagues.[6] Even where women do form a large proportion of the membership, they are seriously under-represented at senior levels. The final contributing factor concerns education and training, which tend to reinforce women's position as low-paid, low-status workers.

Underlying all these factors is the real issue: why are women's jobs almost inevitably poorly paid and poorly valued? A crucial factor has always been the interaction between women's paid work in the workforce and their unpaid family work. This manifests itself in at least four different ways. First, much of the poorest-paid work done by women in the market is an extension of their work done at home: catering, cleaning and child care fall squarely into this category. The fact that this work is so often performed unpaid drives down the pay and status attached to it. The second way in which women's paid work is conditioned by their unpaid work is more concrete: women remain primarily responsible for child care, care of the elderly and domestic work. At the same time, since few families can survive without a second income, women are under intense economic pressure to find paid work as well. They are therefore forced to take whatever jobs are possible in the light of their family responsibilities. The third manifestation of the interaction between family work and paid work is a residue of historical forces. Traditionally, men demanded a 'family wage' while women were expected to work for no more than pin money. This set a pattern of pay scales whereby 'men's' work was substantially better paid than 'women's work'. Many payment systems remain strongly dominated by historical forces, thus retaining the disproportionate differential between men's and women's pay. Finally, the devaluation of women's work extends even to women without children or other family responsibilities.

THE PROBLEMS OF EQUALITY

It is clear from the discussion above that equality as an ideal remains elusive. Yet in the UK, equality rights have been on the statute book for nearly 25 years, in the form of the Equal Pay Act 1970 and the Sex Discrimination Act 1975 (SDA). These are powerfully augmented by European Union (EU) law, in the shape of Article 119 of the Treaty of Rome and a string of directives specifying the equality principle in various contexts. The fact that women's disadvantage has stubbornly resisted such legislative insistence on equality indicates the problematic nature of the principle of equality itself. This section details six weaknesses in the principle of equality, while the following section applies the analysis to the UK statutes and case law.

Structural Inertia: The Male Norm

The first weakness of the equality principle is that because it is tied to a male norm, it is unable to achieve real structural change. Equality does not dictate substantive outcomes, but is essentially a comparative concept. The question is, equal to whom? The answer in anti-discrimination statutes is clear: a woman has the right to be equal[7] to a similarly situated man. At first glance, this formulation appears unchallengeable, drawing as it does on the fundamental Aristotelian maxim that likes should be treated alike. However, such a formulation assumes that there is a gender-neutral test as to when a man and a woman are similarly situated. In reality, however, it is impossible simply to subtract gender from both sides of the equation, leaving two similarly situated individuals. Instead, the situation of each individual is strongly influenced by her or his gender. Indeed, the assumption of neutrality in practice obscures the fact that the norm is emphatically male. Most importantly, the labour market is structured in such a way as to reflect men's experience and marginalize that of women.

This flaw in the principle of equality is well illustrated by considering the relationship between unpaid work in the family and paid work in the market. In this context, the influence of gender on an individual's opportunities is pervasive: since women remain primarily responsible for child care, care of the elderly and housework, a woman's ability to participate in the paid workforce is conditioned by the nature and extent of her responsibilities within the family. For men, on the other hand, family responsibilities are usually separate from labour force participation. This difference in experience becomes problematic because the labour market, reflecting the male experience, emphasizes the dichotomy between the family and the market rather than the interaction between the two. Many benefits and entitlements within the labour market are linked to full-time continuous working patterns, which are only possible for workers who can keep their domestic commitments separate from their paid work. Thus the paradigm worker either has no domestic commitments, or is a man with a wife who has the responsibility for the bulk of the unpaid work in the family. As a simple illustration, women with family responsibilities tend to work part-time in the paid labour force; men in similar situations tend to amass overtime. Part-time work is usually poorly paid and of low status; overtime working, by contrast, attracts large premia. Still more problematic is the fact that this pattern perpetuates itself: the extra pay offered by overtime working encourages men to remain for longer hours in the paid workforce, forcing the women in their families to take on the bulk of the unpaid work of the family and remain marginal in the paid workforce.[8]

This is not to say that the equality principle has no role to play. It has certainly improved the position of those women who are in a position to conform to the male norm. This would include women without family responsibilities, and women with such responsibilities who are either in a position to employ others to perform their family work, or who have partners who take on the primary responsibility for such work. While it is important not to ignore these gains, it is crucial to acknowledge that the movement of a minority of women into positions of advantage in the paid workforce does not change the underlying structure. In fact, statistics show an increasing gulf between the labour market position of women with children and those without.[9] Once in the labour force, women without children are increasingly able to penetrate traditional male occupations, particularly management, while women with children continue to face obstacles to their advancement. Nor is this a static picture: the majority of childless women will go on to have children, and thereby lose their labour market position. Those women with children who do succeed generally do so because their children are cared for by others, who share the same characteristics: they are poorly paid, of low status and women. Because the equality principle does not insist on a reallocation or a re-evaluation of family work, it cannot bring about the structural change necessary to achieve real progress for all women.

The Problem of Difference

The second main weakness of the equality concept is that its coverage is limited to treating likes alike. This is problematic for at least three reasons. First, it assumes that the decision as to whether two individuals are alike is straightforward and value-free. In fact, as Aristotle himself recognized, the decision depends entirely on the context and the measure of comparison.[10] Second, the implications of classification as different rather than equal are profound. Protection is limited to those who are alike; detrimental treatment in cases in which women are held to be different from men is simply legitimated. Likewise, the equality principle does not require that differences be treated proportionately to the degree of difference. Thus a small difference may with impunity be subjected to a disproportionately large difference in treatment. Third, the equality principle creates a false dichotomy, assuming that everything is either equal or different. This is the basis of the 'equality–difference' debate, which has dogged feminist literature in recent years. The long history of adverse treatment of women was invariably justified by the simple assertion that women were fundamentally different from men. The initial and vigorous response of some feminists was to insist that men and women were equal in all relevant respects.[11] Other feminists, however, believed that such a response was merely a call for the assimilation of women to male values and patterns of life, and emphasized instead the difference between women and men.[12] They argued that such difference should attract special rights rather than detrimental treatment. I would argue that this debate is inevitably sterile because of the myopia of the equality principle. It is artificial to divide all characteristics into those which are equal and those which are different. Not only does this obscure the richness of human experience and qualities, but it also continues to use the male norm as a yardstick, even in respect of difference. The focus on this dichotomy thus prevents us from tackling the real disadvantage of women in society.

Equality Guarantees Consistency but not Substance

Equality demands consistent treatment between men and women in similar circumstances, but it gives no guarantees in respect of substantive rights. Thus, provided men and women are treated alike, it is irrelevant whether they are treated equally badly or equally well. In other words, equality is satisfied as much by 'levelling up' as by 'levelling down'. A clear example is found in the controversy over protective legislation. The nineteenth-century debate over whether there should be statutory protection for workers against inordinately long working hours or particularly harsh conditions resolved itself into a question of whether such protection should extend to women only. The aim of many proponents of protective legislation was to raise standards for women, who were often particularly harshly treated, in the hope that similar protection for men would follow. However, the liberals advocated equality even though this meant that all workers, men and women, were equally exploited. Although there is no doubt that some of those who favoured protective legislation did so with the aim of excluding women from the workforce, this stance was not effectively countered by insisting on equality of exploitation. This issue has reappeared in the 1980s: the European Community's insistence that protective legislation contravened the equal treatment directive was met in the UK by a repeal of all such legislation rather than by the extension of protection to male workers.[13] A more useful approach would be first to set substantive standards of health, safety and working conditions, and then to demand that women and men have equal entitlements to such standards.

Equality Individualized

Equality as expressed in legislative form manifests itself as an individual right, exercisable against another individual, often an employer, on the basis of a comparison between two individuals, the woman and a comparable man. The individualism of equality is problematic because it prevents the law from grappling with the collective dimension of discrimination. It is central to the nature of discrimination that although the detriment is felt by a woman as an individual, this is only because she is a member of a group. The limited perspective of equality as an individualized right is manifested in at least two important ways. First, since equality is fashioned in terms of an individual right, the cost of enforcement seems to fall naturally on the individual complainant. Such a cost is, however, frequently beyond the abilities and resources of any individual complainant, especially in the absence of legal aid for proceedings before industrial tribunals. The result is that the number of cases brought before tribunals and courts is disappointingly low. Even more worrying is the fact that a large number of employers are able to ignore the legislation[14] without facing legal challenge of any sort. The second manifestation of the individualization of equality is that remedies flow to the individual alone. Each woman, however similarly situated, is required to bring her own case to prove her point.[15]

Notions of individual fairness also have an important bearing on the way in which the law deals with the question of who should bear the cost of rectifying inequalities. A focus on the individual employer within the strongly fault-oriented frame of reference of the courts and legislature yields a notion of fairness which resists placing the cost on any individual unless he or she can be seen to be in some way 'at fault'. Thus in both the Equal Pay Act 1970, and in the indirect discrimination provisions of the SDA, employers are permitted to defend inequalities by showing that they are justifiable irrespective of sex. There are, however, at least three grounds for criticism of this approach. The first is that the result of relieving the 'innocent' employer of the cost of redressing inequality is simply to leave the whole burden on the shoulders of the victim. The fault model is inappropriate for a situation in which the victim is at least as 'innocent' as the employer. Second, the argument for protecting the employer is not convincing. Not only does the employer often benefit from treating women less favourably than men, but also the employer is in a good position to redress inequalities, for example by appointing, promoting or improving pay. Third, the focus on a bipolar dispute makes it impossible to consider more sophisticated schemes of cost allocation, which could include spreading the cost among different parties, including the state.

Equality Within a Market Order

The principle of equality has the potential of undermining the very basis of a capitalist economy, which is premised on competition and inequality. It is therefore inevitable that legislation embodying the equality principle

limits its reach in such a way as to accommodate, or even to give precedence to, the market order. Yet it is clear from the statistics cited above
that detrimental treatment of women may well be functional to the market. Low wages for women workers, for example, may be a result of an
over-supply of women seeking jobs which can accommodate family
responsibilities. Legal endorsement of such factors as legitimate excuses
for detrimental treatment simply perpetuates discrimination.

The Shifting Meanings of Equality

The concept of equality has several different possible meanings. Many
thinkers have acknowledged the limitations of the equal treatment
model, recognizing that like treatment can in practice yield different
results. Thus a notion of equality of results has been added to equality of
treatment. It has also been recognized that unless starting points are
commensurate, the competition is inevitably unfair; hence a widespread
emphasis on equality of opportunity. Other thinkers have criticized the
symmetrical nature of equality, which insists that likes should be treated
alike regardless of a history of disadvantage. This assumes what has not
yet been achieved: that men and women are social equals. It also makes
it difficult to justify affirmative action to correct disadvantage. To address
this issue, the possibility of asymmetrical models of equality has been considered. Feminist writers have taken the debate past previous frontiers,
and attempted to reconstruct the notion of equality in a manner which
overcomes some of the weaknesses identified above, coining such terms
as 'equality as accommodation', 'equality as acceptance' and 'equality as
empowerment'.[16] I would argue that while the principles and critiques
developed in the literature shed important light on women's position in
society, they gain nothing from a constant stretching of the notion of
equality. The traditional values are so central to the concept of equality
that it is difficult to keep a reconstructed notion of equality from slipping
back into the well-worn tracks. As Finley argues: 'The inherited language
of equality does not easily convey the meanings of those who urge a
broader definition of "equality". The language seduces us into the circu-
larity of the special treatment/equal treatment debate.'[17]

THE WEAKNESSES OF EQUALITY: THE LAW IN CONTEXT

This part of the chapter applies the preceding analysis to the UK anti-discrimination statutes and case law, with the aim of demonstrating some of the reasons why the equality principle has had so little impact on women. The Equal Pay Act 1970 and the SDA are considered in turn.

The Equal Pay Act 1970 (EqPA)

The EqPA gives a woman employee the right to equal pay if she is doing like work or work of equal value with a man currently employed by the same employer in the same establishment or one at which common terms and conditions are observed. The right can, however, be defeated if an employer can show that the difference in pay is genuinely due to a material factor which is not the difference of sex.[18]

The concept of equality utilized here has some positive attributes; but it also manifests several of the basic flaws identified above. On the positive side, the widespread use of differential pay scales prior to 1970 was soon eliminated: the concept of formal equality of women to men doing the same work was sufficient to achieve this much, and the courts and tribunals in the early years of the Act were keen to take a purposive approach.[19] The introduction in 1983 of the right to equal pay for work of equal value[20] was similarly positive. Most importantly, this challenged some of the traditional notions of 'women's work' compared with men's. A good example is the early case of *Hayward* v. *Cammell Laird*[21] in which the work done by a cook was found to be of equal value to that of a carpenter and a joiner. Thus work which has traditionally been women's work unpaid at home was revalued in the light of a comparison with work which is male dominated and has a long history of strong trade union organization.

On the other hand, the concept of equality in the EqPA manifests all the weaknesses identified above. First, the male norm is expressed in its most concrete form: the statute lays down that the right to equal pay only arises if a woman finds a male comparator currently employed by the same employer either at the same establishment or at establishments at which common terms and conditions of employment are observed.[22] Comparison across employers or, in most cases, across establishment is prohibited. Yet, as was mentioned above, one of the major causes of low pay among women is job segregation. Thus for women in segregated workplaces, the promise of equal pay for like work or work of equal value is frequently illusory.[23] Also problematic is the definition of 'value': given that values have always been determined according to the male norm, there is good reason to doubt that the use of value in the equal pay context will be entirely free of male bias. The second flaw, the failure to deal with difference, is also apparent. Where no appropriate male comparator can be found, the statute is silent on pay levels. Thus once the initial judgment that a woman is not 'equal' to a man in the relevant sense has been made, low levels of pay are fully legitimated. It is therefore not surprising that the Act has been of so little assistance to the large number of women who continue to fall into the lowest-paid sectors. The Act also gives a stark illustration of the fact that the equality principle does not require differences to be treated proportionately to the degree of difference. If it is clear that a woman is not doing like work or work of equal value with a man in the same establishment, she is outside the protection of the Act even if her pay is disproportionately low. For example, the EqPA is of no assistance to a woman whose work has been valued at half that of a man at her establishment, but who is paid only a quarter of his pay. The third flaw, namely consistency without substance, is also evident. We have seen that women are over-represented in the lowest-earning categories. Equality is an empty promise for low-paid workers, since the minority of men who work in those areas are equally poorly paid. In this context, a substantive right, such as the right to minimum pay, is of far more use.

The fourth problem, namely individualization of equality, is also manifest in the EqPA. The enforcement process is largely dependent on individuals pursuing claims in adversarial proceedings before a court. The result has been a disappointingly low level of enforcement through the courts, and a widespread absence of either knowledge or commitment on the part of employers to implement the equal value provisions. Thus a mere 240 equal pay cases were completed in 1992–1993, of which only 55 proceeded to a tribunal hearing. Success rates are low: the figure of 38 per cent for 1992–1993 only looks encouraging when compared with 6 per cent in 1991–1992 and 29 per cent in 1990–1991.[24] The equal value provisions have been particularly difficult to fit into an individualized, adversarial system, and cases have taken inordinately long periods to proceed through the courts. It is of course arguable that individualization of this sort is not inevitably part of the concept of equality. There are some important instances of significant progress by means of collective bargaining.[25] In addition, the Equal Opportunities Commission (EOC) has the power to back test cases,[26] a power which has been considerably strengthened by the recent House of Lords declaration that the EOC has standing to challenge primary legislation which may conflict with EU legislation.[27] However, the resources available to the EOC are limited; and the ability of trade unions to achieve equal pay depends heavily on the power balance between employer and union, and within the union itself.

The question of who bears the cost of rectifying inequalities is addressed in the Act by permitting employers to defend an inequality in pay by arguing that the variation is genuinely due to a material factor which is not the difference of sex.[28] On one interpretation of this provision, the employer should be allowed to show simply that the discrimination was unintentional, and therefore he or she was not at fault. The courts have fortunately rejected so simplistic an application of the fault model, insisting instead that there should be an objective purpose for the difference in pay, and that the difference in pay should actually achieve that purpose.[29] However, the pervasive influence of the market order is strongly felt in these cases. In practice, courts have been quick to permit employers to defend a pay disparity by arguing that it corresponds to business needs. The House of Lords in *Rainey* v. *Greater Glasgow Health Board*[30] firmly rejected earlier case law[31] which had held that the defence was confined to personal factors such as skill and seniority. Rather, it held, the defence included factors relating to the efficient carrying on of the employer's business or, in the case of a public authority, its administrative needs. This is somewhat mitigated by the insistence that the disparity corresponds to a real need on the part of an employer, rather than its convenience. Nevertheless, the courts have made it clear that business needs take precedence over the quest for equality. The way in which this perpetuates women's disadvantage is well illustrated by the *Rainey* case itself. Here a health authority found that only women were prepared to work as prosthetists at the level of pay offered, leaving open a number of vacant positions. To attract the predominantly male private sector prosthetists, a higher level of pay was agreed with the latter's trade union. When a woman complained that she was doing the same work as a man for lower pay, the House of Lords held that the disparity was justified by the inability to fill all the posts at the same level of pay. The fact that the lower-paid category was wholly female, while the higher-paid group was predominantly male was, in the view of the court, mere coincidence. A greater commitment to eliminating women's disadvantage would surely have at the very least prompted closer scrutiny of why the two groups were segregated by gender. In particular, market forces should not be accepted as a justification if they themselves perpetuate disadvantage. Yet in the recent case of *North Yorkshire County Council* v. *Ratcliffe*,[32] the Court of Appeal held that it was permissible for a local authority Direct Service Organization (DSO) to pay catering assistants (or 'dinner ladies') 10 per cent less than the collectively agreed rate for such jobs. This departure from the principle of equal pay was justified on the grounds of market forces: competition from private sector contractors was driving down wage rates. The House of Lords overturned this, recognizing that the reason why employers were able to cut the pay of catering assistants was itself due to the women's continuing disadvantage. Yet even this is limited: because the Act does not reach the outside competitors, the DSO may well lose the tender and the women their jobs.

The final weakness in the notion of equality, namely the shifting nature of its connotations, is also evident in the EqPA. Even a careful reading of the Act gives little indication as to whether the Act aims at equal treatment or equality of result. Yet the choice of one or the other has important implications for the extent to which the Act may improve women's position in the workforce. Equal treatment on basic pay may, for example, have insufficient impact on actual pay differentials and therefore on resulting inequalities, since additions to pay such as bonus, shift and overtime payments remain largely within the male domain.[33] Nor does the Act give much indication of how widely or narrowly the lens of equality should be allowed to focus; yet the outcome of a case may depend on this decision. For example, in *Hayward* v. *Cammell Laird*,[34] the key question was whether equal pay requires only that the overall package of terms and conditions be equivalent, or whether it is necessary for each contractual term to be identical. It took a House of Lords decision to resolve this (in favour of the latter); and even then, the result rested purely on statutory construction rather than on a principled decision about the aim of equality. Equality of opportunity is incorporated to some extent by the incorporation of notions of indirect discrimination in the Act.[35] But this is at best partial: equal pay remains illusory for those women who, because of domestic responsibilities or lack of training, do not have the opportunity to earn extra premia.

Direct Discrimination

The principle of direct discrimination, as set out in the SDA, states that a woman must not be treated less favourably on grounds of her sex than a man would have been treated.[36] Direct discrimination is certainly an important principle, and its prohibition by the SDA has had a significant impact on some instances of express prejudice. Thus, for example, a wine bar which refused to serve women at the bar was rightly found to have contravened this principle.[37] Most significantly, prejudice against girls in the provision of grammar school places has been held to be unlawful,[38] thus striking at one of the key causes of continuing gender discrimination.

However, the impact of the direct discrimination provisions has been limited and the flaws in the concept of equality identified above form an important part of the explanation. First, the statutory definition of direct discrimination includes the male norm in express terms: a woman may not be less favourably treated than a man would have been. It is somewhat less concrete than that in the EqPA: there is no need to find an actual male comparator in the same establishment. However, detrimental treatment is still measured by comparison with the treatment given to a man. The effect of this male norm is most glaring in the pregnancy cases, where much of the case law has been devoted to examining whether or not there is a suitable male comparator. Early cases simply held that the provision was inapplicable to pregnancy because no men fell pregnant.[39] This is a clear example of the problem of difference: the decision that pregnancy was a relevant difference merely legitimated detrimental treatment on grounds of pregnancy. In later cases, the male comparator was discovered, in the form of an ill man or a man whose ability to do his work was similarly disrupted.[40] Even when it was acknowledged that adverse treatment on grounds of pregnancy could constitute discrimination regardless of a male comparator, the House of Lords left open an escape route. Employers could defend themselves, it was held, by demonstrating that the detrimental treatment was not on grounds of pregnancy but because the employee was incapable of doing the work for which she was employed.[41] The inability of equality to effect structural change was particularly noticeable here. The social and personal value of childbirth and child-rearing were entirely ignored: instead, the effect of pregnancy on the employer's business was the focus of attention. Such a strong allegiance to the male norm is, of course, not an inevitable consequence of the principle of equality, as is evidenced by the more adventurous jurisprudence of the European Court of Justice (ECJ). In a trilogy of path-breaking cases,[42] the ECJ has held that detrimental treatment on the grounds of pregnancy contravenes the Equal Treatment Directive regardless of the absence of a suitable male comparator. The ECJ has also refused to accept the argument that inability to work is the ground for dismissal, rather than pregnancy.

The third flaw in the equality concept, that of consistency rather than substance, is also evident in the pregnancy cases, particularly those which have utilized the ill male comparator model. Pregnancy and maternity rights, on this model, depend entirely on the existence of comparable rights for illness. If there are no rights in relation to illness, equality is fully satisfied by a total absence of pregnancy or maternity rights. Indeed, in both of the major cases which relied on an ill male comparator, the complaint was dismissed, since an ill man would have fared no better than the pregnant woman.[43] In such cases, substantive rights to protection from dismissal on grounds of pregnancy and to paid parental leave would give far more protection than a vague equality right. Sexual harassment is a further area in which the right to equality is limited because it demands consistency but not substantive rights. If a man can show that he would harass sexually both men and women equally then there is no right to be free from sexual harassment in the workplace.[44] For example, in one case, a woman complained that her employer had unlawfully discriminated against her by requiring her to continue to work with an alleged harasser after an inconclusive inquiry. The Employment Appeal Tribunal (EAT) rejected the complaint on the grounds that the employer would have treated a male complainant in the same way.[45] There is no express provision in the statute prohibiting sexual harassment; indeed, it is to the credit of the courts that a cause of action has been fashioned from the equality provisions. Nevertheless, the process has been tortuous; a substantive right not to be sexually harassed would be clearer and would afford better protection than a broad-brush equality right.

The fourth issue, namely individualization, is also clearly manifest in the law of direct discrimination. So far as the cost of enforcement is concerned, the burden of litigation is primarily born by individual victims of discrimination. This is somewhat mitigated by the fact that the EOC has the power to assist individual complainants[46] or to initiate its own proceedings in relation to discriminatory advertisements, instructions to discriminate and discriminatory practices.[47] However, shortage of resources has made it impossible for the EOC to support large numbers of cases, and levels of enforcement remain low. Indeed, only 1386 SDA claims were dealt with in 1992–1993. The paucity of cases must also be due in part to the fact that remedies provide little incentive to potential claimants. The statute provides for monetary remedies rather than specific performance or reinstatement, reflecting again the reluctance to allow too great a cost to fall on individual employers (or, possibly, third party employees). This view of how the balance of individual fairness should lie as between the employer and the victim of discrimination has been strengthened by the courts and tribunals, which have kept awards of compensation in successful cases low. Thus in 1992–1993, the median award was only £1416, with 54 per cent of awards less than £1500.[48] It is only because of the influence of the ECJ that this pattern is now changing. In the path-breaking case of *Marshal (No. 2)*,[49] the ECJ held that the statutory compensation limit of £11,000 contravened the Equal Treatment Directive because it prevented claimants from receiving an award which reflected the actual loss and damage sustained. As a result, the statutory maximum has been repealed[50] with effect from November 1993. The impact has been immediate, with compensation levels rising markedly. This was especially true in the case of women dismissed from the defence forces on grounds of pregnancy: awards in such cases have averaged £35,478.[51] While progress of this sort must not be underestimated, it is notable that within months of the repeal of the statutory maximum, the EAT has criticized tribunals for awarding compensation at levels which were 'manifestly excessive and wrong'.[52] Thus future awards in these and other cases are likely to be more modest.

The question of who should bear the cost of rectifying inequalities receives a somewhat complex answer in the direct discrimination provisions. By contrast with both the EqPA and the indirect discrimination provisions, there is no statutory defence once a claim of direct discrimination has been made out, suggesting that the legislature intended the equality right to trump other interests in this context. The case law, however, demonstrates a strong ambivalence, even reluctance, on the part of the courts to find that unlawful discrimination has taken place when they perceive that such a finding would be unfair to an employer, either because of the absence of fault, or because there appears to be a good reason for the alleged difference in treatment. Several cases can be used to demonstrate this point. In the context of sexual harassment, it has been held that if an employer has a code of practice prohibiting sexual harassment, this is enough to insulate an employer against a claim based on the sexual harassment of one employee by another.[53] Here the courts seem to be strongly influenced by what they perceive to be an absence of fault on the part of the employer. The fact that the cost therefore falls on the victim of harassment is ignored. A second example of the reluctance to allow too great a cost to fall on the employer is the House of Lords' decision in *Webb*.[54] In this case, an employee, hired as a substitute for a woman on maternity leave, became pregnant herself, requiring leave almost simultaneously with her absent colleague. It was held that her dismissal was not a breach of the direct discrimination provisions, unless EU law held otherwise. The House of Lords paid lip service to the notion that dismissal on grounds of pregnancy constituted discrimination on grounds of sex. Nevertheless, they held that, under UK law, no unlawful discrimination had taken place since her dismissal was not on grounds of her pregnancy but because she was unable to do the job for which she was hired. Although not mentioned explicitly, the cost to the employer was clearly a major factor in this decision. Fortunately, the ECJ has now reversed this decision.[55] Most importantly in this context, the ECJ held that the fact that Ms Webb was initially recruited to replace another employee on maternity leave could not affect the answer given by the national court.

In other contexts, however, the ECJ has been less resistant to the idea that direct discrimination should be open to a defence of justification. A clear example is the case of *Roberts* v. *Bird's Eye Walls*.[56] This case concerned bridging pensions paid by the employer to employees who retired early on grounds of ill health. Mrs Roberts complained of unlawful discrimination on the ground that women between the ages of 60 and 65 were entitled to a smaller payment than men of the same age. Clearly, then, women in this category were treated less favourably than men of the same age. However, the employer argued that the reason for the difference was that women, but not men, between 60 and 65 were entitled to a state pension, and the difference in treatment was intended to achieve the same ultimate result. Therefore, it was argued, the difference in treatment was based on an objective factor beyond the employer's control, namely the fact that women receive a state pension five years earlier than men, rather than on the grounds of their sex alone. The ECJ held that no unlawful discrimination had taken place. The ECJ did not refer expressly to the question of whether direct discrimination could be justified; but the Advocate General made it clear that in his view, discrimination, whether direct or indirect, could always be justified. This time, it is the UK House of Lords which has held the line on the defence of justification. Thus in *James* v. *Eastleigh Borough Council*[57] the House of Lords forcefully held that unequal treatment was unlawful, regardless of the fact that the employer was well intentioned. Perhaps not coincidentally, this case was brought by a man, complaining that women were better treated than men. Here the House of Lords held that it was unlawful for a city council to give concessions on recreational facilities to women over 60 when men were only entitled to such concessions at 65. The court was not prepared to permit the council to justify its position on the grounds that the concessions were intended to assist all old age pensioners, the differential treatment merely reflecting the fact that women were required to retire earlier than men.

The difficulty in reconciling *Bird's Eye Walls* and *James* reflects, too, the final weakness in the notion of equality, namely, its shifting meanings. The answer to the challenge of equality in both cases varies according to which facts are brought into focus. Thus if the focus rests on the treatment itself, it is clear that, in both cases, the treatment of the genders was unequal, to the disadvantage of women in the first case and of men in the second. In *James*, the House of Lords based its decision entirely on this frame of reference. However, if the focus is broader, and includes the substantive result, then the inequality disappears: the bridging pension in *Bird's Eye Walls* was expected to put men, who were not entitled to a state pension, in the same position as women of the same age who were. Similarly, the concession in *James* was intended (possibly too crudely) to be of assistance equally to all people who were thrown into a position of low income because they were past state pensionable age. The ECJ in *Bird's Eye Walls* was prepared to condone unequal treatment in order to

achieve substantive equality of result, whereas the House of Lords in
James insisted on equal treatment, regardless of the fact that this led to
inequality of result: if the concession were extended to men under 65,
the result would be that men who, because they were under the state
pension age, were still earning full pay would be entitled to a concession
to which women under state pension age were not.

Indirect Discrimination

The concept of indirect discrimination has gone further than any of the
other provisions to address the flaws in equality. Most importantly, it
acknowledges that equal treatment can perpetuate existing inequalities,
whether they be biological or social. Transplanted from US Supreme
Court jurisprudence which allows challenges of practices which 'are fair
in form but discriminatory in operation',[58] the concept manifests itself in
the UK statute in the form of a detailed formula.[59] According to this
formula, a woman can succeed in a claim of unlawful discrimination if
she can show that a condition, despite being equally applied to men and
women, excludes a disproportionate number of women and cannot be
justified on grounds unrelated to gender. Its most important impact has
been in the field of part-time workers. As mentioned above, part-time
workers have been chronically disadvantaged in the workforce: hourly
pay is frequently lower than that of full-time equivalents; pension rights
and other important job-related benefits are reserved for full-timers; and
job security rights have been limited or non-existent. Through the concept of indirect discrimination, the courts have been able to recognize the
social fact that the vast majority of the part-time workforce is female.
Part-time workers are therefore able to argue that detrimental treatment
relative to full-time workers amounts to discrimination on grounds of
sex. The result has been to insist on pro rata equal rights for part-timers
as full-timers, subject to the defence of justification.[60]

However, most of the main weaknesses described above are evident in
the concept of indirect discrimination, albeit with less than full vigour.
The part-time cases have made an important dent in the male norm:
women whose unpaid work within the family makes it impossible to conform to the norm of full-time work may improve their position as a result
of these provisions. However, the male norm is by no means demolished.
Most importantly, there has been no change in the fact that women are
primarily responsible for unpaid work in the family. Thus although conditions of part-time workers have been improved, this is not enough to
change the social reality that part-time work is overwhelmingly performed by women. Part-time workers will inevitably earn less than

full-time workers; this in itself gives them less access to social power, and skews power relationships within the family.

Indirect discrimination also displays the second weakness in the equality concept, namely, that it does not address the issue of how to deal with difference. A complainant who fails to convince the court that her case fulfils any one of the many technical elements in the statutory formula is outside the scope of the legislation and may be subjected to detrimental treatment without redress.[61] For example, a complainant who uses the incorrect pool of comparison to prove that a disproportionate number of women are excluded will be unprotected.[62] Indirect discrimination manifests the third weakness too, namely that its aim is merely consistency. For example, if part-time workers work in an occupation that is generally low paid, the pay and benefits to which they have pro rata equal entitlement will remain low.

So far as the fourth issue, individual fairness and cost, is concerned, both the legislature and the courts have found it difficult to reconcile the indirect discrimination provisions with a frame of reference which is intuitively fault-oriented. Instead of perceiving discrimination as a social problem which needs to be rectified, there has been a tendency to regard the legislation as merely aiming to penalize those at fault. Yet the nature of indirect discrimination is such that fault is often difficult to locate. The problem has generally been resolved by weighting the balance in favour of the individual 'innocent' employer. This manifests itself in different contexts. One concerns remedies. As we have seen in respect of direct discrimination, the statute makes no provision for specific remedies, and compensation awards are low. This is repeated in the case of indirect discrimination, but the fault orientation is even more apparent. No compensation is payable at all where the respondent proves that the requirement or condition was not applied with the intention of treating the complainant less favourably on unlawful grounds.[63] A second manifestation is in respect of justification. As in the EqPA, an employer is permitted to justify the discrimination if he or she can show that the offending condition was imposed for reasons unrelated to sex. There has been much case law on the standard of justification. The fact that the UK courts, prompted by the ECJ, have now settled finally on the rigorous standard of business necessity is an important and welcome development. However, it is still the case that an employer can continue to discriminate against women with impunity if he or she can demonstrate this to be necessary for the business. Thus, in the words of the ECJ, if

> the means chosen by [the employer] correspond to a real need on the part of the undertaking, are appropriate with a view to achieving the objectives pursued and are necessary to that end, the fact

that the measures affect a far greater number of women than men is not sufficient to show that they constitute an infringement.[64]

In making the policy decision to spare the employer the cost, the legislature and courts have implicitly accepted that the cost should fall on the victim. This demonstrates, too, the limitations placed on equality by the market order in which it operates.

Finally, it is unclear which of the meanings of equality is embodied in the notion of indirect discrimination. It is often said to encapsulate equality of results. However, while inequality of results is one of the conditions of the formula, equality of results is not necessarily the aim. This is particularly true where there has been a successful defence of justification. Nor does it incorporate equality of opportunity: no attempt is made to commit resources to equalizing the starting points of the different genders.

CONCLUSION

Equality as an ideal has played a central and valuable role in the struggle to emancipate women. These achievements should not be undervalued. However, I hope to have demonstrated that the concept of equality as expressed in the anti-discrimination statutes in the UK is inherently limited and can in fact act as a brake on further progress for women. Similar inherent limitations constrain the effectiveness of the principle of equality which is central to European and international conventions aimed at removing discrimination against women. It is essential now for human rights and anti-discrimination measures to recognize that equality is only an adjunct to substantive values and it is to a change in substantive values that we now need to look. In order truly to transform the position of women in society, we need to change the underlying values which perpetuate our disadvantage. Central to such a re-evaluation is a proper acknowledgment of the true value of unpaid 'family' work, particularly the important work of caring for children, the elderly and the disabled. This entails, for example, a more flexible interface between family and workplace and an accommodation by the workplace of children's needs. Once such a re-evaluation has taken place, equality can play its proper role: ensuring consistency rather than posing as a substitute for proper scrutiny of social values.

NOTES

1. Equal Pay Act 1970, s. 1, and Sex Discrimination Act 1975, s. 1(1).
2. Article 119, Treaty of Rome; Directive 75/117; Directive 76/207; Directive 79/7; Directive 86/378; and Directive 86/613.
3. Convention on the Elimination of All Forms of Discrimination against Women (1979).
4. For a critical analysis of EC law, see S. Fredman, European Community discrimination law: a critique [1992] *Industrial Law Journal* 119; on international law, see H. Charlesworth, C. Chinkin and S. Wright, 'Feminist approaches to international law' (1991) 85 *American Journal of International Law* 613.
5. Statistics in this section are derived from *Equal Opportunities Review* No. 58 (1994) p. 33.
6. See, for example, *Electrolux* v. *Hutchinson* [1976] IRLR 410 (EAT), *Steel* v. *Union of Post Office Workers and the General Post Office* [1977] IRLR 288 (EAT), where it was clear that the unions were colluding in the discriminatory behaviour.
7. This formulation deliberately leaves open the question of whether equality here means equality of treatment or equality of results. See further below.
8. See L. Dickens, *Whose flexibility? Discrimination and Equality Issues in Atypical Work* (London: Institute of Employment Rights, 1992).
9. P. Elias and T. Hogarth, Families, jobs and unemployment. In R. Lindley (ed.), *Labour Market Structures and Prospects for Women* (London: Equal Opportunities Commission, 1994), p. 92.
10. Aristotle, *Politics*, Book III (Oxford, 1995), Chapter 13. Aristotle himself was no advocate of political equality, particularly in respect of women: see *Politics*, Book II (New York, 1995), Chapter 12.
11. For example, M. Wollstonecraft, *Vindication of the Rights of Woman* (1792), ed. C. H. Poston (New York, 1975).
12. For example, C. Gilligan, *In a Different Voice* (Cambridge, MA, 1982).
13. See Employment Act 1989. For a similar example from immigration law, see *Abdulazi 3* v. *UK* (1985) 7 EHRR 471.
14. IRS Research Report, *Pay and Gender in Britain* (London: Industrial Relations Service, 1991) p. 27.
15. *Electrolux* v. *Hutchinson, op. cit.*
16. See C. Littleton, Reconstructing sexual equality, in P. Smith (ed.), *Feminist Jurisprudence* (New York, 1993), pp. 110 ff.
17. L. Finley, Transcending equality theory (1986) 86 *Columbia Law Review* 1118, at p. 1164.
18. Equal Pay Act 1970, s. 1.
19. *Electrolux* v. *Hutchinson, op. cit.*
20. Equal Pay (amendment) Regulations (SI 1983 No. 1794).
21. [1988] IRLR 257 (HL).
22. Equal Pay Act 1970, s. 1(6).
23. Unless 'common terms and conditions' can be established with another establishment of the same employer: see *Leverton* v. *Clwyd CC* [1989] IRLR 28 (HL); but contrast *British Coal* v. *Smith* [1994] IRLR 342 (CA).
24. *Equal Opportunities Review (EOR)*, No. 54 March/April 1994, pp. 22–3.
25. For an account of equal value bargaining in local government, see S. Fredman and G. Morris, *The State as Employer* (London, 1989), pp. 355-7.
26. Sex Discrimination Act 1975, s. 75.
27. *R* v. *Secretary of State for Employment ex p EOC* [1994] IRLR 176 (HL).
28. Equal Pay Act 1970, s. 1(3).
29. *Jenkins* v. *Kingsgate (No. 2)* [1981] IRLR 388 (EAT).
30. [1987] IRLR 26 (HL).
31. *Clay Cross* v. *Fletcher* [1979] ICR 1 (CA).
32. [1994] IRLR 342 (CA) [1995] IRLR 439 (HL).
33. Industrial Relations Services, *Pay and Gender in Britain* (London: IRS, 1991), p. 55.
34. *Op. cit.*

35. *Jenkins* v. *Kingsgate*, *op. cit.*; *Enderby* v. *Frenchay Health Authority* (1994) IRLR 495 (ECJ).
36. Sex Discrimination Act 1975, s. 1(1)(a).
37. *Gill* v. *El Vinos Co. Ltd* [1983] IRLR 206.
38. *R* v. *Birmingham City Council ex p EOC* [1989] IRLR 173 (HL).
39. *Turley* v. *Allders Stores* [1980] ICR 66 (EAT). For a more detailed discussion, see S. Fredman, 'A difference with distinction: pregnancy and parenthood reassessed' (1994) 110 *Law Quarterly Review* 106.
40. *Hayes* v. *Malleable Men's Working Club* [1985] ICR 703; *Dixon* v. *Rees* [1993] IRLR 468 (EAT).
41. *Webb* v. *EMO Air Cargo (UK) Ltd* [1993] IRLR 27 (HL); and see *Dixon* v. *Rees*, *op. cit.*
42. Case C–177/88 *Dekker* [1991] IRLR 27 (ECJ); Case C–32/93 *Webb* [1994] IRLR 482 (ECJ); Case C–421/92 *Haberman-Beltermann* [1994] IRLR 364 (ECJ).
43. *Hayes* v. *Malleable*, *op. cit.*; *Webb* v. *EMO* [1992] 2 All ER 43 (CA).
44. *Strathclyde Regional Council* v. *Porcelli* [1986] IRLR 134.
45. *Balgobin* v. *London Borough of Tower Hamlets* [1987] IRLR 401.
46. Sex Discrimination Act 1975, s. 75.
47. SDA, Part IV.
48. *Equal Opportunities Review* No. 54, (1994) p. 22.
49. [1993] IRLR 445 (ECJ).
50. Sex Discrimination and Equal Pay (Remedies) Regulations 1993.
51. *Equal Opportunities Review* No. 57 (1994), p. 23.
52. *Ministry of Defence* v. *Cannock* [1994] IRLR 509 (EAT).
53. *Balgobin* v. *London Borough of Tower Hamlets* [1987] *op. cit.*
54. *Webb* v. *EMO Air Cargo (UK)*, *op. cit.*
55. Case 32/93 [1994] IRLR 482.
56. Case C-132/92, [1994] IRLR 29.
57. [1990] IRLR 288 (HL).
58. *Griggs* v. *Duke Power Co.* 401 US 424, 434 (1971).
59. Sex Discrimination Act, s. 1(1)(b).
60. *Jenkins* v. *Kingsgate*, *op. cit.*; Case 170/84 *Bilka Kaufhous* [1986] IRLR 317; *R* v. *Secretary of State for Employment*, *op. cit.*
61. See, for example, *Clymo* v. *Wandsworth* [1989] IRLR 241.
62. *Kidd* v. *DRG* [1985] IRLR 190; *Jones* v. *University of Manchester* [1993] IRLR 218 CA.
63. Sex Discrimination Act 1975, s. 66(3).
64. *Bilka Kaufhaus* case 190/84 *op. cit.*; *Rainey* v. *Greater Glasgow Health Board op. cit.*

10

Essential Rights and Contested Identities: Sexual Orientation and Equality Rights Jurisprudence in Canada

Carl F. Stychin

INTRODUCTION

In this chapter, I shall examine sexual orientation as a human rights issue. The reasons why discrimination on the grounds of sexual orientation should be considered an issue of human rights have been articulated by others, and I do not propose to repeat their arguments here.[1] Rather, I seek to examine in a more critical way some of the analytical problems that may arise in fashioning human rights protection. While the substantive goals of human rights struggles are surely commendable – freedom from persecution and from invidious discrimination, or more positively framed claims to the means necessary to live a decent life – the *discourse* of rights has been the subject of critique, for example, by the critical legal studies (CLS) movement in the USA.[2] Rights claims, it has been argued, reinforce the separation of the individual from community. The focus on abstract rights undermines the substantive claims of groups and individuals within society by reifying formal (but ultimately alienating) individual rights.

Of course, the CLS critique itself has been subjected to sustained criticism, particularly from the schools of feminist legal theory and critical race theory (and the intersection of the two).[3] The CLS attack on rights is criticized for its failure to recognize both the substantive and the symbolic impact of concrete rights victories. Furthermore, it has been argued that rights struggles can be contradictory and complex. An apparent rights vindication may not be in all respects a victory for the individuals and groups at the centre of the struggle.[4] Moreover, the analytical tools that are deployed to secure human rights may turn out to be limiting, constraining and inadequate for the task. I seek to elaborate upon this final point by exploring one example of a human rights struggle: namely the question of discrimination on the basis of sexual orientation under the Canadian Charter of Rights and Freedoms. I look first at a number of recent problems that have been encountered and articulated in terms of the methods by which rights are analysed in Canada. In particular, I examine the use of what has been termed categorical thinking in human rights discourse. I then look at the closely related issue of the concept of the immutability of a personal characteristic as the basis of human rights protection. The conceptual difficulties with this approach will be highlighted. Finally, I outline some alternative ideas that might be developed to replace or at least to supplement the categorical approach.

THE CANADIAN CASE LAW

Legislative intervention in Canada to protect 'human rights' is a post-World War II phenomenon. The provincial and federal governments have all attempted to secure some measure of statutory protection of individual human rights in the area of anti-discrimination in both the public and private sectors. In general, this legislation has been comprehensive, in the sense that it has taken the form of single statutes that forbid discrimination on any of a series of enumerated grounds. Human rights tribunals have been granted broad remedial powers in this field across the country. Importantly for my purposes, the general pattern appears to be that discrimination is outlawed exclusively on a series of enumerated grounds. Not surprisingly, rights struggles in the political process have arisen in many jurisdictions based on demands for inclusion of new grounds in the enumerated list of prohibited bases of discrimination.[5]

The scope of human rights protection in Canada expanded dramatically with the enactment of the Canadian Charter of Rights and Freedoms in 1982. Canada was transformed from a system of parliamentary sovereignty (within the confines of a federal form of government) into a country with an enumerated and constitutionally entrenched set of individual and group rights. The focus of this chapter is on the equality provisions of the Charter:

> s. 15(1). Every individual is equal before and under the law and has the right to the equal protection and equal benefit of the law without discrimination and, in particular, without discrimination based on race, national or ethnic origin, colour, religion, sex, age or mental or physical disability.

s. 15(2). Subsection (1) does not preclude any law, program or activity that has as its object the amelioration of conditions of disadvantaged individuals or groups including those that are disadvantaged because of race, national or ethnic origin, colour, religion, sex, age or mental or physical disability.[6]

Clearly, through the use of an enumerated list of prohibited bases of discrimination, the Charter equality rights bear a striking resemblance to the human rights guarantees that had previously been enacted by Parliament and the provincial legislatures. However, fundamental differences also exist. The Charter, unlike the human rights codes, is a constitutionally entrenched document with a difficult amending formula; second, the Charter is limited in its scope to the public sphere, unlike the human rights codes, which all govern private actors; and third, while the enumerated grounds of discrimination in the human rights codes are comprehensive, the Charter equality guarantees were deliberately left open-ended, creating the possibility for constitutional protection against discrimination by the state on grounds not explicitly enumerated within the text of the Constitution.

This openness to new grounds of prohibited discrimination demanded interpretive guidance from the judiciary on how and when other categories of prohibited discrimination might be added to the equality guarantees. In fact, this issue arose in the first s. 15 case considered by the Supreme Court of Canada, *Andrews* v. *Law Society of British Columbia*.[7] This decision has proven to be of crucial importance for a number of reasons. With respect to the grounds of discrimination, the Court devised an interpretive method which it described as purposive. The grounds of discrimination that might be constitutionally prohibited were inextricably tied to the question of what constitutes discrimination. Rejecting both a formal test of discrimination as distinction in law, as well as a 'similarly situated' test, McIntyre J, for the Court, explained the process of determining when constitutionally prohibited discrimination had been perpetrated:

> I would say then that discrimination may be described as a distinction, whether intentional or not but based on grounds relating to personal characteristics of the individual or group, which has the effect of imposing burdens, obligations, or disadvantages on such individual or group not imposed upon others, or which withholds or limits access to opportunities, benefits, and advantages available to other members of society.[8]

From this definition, the Court developed an approach to s. 15 which turns on whether the claim of discrimination rests upon grounds either enumerated within s. 15 or analogous to the enumerated grounds, which were described as 'the most common and probably the most socially destructive and historically practised bases of discrimination'.[9] Thus, an analogy must be drawn between the enumerated ground and the un-enumerated basis in terms of historical or social disadvantage due to discriminatory treatment which has been suffered by individuals as a consequence of membership in the group.[10]

The focus on analogous grounds facilitates the expansion of the bases upon which unconstitutional discriminatory treatment may be found. This was explicitly recognized by Wilson J, writing in the *Andrews* case:

> I believe also that it is important to note that the range of discrete and insular minorities has changed and will continue to change with changing political and social circumstances . . . It can be anticipated that the discrete and insular minorities of tomorrow will include groups not recognized as such today. It is consistent with the constitutional status of s. 15 that it be interpreted with sufficient flexibility to ensure the 'unremitting protection' of equality rights in the years to come.[11]

As Wilson J explained, the determination of whether a group qualifies as analogous depends upon 'the context of the place of the group in the entire social, political and legal fabric of our society'.[12] Thus, individuals, whose basis of identification is not explicitly recognized in s. 15, may still have recourse through the courts.

The reaction to the approach enunciated in *Andrews* generally was highly positive, especially amongst legal academics. The 'disadvantage' test of discrimination, in combination with the analogous grounds approach, was hailed as properly reflecting a purposive and contextual analysis of equality.[13] The formalism and rigidity of US equal protection analysis, it was argued, was rightly rejected as a model.

THE PROBLEMS OF CATEGORICAL THINKING

However, a more critical appraisal has recently emerged, especially in relation to the focus on *categories* of discrimination, which reflects the problems of rigid categorical thinking in law more generally.[14] Categories can become naturalized and essentialized, and a list of

enumerated categories – such as the grounds of prohibited discrimination – may appear historically and socially fixed. As Nitya Iyer has
argued, this approach to anti-discrimination law fails to acknowledge that
social identities are geographically and historically contingent. Moreover,
the existence of a series of categories masks the 'invisible background
norm'.[15] Each category becomes a distinction from the norm, for which
protection is appropriate. The norm, though, remains in place, permanently fixed, immutable, and 'undeconstructed'. The categories of
prohibited discrimination represent mere deviations.

For the claimant of rights, the categorical approach clearly makes
demands on how a case is framed. Obviously, the plaintiff is forced to
make his or her claim in terms of the categories available or to attempt to
put forward a new category which is analogous to the existing ones in
terms of the disadvantage principle. Although in many instances this
approach may not appear problematic, conceptually it demands that differences in terms of disadvantage and social location between individuals
who share membership in the same group are overlooked in the course
of articulating the shared disadvantage. So too, in its focus on categories,
the implications of membership of an individual in more than one category of disadvantage are not easily explained.[16] The categorical
approach demands of individuals that they identify themselves along one
axis of oppression for any particular purpose – to fit themselves within
one grouping that can be labelled disadvantaged. This has also been
described as the minority rights model and an example of legal liberalism, with its focus on pluralism and minority groups who share
characteristics that separate them from the norm.[17]

It is within this system of categories of prohibited discrimination that
arguments were made that 'sexual orientation' constitutes a basis analogous to the enumerated s. 15 grounds. After some initial hesitation, the
uncontroverted trend in Canadian constitutional law has been to hold
that 'sexual orientation' provides an analogous ground within the scope
of s. 15.[18] For example, in *Haig* v. *Canada (Minister of Justice)*, the Ontario
Court of Appeal considered whether the absence of sexual orientation
from the list of proscribed grounds of discrimination in the Canadian
Human Rights Act was discriminatory as being contrary to s. 15.[19] The
factual context of the case concerned the dismissal of a Canadian Armed
Forces officer on the basis of his sexual orientation. The Ontario Court of
Appeal held, first, that the requisite degree of social disadvantage to jus-
tify inclusion within s. 15 was met by the category of sexual orientation:

> The social context which must be considered includes the pain and
> humiliation undergone by homosexuals by reason of prejudice
> towards them. It also includes the enlightened evolution of human

rights social and legislative policy in Canada, since the end of the Second World War, both provincially and federally. The failure to provide an avenue of redress for prejudicial treatment of homosexual members of society, and the possible inference from the omission that such treatment is acceptable, creates the effect of discrimination offending s. 15(1) of the Charter.[20]

The Court held that the Canadian Human Rights Act must 'be interpreted, applied and administered as though it contained "sexual orientation" as a prohibited ground of discrimination'.[21] Thus, by virtue of the use of the analogous grounds approach in interpreting the Charter, sexual orientation has come to be 'read in' as a prohibited ground of discrimination under federal human rights law.

While this developing body of case law is frequently applauded uncritically, especially by liberal legal academics, there are conceptual and theoretical difficulties at work in the reasoning. The use of categories of prohibited discrimination in itself is problematic in the context of sexual orientation (as it is with other prohibited grounds). The approach gives rise to rigid binary classification – the norm (heterosexuality) and the exception (homosexuality) – into which individuals can be 'slotted'. Such an approach is increasingly out of step with much current theory and practice of sexuality. In creating this division, the norm remains invisible and unproblematic. A 'deviation' from the norm is the problem, but one which can be overlooked within liberal human rights discourse.

Categorical thinking, when applied in the context of sexual orientation, also gives rise to an impression that the categories have a historical fixity. Given the emphasis in the *Andrews* decision on social and *historical* disadvantage, it is not surprising that both the category of sexual orientation and discrimination on that basis are not infrequently constructed as both static and universal.[22] The historical specificity of sexual categories is thus overlooked. In particular, the work of theorists who argue that any sexual act 'may have varying social significance and subjective meaning', depending upon how the act is interpreted within a particular cultural and historical location, is neither considered nor applied.[23] Social construction theorists argue that the relationship of sexual act to sexual identity and the construction of identities themselves are not historically fixed, but rather are contingent and thus capable of cultural redefinition.[24]

THE ISSUE OF IMMUTABILITY

Closely related to the universalizing of categories is the focus on their immutability as a justification for constitutional protection of the individual from discrimination. Within the judgments in *Andrews*, there is explicit development of the concept of immutability as both a justification for the categories enumerated in s. 15, and as a basis for determining analogous grounds. While the judgments of McIntyre J and Wilson JJ both referred to membership in a minority as based upon a 'personal characteristic' and to the minority itself as being 'discrete and insular', La Forest J went further down the path of immutability. While the characteristic under consideration in *Andrews* was citizenship, La Forest J justified the acceptance of this category as an analogous ground by drawing upon immutability:

> [T]he characteristic of citizenship is one typically not within the control of the individual and, in this sense, is immutable. Citizenship is, at least temporarily, a characteristic of personhood not alterable by conscious action and in some cases not alterable except on the basis of unacceptable costs.[25]

La Forest J's conception of immutability is interesting because he sees it as sufficiently broad to encompass a characteristic which many people do in fact change – their citizenship – albeit usually only after a period in which entitlement is earned.

The reliance upon immutability as the basis which unites the personal characteristics within s. 15 and any analogous grounds is explicitly adopted in Hogg's *Constitutional Law of Canada*.[26] In this standard textbook, the author unquestioningly accepts that immutability, in the sense that the characteristic 'cannot be changed by the choice of the individual' or that it is 'inherent, rather than acquired', forms the basis of s. 15 protection.[27] Personal characteristics worthy of constitutional protection 'describe what a person is, rather than what a person does. Section 15 prohibits laws that distinguish between people on the basis of their inherent attributes as opposed to their behaviour.'[28] A constitutional remedy thus only is deserving where the individual has been discriminated against 'by reason of a *condition* over which the person has no control'.[29] How this criterion for the determination of grounds applies to sexual orientation is not considered. Hogg does conclude, though, that there are 'very few' legislative distinctions made by the state in law that satisfy the requirement of immutability and therefore amount to prohibited grounds of discrimination.[30] If Hogg has any thoughts on what those grounds might encompass, he keeps them to himself.

In recent s. 15 jurisprudence concerning sexual orientation as a prohibited ground of discrimination, the use of immutability as a basis for
considering what constitutes an analogous ground has on occasion arisen
explicitly. For example, in *Veysey* v. *Correctional Services of Canada*, a decision of the Federal Court Trial Division (affirmed on other grounds by
the Federal Court of Appeal), the trial judge applied the immutability test
and had no difficulty finding that sexual orientation was a personal characteristic which satisfied the requirement:

> Most of the grounds enumerated in s. 15 of the Charter as prohib-
> ited grounds of discrimination connote the attribute of
> immutability, such as race, national or ethnic origin, colour, age.
> One's religion may be changed but with some difficulty; sex and
> mental or physical disability, with even greater difficulty.
> Presumably, sexual orientation would fit within one of these levels
> of immutability.[31]

As this judgment makes apparent, immutability continues to achieve
some popularity in equality jurisprudence, although there are numerous
judgments in which it has not been applied. Others emphasize somewhat
different factors, such as historical disadvantage, patterns of social prejudice, and the 'discrete and insular minority' requirement.[32] The issue is
far from settled.[33]

CONCEPTUAL DIFFICULTIES

The theoretical and practical significance of the choice of test for determining analogous grounds is great. On a theoretical level, the application
of a test of immutability to sexual orientation (or other grounds of discrimination) is highly problematic, particularly in the way that it has been
developed by commentators such as Hogg. In general, a test of
immutability underscores a view of so-called personal characteristics as
essential, neutral, and historically continuous, rather than as historically
specific, culturally changeable, and the outcome of a 'particular pattern
of social relations' based upon oppression.[34] To repeat, under the
immutability approach the personal characteristic becomes an (unfortunate) deviation from a static norm. Individual 'difference' from the
characteristics attributed to members of groups is occluded. The individual is forced to 'take on' the disadvantage suffered by the particular

group of which he or she is a member for the purposes of litigation. Claims of discrimination which arise by virtue of the specific location of the individual agent in a matrix of different social groups become difficult to articulate. In general, the complexity and contradictions of individual subjecthood are obfuscated.

In this way, the legal recognition of a characteristic as a prohibited ground of discrimination might be seen not simply as a neutral, objective vindication of rights, but rather as part of a network of regulation. The creation of categories is a means whereby groups that deviate from the background norm are inscribed with a characteristic which 'regulates, contains, and constitutes them'.[35] Categories, by definition, serve as means of containment, which resist self-definition by members. In fact, the possibility of individual *control* over the meaning of a characteristic is denied by virtue of the reliance upon immutability. At the same time, of course, the norm is neither questioned nor interrogated, nor is it perceived itself as a historically contingent category.

The problems that emerge from this approach are particularly acute in the area of sexual orientation and equality rights. If one subscribes to a social constructionist model, then the close nexus between immutability and sexual essentialism is profoundly problematic. As I have argued to this point, the categorical approach to human rights, to the extent that it emphasizes the historical continuity of immutable categories, is a constraining interpretation on individual and collective identity. In addition, these constraints can be understood through the theoretical divide between essentialism and social construction, particularly as these concepts have been developed in theoretical work on sexuality.[36] Although the terms are themselves far from undisputed in their meaning (thereby demonstrating the social construction of the debate itself), I adopt, for the purposes of this argument, the definitions developed by Epstein:

> Where essentialism took for granted that all societies consist of people who are either heterosexuals or homosexuals (with perhaps some bisexuals), constructionists demonstrated that the notion of 'the homosexual' is a sociohistorical product, not universally applicable, and worthy of explanation in its own right. And where essentialism would treat the self-attribution of a 'homosexual identity' as unproblematic – as simply the conscious recognition of a true, underlying 'orientation' – constructionism focused attention on identity as a complex developmental outcome, the consequence of an interactive process of social labelling and self-identification.[37]

In my view, the approach to equality rights in Canada, particularly in its impact upon sexual orientation, is dominated by an essentialist interpretation.[38] The categories of prohibited discrimination (and the underlying norm) are not seen themselves as problematic, contingent, or socially constructed. Judges and advocates who may well be sympathetic to claims made by lesbian or gay litigants nonetheless frequently 'buy into' a theory that may be very limiting. In particular, by definition this approach denies the possibility of individual agency in determining sexual orientation and practice. Homosexuality becomes defined as an innate inability to realize the heterosexual norm. A prohibition on discrimination in the name of human rights thus becomes justifiable *because* of the construction of sexuality as beyond individual choice. A pre-social urge thus serves as the basis of the constitution of the category. However, within this discourse of human rights, there is little room to articulate a more radical claim about the *ideological* basis of the categories and the process of categorization.[39] While individual sexual identity (which conceptually is problematic, as I will argue shortly) may not be easy for many to alter, the proponents of the understanding of sexual employed within this discourse never consider why it may prove difficult for a *heterosexually* identified individual to change orientation. Either nature or nurture is assumed to create the immutable characteristic; but nowhere is it explained in terms of an *ideology* of compulsory heterosexuality. Furthermore, there is little scope to develop a conception of homosexuality based upon a political theory and practice, which has long been a central aspect of lesbian feminism. Consequently, the human rights model, as it has been developed within the Canadian context, has been criticized as politically conservative from the perspective of sexual politics:

> [T]he minority model is problematic when applied to any group of people; in relation to lesbians and gay men it seems particularly inappropriate. If, as many feminists and others contend, sexuality is socially constructed, and there is no necessary or 'natural' link between reproductive capacities, gender categories, and sexual desire, then representing lesbians and gay men as an immutable minority may restrict rather than broaden our understandings of sexuality. Lesbians and gay men are granted legitimacy, not on the basis that there might be something problematic with gender roles and sexual hierarchies, but on the basis that they constitute a fixed group of 'others' who need and deserve protection. Human rights frameworks thus pull in 'new' identities thereby regulating them, and containing their challenge to dominant social relations.[40]

The focus on immutable categories dampens the possibility of a more politically charged critique of heterosexual institutions and the organization of gender relations. Human rights discourse, particularly in its constitutional form in Canada, thereby becomes a regulatory framework that forces the articulation of claims through the prism of categories.

A related issue is the role of gender in the immutability debate. The observation of many is that the vast majority of subscribers to the immutable/essentialist position within the lesbian and gay community are gay men, while more lesbians consider their sexuality to be socially constructed.[41] This difference highlights two relevant points. The first is sexual politics. The adoption of a social constructionist position is often closely tied to a conception of sexual orientation as highly politically charged; that 'sexual behavior implies a political statement about living outside the mainstream' and the conscious rejection of a system of compulsory heterosexuality within a patriarchal society.[42] Social construction is thus closely linked to feminist theory. Immutability, on the other hand, is related to a theory of the 'sameness' of sexual relations – that 'we are just like you' and that 'we cannot help who we are'. Consequently, if one subscribes to immutability, discrimination on the basis of sexual orientation becomes unjustifiable because it treats similar people differently for reasons beyond their control. The fact that many gay men accept such a view is not surprising, given the differently situated position of gay men as opposed to lesbians in a patriarchal system. For the white, able-bodied gay man, essentialist arguments possess tremendous power if they become widely accepted. If his sexual orientation is considered 'irrelevant' and an 'accident of birth', then the gay man can take on the trappings of male gender privilege.[43] For lesbians, in their position as women, gender privilege is unattainable. Of course, the categorical approach, which unproblematically groups together lesbianism and gay male sexuality, largely ignores this distinction.[44] To argue in favour of the immutability of the characteristic may demand that one speaks from a position of relative privilege within the group under consideration.

However, despite its limitations, the use of essentialist rhetoric retains a strategic usefulness in constitutional rights discourse. In part, this is because immutability, to the extent that it remains unproblematic in its use, provides an easy label through which categories can be made analogous and distinguished in an apparently neutral judicial fashion. Change itself is precluded, since the essentializing of categories prevents the emergence of a vision of radical change in the relationship of norm and deviation (and the transcendence of that binary). It is predictable, therefore, that rights claims framed in terms of immutability may receive a receptive hearing from those sympathetic to liberal pluralist conceptions of difference, particularly since such arguments are at least implicitly framed in terms of gay sexual orientation as 'condition'.

Given that claims to constitutional rights are made for a variety of reasons – to seek an individual remedy, to obtain publicity, to avoid criminal sanction, to realize broader social change – litigation strategies will vary and clearly will not be consistent from case to case. If immutability receives a positive hearing from the judiciary, then one would expect to see it employed again in legal argument. The uses and abuses of immutability in rights litigation are often counterintuitive. This has been particularly true in US constitutional law. Successful claims that distinctions based upon sexual orientation should be subject to heightened scrutiny for the purposes of equal protection analysis (although very rare) have been largely dependent upon arguments that sexual orientation is an immutable characteristic in the sense of being difficult to change.[45] Over the last several years, most courts have denied such claims, often holding that sexual orientation is primarily behavioural, which thereby distinguishes the classification from categories such as race or gender.[46] Sexual orientation cannot be considered an immutable characteristic because it is a *choice* to engage in particular sexual *behaviour*. Thus, in US constitutional jurisprudence, some 'pro-gay' judgments have relied to some extent on immutability arguments, while 'anti-gay' judgments have focused on the mutability and fluidity of sexuality and sexual categories (which resembles social construction theory).[47] The theory and politics of sexual identity thereby assumes a strange dynamic. A conservative theoretical model of sexuality becomes tied to more 'liberal' judgments, while the opposite also holds true.[48]

The fundamental question that remains unexamined in this rights discourse is what constitutes a 'sexual orientation' in the first place. While most courts and commentators find this term relatively unproblematic, its deployment masks its potential political challenge.[49] Lesbian and gay politics and culture in the 1990s is increasingly characterized by a self-reflexive questioning of the meaning and content of sexual orientation and of categorical thinking in general.[50] This introspection, in turn, further undermines essentialist arguments. It has been suggested, for example, that a lesbian or gay identity should be viewed not simply as a question of same sex desire (which is the focus of judicial attention), but rather as turning on the relationship of the individual to heterosexual 'law' and gender identity.[51] Sexuality thus becomes a matter of culture rather than nature, and the politics of gender identity (and non-conformity) replaces anatomy as a primary focus. However, even if one does accept same/opposite sex desire as the basis of sexual orientation, it remains true that the definition of a sexual desire is itself culturally contingent (and socially constructed). The political implications of such a shift are apparent:

> [G]ay history . . . loses the full breadth of its political opportunities when it takes on only the task of deconstructing the taboo on same-

sex desire rather than framing for itself the much larger task of
deconstructing heterosexual law itself.[52]

So, too, a gay legal theory and practice loses its political power through a
narrow focus on sexual difference framed in the language of immutable
categories and essentialism. As Calhoun suggests, the broader political
project is to pose a more fundamental challenge to heterosexuality.

Such a strategy has emerged from the site of 'queer theory' and queer
social practices. The exact parameters of queer theory are difficult to
determine and this of course contributes to its current popularity and
success. Central to the project is the contestation of boundaries and
categories, not only of sexual identity, but more widely to include the
boundaries of normalcy itself.[53] Queerness is in part a rejection of the
minority group categorization. It suggests that the logic of identity is far
more complex 'along dimensions that can't be subsumed under gender
and sexuality at all: the ways that race, ethnicity, postcolonial rationality
criss-cross with these and other identity-constituting, identity-fracturing
discourses'.[54] Moreover, queers constantly seek to reflect upon the contingency and ambiguity of all sexual categories. Rather than constituting
an identity category itself, queerness highlights the contingency of all
boundaries of social practice and identity, including its own. It represents
a subversion of categorical thinking so that 'queer' as a term is capable of
constant reworking to serve new political purposes.[55] Queer theory, then,
is closely related to the critical approaches of deconstruction and post-
structuralism. In fact, the latter has been described as 'a sort of
theoretical wing of Queer Nation'.[56]

The essentialist/immutability model and the categorical approach that
it accompanies are highly problematic from the perspective of queer theory. The categorical approach constrains the challenge posed by queers
to the coherence and stability of identity categories and disguises the role
of relations of oppression in their construction and maintenance. Queers
seek to resist the regime of categorization and the invisible norm(al)
itself. They aim to highlight the failure of the categories fully to 'erect'
boundaries around the subjects within their sphere; to challenge categorization, as a means of creating 'alternative social and political
possibilities'.[56] In a sense, queer theory seeks to deconstruct the categories that are considered essential (and essentialism itself) and,
moreover, at their highest, queers aspire to be sufficiently self-aware to
deconstruct themselves and their queer identities![57] Thus, while queer
theory recognizes that identity categories may be politically useful and
empowering, it also seeks to develop strategies of resistance to the
regimes of power through which such categories are imposed and maintained as stable regimes. Thus, not only is the notion that categories of

individuals are immutable challenged by queer theory, but the idea that categories possess a stability that renders them in some sense fixed also is critically questioned.[58]

Related to the interrogation of the hetero/homo binary that has been developed by queer theory is the challenge to categorization arising from the emerging bisexual rights movement.[59] Here again, the problems raised by immutability- and essentialist-based arguments are apparent. To a large extent, the argument from immutability has some appeal from the perspective of human rights because its focus is on the absence of free choice in sexual objects. Thus, it would be unjust and contrary to the rights of the individual to sanction discrimination on the basis of the gender of one's sexual object choice if it is beyond his or her agency (and therefore not truly a choice at all). Thus, the right is grounded in considerations of fairness.

However, this argument begins to unravel to the extent that an individual acknowledges some degree of free choice with respect to the gender of sexual objects. Bisexuality presents the most apparent example. Even though proponents of categorical thinking acknowledge bisexuality as a subcategory of sexual orientation, its position is problematic. If the self-proclaimed bisexual is capable of true object *choice* (which is part of the basis of the identity), then arguments grounded in fairness, arising out of the immutability position, are inapposite. In other words, why is it unfair – a violation of the rights of the individual – to ask someone who *can* to *make a choice* of the gender of sexual objects?[60] Moreover, if sexual orientation is not immutable for the bisexual, why is it unfair to ask him or her to choose the opposite gender for object choice? Immutability offers nothing as a justification for a right of non-discrimination in this context.[61] Similarly, to the extent that others may view their sexuality as a matter of choice (perhaps a political choice) and capable of alteration and mutability, essentialist-based arguments fail to acknowledge the breadth and diversity of sexuality (which, of course, is the position advanced by queer activists). As Halley argues, 'pro-gay essentialism' is an 'exoneration strategy' in that the demand for human rights arises from the inability of the individual to control or resist what he or she *is*: 'that an individual should not be criminally punished or civilly burdened because he or she helplessly bears a disfavored characteristic'.[62] Proponents of immutability fail to challenge the meaning which has been inscribed on the characteristic within the political process or its coherence as a basis for description. Furthermore, the analysis does not consider the mutability of heterosexuality, which remains the entrenched norm. As Didi Herman has argued, 'while it may be true that a heterosexual's sexual identity is not easily changed, this is not due to an inherent sexuality, but to the context of enforced and privileged heterosexuality that denies people choice'.[63]

Categorical thinking also runs into enormous problems around group definition. Disagreements within groups about membership and the 'true' characteristics of the group render essentialist approaches open to charges of underinclusiveness.[64] Such disagreements over identity are witnessed with increasing frequency within the lesbian and gay communities, particularly in response to the challenges posed by an activist bisexual movement, trans-gendered persons, and the more amorphous queer theory and practice. Immutability of a personal characteristic as a legal argument thus seems alienated from the debates occurring 'on the ground' within the movement.

Finally, the coherence of any identity category and the maintenance of a dominant norm depend upon the existence of an implicit comparison with that which is 'other' to it.[65] Categorical thinking facilitates such a construction because it forces the subject to define himself or herself in terms of subject positions that have already been articulated with a defined content. The focus of Canadian equality law on the articulation of analogous grounds – 'new' categories – may appear to facilitate the voice of the 'other' (those outside the dominant norm). However, the emphasis on bounded categories with an essential and immutable content can facilitate (and demand) the construction of a devalued other in relation to the prohibited ground of discrimination. For example, the increasing acceptance of sexual orientation as a prohibited ground of discrimination in human rights law is in part a strategy to normalize sexual orientation, such that invidious categorization by the state is outlawed. The 'other' is thus made in some sense normal. This position could be described as the 'we are *essentially* the same as you' approach. While such a position has a strategic usefulness because it can easily be wedded to arguments based on fairness, it also readily gives rise to problems of group definition. In particular, I suspect that the process of normalization that occurs through 'pro-gay' human rights discourse amounts to a 'desexualization' of a gay sexual orientation, which increasingly seems to be characterized within this model as an identity rather than as behaviour (to apply Hogg's terminology). Such a move is not unanticipated. The pattern of failure of lesbian and gay rights litigation under US equal protection law has stemmed largely from an inability to persuade courts to characterize the class that experiences discrimination as defined by anything other than a sexual act – sodomy.[66] Thus, because sodomy (between consenting adults in private) is not a constitutionally protected activity under US due process doctrine,[67] lesbians and gay men as a class are not entitled to heightened scrutiny under equal protection. An identity becomes not only completely sexualized, but defined exclusively in terms of one set of sexual practices.

In my view, the Canadian experience is the mirror image of the US approach. The acceptance of sexual orientation as a prohibited ground of discrimination implicitly has a normalizing function such that lesbian or gay male sexual/social practices, to the extent that they are not 'normal' (in the sense of not being readily redefinable as analogous to the dominant norms of heterosexuality), are rendered invisible or defined as 'other' to the protected class deserving of human rights protection. Normalization may thus be indistinguishable from containment and regulation. Queer identity, though, *defines* itself in terms of a rejection of normalcy and a refusal to be entrapped in the categories enunciated from the position of the dominant norm.[68] In that sense, it may well prove a valuable disruptive influence and, in the process, new queer identities may well come to be defined as 'other' to the legally normalized 'good' lesbian or gay man.

CONCLUSION

In this chapter I have sought to intervene in the debates surrounding human rights and sexual orientation by questioning some of the dominant understandings of sexuality as they emerge within legal discourse. In particular, I have focused on categorical thinking in anti-discrimination law and essentialist conceptions of identity.

However, the obvious question that this analysis raises is whether an alternative model can be developed that avoids the pitfalls of the current approach. This point has been touched upon by others. First, Nitya Iyer, in her discussion of categorical thinking, advocates a framework in which the individual must simply 'assert a particular social identity and show that his or her oppression arises from the hierarchical relationship between the dominant social identity and this identity'.[69] Categorical thinking is thus replaced by a focus on fluidity, mutability, contingency and the relational character of all identities. Secondly, Janet Halley, in her critique of essentialist argument in US constitutional law, argues that rather than looking to the personal characteristics of the members of the class under consideration, attention should instead turn to the 'interaction' both among members of the class and between the members of the class and others as to how 'the meaning and value of same-sex erotic desire' has been constructed.[70] Instead of essential definitions, she advocates an open recognition that identities are socially constructed and are both inscribed upon individuals as well as a product of the agency of members of the group. For the purposes of human rights law, the issue

234 Carl F. Stychin

then is the extent to which the state is implicated in the invidious social construction of identities and the social reality that results.[71] Thirdly, Didi Herman argues, from a process-based perspective, that rather than focus solely upon the outcomes of human rights litigation, we need also to look to the '*process* of change' – that is, we should interrogate legal rights struggles in terms of their capacity to provide a forum in which to 'communicate a sexual politics'.[72]

All of this suggests that our approach to human rights law in the area of anti-discrimination should emphasize a greater degree of self-reflexivity about identities, an awareness of their necessarily intersected character, and their social contingency and mutability. I would also advocate a closer relationship between law, legal theory, social theory and social practices so as to challenge the essentialist thinking that currently underpins much of this discourse. Finally, legal doctrine might be informed by a clearer recognition that identity is a product of social relations – that there exists a dynamic relationship between the background norm and identities that have been developed as 'other' to it. The relevance and coherence of any 'personal' characteristic is a social construction with a material reality that emerges through discourses such as law, including 'progressive' human rights law. An awareness of the power of law both to enable and empower as well as to regulate and contain may facilitate a critical awareness of the contradictions within the domain of human rights. As Iris Marion Young has suggested, a vision of a 'democratic cultural pluralism' must be tied to an emancipatory politics where group definition is understood not as essence, but as an ongoing process.[73] This analysis forces a critical re-examination of all categorical thinking to the extent that the fixation with categories may prove not only empowering but also constraining. Heterogeneity replaces the norm – other binary, and group identification, composition and membership become an ongoing political struggle with no logical or fixed outcome.

NOTES

1. See, for example, R. Wintemute, *Sexual Orientation and Human Rights* (Oxford: Oxford University Press, 1995); K. Waaldijk and A. Clapham (eds), *Homosexuality: A European Community Issue* (Dordrecht: Nijhoff, 1993); L. R. Helfer, Lesbian and gay rights as human rights: strategies for a united Europe [1991] *Virginia Journal of International Law* 157.

2. See generally P. Gabel, The phenomenology of rights-consciousness and the pact of the withdrawn selves (1984) 62 *Texas Law Review* 1563; P. Gabel and P. Harris, Building power and breaking images: critical legal theory and the practice of law (1982-1983) 11 *New York University Review of Law and Social Change* 369; D. Kennedy, The structure of Blackstone's Commentaries (1979) 28 *Buffalo Law Review* 209; M. Tushnet, An essay on rights (1984) 62 *Texas Law Review* 1363.

3. See, for example, M. J. Matsuda, Looking to the bottom: critical legal studies and reparations (1987) 22 *Harvard Civil Rights – Civil Liberties Law Review* 323; E. M. Schneider, The dialectic of rights and politics: perspectives from the Women's Movement (1986) 61 *New York University Law Review* 589; P. Williams, *The Alchemy of Race and Rights: Diary of a Law Professor* (Cambridge, MA: Harvard University Press, 1991); R. A. Williams Jr, Taking rights aggressively: the perils and promise of critical legal theory for peoples of color (1987) 5 *Law and Inequality* 103.

4. See generally D. Herman, *Rights of Passage: Struggles for Lesbian and Gay Legal Equality* (Toronto: University of Toronto Press, 1994).

5. For a discussion of one such struggle in Ontario, see D. Herman, The politics of law reform: lesbian and gay rights struggles in the 1990s. In J. Bristow and A. Wilson (eds), *Activating Theory: Lesbian, Gay, Bisexual Politics* (London: Lawrence & Wishart, 1993), p. 245.

6. Canadian Charter of Rights and Freedoms, Part I of the Constitution Act, 1982, being Schedule B to the Canada Act 1982 (UK), 1982, c. 11.

7. (1989) 56 DLR (4th) 1.

8. *Ibid.*, p. 18.

9. *Ibid.*

10. In addition, the rights entrenched in the Charter are subject to explicit limits:

s. 1. The Canadian Charter of Rights and Freedoms guarantees the rights and freedoms set out in it subject only to such reasonable limits prescribed by law as can be demonstrably justified in a free and democratic society.

s. 33 (1). Parliament or the legislature of a province may expressly declare in an Act of Parliament or of the legislature, as the case may be, that the Act or a provision thereof shall operate notwithstanding a provision included in section 2 or sections 7 to 15 of this Charter.

For an analysis of the operation of these sections, see B. McLachlin above, Chapter 2.

11. *Andrews*, p. 33.

12. *Ibid.*, p. 32.

13. See, for example, K. E. Mahoney, The Constitutional Law of Equality in Canada (1992) 44 *Maine Law Review* 229; N. C. Sheppard, Recognition of the disadvantaging of women: the promise of *Andrews* v. *Law Society of British Columbia* (1989) 35 *McGill Law Journal* 207; R. Colker, Section 1, Contextuality, and the Anti-disadvantage Principle (1992) 42 *University of Toronto Law Journal* 77.

14. See N. Iyer, Categorical denials: equality rights and the shaping of social identity (1993) 19 *Queen's Law Journal* 179.

15. *Ibid.*, p. 186.

16. Critical race theorists in the USA have highlighted the position of women of colour in this regard; see, for example, K. Crenshaw, Demarginalizing the intersection of race and sex: a black feminist critique of antidiscrimination doctrine, feminist theory and antiracist politics (1989) *University of Chicago Legal Forum* 139; T. Grillo and S. M. Wildman, Obscuring the importance of race: the implications of making comparisons between racism and sexism (or other-isms) (1991) *Duke Law Journal* 397; A. P. Harris, Race and essentialism in feminist legal theory (1990) 42 *Stanford Law Review* 581. For an analysis of complex inequality claims in the context of sexual orientation, see M. Eaton, Patently confused: complex inequality and *Canada* v. *Mossop* (1994) 1 *Review of Constitutional Studies* 203 (considering the relationship of sexual orientation and family status discrimination); M. Eaton, Homosexual unmodified: speculations on law's discourse, race, and the construction of sexual identity. In D. Herman and C. Stychin (eds), *Legal Inversions: Lesbians, Gay Men, and the Politics of Law* (Philadelphia: Temple University Press, 1995), p. 46 (considering the relationship of race and sexual orientation).

17. See D. Herman, The politics of law reform, *op. cit.*

18. This trend culminated in the unanimous ruling of the Supreme Court of Canada that 'sexual orientation discrimination' by the state falls within the ambit of the equality rights guar-

antees of the Canadian Charter. See *Egan and Nesbit* v. *The Queen*, (1995) 124 DLR (4th) 609.

19. (1993) 9 OR (2d) 495. A similar judgment, turning on the absence of 'sexual orientation' in the Alberta Individual Rights Protection Act, was reached in *Vriend* v. *Alberta* (1994) 6 WWR 414 (Alta. QB).

20. *Haig*, p. 503.

21. *Ibid.*, p. 508.

22. See, for example, the dissenting judgment of Linden J in *Egan et al.* v. *The Queen in Right of Canada* (1993), 103 DLR (4th) 336 (Fed. CA), at p. 355: 'As with enumerated grounds such as race and sex, a person's sexual orientation has been a basis for discrimination and persecution throughout history.'

23. C. S. Vance, Social construction theory: problems in the history of sexuality. In H. Crowley and S. Himmelweit (eds), *Knowing Women: Feminism and Knowledge* (Milton Keynes: Open University Press, 1992), p. 132, at p. 134.

24. See generally E. Stein (ed.), *Forms of Desire: Sexual Orientation and the Social Constructionist Controversy* (New York: Routledge, 1992).

25. *Andrews*, p. 39.

26. P. Hogg, *Constitutional Law of Canada*, 3rd edn (Toronto: Carswell, 1992).

27. *Ibid.*, p. 1167.

28. *Ibid.*, p. 1168.

29. *Ibid.*, (emphasis mine).

30. *Ibid.*, p. 1170.

31. (1989) 1 FC 321, at pp. 370–1.

32. See, for example, J. Bakan, Book Review: Hogg, *Constitutional Law of Canada* (1993) 51 *The Advocate* (*British Columbia*) 607.

33. It has been argued that the recent explosion of 'scientific' explanations of 'homosexuality' is giving rise to a renewed interest in immutability arguments within legal (and other) discourses; see generally J. E. Halley, Sexual orientation and the politics of biology: a critique of the argument from immutability (1994) 46 *Stanford Law Review* 503.

34. N. Iyer, Categorical denials, *op. cit.*, p. 189. The relationship between the concepts of 'immutability' and 'essentialism' is not uncontested. I use the terms in the sense in which they have been employed by Janet Halley. See J. E. Halley, Sexual orientation and the politics of biology, *op. cit.*, pp. 516–7:

> [A]n *essentialist* view of homosexual orientation claims that it is a deep-rooted, fixed, and intrinsic feature of individuals. This essentialist view assumes that homosexual orientation is determined (by nature or nurture), not chosen ... The *constructivist* view of homosexual orientation claims that it is a contingent, socially malleable trait that arises in a person as she manages her world, its meanings, and her desires. The pro-gay argument from immutability is, on these definitions, essentialist. When the pro-gay argument from immutability adds a reliance on biological causation theories, it merely locates the source of determination in nature.

35. D. Herman, The politics of law reform, *op. cit.*, p. 250.

36. It has been argued that the essentialist/constructivist dispute is in fact a cluster of separate controversies, such as realism/nominalism; determinism/freedom; nature/nurture; biology/culture; binarism/pluralism. See generally E. Stein, *Forms of Desire, op. cit.* However, I remain of the view that the essentialist/constructivist divide is a meaningful way of analysing legal discourse in this area.

37. S. Epstein, Gay politics, ethnic identity: the limits of social constructionism. In E. Stein (ed.), *Forms of Desire, op. cit.*, p. 239, at pp. 250–1.

38. I do not mean to suggest by any means that all 'pro-gay' participants in the judicial, activist and political arenas advocate an essentialist approach. On the complexity of the debates in Canada and for examples of anti-essentialist arguments, see B. Cossman, Family inside/out (1994) 44 *University of Toronto Law Journal* 1; J. Freeman, Defining family in *Mossop* v. *DSS*: the challenge of anti-essentialism and interactive discrimination for human rights litigation (1994) 44 *University of Toronto Law Journal* 41.

39. I agree with Susan Boyd that useful insights can be gleaned both from an analysis of

ideology and from discourse theory. See S. Boyd, Some postmodernist challenges to feminist analyses of law, family and state: ideology and discourse in child custody law (1991) 10 *Canadian Journal of Family Law* 79, at p. 98: 'Ideology can not be reduced to discourse because one loses a sense of how discourses have wide ramifications and connections with material relations. Nor can discourse be reduced to ideology, as the concept of discourse allows us to focus on sites in which particular knowledges, including counter discourses, are produced, and is a more particularistic concept in this regard.'

40. D. Herman, The politics of law reform, *op. cit.*, p. 251.

41. See M. S. Kimmel, Sexual Balkanization: gender and sexuality as the new ethnicities (1993) 60 *Social Research* 571, at p. 579, for a discussion of empirical research conducted on essentialist/social construction positions among lesbians and gay men (citing V. Whishman, The social construction of essentialism among gay men and lesbians, unpublished PhD dissertation, New York University, 1992).

42. *Ibid.*, p. 579.

43. I do not mean to suggest that law alone has the power so radically to alter the position of gay men within society. Rather, I aim simply to highlight the different positions occupied by lesbians and gay men within the social order and the logical outcome of essentialist thinking.

44. For an example of this failure to distinguish the material reality of life as a lesbian versus gay man, see the judgment of Linden J in *Egan, op. cit.* note 22, p. 355: 'Gay men and lesbians are legally, economically, socially and politically disadvantaged.' Linden J nowhere seeks to distinguish the ways in which members of the two groups may be differently positioned. While lesbians *qua* women undoubtedly are economically disadvantaged in society (and perhaps are disadvantaged *qua* lesbians), no evidence is provided for the assertion that gay men are economically disadvantaged as men (leaving aside other potential bases of economic oppression such as race and physical ability).

45. See *High Tech Gays* v. *Defense Indus. Sec. Clearance Office*, 909 F 2d 375, 377 (9th Cir. 1990) (Canby J, dissenting); *Watkins* v. *United States Army*, 875 F 2d 699, 726 (9th Cir. 1989) (en banc) (Norris J, concurring); *Jantz* v. *Muci*, 759 F Supp. 1543, 1548 (D. Kan. 1991). Recently, there have been some gay victories through successful arguments that discrimination on the basis of sexual orientation fails 'rational basis' review (which does not require a determination of the immutability of the characteristic); see *Meinhold* v. *US Department of Defense*, 808 F Supp. 1455 (CD Cal. 1993); *Steffan* v. *Aspin*, 8 F 3d 57 (DC Cir. 1993); *Dahl* v. *Secretary of the United States Navy*, 830 F Supp. 1319 (MD Fla. 1993).

46. See, for example, *High Tech Gays* v. *Defense Indus. Sec. Clearance Office*, 895 F 2d 563 (9th Cir. 1990); *Woodward* v. *United States*, 871 F 2d 1068 (Fed. Cir. 1989); *Steffan* v. *Cheney*, 780 F Supp. 1 (DDC 1991). For an interesting and persuasive argument that *both* racial and sexual identities, rather than being essential characteristics, are 'active practices' that are 'ascribed, asserted, avowed, and indeed, disavowed' through 'a constellation of practices,' see K. Thomas, The eclipse of reason: a rhetorical reading of *Bowers* v. *Hardwick* (1993) 79 *Virginia Law Review* 1805, at pp. 1806–7.

47. See, for example, *Woodward* v. *United States* (homosexuals do not constitute a suspect class because the defining characteristic is not immutable); *Jantz* v. *Muci*: 'to discriminate against individuals who accept their given sexual orientation and refuse to alter that orientation to conform to societal norms does significant violence to a central and defining character of those individuals' (at p. 1548).

48. See J. E. Halley, Sexual orientation and the politics of biology *op. cit.*, pp. 513–4, where the author argues that although US courts have displayed a reluctance to accept the immutability argument, 'strong biological evidence . . . might alter future judicial outcomes. Several courts have noted that the *controversy* over biological causation is a reason to reject the argument from immutability, a rationale that might cut the other way if the scientific community were to reach consensus on the etiology of homosexual orientation.'

49. An example of the unproblematic use of the term can be found in R. Wintemute, Sexual orientation discrimination. In C. McCrudden and G. Chambers (eds), *Individual Rights and the Law in Britain* (Oxford: Clarendon Press, 1994), p. 491, at p. 492: 'a person's sexual orientation is the *direction* (to the opposite sex, the same sex, both, or neither) of their attraction to emotional-sexual conduct, or of their actual choice of emotional-sexual

conduct. In addition, each specific instance of emotional-sexual conduct (e.g. a sexual act or a partnership) can also be said to have a sexual orientation, in that (if it involves two persons) it will necessarily be either heterosexual or same-sex'.

50. See D. R. Ortiz, Creating controversy: essentialism and constructivism and the politics of gay identity (1993) 79 *Virginia Law Review* 1833.

51. See C. Calhoun, Denaturalizing and desexualizing lesbian and gay identity (1993) 79 *Virginia Law Review* 1859.

52. *Ibid.*, p. 1872.

53. See M. Warner, Introduction. In M. Warner (ed.), *Fear of a Queer Planet* (Minneapolis: University of Minnesota Press, 1993), p. vii.

54. E. Kosofsky Sedgwick, Queer and now, in *Tendencies* (Durham, NC: Duke University Press, 1993), p. 9.

55. See J. Butler, *Bodies That Matter* (New York: Routledge, 1993), p. 228.

56. S. Seidman, Identity and politics in a 'postmodern' gay culture: some historical and conceptual notes. In M. Warner (ed.), *Fear of a Queer Planet, op. cit.*, p. 105, at p. 131.

57. See J. Butler, *Bodies That Matter, op. cit.*, pp. 226–30.

58. Queer social *practices* also focus on the disruption of boundaries and categories, particularly those centring upon 'space'; see L. Berlant and E. Freeman, Queer nationality. In M. Warner (ed.), *Fear of a Queer Planet, op. cit.*, p. 193.

59. Some trans-gendered persons also claim to challenge rigid categorical thinking in terms of gender. The application of the categories of 'sexual orientation' and 'sex' to discrimination against trans-gendered persons on that basis is an interesting one, but beyond the scope of this chapter.

60. Of course, the idea of sexual 'choice' is itself a contestable concept. Bisexual persons in one sense may have a choice about the gender of their sex partners, but no choice as to the fact that they may experience sexual attraction across the gender divide. Thus, the existence of bisexuality does not *necessarily* advance the social constructivist case. However, my view is that arguments grounded in immutability in general sit very uneasily with bisexuality as a sexual identity.

61. See J. E. Halley, Sexual orientation and the politics of biology, *op. cit.*, pp. 527-8. It should go without saying that demanding such a 'choice' is profoundly unfair, but that is for reasons unconnected with immutability, such as the insult to the dignity of the individual and the security of the person.

62. *Ibid.*, p. 518.

63. D. Herman, Are we family?: lesbian rights and women's liberation (1990) 28 *Osgoode Hall Law Journal* 789, at p. 813.

64. See D. R. Ortiz, Creating controversy, *op. cit.*

65. See generally J. Butler, *Bodies That Matter, op. cit.*, pp. 1-12.

66. See, for example, *Padula* v. *Webster*, 822 F 2d 97, 103 (DC Cir. 1987); *High Tech Gays* v. *Defense Indus. Sec. Clearance Office*, 895 F 2d 563, 571 (9th Cir. 1990); *Ben-Shalom* v. *Marsh*, 881 F 2d 454, 464–5 (7th Cir. 1989).

67. *Bowers* v. *Hardwick*, 478 US 186 (1986).

68. Whether queer culture achieves this goal is open to debate and disagreement. For a critical appraisal of queer political strategies, see A. Wilson, Is transgression transgressive? In J. Bristow and A. Wilson (eds), *Activating Theory, op. cit.*, p. 107.

69. N. Iyer, Categorical denials, *op. cit.*, p. 190.

70. J. E. Halley, Sexual orientation and the politics of biology, *op. cit.*, p. 563.

71. *Ibid.*, p. 566.

72. D. Herman, The politics of law reform, *op. cit.*, p. 260.

73. I. M. Young, *Justice and the Politics of Difference* (Princeton: Princeton University Press, 1990), p. 163. Young argues that 'the politics of difference . . . aims for an understanding of group difference as indeed ambiguous, relational, shifting, without clear borders that keep people straight – as entailing neither amorphous unity nor pure individuality' (at p. 171).

11

A Right To Meritorious Treatment

Donal Nolan

If I were to apply for a job in telesales, and I was rejected on the grounds
that my eyes were blue, I would be aggrieved. If, on the other hand, I
was turned away from a job modelling eye make-up for the same reason,
I might well be disappointed, but I would not consider myself to be a
victim of injustice. Similarly, I would feel that I had been wronged if I was
sacked from a telesales job because of my eye colour, but not if I was dismissed from a modelling job as a result of an absence of products shown
off best by blue eyes. Why do I feel disappointment in the latter cases,
and a sense of having been treated unfairly in the former? The answer,
of course, is that eye colour is (or at least may be) relevant to a modelling
job, but not to a telesales job. My sense of injustice stems from the fact
that I have been judged on something that is not connected with my
ability to do the job. Another way of putting it is to say that I have not
been treated *meritoriously*.[1] Am I right to feel aggrieved? I will argue that
I am, and that I have a right to meritorious treatment which the telesales
company has violated. Whether this violation means that I have any legal
right to redress will depend on my case being covered by enacted legislation on anti-discrimination and unfair dismissal, which can plausibly be
regarded as legal realizations of a right to meritorious treatment.

In this chapter I will argue that a right to meritorious treatment provides an embraceable interpretation of the law of anti-discrimination and
unfair dismissal. The discussion is limited to employment, but is, with
modifications, equally applicable to the allocation of other societal goods,
such as housing and education. I hope to show that this interpretation is
both more intellectually consistent and more politically appealing than
previous theories, and that it fits the relevant legal rules more closely.[2] As
a result of this close 'fit', where I criticize aspects of those legal rules my
claim is that the law is internally inconsistent, and that a particular legal
rule needs to be reformed in order to reconcile it with the principles
underlying the legislation. It seems to me that such an internal critique
has considerable advantages over an external critique which either
openly rejects the principles behind the law, or simply fails to conform
with the fundamental provisions of the legislation. These advantages are

particularly clear where the criticism is directed at judicial interpretation of the legislation, or at the inadequacy of enforcement mechanisms. My argument is that the right these laws protect is relatively uncontroversial, and that it provides powerful support for those who wish to see the scope of the legislation extended, and the protections it affords strengthened.

THE INADEQUACY OF ORTHODOXY

The two main arguments which have been used to justify anti-discrimination legislation are the 'equality' theory and the 'disadvantage' theory. According to the equality approach, everyone is entitled to an 'equal opportunity' to compete for jobs and other societal goods, and they are denied this if they are discriminated against because of their race, gender etc.[3] As Westen[4] has forcefully argued, however, equality is a vacuous concept, and 'equality analysis logically collapses into rights analysis.'[5] Absolute equality of opportunity is not feasible, since recruitment decisions must depend on factors such as intelligence, technical skills and the like. Thus 'equality of opportunity' must, if it is to be coherent, mean a right to be judged on one's merits. As presently formulated, however, this theory simply holds that certain grounds for decisions are illegitimate (e.g. race). This procedural approach makes it inflexible and incapable of distinguishing between discriminatory practices that injure dominant groups (such as white males) and those that injure oppressed groups (such as blacks and women).

The disadvantage theory holds that the purpose of anti-discrimination law is to remedy group disadvantage. MacKinnon defines discrimination as the 'systematic disadvantagement of social groups',[6] and Fiss[7] has argued that the neutral anti-discrimination principle (which states that race- or sex-dependent decisions are presumptively wrongful) is too restrictive, and should be replaced with a 'group disadvantage principle' which would render a practice unlawful if it 'aggravates . . . the subordinate position of a specially disadvantaged group'.[8] The theoretical weakness of the group disadvantage approach is that it fails to explain why only some disadvantaged groups are considered worthy of legal assistance. People with low intelligence, for example, are surely a 'disadvantaged group'. Either *all* disadvantaged groups are to be protected from discrimination, in which case the theory is advocating pure egalitarianism in the distribution of employment opportunities (a recipe for economic catastrophe), or else only those groups which are *unjustifiably* discriminated against are to be protected, in which case, again, the analysis collapses into the claim that people should be treated on their merits. As Tribe points out, the focus on certain groups, and the classification of them as disadvantaged, arises out of disagreement with the judgements that lie behind their treatment.[9] There are also several practical difficulties with this theory. First, it raises the problem of categorization. By focusing on protected *groups* rather than on prohibited *grounds*, the disadvantage approach forces the complainant to slot into one of the disadvantaged categories in order to obtain redress.[10] This is problematic for the individual who is a member of more than one disadvantaged group, and causes difficulties where characteristics are impossible to classify along rigid dividing lines, as with sexual orientation and race. In addition, it may be very difficult to establish whether an individual is a member of a particular group.[11] Second, the theory unduly limits the scope of anti-discrimination law. In order to qualify for protection in the Fiss scheme, for example, a group must have an 'identity' and a 'distinct existence apart from its members', and must be in a position of 'perpetual subordination' and 'severely circumscribed' political power.[12] Those subjected to discrimination on grounds of religious belief, sexual orientation and age would be left without a legal remedy. And finally, the disadvantage theory has political disadvantages because it lacks universality, and because it does not fit with the neutrality of much anti-discrimination legislation (e.g. the Sex Discrimination Act 1975 in the UK).

Theoretical justifications of unfair dismissal legislation are thin on the ground. The argument that such laws are a recognition of an employee's 'property right' in his or her job must fail, since it is plainly contradicted by the ability of management to dismiss for a good reason, and because any such right would have disastrous consequences for the general welfare.[13] The rights-based thesis put forward by Collins[14] is more persuasive, and is close to the view put forward in this chapter, although Collins himself does not identify merit as a foundational concept.

The theoretical weaknesses of all the orthodox theories derive from the way in which they ignore the significance of merit. Merit is the 'missing link', which explains why certain grounds for decision are illegitimate according to the equality theory (they are not relevant to job performance), why certain disadvantaged groups are singled out for protection under the disadvantage theory (they have historically been subjected to negative treatment not founded on considerations of merit), and why certain grounds of dismissal are acceptable and others not (a dismissal is only justified where the employee's behaviour is incompatible with the needs of the job). In practice, the two orthodox theories in the anti-discrimination context present the progressive with a Catch-22 scenario. The equality approach suggests a *widening* of the scope of anti-discrimination law to include more illegitimate factors (such as age), but its inflexibility precludes a *deepening* of protection, since programmes of positive discrimination are in irreconcilable conflict with the neutrality principle, while the disadvantage approach suggests a deepening of protection, but provides no justification for a widening of scope. The right to meritorious treatment provides a way out of this conundrum.

UTILITY, AUTONOMY AND DIGNITY

As Scanlon states,[15] 'rights . . . need to be justified somehow, and how other than by appeal to the human interests their recognition promotes and protects?' A right to meritorious treatment is necessary to protect three valuable human interests, namely utility, autonomy and dignity.[16]

Meritorious treatment is efficient, and therefore promotes the general welfare. Market failures occur as a result of the prejudices and whims of those in positions of economic power, and these are corrected by laws promoting merit. Specifically, discriminatory hiring wastes the skills of those excluded from jobs for irrelevant reasons,[17] while meritorious treatment provides an incentive to acquire the skills necessary for efficient production.[18] Unfair dismissal legislation encourages employers to take more care to select the best people in the first place and may make the workers more committed to the company and therefore more productive, while allowing employers to replace inefficient workers with more efficient ones where necessary. By improving productive efficiency, a right to meritorious treatment increases the overall wealth of society, and this extra wealth can then be used to enhance the autonomy and dignity of those left behind in the meritocratic race.[19] Thus, it is possible to say that the utility interests protected by the right are a moral argument for the recognition of the right.

A right to meritorious treatment also enhances individual autonomy. Raz describes the ideal of personal autonomy as 'the vision of people controlling, to some degree, their own destiny'.[20] If we wish to control our life in work to any meaningful extent we must know on what basis employment decisions will be made. There is an analogy with the rule of law, which, says Hayek,[21] means that 'government . . . is bound by rules . . . which make it possible to foresee with fair certainty how the authority will use its coercive powers . . . and to plan one's individual affairs on the basis of this knowledge'. It is much more difficult for a person 'to bring meaning to his or her life through work'[22] if decisions are made arbitrarily and on the basis of factors which have not been publicized.

Thus, the law of unfair dismissal can increase workers' autonomy by requiring that employers publish disciplinary codes, and apply them fairly.[23] As for recruitment decisions, our expectation that we will be judged by reference to certain criteria induces us to act in the way that we think is most likely to enhance our employment prospects, by studying hard, taking vocational courses, taking care over the application form and so on.

However, this principle of 'legitimate expectation'[24] does not explain why some considerations should be illegitimate and others not – after all, a clear policy that no jobs will ever be given to women, or that employees who are found to be gay will be sacked, would be action-guiding. There are four reasons why meritorious treatment itself enhances autonomy, and is therefore the preferable guiding principle. First, the efficiency of the merit principle means that it creates more wealth, and therefore more jobs, than other systems, thereby enhancing the autonomy of those who would otherwise be unemployed. Second, the variety of jobs available, all of which require different qualities and aptitudes, means that individuals have a wide choice of occupations, and can decide which of their natural skills to develop. A related point is that many of the qualities that are meritorious in a particular field (e.g. typing speed) can be acquired, so the choices available are not limited completely by the need to possess an immutable characteristic (as would be the case in, say, a caste system, where the caste one is born into determines one's occupation). And, finally, by forcing employers to make their personnel decisions solely on the basis of merit, the extent to which the employer can interfere with a worker's behaviour both within and outside the workplace is severely restricted.[25] Individuals will be free to act in whatever way they please, safe in the knowledge that their behaviour will only blight their employment prospects where it can realistically be said to diminish their ability to do a particular job. Thus, an adequate selection of employment opportunities cannot unjustifiably be made to depend upon a reduction in autonomy in other areas of our lives.

Non-meritorious treatment infringes the dignity of the worker because it amounts to a failure to treat him or her with equal concern and respect.[26] As Campbell puts it: 'To be discriminated against . . . is to be insulted.'[27] If a job applicant is turned down because she is a lesbian, this usually indicates that the employer thinks less of her because of her sexual orientation. The employer's contemptuous treatment of the applicant amounts to a denial of due respect for her. Where someone is rejected for reasons of merit, by contrast, the employer's behaviour is grounded not in disrespect for the applicant but in a legitimate concern to promote the interests of his or her business and the general welfare.[28] In the dismissal context, as Collins points out,[29] failure by the employer to give an employee a fair hearing before dismissing him or her for misconduct is also disrespectful. Likewise, objective selection procedures and the application of equal opportunities policies are a form of procedural justice which show concern for the interests of job applicants. Where non-meritorious treatment of one kind is widespread it will be particularly disrespectful, since it will appear to be a community judgment rather than the isolated whim of an irrational individual, and will therefore convey a special social meaning that will stigmatize the affected group, and damage the self-esteem of its members. It is no surprise, then, that the European Commission of Human Rights has held that racial discrimination can constitute 'degrading treatment'.[30]

For all these reasons, and particularly because the losers in the meritocratic race can be compensated from the extra wealth that the merit system generates, it can be assumed that we would all choose merit as the preferred method of allocation of employment opportunities if we were under a 'veil of ignorance' concerning our own individual abilities.[31]

The cost of implementing a general right to meritorious treatment would be prohibitive, so a *de minimis* principle is applied. Whether the right is legally protected in a particular situation will depend on two factors: the interest affected by the non-meritorious treatment, and the amount of discrimination based on the particular characteristic in question. There is a hierarchy of interests, with an existing job at the top, the opportunity of promotion within a company in the middle, and the possibility of a new job at the bottom. This hierarchy is consistent with two of the interests that ground the right to meritorious treatment. Dismissal is a serious threat to an individual's autonomy; he or she may lose money, friends and social status all in one go, and there is no guarantee in present conditions of replacement employment, particularly if the manner of the dismissal harms his or her professional reputation.[32] The time and effort that they have invested in their work may be completely wasted. Where promotions are in issue, the reduction in autonomy is less severe than in dismissal, since the employee retains his or her job, but more severe than in the context of applications, because usually promotion is the most obvious career advance, and therefore employees will invest their energies in seeking promotion, unlike most external job applicants, who will cast their net wider, and be less affected by any one particular recruitment decision. In addition, in both the dismissal and promotion situations, an employee may well have foregone opportunities outside the company in reliance on their expectation that their future treatment by their employer would be meritorious. The catastrophic effect of dismissal makes an unmeritorious or arbitrary dismissal more demeaning and insulting than an unfair recruitment decision, and, again, promotion decisions are in between these extremes; treating someone who applies for promotion unmeritoriously or cavalierly (e.g. by denying them an explanation of a decision not to promote) is more of an infringement of their dignity than it would be if they were an external applicant, and yet not as insulting as it would be in the dismissal scenario.

It is no surprise, therefore, that in the dismissal context the right to meritorious treatment is fully realized. Where applications for employment are concerned, in contrast, the right is realized in a more limited way, and disallows reliance on an irrelevant consideration only where there is evidence of significant (i.e. widespread) discrimination on the basis of it. This is reasonable, since only where there is significant discrimination is legal action worthwhile (the benefits will outweigh the implementation costs) and necessary (because affected individuals may suffer a serious diminution in their employment prospects, and are more likely to feel stigmatized). This explains why different factors are proscribed in different societies; religious belief in Northern Ireland, race in the USA, caste in India and so on. If a society existed where there was widespread discrimination based on eye colour, then legal action against such discrimination would also be required. The distinction between promotion and applications, however, is not reflected in UK law, and has been overlooked in the US case law on positive discrimination, where the courts have tended to treat schemes that detrimentally affect the advancement prospects of existing employees as analogous to those that only affect external applicants.[33]

RECONSTRUCTING MERIT

My definition of merit is a modification of two of the three definitions proposed by Fallon.[34] Merit is 'the possession of those qualities needed to perform a functionally defined task or to produce valued results within a specific context'. In other words, merit means ability to do, or suitability for, the job in question. Merit is by its very nature a social construct. The qualities that are 'meritorious' depend on the nature of the task in question, and it is those in positions of economic power who decide which qualities are needed for which task. It has been forcefully argued, therefore, that since white men have a hugely disproportionate amount of power in society, ideas of merit will inevitably reflect the prejudices and self-interest of this dominant group. The skills of women (which may, of course, be themselves socially constructed) and, to a lesser extent, blacks will be undervalued, and those of white men will be overvalued.[35] It is therefore pointless to try to harness merit as a vehicle for improving the position of the disadvantaged. This is an unduly pessimistic view. The key to the transformation of merit from an instrument of oppression into one of liberation is its reconstruction, or objectification. While completely objective standards may be unrealistic, society as a whole can enunciate fairer guidelines than can those who are presently in powerful positions in the workplace. Attempts to objectify merit have until now been less than successful, but this has been the result of a failure of will on the part of those entrusted with the task (usually the judiciary) rather than proof of the inherent futility of the exercise. By focusing on the concept rather than ignoring it, it is hoped that the process of objectification will be accelerated.

In order to objectify merit, we must objectify the employer. We can do this by reference to Kant's proscription of self-preference in acting. Roughly, this amounts to the principle that you ought not to do to others what you would not do to yourself. We can determine what is meritorious by asking what we would consider to be the relevant skills for a task if we were ignorant of our own personal characteristics (including our gender, race etc. as well as our particular aptitudes), and did not know whether we were employers or employees. Our decisions as to merit in this 'original position'[36] would then be truly objective, for, as Dworkin points out, 'men who do not know to which class they belong cannot design institutions, consciously or unconsciously, to favor their own class.'[37] By objectifying merit in this way, we overcome the problem of dominant group bias. Of course it is impossible to determine exactly what decisions we would make under such a veil of ignorance, but if we are to have just employment laws we must at least try. My argument is that the laws against discrimination and unfair dismissal are attempts to force employers to make the decisions they would make about their workforce composition if they were in the original position.

There are four other points that should be made about the meaning of merit. First, tests that purport to be 'merit tests' (e.g. the Scholastic Aptitude Test used in US university admissions) are clearly nothing of the sort if they are culturally biased in some way. The argument that such tests are unfair is therefore not, properly understood, an argument against merit.[38] In general, there is a danger in adopting an overly scientific approach to the testing of merit, and this chapter is in no way an endorsement of the use of such clumsy devices as IQ tests or psychometric testing in the employment arena. At the same time, my second point is that analytical approaches which separate out the qualities required for a job, and judge applicants on these, are likely to produce more meritorious results than subjective approaches that rely on the employer's 'gut reaction'. This explains why such analytical methods are usually required by equal opportunities policies. Third, since merit is suitability for the job *to be* done, it is forward-looking, and employers should therefore assess the potential of applicants as well as the qualifications and experience that they already possess; this will assist, for example, women in academic jobs who have fewer publications than their peers because they have taken time out of their careers to raise children. And finally, there will be some jobs where factors such as race and gender will be relevant to ability to do the job well, and where they may therefore be legitimately taken into account. As well as the obvious examples, like acting and modelling, this might include jobs involving personal interaction, where being of a particular race or gender might be preferable in order that the employee can better empathize with the client group, or in order to provide 'role models' for students, say, from minority ethnic groups.[39] Indeed, it is possible that ethnic or gender diversity in itself may improve the working atmosphere in a firm, and bring new and valuable insights into the decision-making process.[40] In all these cases the decision is meritorious even though dependent on the race or gender of the applicant or employee; the mistaken belief that these are examples of positive discrimination results from an unnecessarily narrow and insular definition of the job in question.[41]

THREE OBJECTIONS

I want to deal now with three common objections which are made to arguments based on merit. I hope to show that these objections are not insuperable obstacles to the proposition that there exists a right to meritorious treatment.

The first objection is that many of the characteristics that constitute 'merit', such as intelligence, are largely a result of native ability and situational advantages and are therefore no evidence of moral worth. Thus, it is argued that a meritocracy is unjust, because the distribution of resources is made to depend upon criteria that are morally irrelevant.[42] This reasoning is convincing, but it only defeats arguments for meritocracy that are based on desert. My point is not that people should be treated meritoriously because they deserve to have their meritorious qualities rewarded,[43] but rather that meritorious treatment is right because it is efficient and protective of individuals' autonomy and dignity. Furthermore, my position is not that the final distribution of societal wealth should be based on merit, but only that the distribution of employment opportunities should be. Indeed, part of the justification for the merit principle is that the extra wealth it creates can be redistributed to improve the position of the most disadvantaged.

The second objection to merit is that, due to past discrimination and continuing inequalities in the provision of educational services and so forth, the participants in the meritocratic race have unequal starting points.[44] This argument has particular force where one group has consistently been the subject of institutionalized discrimination in educational provision as was the case until recently in South Africa. There are four reasons why this objection does not defeat the argument for meritorious treatment. First, the focus of recruitment decisions should be on the applicant's potential, and the merit principle therefore disallows unjustified reliance on formal qualifications or experience. Second, the interests of efficiency, autonomy and dignity which underlie the right to meritorious treatment also require the state to ensure that the provision of educational resources is fair and equal, and this should, in time, mean that the inequality of starting points is diminished. Third, as I argue below, recognition of the right to meritorious treatment does not rule out measures of positive discrimination which may be used to remedy the problem of unequal starting points. And finally, if inequalities persist, those who suffer from situational disadvantages can be compensated by redistributive measures where necessary.

The third objection relates to discriminatory third party preferences. Suppose that a particular London pub has a clientele which consists primarily of white racists. A position as a bartender in the pub is advertised, and there are two applicants. One of the applicants is black and the other white. The black applicant is a better bartender, but the pub's manager appoints the white applicant, not because the manager is himself or herself a racist, but because he or she knows that if they employ a black bartender they will lose most of their custom.[45] The difficulty for the merit principle here is that the black bartender has not been treated unmeritoriously; after all, suitability for the job depends on race, and therefore race appears to be a legitimate consideration. I hope to show that the right to meritorious treatment does not compel us to accept the counterintuitive proposition that in this case the black bartender should have no legal redress against the pub manager, or the alternative proposition that, if the law compels the manager to accept the black applicant, the white applicant's right to meritorious treatment would be unjustifiably violated.

If we take a formalistic view, the right to meritorious treatment appears to require that the white bartender be taken on, but if we look behind the formal right to the underlying interests that it protects, the picture becomes less clear. First, the utility interest in appointing the white applicant is weak, since doing so is productively inefficient (the black bartender is better at pulling pints, after all), and the 'efficiency' of the white bartender depends upon the irrational prejudice of the customers. Second, it would be a nonsense to say that not appointing the white applicant would infringe his or her dignity, since the decision is simply taken because he or she is not as good a bartender. On the contrary, it is the dignity of the black applicant which is violated if he or she is rejected because of the contempt that the customers feel for black people. And finally, the appointment of the black bartender in such a situation will not significantly affect the autonomy of white jobseekers, whereas satisfying the preferences of racists may compromise the autonomy of blacks who wish to work in service industries. Thus, the interests underlying the right to meritorious treatment seem to point to the appointment of the black bartender, while the formal right itself requires that the white person gets the job.

One way of dealing with this contradiction is to say that it is illogical to invoke the right to meritorious treatment to protect the white applicant in this situation, since to do so would defeat the objects of the recognition of the right in the first place. An alternative approach would be to say that the interests of dignity and autonomy also ground another right, which is separate from, but considerably overlaps with, the right to meritorious treatment, such as a right to be free from adverse treatment grounded in contempt for one's race. In the bartender situation, this new right easily defeats the weakened right to meritorious treatment to justify either a private decision by the pub manager to appoint the black bartender, or a legal rule requiring that he or she be selected.

ANTI-DISCRIMINATION LAW

The Characteristics Subject to Legal Protection

The merit principle points the way to an expansion of the scope of anti-discrimination law, to include all cases where there is significant discrimination. There should be no requirement that the group(s) affected by the discrimination be 'specially disadvantaged'. Discrimination on grounds of religious or political belief, sexual orientation, physical or mental disability, HIV status[46] and age[47] should be made unlawful, if they are not already. Workers should also be protected against discrimination resulting from previous trade union activity or legal action by them in the employment context, and the practice of blacklisting should be outlawed. Other irrelevant factors, such as socio-economic origin, accent[48] and appearance[49] could also be candidates for legislation, although the practical difficulties involved in implementing such laws make their enactment unlikely (consider the difficulties of proof faced by tribunals in the race and sex discrimination fields).

At the moment, British law is woefully inadequate in this respect. Only race, gender and trade union membership[50] (and non-membership) are protected. You are protected against discrimination on the ground that you are married, but not on the ground that you are single. In Northern Ireland religious belief and political opinion are covered (but not race), and these, at the very least, should be extended to the rest of the UK.[51] Parliament looks set to pass legislation against disability discrimination,[52] but action against sexual orientation discrimination seems unlikely in the near future.

In the USA, federal legislation outlaws discrimination on grounds of race, gender, disability and age, and a number of states and cities have banned sexual orientation discrimination. In addition the courts have developed the concept of a 'suspect classification' to determine the extent to which governmental bodies have to come up with a compelling interest to justify discriminatory actions, if they are not to fall foul of the equal protection clause of the constitution. In *Watkins* v. *US Army*,[53] a Circuit Court of Appeals held that sexual orientation was a suspect classification. The reasoning of the court is instructive. Two factors in the decision were that there was a history of discrimination against gays, and that they were lacking in political power. There was thus a *need* for protection, and it was unlikely to come from the legislature. The other two considerations were that sexual orientation is irrelevant to performance in society (i.e. it is not likely to be a meritorious quality), and that it is immutable. This last point is relevant, because where a characteristic is mutable, discrimination based on it is unlikely seriously to reduce the autonomy of those affected in the context of their working lives, since their possession of it is a matter of choice.[54] Mutability is a double-edged sword, however, for where a characteristic is mutable, discrimination on that ground may have the invidious effect of forcing workers to abandon their preferred lifestyles in order to obtain work of a particular kind;[55] it would therefore be quite wrong to suppose that mutability in itself excuses discrimination. Nevertheless, the approach taken in the *Watkins* case is broadly consistent with the right to meritorious treatment.

Direct Discrimination

Discrimination in the human rights context can be defined as unmeritorious treatment. Thus, we do not say that a person who is turned away from an accounts job because of their poor maths has been discriminated against, but we would term the employer's conduct discrimination if they were not chosen because of their race or sexual orientation. Direct discrimination occurs when an employer makes a protected characteristic a criterion for job selection and either it is wholly irrelevant to the work in question or it is given unjustifiable weight in the decision-making process. The neutrality of the legislation (which protects whites as well as blacks and so on) fits well with the merit principle, and the defence of 'genuine occupational qualification' permits the protected characteristic to be used as a criterion where it is relevant to the performance of a particular job. However, the scope of this defence has been too narrow, and in particular the potential significance of gender and race to jobs involving interaction with minority groups, and the benefits of diversity in the work environment, have been ignored.[56]

Two problematic areas within direct discrimination have been pregnancy and sexual harassment. The difficulties have arisen as a result of the use of a 'but-for' test to identify those cases where direct discrimination has occurred.[57] Instead of asking whether, say, gender has been taken into account in an employment decision, courts ask whether the employee would have suffered the detriment in question if they had not been a woman (or man). Thus, dismissing a woman because she is pregnant is direct discrimination,[58] as is failing to protect a female employee against sexual harassment.[59] The strained logic in these types of case has inevitably been used as an argument against the neutral anti-discrimination principle. This 'failure' of the anti-discrimination principle is unsurprising, however, since the principle concerns itself with the issue of merit, which is often not in question in these sorts of situations. Sexual harassment at work usually has nothing to do with merit; if it leads to discrimination in promotion, then having refused to submit to sexual advances by another employee should be added to the list of protected characteristics. Furthermore, where merit is relevant in these cases, the complaint is really one of indirect, rather than direct, discrimination. In pregnancy cases, for example, the employer is not refusing to select the pregnant woman because she is a woman, but is making it a requirement of selection that the applicant not be pregnant, which is, of course, detrimental to more women than men. In practice, however, dealing with pregnancy cases as indirect discrimination is unsatisfactory, because the structure of the legal test for indirect discrimination is unsuitable, the justification defence will limit the rights of pregnant women and, finally, the cost of pregnancy will fall on employers rather than on the state, which may have the effect of increasing discrimination against women at work.

We should recognize, therefore, that while there are important interests at stake in cases of pregnancy discrimination and sexual harassment, they are not necessarily the same interests as those protected by the legislation against sex discrimination, and they should logically be dealt with separately, by banning pregnancy discrimination and making harassment actionable in tort (with employers vicariously liable where appropriate). This 'specific rights' approach ensures that pregnant women, and *all* those people who are harassed at work, are given effective protection; it is reflected in the legislation on pregnancy dismissals in the UK and in the USA,[60] and has been endorsed by academic writers in both fields of law.[61]

Indirect Discrimination

Indirect discrimination consists of a lack of objectivity in the selection of criteria used in employment decisions. It should also include giving undue weight to criteria that prejudice certain groups, but the wording of the indirect discrimination provisions in the UK legislation has been interpreted to exclude this.[62] Although the impugned criteria are not the protected characteristics themselves (as in direct discrimination), they have a detrimental effect on a group which is defined by reference to a protected characteristic, and are not justified by the objective interests of the enterprise. Indirect discrimination can be reconciled with the merit principle by reference to the idea of self-preference discussed above, since it forces a white male employer (say) to take account of the interests of employees and job applicants who are female, black and so on, which he might otherwise ignore, possibly as a result of unconscious bias or ignorance of the circumstances of other groups. The economically powerful are forced to treat others as they would those in their own 'group', and to strive reasonably to accommodate cultures and practices different from their own. This has the effect of objectifying merit, since the extent to which differences must be accommodated is made to depend on the economic needs of the enterprise rather than being left to the self-regarding discretion of the dominant group. Thus, we can see that the contention[63] that direct and indirect discrimination have separate conceptual foundations is incorrect; on the contrary, they share the same theoretical root, namely the right to meritorious treatment.

The issue at the justification stage, therefore, is whether the cost to the company of accommodating the 'difference' is so great that the employer would not accommodate it even if he or she was in the original position.[64] This is a tricky counter-factual enquiry, and various tests have been devised by the British courts to guide their decisions on the justification defence. The test in *Ojutiku* v. *Manpower Services Commission*,[65] that there be 'sound and tolerable reasons' for the discriminatory requirement, has rightly been criticized as too subjective. Balancing the discriminatory effect of the requirement against the reasonable requirements of the enterprise, as recommended by the Court of Appeal in *Hampson* v. *Department of Education*,[66] seems about right, although the approach taken by the European Court of Justice (ECJ) in *Bilka-Kaufhaus* v. *Weber von Hartz*[67] might be preferred on the ground that it stresses the need for the requirement to be objectively justified as necessary in order to meet a real need of the undertaking. This emphasis on objectivity[68] is welcome, and, although it has not always been apparent in the case law in the UK,[69] the decision of the House of Lords in *R* v. *Secretary of State for Employment, ex parte EOC*[70] follows the lead of the ECJ in this respect. In the USA the employer is required to show that the challenged practice is 'job-related for the position in question and consistent with business necessity',[71] and this too is commensurate with the merit approach.

Positive Discrimination

It might be thought axiomatic that a right to meritorious treatment precludes positive discrimination, since those dominant group members adversely affected will not, by definition, have been treated meritoriously. I hope to show that this is an overly simplistic view. The first point is that if we adopt an expansive definition of merit, which recognizes that in many situations race and gender may legitimately be taken into account, then sometimes what has been termed positive discrimination is nothing of the sort. For example, race would be a relevant factor in the selection of students for medical school if the under-representation of minorities in the medical profession diminishes the quality of health care provision to members of those groups, as was argued in *University of California* v. *Bakke*.[72] This is not the end of the matter, however, for it must be recognized that even a broad definition of merit cannot be stretched to cover jobs that involve little personal interaction (an extreme example would be a lighthouse keeper), and that even where race or gender can be characterized as relevant, it would still only be one factor to be taken into account in the overall merit enquiry. Thus, fixed quotas can never be justified on grounds of merit, and only where being of a particular race or gender could realistically be said to be essential to the ability to do the job would a requirement of minority group membership be permissible.

As far as properly defined positive discrimination is concerned, there are two separate but interrelated issues. First, is it wrongful, i.e. does it constitute an unacceptable violation of the right to meritorious treatment? And, second, will it work? In order to determine whether the victims of positive discrimination should be entitled to redress, I wish to refer to the three grounds that Dworkin has argued 'can consistently be used to limit the definition of a particular right',[73] although I would prefer to view them as reasons why an interference with a right is justifiable.

The first reason why an interference may be permissible is that the values protected by the right are not really at stake in the case in question. As Gardner puts it, 'a right is only as powerful as its justification can make it'.[74] We must therefore consider the extent to which positive discrimination affects the interests of autonomy, dignity and utility that ground the right to meritorious treatment. Various factors will determine the amount of autonomy reduced by positive discrimination. Third parties will be hardest hit if they have been led to believe that in a particular career path they will be judged on merit, and then find that access to a considerable proportion of (or all) employment of the type they desire is denied to them by positive discrimination. Another factor will be the extent and form of the discrimination – quotas will usually have a greater effect on the autonomy of third parties than more flexible approaches, and the number of opportunities lost to non-minority persons as a result of the programme will be significant, bearing in mind that the asset which attracts preferential treatment, such as black skin, will usually not be acquirable, unlike many meritorious assets. As for dignity, the benign nature of positive discrimination means that it conveys a social meaning that is very different from that of negative discrimination. It is not disrespectful for the same reason that meritorious treatment is not, namely that it is motivated not by contempt for the affected person, but by concern for the general welfare. Positive discrimination is not stigmatizing and is unlikely to lead to loss of self-respect on the part of those detrimentally affected by it. Finally, if it really *is* positive discrimination, then by definition the most meritorious applicants are not being chosen, and this will be inefficient, at least in narrow economic terms. It may be, however, that this inefficiency is cancelled out by wider efficiency gains brought about by the positive discrimination programme, which might, for example, encourage able minority group members to enter the labour market, thereby unleashing their talents for the benefit of the whole community. Flexible methods will be less inefficient than rigid quotas, since the former permit the employer to vary minority intake over time in accordance with the relative quality of different pools of minority applicants, or to reduce the extent of positive discrimination overall if the general quality of minority applicants is lower than was predicted.

The second reason why the right may be weaker in this context is because it may be in conflict with another right. It is necessary to distinguish between individual and collective rights arguments for positive discrimination. One individual rights argument is that positive discrimination compensates the members of oppressed groups for the discrimination that they have suffered in the past. This argument relies on the assumption that *all* the group's members have been disadvantaged by discrimination. This assumption is problematic, however, since some are bound to have succeeded against the odds, and it does not then seem reasonable to enhance their positions further when disadvantaged members of the 'dominant' group may lose out as a result.[75] This point also weakens the alternative arguments that the dominant group members have been unjustly enriched by discrimination,[76] and that positive discrimination is needed to counterbalance negative discrimination that continues to evade the clutches of anti-discrimination law. The assertion of a *collective* right to compensation for past or present discrimination circumvents this problem, since it is not dependent on there having been a violation of the rights of all the individual members of the group, but is itself reliant on the dubious premise that a group can possess 'rights' which are separate from the collectivity of the individual rights of the group's members. It has been strongly argued that such collective rights are a contradiction in terms,[77] and such a rights claim is therefore an infirm foundation on which to base a violation of the right to meritorious treatment. There are two more general difficulties with rights-based justifications of positive discrimination. First, even if the compensation argument is a valid one, it seems unfair that only some of the dominant group should have to make reparation. And second, the claim that minorities have a *right* to positive discrimination suggests that the adoption of such programmes is compulsory in every society where there has been historical discrimination against a particular group, and that all groups which have suffered mistreatment in the past are entitled to preferential treatment. This conclusion gives rise to insuperable difficulties of identification of responsibility and entitlement, robs policy-makers of the freedom to act in accordance with their perceptions of the practical implications of particular positive discrimination programmes, and raises the unattractive spectre of what has been termed 'a comprehensive system of group allotments.'[78]

The final argument for infringing the right to meritorious treatment is goal-based. It is that the benefit to society of positive discrimination outweighs the rights of the individuals affected. In the light of the potential weakness of those third parties' rights in this context, as revealed by the first argument above, this is entirely possible. The benefits might consist of advantages to society as a whole, an improvement in the position of individuals, or a mixture of the two. This argument assumes, of course, that positive discrimination is indeed beneficial, and the validity of that assumption has been the subject of considerable debate. Utilitarian arguments in favour of positive discrimination focus on the social problems that a permanent underclass creates, such as high crime rates and a

breakdown in community relations. In addition, where a group has been
in a subordinate position for a long time, its members may become pessimistic as to their chances of succeeding in employment, and the existence
of role models in prominent positions could give them renewed hope,
thereby causing them to invest more in their 'human capital'. If so, then
their abilities will be made use of, and this will have the effect of boosting
production. Arguments of individual benefit also focus on the supposed
energizing effect of positive discrimination on members of minority
groups, who may gain autonomy by considering careers which they would
otherwise have thought to be beyond their reach. There are a number of
counter-arguments: that positive discrimination will cast doubt on the abilities of successful members of assisted groups; that it emphasizes, for
example, racial differences and may create resentment of minorities,
thereby increasing (rather than reducing) social tensions and hostility
towards oppressed groups; that it fosters patronage and leads to what
Westen has called 'a crude political struggle between groups seeking
favored status';[79] that it raises the problem of categorization and forces
those implementing the programme to draw clear lines in difficult contexts
(such as race) in order to identify beneficiaries; and that it only really helps
minority group members who are relatively well-to-do in the first place.[80]
This last argument points the way to perhaps the most serious difficulty
with positive discrimination, namely that it is a crude mechanism for the
redress of inequality, since it draws no distinctions within oppressed
groups between those who are personally disadvantaged and those who
are not, and fails to improve the position of those who are disadvantaged
but who happen not to be members of minority groups.

Whether positive discrimination will work or not is therefore a matter
on which opinions will inevitably differ. What implications does the
debate have for a right to meritorious treatment? I would argue that, if a
particular society decides that positive discrimination would be beneficial, it can then permit or mandate such action, provided that the
programme is tailored so as not to interfere unduly with the right of
third parties to meritorious treatment. Thus, where positive discrimination is likely to have a significant impact on the availability to non-
minority candidates of jobs in a particular field, the policy should be publicized well in advance, or phased in, so that third parties are not
prejudiced by the mistaken belief that recruitment in that area will be
based solely on merit. Where the third party is an existing job-holder,
this danger of detrimental reliance is particularly acute, and it will only
be fair positively to discriminate in dismissals where employees are aware
that this will occur from the moment they take up their employment. The
impact of positive discrimination on autonomy and efficiency can also be
limited by the employment of flexible methods (for example, the

factoring of race or gender into the merit enquiry) rather than fixed quotas. And finally, the effect of the policy on the dominant group should be spread as evenly as possible, so that particular individuals are not unjustly burdened with the cost of redistribution. This factor also militates against positive discrimination in dismissals, and suggests that the focus of the programmes should be on benefits (such as basic educational opportunities), the cost of which can be met by society as a whole.[81] Alternatively, it might be thought appropriate to compensate third parties who are particularly burdened by positive discrimination.[82] Only if these sorts of measures are taken will it be possible to say that the rights of third parties have been accorded due weight.

In the UK, positive discrimination is illegal, except in very limited circumstances,[83] and the ECJ has held[84] that preferential treatment of women is a violation of EC Directive 76/207 (the 'equal treatment' directive). However, in the USA 'affirmative action' has been permitted, and in some cases required, in the area of race. The extensive jurisprudence of the US Supreme Court on the subject is somewhat inconsistent, but can broadly be said to reflect the approach taken in the UK. As well as considering the availability of alternative remedies, the Court has been more sympathetic towards short-term programmes, and those that have 'factored in' race rather than laid down strict quotas or absolute bars.[85] Most importantly, the Court has struck down programmes that have threatened the job security of white workers, while permitting preferential hiring and promotion. In *Wygant* v. *Jackson Board of Education*, for example, where a plan which involved laying off non-minority teachers before minority teachers with less seniority was struck down, the Court held that the state could only implement a positive discrimination plan if the burden on innocent third parties was relatively light and diffused among society, Justice Powell remarking that 'denial of a future employment opportunity is not as intrusive as loss of an existing job'.[86]

UNFAIR DISMISSAL

The law of unfair dismissal is designed to implement the right to meritorious treatment in cases where an employee loses an existing job. Because the interest at stake is so fundamental, workers are protected from all unmeritorious treatment in this context, and do not have to establish that the dismissal occurred because the employer used a protected characteristic as a criterion in the decision to dismiss.

Where a dismissal occurs because there is no work for the employee to do, merit is not an issue unless the employer selects only some individuals for redundancy. Considerations of autonomy then require that the selection criteria not be irrational or capricious (see, for example, *Williams* v. *Compair Maxam Ltd*[87]), and that where there are agreed procedures they are complied with.[88] In other cases, a dismissal is unfair if it is unmeritorious. The only significant distinction between what Collins terms 'disciplinary dismissals'[89] and dismissals grounded on such characteristics as race and gender is that in the first type of case the dismissal *may* be unmeritorious (and therefore 'unfair'), while in the latter the treatment *will* be (thus the legislation makes such cases ones of automatic unfairness). Unlike Collins, I do not believe that the restrictions on managerial prerogative in these two contexts are protective of different employee interests; in both instances the justification for intervention is the right to meritorious treatment, and the interests of autonomy, dignity and efficiency which that right upholds.

The rules on procedural fairness in dismissal protect the autonomy and dignity of employees, and mean that a meritorious result is rendered more probable. Companies should publish, and then abide by, a clear disciplinary code so that employees can guide their actions by it. Summary dismissals should be avoided, since they show a lack of respect for the employee, and can add to the sense of disgrace that he or she may feel.[90] Even if the rules are followed precisely, however, the dismissal will still be unfair if the ground for the dismissal is insufficiently related to merit. The rule involved ought to be objectively necessary for the efficient operation of the firm, or else the autonomy of the workers will be unnecessarily compromised. In the UK, this requirement of substantive fairness has led the courts to ask whether the employer's decision to dismiss fell within the range of reasonable responses which a reasonable employer might have made in the circumstances.[91] This is a weak test, and far too often tribunals have ignored the 'reasonable' component, and looked only to the behaviour of the generality of employers to determine whether an employer has acted fairly. The case law has therefore tended to be standard-reflecting rather than standard-setting, and this lack of objectivity has left employees who have been treated unmeritoriously without legal redress. An infamous example is *Saunders* v. *Scottish National Camps*,[92] where the Employment Appeal Tribunal held that the dismissal of a handyman from a job at a children's camp on the ground of his homosexuality was fair, since a considerable proportion of employers would have done likewise. The paramount importance of objectivity in all merit enquiries makes such decisions indefensible; the approach of French law, where the courts use objective criteria in order to decide if a dismissal is founded on 'genuine and serious grounds', is much to be preferred.

It should be added that the failure of either federal or state law to prohibit unfair dismissal in the USA constitutes a serious derogation from the right to meritorious treatment, especially since the decline of organized labour has left the majority of US workers without the protection afforded by collectively agreed grievance procedures.

CORRECTIVE JUSTICE

If a person's right to meritorious treatment is unjustifiably violated, then that person has been wronged, and corrective justice requires that the wrongdoer right the wrong. The best way of doing this is to put the other person in the position he or she would have been in if the wrong had never occurred. This suggests that the remedies for unlawful discrimination and unfair dismissal in the UK should be strengthened. In particular, damages should be available for unintentional indirect discrimination (the objection that this is unfair, since the employer is not at fault, is misconceived, since the finding of indirect discrimination indicates that the employer has failed reasonably to accommodate the interests of other groups) and injunctive powers should be given to industrial tribunals and used widely in the discrimination area (as it is in the USA). Reinstatement should be the usual remedy in unfair dismissal cases, with an award of damages substituted only where this is genuinely impossible; the statutory compensation limit on such an award should also be removed. Technical problems and resource shortages which prevent individuals vindicating their right to meritorious treatment should also be addressed.

FURTHER IMPLICATIONS

Laws against discriminatory treatment and unfair dismissal are not necessarily the only manifestations of the right to meritorious treatment in the employment context. Equal pay laws, for example, are an attempt to redress gendered pay differentials which arise partly as a result of an undervaluation (by a male-dominated market) of the tasks which women perform.[93] The issue here is not the objectivity of the criteria which are used to select workers for jobs, but the extent to which the value attached to the performance of the job is a consequence of the fact that men hold most of the positions of economic power. This type of legal intervention constitutes a much greater threat to market systems than equal treatment laws, and an objective merit approach to the determination of pay for different jobs is very difficult to imagine, since the 'value' of the performance of the task must necessarily refer to the amount of money that will be paid for it in the market-place. This goes some way towards explaining the difficulties that have been encountered in the application of equal pay legislation.[94] If such an objective approach *is* possible, then it could be used outside the gender context to challenge all existing pay differentials on the basis that the market overvalues the skills of the powerful and undervalues those of the weakest in the community. As Campbell points out, 'differences in merit and demerit are seldom as substantial as the differences in situation which characterise people's lots in actual societies'.[95] This in turn offers a vision of a more equal society, which could be realized without recourse to massive *ex post* redistributive taxation.

In the law of tort, the decision of the House of Lords in *Spring* v. *Guardian Assurance*,[96] that an employer may be liable in negligence to a former employee for carelessly writing a negative reference, may also be seen as a realization of the right to meritorious treatment; in this instance the right requires that care be taken to give an accurate account of a worker's merits to those who may be considering him or her for a job.

RIGHTS AND REALITY

Embracing the concept of merit, and redefining it in a way which favours disadvantaged individuals, involves capturing the discourse of the dominant ideology and using it to illustrate the internal contradictions that lie therein. This is what Crenshaw has called turning 'society's "institutional logic" against itself';[97] furthermore, as she points out, 'demands for change that do not reflect the institutional logic . . . will probably be ineffective'.[98] Because the merit principle is objective and colour-blind, it has considerable political appeal, unlike other theories which lack the quality of universality and can thus easily be marginalized as 'special interest pleading'. The claim to meritorious treatment is difficult to refute, and this may explain why measures protective of it have survived even in the least favourable political climates; it is no accident that the Conservative government which has overhauled so much of British labour law since 1979 has left the legislation against discrimination and unfair dismissal more or less unscathed.

The use of rights terminology entrenches the protection that the law provides to the weaker members of society. Legal intervention becomes

more endurable, since rights rhetoric provides a buffer against the political and economic power of dominant groups.[99] At the same time, the
merit principle does not necessitate the sacrifice of radical reform on the
altar of political effectiveness. As we have seen, the flexibility of the right
to meritorious treatment renders it compatible with programmes of positive discrimination, while the internal logic of present anti-discrimination
legislation requires an extension of the scope of legal protection to all
groups that are subjected to significant prejudice in the workplace.
Uniquely, therefore, this theory of anti-discrimination requires a widening of the protection of the law while not ruling out a deepening of it to
further assist the most disadvantaged groups of all.

CONCLUSION

The principal lesson of the merit theory for legislatures is the paramount
importance of extending the scope of legal protection against employment discrimination to groups whose rights may presently be violated
with impunity. As far as the courts are concerned, the right to meritorious treatment will only be adequately protected if the judiciary
(particularly in the UK) apply more objective criteria in determining
such crucial issues as substantive fairness in dismissals, and the operation
of the justification defence to indirect discrimination. Only if the standards applied are vigorously objective will the transformative potential of
the merit principle be realized. Nor should state action be limited to the
provision of formal legal rights. The right to meritorious treatment also
necessitates administrative action designed to ensure that, as far as possible, all the participants in the meritocratic race are given equal starting
points.[100] True equality of opportunity requires, for instance, that educational resources be allocated in a fair and equal way,[101] and that
allocative measures are taken to free women from the shackles of child-
care commitments. Only if such action is taken will true justice in the
workplace be possible.

The right to meritorious treatment is widely recognized throughout
the world, in national legislation on unlawful discrimination and dismissals, in equality provisions of national constitutions, and in all manner
of international human rights conventions. The interests that it protects
are sufficiently important for it to be termed a 'human right', especially
since its implementation does not depend on the society in question having reached a particular stage of economic development. The
recognition that the issues are human rights ones will help to ensure that

the protections afforded to individuals in the employment sphere in the UK and elsewhere are strengthened and improved.

ACKNOWLEDGMENT

I am grateful to Conor Gearty, Maleiha Malik and Rob Wintemute for their helpful comments on an earlier draft. I also owe a debt of gratitude to the participants in the 1992–1993 Oxford BCL seminar on Comparative Human Rights, where I first formed an interest in the matters discussed here.

NOTES

1. I use the word meritorious in this essay to mean 'based on merit', since the latter formulation is unduly cumbersome.
2. The focus of my discussion will be on the law of the UK and of the USA, but it is, I hope, equally applicable to other jurisdictions.
3. See, for example, M. B. Abram, Affirmative action: fair shakers and social engineers (1986) 99 *Harvard Law Review* 1312.
4. The empty idea of equality (1982) 95 *Harvard Law Review* 537.
5. *Ibid.*, p. 560.
6. C. MacKinnon, *Sexual Harassment of Working Women* (New Haven: Yale University Press, 1979), *passim*.
7. Groups and the Equal Protection Clause (1976) 5 *Philosophy and Public Affairs* 107.
8. *Ibid.*, p. 157.
9. L. Tribe, The puzzling persistence of process-based constitutional theories (1980) 89 *Yale Law Journal* 1063, at p. 1075.
10. For a discussion of this point in the context of sexual orientation, see Chapter 10, above
11. For a discussion of the difficulties faced by the Indian authorities in identifying the members of disadvantaged castes for the purposes of preferential treatment, see M. Galanter, *Competing Equalities: Law and the Backward Classes in India* (Berkeley: University of California Press, 1984), Chapter 9.
12. Groups and the Equal Protection Clause, *op. cit.*, pp. 148, 154–5.
13. See H. Collins, *Justice in Dismissal* (Oxford: Clarendon Press, 1992), pp. 9–12.
14. *Ibid.*, especially pp. 15–21.
15. T. Scanlon, Rights, goals and fairness. In S. Hampshire (ed.), *Public and Private Morality* (Cambridge: Cambridge University Press, 1978), p. 93.
16. This analysis is heavily influenced by the approach of H. Collins, *op. cit.*, pp. 15–21.
17. The US government has estimated that the elimination of employment discrimination against people with disabilities will generate increased productivity in the amount of $164 million: see G. Quinn, M. McDonagh and C. Kimber, *Disability Discrimination Law in the United States, Australia and Canada* (Dublin: Oak Tree Press, 1993), p. 8.
18. For the view that anti-discrimination law is unnecessary and inefficient, because the market itself can deal with the problem of irrational bias, see, for example, R. Posner, An economic analysis of sex discrimination laws (1989) 56 *University of Chicago Law Review*

1311. This is contradicted by the prevalence of discrimination in the workplace.

19. The merit approach is therefore compatible with the difference principle of J. Rawls. See J. Rawls, *A Theory of Justice* (Oxford: Clarendon Press, 1972), pp. 75–83.

20. J. Raz, Autonomy, toleration, and the harm principle. In R. Gavison (ed.), *Issues in Contemporary Legal Philosophy* (Oxford: Clarendon Press, 1987), p. 314.

21. F. A. Hayek, *The Road to Serfdom* (London: Routledge & Kegan Paul, 1944), p. 54.

22. H. Collins, *op. cit.*, p. 18.

23. *Ibid.*, p. 20.

24. See J. Rawls, *op. cit.*, p. 103, where he says: 'those who, with the prospect of improving their condition, have done what the system announces that it will reward are entitled to their advantages . . . their claims are legitimate expectations established by social institutions'.

25. See H. Collins, *op. cit.*, p. 20, and Chapter 6.

26. *Ibid.*, p. 16; and see R. Dworkin, *Taking Rights Seriously* (London: Duckworth, 1977), Chapter 9.

27. T. Campbell, Mistaking the relevance of gender. In S. McLean and N. Burrows (eds), *The Legal Relevance of Gender* (Basingstoke: Macmillan, 1988), p. 18.

28. H. Collins, *op. cit.*, p. 16; and see R. Dworkin, *A Matter of Principle* (Cambridge, MA: Harvard University Press, 1985), p. 301.

29. H. Collins, *op. cit.*, p. 16.

30. *East African Asians* v. *United Kingdom (No. 2)* (1973) 3 EHRR 76 (differential treatment on the basis of race may be an affront to human dignity).

31. The 'veil of ignorance' idea is found in J. Rawls, *op. cit.*, pp. 12, 136ff.

32. See H. Collins, *op. cit.*, p. 15.

33. See, for example, *Johnson* v. *Santa Clara Transportation Agency*, 107 SCt 1442 (1988).

34. R. H. Fallon, To each according to his ability, from none according to his race: the concept of merit in the law of antidiscrimination (1980) 60 *Boston University Law Review* 815, at pp. 826–7.

35. See C. MacKinnon, *op. cit., passim* (historical formulation of objective standards is male; ideas of merit are masculine constructs).

36. See J. Rawls, *op. cit.*, Chapter 3.

37. R. Dworkin, *Taking Rights Seriously, op. cit.*, p. 181.

38. For example, S. Fish, *There's No Such Thing as Free Speech* (New York: Oxford University Press, 1994), pp. 63–4.

39. For an interesting example of this, see Note, Race as an employment qualification to meet police department operational needs (1979) 54 *New York University Law Review* 413.

40. For a valuable discussion, see B. Parekh, A case for positive discrimination. In B. Hepple and E. Szyszczak (eds), *Discrimination: The Limits of Law* (London: Mansell, 1992), pp. 268–76.

41. *Ibid.*, p. 273.

42. See, for example, M. Sandel, *Liberalism and the Limits of Justice* (Cambridge: Cambridge University Press, 1982), pp. 72–7.

43. Although they may be *entitled* to meritorious treatment as a result of their reliance on the legitimate expectation that they will receive it.

44. See the discussion of the 'warrior problem' by B. Williams, The idea of equality. In P. Laslett and W. G. Runciman (eds), *Philosophy, Politics and Society*, 2nd Series (Oxford: Blackwell, 1962), p. 121.

45. This would be direct discrimination contrary to the Race Relations Act 1976: *R* v. *CRE, ex parte Westminster City Council* [1984] ICR 770 (Woolf J); affirmed by the Court of Appeal [1985] ICR 827.

46. See Chapter 15, below.

47. See T. Buck, Ageism and legal control. In B. Hepple and E. Szyszczak, *op. cit.*

48. See M. Matsuda, Voices of America: accent, anti-discrimination law, and a jurisprudence for the last reconstruction (1991) 100 *Yale Law Journal* 1329.

49. See Note, Facial discrimination (1987) 100 *Harvard Law Review* 2035.

50. But not previous trade union activism: see *Fitzpatrick* v. *British Railways Board* [1991] IRLR 376.

51. This would have protected the plaintiff in *Dawkins* v. *Department of the Environment*

[1993] IRLR 284, a Rastafarian who was refused a job as a van driver because he refused to cut his hair. Compare *Mandla* v. *Dowell Lee* [1983] IRLR 209 to see how irrational the law is at present.

52. Disability Discrimination Act 1995.

53. 847 F 2d 1329 (9th Cir. 1988); affirmed on different grounds, 875 F 2d 699 (9th Cir. 1989) (en banc).

54. Although the choice may be severely constrained by religious or cultural norms: see the cases in note 51.

55. See Chapter 10, above.

56. For an example from the USA, see *Wygant* v. *Jackson Board of Education*, 476 US 267 (1986).

57. See, for example, *James* v. *Eastleigh Borough Council* [1990] IRLR 288.

58. *Webb* v. *Emo Air Cargo (UK) Ltd* [1993] 1WLR 49. See also Chapter 9, above.

59. *Porcelli* v. *Strathclyde Regional Council* [1984] IRLR 467.

60. In the UK, see now the Trade Union Reform and Employment Rights Act 1993, s. 24; and in the USA, the Pregnancy Discrimination Act 1978.

61. On pregnancy, see S. Fredman, A difference with distinction: pregnancy and parenthood reassessed (1994) 110 LQR 106; and on sexual harassment, see J. Conaghan and W. Mansell, *The Wrongs of Tort* (London: Pluto Press, 1993), Chapter 7, and J. Dine and B. Watt, Sexual harassment: moving away from discrimination (1995) 58 *Modern Law Review* 343.

62. See *Perera* v. *Civil Service Commission* [1983] IRLR 136.

63. See C. McCrudden, Changing notions of discrimination: In S. Guest and A. Milne (eds), *Equality and Discrimination (Archiv fur Rechts- und Sozialphilosophie*, supplement 21); and J. Gardner, Liberals and unlawful discrimination (1989) 9 OJLS 1. Compare A. Morris, On the normative foundations of indirect discrimination law (1995) 15 *Oxford Journal of Legal Studies* 199.

64. There are similarities here with the 'reversing the groups' test devised by D. A. Strauss: see D. A. Strauss, Discriminatory intent and the taming of *Brown* (1989) 56 *University of Chicago Law Review* 935.

65. [1982] ICR 661.

66. [1989] IRLR 69.

67. [1986] IRLR 317.

68. See also the *Nimz* case [1991] ECR I-297.

69. See, for example, *Briggs* v. *North East Education and Library Board* [1990] IRLR 182, and *Brook* v. *London Borough of Haringey* [1992] IRLR 478.

70. [1994] ICR 317.

71. Civil Rights Act 1991, s. 105.

72. 438 US 265 (1978).

73. R. Dworkin, *Taking Rights Seriously, op. cit.*, p. 200.

74. J. Gardner, Freedom of expression. In C. McCrudden and G. Chambers (eds), *Individual Rights and the Law in Britain* (Oxford: Clarendon Press, 1994), p. 210.

75. See G. Pitt, Can reverse discrimination be justified? In B. Hepple and E. Szyszczak, *op. cit.*, p. 285.

76. K. O'Donovan, Affirmative action: fair shakes and social engineers. In Guest and Milne, *op. cit.*

77. See, for example, W. Kymlicka, *Liberalism, Community and Culture* (Oxford: Clarendon Press, 1989), p. 140, where he says that there is 'no room in the moral ontology of liberalism for the idea of collective rights'. See also the discussion of the issue in Chapter 7, above.

78. M. Galanter, *op. cit.*, p. 567.

79. K. O'Donovan, *op. cit.*, p. 1321.

80. This has been a recurrent criticism of the Indian programme of positive discrimination in favour of the lower castes; see M. Galanter, *op. cit.*, p. 548 ('the better situated among the beneficiaries enjoy a disproportionate share of program benefits').

81. M. Galanter, *op. cit.*, p. 566.

82. This is advocated by J. H. Verkerke, Compensating victims of preferential employment discrimination remedies (1989) 98 *Yale Law Journal* 1479.

83. The exceptions are to be found in ss. 33–4 and 47–9 of the Sex Discrimination Act 1975.

84. *Eckhard Kalanke* v. *Freie Hansestadt Bremen*, case 450/93.

85. *Bakke*, per Justice Powell (pp. 316–9) but cf. Justice Blackmun, p. 406 (constitutionally the distinction between factoring in race and quotas seems irrelevant).

86. 476 US 267 (1986) pp. 282–3. See also *Firefighters* v. *Stotts*, 104 SCt 2576 (1978). Only where the beneficiaries of the programme are identifiable victims of past discrimination by the firm will an award of retroactive seniority be permissible: e.g. *Franks* v. *Bowman Transportation Co.*, 424 US 147 (1976).

87. [1982] ICR 156.

88. The repeal (by s. 36 of the Deregulation and Contracting Out Act 1994) of s. 59 (1) (b) of the Employment Protection (Consolidation) Act 1978 (which rendered unfair a selection for dismissal in contravention of a customary arrangement or an agreed procedure) is therefore to be regretted.

89. H. Collins, *op. cit.*, p. 53.

90. *Ibid.*, pp. 15–16.

91. See, for example, *Iceland Frozen Foods* v. *Jones* [1983] ICR 17, at p. 25.

92. [1980] IRLR 174; affirmed by the Court of Session [1981] IRLR 277.

93. See S. Dex, Gender in the labour market. In D. Gallie (ed.), *Employment in Britain* (Oxford: Blackwell, 1988).

94. See, for example, *Enderby* v. *Frenchay Health Authority* [1992] IRLR 15.

95. T. Campbell, *Justice* (London: Macmillan, 1988), p. 32.

96. [1994] ICR 596.

97. K. Crenshaw, Race, reform and retrenchment: transformation and legitimation in antidiscrimination law (1988) 101 *Harvard Law Review* 1331, at p. 1366.

98. *Ibid.*, p. 1367.

99. See the essays by R. Delgado and P. J. Williams in (1987) 22 *Harvard Civil Rights – Civil Liberties Law Review* 301, 403.

100. For a discussion of the limits of formal legal intervention as a strategy for reducing racial discrimination, see L. Lustgarten, Racial inequality and the limits of law (1986) 49 *Modern Law Review* 68.

101. See J. Rawls, *op. cit.*, p. 73.

12

Equality or Self-determination?

Clíona J. M. Kimber

INTRODUCTION

While it is gradually becoming accepted that it is a legitimate and desirable objective that women and disadvantaged groups should be able to participate to the full in society and pursue their conception of a truly good life, there is considerable disagreement as to how such an objective can best be achieved. Many different approaches have been taken to the problem of creating a society in which the values and desires of women and other dominated and disadvantaged groups can be seen as legitimate and as worthy of expression and achievement. Foremost among these has been the use of the principle of equality of individuals and groups, whether contained in international human rights documents or enacted in national constitutions and bills of rights. The equality principle, however, contains central flaws and these restrict its effectiveness in achieving its ultimate objective. In this chapter I suggest that, by contrast, the principle of self-determination overcomes many of these defects and has greater potential to create a more just society. Furthermore, I will argue that such has been the development of the principle of equality away from its doctrinal roots that it is now more properly described as a principle of self-determination.

This point will be developed by exploring the parameters of three models of equality: strict identical treatment; identical treatment combined with special treatment; and the subordination principle. All three will then be contrasted with the principle of self-determination.[1] The models are, of course, ideal types and do not exist in pure form in any of the jurisdictions discussed. Nevertheless, various jurisdictions have enacted legislation which conforms very nearly to these models, although it cannot be said that such legislation has ever been designed specifically with the objective of putting into concrete form any of these models.

MODEL 1: STRICT IDENTICAL TREATMENT

The first model of equality is that of strict identical treatment. It is also described as the sameness approach or as formal equality. The central principle is that like should be treated alike and different should be treated differently. This model of equality is premised on the idea that there are no important and immutable differences between individuals which justify their different treatment. Therefore all legal and other distinctions based on gender, race, religion and so on should be eliminated. The model is assimilationist in that its ideal is a society where classifications such as race or gender would be 'the functional equivalent of the eye colour of individuals'.[2]

This approach to equality, based on identical treatment, can be seen in the many jurisdictions which have enacted legislation incorporating a general principle of non-discrimination. In Britain this can be seen in the Race Relations Act 1976 and the Sex Discrimination Act 1975. In Ireland one can look at the Anti-Discrimination (Pay) Act 1974 and the Employment Equality Act 1977. At the European level, Article 119 of the Treaty of Rome deals with pay equity by providing that 'Each Member-State shall . . . ensure and maintain the application of the principle of equal remuneration for equal work as between men and women workers.' The identical treatment approach is continued in subsequent legislation, in particular the Equal Treatment Directive, where the basic principle is that 'the principle of equal treatment shall mean that there shall be no discrimination whatsoever on the grounds of sex either directly or indirectly by reference in particular to marital or family status.'[3]

In the USA, the federal law concerned with discrimination in employment, Title VII of the Civil Rights Act 1964, also requires identical treatment. It provides *inter alia* that it is an unlawful employment practice for an employer 'to discriminate against any individual with respect to his compensation, terms, conditions, or privileges of employment, because of such individual's race, colour, religion, sex or national origin'.[4]

Analysis of Model 1

The attractions of this model are obvious. First, it is clear and simple to apply, and is very effective in removing overt and explicit discriminatory legislation and policies. As a first step towards achieving basic rights, this principle is extremely useful as long as women and other marginalized groups can show their sameness to men or to the dominant groups and are happy to do this.[5] The effect is that the most blatant discriminatory and exclusionary practices can be ended. Legal restrictions which prevent members of certain groups from entering and participating in various aspects of public life can be removed. Similarly, legislation which places members of certain groups under a legal or other disability can be repealed. As Bacchi points out, this model of formal equality was first espoused by women in the nineteenth century who sought, among other rights, freedom from legal restriction in access to education and employment, and the right to vote.[6] Second, it fits well within the political and legal frameworks of most Western democracies. That a jurisprudential tradition based on this model of equality has been established can be seen from the brief description of equality legislation in the previous section. In the common law some minimum level of procedural equality has been accepted from Dicey onwards.[7] The establishment and acceptance of this tradition means that it is easier for legal argument based on this model to succeed.

The defects and limitations of this model are numerous, however, and do not compensate for its advantages. First, the principle of equality is itself empty of any normative content. It contains no minimum content of fairness or justice, and no minimum standards of treatment. As long as those who are classified as like are treated alike, it does not matter how harsh or unjust that like treatment is. A sort of procedural equality is therefore created but the substance of laws is not affected. A legal order may therefore sanction any treatment of what is equal and what is different without violating the equality principle as formulated in this model.[8] This model of equality does not attempt to formulate any normative standards of treatment. Second, this model does not provide answers to the question of what is like and what is unlike for the purpose of applying the principle. For example, what is equal work? Does it mean exactly the same job, similar jobs, or jobs which though in substance very different are in effect of similar status?[9] The classification of pregnant women is particularly difficult. Who are pregnant women like and who are they unlike for the purpose of securing a certain level of treatment? Are pregnant women and non-pregnant men alike?[10] The attempt to answer these and similar questions has led US jurisprudence down the long road of deciding which individuals are similarly situated and which are not for the purposes of Title VII of the Civil Rights Act, briefly mentioned above. In European Union legislation there has been a similar questioning of the justification for dissimilar classification leading to dissimilar treatment, and the same has been true in Britain. In order to overcome the difficulties presented by pregnancy, the requirement to find similarities has led to the drawing of unsatisfactory analogies in all jurisdictions mentioned between pregnant women and men with an illness or temporary disability.[11] This has also been the case for other differences which do not admit of an easy comparison.

Third, as Fredman points out, to apply the equal treatment principle, one must answer the question, 'equal to whom?', and for sex equality, the answer is 'equal to a man'.[12] For other groups, the answer is equal to what you are not, where what you are not is defined as difference from the dominant group in the society in which you live. In practice this means for non-whites living in a white society, equal to white people, for disabled people, equal to able-bodied people, for Muslims living in a Christian society, equal to Christians, and for Muslims living in a Jewish society, equal to Jews. The list is of course as endless and various as the societies and circumstances in which people find themselves. The overall limitation is the same, however. One must find a suitable comparator and show that one is the same as that comparator and therefore entitled to the same treatment as that comparator. Thus the equality principle as applied in this model falls down where there is no comparator, as can be seen from the difficulties with pregnancy, part-time workers, and people with disabilities.

A fourth limitation is that the principle can only reach situations where there is a comparator whose treatment an individual wishes to claim.[13] Individuals can only advance therefore to the extent that this is possible. Where this is not possible, the treatment afforded to individuals is subject to no scrutiny whatsoever. People with disabilities in particular suffer from this limitation. Asserting sameness with able-bodied people increases in difficulty in proportion to the level of disability, and yet if this sameness cannot be shown, then under this model of equality, there is nothing which can be done regarding detrimental treatment. A fifth limitation, and this follows on from the fourth, is that even if an individual can show that he or she is similarly situated to someone whose rights or benefits he or she would like to have, he or she is only entitled to that level of rights, inadequate though that may be. For example, a pregnant woman is only entitled to the rights a man with a disability or illness is entitled to: 'a woman's rights are entirely dependant on the extent to which comparable rights are afforded to comparable men'.[14] This is also true of those with disabilities, or requirements for special schooling or schooling in a different language.

A sixth limitation is that this model accepts current social and political structures and assumes their continued existence. It contains no suggestion that existing political bodies and structures need to be reorganized. However, existing structures can act as significant barriers to the achievement of an equal society simply because they have not been designed with members of disadvantaged groups in mind. For example, buildings designed with access only for the able-bodied can restrict the equality of opportunity of access for the disabled. In the workplace, established procedures of recruitment, hiring and promotion can result in discrimination through the continual selection of similar types of employees, even though the procedures are not designed to promote discrimination and are not overtly discriminatory. This model also measures equal treatment by established norms and values, many of which have been created without members of disadvantaged groups in mind. If equality of result is to be achieved, these social and political structures and existing norms and values would have to be questioned and reformed.

MODEL 2: IDENTICAL TREATMENT COMBINED WITH SPECIAL TREATMENT

This second model is a development of the first and has many of the same premises and applications. The central principle remains that like should be treated alike and different differently. It acknowledges, however, that there are differences which are immutable and unchangeable and which must, paradoxically, be given special treatment in order to achieve equal treatment. Where these differences would lead to different treatment under model 1 and this different treatment would lead to substantive inequality, then these differences must be taken into account in formulating policy and legislation and special provision must be made. The differences acknowledged can be limited to biological differences alone, in the case of women, or can extend to all the differences between people of a different gender, race, religion, ability and so on. The model effectively acknowledges that there are exceptions to the strict equality principle and that special treatment may be required in certain circumstances to achieve equality of results.

Special treatment takes many forms. There can be specific provision for a specific circumstance such as disability,[15] minority language schooling, or pregnancy. As regards pregnancy, special treatment of this kind can be seen in the UK with the Employment Protection (Consolidation) Act 1978, the Social Security Act 1986 and the Trade Union Reform and Employment Rights Act 1993, which provide, *inter alia*, job security and maternity leave for pregnant women. The EU added special treatment to its non-discrimination or identical treatment model only in 1992 with the Pregnant Workers Directive,[16] and the USA even more recently with the Family Leave Act 1993. Special treatment can also take the form of protective legislation, e.g. in the UK, the Factories Act 1961, limiting hours of work for women. Affirmative action programmes, ranging from monitoring of numbers to the setting of loose goals to fixing strict quotas, can be justified as special treatment. This model therefore can be said to have moved from a purely assimilationist view of equality to a recognition that there are differences which must be accommodated, and as such it represents a step along the road from equality of opportunity to equality of results.

Analysis of Model 2

This model has a number of advantages over the first model outlined above. It is broader in scope and contains an acceptance of the fact that there must be exceptions to the identical treatment of the strict equality model if equality of results is to be achieved. This has a number of consequences. First, identification of appropriate comparators or similarly situated individuals is not a prerequisite to obtaining rights. The reach of the principle is not therefore limited to those who can show that they are the same as or similarly situated to someone whose rights or benefits they wish to have. Second, the use of affirmative action or positive discrimination can be legitimated. Under the identical treatment rubric, such action violates the principle of sameness of treatment. Third, the model is aimed more carefully at producing equality of results by targeting measures and provisions at specific problems which have been identified. This is particularly true in the case of affirmative action. Fourth, this model also has a perceptive advantage in that it is respectful of difference and does not try to eliminate diversity through assimilation.

Nevertheless, despite these advantages, the model also has considerable weaknesses which limit its potential for achieving the ultimate objective outlined above. First, by characterizing issues of equality in terms of sameness and difference it falls prey to many of the limitations of the first model concerning the classification of sameness and difference. The model contains no method of deciding which differences are significant enough to merit special treatment and which are not. Second, this model does nothing to challenge the assumption that the standard for comparison remains the man, in the case of women, and for other groups, the dominant group in society. As Thornton observes in the case of women:

> Although the special treatment model adopts a qualified substantive, rather than a formalistic, interpretation of equality, the model is still constrained by the liberal legal view that it is equality with men which

is the ideal. Furthermore the discourse of 'difference' and 'special-ness', as applied to women, serves to endorse maleness as the norm.[17]

For other marginalized groups, it is fair to say that it is equality with the dominant groups which is the ideal. Third, where difference is such that it requires special treatment, this can lead to the view that those in receipt of special treatment are somehow inferior or remedial and could not suc-ceed in the real world without this special help. This has been a particular weakness with affirmative action programmes, and has led to their rejection as an effective tool by many scholars.[18] Fourth, no method is provided for distinguishing invidious special treatment from beneficial special treatment. Special protection for women workers based on the protection of their reproductive capacities and imbued with assumptions of the primacy of the domestic role is a good example of this limitation. While the enactment of protective legislation was a victory for those con-cerned for the welfare of women and children in the nineteenth century, it also operates to prevent women from working in certain occupations and can act as a barrier to their full participation in the labour market. In some cases the reproductive capacity of men is also at risk, but as yet no protective legislation is in place.[19] This model therefore does not pre-vent a paternalistic attitude to special treatment which prevents rather than achieves substantive equality.

Fifth, there is also the danger that this model of equality could oper-ate to entrench differences, where differences are based on stereotypical views of women and similar groups, or where these differences result from socialization into a subordinate position. The differences model makes no attempt to question why differences exist, why they are con-structed, viewed and classified as they are, and, furthermore, it does not question the social and political structures which have meant that differ-ences have become barriers to full participation in society. Finally, if difference is recognized as a basis for special treatment, it can also be used to justify invidious discrimination in other circumstances.[20] The *Sears* case in the USA provides an excellent example of the tensions inherent in this approach.[21] In this case the Equal Employment Opportunity Commission (EEOC) brought an action against Sears, Roebuck and Co., alleging that the company had discriminated against its women employees in that women were substantially under-represented in the lucrative commission sales positions even though women were well represented in other sales categories. Sears argued that this under-representation was not due to discriminatory policies or prac-tices on its part, but was due to the fact that women did not seek these higher-paid positions because of the added stress, competition and risk associated with these positions, and because women were different from men in their career aspirations and interests; they preferred to take lower-paid, but more secure, jobs while channelling their energies into home and family. Sears was successful in this argument and no discrimination was found.

MODEL 3: THE SUBORDINATION PRINCIPLE

It is fair to say that this third model of equality is the most recent in terms of scholarly articulation and adoption in the jurisprudence of a legal system. This model differs fundamentally from those described above in that it sees issues of equality as issues of hierarchy and dominance. Policies or legislation that facilitate and reinforce the subordination of one group to another or the domination of one group by another are seen as morally illegitimate and as being required to be legally prohibited.

This model of equality does not involve as a precondition of its application that an appropriate comparator or a person similarly situated be identified, as is the case with the first model. Nor does it carve an exception away from the identical treatment principle and give that group of individuals special treatment, as the second model does. Instead, the impact of a particular piece of legislation or classification is assessed. The central question asked is whether such a measure operates to increase or decrease the conditions of disadvantage of a disadvantaged group. This principle is, therefore, quite clearly oriented towards equality of results.[22]

As is immediately obvious, this involves a much wider analysis, involving a consideration of the historical origin of the policy, its social and economic effects, and the experience of those affected by it, if that experience can be ascertained. These are not the kinds of questions which courts of law have traditionally felt themselves authorized or even qualified to answer, requiring as they do a detailed sociological analysis of the society in question, an individual's place in that society and the political and sociological effect of law in its broadest sense. Under this model, the equality principle has been interpreted as requiring that practices and policies which keep women and other groups in a position of subordination must be eliminated. Laws or policies which deprive a group of control over its own development are seen as contrary to the principle of equality.[23] It is also seen as requiring the changing of social and political structures so that the barriers to the participation of women and other groups can be removed.[24] Finally, it has been interpreted by academic commentators as requiring that the values and goals of hitherto subjugated and dominated groups be respected and recognized as having an inherent value and worth, and that these groups be allowed the freedom to determine the course of their own lives.[25]

The subordination principle is the model of equality which is currently used to interpret the equality guarantee in s. 15 of the Canadian Charter of Rights and Freedoms[26] and its use in that jurisdiction is illustrated by a consideration of *Andrews* v. *Law Society of British Columbia*, which expressly adopted this interpretation. *Andrews* involved a challenge to the British Columbia Barristers and Solicitors Act, which provided that only Canadian citizens could practise law in British Columbia. This requirement was challenged as a violation of the equality rights in s. 15 of the Charter. The court found for Andrews, holding that non-citizens were a historically disadvantaged group in Canada, and that their exclusion from the practice of law had the effect of denying them access to opportunities available to citizens. This broad interpretation of equality which focused on the effect of impugned legislation, not simply on their intent, can be seen in the leading judgment of McIntyre J:

> [D]iscrimination may be described as a distinction, whether intentional or not but based on grounds relating to the personal characteristics of the individual or group, which has the effect of imposing burdens, obligations or disadvantages on such individual or group not imposed on others, or which withholds or limits access to opportunities, benefits and advantages available to other members of society.[27]

The adoption of this model of equality was welcomed and seen as a significant advance on previous models.[28]

Analysis of Model 3

The subordination principle as a model of equality has considerable advantages over the first two models described. Its chief characteristic is that it moves away from seeing equality as issues of sameness and difference and instead sees equality as involving issues of hierarchy and dominance. This formulation of equality has a number of consequences.

First, the subordination principle offers a way out of the often intractable sameness–difference debate, because the classification of individuals in these terms is not a prerequisite for the application of the equality principle. Second, the model contains within itself a clearer articulation of its ultimate objective, namely, ameliorating conditions of disadvantage, and ending relationships of hierarchy and dominance. This provides a clearer standard for decision-makers to apply in deciding whether a policy or a practice violates the equality principle. Third, it is a clear statement that equality of results is the ultimate objective, not simply equality of opportunity. Thus a formal interpretation of equality is rejected for a substantive one, rather than a qualified substantive approach which is taken in the second model. Fourth, the requirement to end relationships of hierarchy and dominance brings with it the requirement to contemplate change in social and political structures. Thus this model is a considerable advance on models in which the social and political *status quo* is assumed and accepted. Finally, it enables the whole range of problems which beset women and marginalized groups, such as abortion, reproductive questions, gender and race bias in the law and in the courts, to be seen as issues of equality and non-discrimination.[29]

This model still suffers from a number of crucial limitations, however, which in the end I would argue limit its advantages. The most significant of these is that the subordination principle has pushed out the doctrinal boundaries of the equality principle so far that it is almost unrecognizable as equality. The conceptual basis of the subordination model gains nothing from its adherence to the equality principle and in fact is probably considerably limited by its doctrinal structure, so that more radical policies are likely to be seen as contravening the equality principle. Neither does the principle provide answers to such questions as which groups have been disadvantaged and subordinated to the extent that policies which further this disadvantage ought to be invalidated. Are white middle-class women, for example, a group which has been disadvantaged or exploited? Even if they have been in the past, is this still the case today? Are such questions to be answered by examining statistical indicators of wealth, poverty, income, representation in the criminal population, and membership of the professions, courts and parliament, and if so are courts of law the proper bodies to do this? Finally, it is still the courts which decide whether a policy or law facilitates or prevents disadvantage, and this decision may be different from the views of those affected by such a policy.

SELF-DETERMINATION

Having explored the concept of equality, I now return to the claim made at the outset, that the development of the equality principle has been such that what is now sought is more properly described as self-determination. What is meant by self-determination? The principle of self-determination which I put forward is composed of the core of the principle of self-determination at international law together with instinctive conceptions of self-determination implicit in much human rights, philosophical and feminist scholarship. This is self-determination shorn of the concept of the self in UN practice, namely a colonial and territorial self,[30] and the methods of self-determination such as independence or secession which have necessarily resulted from that definition of self. This is self-determination transposed into national law and based on the same premises as the concept of internal self-determination in the jurisprudence of international law.[31] Self-determination as thus enunciated is what I believe is implicitly desired, argued for and groped towards in both feminist scholarship and scholarship which has as its objective the legal accommodation of the rights of other subordinated groups.

What, therefore, is the core of the right to self-determination in international law? As a right, self-determination is well established in international law. It is one of the principles and purposes listed in the Charter of the United Nations (Article 2.1). The 1960 Declaration on the Granting of Principles of Independence to Colonial Countries and Peoples[32] is central to the establishment of the right. It declares that the subjection of peoples to alien subjugation, domination and exploitation constitutes a denial of fundamental human rights. It goes on in Article 2 to provide that 'all peoples have the right to self-determination; by virtue of that right they freely determine their political status and freely pursue their economic, social and cultural development'. This definition of the right to self-determination has since been incorporated in numerous international instruments; indeed, Common Article 1 of the 1966 Covenants on Civil and Political Rights and Economic and Social Rights reproduces the language of Article 2 of the colonial declaration exactly.[33]

The central core of the right to self-determination is brought into sharper focus by academic commentators. Thornberry has observed that the distinctive and defining characteristic of the right to self-determination is that it recognizes the right of those under alien subjugation and domination to have control over their own development and determine for themselves how that development should be pursued. It is the ending of subjugation and domination of one group by another.[34] The core of the right is described by Brownlie as the right of a community which has a distinct character to have that character reflected in the institutions of government under which it lives.[35] Again, in the *Western Sahara* case, a central case in the development and implementation of the right to self-determination, we see the assertion that 'the essence of self-determination is method, not result: the need to pay regard to the freely expressed will of peoples'. The core of the right can also be seen by what it requires for its fullest implementation, namely participatory democracy,[36] representative government,[37] participation in political control[38] and respect for fundamental human rights.[39] It is worth emphasizing the crucial characteristics of self-determination, namely that it sees the bearers of the right as autonomous, self-directing and self-governing, pursuing their own development, based on values they have chosen for themselves and goals they have set for themselves.

In summary, therefore, the principle of self-determination in international law jurisprudence can be described as follows: it is the right to be recognized and respected as a centre of autonomous choice and valuation, and to pursue the development of the centre according to the value system of that centre and the goals it has set for itself. It is the right to be free from subjugation and domination, and to be self-directed and self-governing. This respect has both positive and negative aspects. The negative aspects are the duty not to destroy or impair the capacity for and the opportunity to pursue self-determination by subjecting a group or individual to exploitation or domination. In its positive aspect, it is an acknowledgment that differing value systems will make for different conceptions of what is a worthwhile and meaningful life, and a requirement to provide the material and social conditions necessary to pursue the goals set, and abolish or change those social institutions and practices which impair or destroy the right to self-determination.

Equality and Self-determination Compared

It is my contention that the expansive interpretation of the equality principle which is particularly apparent in the subordination principle is at odds with the doctrinal basis of equality and, furthermore, that it is more correctly identified as self-determination. There is a correlation and fit between the two, which is not the case with a strict application of the equality principle. This can be seen from a direct comparison of some of the core characteristics of both principles.

First, the characterization of the problem and method of analysis are similar for both principles. Injustice is seen as being caused by alien subjugation and domination on the one hand, and by relationships of hierarchy and dominance on the other. Second, the chief demand of both self-determination and the subordination principle mirror each other. Self-determination requires the ending of subjugation and domination of one group by another. The subordination principle requires the elimination of hierarchy and dominance. Third, one of the central requirements of self-determination is that peoples must be given the freedom freely to pursue their own development. Expansive interpretations of the equality principle claim this freedom for groups. This emphasis is lacking in strict equality models, which are profoundly other-determinative. Fourth, there is a congruence of methods of implementation. The principle of self-determination requires the returning of control, and in particular political control, to hitherto dominated groups. The expansive interpretation of equality requires the elimination of practices and policies which deprive marginal groups of control over their own development, and block their access to participation in political control. This is notably absent in strict equality models, where control remains firmly with the dominant groups in society.

Finally, there is a similarity of results. Self-determination requires representative government, participatory democracy, the right to participation in the political processes, structures and institutions as an end in themselves and as a precondition for the enjoyment of other human rights. An expansive interpretation of equality is said to require the full participation of marginalized groups in society's major institutions of political and social control and condemns social and political structures which preclude this.

It is fair to say that there are striking similarities between the core characteristics of self-determination and the subordination principle. At the same time it has become difficult to maintain the relationship between the expansive interpretation of the equality principles and its doctrinal roots, namely that what is like should be treated alike, and what is different, differently. To continue to adhere to the equality principle requires ever more expansive interpretations. Indeed, the weight of tradition and the inability of equality analysis to abstract itself from questions of sameness and difference would seem to make the effort doomed to failure. It would be better, therefore, to cut loose and adopt the principle and language of self-determination. Indeed, there is some indication that this process has already begun. Some feminist scholars are already beginning to use the language of self-determination.[40] This is also true of other groups such as homosexuals[41] and people with disabilities. Indigenous peoples have also abandoned the equality principle and are articulating their rights in the language of self-determination.

Analysis of Self-Determination

If this contention is accepted and the rights of women and other groups are articulated using the legal principle of self-determination, what would the advantages of this approach be? One of the central advantages is that the principle of self-determination states as its clear objective the ending of relations of hierarchy and domination. In international law jurisprudence this is seen as a precondition for the full enjoyment of all other human rights. This requirement is one which has been identified again and again by writers on equality as essential for the achievement of full equality, but it is not a requirement which sits easily with the equality principle. Second, self-determination is also an advance on equality in that it affirms the values of a group or individual, recognizing both as having an inherent worth in themselves and as being entitled to respect on that basis. Third, self-determination is a process as well as a substantive right. This can be seen in the rights to participation, representation and political control and to involvement in ongoing decision-making power.

Fourth, and perhaps most importantly, self-determination requires the returning of autonomy, decision-making power, and also the power to set goals according to one's own values, to groups who were hitherto deprived of this power. It is essentially a right of self-determination, not other-determination. This would have the effect of providing a tool whereby paternalistic or well-meaning but misguided policies could be criticized by showing that they were not what a group itself required or wished for its development. The legal principle of equality does not have this capability.

Implications of the Adoption of a Right to Self-determination

What exactly would be required in terms of specific legislation by the adoption of the principle of self-determination in national law? The process of answering this question necessitates a return to the distinctive and defining characteristic of the international law right to self-determination stated earlier, namely the right of a group with a distinct character to be recognized and respected as a centre of autonomous choice and to pursue the development of the centre according to the value system of that centre and the goals it has set for itself.

What would this require, then, in terms of specific measures in a particular jurisdiction? The minimum which would be required would be fourfold, first the creation of structures where decisions are taken to the greatest extent possible either by or in consultation with those affected by them; second, the reconstruction of existing decision-making bodies so that their membership contained representatives of all groups in society; third, the making freely available the information necessary for choices and evaluations to be made and decisions to be taken; and fourth, the enactment of legislation making void any policies or practices which would increase the disadvantage of an already disadvantaged group.

The idea that decisions should be taken at the lowest practical level by the individuals themselves or by the social grouping to which they belong is not a new idea. It can be seen in the principle of subsidiarity in the European Union (EU). Subsidiarity as a principle is not yet capable of being defined precisely as it has been introduced into EU law only recently by Article 3b of the Treaty on European Union.[42] At its most abstract it requires that decisions be taken at their lowest level to enable individuals and social groupings to fulfil their part in society. The principle also aims to guard against over-centralization of power. In EU law it is used to achieve a satisfactory division of powers and functions between the EU and the member states so that excessive power is not taken by the EU.[43] Returning decision-making to the lowest level, and bringing power and decisions closer to the people, is also part of the reasoning behind the division of power between levels of government in federal systems and between central and local government in unitary systems.[44]

Returning decision-making to the people affected by the decisions is crucial and central to the implementation of the principle of self-determination in national law. The core of self-determination is the right of peoples freely to determine their own status and development – the power to take and implement decisions is a prerequisite for the exercise of this right. If this power to take and implement decisions is to be made real within an existing state, bodies composed of members of a particular group and representing that group would have to be given power to take decisions and formulate policy to the greatest extent possible, and thereafter be given the right to be consulted prior to the making of decisions which would have a significant impact on the group. Certain representative bodies which could perform such functions are already in existence, for example the disability council, women's groups and other centres which act as lobby groups or information centres for language, religious or cultural groups, and as a focus for members of groups. These bodies provide information, conduct research into relevant issues, identify problems and difficulties and suggest solutions. In the process the values, concerns and objectives of the groups and group members are clarified and articulated, and, in some cases, goals are achieved. At present, however, this happens only on an *ad hoc* and unsystematic basis. To further self-determination, this type of group activity would have to be developed and representative entities would need to be set up where these do not already exist. Entities would need to be given a more formal status, funding would have to be provided for their work, and, most importantly, decision-making power would have to be given where possible, or at a minimum a right to be consulted before policies were formulated and decisions taken.

Also crucial to the implementation of the principle of self-determination at national law would be the restructuring of existing decision-making bodies so that they contained representatives of all groups in society rather than simply a few. It is clear that such reconstitution is required by the principle of self-determination – a people or group who are denied membership of and the opportunity to participate in government and the decision-making process cannot be said to be self-determining. At present, women, the disabled and members of ethnic and minority groups are under-represented in the bodies which make decisions in the state, such as Parliament, the executive and the judiciary and also at lower levels of power.[45] A vigorous and positive programme of action would be required to redress such imbalances, proceeding through a process of policy statement, data collection with detailed audits of membership of existing bodies and identification of barriers to access, followed by the setting of general objectives as well as specific targets to be achieved in terms of representation of members of disadvantaged groups on specified decision-making bodies. The process would then have to be monitored and the level of achievement measured. Such a policy has been called for by Justice in order to increase the numbers of women and ethnic minorities on the bench,[46] and has been used in Canada and Australia to increase the numbers of disadvantaged groups in employment.[47]

A third implication of the adoption of the principle of self-determination in national law would be that greater freedom of access to information would be required. Access to information is a prerequisite for the exercising of choice, the making of decisions and participation in decision-making.[48] Groups cannot meaningfully make the decisions necessary to be self-determining without being in possession of accurate information relating to their decision. Neither can they adequately promote or defend their interests against a state or against other groups without such information. The ready availability of sufficient and accurate information for the evaluation of options and the making of decisions is of central importance. That such information is crucial to both participation and dissent is recognized by many writers on democracy.[49] For this reason many jurisdictions have enacted legislation which gives access to the files and records of designated information holders.[50]

Providing for access to information is not without its difficulties, however. Decisions must be made as to which information will be made available to whom and on what conditions. Many existing legislative schemes make available only information held by governmental institutions, or by agencies funded by the state or acting on behalf of the state.[51] Most systems have important grounds on which access to information can be refused, for example commercial confidentiality or trade secrets.[52] In some cases the form in which the information is made available, or the cost of obtaining it, can make the right to access meaningless.[53] It is not proposed here to rehearse the debate on freedom of access to information. It is important to point out, however, that for the effective implementation of the principle of self-determination, the wider the delimitation of designated information holders and those entitled to demand information and the narrower the framing of exceptions, the greater the opportunity for self-determination through informed decision-making. The ability to make meaningful choices will depend directly on the amount of information available.[54]

Finally, the principle of self-determination would require a legislative or constitutional provision providing that any legislation or policies or practices which increased the disadvantage of an already disadvantaged group or of an individual who is a member of such a group would be void. This is the most radical extension of the equality principle and the development which I have argued earlier moves the interpretation of the equality principle so far away from its doctrinal basis that it is more properly called self-determination. The points discussed above, returning decision-making to the groups themselves, restructuring existing decision-making entities and providing for access to information, are the positive implications of the implementation of self-determination. The prohibition of measures which increase the disadvantage of already disadvantaged groups is the negative aspect, that is, it is the prevention of all measures which would have the effect of removing the power of groups to be self-determining. Such a legislative provision would operate in domestic law in a similar fashion to the subordination principle discussed above. The difference in operation between such a provision under the principle of self-determination and under the principle of equality is best illustrated, for example, considering an action against an employer for refusing to employ a person because of his or her ethnic background. Under the equality principle the argument would be made that such a practice is discriminatory in that it fails to treat people from ethnic minorities equally, i.e. the same as white people. Using the principle of self-determination, the argument against this practice would be constructed differently. The analysis of the situation would begin with a recognition that, in the particular society in question, individuals from certain ethnic backgrounds have been historically disadvantaged. The effect of the refusal to hire a person from a particular ethnic background would be characterized as a practice excluding members of that group from participating in economic and vocational opportunities provided by society and thereby increasing the economic and social disadvantage of this group. Furthermore, it would be seen as an exclusion of members of that group from the opportunity to accumulate the economic resources necessary to exercise choice and pursue their goals in society and therefore increasing their conditions of disadvantage. For this reason such a practice would be considered a violation of the right of members of that group to self-determination. Classification into categories of sameness and difference would not be necessary for the purposes of application of the principle.

Problems of Implementation

Some arguments can be made, however, against the implementation of a principle of self-determination in municipal systems. The first concern is that the adoption of a principle of self-determination would add to the confusion surrounding the principle in international law. The precise ambit of the principle in international law is by no means certain. Considerable disagreement exists as to the scope of the principle, the definition of peoples entitled to self-determination, methods of self-determination, and many other aspects of the right.[55] As has been discussed above, some writers are of the view that self-determination is tied to colonial, ex-colonial and analogous situations.[56] Other writers argue for a much broader interpretation.[57] The implications of the recognition of the right are also subject to debate. The argument could therefore be made that any attempt to widen the application of the principle to municipal law would only increase the confusion in this area of the law and that this consequence would be undesirable. In light of this potential for confusion, would it not be better to leave the name self-determination to the right at international law and create a principle of self-definition or self-development at national level? While this argument certainly deserves consideration, to take this approach would defeat the central objective of the adoption of the principle and language of self-determination, which is to harness the powerful principle of self-determination in international law for the improvement of the human rights of groups within an existing state. To use the language and rhetoric of self-determination is to subject the internal organization of a state, the process of government and the exercise of power to scrutiny and to ask the question, why should significant entities or groups of people be excluded from participating in governing and shaping the society in which they live, to make it more in accord with their values and aspirations. This would be lost if a principle of self-development or self-definition were adopted.

In practice, I would suggest that the likelihood of confusion is probably overstated. I would argue that it would be relatively easy to distinguish between on the one hand *external* self-determination and its concern with restructuring existing territorial boundaries, organization of states and the external relations between them, and *internal* self-determination on the other hand, which starts from the premise that the existing boundaries and legal personality of a state are to remain unchanged, and that it is the internal organization that is to be restructured.

A stronger fear concerning the adoption of the principle of self-determination in national law is that it will lead to the fragmentation of society into a number of different groups with competing interests, with the adverse effects this would have for the stability of the state and society. Fear of the fragmentation of society and the consequent destruction of the stability of the state have also been expressed in regard to self-determination at the international level.[58] Certainly such fears must be taken seriously. I would suggest, however, that the implementation of the principle as outlined in this chapter is more likely to foster social cohesion than social fragmentation. By improving the human rights of oppressed and disadvantaged groups within a state and facilitating their participation in society, by fostering a sense of allegiance through the integration of groups into society and their inclusion and participation in the decision-making process, social cohesion and a sense of identity within a state is promoted. By altering the composition of the decision-making institutions to incorporate the interests, values and objectives of hitherto excluded groups, their legitimacy as bodies entitled to make decisions for all groups would be enhanced. The result would be the strengthening of central institutions which would operate as a focus point for a wider conception of society, for the idea of the state, but in a manner which respects the right to self-determination of all who comprise society. There is therefore a greater likelihood that the civil unrest which stems from frustration and alienation from society would be avoided.[59] On the other hand, power structures in society at present, which fail to adequately include women, the disabled or members of religious and ethnic minorities, can lead substantial numbers of people to feel alienated from the state and to distrust the established power structures to the extent that any sense of civic or societal responsibility has been lost.[60] It is surely the case that such a situation is a greater danger to the stability and coherence of the state and society than the implementation of the principle of self-determination, which, it must be remembered, seeks to include members of such groups in the decision-making process in a society.

The criticism that the implementation of the principle of self-determination in the domestic law of a state will lead to the division of society into groups with competing interests also fails to recognize that society is in fact already divided into groups on the basis of colour, race, religion, sex and disability. These groups can often have little interaction with each other, and there already exists tension between them on a political and social level. If society is already divided in fact, with some groups dominant over others, then the introduction of a legal principle which recognizes this *de facto* division, and seeks to redress some of the harms done by this division and consequential diminution of human rights, must surely operate to decrease fragmentation and alienation rather than increase it. In such circumstances, if we wish to use law to advance human rights, surely law can be more effective if it sees society as it is, namely composed of groups and individuals who are members of these groups, rather than simply as autonomous unconnected individuals?[61]

There does remain, however, the difficulty of adequately defining the group and the membership of it, and in addition deciding which entities represent particular groups, especially if there is more than one body which claims this status. In international law, the delimitation of the groups entitled to self-determination has given rise to a considerable difficulty.[62] In other contexts, defining such groups as women and the disabled has also been difficult.[63] In delimiting membership of a group entitled to self-determination at national level, there are three approaches which could be taken. The first would be to allow for subjective or self-definition – a person is a member of a group if he or she regards himself or herself as so being and identifies with that group. The second approach is to have objective criteria of membership set out in legislation – a person is then regarded as a member of that group if he or she complies with the criteria of membership. The third approach would be to combine the two and have certain external and objective criteria of membership, but allow an individual to dissociate himself or herself from membership of the group if he or she does not identify with the group or does not regard himself or herself as being a member of that particular group. This third approach is preferable for the following reasons: the detailing of objective criteria, if not too rigid and inflexible, would bring a degree of certainty to the law, while the retention of a subjective element would allow individuals to dissociate themselves from membership of a group if they did not regard themselves as belonging. This would overcome the difficulty experienced by those formulating policy and legislation for the improvement of the situation of the disabled in Canada, whereby some individuals did not want the stigma of being formally and legally labelled disabled.[64] Such a combination of objective and subjective criteria is the method used to define 'ethnic group' by courts in the UK for the purposes of s. 3 of the Race Relations Act 1976.[65]

CONCLUSION

The question of how to improve the human rights of all groups in society is one which has been the subject of much argument and discussion. This chapter has attempted to move this debate forward by arguing that one method used to improve human rights, namely the application of the equality principle, has reached the limits of its effectiveness as a legal tool for ending the domination and disadvantage of oppressed groups in society, and that instead the principle and language of self-determination should be adopted. I have also attempted to delineate the implications of such an approach in terms of specific national legislation and practical application. In my view, to take such an approach would result in a significant advance in the understanding of human rights as a good to which we are entitled by our very nature as people, but the proof of this assertion can only lie in its application to the lives of the disadvantaged in society.

NOTES

1. The taxonomy I adopt is based on that put forward by E. A. Sheehy for the Canadian Advisory Council on the Status of Women, but conflated in some respects. See E. A. Sheehy, Background Paper, *Personal Autonomy and the Criminal Law: Emerging Issues for Women* (Ottawa: Canadian Advisory Council on the Status of Women, 1987).

2. R. Wasserstrom, Racism, sexism and preferential treatment (1977) 24 *UCLA Law Review* 600.

3. Directive 76/207/EEC on the Implementation of the Principle of Equal Treatment for Men and Women as Regards Access to Employment, Vocational Training and Promotion and Working Conditions. See also Equal Pay Directive 75/17/EEC and the Equal Treatment (Social Security) Directive 86/378/EEC as amended.

4. 42 USC 2000e-2(a)(1).

5. The chief proponent of this approach is W. Williams; see W. Williams, Equality's riddle: pregnancy and the equal treatment/special treatment debate (1984) 13 *NYU Review of Law and Social Change* 325.

6. C. Bacchi, *Same Difference: Feminism and Sexual Difference* (Sydney: Allen & Unwin, 1990), Chapter 1. See also K. O'Donovan, *Sexual Divisions in Law* (London: Weidenfeld and Nicolson, 1985), pp. 160–1.

7. See A. V. Dicey, *The Law of the Constitution*, 1st edn (London: Macmillan & Co., 1885), and in particular pp. 200–3, where Dicey writes that the rule of law 'means, again, equality before the law, or the equal subjection of all classes to the ordinary law of the land administered by the ordinary law courts'.

8. H. Kelsen, *What is Justice? Collected Essays* (Berkeley: University of California Press, 1975). See further Chapter 9, above.

9. See *Enderby* v. *Frenchay Health Authority* [1994] 1 CMLR 8.

10. See *Turley* v. *Allders Stores Ltd* [1980] ICR 66; *Gedulgig* v. *Aiello*, 417 US 484 (1974); *General Electric* v. *Gilbert*, 429 US 125 (1976).

11. See, for example, US *Pregnancy Discrimination Act* 1978, *Webb* v. *EMO Air Cargo (UK)*

Ltd [1992] 2 All ER 43. The European Court of Justice has since rejected the analysis in *Webb* that a pregnant woman is comparable with a sick man. See *Webb* v. *EMO Cargo (UK) Ltd* Case C-32/93 and the discussion by B. Napier, Webb in Europe (1994) 144 *New Law Journal* 1020.

12. S. Fredman, A difference with a distinction: pregnancy and parenthood reassessed (1994) 110 *Law Quarterly Review* 106.

13. *Ibid.*, p. 110.

14. *Ibid.*, p. 111.

15. For a discussion of the special provision made for people with disabilities in the US by the Americans with Disabilities Act 1990, see G. Quinn, Disability discrimination law in the United States. In G. Quinn, M. McDonagh and C. Kimber, *Disability Discrimination Law in the US, Australia and Canada* (Dublin: Oak Tree Press, 1993).

16. Council Directive 92/85.

17. M. Thornton, Feminist jurisprudence: illusion or reality (1986) 3 *Journal of Law and Society* 5, at p. 13. Of further interest in this context is *Kalanke* v. *Freie Hansestadt Bremen* (ECJ), *The Times* 26 October 1995 (national rules guaranteeing women absolute and unconditional priority for appointment as promotion went beyond promoting equal opportunities).

18. For a discussion of the advantages and disadvantages of affirmative action, see M. Thornton, Affirmative action, merit and the liberal state (1985) 2(2) *Australian Journal of Law and Society* 28; C. Edley, Affirmative action and the rights rhetoric trap. In R. K. Fullinwider and C. Mills (eds), *The Moral Foundations of Civil Rights* (Totowa, New Jersey: Rowman and Littlefield, 1986); M. Matsudi, Looking to the bottom: critical legal studies and reparations (1987) 22 *Harvard Civil Rights – Civil Liberties Law Review* 323.

19. See *Page* v. *Freight Hire Limited* [1981] 1 All ER 394; K. O'Donovan, *op. cit.*, pp. 163–6.

20. For example, in *Johnston* v. *RUC* [1986] ECR 1651.

21. *EEOC* v. *Sears, Roebuck and Co.*, 628 F Supp 1264 (1986).

22. The originator of this interpretation is C. MacKinnon; see C. MacKinnon, *Toward a Feminist Theory of the State* (Cambridge, MA: Harvard University Press, 1990); Reflections on sex equality under the law (1991) 100 *Yale Law Journal* 1281.

23. MacKinnon's characterization of the laws surrounding reproduction are an example of this: 'any constitutional interpretation of a sex equality principle must prohibit laws, state policies, or official practices and acts that deprive women of reproductive control'. Reflections on Sex Equality, *op. cit.*, p. 1319.

24. E. Ellis, *European Community Sex Equality Law* (Oxford: Clarendon Press, 1991). Young's description of social equality is illustrative here as it is seen as 'the full participation and inclusion of everyone in a society's major institutions and the socially supported substantive opportunity for all to develop and exercise their capacities and realise their choices'. See I. Young, *Justice and the Politics of Difference* (Princeton: Princeton University Press, 1990) as quoted in S. Fredman, *op. cit.*, p. 121.

25. D. Greschner, Abortion and democracy for women: a critique of Tremblay and Daigle (1990) 35 *McGill Law Review* 634.

26. Section 15(1) provides as follows: 'Every individual is equal before and under the law and has the right to the equal protection and equal benefit of the law without discrimination, and in particular, without discrimination based on race, national or ethnic origin, colour, religion, sex, age or mental or physical disability.'

27. *Andrews* v. *Law Society of British Columbia* [1989] 1 SCR 143, at 184. This approach has been affirmed by subsequent decisions. See *Rudolph Wolff* v. *Canada* [1990] 1 SCR 695, and *R* v. *Turpin* [1989] 1 SCR 1296. For a critique of the operation of section 15, see Chapter 10, above.

28. See, for example, N. C. Sheppard, Recognition of the disadvantaging of women: the promise of *Andrews* v. *Law Society of British Columbia* (1989) 35 *McGill Law Review* 207.

29. C. MacKinnon, Reflections on sex equality, *op. cit.*

30. M. Pomerance, *Self-Determination in Law and Practice: The New Doctrine in the United Nations* (The Hague: Martinus Nijhoff, 1982).

31. A. Michalska, Rights of peoples and human rights in international law. In G. Kutukdjian and A. Papisca (eds), *Rights of Peoples* (Padova, CEDAM, 1991), p. 31.

32. GA Resolution 1514 (XV), 14 December 1960.

33. Two of the more important such instruments are GA Resolution 2625 (XXV), 24 October 1970, *Declaration on Principles of International Law Concerning Friendly Relations and Co-operation Among States*, and Principle VIII of the Final Act of the Conference on Security and Co-operation in Europe, Helsinki, 1975. See also GA Resolution 1541 (XV) 15 December 1960, *Principles Which Should Guide Members in Determining Whether or Not an Obligation Exists to Transmit the Information Called for Under Article 7(3)e of the Charter*.

34. P. Thornberry, Self-determination, minorities, human rights: a review of international instruments (1989) 38 *International and Comparative Law Quarterly* 867, at p. 870.

35. I. Brownlie, The rights of peoples in modern international law. In J. Crawford, *The Rights of Peoples* (Oxford: Clarendon Press, 1988), p. 1, at p. 6.

36. E. M. Morgan, The imagery and meaning of self-determination (1988) 20 *NYU Journal of Law and Politics* 355.

37. I. G. Shivji, State and constitutionalism in Africa: a new democratic perspective (1990) 18 *International Journal of the Sociology of Law* 381; W. Reisman, Sovereignty and human rights in contemporary international law (1988) 84 *American Journal of International Law* 866.

38. P. Thornberry, *op. cit.*, p. 860.

39. A. Michalska, *op. cit.*, p. 45.

40. See, for example, D. Greschner, *op. cit.*

41. B. Epstein, Gay politics, ethnic identity: the limits of social constructionism (1987) 17 *Socialist Review* 11.

42. For a discussion of the principle, see D. Lasok, *Law and Institutions of the European Union*, 6th edn (London: Butterworths, 1994), p. 36 *et. seq.*

43. See *The Principle of Subsidiarity: Communication of the Commission to the Council and the European Parliament*, SEC (92) 1990 Final.

44. D. Oliver, *Government in the United Kingdom: The Search for Accountability, Effectiveness and Citizenship* (Buckingham: Open University Press, 1991), Chapter 5.

45. As regards membership of women and ethnic groups in the judiciary, see the report by Justice, The Judiciary in England and Wales (London: Justice, 1992), Appendix 6.

46. *Ibid.*, p. 23.

47. For Australia, see Affirmative Action (Equal Opportunity for Women) Act 1986, Cth, Equal Employment Opportunity (Commonwealth Authorities) Act 1987, and in Canada, Employment Equity Act L. 23 RSC 1985.

48. See R. Austin, Freedom of information: the constitutional impact. In J. Jowell and D. Oliver, *The Changing Constitution*, 3rd edn (Oxford: Clarendon Press, 1994), Chapter 14.

49. See D. Held, *Models of Democracy* (Stanford: Stanford University Press, 1987) p. 262 *et seq.*; B. Barber, *Strong Democracy: Participatory Politics for a New Age* (Berkeley, California: University of California Press, 1984), p. 276 *et. seq.*; R. Austin, *op. cit.*, pp. 400–1. I am grateful to Katrina Kelly, University of Aberdeen, for her comments on access to information in the context of self-determination.

50. For the USA, see Freedom of Information Act 5 USC s. 552 (1988), and for Canada see Access to Information Act RSC 1980–81–82–83 c. 111 Sch. I. As regards access to information on the environment in the EU see EC Directive 90/313 *Freedom of Access to Information on the Environment*.

51. For Canada, see Access to Information Act, s. 2; for Texas, see Open Records Act, Texas Civ. Stat. Art. 6252-17a, s. 2(1)(F).

52. For Canada, see Access to Information Act, s. 20.1; see EC Directive 90/313, Article 3(2).

53. For the UK experience with water registers, see T. Burton, Access to environmental information: the UK experience of water registers (1989) 1 *Journal of Environmental Law* 192.

54. This point is supported by R. Austin, *op. cit.*, p. 400, where he argues that 'the value of the participant's role as measured by his ability to affect the outcome of the decision-making process is dependant on his degree of access to official information'.

55. For a discussion of many of the areas of disagreement, see M. Pomerance, *op. cit.*; W. Ofuatey-Kodjoe, *The Principle of Self-Determination in International Law* (New York: Nellon, 1977); A. Rigo-Sureda, *The Evolution of the Right to Self-Determination: A Study of UN Practice*

(Leiden: Sijthoff, 1973).

56. A. Rigo-Sureda, *op. cit.*, pp. 104–11.

57. M. Pomerance, *op. cit.*, Chapter III.

58. See J. Schumpeter, *Capitalism, Socialism and Democracy* (New York: Harper, 1942).

59. D. Oliver, *op. cit.*, Chapter 9.

60. *Ibid.*, p. 38.

61. For a critique of legal theory taking an individualistic view of society, see C. Pateman, *The Problem of Political Obligation: A Critique of Liberal Society* (London: Wiley & Sons, 1979); C. B. McPherson, *The Life and Times of Liberal Democracy* (Oxford: Oxford University Press, 1977); O. Fiss, Groups and the Equal Protection Clause (1975) 5 *Philosophy and Public Affairs* 105.

62. Brownlie points out in this respect that 'the establishment of a definition of membership, the analog of nationality is a delicate matter'. I. Brownlie, *op. cit.*, p. 7.

63. See E. Spelman, *Inessential Woman* (Boston: Beacon Press, 1988); Quinn *et al.*, *op. cit.*, pp. 47–53, 124–128 and 209–210 for the definitions of disability in the US, Australia and Canada respectively.

64. See C. Kimber, Disability Discrimination law in Canada. In G. Quinn *et al.*, *op. cit.*, p. 209.

65. *Mandla* v. *Dowell Lee* [1983] 1 All ER 1062.

PART FOUR:

RIGHTS AND PERSONAL LIBERTY

13

Human Rights, Sexual Orientation and the Social and Legal Impact of Law and Law Reform

Nicholas Bamforth

Oscar Wilde pointed out that one cannot make men moral by law, that all that one can do is criminalise their preferences. (Edwina Currie MP, House of Commons, 21 February 1994)[1]

[K]eeping the law in a discriminatory fashion ... automatically means that young gay men will be set apart from society. If we remove that discrimination from the statute-book, it may go some way towards giving young gay men the self-respect and the self-dignity to which they are entitled and should have. (Chris Smith MP, House of Commons, 21 February 1994)[2]

INTRODUCTION

During the House of Commons debate on the clauses of the then Criminal Justice and Public Order Bill 1994 which affected the age of consent for sexual acts between men,[3] many obvious arguments were raised about the proper functions and limits of the criminal law. MPs who supported a common age of consent for homosexual and heterosexual acts set at 16 argued, for example, that the law should respect privacy and should treat like cases alike. A higher age of consent for homosexual than for heterosexual acts constituted, they argued, an undue invasion of the privacy of young gay men, and would be to treat them less favourably than their heterosexual counterparts.[4] By contrast, most supporters of a higher age of consent for homosexual than for heterosexual acts, whether set at 18 or at 21, argued that the criminal law should assume a protective role towards young men alleged to be uncertain about their sexual orientation, and should therefore prohibit them from engaging in homosexual activity.

Whatever one's view of the merits of these competing arguments, it should be clear that they go only to the normative issue of the proper *function* of the law, in this case in relation to non-heterosexual sexual orientations and conduct.[5] However, an assessment of the worth of most proposals to alter the law will usually also involve, if only at a common-sense level, an evaluation of the proposal's likely *impact* on social behaviour if it is implemented[6] – after all, there is little point in amending the law, especially via statutory reform, if that amendment lacks even symbolic effect in society as a whole. The significance of the social impact of law was not lost on the two MPs – both supporters of an equal age of consent at 16 – who made the comments set out above: the first comment addresses the *ineffectiveness* of the criminal law in altering a person's sexual orientation, while the second suggests that the criminal law can play an *effective* role in stigmatizing certain groups and in setting them apart from the rest of society.

This distinction – between arguments about the proper functions of law and arguments about its impact – has important consequences not only for debate about the legal regulation of lesbian, bisexual and gay sexual orientations, but also more generally for debate over whether an enforceable human rights code – such as an entrenched bill of rights – should be enacted in the UK. For evaluation of arguments concerning the impact of law, in addition to those concerning its proper functions, is vital at a practical level if we wish to formulate viable tactics either for eliminating social hostility and prejudice directed towards people who are or who are perceived as being of non-heterosexual sexual orientations, or more generally for promoting greater awareness of and respect for notions of human rights (however defined) in our political culture. A central and often overlooked question is, *if* we are concerned to ensure the eradication of what we deem to be unjustifiable prejudice or other unfair treatment directed at a particular group, or if we wish to combat what we identify as an absence of respect for notions of human rights more generally, *and* if we decide that it is – according to our view of law's normative function – justifiable to use law to pursue these ends, will law and law reform be *effective* means of achieving our policy goals? It may be the case, for example, that the options for reform on offer are so toothless, or that law would, *per se*, be so ineffective in altering hostile or prejudiced social behaviour, that our policy goal would be better or more easily fulfilled by investing time and resources in outreach or educational work.[7] A supplementary issue is whether law reform is likely to take us closer to our policy goals if effected by statute or by case law, by a general rights code or by a judicial discretion.

Equally, failure to recognize the importance of arguments concerning the impact of law is likely to produce an incomplete or blurred analysis. As Otto Kahn-Freund has pointed out:

> Many people have something like a magic belief in the efficacy of the law in shaping human conduct and social relations. It is a superstition which is itself a fact of political importance, but a superstition it is all the same ... where there are strong forces or traditions favouring a pattern or action ... the role which the law can play in improving the situation, though not negligible, can never be decisive. [8]

This observation is reinforced by recent literature on racial discrimination legislation, which shows that the mere existence of legislation prohibiting racially discriminatory practices in specified circumstances has not in reality resulted in the eradication of such practices, or in anything approaching racial equality.[9] Finally, the importance of debate about the impact of law has been underlined by Roger Cotterrell's observation that law is seen in contemporary Western societies as an instrument of state power.[10] As swathes of post-World War II legislation in the UK show, law has been used by successive governments as a tool in their attempts to achieve certain policy goals.[11]

The notion that law reform (whether affecting non-heterosexual persons or issues of human rights more generally) is usually motivated by the assumption that it can have an impact of some sort, either on society or on the legal system, carries an important implication for our understanding of 'human rights'. Many of us will have views, in the form of moral theories or theories of justice, about the things to which we feel people are morally entitled and about the ways in which they should be able to behave. Our views at the moral level may not, however, be reflected in people's entitlements under existing law, and it is also possible to imagine types of behaviour which may be legally permissible but which would attract social reprimand if they occurred in everyday life. Perceived disparities of this sort – between moral, legal and social levels of entitlement – are usually the focal point of calls for law reform, whether to protect 'human rights' generally, or to protect a specific group of people or type of 'human right' (whatever substantive interests each of us counts as human rights). If we feel that people are morally entitled to behave in a certain fashion, if we have decided that this type of behaviour is sufficiently important to count as a 'human right' under our own moral theory, and if the law fails to allow people to behave in the manner concerned, then we are likely to identify the disparity as a 'human rights issue' and to feel that the law should be changed. If the law

is changed but severe social penalties are still imposed upon people identified as behaving in the relevant manner, we might well say that they
were being prevented from exercising their 'human rights'. We would
also identify as a 'human rights issue' a government's more general
denial, to the population or to individuals, of things to which we felt the
population was morally and/or legally entitled. Calls for law reform to
protect 'human rights' therefore presuppose a theory of moral entitlement to the 'human right' in question, and tend to assume that law
reform will have some impact at the social level as well as the legal.

In this chapter, I wish to re-examine some existing theories of the
impact of law and law reform, and to draw some conclusions from this
about the protection of human rights – however defined – through law.
This examination will focus particularly on the development and practical effects of laws and law reform measures affecting lesbians, bisexuals
and gay men. There are two reasons for this. First, the 1994 age of consent debate highlighted many of the assumptions commonly made by
legislators and members of the public about the impact of law and law
reform, and is therefore a good contemporary case study. Second, the
acute social sensitivity which still attaches to non-heterosexual sexual
orientations in the UK means that the attitudes about law reform displayed in this context tend to stand in starker relief than in other law
reform debates, highlighting more clearly the difficulties in existing
theories about the impact of law reform. The word 'law' will be taken
here to cover both statutes and case law, although distinctions between
the two will be drawn where appropriate. The term 'law reform' is used
in a neutral sense, that is, it is taken to refer to any deliberate change in
the law, whether or not such a change is considered at a normative level
to be progressive.[12]

THEORIES OF LAW'S IMPACT

It seems plausible to suggest that the impact of law or of law reform will
be felt at two important levels. The first is within the legal system: a legal
rule, whether embodied in statute or common law, is supposed to resolve
authoritatively any dispute falling within its scope. Introducing a new
rule or reforming an existing one should therefore directly affect the way
in which disputes falling within the scope of that rule are resolved in
court. In other words, the legal rights of the parties are determined by
the existence of rules governing the situation concerned, and can be
altered by reform of those rules. This model is, however, a little blunt,

since jurisprudential controversies over theories of adjudication (i.e. the way in which judges decide cases), 'gaps' in the law and rules of precedent all play a role here. And, as Doreen McBarnet has shown, judges can happily use the case law technique to erode broader rules of law which they dislike.[13] As such, the mere existence of a rule is unlikely to have an automatic and decisive effect on the outcome of cases falling within its scope: instead, we must also take account of the effect of judicial interpretation or manipulation of the rule in assessing its precise impact on the legal system. Within these parameters, it is clear that rules of law do nevertheless have considerable impact within our own legal system, for judges usually feel obliged to take account of them in their reasoning, whether the reasoning is designed to apply, extend, qualify or deny the relevance of the rule concerned.[14]

The second and more difficult level of impact is within society as a whole, a key aspect of which is the relationship between law and social stability or social change. These concepts can be explained more precisely. Yehezkel Dror has suggested that:

> Society is always undergoing processes of change; human generations follow one another and different persons fulfil various social roles. The concept 'social change' does not refer to this constant change in the population of every society, but refers to changes in the society as such, including the various social institutions, roles and status definitions, accepted ideologies, value patterns, pattern variables and value-profiles. In other words, the concept of social change refers to changes in social structure or in culture.[15]

And William Evan has noted that:

> Law emerges not only to *codify* existing customs, morals, or mores, but also to *modify* the behaviour and the values presently existing in a particular society. The conception of law as a codification of existing customs, morals, or mores implies a relatively passive function. On the other hand, the conception of law as a means of social change, i.e., as a potential for modifying behaviour and beliefs, implies a relatively active function.[16]

We should note that this argument is analytical rather than prescriptive, for Evan makes no attempt to prescribe which modifications of behaviour and belief law should bring about in its active function. As such, a law which encouraged social discrimination against a particular group would, if successful, be acting as an agent of social change as much as a law which successfully discouraged such conduct. It is also important to notice that the argument does not fall foul of Kahn-Freund's 'magic belief' objection, for Evan does not assume that a legal change *automatically* ensures a corresponding social change. Rather, law in its active function is seen as having the *potential* for modifying behaviour and beliefs. This brings us to the central issue, namely how, at a theoretical level, law is thought to be capable of doing so, and what obstacles are seen as standing in its way – in other words, if law and law reform can have a social impact, what form(s) does this assume?

We can argue that one way in which law can have a social impact is by guiding behaviour patterns outside the courtroom. This analysis covers both 'technical' rules of law and those directly concerned with our civil liberties. In the technical area, we can argue, for example, that conveyancing formalities in real property law encourage the use of approved and standard procedures in the buying and selling of interests in land.[17] In the civil liberties sphere, public order legislation enables citizens to distinguish lawful from unlawful forms of public protest.[18] From this perspective, a court case can usually be seen as a device of the last resort; in general, the aim of law is for people to obey its strictures without the need for actual enforcement and, as such, a court case – at least in an area where the law is clear – is a failure of law's guidance function.[19] The social impact of law as a guidance device can presumably be affected by, among other things, the clarity of the rule concerned and the degree to which the public is aware of it. A difficulty in terms of guidance is the degree to which relevant laws have an impact on the negotiation and terms of out-of-court settlements.[20]

The alleged social impact of law as a guidance device is concerned simply with law's effect on people's behaviour. What, however, of people's beliefs? Roger Cotterrell has suggested that 'educative' legislation is intended '*to change ideas* by influencing behaviour', an example being the original race relations legislation in the UK.[21] This is to be distinguished from 'symbolic' legislation, which, he suggests, has no role in promoting social change, existing merely with the object of 'placating opposed interests of various sections of society while avoiding change'.[22] In addition, no realistic consideration may have been given to the possibility of enforcing symbolic legislation.[23] Such legislation might include general but unenforceable aspirations contained within a human rights code, whose effect could be to dampen down demands for further change by giving the appearance of granting greater freedom to citizens.[24] We should note, however, that the failure of a piece of legislation to promote social change does not prevent it from having a social impact, such impact being the curtailing of demands for further legal reform. In addition, it is not necessarily true to say that symbolic legislation is always *intended* to avoid change: a legislature which wished to make a statement

of its support for human rights notions might introduce an unenforceable human rights code because it was worried by the political power
which an entrenched bill of rights would confer on the judiciary. The
code itself would be intended, in these circumstances, as a statement of
support for human rights notions and as an exhortation to others to
support them.

Theorists are much less clear about how, exactly, law is supposed to
educate. Anthony Lester and Geoffrey Bindman, writing on the impact
of race relations legislation, simply asserted that '[c]ontrary to the belief
of some critics, legislation and education are not incompatible; legislation
is a powerful form of education, and legislation and education depend
upon each other.'[25] Evert van der Veen and Adrianne Dercksen have
argued that social discrimination against persons who are or are perceived to be lesbian or gay results from negative views of lesbian and gay
sexual orientation conveyed, at least in European Union member states,
by legislation and by prevailing religious and medical doctrines which
marginalize or stigmatize such sexual orientations in a socially relevant
fashion.[26] Unfortunately, the authors fail to explain how this process
actually works, or the precise role played by any of their three factors.
Finally, William Evan, in explaining his 'active function' for law, suggests
that:

> As an instrument of social change, law entails two interrelated
> processes: the institutionalization and the internalization of
> patterns of behavior. In this context, institutionalization of a pattern
> of behavior means the establishment of a norm with provisions for
> its enforcement, and internalization of a pattern of behavior means
> the incorporation of the value or values implicit in a law. *Law . . . can
> affect behavior directly only through the process of institutionalization; if,
> however, the institutionalization process is successful, it, in turn, facilitates
> the internalization of attitudes or beliefs.*[27]

While being a little more precise about the mechanics of the educative
process, this still fails to explain how the mere fact that something has
been successfully established as a norm can alter people's attitudes or
beliefs.

In fact, the notion that law can, on its own, miraculously 'educate' a
grudging or hostile populace seems as simplistic as many theories about
the alleged deterrent effect of law.[28] As mentioned earlier, recent
literature has shown the lack of 'bite' which the race relations legislation
has had, despite the optimism of Lester and Bindman in the early
1970s.[29] The importance of law in people's day-to-day moral evaluations
of social situations should also not be overstressed. An obvious example

is that despite the existence of well-publicized traffic speed limits, such limits are disregarded on a casual and near-universal basis, without any moral qualms at the fact that the law is thereby broken. Equally, one suspects that most people's instinctive revulsion at the idea of intentionally killing another human being is not dependent solely on the existence of a law against murder. Popular reactions to news of an intentional killing tend to take the form of anger at the fact that the victim has been killed. That the killing involved the law of murder being broken is simply irrelevant.[30] In short, blandly asserting that the creation or existence of law is capable of 'educating' people, in the sense of altering their beliefs, is a serious underestimation of the variety and the independence of human responses to social situations involving law. People's conceptions of moral right and wrong seem frequently to be shaped not by the present law, but by their assumptions about what one is socially (and maybe morally) entitled to do.[31] For example, while sexual harassment at work contravenes the Sex Discrimination Act 1975,[32] sexual harassment is still rife in the workplace. This suggests that many male employees either feel that it is socially acceptable to treat women in this way, or assume that they can do so and escape unpunished – the assumption behind either state of mind being that male employees are socially entitled to harass women.

In addition, various other factors would seem to affect the social impact of law, whatever form that impact takes. First, Yehezkel Dror has argued that 'whether law-enforcing agencies prosecute or refrain from prosecuting certain offences affects the impact of the law on society, although the law itself is not changed'.[33] This argument can be developed to cover the enforcement of law more generally, including (if appropriate) decisions about whether to arrest and decisions as to the level of penalty, civil or criminal, to be imposed on an unsuccessful defendant. While the concept of 'dead letter' laws is well known, we will see below that the mere non-enforcement of a law might not necessarily deprive it of all social impact.[34] Second, judicial emasculation of a law may blunt the social message which that law conveys, thereby diluting its social impact.[35] One can therefore say that, in this sense, the legal impact of a law can affect its social impact. Third, as Dror notes, '[b]asic institutions rooted in traditions and values, such as the family, seem to be extremely resistant to changes imposed by the law.'[36] This ties in with the point made above about the danger of overstressing the social importance of law; if we are concerned with institutions with a special place in our culture, such as the family, popular moral evaluations are particularly unlikely to be altered by the mere existence of a law. These three factors are, of course, mutually reinforcing, in that popular prejudice will be engaged or affected even less by a law which is not effectively enforced, whether by an enforcement agency or in the courts.

Unfortunately, the picture is clouded by another group of important factors. Law clearly possesses a certain importance in popular imagination – the oft-heard assertion that 'there ought to be a law against it', 'it' referring to any practice of which the speaker disapproves, suggests that people do think of law, at least sometimes, as having a practical and/or moral role. And if law did not have this importance, law reform debates, at least where sensitive social issues such as ages of consent or anti-discrimination laws are concerned, would not assume the significance which they do, whether for supporters or opponents of the law reform measure concerned. The European Court of Human Rights has asserted that law can have a social impact, in its acceptance of the argument that the mere existence of a law which singles out a particular group for unfavourable treatment may, even if it is not enforced (whether against the applicant or more generally) nevertheless affect members of that group to the extent that they can claim to be 'victims' under Article 25 of the European Convention on Human Rights (ECHR), with standing to litigate.[37] This suggests that the notion of symbolic legislation can be taken further, and deployed less cynically than Cotterrell would suggest. Cotterrell admits that his notions of symbolic and educative legislation 'cannot always be clearly separated';[38] the ECHR case law in fact suggests that where laws mark out particular groups of people for special treatment of some sort, they can reinforce how other people see these groups, *and how members of them see themselves*. Even if not enforced, such laws might therefore have a symbolic social impact. If this is so, it follows that a law can both stigmatize and, if deployed for positive social purposes, perhaps socially empower members of the directly affected group.

A still stronger argument has been developed by Kendall Thomas, in his analysis of the legal and social position of bisexual and gay men in the USA. Oral and anal intercourse between men is prohibited under the criminal law of approximately half the US state jurisdictions. While avoiding any claim that the widespread legal prohibitions directly *cause* homophobic attacks, Thomas nevertheless suggests that they tend to *legitimize* such violence – he asserts that 'homosexual [anti] sodomy statutes express the official "theory" of homophobia; private acts of violence against gay men and lesbians "translate" that theory into brutal "practice". In other words, private homophobic violence punishes what homosexual sodomy statutes prohibit.'[39] Under this theory, criminal prohibitions on homosexual behaviour contribute to the development of a social climate in which homophobic violence is accepted and even celebrated.

A final argument for the view that law can have a social impact is that not even the strongest critics of the weakness of existing anti-discrimination legislation have advocated its repeal.[40] This suggests that they see the potential social impact of such a law reform measure as disastrous, despite the poor legal impact of the relevant laws at present.

This analysis leaves us, then, with an apparently contradictory picture. On the one hand, the notion that law, acting alone, can have a social impact as an educative agent is clearly too simplistic, and we can see that law plays a much smaller role in popular moral evaluations than some lawyers have tended to assume. On the other hand, law is popularly perceived as having some role to play, we have indications that it can play a symbolic role or a role which reinforces the social disempowerment of particular groups, and most of us tend to feel that law reform is an important political issue.[41] We will now attempt to clarify the picture a little by conducting a more detailed examination of legislators' and judges' stated feelings about law reform as it affects the position of lesbians, gay men and bisexuals. We will then use this to draw some more general conclusions about the social impact of law and human rights codes.

LEGAL REGULATION OF SEXUAL ORIENTATION

Robert Wintemute has noted that legal tactics to promote the elimination of discrimination against people on the ground of their sexual orientation tend to start with reform of the criminal law.[42] As such, the fact that in the UK two of the three major parliamentary law reform debates about sexual orientation in the last 25 years have concerned the criminal law as it affects gay men, while the third, concerning s. 28 of the Local Government Act 1988, led to a restriction in the ability of local authorities to break down social prejudice against non-heterosexuals, is a sign of the very limited extent to which even the legal position of lesbians, gay men and bisexuals has been improved, especially by comparison with other European Union member states. I do not, however, intend here to embark on a detailed examination of the legal regime in force in the UK:[43] rather, I intend to examine the significance attached to law reform by participants in the various debates on this topic.[44]

The richest source of material on political attitudes to the likely social impact of law and law reform can be found in: the 1957 Wolfenden Committee Report[45] which originally recommended the partial decriminalization of male homosexual acts; the parliamentary debates and the reactions to the proposals enacted as the Sexual Offences Act 1967 and s. 28 of the Local Government Act 1988; and the House of Commons debate on the age of consent sections of what became the 1994 Criminal Justice and Public Order Act. It should be noted that the arguments about impact which can be extracted from these sources all presuppose a view about the moral propriety or otherwise of homosexual conduct, and most assume a view about the appropriate function of the law in this area. As such, one's view of the likely impact of law or law reform may well be shaped by, and is unlikely to be capable of complete separation from, one's views on these other issues.

This is particularly clear from some of the more extreme arguments put forward by opponents of the 1967 and the 1994 Acts. Such arguments tended to focus upon the idea that a change in the law would give the state's blessing to homosexual behaviour,[46] or even result in a direct increase in its occurrence[47] – notions which, even if they were true, would clearly only be important to a person who was opposed to such behaviour *per se*. We have already seen, at a theoretical level, that there are great difficulties in the view that law can encourage or educate. Many of the opinions expressed in the various law reform debates not only support this, but also help provide an answer to some of the problems considered in the previous section.

To go back to 1957, the Wolfenden Committee was of the opinion that it was unlikely that partial decriminalization of male homosexual acts would bring about a substantial increase in their occurrence. Such an argument, the Committee felt, 'seems to us to exaggerate the effect of the law on human behaviour'.[48] And Lady Gaitskell, during the House of Lords debate on what became the 1967 Act, declared that 'I do not believe that the present laws keep homosexuality in check, and I do not believe that homosexuality would be increased if the laws were liberalised.'[49] Of particular interest here is Edwina Currie MP's assertion during the debate on the 1994 Act that 'one cannot make men moral by law, that all that one can do is criminalise their preferences'.[50] This seems, at least partly, to rest on the widely supported medical opinion that sexual orientation is (at least for men) either genetic or becomes determined at an early age, so that law is incapable of affecting it.[51] Equally, as Stephen Jeffery-Poulter has pointed out, in every Parliamentary debate on what became the 1967 Act 'even the most fervent of the Bill's supporters had repeatedly asserted that they did not wish to suggest that Parliament was encouraging or approving of homosexual activity by removing criminal sanctions against it'.[52] And, as the history of the period after 1967 shows, the growth of organized gay clubs, cafés, helplines and associations occurred very slowly, being met with ongoing hostile reactions.[53]

This suggests two things. First, a characteristic as central to a person as their sexual orientation will not be altered by the law, and its actual incidence, as opposed to openness about its incidence, is unlikely to be altered dramatically.[54] Law might encourage people to hide or even to ignore their sexual orientation for fear of being caught, but it cannot alter it or snuff it out. This constitutes an in-built limitation on the social impact, if any, of law.[55] Second, it is not the mere fact that the law has been altered which will bring about a change in public opinion, i.e. have an educative impact. To expect it to do so, especially in an area where the populace is hostile to the law reform measure in question, is to take a very simplistic view of human nature. The process is in fact much more subtle, and varies from case to case and from society to society. The debate surrounding any change in the law will clearly be important, for this enables both law-makers and members of the public to express opinions which would not otherwise be heard. This openness can, in turn, encourage members of the public to re-think their attitudes, regardless of the actual success or otherwise of the law reform measure concerned, and may encourage those who, in social life, wish to assert their own non-heterosexual sexual orientation more openly. At a more indirect level, the visibility of the topic created by the public debate may mean that the activity will come to appear more 'normal', or at least more understandable; one of the greatest causes of human prejudice is, after all, ignorance, and if hard data and argument on a topic are presented, it is harder for opinions based on ignorance to be sustained. Bigotry is always likely, to some extent, to remain – another in-built limitation on the social impact of law and any debate surrounding its alteration – but the impact, extent and social tolerance of bigotry may diminish.

This argument about the relevance of debate can be supported by a number of examples. Edwina Currie, for example, was clear that one effect of the House of Commons debate on the 1994 Act was that 'the taboo of silence that has denied the sexuality of young gay men has been decisively broken. Tonight's debate establishes the question as a matter of conscience – as it should be',[56] and that 'it is interesting that once respondents know a gay man, attitudes change dramatically and bigotry disappears'.[57] And, in a courageous letter which appeared in the *New Statesman* in 1960, three gay men – Roger Butler, Raymond Gregson and Robert Moorcroft – making what Stephen Jeffery-Poulter describes as one of the earliest gestures of 'coming out' in the British press – welcomed the then debate about the Wolfenden Committee proposals because:

> Over the past few years an enormous amount has been spoken and written about the homosexual situation. Most of it has been realistic and sensible, some has been vicious and ill-informed. But whatever its form we welcome it because we must welcome anything which brings this topic, for so long taboo, into open discussion. Only in this way can prejudice, which is born of fear and ignorance be overcome.[58]

Two points suggest, however, that certain refinements need to be introduced into our argument. First, the authors of the 1960 letter were clear
that homosexuality, at the time, was 'a problem only because of the prevailing attitude towards it, and because the law encourages such an
attitude and hinders every attempt to overcome it'.[59] Second, we must
remember the point – which we characterized as concerning the symbolic
impact of law – developed by the European Court of Human Rights
when it was considering laws directed against gay male sexual activity in
the *Dudgeon*, *Norris* and *Modinos* cases.[37] The Court was clear that laws
marking out particular groups of people for especially unfavourable
treatment could reinforce how other people saw those groups, and how
members of the groups saw themselves, regardless of whether such laws
were actually enforced. And, prior to the debate over the age of consent
provisions of the 1994 Act, the lesbian and gay community itself organized the campaign which produced and influenced that debate, via the
lesbian and gay press and several pressure groups. It is clear that without such a campaign – i.e. without lesbians and gay men themselves
feeling sufficiently affected by the existing legislation that they decided to
do something about it – no such debate would have happened. Also relevant here is Chris Smith MP's assertion in the 1994 House of Commons
debate that a higher age of consent for homosexual than for
heterosexual acts

> automatically means that young gay men will be set apart from soci-
> ety. If we remove that discrimination from the statute-book, it may
> go some way towards giving young gay men the self-respect and the
> self-dignity to which they are entitled and should have.[60]

All this suggests that law does, in some circumstances, have a symbolic
social impact, in the sense discussed at the end of the last section. The
crucial issue is, therefore, when law is, and is not, likely to have a symbolic and/or educational impact, and which segments of society are likely
to feel that impact. The material considered so far prompts certain tentative suggestions. The central observation must be that the social impact
of law and law reform is, in reality, somewhat lopsided. It seems that law
reform *alone* is, in the main, unlikely to have much impact, educationally
or otherwise, on the bulk of the population. *Debate* about law reform may,
however, have an educational effect, although this will depend on the
subject and the degree to which the listener's prejudice is in-built or
encouraged by the surroundings; the impact here is, anyway, likely to be
felt only gradually. Equally, in areas of life where certain moral reactions
are simply taken for granted, for example people's usual moral reaction
to an intentional killing, or to exceeding a speed limit, the existence of a

relevant law has little if any role to play.

I would submit, however, that the key to the social impact issue lies in differing popular reactions to laws which could be seen as empowering socially weak groups and laws which are identified as weakening the position of those groups still further, and between the differing reactions to each type of law from members of the weak group and from other members of the public. Important here are the sensitivities which the role of the weak group in issue raises within popular culture. For a group which raises sensitivities of a particularly acute sort in the popular imagination – and lesbians, bisexuals and gay men certainly fall into this category – the existence of a law which specially penalizes members of that group can help in reinforcing existing attitudes.[61] The law itself, in this situation, is an ingredient of popular culture. Equally, the mere existence of that law, when set against a prevailing background of social prejudice, will have a strong symbolic impact for those who are aware of their membership of the group concerned – hence the recent campaign for the equalization of the age of consent. In similar vein, reform of the law to the advantage of a disempowered group may have the effect of giving that group greater confidence and making its members more assertive. We should note, however, that the introduction of a hostile law can galvanize the group affected into action as much as a campaign to improve the existing law, the lesbian and gay community's campaign against s. 28 of the Local Government Act 1988 being clear evidence of this.[62] Equally, the fact that debate is thereby generated can give members of the group concerned a chance to air their viewpoint, and participating in or being the subject of debate may cause members of the group to refine their own position and future strategy.

What this suggests is that the social impact of law, law reform or debate about these topics can never be divorced from the relevant social background, and that, while law may reinforce existing sensitivities directed at a particular group,[63] debate and information, which might be associated with a move to alter the law, can help in eradicating the sensitivities and consequent prejudice. Even then this will be a slow process, and the extent to which debate surrounding the process of law reform impacts upon a particular society will clearly vary depending on the strength of pre-existing feelings about the topic in the society concerned. Regardless of the social impact of law in this sense, however, its mere existence can clearly contribute at a symbolic level to feelings of disempowerment among its victims, and an alteration in the law in that group's favour can assist, as Chris Smith MP suggested, in making that group feel more socially accepted. Law thus seems to have a variety of social impacts which vary according to the viewer's perspective and pre-existing feelings of social empowerment or disempowerment.

A further qualification must be made. This is that it is perhaps artificial to attempt to scrutinize individual laws for their social impact. Particular, well-publicized law reform issues – and debate surrounding law reform by case law can do this as much as law reform by legislation[64] – may focus attention on an area of social sensitivity more generally. But outside this particular forum, it is likely to be the whole body of laws, or laws of which the public is aware, which will produce any social impact. For example, the recent House of Commons debate about ages of consent enabled positive images of gay men to be presented, yet the existence of s. 28 of the Local Government Act 1988 still attaches a strong stigma to non-heterosexual sexual orientations. It will be interesting to see whether, with hindsight, the social impact of the debate over the 1994 Act comes to be identified as positive, in that it enabled favourable arguments about gay male sexuality to be heard (especially since these concerned the particularly sensitive area of sexual activity and young men), or as negative, in that a regime of unequal treatment was reaffirmed.

CONCLUSION

What can we learn from the above arguments about the value of law reform exercises, first, in eradicating social discrimination directed against lesbians, gay men and bisexuals, and second, as a means of promoting respect for notions of human rights more generally?

The answer to the first question seems to be that law reform, whether by legislation or case law,[65] can have some positive impact on the sense of security and self-worth of those who are lesbian, gay or bisexual. In this sense, law is assuming a symbolic social role. Debate about law reform may have some impact, in an educative sense, on heterosexuals; this cannot, however, be taken for granted, and any impact is likely to be over the long term. This seems to suggest that the reasons for law reform must be spelt out very clearly, and that education of the public, via outreach programmes and the like, is probably the more important element in any programme designed to eradicate discrimination as a matter of social practice. Among possible law reform measures, those which convey a clear message are also to be preferred over those which are ambiguous. Our conclusion here must therefore be that if we believe that lesbians, bisexuals and gay men are morally entitled to respect for and freedom to follow and express their sexual orientations,[66] then protecting these entitlements through law is unlikely, on its own, to eradicate social discrimination. This should not be taken as a reason for resisting law reform proposals, for the law reform process may, as suggested above, play some useful social role. Rather, it is an argument for placing law reform campaigns in proper perspective: as a sometimes, but not always, useful – and by no means the only – tactic in combatting discrimination as a matter of everyday social practice.

At the level of human rights codes more generally, Ronald Dworkin has suggested – in his argument for incorporating the ECHR into UK law – that without an enforceable code, Britain's 'culture of liberty' is at risk, in that the importance attached to liberties such as freedom of expression and the right to a fair trial is diminished.[67] While Dworkin suggests that with a bill of rights, respect for such liberties will grow within the culture of the legal system,[68] it is not clear whether he believes them currently to be at risk primarily from the government, from public indifference to their role, or from some mixture of the two. The material considered in this chapter suggests that it is a little simplistic to argue – if this is what Dworkin is arguing – that an enforceable human rights code would, in and of itself, have a social as well as a legal impact. First of all, any impact on social behaviour or attitudes to human rights generally will surely depend on the debate and publicity surrounding the introduction of the code. It will take time – and judicial decisions – to explain the exact meanings and strength of the entitlements the code protects, and still further time for this to filter down into popular consciousness. Second, it is likely that the social and possibly the legal impact of the different sections of any code will vary according to pre-existing social sensitivities about the entitlements each section protects. It is unlikely, for example, that a population (and a judiciary) which is largely hostile to lesbians, bisexuals and gay men will suddenly be converted to their cause by the enactment of a bill of rights which claims to protect them. While such a population would be more likely to value or even to celebrate the uncontentious sections of the new code, much educational work would be needed for the provisions affecting socially sensitive groups to have a beneficial social impact. Third, however, the failure to include sensitive topics such as sexual orientation in a code which claims to protect people from race and sex discrimination will carry a negative message for those suffering social discrimination because of their sexual orientation, whereas including such a topic would have a positive, empowering effect on the group concerned. Fourth, judicial and enforcement agency activity may affect the social impact of a human rights code, and may affect the decision whether or not such a code should take the form of an entrenched bill of rights.

Law reform and human rights codes are not, therefore, guaranteed to generate respect, in day-to-day social life, for the substantive entitlements and interests they claim to protect. Given that the social and legal impact of a law reform measure – even one bearing the emotive label 'bill of rights' – is likely to be a complicated and variable phenomenon, it seems fair to conclude that we cannot rely on law alone if, at a normative level, we deem a particular form of social change to be desirable. Exercises in law reform may well be useful in a variety of ways in the human rights field, but cannot be seen as ends in themselves.

ACKNOWLEDGMENTS

I should like to thank Conor Gearty and Adam Tomkins (the editors), Leslie Moran and Carl Stychin for their helpful comments and suggestions in relation to earlier drafts of this chapter.

NOTES

1. HC Debs, 21 February 1994, Col. 76.
2. *Ibid.*, Col. 111.
3. Now Criminal Justice and Public Order Act 1994, ss. 143–148.
4. See, for example, the comments at HC Debs, 21 February 1994, col. 75. The speaker referred to at col. 75 is *Mrs E. Currie*.
5. Any such argument will, however, entail the adoption by its author of a moral position on the issue of non-heterosexual orientations or conduct more generally – for further analysis, see N. Bamforth, *Sexuality, Morals and Justice* (London: Cassell, 1996).
6. The precise importance assumed by each issue will vary according to the law reform debate in question.
7. As the phrases 'better' and 'more easily' show, the impact issue cannot be divorced from normative considerations, and is sometimes in fact merged with the normative issue of function – for example, in the argument that law should not be used unless there is utterly clear evidence, rather than just suspicion, that it will bring about the desired end.
8. O. Kahn-Freund (1969) 17 BJIR 301–316, at p. 311. For a view which assumes the efficacy of law, at least in co-operative societies, see A. M. Honoré, The dependence of morality on law (1993) 13 *Oxford Journal of Legal Studies* 1; A. M. Honoré, Nécessité oblige. In A. M. Honoré, *Making Law Bind: Essays Legal and Philosophical* (Oxford: Clarendon Press, 1987), Chapter 6.
9. See, for example, L. Lustgarten, Racial inequality and the limits of law (1986) 49 *Modern Law Review* 68; D. Bell, An allegorical critique of the United States Civil Rights Model. In B. Hepple and E. Szyszczak (eds), *Discrimination: the Limits of Law* (London: Mansell, 1992), Chapter 1. B. Hepple, Have twenty-five years of the Race Relations Acts in Britain been a failure? In B. Hepple and E. Szyszczak (eds), *op. cit.*, Chapter 2.
10. R. Cotterrell, *The Sociology of Law: An Introduction*, 2nd edn (London: Butterworths, 1992), p. 45.
11. The enactment of laws in attempts to resolve perceived labour relations and public order problems provide examples of this.
12. See also Laurence Lustgarten's definition of 'legal change': L. Lustgarten, *op. cit.*, p.

70.

13. D. McBarnet, Legal form and legal mystification: an analytical postscript on the Scottish Criminal Justice Act, the Royal Commission on Criminal Procedure, and the politics of law and order (1982) *International Journal of the Sociology of Law* 409, especially p. 414.

14. The impact on a legal system of rules which are not directly enforceable in domestic courts may be much more sporadic – for an example, see L. Flynn, The significance of the European Convention on Human Rights in the Irish legal order [1994] *Irish Journal of European Law* 4.

15. Y. Dror, Law and social change (1959) 33 *Tulane Law Review* 787, at p. 788; see also R. Cotterrell, *op. cit.*, pp. 47–8.

16. W. Evan, Law as an instrument of social change. In A. W. Gouldner and S. M. Miller (eds), *Applied Sociology – Opportunities and Problems* (Glencoe, Illinois: The Free Press, 1965), p. 286. The model proposed by Evan on pp. 288–92 is clearly artificial – see L. Lustgarten, *op. cit.*, p. 70, fn. 11. Lord Devlin's (conservative) discussion might be seen as invoking the likely normative aspects of Evan's passive function: Lord Devlin, Judges and law-makers (1976) 39 *Modern Law Review* 1.

17. Cf. Law of Property Act 1925; Land Registration Act 1925; Land Charges Act 1972.

18. Cf. Public Order Act 1986; Criminal Justice and Public Order Act 1994.

19. A good example is the Highway Code – the sections with a statutory basis are capable of enforcement in the courts, but potential motorists are tested on the Code before being issued with a driving licence. Such a test would be superfluous unless it was intended that the motorists' knowledge of the relevant sections would subsequently guide their driving and *prevent* them from breaking the law. The Wolfenden Committee was clearly of the opinion that the criminal law played a preventive role in the field of sexual offences – *Report of the Committee on Homosexual Offences and Prostitution* (1957 Cmnd. 247, reprinted 1968), para. 213.

20. See P. Cane, *Atiyah's Accidents, Compensation and the Law*, 5th edn (London: Butterworths, 1993), Chapter 10, for discussion of disparities between rules of tort law and methods of out-of-court settlement pursued by insurance companies in tort cases.

21. R. Cotterrell, *op. cit.*, p. 55 (my italics); see also B. Hepple, *op. cit.*, pp. 27–8; A. Lester and G. Bindman, *Race and Law* (London: Longman, 1972), pp. 85–7.

22. R. Cotterrell, *op. cit.*, p. 54; see also *ibid.* pp. 102–6.

23. R. Cotterrell, *op. cit.*, p. 54.

24. Another example could be the Consumer Protection Act 1987.

25. A. Lester and G. Bindman, *op. cit.*, pp. 85–6.

26. E. van der Veen and A. Dercksen, The social situation in the member states. In K. Waaldijk and A. Clapham (eds), *Homosexuality: A European Community Issue* (Dordrecht/Boston/London: Martinus Nijhoff Publishers, 1993), pp. 137–40, 142, 159.

27. W. Evan, *op. cit.*, pp. 286–7 (my italics).

28. See Andrew Ashworth's discussion in A. Ashworth, *Sentencing and Criminal Justice* 2nd edn (London: Butterworths, 1995), pp. 62–6.

29. A. Lester and G. Bindman, *op. cit.*

30. Although the legal term 'murder' has an emotive appeal which 'manslaughter' does not possess, both terms are the creatures of law rather than popular imagination.

31. While different assumptions prevail in different social groups within any society, the parameters of such groups turning on factors such as employment hierarchy, sexual orientation, notions of social class, etc., the political cultures of the UK and USA tend to be influenced by a particular set of assumptions epitomized by morally laden phrases like 'family values'. No hard-and-fast rule can be laid down concerning which assumptions are likely to be most dominant in particular circumstances, although the assumptions of stronger social groups would seem to start from an advantageous position in influencing people who do not feel themselves to be in any way distinct from the social mainstream.

32. *Strathclyde R.C. v. Porcelli* [1986] IRLR 134; *Bracebridge Engineering v. Darby* [1990] IRLR 3.

33. Y. Dror, *op. cit.*, p. 794. See also R. Cotterrell, *op. cit.*, p. 56.

34. Cf. R. Cotterrell, *op. cit.*, pp. 105–6.

35. Although see D. McBarnet, *op. cit.*

36. Y. Dror, *op. cit.*, p. 801. See also O. Kahn-Freund, *op. cit.*, p. 311; W. Evan, *op. cit.*, pp. 287–8.

37. *Norris* v. *Ireland* (1989) 13 EHRR 187, at 194–6; *Dudgeon* v. *United Kingdom* (1981) 4 EHRR 149, at 160–2; see also the analogous argument in *Modinos* v. *Cyprus* (1933) 16 EHRR 485, at 493–4.

38. R. Cotterrell, *op. cit.*, p. 54.

39. K. Thomas, Beyond the privacy principle (1992) 92 *Columbia Law Review* 1431, at pp. 1485–6; the thesis is developed further on pp. 1435, 1475, 1477, 1485–6 (especially fn. 194), 1490–2 (especially fn. 206), 1508, 1514.

40. N. Lacey, From individual to Group? In B. Hepple and E. Szyszczak (eds), *op. cit.*, p. 121. Reading D. Bell, *op. cit.*, in the same volume provides a good test of the importance one attaches to the social role of legislation.

41. For a theory about the value of law for socially disempowered groups, see V. Kerruish, *Jurisprudence as Ideology* (London: Routledge, 1991), especially Chapters 6 and 7.

42. R. Wintemute, Sexual orientation discrimination. In C. McCrudden and G. Chambers (eds), *Individual Rights and the Law in Britain* (Oxford: The Law Society/Clarendon Press, 1994), p. 530.

43. For which see R. Wintemute, *op. cit.*; P. Crane, *Gays and the Law* (London: Pluto Press, 1982), although this is now a little outdated; E. Van der Veen and A. Dercksen, *op. cit.*

44. An especially useful study in this respect is S. Jeffery-Poulter, *Peers, Queers and Commons: The Struggle for Gay Law Reform from 1950 to the Present* (London: Routledge, 1991), especially Chapters 2–4, 10, 11.

45. *Report of the Committee on Homosexual Offences and Prostitution*, *op. cit.*

46. Cf. S. Jeffery-Poulter, *op. cit.*, pp. 33, 41, 50, 124, and, by analogy, HC Debs, 21 February 1994, cols 114–115.

47. Cf. S. Jeffery-Poulter, *op. cit.*, pp. 51, 72.

48. *Report of the Committee on Homosexual Offences and Prostitution*, para. 58. See also para. 59.

49. S. Jeffery-Poulter, *op. cit.*, p. 89.

50. HC Debs, 21 February 1994, col. 76.

51. HC Debs, 21 February 1994, cols 79, 82, 98. See also R. Wintemute, *op. cit.*, p. 495 fn. 5 (the phrase 'at least for men' is used in the text since some lesbians would argue that their sexual orientation is the product of a rational political choice). See further, Chapter 10, above.

52. S. Jeffery-Poulter, *op. cit.*, pp. 81–2.

53. Cf. S. Jeffery-Poulter, *op. cit.*, Chapters 5–10; R. Wintemute, *op. cit.*

54. The reasons for a person's sexual orientation are, of course, open to fierce medical/political debate.

55. An interesting feature here is the subtle shift in argument, between 1967 and 1994, on the part of those opposed to, respectively, partial decriminalization and reduction in the age of consent to 16. In 1967, opponents' arguments looked at the direct message which they believed a change in the law would give, i.e. one of moral approval. In 1994, the main argument was that law should 'protect' an alleged group of young men, uncertain of their sexual orientation, from exploitation *by* others who sought to 'convince' them.

56. HC Debs, 21 February 1994, col. 74.

57. HC Debs, 21 February 1994, cols 75–76.

58. *New Statesman*, 4 June 1960. Reprinted in S. Jeffery-Poulter, *op. cit.*, pp. 66–7.

59. See note 58. For contemporary evidence, see G. Westwood, *A Minority – A Report on the Life of the Male Homosexual in Great Britain* (London: Longmans, 1960), pp. 144–7.

60. HC Debs, 21 February 1994, col. 111.

61. See Kendall Thomas's analysis of the US position in K. Thomas, *op. cit.*

62. Cf. S. Jeffery-Poulter, *op. cit.*, Chapter 11; R. Wintemute, *op. cit.*, pp. 507–10. Another example may be the widespread protest – among many strands of youth culture – during the passage through Parliament of the then Criminal Justice and Public Order Bill 1994, due to its restrictive public order and trespass provisions.

63. Cf. M. Burke, Homosexuality as deviance: the case of the gay police officer (1994) 34 *British Journal of Criminology* 192, especially pp. 196–7, for further analysis of this point.

64. Marital rape is perhaps an example.

65. An example of law reform by case law can be seen in the redefinition, in *R* v. *Birmingham City Council, ex parte Equal Opportunities Commission* [1989] 1 AC 1155, and *James* v. *Eastleigh B.C.* [1990] 2 AC 751, of the meaning of direct discrimination within s. 1(1)(a) of the Sex Discrimination Act 1975, a consequence of which was an apparent widening in the range of groups potentially able to claim protection under the Act. See N. Bamforth, The changing concept of sex discrimination (1993) 56 *Modern Law Review* 872; *ibid.*, Sexual orientation and dismissal from employment (1994) 144 *New Law Journal* 1402.

66. See further N. Bamforth, *op. cit.*

67. R. Dworkin, *A Bill of Rights for Britain* (London: Chatto & Windus, 1990), especially pp. 10–12.

68. *Ibid.*, pp. 22–3, 45–51.

14

The Homosexualization of Human Rights

Leslie J. Moran

INTRODUCTION

This chapter is a study on the theme of homosexuality and human rights. It focuses upon two incidents. The first is a letter of 5 November 1955 from W. C. Roberts, the Secretary to the Wolfenden Committee, created by the UK government in 1954 to investigate the law relating to 'homosexual offences'.[1] Roberts wrote to the chairman of that committee, Sir John Wolfenden, on the topic of human rights and homosexuality. He drew Wolfenden's attention to the fact that human rights had been used in aid of an argument for the decriminalization of certain 'homosexual acts'. In responding to that claim Roberts pointed out that various qualifications and silences found, in particular, in the European Convention on Human Rights could be read as the effective denial of homosexual rights claims. This letter appears to have brought to an end any further consideration of the connection between homosexuality and human rights in the Wolfenden review. The second incident occurred in 1981. In that year the European Court of Human Rights concluded that the total criminalization of 'homosexual acts' in Northern Ireland (a part of the UK unaffected by the Wolfenden reforms enacted in the Sexual Offences Act 1967, which decriminalized certain 'homosexual acts' in limited circumstances)[2] was a violation of human rights under the European Convention on Human Rights. In general, my concern here is to develop an analysis that seeks to explore how the sense of these two positions relating to homosexuality and human rights became not only thinkable, but thinkable in such a way as to render other solutions impossible.

Homosexual(ity) connects the two moments. In both instances homosexual(ity) operates as a term through which a possible subject of human rights might be imagined. In both situations homosexual(ity) relates to a very particular way of imagining the subject. It is a way of making the sense and non-sense of the subject of human rights by reference to the body and its desires. More specifically, that embodied subject is imagined by reference to the genital and inter–genital relations. In both instances the sense of that subject is made by reference to that genital body and its desires as a specific sexed body. It is the body as male. Thus in both instances through homosexual(ity) the possible subject of human rights is imagined as the male genital body in its genital relations with other male bodies. However, homosexual(ity) is also the thing that separates these two moments. In each instance it produces different effects. In the first instance, homosexual(ity) appears as the impossible embodied subject of human rights. In the second instance, homosexual(ity) appears as the viable embodied subject of human rights. My concern here is to understand the different ideas through which the sense and non–sense of this embodied male genital subject is made and deployed in the production of the two different conclusions relating to the connection between homosexual(ity) and human rights.

To achieve this objective the first section of the chapter offers an analysis of the history and practices of the idea of homosexual(ity) in general. In the second section I return to the brief exchange of correspondence which, during the course of the Wolfenden Committee's deliberations, considered the connection between homosexuality and human rights. Having set out the terms of that exchange, I will consider the particular ideas of homosexual(ity) that informed the Committee's deliberations and explain how these ideas worked to make the conclusions put forward by Roberts not only thinkable, but thinkable in such a way as to render other solutions impossible. The final section of the analysis will consider the idea of homosexual(ity) that informs the decision of the European Court of Human Rights in *Dudgeon* v. *UK*.

HOMOSEXUALIZATION

In this section I want to introduce the key features of the idea of homosexuality. Recent histories of male identity in general and male sexuality in particular have pointed to the novelty of homosexuality as a way of imagining the subject.[3] This is not to suggest that the male genital body is a new focus of practices of identity or that male-to-male genital relations and male-to-male eroticism are a new invention. Its significance is that it draws attention to the novelty of the term homosexual(ity) as a way of making the sense and non-sense of the male subject as a genital body in its genital relations with other male bodies.

In the context of human rights, the history of (homo)sexuality has particular significance. The use of homosexual to name the subject seeks to attach specific characteristics to that subject. Michel Foucault has provided us with a significant insight into the attributes that have been connected to the subject through the new term homosexual(ity). It is a way of producing the sense and non-sense of the embodied subject that purports to speak of its fundamental nature (its ontology). Foucault suggests that the emergence of this idea of homosexual(ity) marks a transformation in Western culture. Prior to the inauguration of the term, the male genital body in its inter-genital contacts with men had been imagined as a concern with forbidden acts (that are within the capacity of all human subjects). In homosexuality the sense of that body was to be understood as a matter of specific, unique, perverse identity (characterized as limited and specific to certain individuals).[4] Foucault suggests that the focus on forbidden acts as a manifestation of a universal subject is articulated through the terms buggery and sodomy and the focus upon the unique and perverse subject is emblematized through terms such as Uranian, invert, the third sex, and homosexual.

In attempting to understand the particularity of the sense and the non-sense of the embodied subject that it produced through the two articulations of homosexual(ity) referred to above, there is a need to engage with Foucault's invaluable insight with some caution. It is important not to read Foucault's insight as a suggestion that one way of imagining this male body, its desires and practices, (homosexual), has totally eclipsed all others. While it is important to locate the rise of homosexual(ity) as a particular way of making the sense of the male body and male identity, it is also important to situate this in the context of a more complex picture of other terms and schemes of sense that have been viable and that continued to be used to name this body, its desires and practices. Homosexuality must be placed in the context of these other ways of making the sense of this embodied subject, such as, bugger, sodomite, hermaphrodite, Uranian, invert, pervert, the third sex, pansy, queer. The current strangeness and familiarity of these other terms draws attention not only to the need to pay particular attention to the distinctive inflections produced through the deployment of the term homosexual(ity) as the current privileged and distinct practice of subjection but also to the need to be sensitive to the connections made between homosexual(ity) and these other possible sensibilities of the male body.

A second note of caution must be sounded in the context of the use of homosexual. The repetition of the term homosexual(ity) in different places over different points in time should not be understood to illustrate the fixity of the term homosexual(ity) or to signify the ability of the term homosexual(ity) to capture the fixed essence of the phenomenon that it purports to name or its ability exhaustively to define the thing it represents. Its ability to be repeated in different places at different times points more to the impossibility of these characteristics of the term homosexual(ity). The success of homosexual(ity) lies in its ability to be repeated in different contexts in different times. This draws attention to the possibility of deploying the term beyond the cultural and temporal specificity of its production and deployment.[5] At best homosexual(ity) should be understood as expressive of a rich shifting matrix of cultural and temporal concerns.[6]

The shifting matrix of cultural and temporal concerns that is of particular significance in this study is articulated in the connection between the embodied subject and the juridical. As human rights these concerns are most frequently presented not as Uranian rights, inverts rights or the human rights of sodomites or pansies but as a demand for the recognition of gay rights or homosexual rights as human rights. In part this popular formulation is a reflection of the currency of the terms 'homosexual' and 'gay'. I want to focus upon two aspects of the cultural and temporal concerns articulated through these specific conjunctions of the subject and the juridical. The first theme I want to pursue relates to the general history of the use of homosexual and gay. This is undertaken in order to understand their present deployment. The second relates to the specific way in which these terms have been fabricated to imagine juridical relations. This will draw attention to the relatively short but complex history of the use of these terms to imagine the juridical past, present and future. For example, homosexual has been invoked to generate demands for the criminalization of the male body, and for its decriminalization, and invoked as the basis for a claim of human rights. It is to these matters that I now turn.

Homosexual(ity) and more recently gay are both terms that can be located within a particular tradition. In general they are terms that have been fabricated in order to name oneself; they emblematize autonomy.[7] 'Homosexuality' is a term first invented by a Hungarian doctor, Benkart (who used the pseudonym K. M. Kertbeny) in the mid-nineteenth century.[8] The juridical had a special place in his articulation of this emblem for an autonomous subject. Homosexual was made in response to an imminent threat of criminalization. It was first put to use to express defiance and indignation at bigotry, ignorance and intolerance towards male-male genital relations. It was used to imagine a celebration of the present by reference to a past: a huge catalogue of Western cultural icons were named homosexual; from general aspects of a venerated epoch within Greek culture,[9] to specific individuals, such as Michelangelo, Byron, Newton, Louis XVIII and Shakespeare (to name but a few). It was also coined as a term that demanded a 'rational' and a 'progressive' approach to such relations in law, or more specifically it was a term through which the non- or de-criminalization of those relations might be imagined. It was also a term through which this juridical arcadia might be given a history, by specific reference to the Code Napoleon.[10] Finally, it was deployed as a term that imagines the male genital body in its genital relations with other male bodies as a specific subjectivity (ontology) with certain causes (aetiology). This homosexual(ity) was an identity fundamental to the sense of self. It was to name that which is natural and inborn. These ontological and aetiological themes had a particular place in imagining the juridical arcadia. If homosexuality was fundamental to the sense of self and inborn, its punishment could not be regarded as rational by persons who respect the laws of nature.

Contemporaries of Benkert (and others that followed him) not only deployed the term that marks this specific attempt to produce a sense of the subject as the male genital body in its inter-genital relations, but also translated its themes into other contexts, inventing other terms having different inflections. For example, Karl Heinrich Ulrich, who coined the term 'Uranian',[11] produced a vast body of work that both echoed the themes articulated by Benkert and gave them a particular inflection. In particular, Ulrich appears to have focused upon the theme of ontology. He used Uranian to imagine this particular embodied genital male subject as an identity that might be explained as a woman's mind in a man's body. In turn we could follow the development of these themes and map further twists and transformations into other terms such as inversion, which is a term closely associated with the work of Havelock Ellis.[12] In this context it is of particular importance to note that this rehearses ontological and aetiological claims similar to those already outlined in the context of homosexual and Uranian. Space does not permit an excursion to explore the many other matters spoken by these authors by way of these terms.

Gay is similar to the homosexual outlined above, in that it has been deployed as a vehicle through which in a different time (historians have tended to locate the deployment of 'gay' as a term through which male-to-male genital relations might be celebrated as post-war) and a different cultural context (inaugurated in the USA,[13] disseminated via the globalization of the USA) defiance and indignation at bigotry, ignorance and intolerance towards same sex genital relations has been expressed. Furthermore, like homosexual before it, gay was mobilized to imagine a celebration of the present by reference to a past.[14] The Introduction to the UK Gay Liberation Manifesto provides a good example of the articulation of these themes to 'gay':

Throughout recorded history, oppressed groups have organised to claim their rights and obtain their needs. Homosexuals, who have been oppressed by physical violence and by ideological and psychological attacks at every level of social interaction, are at last becoming angry.

> To you, our gay sisters and brothers, we say that you are the oppressed; we intend to show you examples of the hatred and fear with which straight society relegates us to the position and treatment of sub-humans, and to explain their basis. We will show you how we can use our righteous anger to uproot the present oppressive system with its decaying and constricting ideology, and how we, together with other oppressed groups can start to form a new order, and a liberated life-style, from the alternatives which we offer.

At the same time this particular deployment of 'gay' imagines the embodied subject by way of a different grammar. 'Gay' avoids the disqualification and the negativity that is said to be associated with homosexual. More specifically, the body and its desires as 'gay' is set up in contrast to the homosexual subject produced by other homophile practices.[15] In the UK, 'gay' emerged within a leftist agenda, a particular, Marxist-inspired, analytical perspective and a programme of revolutionary change. As a project of liberation, 'gay' imagines its embodied subject as an authentic ontology which precedes the structurally determined cultural practices of oppression and repression.[16] As such, it imagines a subject that awaits liberation. As a term through which a conjunction between that subject and a juridical arcadia might be uttered, the juridical is no longer defined by an agenda limited to (de)criminalization. This is a subject as lifestyle. As a subject awaiting liberation it is connected to a more diverse juridical project of rights through which that broader agenda of a sexualized lifestyle might be produced and secured.

In general, when coupled to rights talk, homosexual and gay can be understood as attempts to conjoin particular ways of imagining the male genital body desires and actions to a particular way of imagining juridical relations. In calling these rights human rights, this embodied subject is conjoined to a very particular rights project. More specifically, this subject is connected to a juridical agenda that has been described as 'one of the monumental legacies left by the Enlightenment'.[17] Thereby homosexual and gay as emblems of autonomy, as articulations of identity and desire, and as expressions of indignation, defiance and celebration, are mobilized in intimate association with juridical themes of personality, authenticity, final truth, rationality, humanity and legitimacy.

Before proceeding to focus upon the two specific instances of an engagement between the practices of homosexual, gay and human rights referred to in the opening paragraph of this analysis, it is important to place the ideas of the body and its pleasures that I have outlined in the context of other ways of making sense of this male body in its male to male genital relations. These other ideas also deploy the term homosexual but give it a very different inflection. They are particularly important in that they draw attention to the fact that it would be wrong to conclude that terms such as homosexual (and to a lesser extent Uranian, and inversion) were univocal, particularly with respect to the ontological, aetiological or juridical themes already outlined. As Butler has noted:

> As much as it is necessary to assert political demands through recourse to identity categories, and lay claim to the power to name oneself and determine the conditions under which that name is used, it is also impossible to sustain that kind of mastery over the trajectory of those categories within discourse.[18]

So it is important to note other ways of making the sense and non-sense of the embodied male genital subject by way of homosexual and gay.

Krafft-Ebing's[19] work is of importance here for various reasons. On the one hand, his writings illustrate other ways of making sense of the male genital body that are remote from those already considered. On the other hand, he resorts to those other prior and coextensive imaginings of this body already referred to. He uses and reworks the terms inversion and homosexual in order to produce a different male genital subject.

In Krafft-Ebing's scheme of things the male genital body and its male inter-genital relations are imagined through the general term, perversion. This category is then split into two categories: the congenital and acquired perversion. (The latter is further divided into pathological and moral perversity.) Of the first category, the congenital, Krafft-Ebing explained that 'congenital sexual inversion occurs only in predisposed (tainted) individuals'[20] and went on to declare that his primary concern was with these 'homosexuals'. As such he appears to continue the tradition of using homosexual to speak of a very distinctive ontology. However, while this suggests that the terms perversion, inversion and homosexual[21] are separate and distinct, his scheme of classification also suggests that these terms have a certain interchangeability. Although there seems to be some attempt to secure a formal association between 'homosexual' and 'congenital' homosexual appears no longer to be limited to the congenital but might now be used to name perversion that is acquired. As such homosexual is now made to stand for at least two possible psychic and somatic states, the congenital and the acquired. Of particular importance here is the way in which the conflation of congenital and acquired in the common term homosexual masks the fragmentation of the ideas relating to the nature of that embodied subject (ontology) and the causes (aetiology) of that identity associated with the new use of the term.

Despite the reworking of this language of male-to-male genital relations, Krafft-Ebing's writings demonstrate that his deployment of a different homosexual(ity) still works as a vehicle through which, in general, it might be possible to emblematize an autonomy through which defiance and indignation at bigotry might be articulated and through which a different social order might be imagined. Furthermore, this new homosexual might still be deployed as a term to invoke the naturalness of abnormality.[22] Finally, this homosexual still works as an appellation through which a reform of the law might be staged:[23]

> The jurist could not consent to [a repeal of the law], if he is to remember that pederasty [which here refers to 'Sodomy in its strict sense ... inserting the penis into the anus'] is much more frequently a disgusting vice than the result of a physical and mental infirmity; and that, moreover, many homosexuals, though driven to sexual acts with their own sex, are yet in nowise compelled to indulge in pederasty – a sexual act which, under all circumstances, must stand as cynical, disgusting and when passive, as decidedly injurious.[24]

Here he draws attention to the importance of the interface between the law and the various ways of making the sense and non-sense of the embodied subject of law as the male genital body, its desires and practices. His observations suggest that the success of law reform is closely connected to the installation of a particular idea of the embodied male genital subject: homosexual as the congenital. Within this juridical future, homosexual as acquired perversion might be problematic, being remote from the ontology (the naturalness of homosexual(ity)) that grounds the claim for reform. In this scheme of things, Krafft-Ebing puts homosexual as acquired perversion to another use. Homosexual as acquired becomes a vehicle through which he articulates a different reform agenda – one that is concerned with returning the perverted back to its original position. For Krafft-Ebing this is not so much a juridical project but a project of medicine.

THE HOMOSEXUALIZATION OF HUMAN RIGHTS IN ENGLISH LAW; THE WOLFENDEN REVIEW

However, the purpose here is not to pursue the more general debate[25] relating to the competing and conflicting ideas of this genital subject but to focus upon the trajectory of homosexual as an embodied genital subject in the context of two exchanges relating to homosexuality and human rights. The first example appeared in a brief exchange found in the Wolfenden correspondence. The matter of homosexuality and human rights arose early in October 1955.[26] Professor Waldock, a member of an international committee investigating breaches of human rights, had received a petition which had argued that the conviction and sentencing of a man for genital relations with another man was in breach both of human rights provisions that protected private life and other such provisions which purported to prohibit discrimination on the basis of sex. Waldock's purpose appears to have been not so much to suggest that there was a valid human rights claim here but to suggest that the committee undertake a comparative analysis of the law relating to homosexual behaviour. Wolfenden addressed the matter in a letter to Waldock of 2 November 1955, where he noted that 'the kind of plea your letter mentions has . . . always been dismissed for fairly obvious reasons'. These are made clear in a note from Roberts, the secretary to the committee,[27] to Wolfenden of 5 November 1955. Roberts noted that the relevant articles of the European Convention on Human Rights were Articles 8 (the right to respect for private life) and 14 (dealing with discrimination). He continued:

> You will observe that Article 8 allows public authorities to interfere with the exercise of the right concerned where this is necessary not only '. . . for the prevention of . . . crime' but also . . . 'for the protection of morals'.

> It seems to me that there is nothing in Articles 14 or elsewhere to prevent any state from deciding an act of gross indecency between male persons should be a crime even though an act of indecency between females may not be an offence.

> Even if the law were changed in such a way that homosexual acts between consenting adult males were no longer criminal 'the protection of morals' would cover quite a lot.

On 21 December 1955 Waldock wrote to Wolfenden that after a long and interesting debate he was 'glad to say that [the international committee] were unanimous in dismissing the claim'. This brought to an end further consideration of homosexuality and human rights. My concern here is to attempt to understand this exchange. More specifically, my concern is to understand the idea of homosexual(ity) that works to produce the sense of the conclusions. This exchange took place in the context of a series of deliberations that spanned a three-year period. In order to consider the homosexual(ity) at work in this particular exchange, it is necessary to look at the production of homosexual(ity) in the wider context of the Wolfenden conversations.

The review was inaugurated on 24 August 1954. The committee was required to consider the law and practice relating to homosexual offences and the treatment of persons convicted of such offences by the courts.[28] The committee had particular difficulty with the theme of 'homosexual offences'. It found that the phrase was not defined by the government ministers who set the agenda for the committee,[29] and nor was it a phrase that was already known within the law. It referred neither to a particular named offence nor to a discrete category of criminal offences known to English or Scots law.[30] Nor was the task of the committee assisted by the formal existence of a wider general legal category of 'sexual offences'. The category of sexual offences did not come into existence in English law until 1956 with the Sexual Offences Act (towards the end of the Wolfenden Committee's deliberations). Nor did the creation of a discrete category of sexual offences give much assistance to the committee. While the Sexual Offences Act 1956 purported to bring together all of the existing offences in England and Wales relating to the sexual, it did not organize those offences by way of a division between heterosexual and homosexual.

Two factors are of immediate importance here. The first is the discovery of the formal absence from the law of the category of homosexual. The second is the peculiarity of the use of homosexual in the phrase 'homosexual offence' that the committee went on to outline. The committee's attention focused on the conjunction of 'homosexual' and 'offence'. It expressed the problem in the following way:

> It is important to make a clear distinction between 'homosexual offences' and 'homosexuality' . . . homosexuality is a sexual propensity for persons of one's own sex. Homosexuality, then is a state or condition, and as such does not, and cannot come within the purview of the criminal law.[31]

While the word 'offence' might refer to wrongful acts and thereby bring the specific object of the committee's attention within the general agenda of the criminal law, the addition of 'homosexual' rendered that problematic. As the committee pointed out, 'homosexual' seeks to define the wrongful acts by way of 'homosexuality', a term that refers to a 'state or condition'. As such, 'homosexuality' was not and never had been illegal and therefore was not the concern of either the law in general or the criminal law in particular. The conjunction of 'homosexual' and 'offences' brought together one term that was primarily a reference to matters outside the legal interests of the committee with another term that referred to an object firmly within the purview of their investigations. The combination of the terms threatened to name an object that was unintelligible within their agenda.

However, not only was the committee confronted with 'homosexual offences' in its terms of reference but the phrase occurred repeatedly in the papers presented and in the debates organized and conducted by the committee. As such, there appeared to be clear evidence that the phrase 'homosexual offences' had a certain currency. In particular, the use of the phrase 'homosexual offence' in the original terms of reference suggested that it had a currency that preceded the Wolfenden debate. In the final instance, the committee found the key that unlocked the riddle of the pre-existence of this oxymoronic phrase and its meaning in the government's original directions to the committee. The answer lay in the reference to treatment. The 'homosexual', 'homosexuality' and 'homosexual acts' of these deliberations had a meaning within the context of the treatment of offenders. They already had a legibility in the day-to-day practices of the prison medical service and in general in the practices of individuals in other related contexts prior to the Wolfenden review.

Evidence presented to the committee demonstrated that the homosexual(ity) of these practices of the prison medical services arose by way of the deployment of a particular way of imagining male-to-male genital relations which, as the committee noted, focused upon the nature and origins of the individuals who engaged in certain acts. The committee also noted here homosexual(ity) was deployed for the classification of a different and distinct subject. Furthermore this homosexual(ity) was a way of making the sense and non-sense of that subject fabricated and deployed by particular specialists, doctors and other medical experts. In turn, the committee resorted to its own medical experts, the psychiatrists Drs Curran and Whitby,[32] in order to interrogate the sense of this particular knowledge of the embodied subject. They found that a particular configuration of associations made up the idea of homosexual(ity) practised through these treatment regimes. In turn it was this particular idea of homosexual that had been used to name a specific calendar of criminal wrongs, 'homosexual offences'.

The evidence presented to the committee suggests that the idea of homosexual that had appeared in connection with the law owed more to the imaginings of Krafft-Ebing than to those of Benkart or Ulrich. For example, a dominant theme in the committee's deliberations was a struggle to make sense of the various dichotomies, invert and pervert, congenital and acquired, which in their various ways fragmented the ideas about the nature (ontology) and causes (aetiology) of male-to-male genital relations.

These themes are expressed both in the committee's general conclusions and in its specific proposals to decriminalize certain homosexual relations. They appear in its obsessive concern with the causes of acquired perversion and in particular with the focus upon seduction. They take shape in an apparently endless search for effective treatment regimes in the face of repeated failure.

The idea of homosexual(ity) that the committee works with the dichotomies invert–pervert, congenital–acquired, are violent oppositions where one of the terms of each opposition is privileged: pervert and acquired. From this perspective the invert and the congenital (both terms associated with the ontology of naturalness) are given a specific role to play. Here the invert and congenital are not so much the abnormal-as-natural but that which is the always already corrupt. In this scheme of things they function to symbolize the origin of corruption that will be made manifest in another place, another body.

Through the emphasis upon homosexual as 'pervert' and 'acquired', homosexual becomes a means through which demands can be articulated for regimes of protection. This homosexual becomes a vehicle for the articulation of demands for treatment for all. It is a vehicle for the representation of the embodied subject as a vulnerable subject, an unstable subject, a subject always already at risk. This homosexual is deployed to imagine the embodied male genital subject as one that has fallen from grace and stands in need of reform. It is used to imagine male inter-genital relations as human relations of no social worth. Here homosexual is used to imagine a project of the eradication of a particular male genital subject. As such this homosexual(ity) of the Wolfenden Committee is not so much a homosexual(ity) that might emblematize an autonomy, or work as the expression of defiance and indignation at bigotry. This homosexual is more a vehicle for the articulation of a particular practice of bigotry; of a tyrannical, anxious heterosexuality. This homosexual is used to imagine the techniques necessary for the successful installation of a certain compulsory embodied subject (a male heterosexual subject). This homosexual mobilizes an authoritative set of professional practices that name an interface between classificatory schemes and treatment regimes. In the final instance the committee

concluded that the citation of homosexual in the initial terms of reference referred to the accumulated force of these practices in law for the
categorization of wrongful acts. These practices deployed a very specific
idea of homosexual. They purported to define wrongful acts by way of a
set of practices of classification mobilized through specific (medical) inter-
rogations dedicated to the production of identity and desire, connected
to treatment programmes dedicated to the erasure of that identity and
the eradication of that set of desires.[33]

This is not to suggest that other ways of making sense and non-sense
of this male body and its desires and practices were not heard by the committee. Much of the evidence presented by men who engaged in genital
relations with other men or who advocated reform deployed other senses
of homosexual as the male embodied subject in order to imagine a
different juridical order.[34] While these other ways of imagining this body
did receive a hearing, I would suggest that in the final instance the committee's reform proposals were informed by an idea of homosexual that
prioritized the pervert and the acquired, and imagined homosexual as a
project of eradication of a particular male body and the termination of
specific desires and practices.

What remains to be explained is first, the way this idea of homosexual
led to the denial of human rights, and second, the way that, at the same
time, this idea of homosexual led to proposals to decriminalize certain
male-to-male genital practices. The priority given in Robert's analysis of
the homosexual human rights connection to the references to 'protection
of morals' and 'prevention of crime' that appear in the European
Convention on Human Rights suggest that it is homosexual as danger
and risk that is invoked here. It is a use of homosexual that allows stories
of seduction and corruption to make sense. It imagines the embodied
subject as threatened and thereby as a threat to public morality. Through
these stories this homosexual celebrates the perverted and fragmented
ontology and imagines an aetiology of vulnerability. It is a denial of
homosexual as a subject of human rights through an emphasis upon
homosexual as acquired. This homosexual facilitates the articulation of
an idea of a heterosexuality at risk. Homosexual is the impossible subject
of human rights when, as here, homosexual is a rehearsal of demands for
control in the name of eradication of male-to-male genital practices, not
their celebration. In the final instance the impossibility of this homosexual for a subject of human rights is made sensible by way of a homosexual
that is a project for the eradication of that subject. The focus on risk also
mobilizes an idea of homosexual that celebrates the naturalness of the
perverse. But in this instance nature is celebrated in order to extinguish
nature.[35]

But how at the same time does this idea of homosexual lead to recommendations to decriminalize certain genital acts between men? Again the answer lies in part in the emphasis on homosexual as acquired and the project of eradication. The project of eradication contained in the proposals for reform has two dimensions. The committee hoped that decriminalization would enable more men to publicly seek treatment. (The Wolfenden Committee also demanded more information on homosexuality in order that a project of eradication might be further advanced.) A second mode of eradication has a specific juridical quality. The committee proposed to decriminalize certain consensual relations in private; certain genital acts performed by no more than two persons over the age of 21 in private were no longer to be criminal. In proposing to create such a private realm beyond the purview of the law, the committee proposed the creation of a certain juridical invisibility. As such, decriminalization suggested a certain juridical eradication. The proposals to decriminalize are also informed by another factor. The committee found that the oppositions between innate and acquired, and pervert and invert, could give rise to an almost endless set of permutations of distinct ontologies and aetiologies. While this might produce an elaborate classification of subjects and thereby signify the success of this idea of homosexual (as it appears to explain more and more) at the same time it was also recognized as its failure. Through this proliferating fragmentation of perverse subjects, homosexual(ity) begins to lose its capacity to express any general characteristics; the general disappears behind an individualizing tendency.[36] Thereby, this homosexual(ity) appeared to be able to explain all male behaviour, not just the behaviour of a discrete class of perverts.[37] As such it became more difficult to imagine this homosexual as the abnormal. It is perhaps in both its success (its proliferation of subcategories) and its failure (being unable to single out distinct common characteristics) that this idea of homosexual worked to promote decriminalization. Decriminalization would appear to lie in the space between this homosexual(ity) as an endlessly proliferating category of subjectivity and as a project of eradication. A factor that joins the denial of homosexual as the subject of human rights and the project of the decriminalization is the fact that this homosexual is the impossible subject of juridical relations. From this it is clear that decriminalization is not dependent upon a homosexual(ity) that seeks to articulate a new epoch of respect for genital relations between adult men.

THE HOMOSEXUALIZATION OF HUMAN RIGHTS; *DUDGEON* v. *UNITED KINGDOM*

I now want to turn to the second reference to homosexual and human rights in the *Dudgeon* decision of the European Commission of Human Rights[38] and the European Court of Human Rights.[39] The Commission and the Court concluded that the criminalization of homosexual conduct carried out in private between consenting adults was an interference with the right to respect for private life (Article 8 of the European Convention on Human Rights) and was not justified as necessary in a democratic society. These decisions have a particular connection with the Wolfenden review in that the result of the case effectively mimics the Wolfenden reform proposals to decriminalize certain genital acts between men. At the same time they differ from that review in something of a radical way in that they frame that project of decriminalization as a project of recognition and respect for human rights, a context that was specifically dismissed in the Wolfenden review.

In the majority opinion in support of Dudgeon's application in the Court, a particular homosexual(ity) is deployed with a particular inflection. It appears in the judgment as follows:

> The applicant has, on his own evidence, been consciously homosexual from the age of 14.[40]

> . . . his private life (which includes his sexual life) . . . is disposed by reason of his homosexual tendencies . . .[41]

> The Convention right affected by the impugned legislation protects an essentially private manifestation of the human personality . . .[42]

These oblique and direct references to a homosexual(ity) for human rights are of especial interest. Judge Walsh in his dissenting judgment comments on the use of this homosexual in the opinion of the majority:

> However it is to be acknowledged that the case for the applicant was argued on the basis of the position of a male person who is by nature homosexually predisposed or orientated. The Court, in the absence of evidence to the contrary, has accepted this as the basis of the applicant's case and in its Judgment rules only in respect of the males who are so homosexually orientated (see for example paras 32, 41 and 60 of the Judgment).[43]

While this use of homosexual does not provide evidence of the production of an idea of homosexual(ity) that directly addresses and resolves or refuses the invert–pervert congenital–acquired distinction as found in the Wolfenden review, it does suggest instances of a use of homosexual where those distinctions have been displaced in a particular way. The dichotomy between the invert and pervert, or congenital and acquired, of homosexual has been displaced and homosexual is imagined only as the congenital.

The homosexual(ity) that appears in the majority opinion is given a particularly vivid profile when considered against the homosexual(ity) cited in the six dissenting judgments. In the dissenting judgments, that which is displaced in the opinion of the majority returns. For Judge Zekia the homosexual is a category through which he invokes human suffering. In part it is a suffering that all are to be subjected to; it is the turmoil and public outcry that will inevitably meet any change to the laws that criminalize all male-to-male genital behaviour. Homosexual is in part a way of imagining a suffering of the majority; the opinions of the majority (who are against unnatural and immoral practices) will be violated by a decision in support of Dudgeon. Homosexual is also invoked as a particular suffering attributed to physiological or psychological causes which echo the congenital–acquired dichotomy. Homosexual is also a way of relieving these sufferings through continued criminalization and the enactment of that law in the name of the will of the majority. The suffering of the individual is intelligible here only in terms of exculpation (self-management/control) or mitigation (eradication/treatment).

Judge Matscher began his dissenting opinion with the following assertion:

> Article 8 by no means requires any society in the form of a State to consider homosexuality – however it is manifested – as a variant equivalent to heterosexuality and consequently that its legislation should treat both equally.[44]

Here homosexual(ity) is invoked to name that which is other than and lesser than heterosexual. This is repeated in the citation of homosexual in a description of Dudgeon's claim:

> The applicant and those supporting him also seek the express, formal repeal of legislation in force, i.e. a 'charter' declaring that homosexuality is a variant equivalent to heterosexuality, with all the consequences that would entail (for example concerning sex education). However, this is certainly not required by Article 8 of the Convention.[44]

The reference to 'sex education' is of particular interest; here homosexual is imagined as seduction and corruption. Judge Matscher elaborates this theme in the following paragraph:

> It is well known that this tendency [homosexual relations with minors] is widespread among homosexuals and the fact that the applicant himself was engaged in a campaign for lowering the legal age of consent indicates the same thing.[45]

Judge Matscher deploys homosexual to invoke particular ideas of the ontology and aetiology of identity and desire. Here homosexual is a name for the acquired, the corrupted and the unnatural (the always already corrupted). This homosexual in human rights is cited as a vehicle by which a particular (heterosexual) indignation and defiance is imagined. Here a homosexual of human rights is imagined as a project aligned with the trajectory of eradication.

Judge Walsh imagines homosexual in the following way:

> It is not essentially different to describe the 'private life' protected by Article 8(1) as being confined to the private manifestation of the human personality. In any given case the human personality in question may in private life manifest dangerous or evil tendencies calculated to produce ill-effects upon himself or upon others.[46]

For Judge Walsh homosexual as authenticity of personality (congenital) is contingent in its significance. Homosexual is mobilized here to name the ontology and aetiology of danger and evil. That danger and evil are then put to work to imagine homosexual as the dichotomy of acquired and congenital, pervert and invert:

> The fact that a person consents to take part in the commission of homosexual acts is not proof that such person is sexually orientated by nature in that direction. A distinction must be drawn between homosexuals who are such because of some kind of innate instinct or pathological constitution judged to be incurable and those whose tendency comes from a lack of normal sexual development or from a habit or from experience or from other similar causes but whose tendency is not incurable.[43]

A stark contrast is drawn here between Judge Walsh's use of homosexual where acquired–pervert is celebrated and the homosexual of the majority opinion. Judge Walsh engages in a celebration that has particular characteristics. It demands the congenital, as it is the congenital that stands for the always already of the corrupt state that makes it possible to imagine the possibility and inevitability of that other state, of future corruption. Congenital here stands for identity as corruption. But another image of corruption haunts this imagining: 'It is known that many male persons who are heterosexual or pansexual indulge in these acts not because of any incurable tendency but for sexual excitement.' Here corruption is imagined as being more closely aligned with desire itself. Here homosexual as corruption appears in the figure of the heterosexual or the pansexual who may engage in male-to-male genital relations for sexual pleasure.

It is this homosexual for human rights that is connected with treatment and eradication. As Judge Walsh demonstrates, this is homosexual as victim twice over. The homosexual is first made victim by an anonymous actor:

> So far as the incurable category is concerned, the activities must be regarded as abnormalities or even as handicaps and treated with the compassion and tolerance which is required to prevent those persons from being victimised in respect of tendencies over which they have no control and for which they are not personally responsible.[43]

The homosexual is then victimized a second time in the name of human rights:

> However, other considerations are raised when these tendencies are translated into activities. The corruption for which the Court acknowledges the need for control and the protection of the moral ethos of the community referred to by the Court may be closely associated with the translation of such tendencies into activities.[43]

This is the legitimate victimization of state-sponsored control.

This analysis draws attention to the fact that two very different but related ideas of homosexual(ity) are put to work in the various opinions dealing with the deployment of homosexual in the context of human rights. How might we explain the distribution of ideas across the judgments? Again, we might start with an astute observation made by Judge Walsh on the majority position. He suggested that:

> The judgment of the Court does not constitute a declaration to the effect that the particular homosexual practices which are subject to penalty by the legislation in question virtually amount to fundamental human rights. However, that will not prevent it being hailed

as such by those who seek to blur the essential difference between homosexual and heterosexual activities.[47]

Judge Walsh is right to point out that the use of homosexual in the judgment of the majority need not be read as a declaration either of homosexual rights or more specifically of homosexual rights as human rights. The juridical subject of human rights in general and of the human right to respect for private life in particular is the juridical subject as human subject. Article 14 of the European Convention on Human Rights suggests that this juridical subject is neither sexed, gendered, raced nor to be defined over against any other of the categories of otherness listed therein. As the majority judgment of the Court in *Dudgeon* suggests in its rejection of an argument based upon Article 14, the juridical subject of Article 8 has not been divided by way of homosexual as a category of the other, and therefore there is no need to give specific attention to the prohibition that is placed upon such attempts to fragment the ontology of the juridical subject. Thus the subject of the right articulated in the *Dudgeon* decision need not be thought of as the embodied male genital subject.

However, Judge Walsh's earlier point about the importance of the homosexual as congenital is still of consequence here. Even within an explanation that seeks to take the human subject as the subject of human rights, homosexual as a specific set of ontological and aetiological claims, as the natural and the inborn, remains significant. These attributes resonate with the rhetoric of legal humanism that forms the juridical subject of human rights. This is a rhetoric that imagines the juridical subject of rights as a position grounded in the true self, and authentic identity, and in humanity as a natural order that precedes the social that provides the ontological grounding for certain rights.[48] As such, the discursive condition of social recognition of homosexual as authentic subject precedes and conditions the formation of that subject.[49] Within this scheme of things, the *Dudgeon* decision demonstrates that the homosexual as congenital is in its authenticity always already the subject of human rights.

Judge Walsh's observation perhaps has another significance here. The homosexualization of human rights that Judge Walsh recognizes as a possibility arising out of the *Dudgeon* decision might also be the end of homosexualization, in that the juridical subject that is imagined there in the success of the claim is not a sexualized subject. Finally, Judge Walsh's observation draws attention to the fact that subject position is not only that which must precede the subject but also the moment of its citation. Judge Walsh seeks not only the power to name but also the capacity to determine the condition under which that name is used. However, he draws our attention to the problematic nature of such attempts at mastery. It is impossible to sustain that kind of mastery over the trajectory of categories within (legal) discourse. Thus the connection of authenticities (of humanness and homosexual) is both the impossibility and possibility of homosexual rights as human rights in this instance. That possibility and impossibility are not only repeated in the imaginings of those outside the law who cite the homosexual of *Dudgeon*, but also form a part of the practices of the Court in subsequent judgments such as *Norris* v. *Ireland*.[50]

The *Dudgeon* decision also demonstrates something more. Another use of homosexual is imaginable within human rights. This produces very different effects. Here homosexual is put to work to instal the juridical subject as the heterosexual subject. As such the subject of human rights is not so much the possible victim of state power but the potential victim of a corruption and a perversion that is attributed to homosexuality. Here the state takes up the position of the protector and the one who preserves the human rights of the subject.[51]

CONCLUSION

This analysis is not concerned with the either/or or the for/against homosexual or gay rights as human rights, or the correctness or incorrectness of the conclusions drawn in the context of the Wolfenden review, the *Dudgeon* decision or any other decision. My interest in each instance referred to above lies in an attempt to understand the nature of the claims and the counterclaims that are made in the will to politicize identity and desire. The focus of this chapter is upon the historicity of the naming practices. The history of usage draws attention to the fact that the act of naming is always already an engagement with the histories of usage that one never controlled, that constrain but also that create the very possibility of emblematizing subjectivity both within the law and beyond. This chapter has been concerned with analysing those practices through which the thinkability and unthinkability of the various identity claims in law become thinkable, and with how the particular coherence and incoherence is made, deployed and in the final instance installed and enforced. The chapter does not purport to be an exhaustive analysis of this complex shifting terrain. It is offered more as a fragment of an analysis that is ongoing.

While homosexual has long been associated with imagining law as a project of rules and the rationalization of social order, my focus upon homosexualization seeks to challenge and escape the particular debates that focus upon law as a matter concerned with rules and rationality. The focus on homosexual seeks to draw attention to the importance of considering human rights in particular and law in general as a matter of representation. It is as two instances of struggles over representation of the body as a locus of juridical relations that the Wolfenden denial of human rights and the *Dudgeon* declaration of human rights can be best understood. The analysis offered suggests that these struggles over rights take a particular form. They are produced through the articulation of different and shifting sensibilities of the body which is the enunciation of a rich and changing matrix of cultural and temporal concerns. What connects the Wolfenden denial of homosexual human rights to *Dudgeon* is homosexual(ity). What separates these two moments is the diverse sensibilities and the different cultural and temporal concerns that are articulated through these homosexual(ities).

ACKNOWLEDGMENTS

Special thanks are due Carl Stychin and Didi Herman who were subjected to earlier drafts of this chapter, and to those who participated in discussions on homosexuality and human rights at seminars in Phoenix and Calgary and at the Hart Workshop in July 1994.

NOTES

1. Sir J. Wolfenden, *Report of the Departmental Committee on Homosexual Offences and Prostitution* (London: HMSO, 1957) Cmnd 247. This event has been the subject of several recent histories: see S. Jeffrey-Poulter, *Peers, Queers and Commons* (London: Routledge, 1991); A. Grey, *Quest for Justice: Towards Homosexual Emancipation* (London: Sinclair–Stevenson, 1992). Other recent histories that deal with a wider agenda of sexual politics in the UK during this period include D. T. Evans, *Sexual Citizenship: The Material Construction of Sexualities* (London: Routledge, 1993); and T. Newburn, *Permission and Regulation: Law and Morals in Post–War Britain* (London: Routledge, 1992).

2. The provision in the Sexual Offences Act 1967 was in the first instance applicable only to England and Wales. It was extended to Scotland in the Criminal Justice (Scotland) Act 1980. For an analysis of the peculiarities of the 1967 Act, see L. J. Moran, Buggery and the tradition of law (1993) 19 *New Formations* 110.

3. For example, see A. Bray, *Homosexuality in Renaissance England* (London: Gay Men's Press, 1982); M. Foucault, *The History of Sexuality*, Vol. 1: *An Introduction* (London: Penguin, 1978); J. Weeks, *Coming Out* (London: Quartet, 1977); J. Weeks, *Sex, Politics and Society: The Regulation of Sexuality since 1800* (London: Longman, 1981); J. Weeks, *Sexuality and its Discontents* (London: Routledge and Kegan Paul, 1985); M. McIntosh, The homosexual role. In K. Plummer (ed.), *The Making of the Modern Homosexual* (London: Hutchinson, 1981).

4. M. Foucault, *op. cit.*

5. Derrida develops the point in J. Derrida, Signature event context. In *Margins of Philosophy*, (translated by Alan Bass) (Hemel Hempstead: Harvester, 1982) pp. 315–17: ' "written communication" must . . . remain legible despite the absolute disappearance of every determined addressee in general for it to function as writing, that is for it to be legible. It must be repeatable – iterable – in the absolute absence of the addressee or of the empirically determined set of addressees. . . The possibility of repeating, and therefore of identifying, marks is implied in every code, making of it a communicable, transmittable, decipherable grid that is iterable for a third party, and thus for any possible user in general . . . a written sign carries with it a force of breaking with its context, that is, the set of presences which organise the moment of its inscription' (pp. 315–16).

6. For example, in my own work see L. J. Moran, The uses of homosexuality: homosexuality for national security (1991) 19 *International Journal of the Sociology of Law* 149–70; L. J. Moran, Buggery and the tradition of law, *op. cit.* Other examples include R. Dyer, *The Matter of Images: Essays on Representation* (London: Routledge, 1993); S. Watney, *Policing Desire: Pornography, Aids and the Media* (London: Methuen, 1987); K. Theweleit, *Male Fantasies*, Vol. 1 (Translated from German by S. Conway, E. Carter and C. Turner) (Cambridge: Polity Press, 1987); K. Theweleit, *Male Fantasies*, Vol. 2 (Translated from German by C. Turner, E. Carter and S. Conway (Cambridge: Polity Press, 1989).

7. J. Butler, Critically Queer (1993) 1 *GLQ: A Journal of Lesbian and Gay Studies* 17–32, 19.

8. J. Lauritsen and D. Thorstad, *The Early Homosexual Rights Movement (1864–1935)* (New York: Times Change Press, 1974).

9. For example, see J. A. Symonds, A problem in Greek Ethics. In *Sexual Inversion* (New York: Bell Publishing, 1984).

10. The problematic nature of this particular history is raised in A. Copley, *Sexual Morality in France 1780–1980* (London: Routledge, 1989).

11. The term 'Uranian' is located within the theme of celebrating a present by reference to a past in that it invokes a particular aspect of an icon of Greek culture and the philosophical writings of Plato, particularly in the *Symposium*, deploying them as a way of naming genital relations between men.

12. See especially H. Ellis, *Studies in the Psychology of Sex*. Vol. 1 *Sexual Inversion* (London: The University Press, 1897). Also see H. Ellis, *Studies in the Psychology of Sex*. Vol. 2 *The Evolution of Modesty, The Phenomena of Sexual Periodicity, Auto-erotism* (Leipzig: The University Press, 1900).

13. For example, see D. Altman, *The Homosexualisation of America* (Boston: Beacon Press, 1982), and for a slightly different narrative of its genesis see J. Bristow, Introduction: texts, contexts (1990) 4 *Textual Practice* 1.

14. In the UK the Gay Left Collective was prominent in the genesis and circulation of such ideas. An excellent example is to be found in Gay Left Collective, *Homosexuality: Power and Politics* (London: Allison and Busby, 1980).

15. See, for example, S. Watney, Ideology of GLF. In Gay Left Collective. *op. cit.*

16. See D. Fernbach, Ten years of Gay Liberation. In Gay Liberation Front (ed.) *Politics and Power* Vol. 2 (London: Routledge and Kegan Paul, 1980), pp. 169–88, and S. Watney, On Gay Liberation: A response to David Fernbach. In *Politics and Power*, Vol. 3 (London: Routledge and Kegan Paul, 1981), pp. 295–304.

17. R. Gaete, *Human Rights and the Limits of Critical Reason* (Aldershot: Dartmouth Publishing Company Ltd, 1993), p. 1.

18. J. Butler, *op. cit.*

19. R. Krafft–Ebing, *Psychopathia Sexualis* (New York: Pioneer Publications, 1948).

20. *Ibid.*, p. 382.

21. Another term used by Krafft–Ebing is antipathic sexual feeling. Other schemes of categorization are also found in operation within Krafft-Ebing's scheme of things, such as neuropathic and psychopathic.

22. Krafft-Ebing described it as 'an abnormal condition natural to him' and wrote 'from his [the homosexual's] morbid standpoint, it is natural'. R. Krafft-Ebing, *op. cit.*, p. 382.

23. This is echoed in the nature/nurture debate within lesbian and gay politics. A par-

ticularly interesting analysis of this dichotomy is to be found in J. Dollimore, *Sexual Dissidence: Augustine to Wilde, Freud to Foucault* (Oxford: Clarendon Press, 1991), and D. Fuss, *Essentially Speaking: Feminism, Nature and Difference* (London: Routledge and Kegan Paul, 1989).

24. R. Krafft-Ebing, *op. cit.*, pp. 381, 386.

25. I pursue that debate in the context of *The Homosexuality of Law* (London: Routledge, 1996).

26. The discussion is to be found in correspondence between the secretary of the committee and Sir John Wolfenden in November 1955. Public Records Office, HO345/2.

27. Roberts had particular knowledge of the issue, having been a civil servant in the international branch of the Home Office.

28. A second theme of the committee's work was to consider the law and practice relating to criminal offences in connection with prostitution and solicitation for immoral purposes.

29. Sir J. Wolfenden, *op. cit.*

30. English law refers to the law applicable to England and Wales. The terms of reference of the committee did not include Northern Ireland, the Isle of Man or the Channel Islands.

31. Sir J. Wolfenden, *op. cit.*, para. 11. For further discussion see L. J. Moran, *The Homosexuality of Law, op. cit.*

32. Evidence from the prison medical authorities has particular significance in the committee's attempts to understand the phrase 'homosexual offence'. See generally Sir J. Wolfenden, *op. cit.* For further discussion see L. J. Moran, *The Homosexuality of Law, op. cit.* At the start of the Wolfenden proceedings none of the wrongful acts collected under the title 'homosexual acts' formally either referred to sexuality in general or to the homosexual–heterosexual divide in particular. By the time of the final report these wrongful acts not only had come to speak of sexuality in general but to speak of homosexuality in particular.

33. For a more detailed discussion of this, see L. J. Moran, The homosexualisation of English Law. In C. Stychin and D. Herman (eds), *Legal Inversions* (Philadelphia: Temple University Press, 1995).

34. PRO.HO 345/8 CHP/51, 59, 68 and 70.

35. Sir J. Wolfenden, *op. cit.*, Chapter 3.

36. See L. J. Moran, The homosexualisation of English Law, in C. Stychin and D. Herman (eds), *op. cit.*

37. Sir J. Wolfenden, *op. cit.*, para. 20.

38. *Dudgeon* v. *United Kingdom* (1981) 3 EHRR 40.

39. *Dudgeon* v. *United Kingdom* (1982) 4 EHRR 149. All subsequent references refer to specific paragraphs in this report.

40. *Ibid.*, para. 32.

41. *Ibid.*, para. 41.

42. *Ibid.*, para. 60.

43. *Ibid.*, para. 12 of Judge Walsh's dissenting opinion.

44. *Ibid.*, para. 12 of Judge Matscher's dissenting opinion.

45. *Ibid.*, para. 13.

46. *Ibid.*, para. 8 of Judge Walsh's dissenting opinion.

47. *Ibid.*, para. 19.

48. This theme is developed and explored in R. Gaete, *op. cit.*

49. J. Butler, *op. cit.*, p. 18.

50. (1988) 13 EHRR 186 and *Modinos* v. *Cyprus* (1993) 16 EHRR 485.

51. Not only is this demonstrated in the dissenting judgments in *Dudgeon*, but it is the dominant theme in the various decisions that have addressed the issue of homosexuality and the 'age of consent'. For example, see *X* v. *United Kingdom* (1978) 3 EHRR 63. For a general review of the decisions addressing this theme, see L. R. Helfer, Finding a consensus on equality: the homosexual age of consent and the European Convention on Human Rights (1990) 65 *New York University Law Review* 1044–100.

15

Human Rights, HIV and AIDS

Anne Scully

AIDS is the name for a syndrome of illnesses which develop from HIV, a virus which debilitates the human immune system and can be fatal. Medical research has established the existence of the virus and can test for its presence. Currently there is no cure; nor is there a vaccine. The virus is transmitted via bodily fluids, during either sexual intercourse, intravenous drug use or blood transfusion.

In the UK the existence of the HIV virus became a matter of widespread public knowledge in the mid-1980s, due to a vigorous public health campaign organized by the Health Education Authority (HEA). The campaign consisted of information leaflets distributed to every home in 1985, and was backed up by television commercials depicting the terminal and random nature of the virus, either by way of granite tombstones inscribed with gloomy slogans or by showing the virus as a bowling ball knocking down human skittles. Similar campaigns were used across the Western world; notably in an Australian television commercial, in which death, the grim reaper, was shown scything his way through a happy and blissfully ignorant population.

Most of the earliest reported cases of HIV positivity concerned gay men,[1] some such cases dating from as early as the late 1970s, and growing in number by 1982. Indeed, the public health leaflets that were distributed, while asserting that the HIV virus was not exclusive to the gay community, detailed means of sexual transmission which were linked directly to gay sex. Despite the fact that by the late 1980s the spread of the virus amongst gay men had not continued to increase[2] as rapidly as was first expected, and that the increase in transmission amongst the heterosexual community was growing at an ever-increasing rate, the virus had been connected in the minds of the public with homosexuality or drug addiction. One example of the link between HIV/AIDS and homosexuality and the press can be seen in *Gilberthorpe* v. *Hawkins and others*.[3] Gilberthorpe was a Conservative councillor on both the city and county councils of Gloucestershire. Allegations that he had been tested for the HIV virus and was receiving treatment forced him to resign from public office. This is an issue in itself, but what is most relevant here is the way in which the press reported the event. The *Daily Mirror*, on 16 January 1987, reported that 'A *bachelor* [my emphasis] Tory councillor is to resign over allegations that he is being treated for AIDS.' Although there is no overt link here with homosexuality, one wonders why the newspaper felt it necessary to mention that Gilberthorpe was a bachelor? Another publication, a local Gloucester paper, *The Citizen*, on the same day reported that 'Councillor Anthony Gilberthorpe ... said yesterday that he is resigning from his seats on the City and County councils amid allegations that he is a homosexual and has the killer disease AIDS.' Again, although the link between homosexuality and HIV is not made as explicit as in some of the worst headlines, for example 'AIDS: The Gay Plague', the association between allegations concerning HIV status and sexuality is still present.

Further, despite the initial slogan of the HEA's campaign, 'Don't die of ignorance', fear of contagion by means which were medically almost impossible continued to grow. In one road traffic case, *Director of Public Prosecutions* v. *Kinnersley*,[4] the defendant refused to take a breathalyser test. The defendant was requested to give specimens of breath both when stopped on the highway by a police constable and when presented to the custody officer at the police station. Under s. 6 and s. 7 of the Road Traffic Act 1988, a person may refuse to give specimens of breath in both of these situations without being guilty of an offence if he or she has a reasonable excuse. Although the defendant did not mention it at the time, it later became apparent that his reason for failing to take the tests was 'that he feared contracting the Human Immunodeficiency Virus which was believed to lead to AIDS. In support of that it was argued that he could not be sure that the mouthpieces of the respective breathalyser test devices were sterile.'[5] The court did not accept the defendant's subjective fear of contracting the virus. When looked at in the light of objective knowledge concerning transmission of the virus, the defendant's beliefs could not be accepted as being a reasonable excuse.

Returning to the Gilberthorpe case, the *Sun* showed further evidence of the panic that surrounds HIV transmission in the headline which ran 'AIDS Man Kissed Maggie'.[6] These cases adequately illustrate the misconceptions concerning the transmission of the HIV virus, despite a widespread public education campaign.

Although AIDS exists within the medical discourse of epidemiology, its development as a virus has been traced through several mutations, and its modes of transmission are clearly recognized in medical terms, it would be a mistake to suggest that this is the way in which society at large perceives the HIV virus. In the public information broadcasts from the HEA, the grim reaper scything down unsuspecting families carries connotations of the plague and this became a metaphor for AIDS.[7] AIDS had effectively moved from the medical arena, where rigid adherence to facts was paramount, to the media circus and stylized sensationalism. The metaphor of the plague continued, being used most damagingly in the context of AIDS as a gay plague. The fear encapsulated in the figure of the grim reaper took hold and demanded a scapegoat. What followed is what Stanley Cohen[8] has described as a moral panic:

> A condition, episode, person or group of persons emerges to become defined as a threat to societal values and interests, its nature is presented in a stylised and stereotypical fashion by the mass media: the moral barricades are manned by editors, bishops, politicians and other right thinking people, socially accredited experts pronounce their diagnoses and solutions; ways of coping are evolved or (more often) resorted to; the condition disappears, submerges or deteriorates and becomes more invisible.

People living with AIDS (PWAs) or those who are HIV+ have found themselves in situations where they are discriminated against on the grounds of their serostatus. Human rights are often said to exist to protect the fundamental freedoms of society at large, and in particular are said to exist to protect minorities and those who cannot enforce their own liberty and basic rights. Where instances of infringement of the rights of PWAs and those who are HIV+ occur, it would seem appropriate to apply human rights law in this situation. Examples of the contravention of the rights of UK subjects include refusal of re-entry into another country[9] and dismissal from employment[10] based on an assumption of serostatus. At the International Forum on Policy, Politics and AIDS, the relevant human rights were thus enumerated: 'Among the rights of individuals which may be threatened by AIDS are the rights to privacy and confidentiality, the freedom to associate with whomever one pleases and the right to non-discrimination in employment, housing and social services.'[11] In addition to these I would like to add another: the right to bodily integrity. This last is particularly relevant when considering the issue of testing for HIV.

However, I shall argue that while at present it is of paramount importance that this form of discrimination is dealt with as effectively and stringently as possible, human rights discourse is not in itself the most efficient means of promoting a system of equality with regard to AIDS and HIV.

Before considering the problems inherent in human rights discourse about HIV/AIDS, I shall consider the protection afforded by human rights law to PWAs and those who are HIV+. Within the field of human rights law there are several different instruments which feature fundamental and universal human rights. For the sake of clarity, the instruments which I shall deploy as a yardstick of human rights protection are the Universal Declaration of Human Rights (UDHR) and the European Convention on Human Rights and Fundamental Freedoms (ECHR). There are significant areas of substantive overlap in these two instruments. Where a fundamental right, for example the right to privacy, is given in different terms in the two documents, I will consider the possible consequences of each. It should also be noted that neither of these documents were concluded with AIDS or HIV in mind. However, the ECHR does raise the issue of the public interest with regard to infectious diseases, and it is this point which I will refer to when dealing with the incidence of the virus.

ISSUES ARISING FROM AIDS/HIV AS A DISCRETE CONSIDERATION IN HUMAN RIGHTS LAW

Issues specific to AIDS and HIV include: mandatory testing, that is obtaining a sample of blood from an individual without his or her consent; isolation or detention of PWAs or those who are HIV+; disclosure of information about an individual's serostatus; and unfair dismissal from employment. While this list is not exhaustive, these issues reflect the significant concerns of those affected by the HIV virus and by AIDS.

Testing for HIV/AIDS

The right to bodily integrity is a hybrid term, rather than a single right, which has been adopted by Feldman[12] to cover a variety of circumstances under which a threat of physical interference occurs. These range from freedom from torture and physical assault to access to minimum standards of health care. The sources of this right are predominantly Article 5 of the UDHR, 'No one shall be subjected to torture or to cruel, inhuman and degrading treatment or punishment', and Article 12 of the same document: 'No one shall be subjected to arbitrary interference with his privacy, family, home or correspondence, nor to attacks upon his honour and reputation. Everyone has the right to the protection of the law against such interference or attacks.' The combination of the rights to privacy and freedom from cruel, inhuman or degrading treatment presents a persuasive defence against mandatory testing for the HIV virus. Mandatory testing has been considered as a way of collecting information with regard to the spread of the virus, with a view to prevention of any further infection. Mandatory testing, therefore, can be defended as a public health matter. Indeed, Article 5(1)(e) of the ECHR does allow for exceptions to liberty and security of person: no-one shall be deprived of his liberty except, among other exceptions, when necessitated by 'the lawful detention of persons for the prevention of the spreading of infectious diseases'. Although the UDHR offers an unqualified right, the ECHR balances that right and qualifies it by reference to the public interest in prevention. But public health experts are generally against the use of testing in order to prevent further spread of the disease, for a number of reasons. One of these is that the test is not totally accurate, and while the number of errors are small the consequences of a false-positive test result would be traumatic for the patient. It could even be said to result in a contravention of our right to be free from mental torture.[13]

Further to this, the premise of the test as a means of prevention is flawed. It is thought that if an individual is aware of his or her HIV status then he or she may alter his or her behaviour, particularly sexual behaviour. However, the test will not detect the antibodies produced in the blood by the immune system as a response to the virus for anything up to six months. After this time, any result can only indicate that one is not HIV+ on that day. To encourage society to change its behaviour depending on serostatus is of limited effect as a preventative measure. Behavioural change should not be linked too closely to the antibody test result.

Second, there is currently no cure for either the HIV virus or ultimately for AIDS-related illnesses. To argue that compulsory screening takes place as a means of public information and as a means of prevention in relation to other diseases such as tuberculosis, and should for this reason occur here as well, ignores this fact. With regard to tuberculosis, the aim of the test is to diagnose, treat and cure the patient.[14] With an HIV antibody test, one may only diagnose, as there is no cure. However, the trauma related to HIV testing is sited not only in finding out that one faces a potentially life-threatening disease. The corollary to this is social stigma.[15] The consequences of HIV screening are far-reaching, affecting not only the person tested but also all those who know him or her. To draw an analogy with tuberculosis is to ignore the complexity of issues surrounding HIV/AIDS. In addition to the changes a positive result may make to relationships, there is also the possibility that employment may be adversely affected.

Perhaps of greatest concern is the likelihood that if everybody, or members of high-risk groups,[16] is compelled to undergo testing, those who are most in need of medical care or counselling will be deterred from seeking it.

It seems that the arguments presented by public health experts are clearly not in favour of mandatory testing, for the purposes of either prevention or data-gathering. There is, however, one aspect of mandatory testing on which they are less clear: screening blood and organ donors. Screening individuals, so that they may know their serostatus and act accordingly, is of limited use.[17] Nevertheless, to screen the donor of a blood product or organ is an efficient means of preventing the facilitation of the spread of the virus. Although this testing still requires a breach of bodily integrity, it may be justified in two ways. First, it has been suggested that for people who 'choose to engage in that act of donation then mandatory screening is appropriate'.[18] The reason for this rests upon the voluntary aspect of donation. There is no requirement to donate, and nor is it necessary in order for the donor to subsist. If people do not want to undergo HIV antibody tests, they need not offer to donate blood. This defence would be inadequate in countries where blood donation is a paid occupation, as the necessity of giving blood in an economic climate where that may be the only source of income for a family, for example in some poorer parts of Pakistan and India, would ensure that an antibody test would not be a matter of choice. Should people lose their right to bodily integrity because they do not have any economic choice other than to submit to the screening process? This perhaps highlights the difficulties of a universal right which does not look at a person's specific circumstances. Returning to blood donation in the UK, it is justifiable in a voluntary undertaking, on the grounds of the area health authority's duty to provide uninfected blood and blood products,[19] to impose requirements concerning the serostatus of the blood or blood product. In this scenario the donor does not have to waive his or her right to bodily integrity in order to achieve financial remuneration, but can decide whether or not he or she wishes to be screened for the HIV virus.

The second justification for mandatory testing in this respect is that forwarded by the World Health Organization: any donor must give informed consent to an HIV test, for the purpose of prevention, with an assurance of confidentiality and counselling. Once these three requirements are complied with, the test may no longer be viewed as mandatory, but is in fact voluntary.

To summarize, mandatory testing as an infringement of the right to bodily integrity is on the whole prohibited. However, the exception in Article 5(1)(e) of the ECHR poses a problem. Where there is a possibility that the public interest in preventing the spread of the disease may be balanced against the right of the individual, and the public interest is given priority, it is not true to say that the right to bodily integrity is sufficiently well protected by human rights law. Should the moral panic surrounding HIV escalate, or the rate of transmission increase rapidly again, there is no complete protection of the individual against mandatory testing. Whether the prohibition rests upon the nature of the right, or on the prevailing opinion of public health experts, is an important question for future consideration.

Other problems arise within the issue of mandatory testing which also relate to the right to privacy under Article 12 of the UDHR. In this instance the right to privacy is not a right to physical privacy, but instead concerns public knowledge of an individual and his or her reputation.

Disclosure of HIV Status

What will be done with the test results once they are known? Disclosure of such information, either to a spouse or partner, to an employer or to the general public via the media, may rightly be said to contravene one's right to respect for one's private life. This issue is of relevance to AIDS/HIV in the context of contact tracing, employment, health care and compulsory registration of those who are HIV+.

The usefulness of contact tracing can be seen in relation to other sexually transmitted diseases (STDs) where contact tracing is the accepted norm. The primary motive in this respect is to treat and cure the sexual partners. Prevention is a byproduct of treatment. In the case of HIV, while treatments to slow the progress of the virus are available, prevention must be the motivating force in contact tracing. Again, it is important to consider the differences between HIV and other illnesses. Furthermore, to insist upon contact tracing would be to presume automatically that the rights of the contact to be informed have priority over the right to privacy of the client.

This raises a thorny problem, embodied in Article 8 of the ECHR. This Article relates to privacy, but provides a qualified rather than absolute right to privacy:

> There shall be no interference by a public authority with the exercise of this right except such as is in accordance with the law and is necessary in a democratic society . . . for the protection of health or morals, or for the protection of the rights and freedoms of others.

Within the ECHR it is assumed that the rights of the client will be subordinated to the rights of others in certain circumstances, particularly for health reasons. Although the UK is a signatory to the ECHR, Article 8 has not yet been raised as a means of protection against a breach of confidentiality concerning serostatus. However, there have been two important statements of policy concerning the balance between the public interest in knowledge of the incidence of the virus and the public interest in maintaining respect for one's private life. These two statements are of interest in that they are analogous to the reasoning that would be employed by the European Court with regard to HIV and privacy.

The first such statement emanates from the General Medical Council. Where a doctor is aware of a colleague's seropositivity, and that colleague fails to alter his or her practice, or is negligent in following hygiene routines, a doctor would not be infringing his or her colleague's right to privacy by divulging his or her serostatus to either a superior or to a disciplinary committee.[20] In this event, the public interest in knowing of HIV infection only outweighs the interest in respect for one's private affairs where the individual concerned is in a position to inadvertently infect another and where the infected person has not acted in a responsible manner so as to prevent transmission. It would seem that this balance is not unnecessarily harsh, as the employee is not asked to divulge his or her serostatus as a matter of course but is only asked to modify his or her practice. There is not a hint of compulsion or of any loss of benefit.

The second statement concerning the conflict between the two forms of public interest arises from the English case of *X* v. *Y*.[21] In this instance the necessary level of hygiene precaution was taken by the doctor/health worker, and so disclosure of the information was said to be in breach of confidentiality. While at present English law does not explicitly recognize a right to privacy, an analogous remedy is available in breach of confidentiality. In *X* v. *Y*, health authority employees gave records of two doctors who were HIV+ to a reporter. The records were paid for by the reporter's newspaper. The newspaper ran the story despite an injunction prohibiting the publication of the details contained in the records. It was held that the public interest in the confidentiality of the records of AIDS sufferers outweighed the freedom of the press. Here there was no evidence of recklessness as to the future transmission of the virus and thus the public interest in confidentiality was stronger. The gain made from the publication of the details of the employees was based neither on prevention nor on adding to knowledge about the virus for the purposes of research. In this sense disclosure would not be a benefit.

Although these are two instances of decisions outside of the human rights discourse, they are important in that they illustrate the manner in which the conflicting public interests can be calculated. It would seem that the emphasis is on personal responsibility. However, given the power of the moral panic to scapegoat a whole section of society, it is doubtful that the decision as to whether someone is to be held personally responsible can ever be a value-free judgment. Therefore, where human rights conflict, several factors must be taken into account: the health care of contacts, and their right of access to medical treatment; the likelihood of abuse of the information; whether a culture of disclosure of information will force underground those who are most in need of help; and, more worryingly, what type of person it is whose privacy will be infringed.

A further consideration is that of the transmission of the virus from patient to health worker, rather than vice versa. Due to the nature of this relationship it is likely that health workers will be in a position to be exposed to infected bodily fluids. As mentioned earlier, health workers must use specific safety and hygiene procedures to prevent transmission of a variety of diseases, not only HIV. A requirement of disclosure of a patient's serostatus before agreement is given to treat him or her would not serve any constructive purpose, due to the safety procedures. Thus to allow for a breach of the patient's privacy in this instance would be indefensible.[17]

Similarly, it has been suggested that a register of those who test positive would be of use in both a preventative manner and as a research resource. This would fit within the exception in Article 8 of the ECHR. To move outside of the jurisdiction of the ECHR, a US example shows that freedom of information concerning the incidence of the virus need not require an individual's rights to be adversely affected. This was done in Colorado, USA in the late 1980s.[22] The administration of the register was exercised under a strict ethic of confidentiality, although information given was used for contact tracing by the public health authority. The programme has been defended by the Executive Director of the Colorado Department of Public Health on a two-fold basis: it is acceptable to give a false name on presenting oneself for the antibody test; and knowledge of the way in which HIV occurs in any given community will result in further understanding of the development of the HIV virus. To manage the register in this way obviates the need for a conflict of rights, as it allows knowledge to be gathered and counselling to be given without imposing the burden of public knowledge of serostatus upon an individual.

To summarize, it seems that human rights law supports a variety of positions with regard to disclosure of HIV status. Either one has an absolute right to privacy which may not be breached, as with the UDHR, or a right that one may exercise only if one acts in a 'responsible' manner, or, lastly, a right to privacy/confidentiality which will always be balanced against the rights of other individuals or against public health policies. These last two alternatives are different interpretations of the European Article (Article 8 of the ECHR), depending upon the level of autonomy granted to the individual.

Because of the qualified rights to privacy and freedom from physical interference, should the health experts' opinion of the validity of testing in relation to prevention change, mandatory testing may become possible in the case of public health. Should this occur, it would be likely that the concept of high-risk groups would be utilized. Although sources ranging from the HEA to the radical US group Gay Men's Health Coalition have repeatedly stated that what is significant in thinking about AIDS/HIV is high-risk behaviour and not what group one belongs to, high-risk groups are still used as a means by which to explain transmission of the HIV virus. I suggest that the reason for this is not medically justified but is rather derived from the fact that they are seen as different, on the basis of sexuality, race or gender stereotypes. These groups will also be equated with difference in relation to HIV; that is, they will be assumed not to have 'normal' HIV status, but will be assumed to be HIV+.

On a more practical level, testing, and deprivation of liberty in order to compel someone to undergo a blood test, depend upon the ease of targeting specific groups. In this instance, those who are not nationals, or appear to be racially different, or those women typically classified as 'not good' women, perhaps prostitutes, would be most at risk due to their high-profile 'otherness'.

Detention and Isolation

In addition to the question of disclosure of information, a further corollary of mandatory testing is that of detention of those suspected of being HIV+ and of those who are known to be so. Flaws in the antibody test mean that most often several tests at intervals of up to three months will have to be carried out. Where multiple tests are required, the person undergoing the test might have to be detained to ensure that he or she would be present for the whole series of tests. This, however, would be to contradict Article 3 of the UDHR, which states that 'Everyone has the right to life, liberty and security of person', and, furthermore, Article 9, which reads 'No one shall be subjected to arbitrary arrest, detention or exile.'

The right to liberty and to freedom from detention are also enshrined in the ECHR, under Article 5. This Article, as was the case concerning the ECHR provision for privacy, does not offer as extensive protection as the UDHR. The right to liberty under the ECHR is a qualified one. As we have seen, Article 5(1)(e) limits the right to liberty so that it does not apply in cases of 'lawful detention of persons for the prevention of the spreading of infectious diseases'. For detention on this ground to be lawful, the burden of proving that mandatory testing and isolation do prevent further spread of the virus is with the state. In the case of *X* v. *Austria*[23] the European Commission found that a compulsory blood test constituted a deprivation of liberty, even if the detention was of only a minute's duration. This source provides a strong defence against detention and deprivation of liberty for reasons associated with antibody testing. There are, however, limits to this defence.

As I have discussed already, testing has a negligible preventive effect. In fact, the threat of detention would further encourage an unwillingness to approach the authorities for help. Furthermore, public health experts are as sceptical about the value of isolation as they are about mandatory testing: 'it would be a dangerous illusion to believe that we will break the back of HTLV III infection by controlling those who behave publicly in ways that spread the virus'.[24]

There are two probable reasons for a state to isolate someone linked with HIV. The first of these grounds would be simply because the person is HIV+, and in the light of a moral panic may be seen to constitute a risk, either to the public health or to the moral fibre of the country. The second reason may be that the HIV+ individual may be seen to be taking part in high-risk behaviour. Isolation would require the serostatus of each person to be ascertainable. Thus mandatory testing would be a prerequisite. This is acceptable in human rights law under the ECHR. Further, HIV transmission takes place largely in private and intimate circumstances, that is either when drugs are being taken intravenously or in sexual intercourse. How would transmission of the virus be policed, and how would the authorities know whom to test? In the situation where transmission is via drug-taking, the problem arises that most intravenous drug use involving unhygienic needles is illegal. The act itself is already proscribed and yet goes on. If the offence of taking illegal drugs cannot be adequately policed, then how will this form of 'reckless behaviour' be prevented? One way in which this could happen would be to gain access to a doctors' register of drug addicts. However, this would raise similar issues of disclosure of confidential information to those I have already discussed. Detention in order to test would depend on disclosure of this information, but, far more importantly, detention due to the fact that someone is a HIV+ drug user and therefore could infect someone else is a form of detention which is of a longer duration. The virus is not going to leave a person's system. It would perhaps be possible for a drug rehabilitation programme to be required to prove that the drug user would no longer participate in what could be a habit dangerous for others around him or her. However, what would be the penalty if the user began to take drugs again?

If only those who threaten to transmit the virus so as recklessly to endanger public health can be lawfully detained, as Article 5(1)(e) of the ECHR would seem to suggest, it will be essential for the state to show that each individual who is HIV+ does not intend to conduct himself or herself so as to cause transmission. If the state wishes to show either that such individuals will not take any precautions or that they positively intend to act in a reckless manner, how will their malicious intent be distinguished from the intentions of those who are HIV+ and have no such intention? Given that the other main mode of transmission is sexual, the state would have to identify high-risk behaviours and then attempt to police them. The implications are that freedom of sexual expression would be curtailed, and that discrimination against specific groups would be increased, with consequent intrusion into the lives of gay men. This would stem from the prevailing attitude that HIV is linked to high-risk groups rather than high-risk behaviour. Again, detention in order to test against someone's will is prohibited in *X* v. *Y*, but is not ruled out in the ECHR. Given that a consensual sexual relationship is not, unlike drug abuse, illegal, detention in order to protect public health would be more difficult to organize. There is no register, such as that of drug addicts, to use as a starting point for identification. Also, there is the issue that the partner of someone who is HIV+ may opt to take the risk that the virus will not be transmitted between them. This is a completely different issue from that of someone who intends to infect another person.

While cases of isolation have not yet been confirmed, despite suggestions that it is already happening in some countries, for example Cuba, it is true that people who are HIV+ are not being granted entry into some countries, even if they are not yet being prevented from leaving their own. In *Re T (Minors) (Care Proceedings: Wardship)*,[25] a mother who had lived in the USA with her American partner and child left her partner and during divorce proceedings came to live in Britain. While she was living in Britain she found out that she was HIV+. The mother wished to return to the USA in order to be present at the hearing concerning the custody of her child. Her visa was not extended to allow her to do this. On enquiry by the Court of Appeal, it was suggested by the US embassy that her HIV status had been significant in this decision, particularly with a view to returning to the state of New York. Although under the ECHR in Article 1 protection of human rights is extended to each person within the jurisdiction of the state, this would not apply in this case. Under the UDHR in Article 13(2): 'Everyone has the right to leave any country, including his own, and return to his country.' In this case the mother would not be able to claim any right to re-enter the USA, and thus the discrimination against her on the basis of her HIV status stands.

To summarize, the qualified right to liberty afforded by the ECHR in relation to infectious diseases adversely affects those who are HIV+ or

PWAs disproportionately to the likelihood of transmission of the HIV virus. Freedom of movement is already infringed around the world. The breach of fundamental rights and freedoms is based on misconceptions surrounding HIV/AIDS.

A deconstruction of the freedom of movement raises problems which otherwise might be overlooked. Isolation as a public health policy would necessitate utilization of the 'high-risk group' classification in much the same way as would be required by mandatory testing. As can be seen from Hummel,[26] the implication is that there are certain people who can be identified as being a public threat. It can only be assumed that this is a reference to prostitutes, and reinforces the argument that isolation is a mechanism which would marginalize further those who are already outside of the accepted social norms. If instead the prostitute's experience of AIDS/HIV were to be used to contextualize discussion of isolation, we could see a historical pattern emerging. At the height of the syphilis epidemic, prostitutes were detained in locked hospitals while their military clients were free to do as they pleased.[27] It would seem that once again we are targeting those in positions of powerlessness rather than confronting the idea that a white, heterosexual man may be responsible for the spread of HIV.

A somewhat different situation can be seen to be in train with regard to refusal of entry into certain countries. Sontag[7] depicts AIDS as an invasive force, and indeed the disease has been categorized in some instances as a threat to a nation's health from outside. But is this fear of the spread of AIDS, or is it racism? Public health experts have accepted that we are not going to prevent the spread of the virus by isolation. Is it any more likely that in a country where the virus is already present, restrictive entry requirements will hinder the spread of AIDS? In this situation the context of an East African's experience of AIDS will differ greatly from that of a Western gay man. In fact, freedom of movement is unlikely to be infringed with regard to a homosexual.

Employment

The right to work is enshrined in Article 23(1) of the UDHR.[28] As with all formulations of rights, there are differences in interpretation. Different interpretations of the right to work vary from socialist to free market versions.[29] The interpretation I shall use here means that the state shall not prevent any of its citizens from seeking gainful employment.

Discrimination in the workplace against PWAs and those who are HIV+ occurs in at least two different ways. First, it has been claimed that the presence of someone who is HIV+ may give rise to complaints from co-workers or other third parties. This was the case in *Buck* v. *Letchworth Palace*.[30] Although Mr Buck's colleagues did not know for certain that he was HIV+, they assumed that he was because he was homosexual. They also feared that they too would become infected by working with him. Despite a decision in an earlier case, *Cormack* v. *TNT Sea Lion*,[31] which came down in favour of the employer, in *Buck* the employee won his case. As WHO has stated, 'HIV infection is not spread through casual contact or routine social contact in... the workplace.'[32]

A further consideration is whether the employer should be made aware of an employee's serostatus. The case with regard to health workers and medics has already been discussed. Of other occupations, the ILO, together with WHO, have stated 'There should be no obligation on the employee to inform the employer of his/her HIV status.'[33] Nor, it seems, having considered mandatory testing, should an HIV test be a pre-employment requirement. After all, seeking employment is not of the same voluntary nature as a blood donation.

Turning to the second way in which discrimination in the workplace is characterized, it has been claimed that being HIV+, with the long-term possibility of developing full-blown AIDS, may affect the employee's capacity to work. Cases in the USA have not on the whole dealt with HIV positivity, but have instead claimed protection by drawing a parallel with treatment of disabled people in the workplace. To categorize HIV/AIDS as a disability means that as long as the employee is still able to perform his or her job satisfactorily he or she may not be dismissed. The ILO has stated that 'HIV infection is not a cause for termination of employment. As with many other illnesses, persons with HIV-related illnesses should be able to work as long as medically fit for available appropriate work.'[34] Where HIV-related illnesses may affect an employee's work, alternative arrangements are required of the employer. This is current practice in the NHS, which would suggest that to fail to do this would constitute unfair dismissal.

To summarize, employment protection offered by human rights law and employment law would seem to be adequate. Some changes in working arrangements may be necessary, and a portion of the protection afforded to employees derives not from anti-HIV discrimination clauses, but from anti-disability policies. However, the overall result is favourable to those who are HIV+ or PWAs.

Several issues of difference are raised in considering the right to work. First, returning to the *Cormack* case, it is clear that prejudices concerning HIV and homosexuality are interlinked. Cormack's employees knew that he was gay, and jumped to the conclusion that he must therefore be HIV+. In addressing the issue of Cormack's right to work under human rights law it is possible to adopt a position in which Cormack would be able to stay at work. But if we ignore the part that his sexuality played as a target for AIDS discrimination, it is unlikely that his working environment would be much changed. A second point which arises from this is that Cormack was not HIV+. If this is the case, then how can a plaintiff prove that the discrimination against him is based on HIV/AIDS without being able to show the link between homosexuality and AIDS in the minds of those who are discriminating against him? It is vital that human rights law does not view AIDS/HIV as a discrete consideration in cases like this.

The requirement that an employer finds alternative work for an employee who is no longer able to carry on in the same position due to HIV infection reflects a final point with regard to the way in which the right to work is defended under human rights law. It is suggested that this particular protection of the individual's rights is appropriate only in the context of middle-class professions. While an articulate, professional gay man may be able to use these provisions to protect himself, the experience of a woman whose sole source of income is from prostitution will be very different. To consider AIDS as a totalizing force would be to ignore the difficulties that are faced by several sections of society in utilizing human rights protection. For example, although a gay man may stand more chance of manipulating the discourse effectively, it may be that to bring an action for unfair dismissal would be too traumatic given the stigma which is currently attached to AIDS/HIV.

To return to the example of the prostitute, in accepting HIV status as a unifying characteristic in cases of breach of human rights, it is the case that appropriate ways in which to help particular groups of people are overlooked. To insist on a right to work will not help a prostitute who is already working on the wrong side of the law. However, to bear in mind the specificity of her situation would allow us to look beyond the slogan 'the right to work' and to create a remedy within the context of her particular situation. For example, legalized brothels in which safer sex is the rule would be more effective in terms of employment for the prostitute than defining interpretations of AIDS in the workplace.

CONCLUSION

Existing human rights law does to some extent protect those affected by the HIV virus. However, to ignore the moral panic which creates the stigma surrounding AIDS is to fail to provide adequate protection. By contextualizing, rather than totalizing, the experience of different people affected by AIDS/HIV it is possible to arrive at an understanding of the more complex issues involved, and thus it is hoped to address them in a more effective manner. To view AIDS/HIV within the context of an individual's experience of HIV positivity enables us to see the flaws inherent in the protection afforded to that individual under human rights law. The identification of a moral panic surrounding AIDS/HIV rebuts the validity of addressing AIDS as a discrete entity within human rights law. The transformation of AIDS from a medical phenomenon to a moral panic brought to the forefront a variety of fears and prejudices already inherent in society's psyche. For example, Philip Thomas[35] argues that the AIDS panic was triggered by homophobia; that without an existing deep social concern about homosexuality, and its effect on the nuclear family, AIDS would not have been transformed from an epidemiological fact into a sensationalized gay plague. The implication arising from this is that by developing AIDS as a moral issue, the conservative constituency was furnished with a smokescreen under which homophobic discrimination could be perpetuated and reproduced, supported by popular opinion. It is precisely the use of AIDS as a smokescreen which presents the possibility that to address AIDS as a discrete entity within human rights law is to be mistaken as to the quality and extent of discrimination faced by PWAs, those who are HIV+, and those who are suspected of being so. How then is this smokescreen created and sustained? It is suggested that we are distracted from seeing the true nature of discrimination against a variety of social groups because of our attraction to what Young[36] calls the logic of identity. This can be understood as an attempt by the rational part of ourselves to understand, and therefore to gain some control over, the multiplicity of differences which surround us. This is facilitated by a process of categorization. We identify the unifying qualities in any group of objects/people and name that group by their similarities, giving greater value to the shared characteristics. In other words, in order to understand we must to some extent generalize, and in doing so we also prioritize.

With reference to the subject of AIDS we categorize people as those who are normal and those who are infected. While this is a valid medical distinction, once transferred to the moral, social world it becomes meaningless. To categorize society within this duality is to ignore, or, even worse, to suppress the recognition of the variety of people and experiences contained within each part of the duality. Thus attempts to protect HIV+ people from the discrimination that they face must necessarily be incomplete. HIV status has become a totalizing force, addressing only one aspect of each individual's experience of living with AIDS/HIV whilst other strands of his or her identity which may also be a focus for discrimination are submerged. To accept AIDS as a totalizing quality means that other contributory modes of discrimination (race, gender, sexuality) are not addressed. The question may be asked: why not address each mode of discrimination separately? Human rights law, after all, recognizes a myriad of bases for discrimination. The answer lies in the closure which occurs once a discrete characteristic, such as HIV status, is identified as a source of powerlessness. By concentrating on a person's HIV status, a medically proven fact, it is possible to maintain a multiplicity of prejudiced attitudes behind a drive for prevention of the spread of the virus. As mentioned earlier, Philip Thomas has looked behind the smokescreen to name homophobia as a form of prejudice legitimized by the AIDS panic. Without detracting from the violent and brutal backlash faced by the gay community in the wake of the AIDS panic, to equate AIDS/HIV discrimination with homophobia still suppresses the various differing experiences of those touched by the AIDS panic. Other dualities of power which must also be taken into account include good women/other or bad women; Westerners/non-Westerners; worthy/ unworthy AIDS victims.[37]

It is important to consider the role played within the AIDS/HIV discourse by the duality of worthy/unworthy AIDS victims in more detail. To say that it is possible, and indeed desirable, to look at HIV status as a discrete entity must become impossible in the light of this dichotomy. If HIV infection is an impartially assessed characteristic, why then are there those who are said not to deserve to be infected, and others who are said to deserve it? The answer must lie in notions of morality; some people were not within a group constituted as 'other' at the time of infection, while others were. This pattern can be seen to be true if one considers modes of transmission. A person who was infected by means of sexual intercourse may be considered as worthy or unworthy, depending on their sexuality and on questions relating to fidelity or promiscuity. For those infected by blood transfusion, no such analysis of character is ever undertaken. This is not to say, however, that they are free from discriminatory behaviour. It is simply to say that in this case it is perhaps easier to view HIV status as a discrete ground of infringement of human rights. Last, the fear of disease or illness (as a veil for existing prejudices) should not be denied when discussing AIDS. Fear of contagion is very real. It is, however, problematic, in that it has become inextricably linked to existing fears of difference.

While considering the many and varied aspects of human rights and AIDS, this chapter has found repeatedly that the question of the exercise of rights by PWAs or those who are HIV+ is placed in conflict with the exercise by others of their rights. I would suggest that by reviewing AIDS and the relationship it has to human rights protection as a complex web of fears and prejudices, it would perhaps be possible to open up the conflict of rights, and by contextualizing them remove many conflicting factors from the debate.

NOTES

1. *Health Update: Sexual Health*, vol. 4 (Health Education Authority, 1994), table 1.1.
2. *Ibid.*
3. (1989) 139 *New Law Journal* 1039. Case heard on 25 May 1989.
4. [1993] RTR 105.
5. *Ibid.*, p. 108.
6. *Sun*, 16 January 1987.
7. S. Sontag, *AIDS and its Metaphors* (Harmondsworth: Penguin, 1990).
8. S. Cohen, *Folk Devils and Moral Panics* (Oxford: Basil Blackwell, 1987).
9. *T (Minors) (Care Proceedings: Wardship), Re* [1989] 1 FLR 313 CA.
10. *Cormack* v. *TNT Sea Lion*: cited in IRLIB (Industrial Relations Legal Information Bulletin) 354.
11. R. F. Hummel, W. F. Leary, M. Rampolla and S. Chorost (eds), *AIDS: Impact on Public Policy* (New York: Plenum Press, 1986), p. 18.
12. D. Feldman, *Civil Liberties and Human Rights in England and Wales* (Oxford: Clarendon Press, 1993), p. 127.
13. R. F. Hummel *et al.*, (eds), *op. cit.*, p. 19.
14. P. Sieghart, *AIDS and Human Rights: A UK Perspective* (London: British Medical Association, 1989), p. 31.
15. R. F. Hummel *et al.*, (eds), *op. cit.*, p. 23.
16. I have used 'high-risk group' at this point in the chapter, as this is the common term. I will address the difficulties that this terminology presents later.
17. See World Health Organization, *AIDS Diagnosis and Control: Current Situation* (Geneva: WHO, 1987).
18. R. F. Hummel *et al.*, (eds), *op. cit.*, p. 30.
19. *Re HIV Haemophiliac Litigation CA* 20 September 1990. The plaintiffs had been infected by blood products imported from the USA by the National Health Service. It was held that, under the National Health Service Act 1977, the Department of Health was negligent in failing to achieve self-sufficiency in blood products for England and Wales. Further, the Department should have known of the risk to the plaintiffs in using blood concentrate from the USA; practicable steps should have been taken to reduce that risk. The Court of Appeal found that if it could be proved that the person with discretion to make these decisions had in fact been aware of the risk, then the Department was negligent.
20. General Medical Council, *HIV and AIDS: The Ethical Considerations* (London: British Medical Association, 1988), p. 2.
21. [1988] 2 All ER 648.
22. R. F. Hummel *et al.*, (eds), *op. cit.*, pp. 25–7.
23. *X* v. *Austria* (8278/78) (1979) DR 18, 154.
24. R. F. Hummel *et al.*, (eds), *op. cit.*, p. 16. I will return for further examination of this sentiment later in the chapter. However, for now let it stand as proof of the invalidity of isolation and nothing more.
25. [1989] 1 FLR 313, CA.
26. See note 24.
27. J. Weeks, *Sex, Politics and Society: the Regulation of Sexuality Since 1800*, 2nd edn (New York: Longman, 1989).
28. 'Everyone has the right to work, to free choice of employment, to just and favourable conditions of work and to protection against unemployment.'

29. P. Sieghart, *op. cit.*, p. 54.

30. *Buck* v. *Letchworth Palace* (1987) COIT 1862/79.

31. Reported in IRLIB (Industrial Relations Legal Information Bulletin) 355. The facts are identical except that the tribunal in *Cormack* held that it may be a material fact that Mr Cormack's work required that he get along with his colleagues.

32. World Health Organization (in conjunction with ILO) *Statement from the Consultation on AIDS and the workplace* (Geneva: WHO, 1988).

33. Cited in P. Sieghart, *op. cit.*, at p. 56.

34. *Ibid.*, p. 56.

35. P. A. Thomas, The nuclear family, ideology and AIDS in the Thatcher years (1993) 1 *Feminist Legal Studies,* 23–44.

36. I. M. Young, *Justice and the Politics of Difference* (Princeton: Princeton University Press, 1990).

37. Whilst I dislike this terminology, it serves to present the dichotomous nature of AIDS/HIV power structures.

PART FIVE:

NEW FRONTIERS

16

The Utility of 'Rights Talk': Employees' Personal Rights

Simon Deakin

INTRODUCTION: EMPLOYEES' PERSONAL RIGHTS AND THE 'CONSTITUTIONALIZATION' OF LABOUR LAW

The concept of the individual or 'personal' rights of the employee, which is well known in the labour law systems of mainland Europe, is scarcely acknowledged in British labour law.[1] This does not mean that legal protection for certain human rights at work is completely lacking here. The UK has acquired a substantial body of legislation on equal treatment in employment and on data protection, and the common law of the contract of employment and the statutory law of unfair dismissal have between them achieved a limited recognition that certain employee rights should prevail over managerial interests.[2] However, these are fragmentary protections which disclose no general legal principle. What is missing is a unifying conception of the right of the individual to the protection of his or her personal dignity and autonomy in relation to employment. Although the potential value of this idea as a justification for dismissal protection, for example, has been identified,[3] it is much more difficult to argue that it is adequately reflected in the existing body of the law. In the mainland systems, by contrast, the idea of the employee's personal rights is increasingly used to link together such issues as equality of treatment, freedom of expression and opinion, employee privacy and the protection of family life and time, which all have in common the definition of a private sphere for the individual employee, free from managerial prerogative. There is more involved here than the negative sense of 'the right to be let alone', which is characteristic of common law attempts to define privacy.[4] In the civilian systems, it is described in terms of broad affirmative notions such as the 'self-determination of the employee' and the 'humanisation of the employment relationship'.[5]

In addition to its substantive importance, the notion of the employee's rights as an individual raises fundamental questions concerning the relationship between labour law regulation and constitutional principle. Personal rights have assumed a growing importance in the mainland European systems partly because they represent the 'infiltration' of constitutional law into labour law, or the 'constitutional recomposition of the employment relationship'.[6] Rights conferred upon individuals in their status as citizens may be invoked to protect them as employees, either directly by way of express provision in constitutional texts, or as a consequence of the principle of *Drittwirkung* or third party effect, through which the obligation to respect fundamental rights, which is initially imposed on the state, is applied to certain private relationships.[7] This process has been said to represent

> the highest degree of juridification of labour relations . . . it marks the transition to a new epoch in the history of labour law, a period characterised by the gradual rediscovery of the individual and thus by the ever increasing individuation of employees.[8]

The constitutional texts of mainland Europe are unusual in containing a number of references to basic social rights, of the kind which are absent from many other liberal-democratic constitutions. The Italian Constitution of 1947 is the most extensive in this regard, recognizing 'all citizens' right to work' as one of a number of 'Basic Principles',[9] and under the Title of 'Economic Relations' acknowledging the existence of a right to an equitable wage, the right to equal pay for equal work between men and women, the right to social assistance, the right to trade union organization and the right to strike.[10] The Preamble to the French Constitution of 1946 also embodies the right to work, the right to strike and the principle of trade union freedom.[11] However, these provisions, which are specific to labour and social law, are not the foundation of the notion of the employee's personal rights. Instead, that notion is derived from provisions which are general in character but which have acquired a particular meaning within the context of the employment relationship. Much of the discussion of personal rights has been directly or indirectly inspired by the Basic Law of the German Federal Republic, the first article of which guarantees the 'Protection of human dignity', and the second of which states that 'Everyone shall have the right to the free development of his personality in so far as he does not violate the rights of others or offend against the constitutional order.' These provisions, together with Article 4 on freedom of opinion, conscience and religion, Article 5 on freedom of expression, and Article 6 on the protection of marriage and the family, have had an extensive influence on labour law.[12] The model provided by the German Basic Law influenced the Spanish Constitution of 1978, and it is the latter's general guarantees of freedom of belief and of religion, the right to privacy, freedom of expression and communication and the presumption of innocence which have provided the means for the 'constitutionalization' of labour law in that country.[13]

In the UK, with no constitutional code or bill of rights, there is the familiar situation of isolated statutes, courts' decisions and codes of practice, from which it may be possible to deduce the existence of certain substantive legal rights; or not, as the case may be. However, to a certain extent the current body of law governing the employment relationship fulfils many of the same functions as constitutional texts perform in some of the mainland systems. Where 'rights talk' is concerned there are three essential functions to be performed. First, it is necessary to identify *which rights* of the employee are recognized as deserving legal protection. Rights which might elsewhere be spelled out in a bill of rights largely take a legislative form in Britain, the common law of employment contributing a little but not much. Second, the law must determine how far the exercise or assertion of rights in particular cases may be limited by *instrumental factors*, such as industrial efficiency or a wider 'public interest'; and third, it may be necessary to resolve *conflicts* between employees' rights and the protected rights of other relevant parties (including employers, fellow employees and trade union members, and consumers). Again, balancing acts of this kind which are to some extent the province of constitutional tribunals in other systems are completely familiar to the courts of the UK, albeit in the more parochial context of the interpretation of social legislation and its relationship to the common law.

The central question for British labour law, however, is whether employment rights can be adequately protected using the existing instruments provided by the common law and social legislation, or whether 'rights talk' of a more formal, constitutional kind is needed. In this chapter the substantive law of the employment relationship will be examined to see how far the common law and social legislation are capable of generating and defining the necessary guarantees for employees, guarantees which are capable of opposing or possibly 'overriding any countervailing welfare considerations'.[14] It will be suggested that while the outcome is unsatisfactory from this point of view, the result owes more to the lack of a comprehensive labour code than it does to the absence of a bill of rights. This does not mean that the enactment of a bill of rights would necessarily be without value; but it should caution us against any belief that a bill of rights would achieve much without wider reforms of procedure and substance in labour law.

SPELLING OUT EMPLOYMENT RIGHTS: THE ROLES OF THE LEGISLATIVE AND JUDICIAL BRANCHES

The long tradition in Britain of doubting whether it is useful to express the rights of the individual in the form of a 'basic law' or constitutional declaration, which Dicey expressed so clearly, remains central to the debate about the role of rights in labour law. Dicey thought that the rights or interests incorporated in the common law, what he called 'the ordinary law of the land', enjoyed a kind of fundamental protection against arbitrary removal by executive action or even by statute.[15] Although this view has obviously not withstood the enormous growth in the present century of regulatory legislation intruding into areas previously governed by the common law and in many cases limiting private rights in significant ways, it is not entirely misleading either. The idea that the common law *is* the law of the land, from which Parliament is only able to carve a series of limited exceptions which must themselves be strictly construed, lies at the heart of the judges' restrictive approach to the interpretation of modern legislation establishing social and collective rights.[16] It is almost as if private common law rights (in particular certain property and contract rights) are close to being 'inderogable' in the sense that social legislation may not readily be interpreted as limiting them: there is a presumption that legislation is not intended to encroach on the common law if this is not clearly stated.[17] Inderogability is a concept developed primarily in civilian labour law systems to explain the legal priority of certain sources of law over others, and in particular the supremacy of norms laid down in legislation and collective bargaining over individual contracts. It is a major weakness of labour law in Britain that this notion is capable of working in reverse, to privilege freedom of contract and the employer's property rights.

Within modern labour law it is social legislation rather than the common law which is the principal source of protection of the employee's personal rights, a complete inversion of Dicey's position. In the 1960s and 1970s the quantity and scope of individual employment legislation in Britain grew considerably, in the linked but separate forms of *employment protection* and *equal treatment* legislation. The Data Protection Act 1984, derived from a Council of Europe convention, is also an important source of protection against abuse of information for individuals generally and necessarily has an impact upon the employment relationship, although its provisions are not always well adapted to it: 'the processing of data in the employment sphere is . . . only one, relatively small part of a much larger picture'.[18]

Employment legislation (including for this purpose the Data Protection Act 1984) has in many senses made only small inroads into the common law core of employment law in Britain, and the employee's civil rights are generally acknowledged to be poorly protected.[19] Unfavourable comparisons could easily be drawn between Britain and the explicit constitutional guarantees of mainland Europe. Keith Ewing has argued, however, that a bill of rights would be counterproductive from the point of view of British labour law.[20] This is not just because virtually all models so far advanced for a British bill of rights, in common with the European Convention on Human Rights (ECHR), stress civil or political rights, such as freedom of expression and assembly, at the expense of social and economic rights such as the right to an equitable wage. Nor is it solely because opponents of *collective* labour rights used the freedom of association provisions of the ECHR to undermine legislation supporting the institution of the closed shop (or compulsory union membership) in the early 1980s.[21] It is also because of a deep scepticism about the utility of enacting rights in *general* terms and leaving their precise interpretation in hard cases up to the judges.

The respective roles of Parliament and the courts are at the heart of this argument. Since constitutional provisions are by their nature open-textured and are not self-executing but depend upon judicial interpretation to give them meaning in specific contexts, a bill of rights would transfer to the judges the responsibility of making 'major political decisions . . . without having to account for what they have done'.[22] This argument applies equally to any judicial power to assert individual constitutional rights against private powers, via *Drittwirkung*, as it does to a power to strike down legislation. But if the judges cannot be entrusted with this task, to what extent is it better fulfilled by social legislation of a *specific* kind? Will legislation be effective in excluding the common law and limiting judicial discretion, as it should according to the doctrine of parliamentary sovereignty? As we have seen, one difficulty here is the principle of interpretation that a statutory rule which purports to oust the common law must be strictly construed. If legislation is detailed enough and comprehensive enough, however, it should be made to prevail over the most reluctant court. In the end, even the prolonged judicial resistance to the broad trade dispute formula contained in ss. 13

and 29 of the Trade Union and Labour Relations Act 1974 collapsed out of recognition for this basic constitutional principle, albeit when it was already clear that Parliament would itself act to restrict the scope of trade union immunities.[23] The more problematic question which will be considered next is whether social legislation can be effective in articulating fundamental rights which apply across the range of issues which affect the individual employment relationship.

CONTRASTING MODELS OF EMPLOYEE RIGHTS: COMMON LAW, EMPLOYMENT PROTECTION AND EQUAL TREATMENT

The Common Law

The common law recognizes very little by way of inderogable or entrenched rights of the employee, largely because it places few if any restrictions on the employer's right to use his or her normally superior bargaining power to fill in what Alan Fox calls the 'empty boxes' of the contract of employment in his or her favour.[24] However it is not freedom of contract alone which underpins managerial prerogative; the common law has long recognized an element of subordination which is grafted onto the contractual form of the relationship, in modern cases in the legal form of implied terms expressing the employee's duties of obedience, cooperation, fidelity and loyalty. In many instances these 'status obligations'[25] are the descendants of restrictive nineteenth-century legislation regulating the service relationship, whose influence has lingered on in the common law long after its formal repeal in the liberalizing reforms which began in the 1870s.[26] The inherent flexibility of the contract of employment from the employer's point of view is expressed in the wide-ranging notion of the duty of cooperation, which explains, for example, why employees in the Inland Revenue were under an implied duty to go along with the introduction of new technology which greatly affected their working conditions and which would lead to some of them being made redundant,[27] and why schoolteachers were under a responsibility to cover for absent colleagues even though the classes in question were not contained in their school timetable or in the schedule of their working hours.[28]

There has, nevertheless, been a significant development in recent years in the use of these implied terms to limit the apparently open-ended powers of the employer. The common law increasingly recognizes the essential reciprocity of the contract of employment, a view which is not consistent with an open-ended contractual power for the employer. The duty of obedience, for example, is no longer expressed in the unconditional terms of certain nineteenth-century decisions,[29] but takes into account the position, skills and seniority of the employee as well as the employer's responsibility to treat the employee with a basic degree of personal respect.[30] Just as an isolated act of disobedience or dissent will now rarely justify a summary dismissal at common law, so an employee will be entitled to resign and claim constructive dismissal if subjected to arbitrary or oppressive discipline or verbal abuse by an employer.[31] The employer's duty to cooperate has been held to extend to a requirement to act in good faith in the exercise of a power to raise pension payments under the terms of a pensions trust[32] and to give an employee adequate notice of a transfer to a different branch of the company under a mobility clause.[33] Other cases are more directly concerned with what may be regarded as personal as opposed to economic rights of the employee. Thus in general 'an employer must not destroy the mutual trust and confidence on which co-operation rests';[34] examples include directing the employee to work overtime which, although agreed to in the contract, could endanger his or her health through exposure to excessive working hours,[35] failing to deal with sexual harassment of the employee by a senior manager[36] and making a false and ill-informed accusation of theft against the employee.[37]

Notwithstanding these advances in the common law, two overwhelming weaknesses remain. One concerns remedies: with the exception of certain public sector workers whose status in this regard is unclearly defined,[38] a specific order to maintain the contract of employment and the vested rights attached to it is not available to an employee disciplined or dismissed in breach of contract. Normally the employee will only receive damages representing wages or salary for the notice period and possibly for any period during which a disciplinary procedure would have operated.[39] This in turn is the result of a common law rule that an employer can always end the contract of employment by giving notice for any reason, including a mistaken or 'abusive' one,[40] or for no reason at all.[41] This fragility of the individual contract means that few if any rights of the employee can survive an employer's determination to end the relationship. Second, in the last resort the court's willingness to uphold the employer's residual managerial prerogative will almost certainly prevail in cases where the interests of the business are seen as conflicting with the rights of the employee to freedom of expression or opinion, for example. In such cases the common law soon reaches its limits, which is after all why there has been such extensive statutory intervention in this area.

Employment Protection

Employment protection legislation injects an element of 'formal rationality' into the employment relationship by requiring the employer to give reasons for a dismissal, to show that the reason principally relied on falls within a category of 'potentially fair reasons' listed by statute and, finally, to demonstrate that in the actual circumstances the employer 'acted reasonably' in treating the reason as sufficient for dismissing the employee.[42] Failure to produce a potentially fair reason or to show that dismissal was reasonable in the circumstances will result in a finding of unfair dismissal, which in turn will lead either to an award of compensation normally in excess of anything available at common law or to an order of re-employment. These more effective remedies indirectly strengthen the common law since, for the purposes of the Employment Protection Consolidation Act 1978 (EPCA), an employer's repudiatory breach of contract amounts to constructive dismissal, allowing the employee to quit and bring an unfair dismissal claim for compensation. A constructive dismissal, even a repudiation of express contract terms, is not necessarily unfair, but in most cases it will be, so that an employer's refusal to treat the employee with dignity and respect in breach of the contract of employment may be penalized by this indirect route.

However, unfair dismissal legislation marks less of an advance on the common law than might at first sight be supposed. In the first place this is because the categories of potentially fair reasons for dismissal are very widely defined, to include not only the grounds of misconduct, lack of capability or qualifications, statutory prohibition and redundancy, but also the catch-all of 'some other substantial reason of the kind such as to justify the dismissal of an employee holding the position which that employee held'.[43] Second, the test of reasonableness or 'fairness' under the EPCA, s. 57(3), while enabling the tribunal to weigh a number of factors in the balance which go far beyond the terms of the contract, is not well designed to protect the employee's personal rights in cases of conflict with the employer's business interests (or, if one prefers, the employer's *property rights*). The Employment Act 1980 removed a provision shifting the burden of showing reasonableness on to the employer; now the burden is 'neutral' as between the two sides, which does not assist the employee. Nor is it an accident that the Act phrases the test of fairness in terms of whether the employer '*acted* reasonably' (emphasis added). The focus is on conduct, and not on the result; the criteria to be applied are those of procedural as opposed to substantive justice. This may benefit the employee in a case where the employer fails to observe the requirements of due process, as these are loosely laid down for the guidance of tribunals in the advisory Code of Disciplinary Practices and

Procedures; not allowing the employee to put his or her case or to be represented by a trade union may lead to a finding of unfairness regardless of whether the end result would have been any different[44] (although if the tribunal considers that the employee would have been dismissed in any event, compensation will be substantially reduced).

But in other cases, the opposite happens: the employee may be lawfully dismissed even though it can be shown, after the event, that he or she was not guilty of an alleged act of indiscipline or misconduct, for example if *at the time of dismissal* the employer did all that he or she reasonably could to ascertain the facts of the case and to judge the appropriate penalty.[45] A particularly low standard of procedural propriety will operate if the business is a small one in terms of size and resources. The emphasis here is on ensuring that the exercise of managerial power is legitimized and, in a fundamental sense, strengthened.[46] Far from supporting the employee's expectation of receiving 'industrial justice' regardless of the resources at the employer's disposal, the law protects the employer against the imposition of an unduly onerous burden in determining the rights and wrongs of individual cases. With such a partial emphasis on due process, it is not surprising that unfair dismissal offers such a weak form of protection for fundamental substantive rights.

Discretion in the operation of standards is built into the EPCA. The emergence of a set of clearly protected employee rights has been stymied by the wide discretion reserved to the industrial tribunals at first instance; early attempts of the Employment Appeal Tribunal (EAT) to lay down general guidelines for tribunals to follow were rebuffed by the Court of Appeal.[47] The greatest limitation upon unfair dismissal arises from the wide area of legitimate authority left to employers by the 'band of reasonableness test'.[48] This means that as long as an employer can show that his or her behaviour fell within a range of responses which reasonable employers could have taken, he or she will not be found to have contravened the statute. The standard is reactive in the sense of incorporating not the best employer practice, but an ill-defined 'middle ground'. Its most controversial application is the decision of the EAT in *Saunders*, to the effect that the dismissal of an attendant in a boys' camp on the grounds solely of his homosexuality was fair, even though he regarded his sexuality as an entirely private matter and there was no evidence of its affecting the way he performed his job; the industrial tribunal nevertheless considered that most employers would have taken the view that the applicant should not have been employed in close proximity to children, and this judgment was upheld on appeal.[49]

There is, moreover, the point that unfair dismissal remedies are stronger in theory than they are in practice, and (cases of trade union and sex or race discrimination aside) are not intended to be exemplary but merely to compensate the employee.[50] Orders of re-engagement and reinstatement have amounted to around only 5 per cent of successful unfair dismissal claims since the introduction of the remedy in the 1970s and the average award of compensation is much less than the statutory maxima allow (currently £11,000 for the compensatory award and £6150 for the basic award which represents loss of acquired seniority). In 1993-1994 the median award was £2773; in 1990-1991 it was £1773; and in 1986-1987 it was £1676.[51]

Unfair dismissal protection is strengthened in a number of cases in which dismissal for a particular reason is classified as 'automatically unfair'. Once the reason is established, the tribunal no longer has any discretion: it must find the dismissal unfair. Nor is there a qualifying period of service in these cases, which apply to dismissals on the grounds of trade union membership or activities,[52] of pregnancy,[53] or of assertion of a statutory right,[54] for taking steps to avoid a danger to health and safety[55] and, in the case of certain retail employees, for refusing to work on Sundays.[56] Extra compensation is also available if the dismissal is for trade-union-related reasons or for reasons related to sex or race discrimination (even though the latter is not, formally, automatically unfair under the 1978 Act).[57] There are, however, some obvious omissions from the list of inadmissible reasons: no reference is made to dismissal related to the expression of political or religious opinion, for example. As things stand at present, the list can only be added to piecemeal; the vast majority of dismissals fall under the general provisions of ss. 55 and 57 of the Act.

Free speech is, nevertheless, better protected in relation to those matters which are the subject of specific provision to make certain dismissals automatically unfair. Participation in the activities of an independent trade union is such a reason, and action short of dismissal or the subjection of an employee to a detriment on trade union grounds is also prohibited.[58] This protection is limited, however, by the requirement that the activities should take place at an 'appropriate time', which normally means outside working hours, and by the exclusion of participation in industrial action from the scope of protected activities:[59] the selective dismissal of employees taking part in an unofficial industrial action is automatically fair, while in the case of an official strike the employer may equally well obtain an immunity by dismissing *all* those taking part at any given time (while also retaining the right selectively to re-engage after only three months).[60] There is no exception here for industrial action involving picketing, notwithstanding the implications of that form of industrial action for the exercise of free speech. Strikes aside, the courts have encountered difficulty in cases where protests and representations by employees were not clearly supported or authorized by the union of which they were members. In *British Airways Engine Overhaul*

v. *Francis*[61] a shop steward issued a statement to the press to the effect that the union was not dealing adequately with the complaint of its women members for equal pay; for taking this action she was subsequently reprimanded by her employer. She was held to have been acting in relation to the activities of the union and the employer was declared to have acted unlawfully. But in other cases the distinction between the actions of an individual employee and those of the union has been firmly maintained, partly on the grounds that union support is evidence that the complainant is not just a 'troublemaker'.[62]

Section 57A of the 1978 Act, inserted in 1993 in order to ensure compliance with EC Framework Directive 89/391 on Health and Safety, makes it automatically unfair to dismiss an employee for carrying out health and safety activities as a statutory safety representative (a position akin to being a shop steward in a recognized trade union, if not actually held by a shop steward as part of his or her duties) or as an employee designated to do so by the employer. An employee may not be dismissed for bringing a danger to health and safety to the employer's attention where there is no such representative, or where it was not reasonably practicable to make representations through him or her; and an employee is also protected where he or she leaves work, or refuses to return, in circumstances where he or she reasonably believes that there is a serious and imminent danger. Finally, and most importantly for present purposes, an employee is protected where 'in circumstances of danger which he reasonably believed to be serious and imminent, [he] took, or proposed to take, appropriate steps to protect himself or other persons from the danger'. This could include informing fellow employees or, perhaps, 'whistleblowing' to outside bodies such as a regulatory authority or (less likely, perhaps) the media. The tribunal must judge what steps were appropriate, taking into account all the circumstances 'including, in particular, [the employee's] knowledge and the facilities and advice available to him at the time'; but the employer has a defence if it can be shown that the steps which the employee took or proposed to take were so negligent that 'a reasonable employer might have dismissed him for taking, or proposing to take, them'. This reintroduces the 'band of reasonableness' test and with it the tribunal's wide discretion, making an apparently inadmissible reason for dismissal much more like the dismissal under the general test of fairness.

Whistleblowing on grounds other than health and safety enjoys no special protection in law, however. The contracts of many private sector and public sector workers contain confidentiality clauses; doctors and nurses in the NHS are formally required both by their conditions of service and by the codes of their professional associations to maintain patient confidentiality.[63] This is part of a growing trend for public sector employers to impose general confidentiality clauses on their employees, prohibiting them from discussing with outside persons matters of general importance to the service or business in question. An employer may be able to obtain an injunction to prevent the release of information deemed by the contract, or by general principles of law, to be confidential and there is only a very limited public interest exception which permits disclosure to a responsible person, which will sometimes but need not always cover the case of talking to the media.[64] Nor will dismissal of the employee be automatically unfair; to succeed under the general provisions of unfair dismissal law, the employee will have to show that he or she has the required two years' continuous qualifying service and that dismissal was unfair in the circumstances. Employees have won compensation in some instances such as that of the nurse Grahame Pink, who was dismissed after revealing evidence of a lack of care for elderly patients in a NHS hospital; but in other cases whistleblowing has been regarded as a breach of the employee's obligation of trust and confidence.[65]

A particular failure of employment protection legislation concerns employee privacy. An employee who conceals his or her past or out-of-work activities at the recruitment stage is open to dismissal on the ground of misrepresentation, however irrelevant the matter might be to the performance of the job.[66] The Data Protection Act 1984 provides only limited protection against abuse of information collected by the employer. Although it imposes a requirement to register with the Data Protection Registrar upon all 'data users', including employers, who hold 'personal data' which may be processed automatically, and to abide by the principles which are derived from the Council of Europe Convention on Data Protection, it permits an even wider degree of self-regulation than unfair dismissal law does. Whereas under the Employment Protection (Consolidation) Act 1978 the relevant standard is that of the 'reasonable employer', under the Data Protection Act 1984 the employer itself, as data user, can expand its freedom of action simply by declaring a wide range of purposes for which it is holding the data; to a large extent, an employer which limits the use of the information to these self-declared purposes will have complied with the Act. There are also numerous and wide-ranging exemptions from the requirements of the Act: these cover information relating to national security (this particularly affects civil servants and other public sector employees), payroll and accounts, crime and taxation, health and social work matters and information covered by legal and professional privilege.

The Act does not even purport adequately to protect privacy as such. A power[67] to adopt more stringent regulations to regulate the use of information concerning an individual's racial origin, their political, religious or other beliefs, their physical or mental health or sexual life and their criminal convictions has not been exercised. Even the Data Protection Registrar has noted that, unlike the Convention on Data Protection, 'the Act does not refer to privacy, it is simply a statute "to regulate the use of automatically processed information relating to individuals" '.[68] Indeed, it seems that 'a principal reason for the introduction of the [Act] in the first place was government concern that absence of domestic regulation would mean loss of lucrative business in international data processing'.[69]

Equal Treatment Legislation

Equal treatment legislation is potentially a more effective route to protection of the employee's personal rights, for a number of reasons. Most importantly, substantive justice, in the sense of the achievement of greater 'horizontal' equality, is of the essence here. This affects the entire structure of the legislation, which places much less emphasis on the employer's business interest as a potential opposing factor or defence to the infringement of rights. Few defences are available to a claim of adverse treatment or 'direct discrimination', in which openly sex- or race-related criteria form the basis for an employer's decision; a certain number of 'genuine occupational qualifications' for posts are listed in the Sex Discrimination Act,[70] for example, but these form an exhaustive list and may not be added to by judicial interpretation. The employer's defence of justification is a great deal broader and more open-ended in cases of adverse impact or 'indirect discrimination', but under the influence of European Union law a far more critical attitude to employer's claims is becoming evident: it is not enough to show that the employer's alternative aim is reasonable; instead, the employer must show objective grounds for departing from equal treatment and satisfy the court that the arrangements chosen were essential for the achievement of the alternative goal and, by extension, that they contravened the equality principle as little as possible (or as little as any feasible alternative).[71] Remedies for discriminatory action are stronger than those for unfair dismissal, largely because the upper ceiling on compensation in discrimination cases has been removed on the grounds of its incompatibility with EC Directive 76/207,[72] and the equality principle is also broader in scope than employment protection in the sense of conferring rights on job applicants and not simply on those who are already employed as employees.[73]

There is one aspect of respect for the personal dignity of the employee which is recognized under this head of legislation, in so far as it is now clearly established that an employer who permits sexual or racial harassment to go on will most likely be in breach of the equal treatment legislation, since the mistreatment of the employee will be regarded as related to his or her sex or race, as the case may be.[74] An isolated act of harassment can amount to a 'detriment' for the purposes of the definition of employment discrimination, at least if the employer does nothing about it; under these circumstances an employee would also be entitled to resign and claim compensation for unfair dismissal on the basis that the employer has acted in breach of the duty of mutual trust and confidence under the contract of employment.[75]

There are, nevertheless, some substantial difficulties in applying the equal treatment model to the wider categories of the employee's personal rights to privacy and dignity. As explained above, the statutes on sex and race discrimination are specific to *those* sources of social discrimination, and do not extend to discrimination on the grounds of age, sexuality or disability, for example. This has led to some rather strained attempts to fit cases of personal rights into the framework of sex and race discrimination. If an employer refuses to hire a homosexual male on the grounds of his sexual orientation, can this be seen as sex discrimination? A major problem here is the need to find a 'comparator' who is treated differently on the grounds prohibited by the two Acts, that is to say sex or race. The problem of comparison is inherent in the notion of 'horizontal equality' which underlies the equal treatment model. Section 5(3) of the Sex Discrimination Act 1975 requires the comparison of the 'cases of persons of different sex or marital status' to be 'such that the relevant circumstances in the one case are the same, or not materially different, in the other'. An employer who refuses to employ a homosexual male may argue that the relevant circumstances are that this particular person is attracted to members of the same sex, and that the employer would not have recruited a woman similarly so inclined. In reply, one could only contend that a person's sexuality should not be considered as a 'relevant circumstance'.[76] While this last point would seem to be correct in principle, the Sex Discrimination Act 1975 has not been consistently invoked to prevent anti-homosexual discrimination.

The same problem arises in cases concerning transsexuals. In a case involving an employer's refusal to recruit a preoperative male-to-female transsexual, an industrial tribunal invoked s. 5(3) of the Sex Discrimination Act 1975 to reject the applicant's claim of sex discrimination, on the grounds that the same treatment would have been applied to a female to male transsexual.[77] The problem will probably only be solved by extending the substance of the equal treatment principle to make the homosexuality or transsexuality of the employee or applicant a prohibited ground of discrimination.[78]

An example of such an extension, in a different context, is the Fair Employment (Northern Ireland) Act 1976 as amended in 1989; this prohibits both direct and indirect discrimination on the grounds of reli gious belief and political opinion. It is surprising, to say the least, that the principle of freedom of religion and political expression which the Act embodies has no application in the rest of the UK.[79]

CONCLUSION: THE ROLE OF 'RIGHTS TALK' IN LABOUR LAW

We may now return to the question posed earlier: how successfully has labour law in Britain served to define fundamental employee rights in the absence of a constitutional code, and how has it fared in resolving the conflicts between employee rights and instrumental considerations and between the employee's personal or individual rights and the employer's property rights? One part of the answer is that 'rights talk' of this kind already exists in British labour law. In particular, the model provided by existing equal treatment legislation is a valuable one from the point of view of resolving these conflicts. However, the wider assessment is not so positive. A number of important rights are not respected as such and a preponderant weight is still given to managerial prerogative in the common law and the law of unfair dismissal.

In terms, first of all, of the definition of employees' rights, the dependence on legislation means that a number of important guarantees simply fall through the gaps between the existing statutes. The list of matters protected by the principle of automatically unfair dismissal under the Employment Protection (Consolidation) Act 1978 is as much a product of political pressure at various times and historical accident as anything else. It is not a coherent account of those rights of the employee which are of sufficient importance clearly to rank above instrumental factors. Nor is there any particularly compelling logic to the existing categories of equal treatment legislation. Relying on legislation as opposed to a bill of rights certainly has the effect of limiting judicial discretion; the courts of the UK have no opportunity to exploit the open-textured quality of constitutional statements of rights. But equally, strive as they might to give extended interpretations to the rights contained, for example, in the Sex Discrimination Act 1975, they soon reach the limit of what is constitutionally permissible. This means that certain aspects of discriminatory treatment are simply beyond the scope of the law, and will remain so as long as Parliament fails to act.

Second, in relation to the resolution of conflicts between rights and instrumental factors, or between the employee's personal rights and the property rights of the employer, the gravest deficiency in the current law is the priority accorded to managerial efficiency (as the courts see it) by the unfair dismissal provisions of the Employment Protection (Consolidation) Act 1978. The protection of employee rights is a secondary consideration when set against the corporatist aims of unfair dismissal legislation, of formalizing employment procedures and of legitimizing the exercise of managerial prerogative within the workplace.[80]

But the inadequacy of British labour law in this regard cannot be solely attributed to the failure to articulate fundamental rights in a constitutional text. What also marks the British system apart from its mainland counterparts is the piecemeal nature of social legislation and the importance still placed on the employer's common law contract and property rights. This is part of the legacy of voluntarism, the principle that employer power should be offset, in the first instance, by the collective social power of organized labour rather than by a comprehensive statutory framework of employment regulation. Where Dicey saw the common law as the 'law of the land' from which Parliament could not legitimately derogate, Kahn-Freund saw organized labour's right to a collective voice as similarly 'inderogable' precisely because it did not rest on a statutory footing of explicit rights; since the strength of organized labour lay beyond the law, what the state had not conferred the state could not take away.[81] But the collective *laissez faire* described by Kahn-Freund has turned out to be no more immune to change than Dicey's individualist version was. With the erosion of organized labour's collective voice in the 1980s, collective bargaining is no longer capable of reaching more than about half of the employed labour force.[82]

In both respects, significant contrasts may be made with other systems in western Europe.[83] The use of constitutional law to control abuses of employer power is most extensive in Germany and Spain. Because the courts have the power to intervene in this way, matters which may not be dealt with in legislation may nevertheless be subjected to legal control; in Germany, these have included the installation of closed circuit television to monitor employees during working hours, the automatic processing of information on employees and the use of graphological tests to measure the suitability of job applicants.[84] In Spain, a wide range of issues concerning the question of dress codes and employees' physical appearance, freedom of expression and opinion, and the form of enterprise-level disciplinary procedures have come before the Constitutional Court.[85] The balance struck between employee rights and the business interests of the enterprise necessarily differs from case to case, but what is most relevant for present purposes is that a legal space exists in which rights can be defined and tested, in contrast to the position in Britain, where any residual space of this kind is occupied only by the common law.

It is also the case, however, that in both these systems the constitution is supplemented by extensive statutory regulation. Laws on data protection are more far-reaching than the equivalent measure, the Data Protection Act 1984, in Britain, and more clearly orientated towards protection of employee privacy. In Germany this is partly because the detailed statutory rules are underpinned by the Federal Constitutional Court's decision of 1983 recognizing a fundamental individual right to control over the processing of personal data,[86] which was based on its interpretation of Articles 1 and 2 of the Basic Law concerning the dignity of the person and the right to protection of the personality respectively.[87]

In short, the constitutional codes have not operated in isolation from labour law as a whole; they have underpinned and not replaced more specific social legislation on the employment relationship. Indeed, in Germany there has been a substantial debate on the meaning of the *Drittwirkung* principle, in which one school of thought has argued that the provisions of the Basic Law 'do not place obligations directly on individuals, but do so indirectly by filling out the general clauses of the Civil Code',[88] or, in the present context, of statutes in the area of labour and social law. It has been suggested that the difference between the two sides is 'not very great' and that the debate sometimes has a 'byzantine' air to it.[89] Nonetheless, it is arguable that the role of the Basic Law in employment cases is closely interdependent with that of social legislation. Without the latter,

> abstract statements about the 'dignity' of the employee or the responsibility to respect his or her 'personality' are . . . of no help. The guarantees of self-determination are not appeals, they are instructions. They must contain clear prohibitions as well as precise regulations constraining especially the employer to act in a certain way.[90]

In France and Italy legislation plays the principal role in the articulation and protection of rights, but nonetheless achieves a broader degree of regulation than in Britain. The French law on data protection dates from 1978[91] and is based on the principle that data processing shall not impose on 'personal identity, the rights of man, privacy or individual and public liberties'.[92] More recently, a law of 1992 concerning (*inter alia*) the recruitment of employees states that the employer may not impose on the rights of the person or on individual or collective liberties 'any restrictions which may not be justified by the nature of the task to be achieved or which are not proportionate to the end to be accomplished'.[93] No information may be required of an applicant for employment which is not aimed at establishing either his or her capacity for the job in question or his or her professional capabilities;[94] and no person may be excluded from a process of hiring, nor any employee disciplined or dismissed, 'by reason of his origin, sex, customs, family situation, ethnic, national or racial origin, political opinions, trade union activities, religious beliefs, or, unless his lack of capability is medically established . . . by reason of his state of health or any handicap'.[95] In Italy, the principal source of protection in this area is Title 1 of the Workers Statute,[96] legislation which as long ago as 1970 regulated the 'remote monitoring' of workers' activity by televisual or control equipment.[97] The Workers' Statute also provides for freedom of expression at the workplace[98] and makes it unlawful for an employer

> for recruitment purposes or during the course of the employment relationship, to make enquiries or have enquiries made into the political, religious or trade union opinions of a worker or into facts that are not relevant to the assessment of a worker's approach to his work.[99]

Much of the debate about individual rights in the civilian system assumes that social legislation and collective bargaining have already achieved basic levels of social protection in terms of wages, working time and health and safety for employees. For British labour law, on the other hand, the immediate priority for any reform must be the use of legislation to restore this floor of *social* rights within the employment relationship which is taken almost for granted elsewhere in Europe. According to the Organization for Economic Co-operation and Development, Britain currently has the weakest labour standards with regard to minimum wages, working time, employment protection and employee representation of any advanced industrialized country, with the exception of the USA.[100] The construction of the right to 'employee self-determination' will not proceed very far until these more basic rights are guaranteed, once again, in respect of the vast majority of the employed labour force.

But the restoration of a social floor of rights should not be the only ambition of labour law reform in Britain. The wider questions of individual employee autonomy of the kind analysed here must also be addressed. In this respect, a fundamental lesson from the experience of the mainland European systems is that employee rights, to be effective, need to be part of an integrated and comprehensive system of labour standards, in which *substantive* rights are supported by a procedural framework of *collective participation*. Hence, infrastructural reform along the lines of a revised labour court system, an enlarged role for a labour inspectorate and, conceivably, a statutory underpinning for workplace representation[101] is vital if a meaningful debate on the content of employees' rights, and the balancing of those rights against competing interests, is to take place. Any reform must recognize that employee rights, whether in a constitutional or statutory form, are not *economically and socially* self-executing.

Where does this leave the case for a bill of rights? The French and Italian examples given above indicate that broad statements of principle can be embodied in legislation, and that the advantage of doing this is that the enforcement of rights can then take place using the procedures and sanctions which apply to other labour law rights (assuming, of course, that the latter are broadly effective for their purpose, or can be made to be); the rights in question are not just fine-sounding expressions. In the British context, the expansion of the equal treatment principle could be achieved using the model of the sex and race discrimination legislation. While some aspects of the framework are in need of improvement,[102] the essential conceptual structure is already in place.

It could be argued that the introduction of the principle of third party effect or *Drittwirkung* is unnecessary once a comprehensive legislative code is put in place, and, moreover, that intervention of this kind should be reserved for the democratically accountable legislative branch.[103] However, it is important to remember, in this context, the reason for the inclusion of the third party effect in the Basic Law and its extension to all courts (and not just specialized tribunals) of a constitutional jurisdiction. The Basic Law was designed not simply to enshrine individual rights, as an expression of democratic and anti-totalitarian values, but also to make those rights legally effective, avoiding the 'programmatic' approach of the post-1918 Weimar Constitution.[104] In common with the other post-War constitutions of western Europe, the Basic Law used the language of human rights with the aim of establishing a broader political consensus on the content of fundamental democratic rights, both civil and social.

In the continuing debates about constitutional reform in Britain, this is a role for a bill of rights which must not be neglected. More than any other industrialized country, Britain in the past 30 years has suffered from an absence of consensus on the issue of labour and social rights; the adverse consequences for social cohesion and, arguably, for economic efficiency are now clear.[105] If a system of labour law which respects these rights is to be reconstructed, all mechanisms for ensuring that its values endure must be taken into account. Much attention has rightly been given to the negative consequences for labour law of constitutional 'infiltration' in the USA and Canada,[106] but this should not be at the expense of further consideration of constitutional models much closer to home.

NOTES

1. See the collection of essays on the theme of personal rights and labour law in Vol. 15 of the *Quaderni di Diritto del Lavoro e delle Relazione Industriale* (1994).

2. On freedom of speech, see Chapter 17.

3. See generally H. Collins, *Justice in Dismissal* (Oxford: Clarendon Press, 1992).

4. On this, see B. Markesinis, Our patchy law of privacy – time to do something about it (1990) 53 *Modern Law Review* 802.

5. S. del Rey Guanter, Contrato de trabajo y derechos fundamentales en la doctrina del tribunal constitucional. In R. M. Alarcón Caracuel (ed.), *Constitución y Derecho del Trabajo: 1981-1991. Análasis de diez años de Jurisprudencia Constitucional* (Madrid: Marcial Pons, 1992); S. Simitis, The rediscovery of the individual in labour law. In R. Rogowski and T. Wilthagen (eds), *Reflexive Labour Law* (Deventer: Kluwer, 1992). The notion of the 'humanization' of the employment relationship originates in German labour law: W. Däubler, *Das Arbeitsrecht* (Reinbek: Rowohlt, 1990), p. 321.

6. S. del Rey Guanter, *op. cit.*, p. 32 ('una recomposición constitucional del contrato del trabajo').

7. On *Drittwirkung* in the context of labour law, see Sir Otto Kahn-Freund, The impact of constitutions on labour law (1976) 35 *Cambridge Law Journal* 240, at p. 267 *et seq.*; M. Forde, Who can remedy human rights abuses? The 'state action' question. In K. D. Ewing, C. A. Gearty and B. A. Hepple (eds), *Human Rights and Labour Law* (London: Mansell, 1994), Chapter 9. See also more generally Chapter 23, below.

8. S. Simitis, *op. cit.*, pp. 183, 184.

9. Constitution of the Italian Republic, 22 December 1947, Article 4.

10. *Ibid.*, Articles 35-40.

11. Under the Constitution of 1958, the Preamble to the 1946 Constitution continues to be a source of constitutional norms.

12. W. Däubler, *op. cit.*, Chapter 15.

13. S. del Rey Guanter, *op. cit.*, pp. 33, 91.

14. This phrase is used by H. Collins, *op. cit.*, p. 20.

15. A. V. Dicey, *An Introduction to the Study of the Law of the Constitution*, 7th edn, 1908, reprinted with an introduction by E. C. S. Wade (London: Macmillan, 1959), p. 201.

16. See, among many such examples, the judgment of Astbury J in *Valentine* v. *Hyde* [1919] 2 Ch. 129, 153.

17. See Lord Wedderburn, Inderogability, collective agreements and Community law (1992) 21 *Industrial Law Journal* 245, at p. 249.

18. B. Napier, Computerisation and employment rights (1992) 21 *Industrial Law Journal* 1, at p. 13.

19. G. Pitt, Justice in dismissal: a reply to Hugh Collins (1993) 22 *Industrial Law Journal* 251.

20. K. D. Ewing, *A Bill of Rights for Britain?* (London: Institute of Employment Rights, 1989); The Bill of Rights debate: democracy or juristocracy in Britain? In K. D. Ewing *et al.*, *op. cit.*, Chapter 7.

21. *Young, James and Webster* v. *United Kingdom* [1981] IRLR 408.

22. K. D. Ewing, in K. D. Ewing *et. al.*, *op. cit.*, p. 181.

23. *Duport Steels Ltd* v. *Sirs* [1980] IRLR 116. At the time the House of Lords decided this case, a newly elected Conservative government was already pledged to placing limits on the broad trade dispute formula in the 1974 Act.

24. A. Fox, *Beyond Contract: Trust, Power and Work Relations* (London: Faber, 1974).

25. A phrase used by J. B. Atleson, *Values and Assumptions in American Labor Law* (Amherst: Massachusetts University Press, 1982).

26. See S. Deakin, Logical deductions: wage protection before and after *Delaney* v. *Staples* (1992) 55 *Modern Law Review*, 848.

27. *Cresswell* v. *Board of Inland Revenue* [1984] IRLR 90.

28. *Sim* v. *Rotherham MBC* [1987] Ch. 216.

29. E.g. *Turner* v. *Mason* (1845) 14 M. & W. 112.

30. *Laws* v. *London Chronicle* [1959] 1 WLR 698; *Garner* v. *Grange Furnishing Ltd* [1977] IRLR 206.

31. *Pepper* v. *Webb* [1969] 1 WLR 514; *Wilson* v. *Racher* [1974] ICR 428.

32. *Imperial Group Pension Trust Ltd* v. *Imperial Tobacco Ltd* [1991] IRLR 66.

33. *United Bank Ltd* v. *Akhtar* [1989] IRLR 507.

34. B. A. Hepple and P. O'Higgins, *Employment Law*, 4th edn (London: Sweet and Maxwell, 1980), p. 134.

35. *Johnstone* v. *Bloomsbury AHA* [1991] IRLR 118 (Browne-Wilkinson VC; the two other judges decided the case on different grounds).

36. *Wood* v. *Freeloader Ltd* [1977] IRLR 455; *Western Excavating (ECC) Ltd* v. *Sharp* [1978] ICR 221, at 229.

37. *Robinson* v. *Crompton Parkinson Ltd* [1978] ICR 401.

38. See S. Fredman and G. Morris, *The State as Employer* (London: Mansell, 1989), Chapter 8; Public or private? State employees and judicial review (1991) 107 *Law Quarterly Review* 298.

39. *Gunton* v. *Richmond-upon-Thames LBC* [1980] ICR 755.

40. *Boston Deep Sea Fishing Co. Ltd* v. *Ansell* (1889) 39 Ch.D. 339.

41. *Allen* v. *Flood* [1898] AC 1, 173 (Lord Davey).

42. Employment Protection (Consolidation) Act 1978, ss. 55, 57.

43. *Ibid.*, s. 57(1)(b).

44. The leading case is a decision of the House of Lords on unfair procedure in redundancy selection which nevertheless applies generally to unfair dismissals: *Polkey* v. *A.E. Dayton (Services) Ltd* [1988] AC 344; see also the decision of the Court of Appeal in *Duffy* v. *Yeomans & Partners Ltd* [1994] IRLR 642.

45. *BHS* v. *Burchell* [1978] IRLR 379; *Weddell* v. *Tepper* [1980] ICR 286; *Scottish Midland* v. *Cullion* [1991] IRLR 261.

46. H. Collins, Capitalist discipline and corporatist law (1982) 11 *Industrial Law Journal* 78, 170; *Justice in Dismissal, op. cit.*, p. 140.

47. *Bailey* v. *BP Oil (Kent Refinery) Ltd* [1980] ICR 642.

48. *Iceland Frozen Foods Ltd* v. *Jones* [1983] ICR 17.

49. *Saunders* v. *Scottish National Camps Association* [1980] ICR 174; see also *Boychuk* v. *H.J. Symons Holdings* [1977] IRLR 395 (dismissal of accounts clerk who wore lesbian badges: held, the dismissal was fair since the badges could cause offence to fellow employees and customers).

50. L. Dickens, M. Hart, M. Jones and B. Weekes, *Dismissed: A Study of Unfair Dismissal and the Industrial Tribunal System* (Oxford: Blackwell, 1986), Chapter 5.

51. Industrial and Employment Appeal Tribunal Statistics 1992–93 and 1993–94, *Employment Gazette*, October 1994, p. 369; House of Commons Written Answers, *Hansard*, 30 June 1992, col. 542.

52. Trade Union and Labour Relations (Consolidation) Act 1992, s. 152.

53. Employment Protection (Consolidation) Act, s. 60, as amended by the Trade Union Reform and Employment Rights Act 1993.

54. Employment Protection (Consolidation) Act, s. 60A.

55. *Ibid.*, s. 57A.

56. Sunday Trading Act 1994, Schedule 4; S. Deakin, Open for business (1994) 23 *Industrial Law Journal* 33.

57. Trade Union and Labour Relations (Consolidation) Act 1992, s. 158; Employment Protection (Consolidation) Act 1978, ss. 71 (2), (3), 75A.

58. Trade Union and Labour Relations (Consolidation) Act 1992, ss. 146, 152.

59. *Drew* v. *St. Edmundsbury BC* [1980] ICR 513.

60. Trade Union and Labour Relations (Consolidation) Act 1992, ss. 237, 238; on the meaning of official and unofficial action, see ss. 20–21.

61. [1981] ICR 278; H. Collins, *Justice in Dismissal, op. cit.*, p. 207.

62. *Gardner* v. *Peaks Retail Ltd* [1975] IRLR 444; *Chant* v. *Aquaboats Ltd* [1978] ICR 643.

63. J. McHale, Whistleblowing in the NHS [1993] *Journal of Social Welfare and Family Law* 363; Whistleblowing in the NHS revisited [1994] *JSWFL* 52.

64. *Initial Services* v. *Putterill* [1968] 1 QB 396; *Lion Laboratories* v. *Evans* [1984] 2 All ER

47; J. McHale, Whistleblowing in the NHS, *op. cit.*, p. 366.

65. *Thornley* v. *Aircraft Research Association Ltd* 1.5.77 unreported; Y. Cripps, *Legal Implications of Disclosure in the Public Interest*, 2nd edn (London: Sweet and Maxwell, 1994), pp. 315–17.

66. *O'Brian* v. *Prudential Assurance Co.* [1979] IRLR 140. The only occasion on which the law explicitly permits an applicant for employment to lie at the recruitment stage concerns 'spent' convictions under the Rehabilitation of Offenders Act 1974.

67. Data Protection Act 1984, s. 2(3).

68. Data Protection Registrar, *Ninth Report* (London: HMSO, June 1993), p. 8.

69. B. Napier, *op. cit.*, pp. 12-13.

70. Sex Discrimination Act 1975, s. 7.

71. See, in particular, *R* v. *Secretary of State for Employment, ex parte Equal Opportunities Commission* [1994] IRLR 176 (HL).

72. SI 1993/2798 passed following the decision of the European Court of Justice in *Marshall* v. *Southampton and South-West Hampshire AHA (No. 2)*, Case C-27/91 [1993] IRLR 445. Legislation has also removed the upper limit in racial discrimination cases (the Race Relations (Remedies) Act 1994).

73. A slight extension of the employment protection model was made by the Employment Act 1990 to cover discrimination at the hiring stage on the grounds of trade union membership or non-membership (see now Trade Union and Labour Relations (Consolidation) Act 1992, s. 137), but the main purpose of this was to render ineffective the pre-entry closed shop.

74. Under draft legislation proposed in 1994 (the Racial Hatred and Violence Bill 1994) racial harassment would have become a criminal offence, with a specific civil action for compensation also available to the victim of harassment.

75. *Bracebridge Engineering Ltd* v. *Darby* [1990] IRLR 3; see also *Porcelli* v. *Strathclyde RC* [1984] IRLR 467; *De Souza* v. *Automobile Association* [1986] IRLR 103.

76. J. Earnshaw and P. Pace, Homosexuals and transsexuals at work: legal issues. In M. J. Davidson and J. Earnshaw (eds), *Vulnerable Workers: Psychosocial and Legal Issues* (Chichester: Wiley, 1991), p. 248. See generally Chapter 10, above.

77. *Calvin* v. *Standard Telephone and Cables plc*, 16 January 1986 unreported, discussed by J. Earnshaw and P. Pace, *op. cit.*, p. 249.

78. J. Earnshaw and P. Pace, *op. cit.*, p. 255.

79. This is not to say that the Northern Ireland Act does not suffer from certain other weaknesses. For discussion of the White Paper which preceded the 1989 Act, see C. McCrudden, The Northern Ireland Fair Employment White Paper: a critical assessment (1988) 17 *Industrial Law Journal* 162.

80. H. Collins, Capitalist discipline and corporatist law, *op. cit.*

81. O. Kahn-Freund, Labour law. In M. Ginsberg (ed.), *Law and Public Opinion in England in the 20th Century* (London: Stevens, 1959), pp. 215–63.

82. See S. Deakin, Labour law and industrial relations. In J. Michie (ed.), *1979–1992: the Economic Legacy* (London: Academic Press, 1992), Chapter 8.

83. A more complete review is beyond the scope of this chapter; for further detail, see *Quaderni di Diritti del Lavoro e delle Relazione Industriali*, Vol. 15 (1994).

84. W. Däubler, *op. cit.*, Chapter 14.

85. S. del Rey Guanter, *op. cit.*

86. BVerfG, DB 1984, 311.

87. On the legislation, see S. Simitis, Developments in the protection of workers' personal data (1991) 10/2 *ILO Conditions of Work Digest* 7; and on the Spanish law 5/1992 on regulation of automatic processing of personal data, see S. del Rey Guanter, Tratamiento automatizado de datos de carácter personal y contrato de trabajo (1993) 15 *Relaciones Laborales* 7.

88. M. Forde, *op. cit.*, p. 225.

89. U. Zachert, Les droits fondamentaux des salariés en droit allemand (1994) 15 *Quaderni di Diritto del Lavoro e delle Relazione Industriale* 119.

90. S. Simitis, The rediscovery of the individual in labour law, *op. cit.*, p. 204.

91. Loi No. 78/17 du 6 janvier 1978 relative à l'informatique, aux fichier et aux libertés,

(*Journal Officiel* du 7 janvier 1978 et *JO* du 25 janvier 1978).

92. *Ibid.*, Article 1: 'L'informatique . . . ne doit porter atteinte ni à l'identité humaine, ni aux droits de l'homme, ni à la vie privée, ni aux libertés individuelles ou publiques.'

93. Loi No. 92-1446 du 31 décembre 1992 (*JO* du 1er janvier 1993), amending Code du Travail, Article L. 120-2, which now reads: 'Nul ne peut apporter aux droits des personnes et aux libertés individuelles et collectives de restrictions qui ne seraient pas justifiées par la nature de la tâche à accomplir ni proportionées au but recherché.' The 1992 law was preceded by a report to the Ministry of Labour by Professor G. Lyon-Caen, *Les Libertés Publiques et l'Emploi* (Paris: La Documentation Francaise, 1992).

94. Code du Travail, Article L. 121-6, as amended: 'Les informations demandées, sous quelques forme que ce soit, au candidat à un emploi ou à un salarié ne peuvent avoir comme finalité que d'apprécier sa capacité à occuper l'emploi proposé ou ses aptitudes professionelles'.

95. Code du Travail, Article L. 122-45, as amended: 'Aucune personne ne peut être écartée d'une procédure de recrutement, aucun salarié ne peut être sanctionné ou licencié en raison de son origine, de son sexe, de ses moeurs, de sa situation de famille, de son appartenance à une ethnie, une nation ou une race, de ses opinions politiques, de ses activités syndicales ou mutualistes, des convictions religieuses ou, sauf inaptitude constatée par le médecin du travail . . . en raison de son état de santé ou de son handicap.'

96. Statuto dei Lavoratori, Legge 20 maggio 1970 No. 300.

97. *Ibid.*, Article 4.

98. *Ibid.*, Article 1.

99. *Ibid.*, Article 8: 'E fatto divieto al datore di lavoro, ai fini dell'assunzione, come nel corso dello svolgimento del rapporto di lavoro, di effettuare indagini, arche a mezzo di terzi sulle opinioni politiche, religiose o sindicali del lavoratore, nonché su fatti non rilevanti ai fini della valutazione dell'attitudine professionale del lavoratore.' On the notion of privacy in Italian law more generally, see S. Rodotá, *Privacy* e construzione della sfera privata. Ipotesi e prospettive (1991) 22 *Politica del Diritto* 521.

100. OECD, Labour standards and economic integration, *Employment Outlook*, 1994, p. 154. On a 'synthetic index' of the strength of labour standards, the UK and USA both scored '0', compared to a score of '6' for both France and Germany.

101. This issue has been given added urgency by the decisions of the European Court of Justice in Case C-382/92 and Case C-383/92 *Commission* v. *UK* [1994] IRLR 392, 412 (noted by P. Davies (1994) 23 *Industrial Law Journal* 272) and by the response of the TUC, *Representation at Work. Interim Report to the 1994 Congress* (1994). See now SI 1995/2587.

102. See, in particular, B. Hepple, Have twenty-five years of the Race Relations Acts in Britain been a failure? In B. Hepple and E. Szyszczak (eds), *Discrimination: the Limits of the Law* (London: Mansell, 1992), pp. 19–49.

103. K. D. Ewing, The Bill of Rights debate: Democracy or juristocracy, *op. cit.*

104. U. Zachert, *op. cit.*

105. On deregulation and economic efficiency, see S. Deakin and F. Wilkinson, Labour law, social security and economic inequality (1991) 15 *Cambridge Journal of Economics* 125.

106. K. D. Ewing, The Bill of Rights debate: Democracy or juristocracy, *op. cit.* See also Chapter 3, above.

17

Rights and Employee Rights – the Case of Free Speech

Gwyneth Pitt

Discussions of rights take place in different contexts. We may be referring to rights recognized by the municipal legal system and capable of legal vindication. We may mean rights which are recognized at a different level, for example in international treaties or even, perhaps, natural law. Or we may use the term in a more rhetorical sense, for things which we believe ought to be recognized as rights (or entities we think should be recognized as holding rights – such as animal rights). This discussion is concerned with those generally recognized human rights which are guaranteed by international instruments such as the Universal Declaration of Human Rights (UDHR), the International Covenant on Civil and Political Rights and the European Convention on Human Rights (ECHR) – such as freedom of association, freedom of assembly, freedom of religion, freedom of expression and freedom from discrimination. While there may be debate about their precise content, these are rights which the UK has accepted through its ratification of these instruments, and consequently a commitment to them should be enshrined in British law. The principal argument in this chapter is that citizens should not leave their rights at the factory or office door: rights should be guaranteed for employees in the workplace. The general position will be related particularly to freedom of speech.

HUMAN RIGHTS AND EMPLOYEE RIGHTS

It is first necessary to consider whether it is appropriate to deploy the language of human rights in an employment context. A number of objections may be made to this, on the grounds either that rights are essentially about the citizen's relationship with the state and have no place in a private contractual relationship,[1] or that the employment relationship is significantly different from citizenship in ways which render rights inappropriate for incorporation.

While it may be true that in general terms human rights call for restrictions on governmental power, many well-established civil rights have greatest impact in a work setting. Injunctions against slavery are usually cited as justification for the general principle that there can be no specific performance of contracts of employment.[2] Freedom of association is guaranteed not only in human rights treaties but also in the conventions of the International Labour Organization (ILO),[3] which are especially relevant to the freedom to form and join trade unions.

There may be certain political liberties which have no real counterpart in a workplace setting, but it is submitted that they are few. A right to vote might be one. Even there, however, there is a powerful body of opinion that there should be some measure of industrial democracy, with workers involved in decision-making,[4] and the requirement that unions should hold a secret ballot before organizing industrial action may also be noted. If rights were to be regarded as irrelevant to the employment relationship, we would be significantly reducing the importance and universality usually claimed for human rights: work absorbs much of the time, efforts and energy of most of the population. It has a powerful impact on social life as well. Could a society which denied human rights in the workplace be genuinely regarded as one which placed much value on human rights?

Turning to the second objection, are there any critical differences between one's status as a citizen and one's status as an employee which suggest that the application of rights language in an employment context is inappropriate? The obvious contrast is in the degree of choice that exists. In practical terms, we have no choice about our status as citizens. To suggest that if we do not like the society in which we find ourselves we can go somewhere else is unrealistic: most people are unfitted by language, education, culture and family ties to move elsewhere. Even if they wished to do so, the state of their choice might well be unwilling to receive them and, more importantly, any state to which someone might be able to migrate will have rules which dictate certain patterns of behaviour. It is impossible to opt out of state regulation altogether, and this is the strongest argument in favour of limits on state power positively expressed as rights.

But is not the employment context very similar? In reality, most people do not have a choice whether to work or not. True, it is possible to change employers, although the possibility of doing this is restricted according to the state of the economy, and if full employment will not be a realistic aspiration in future, perhaps the state of the economy will always constrain the possibility of job mobility. Not only general economic conditions but also factors such as qualifications, trade or profession and family circumstances mean that, for many people, changing employers is not at all a realistic proposition, any more than changing states is. Again, as with states, it is the case that moving from one employer to another will mean exposure to another set of regulations.

It is true that in the employment context there is the possibility of becoming self-employed – the equivalent of finding an uninhabited island free of government – which provides a choice in employment which does not exist in civic life. But despite the best efforts of successive Conservative administrations, the entrepreneurial spirit does not animate every breast, and the failure rates of small businesses do not seem calculated to alter this. Self-employment is not a realistic choice for the majority of people, and the theoretical possibility does not constitute a sufficient difference to invalidate the analogy between human rights and employee rights.

Freedom of contract may be invoked as a competing value which should not be overridden lightly in favour of employee rights. But this is seen on closer reflection to be a weak argument. It has long been recognized that the bargaining position between employer and employee is inherently unequal and that the vast majority of employees have to contract on the terms offered by the employer: their choice is strictly to take it or leave it. This provides the conventional justification for trade unions and collective bargaining and also for the employment protection legislation which has burgeoned since the early 1960s. Indeed, it highlights an important similarity between the state–citizen and employer–employee relationships, for civil liberties are designed to protect individuals from the more powerful state in the same way that employment protection legislation is intended to protect individual employees from the more powerful employer.

Traditionally, the power of management was balanced by the combination of labour in the collective bargaining process, which was meant to ensure a rough equality of bargaining position and also to serve the value of freedom of contract, since it entailed no intervention in the substantive agreements made by the parties. The role of the law was to encourage voluntary collective bargaining and to extend to weak or unorganized groups of workers the benefits of generally observed norms. However, as things stand at present, this is increasingly unlikely to occur. The Conservative administration takes the view that collective bargaining hampers flexibility and creates a disincentive to individual effort[5] and has therefore dismantled the laws which supported and encouraged collective bargaining,[6] culminating in the removal of 'promoting collective bargaining' as one of the statutory purposes of ACAS by the Trade Union Reform and Employment Rights Act (TURERA) 1993.[7] It is estimated that the number of employees covered by collective agreements has gone down from 75 per cent in the mid-1970s to about 45 per cent at the beginning of the 1990s. Thus to rely on collective bargaining alone as a safeguard for employee rights may be unduly sanguine. In any case, even a robust system of collective bargaining would not guarantee that adequate substantive safeguards would be agreed in relation to rights issues, since such matters did not customarily appear on bargaining agendas.[8]

Other recent developments make the argument for greater employment protection through the recognition of rights more compelling. Alongside the trend towards individualized contracts, it is also the case that employers are seeking greater flexibility. It has become common to stipulate that employees can be moved to other jobs, provided that they are reasonably within the employee's capabilities,[9] and it is not at all unusual to find contracts providing a power for the employer to vary the terms at will in the future without even any consultation with employees, much less with their agreement. While it could perhaps be argued that such a contract is so lacking in certain content that there cannot be said to be an agreement, this would be an unlikely interpretation when, as will frequently be the case, the parties have acted on it for a considerable period. But if such a term is valid, it renders the employee enormously vulnerable. It is by no means clear that the courts will restrict such powers by reference to a concept of what is reasonable. Hence, it is submitted, there is a need for greater control over the substantive terms of the contract of employment.

IMPLIED TERMS IN CONTRACTS OF EMPLOYMENT

Another powerful argument in favour of enforceable employee rights is that it would counteract the growing tendency on the part of the courts to develop implied terms in the contract of employment to a level where employees have an affirmative duty to promote the interests of the employer way beyond the express terms of the contract and seemingly at the expense of their own interests.

The starting point for this development, which has been mainly, but not exclusively, in the context of industrial action, is *Secretary of State* v. *ASLEF* (*No. 2*),[10] where a work-to-rule by railway workers was held to be a breach of contract either because it was in breach of a duty of good faith or because it was in breach of an implied term not to obey orders in an unreasonable manner. In *Cresswell* v. *Inland Revenue*[11] a duty to cooperate was held to exist to the extent that staff could be expected to adapt to using computers instead of keeping records manually, and in *Sim* v. *Rotherham BC*[12] it was held that teachers had a duty to cooperate with the headteacher in running the school, and that this could include duties beyond their contractual requirements, such as covering for absent staff, mealtime supervision and so on. The apotheosis of this line of cases is *Ticehurst* v. *British Telecom*,[13] where the Court of Appeal held that an employee performing duties within her contract but which were intended to cause disruption to the employer's business (in pursuance of a withdrawal of goodwill which had been called by her trade union) was thereby in breach of the duty to give faithful service even though no independent breach of contract had been shown and even though no actual disruption of the employer's business had been demonstrated.

It is easy to see how a duty to give faithful service, which used to be composed of a number of 'thou shalt nots', can be turned around into a positive obligation actively to promote the employer's interests. However, this could be to the substantial detriment of the employee. A statement of employee rights would not necessarily prevent such decisions, since rights would have to be interpreted, but it would at least focus on the need to take the employee's interests into account also.

RIGHTS ARGUMENTS IN THE EMPLOYMENT CONTEXT

Because there is nothing equivalent to a bill of rights for employees, when cases involving human rights issues have arisen there has been no systematic consideration of the relevance of international standards. It has often been a matter of chance whether the issues have even been identified and considered, even though it can be argued that consideration of reasonableness in unfair dismissal, for example, could without difficulty involve reference to international standards of good practice. The point may be illustrated by reference to cases involving freedom of religion, privacy and freedom of speech.[14]

In *Ahmad* v. *ILEA*,[15] an unfair dismissal case, reliance was placed on Article 9 of the ECHR, guaranteeing freedom of thought, conscience and religion. A Muslim teacher resigned when refused time off on Friday afternoons to enable him to attend mosque in accordance with the requirements of his religion, and claimed that he had been constructively dismissed. By a majority the Court of Appeal held that there had been no constructive dismissal. Lord Denning said:

The Convention is not part of our English law, but, as I have often said, we will always have regard to it. We will do our best to see that our decisions are in conformity with it. But it is drawn in such vague terms that it can be used for all sorts of unreasonable claims and provoke all sorts of litigation.[16]

Orr LJ pointed out that Article 9 is itself qualified:

The right so declared is, however, expressly made subject to such limitations by the State as are prescribed by law and are necessary in a democratic society for the protection of the rights and freedom of others and in my judgment it cannot be construed as entitling an employee to absent himself, for the purpose of religious worship, from his place of work during working hours and in breach of his contract of employment.[17]

Only Scarman LJ, dissenting, placed emphasis on Article 9, using it to underpin a wide interpretation of the relevant Education Act, which would have entitled the teacher to time off.

It has long been settled that employees owe a duty not to disclose confidential information belonging to their employer, and it was by analogy to this (rather than by reference to considerations of privacy) that in *Dalgleish* v. *Lothian & Borders Police Board*[18] Lord Cameron held that an interim interdict should be granted to prevent an employer disclosing names and addresses of employees without their consent. The information had been requested by the Lothian Regional Council, which wanted to find out which public employees had not paid their community charge, or poll tax. If there were recognition of a right to privacy in this context, it is unlikely that such a case would even have arisen.

The necessity for protected rights is highlighted in unfair dismissal law, since tribunals have shown reluctance to pronounce upon the substance of an employer's rules. If a dismissal is carried out in accordance with a term of the contract, it is highly unlikely that it will be found to be unfair because the tribunal considers the term to be unreasonable. A good example is furnished by *Bright* v. *Coutts & Co*,[19] where the employee was dismissed for breach of a rule that staff should have a current account at the bank and should not have accounts elsewhere or engage in any outside borrowing. This seems a considerable intrusion on the private life of an employee, and it was argued on behalf of the applicant that other banks would not insist on such a rule and therefore the employer was being unreasonable in using it as a reason to dismiss. This was the closest it was possible to come to arguing that the dismissal was unfair because the rule was unfair. The Employment Appeal Tribunal (EAT) upheld the tribunal's decision that the employer had acted reasonably. Privacy was not discussed.

One of the most controversial innovations in TURERA was the requirement that a union balloting its members before industrial action should send a notice to their employer 'describing (so that he can readily ascertain them)' the employees who would be entitled to vote in the ballot – and therefore likely to be involved in any ensuing industrial action.[20] Predictably, in the first case on the section it was held that this meant naming the relevant employees.[21] The fact that this section constitutes a gross infringement of employees' privacy by disclosing the fact of their trade union membership to their employer seems not to have been considered by Parliament when the Act was going through. This again demonstrates the need for recognized rights which will weigh effectively in the balance against administrative convenience.

FREE SPEECH AND EMPLOYMENT

The Common Law

There has been an interesting recognition of rights to free speech in *Middlebrook Mushrooms Ltd* v. *TGWU*.[22] The plaintiffs sought an injunction to stop the union engaging in consumer picketing. Members of the union were proposing to hand out leaflets outside supermarkets exhorting customers not to buy mushrooms produced by the plaintiffs because they had dismissed 89 employees in the course of a trade dispute. There was no attempt to persuade the supermarkets to stop dealing with the plaintiffs. The Court of Appeal held that there was no tortious conduct in this case, on the grounds that the union's action could not be regarded as a direct interference with the plaintiff's contracts. The distinction between demonstrating and picketing has never been clear-cut, but Neill LJ at least recognized the freedom of expression aspect of this case, commenting:

> Though counsel for the [union] did not place any specific reliance on Article 10 of the European Convention on Human Rights and Fundamental Freedoms, it is relevant to bear in mind that in all cases which involve a proposed restriction on the right of free speech the court is concerned, when exercising its discretion, to consider whether the restraint is necessary.[23]

However, it seems unlikely that Article 10 would avail an employee who has contravened an employer's rule prohibiting certain kinds of speech, for the reasons already discussed. A typical example would be *British Airways Engine Overhaul Ltd* v. *Francis*[24] where company regulations provided that employees had to get permission before making any statement about the company's business or their own duties. The employee was disciplined because she gave an interview to a local paper criticizing her *union* for not doing enough for workers in her grade. As she was a shop steward, she was able to argue that this was a protected union activity; had this not been the case, there can be no doubt that this would have been regarded as within the employer's disciplinary powers. The employer's freedom to define its own needs for protection and the unwillingness of tribunals and courts to consider the substantive content of the employer's rules combine to outweigh the employee's interest in freedom of expression.

The same would seem to hold true also for free speech in trade unions. It is often instructive to compare the standards of behaviour required of employers in relation to employees with those imposed on the relationship between a trade union and a member. Both relationships are based on contract; both are situations where freedom of contract is more apparent than real. However, this is less the case when a worker is relying on status as a trade union member rather than status as an employee. Since the closed shop is no longer enforceable,[25] there is no compulsion to join a trade union in order to preserve one's job. To that extent, then, trade union membership is genuinely voluntary. However, if a trade union is recognized as the bargaining representative for a group of staff, membership becomes a prerequisite for having influence on the bargaining process, and to that extent there are sound practical reasons for belonging,[26] although it might go rather far to say that it amounts to compulsion. In both cases, the member/employee has to accept the terms of the contract offered by the other party, with few opportunities to negotiate entry (less for union membership than for employment entry, although there is more chance of changing the rules of a union to your liking than of persuading your employer to change your contract). Finally, expulsion from a trade union is of much less importance than dismissal: effectively, one may lose some friends but save a bit of money. It is not the personal and financial disaster that dismissal is for the vast majority of employees.

Paradoxically, however, there has always been greater control at common law over the union membership contract than over the contract of employment, and this is now mirrored by statutory developments. However, so far as free speech is concerned, it seems unlikely that a court would strike down a rule that, say, rendered a member liable to be disciplined for criticizing the union, provided that the disciplinary power was contained in the rules[27] and the rules had been properly interpreted by the internal tribunal.[28]

This is illustrated by *Losinska* v. *CPSA*.[29] The plaintiff was president of one of the civil service unions. She published an article in the *Reader's Digest* (part of a series called 'The Marxist Battle for Britain') saying, *inter alia*, that 'nearly 10 per cent of the *active* membership of my union are now supporters of the militant left' and much else in the same vein. Having received a number of protests from union members, the National Executive Committee passed a resolution deploring the views expressed. The Committee proposed that an article reporting the resolution and correcting the inaccuracies in the *Reader's Digest* piece should appear in the union journal. The annual conference of the union was also imminent and a number of motions were proposed censuring the plaintiff's conduct. The plaintiff obtained interlocutory injunctions to prevent the circulation of the NEC resolution and an agenda containing the censure motions on the grounds that they would prejudice potential disciplinary proceedings against her. The Court of Appeal upheld the interlocutory injunctions, but in a more limited form because of their recognition of the needs of free speech – albeit it was the freedom of the union that concerned them. Lord Denning put the issue as follows:

> The solution of this case must depend on the rules of the union. . . Unless there is something in the rules which would prohibit it, there is no doubt whatever that this trade union and its members can reply to the article which Mrs Losinska wrote with just the same force as that with which she herself wrote it. If there is nothing in the rules to prevent it, they too can condemn her as she condemned them. This is the elementary principle of free speech which means not only freedom to express those views of which we approve, but also those views which we wholeheartedly detest. So, unless there is something in the rules to stop it, the union can certainly go ahead with their motion, their resolution, their censures and the like, subject only to the limitations imposed by the law of libel.[30]

The implication of this decision is that the union could, by appropriate rules, limit the rights of members to engage in critical speech in the sense that there could be valid expulsions on this ground.[31]

Free Speech in Employment: the Statutory Context

The common law on free speech in trade unions, which could be regarded as relatively similar to the employer–employee position, has been altered significantly by statute. The Employment Act 1988 introduced a concept of 'unjustifiable discipline',[32] and TURERA prohibits exclusion or expulsion from a trade union except where an individual no longer fulfils an objective trade/occupational/geographical qualification for membership or where the exclusion or expulsion is entirely attributable to his or her conduct.[33] Conduct considered to be unjustifiable discipline will not justify exclusion or expulsion for the purposes of s. 174, and it includes certain kinds of critical speech. Thus indicating opposition to or lack of support for industrial action, asserting that the union, its officials or representatives are in breach of the law or of union rules and encouraging other workers to perform their contracts of employment are all speech activities which are now protected.[34]

It is conceivable, however, that the new formulation of s. 174 is actually narrower than the provision it replaced. The original s. 174 (derived from the Employment Act 1980, s. 4) only applied in closed shop situations, but it prohibited any *unreasonable* exclusion or expulsion – and specifically provided that compliance with the union's own rules was not conclusive of reasonableness. Suppose a union had a rule specifically providing that members should not criticize the union's constitution. Assuming that such criticism would not amount to protected speech within the parameters of s. 65, it seems that the union would be able to expel a member who was in breach of the rule. As such an expulsion would be entirely on account of the member's conduct, it would seem to be permitted by s. 174. However, it is certainly possible that a tribunal testing it against a reasonableness criterion would have concluded that it was unreasonable. Section 174 is in addition to any common law rights of the trade union member, but if the rule is clearly drawn it is submitted that it could not be struck down, at least according to current jurisprudence on union rule books.

There is now, also, a limited statutory protection against retaliatory action by the employer in response to certain kinds of speech by employees. The first category to receive protection was trade union activities. It is automatically unfair to dismiss or treat an employee less favourably for taking part in trade union activities at an appropriate time, and it is clear that this can protect speech.[35] The protection is incomplete in a number of respects: at the point of entry to employment only discrimination on grounds of union *membership*, not union *activities*, is outlawed,[36] apparently dismissal for trade union activities with another employer, prior to this employment, is not covered,[37] and it does not provide protection for union-like activities where there is no union or where the employee has no official union status.[38]

Under the Sex Discrimination Act 1975, s. 4, and the Race Relations

Act 1976, s. 2, it is unlawful for an employer to victimize an employee for certain activities related to sex or race discrimination. These include giving evidence or information in connection with a discrimination claim or making (in good faith) an allegation that a breach of the legislation has occurred. These categories of speech obviously require protection for public policy reasons, and the only surprise is that the protection has been limited to sex and race discrimination. Recently the same policy reasons have led to a welcome extension of anti-victimization provisions, although the impetus has come from the European Community.

The 1989 Framework Directive on Health and Safety at Work[39] requires that safety representatives – whether appointed by the employer or by the workers – must not be disadvantaged because of activities related to the protection and prevention of occupational risks. This has been translated into new provisions in the Employment Protection (Consolidation) Act 1978[40] which are designed to protect employees from detrimental action, dismissal or selection for redundancy on certain health and safety grounds. These include activities as a safety representative, but also taking 'appropriate steps' in 'circumstances of danger which he reasonably believed to be serious and imminent'. 'Activities' will clearly include speech, and it would appear that the category of activity protected in cases of serious and imminent danger would include 'blowing the whistle' on the employer – although it is doubtful that 'appropriate steps' would justify an employee in going further outside the organization than the Health and Safety Executive.

While TURERA was going through Parliament, another area of protection was introduced on the back of the health and safety grounds. The new Employment Protection Consolidation Act (EPCA) s. 60A[41] makes it automatically unfair to dismiss an employee for asserting that the employer has infringed one of the employee's statutory rights.[42] The allegation by the employee need not be correct – but it must be made in good faith. This makes another category of protected speech, although the protection is incomplete, in that it does not give a remedy for detrimental action short of dismissal (contrast the position for sex and race discrimination, above).

Free Speech and Employment – Four Problems

As shown above, the present state of the law of employment, in relation to rights in general and free speech in particular, is a picture of only intermittent protection with no systematic justificatory underpinning. This is particularly noticeable in an examination of statutory protection for free speech, where the reasons for some aspects receiving protection rest on very different philosophies: a desire to control the internal affairs of trade unions, pressure from Europe and prevention of discrimination all figure, but there is no common denominator. It may be that protection of a right of free speech for people in their capacity as employees can justifiably be more limited than their rights as citizens. However, it is submitted that the present position permits too much restriction. In the rest of this chapter, some of the problems likely to arise in attempting to frame a right to free speech for employees will be examined by reference to real and hypothetical cases, and a possible formula for protected speech will be proposed. Limitations on speech are of course provided by the general law – in particular the law of defamation. The question then is what other limitations, if any, there should be where speech is made in the context of employment. In what follows, it will be assumed that the employee is acting in good faith, unless the contrary is stated.

THE IDENTITY OF THE EMPLOYEE

In January 1993 it was reported that a Crown Prosecution Service (CPS) manager had been suspended from his job after making a speech at a university in which he said that criminals should be liable to hanging and flogging.[43] As a public employee, he would of course be subject to the notoriously restrictive regime for civil servants,[14] but leaving this aside and treating the question hypothetically, as if he had been a private employee, should he have been disciplined for this?

In the USA, where public employees receive First Amendment protection,[44] two limitations have been recognized on their rights to free speech: first, where the employee's speech is likely to be attributed to the employer, and second, where the employer is an 'amplifying organization' – one which exists expressly to propound a particular point of view, as many campaigning organizations do.[45] The first category comprises not only employees employed as spokespersons for their organizations but also employees who are sufficiently high-ranking that their speech is likely to be attributed to the organization, whether they are on or off the job.[46]

It is submitted that there is no real difficulty in relation to someone employed as a spokesperson, where freedom of expression is confined only in relation to the work. The limitation in such a case would go no further than is necessary, assuming that there is no attempt to restrict the employee's freedom of speech outside work. The high-ranking or policy-making employee is more difficult, however. Can it be right effectively to say that such a person has no private existence for free speech purposes, and can the employing organization properly claim an interest in the employee's publicly expressed views on any issues, even if unrelated to

the business? If the chief executive of a retail chain makes a speech arguing in favour of Sunday trading, it is reasonable to assume that this view
will be attributed to the company and that therefore he or she should not
express it unless it is in accordance with company policy. This should be
distinguished from views on the subject expressed by the chief executive
at a private dinner party, even if a journalist is among the guests. But
what if the chief executive expresses in public his or her views on immigration or single-parent families? This can scarcely be a situation where
the company's policy will be contradicted or undermined, since the company is not likely to have a policy on such matters.

A possible rule might be that such speech should not be subject to
restraint unless damage to the business is likely to result from it. This
would accord with the general position in unfair dismissal law relating to
conduct outside employment.[47] However, it is submitted that this would
be too restrictive. If the chief executive's views were likely to cause
offence to a recognizable group who might boycott the company and its
products, damage would have been demonstrated. But if offensiveness to
the public is a justification for restraining the expression of controversial
opinions on matters unrelated to the employer's business, there really
would be no freedom of speech for someone in that kind of position.

There is a further problem in that the public may be apt to attribute
an employee's views to the employer even where the employee is not particularly high-ranking. Let me return to the CPS manager. There must
be a large number of officials at this level in the CPS: they may have some
input into policy-making, but probably their task is primarily implementing policy decided at a higher level. If one were to adapt the alter
ego test used in criminal law in deciding whether the employee's actions
can be regarded as those of a company for the purpose of rendering the
company criminally responsible,[48] it is submitted that the CPS manager
would count as a hand rather than a directing mind. No doubt he would
not have been invited to the university to give a speech if he had not been
employed in this particular capacity, but it might be stretching things to
describe him as a spokesperson for the employer on this particular occasion. What he talked about was connected with his work although it is not
clear that it actually constituted a disagreement with CPS policy (in the
sense that the CPS might not have any particular policy on the subject).
The news report does not make clear whether he entered a disclaimer to
the effect that he was putting forward personal views, although it is submitted that this must have been perfectly obvious.

It seems likely that the manager's speech *was* seen as in some way
reflecting on the CPS and it caused sufficient furore to result in the suspension. Yet if, as suggested above, he is neither a spokesperson nor
sufficiently high-ranking to be identified with the organization, it is

submitted that his speech ought to be protected. A final possible factor may be whether there is damage to the employer as a result. Presumably, no one would boycott the CPS as a result of his speech. It might be argued that damage resided in the risk of public confidence in the CPS being undermined by the revelation that one of its employees favoured punishments harsher than those presently prescribed by the law. But on closer examination, such an assertion is not convincing. It seems reasonable to guess that for as many people who were offended by what he said a similar number would agree with him. Furthermore, it is not clear that his view of what the law ought to be would necessarily affect his ability to work within the law as it is. It is possible that his views might be taken to indicate a person who would exercise the discretion to prosecute in a biased manner – but merely to articulate the objection is to reveal its flimsiness. This would be an unduly remote extrapolation from the evidence. Finally, the objection might be that the CPS should not employ people holding those kinds of opinions. If so, I would have to disagree. It would be an undesirable infringement of freedom of speech, conscience and privacy to apply such a political test to employment. It is permissible to insist that employees do not allow their political judgments to affect their work, but that is quite another matter.

Another example, also drawn from the CPS, is provided by the case of Neil Addison, employed as a barrister by the CPS, who wrote an article in *The Times* on 1 November 1994 arguing against the possible privatization of the CPS. The article carried a footnote making it clear that he was writing in a personal capacity. As a result he was suspended from his post and threatened with disciplinary proceedings. Interestingly, it was reported that in negotiations over his suspension, his solicitors argued that the CPS was in breach of Article 10 of the ECHR. The matter ended with a settlement that involved Mr Addison resigning his post and returning to private practice – part of the agreement being that neither party would make further comment on the affair.[49]

Hence, the provisional conclusion is that it is reasonable to restrict the speech of an employee when he or she is acting as a spokesperson for the employer. It is reasonable to restrict those employees who can be regarded as the alter ego of the organization when dealing with matters which relate to the organization and its business. The speech of other employees should not be restricted where it is presented only as a personal view, subject to what is said about types of speech, below.

WHISTLEBLOWING

Whistleblowing is usually defined as going public on corporate wrongdoing. The term is used by analogy with a referee blowing the whistle to stop the game when a foul is committed, or a police officer calling public attention to a crime by blowing a whistle. Legally and morally, this is rarely required conduct: it is a cliché of English law that we are not required to be Good Samaritans and save others, even when we could do so by minimal effort. There might be general agreement on a moral obligation for employees to reveal wrongdoing when there is a serious risk to health and safety; arguably, s. 7 of the Health and Safety at Work Act 1974 could be read as imposing a legal duty to that effect,[50] although it is unlikely that revealing the employer's wrongdoing could be described as cooperating with the employer. A close analogy to a legal duty to blow the whistle may exist for professionals subject to a code of ethics, who may be subject to disciplinary action by their professional association if they fail to reveal shortcomings.[51] More difficult, however, are the cases where it is merely argued that whistleblowing is morally justified and therefore ought to be permissible.

The few reported English cases on whistleblowing have mainly arisen where employers have sought to prevent the publication of information by a whistleblower on grounds that it would entail disclosure of confidential information.[52] The employee in all these cases had already left the organization and the debate in each case was whether there was sufficient public interest at stake to override the prima facie obligation of confidence. There are no reported cases on whistleblowing and unfair dismissal, although in *Thornley* v. *British Aircraft Corporation*[53] the EAT held the dismissal of a research scientist for publishing confidential data to be fair, because it was a breach of confidence as well as a breach of the Official Secrets Act.

Discussions of whistleblowing in the literature on business ethics suggest that in order to be justified, whistleblowers should: be correct in their allegations (accuracy); have first tried internal avenues of redress (complaint to proper person); and be acting in good faith (disinterested motive).[54] However, on closer examination, it may be found that these seemingly reasonable conditions are too stringent.

Accuracy
The potential for harm to the organization's business from false disclosures seems a powerful reason for the first condition; however, in reality employees may not have sufficient access to information to be absolutely certain of the correctness of their fears. Rather than insisting on accuracy, distinctions should be drawn between different kinds of disclosure, according to whom the disclosure is made, the status of the employee making it, and the kind of information disclosed.

In some circumstances, there may be a proper authority to whom disclosure can be made: the Health and Safety Executive, or a regulatory organization such as the PIA or FIMBRA or Oftel. It is submitted that where there is an impartial outside body with authority to investigate complaints, an employee would be justified in making disclosure to it even if unsure of the facts. This approach is implicitly endorsed in *Re a Company's Application*,[55] where a financial services company failed to get an injunction to prevent a former employee disclosing to FIMBRA and the Inland Revenue allegations that the company was helping clients to evade tax. The employee could not demonstrate conclusive evidence of breaches of the law, but the judge considered that the employer's interests were sufficiently protected by an injunction limiting disclosure to these bodies.

The status of the employee involved should also be relevant. It would be justifiable for an employee who may be held responsible, either contractually, in tort or by a professional disciplinary tribunal, to go public on reasonable suspicions, where someone less closely implicated might be required to have harder evidence. However, this is not to say that whistleblowing by an employee wholly unconnected with the issue on which he or she went public would not be justified. In *Geary* v. *US Steel Corporation*,[56] one of the US cases where the employment-at-will doctrine was challenged on the grounds that the dismissal was contrary to public policy, the discharged employee was a salesman who complained to senior management that a tubular casing had not been adequately tested and was potentially dangerous. He was right, and the product was withdrawn but he was dismissed for complaining. The court held that this did not violate public policy because, as a salesman, it was not his function to pick this up: hence there was no danger that his dismissal would have a 'chilling' effect which might reduce the vigilance of those employed to check such things. However, on my argument, this would clearly be protected speech.

The final point here is in relation to the information itself. Issues about the safety or quality of a product may not be clear-cut questions of fact but rather questions of opinion, on which experts can reasonably differ. In these circumstances, accuracy is an elusive concept. In *Pierce* v. *Ortho Pharmaceutical*[57] the plaintiff doctor was in charge of a research team developing an anti-diarrhoea drug for use by children and old people to which saccharin was to be added to make it more palatable. She opposed this on the grounds that the safety of saccharin was 'controversial', and ultimately resigned, saying that she could not square continuing to work on the project with her Hippocratic oath. The court held that this revealed merely a difference of opinion between the plaintiff and her equally qualified superiors; thus even if they had been prepared to accept a concept of constructive dismissal, this would not have constituted a violation of public policy. Would Dr Pierce be justified in going public on these facts? Arguably it should be enough if the opinion expressed by the whistleblower is honestly held on reasonable grounds – the latter requirement embracing a consideration of the employee's own expertise as well as that of general informed opinion.

Complaint to Proper Person

Where a proper recipient of information exists, then it seems reasonable to argue that disclosure to anyone else (such as the media) would not be justified. As discussed above, the accuracy of the information should be taken into account in relation to this also. Alternatively, or perhaps additionally, many would argue that a complainant would not be justified unless he or she had tried internal avenues of complaint first. However, this cannot be an unconditional requirement either. It would be important to know whether or not the regulatory authority had shown itself to be effective. Similar considerations apply in relation to whether the employee should be expected to use internal avenues of redress first: it is conceivable that the employee could justifiably lack confidence in internal procedures, or could fear that this would simply provide the employer with enough warning to be able to conceal any evidence of wrongdoing or to retaliate in some way against the employee.[58]

In English law it is not clear whether there is a requirement that disclosure must be to the proper bodies. In *Initial Services* v. *Putterill* (where an ex-employee had gone to the *Daily Mail*, alleging that the company was engaged in price-fixing contrary to the Restrictive Practices Act), Lord Denning said:

> The disclosure must, I should think, be to one who has a proper interest to receive the information. Thus it would be proper to disclose a crime to the police; or a breach of the Restrictive Trade Practices Act to the registrar. There may be cases where the misdeed is of such a character that the public interest may demand, or at least excuse, publication on a broader field, even to the press.[59]

On a motion for striking out, the Court of Appeal held for the employee. In *Lion Laboratories* v. *Evans* it was argued that ex-employees concerned about the accuracy of the company's breathalysers, which were being used by the police, should have gone to the Home Office rather than the *Daily Express*, but Griffiths LJ took the point that the Home Office was 'an interested and committed party', and would perhaps be reluctant to be convinced by the evidence.[60]

Disinterested Motive

In general I have been arguing for free speech where the employee's speech is made in good faith on reasonable grounds. However, in relation to whistleblowing where the allegations are in fact true, it is difficult to see why purity of motive should be a requirement. As a practical matter, it may be the case that evidence will be more convincing from someone who has no financial interest in the outcome or who is not acting out of malice. It has been pointed out that one of the first tactics used by employers against whistleblowers is to discredit them personally by attacking their competence, personality or motives for action.[61] However, whether this means that a whistleblower will only be justified if personally above suspicion is a different matter. It is submitted that this is a matter which goes only to credibility, not to justification. Given that many whistleblowers end up out of a job, it seems over-harsh to prevent them from at least profiting in some sense from their disclosures. This seems to be recognized in the case law on the subject. While a number of judges express distaste for what they see as the disloyalty involved in whistle-blowing, it has been held that the receipt of money has no bearing on legal justification.[62]

CONFIDENTIAL INFORMATION

Discussions of whistleblowing usually argue for better protection for whistleblowers, but on the basis of the public interest in their disclosures rather than as a vindication of their right to freedom of speech.[63] No doubt the public interest in certain kinds of information raises special issues which require separate consideration. The most important of these is that whistleblowing invariably entails disclosure of confidential information. Since an employer has a right to keep confidential information secret, there have to be very good reasons to override this equitable and contractual obligation. However, this leaves us with two problems concerning other kinds of critical speech: first, the concept of 'confidential information'; and second, how far critical speech should be permitted even where there is no public interest at stake.

When an employee leaves employment, courts have shown themselves astute in restricting the concept of what is confidential information to ensure that an employer is not getting the benefit of a restrictive covenant without having included it in the contract[64] and to ensure that the employer is not just stifling competition and preventing the employee from working in his or her chosen field of employment.[65] But it seems that while the contract is ongoing, it is possible for an employer to designate just about anything as confidential information and to make it a term of the contract that employees are not to say anything about the business to anyone outside:

We would venture to state these principles:

(1) Where the parties are, or have been, linked by a contract of employment, the obligations of the employee are to be determined by the contract between him and his employer.

(2) In the absence of any express term, the obligations of the employee in respect of the use and disclosure of information are the subject of implied terms.

(3) While the employee remains in the employment of the employer the obligations are included in the implied term which imposes a duty of good faith or fidelity on the employee . . . the extent of good faith will vary according to the nature of the contract.[66]

The fact that any restriction can be upheld as long as it is expressly stated in the contract constitutes the main threat to free speech for employees. All-embracing gagging clauses can be included, no matter how un-realistic, leaving the employer a wide discretion as to how they are implemented. *British Airways* v. *Francis*,[24] discussed above, is a good example of this. The danger of implied terms of good faith and fidelity being used to impose affirmative duties on employees over and above the contract has also been noted already.

It is submitted that the basic values served by the right to freedom of speech, namely, the benefits of self-expression and the public interest in the free flow of information, mean that the speech of employees should not be restrained even where there is no demonstrable public interest in the content, unless it would involve the disclosure of confidential inform-ation in the limited sense in which the concept is used in actions for breach of confidence or in respect of the implied obligations of ex-employees – that is, trade secrets or customer connection. Debate and criticism should be permitted, regardless of whether a direct public benefit can be shown.

CRITICAL SPEECH WHICH DOES NOT DISCLOSE WRONGDOING

What if the employee is critical of the employer, although not actually dis-closing confidential information nor indeed matters in the public interest? An example might be Gerald Ratner's notorious denunciation of his company's products – although he would fall into the category of an employee identified with the organization, and liable to restriction on that ground. It is submitted that a fair balance would be achieved if such speech was subject to restraint only if *actual* damage to the business could be shown.

As a recent example to illustrate the point, let us consider how Terry Drew's book, *Accounting for Growth*, led to his dismissal from UBS Phillips

& Drew when it was published in 1992. The book did not reveal wrong-doing in the sense discussed above on whistleblowing, but it did lay out the ways in which current accounting practice could be used to 'flatter' profits and generally make a company look a better bet than it actually was. The book upset some of the firm's clients, and he was dismissed for breach of a rule that the text should have been submitted to the firm for prior approval. Now, it is possible that in this case genuine confidential information was involved, although the point was never tested. Suppose, however, that this was not the case. In this situation, the value of the information being put into the public domain is obvious, given the number of high-profile collapses of businesses in recent years (of which BCCI is but one example) where accounts had passed the auditors. Interestingly, no criticism of his employers was involved. While clients may have been upset, there was no evidence that any had actually changed their accountants as a result. It is submitted that only if there was real evidence that the company risked losing clients as a result would there be sufficient damage to restrain the employee's publication.

CONCLUSION

In arguing that employees should have a right to freedom of speech, it is important to indicate what such a right would entail. What is here proposed is a right in the sense that the employee should not be subject to retaliatory action by the employer as a result of exercising, or intending to exercise, the right. In practice, this is not unduly problematic, given the now fairly extensive experience of non-discrimination law in relation to sex, race and trade union activities. In TURERA, the strategy of adding new grounds to employee protection against discrimination was accepted. (For dismissals on health and safety grounds and for asserting a statutory right, see p396 above.) It is submitted that the same strategy could be used to give protection to employee rights: thus not only dismissal, but detrimental action short of dismissal, would be prohibited, with the employee having a right of recourse to an industrial tribunal. There would perhaps be difficulties around proving that the reason for the retaliatory action was indeed the exercise of a right by the employee rather than, say, incompetence or misconduct, but these would be no worse than they are for other discrimination actions.

A formulation of an employee's right to free speech is suggested in the following terms: Employees should have a right to redress where they have suffered unfavourable treatment on grounds of their public or private utterances, except in the following circumstances:

> 1 Where the employee is employed as a spokesperson or advocate
> and in that capacity expresses views contrary to the policy of the
> organization.
> 2 Where the employee is sufficiently high-ranking to be properly
> regarded as the alter ego of the organization and makes public pro-
> nouncements on matters relating to the organization and its business.
> 3 Where the employee publicly accuses the employing organization
> of wrongdoing and *either* does not have reasonable grounds for
> believing the allegation to be correct *or* has not reported the allega-
> tions to a proper independent authority.
> 4 Where the employee discloses confidential information (in the
> sense of trade secrets or customer connection) which is not justified
> by reference to the public interest.
> 5 Where the employee makes any other criticisms of the employing
> organization which cause damage to its business.

Where the employee should reasonably appreciate that there is a risk of
his or her views being attributed to the employing organization, even
though the speech is not within the categories noted above, he or she will
not be protected unless he or she made it clear that he or she was acting
in a personal capacity.

While this is far from being an unrestricted right of free speech for
employees, it would have the effect of increasing protection substantially
from the present position and, it is submitted, would strike a fair balance
between the interests of management and those of the individual worker.

NOTES

1. The public-private divide, and how it is used to deny rights in the workplace, is discussed in H. Collins, *Justice in Dismissal* (Oxford: Clarendon Press, 1992), pp. 187-96. For a
general overview and a comparative perspective, see Chapter 16, above.
2. See the Trade Union and Labour Relations (Consolidation) Act 1992 (TULRCA), s. 236.
3. ILO conventions No. 87, 98.
4. See Lord Wedderburn, *The Social Charter, European Company and Employment Rights*
(London: Institute of Employment Rights, 1990), Chapter 5.
5. See the White Paper, *People, Jobs and Opportunity*, Cm 1810, 1992, Chapter 4, and the
Green Paper, *Industrial Relations in the 1990s*, Cm 1602, 1991, Chapter 8.
6. See the repeal of Fair Wages Resolutions and Employment Protection Act 1975,
Schedule 11; the abolition of statutory recognition procedure: and the abolition of wages
councils.
7. Trade Union Reform and Employment Rights Act 1993, s. 43.
8. Cf. H. Collins, *op. cit.*, pp. 194–5.

9. See *Cowen* v. *Haden* [1983] ICR 1 (CA).

10. [1972] 2 QB 455 (CA).

11. [1984] 2 All ER 713.

12. [1986] ICR 897.

13. [1992] IRLR 219 (CA); it should be noted that the employee had supervisory responsibilities.

14. The discussion is limited to the position of private employees: public employees are subject to different rules. The rules governing certain categories of public service are generally held to be too strict, but a discussion of the issues is beyond the scope of this chapter. See S. Fredman and G. Morris, *The State as Employer* (London: Mansell, 1989), pp. 215–44.

15. [1978] 1 All ER 574 (CA).

16. *Ibid.*, p. 577g.

17. *Ibid.*, p. 581(b)–(c).

18. [1991] IRLR 422 (Court of Session, Outer House).

19. EAT 8 October 1993; IDS Brief 512, March 1994.

20. New Trade Union and Labour Relations (Consolidation) Act 1992, s. 226A(2)(c), introduced by Trade Union Reform and Employment Rights Act 1993, s. 18.

21. *Blackpool & Fylde College* v. *NATFHE* [1994] IRLR 227 (CA).

22. [1993] ICR 612 (CA).

23. *Ibid.*, p. 620C. See also *Spring* v. *Guardian Assurance* [1994] IRLR 460 (HL), where Article 10 was unsuccessfully invoked on behalf of an employer who had negligently prepared a reference on a former employee; see Lord Lowry at p. 470, para. 54, and Lord Woolf at pp. 480–1, para. 142.

24. [1981] ICR 278 (EAT).

25. TULRCA, ss. 137, 146, 152.

26. Other reasons are that only recognized unions (at present) are entitled to consultation over redundancies and transfers and are able to appoint safety representatives.

27. *Luby* v. *Warwickshire Miners' Association* [1912] 2 Ch. 371.

28. *Lee* v. *Showmen's Guild of Great Britain* [1952] 2 QB 329.

29. [1976] ICR 473 (CA).

30. *Ibid.*, p. 489 A-C.

31. See also *Maclean* v. *Workers' Union* [1929] 1 Ch 602: member could be disciplined for disseminating circulars critical of union officers as he had not complied with a rule requiring circulars to be cleared by the executive first.

32. Now in TULRCA, s. 65 (as amended by TURERA).

33. TULRCA, s. 174 (as amended by TURERA).

34. TULRCA, s. 65(2); there is no protection for false assertions made in bad faith: s. 65(6).

35. *Zucker* v. *Astrid Jewels* [1978] ICR 1088 (EAT).

36. TULRCA, s. 137; but see *Harrison* v. *Kent CC*, 8 March 1995, *The Times* (EAT).

37. *Fitzpatrick* v. *BRB* [1990] ICR 674 (EAT).

38. *Chant* v. *Aquaboats* [1978] ICR 643 (EAT) – but see below for dismissal on health and safety grounds.

39. EC/89/391 Article 7(2).

40. Employment Protection Consolidation Act (EPCA), ss. 22A, 57A, 59, introduced or amended by TURERA, s. 28, Schedule 5.

41. Introduced by TURERA, s. 29.

42. Rights under the Wages Act, under the EPCA itself, and individual rights given in TULRCA.

43. (1993) 7/4 *The Lawyer* 3.

44. *Pickering* v. *Board of Education*, 391 US 563 (1968) (SCt).

45. Note, 'Free speech, the private employee and state constitutions (1982) 91 *Yale Law Journal* 522.

46. *Mitchell* v. *King*, 537 F 2d 385 (1976).

47. Cf. *P* v. *Nottinghamshire CC* [1992] ICR 706 (CA); ACAS Code of Practice No. 1, para. 15(c).

48. *Tesco Supermarkets* v. *Nattrass* [1972] AC 153 (HL).

49. See *New Law Journal* 4, 11, 24 November 1994; 16 December 1994; 13 January 1995.

50. Health and Safety at Work Act 1974, s. 7:
It shall be the duty of every employee while at work –
(a) to take reasonable care for the health and safety of himself and of other persons who may be affected by his acts and omissions at work; and
(b) as regards any other duty or requirement imposed on his employer or any other person by or under any of the relevant statutory provisions, to co-operate with him so far as is necessary to enable that duty or requirement to be performed or complied with.

51. J. McHale, Whistleblowing in the NHS [1992] *Journal of Social Welfare and Family Law* 363; Whistleblowing in the NHS revisited [1993] *Journal of Social Welfare and Family Law* 52. This was also an issue in the *Addison* case, where it was agreed that attempts to gag him were inconsistent with his duty as a barrister.

52. *Initial Services* v. *Putterill* [1968] 1 QB 396 (CA); *Lion Laboratories* v. *Evans* [1985] QB 526 (CA); *Re a Company's Application* [1989] ICR 449. On this generally, see Y. Cripps, *Legal Implications of Disclosure in the Public Interest* 2nd edn. (London: Sweet and Maxwell, 1994).

53. EAT 669/76, discussed in Y. Cripps, *op. cit.*, pp. 141–5; 314–17.

54. For example S. Bok, Whistleblowing and professional responsibility (1980) 2 *New York University Education Quarterly*; R. T. De George, *Business Ethics* (New York: Macmillan, 1982), p. 161, adds that the potential harm must be serious and that the whistleblower should have reasonable grounds for believing that the necessary changes will result from disclosure.

55. [1989] ICR 449.

56. 319 A 2d 174 (Penn. 1974).

57. 417 A 2d 505 (NJ 1980).

58. This is one of the major criticisms of the health service guidelines proposed after well-publicized cases of retaliation against whistleblowers such as Dr Helen Zeitlin and Graham Pink.

59. [1968] 1 QB 396, 405-6 (CA). See also Salmon LJ at p. 409 and Winn LJ at p. 411.

60. [1985] QB 526, 553 (CA).

61. T. Devine and D. Aplin, Whistleblower protection – the gap between the law and reality (1988) 31 *Howard Law Journal* 223. The case of Dr Helen Zeitlin is particularly instructive on this: see the account in *The Times* 6 August, 7 August ('Sacked NHS doctor "had a reputation for being disruptive" ') and 4 November 1992.

62. For example *British Steel* v. *Granada* [1981] AC 1096, 1202; *Lion Laboratories* v. *Evans*, *op. cit.*

63. For example H. Collins, *op. cit.*; Y. Cripps, *op. cit.*; J. McHale, *op. cit.*

64. *Faccenda Chicken* v. *Fowler* [1986] ICR 297 (CA).

65. *Herbert Morris* v. *Saxelby* [1916] 1 AC 688 (HL).

66. *Faccenda Chicken* v. *Fowler* [1986] ICR 297 *per* Neill LJ at pp. 308–9.

18

Can Rights Extend to Animals?

Mike Radford

INTRODUCTION

The purpose of this chapter is to provide a brief overview of the debate concerning the moral status of animals and the consequential obligations which humans may have towards them. It is not my intention to act as a proponent for any particular view, but, by considering the ways in which attitudes to animals have developed over time, I hope to add an additional dimension to our understanding of the nature of *human* rights. Put simply, the issue is this: are moral rights – assuming that they exist at all – restricted to humans, or can they be extended to other species?

TRADITIONAL ATTITUDES

The origins of European attitudes towards animals are to be found in the combined influences of Judaism, classical Greek philosophy, and Christianity. According to the Book of Genesis, God made the heaven and the earth, and everything on it, in six days. This culminated with the creation of man in God's own image, to whom He gave 'dominion over the fish of the sea, and over the fowl of the air, and over every living thing that moveth upon the earth'.[1] 'Dominion' could, of course, have been interpreted in this context to mean 'stewardship' or 'responsibility' for other species, but these are essentially modern concepts. Historically, it was taken to mean that God had given man *power* over the animal and plant kingdoms: for dominion, read dominance. There is a suggestion in the biblical creation story that, prior to the Fall, Adam and Eve were in fact vegetarian, and it was only after that event that the killing and eating of animals became the normal practice. In any event, after the Flood, God specifically told Noah that: 'Every moving thing that liveth shall be meat for you; even as the green herb have I given you all things.'[2]

A number of classical philosophers considered the nature of man's relationship with animals. The Cynics, for example, considered animals to be superior to humans; and Pythagoras, a committed vegetarian, recognized a kinship between humans and other animals, and is credited as the originator of the view that cruelty to animals leads inexorably to the infliction of cruelty on humans. However, the most influential contribution was that of Aristotle. He saw nature as a hierarchy, based upon the ability to reason, with those lower down the hierarchy existing to serve those above. Humans were, unsurprisingly, at the top, on the basis of their possession of language and rationality (they were then subdivided into a further hierarchy, with slaves and women existing to serve men). Animals did no better under this scheme than they had in the Old Testament. According to Aristotle: 'Now if nature makes nothing incomplete, and nothing in vain, the inference must be that she has made all animals for the sake of man.'[3]

Turning to Christianity, the New Testament makes little specific mention of the treatment of animals. There are some suggestions about the extent of God's concern for His creation, but the emphasis is on the importance of humans:

> Are not five sparrows sold for two farthings, and not one of them is forgotten before God? But even the very hairs of your head are all numbered. Fear not therefore: ye are of more value than many sparrows.[4]

Clearly, the nature of Christianity served to highlight the uniqueness and sanctity of human life, particularly by stressing the importance of the soul and the espousal of life after death.

These three unrelated views of the proper relationship between humans and other species were brought together in the theology of St Thomas Aquinas (1225–1274). He, like Aristotle, saw nature as hierarchical, with plants having vegetative souls; animals, sensitive (mortal) souls; and humans, rational (immortal) powers. From this, he concluded that humans could use animals for their own ends, and there was nothing intrinsically wrong with causing animals to suffer,

> for by the divine providence they are intended for man's use according to the order of nature. Hence it is not wrong to make use of them, either by killing or in any other way whatever.[5]

There was, however, one important caveat to this general rule – a reiteration of the Pythagorean fear that cruelty to animals might lead to the mistreatment of humans:

> And if any passages of Holy Scripture seem to forbid us to be cruel
> to brute animals, for instance to kill a bird with its young, this is
> either to remove man's thoughts from being cruel to other men, lest
> through being cruel to animals one becomes cruel to human beings;
> or because injury to an animal leads to the temporal hurt of man,
> either of the doer of the deed, or of another.[5]

Accordingly, humans may owe an *indirect* duty to animals, because of the
possible effect that mistreating them may have on the perpetrator, or on
other humans.

Historically, the Thomist attitude to humans' proper relationship with
animals has been extremely influential, and continues to be so. It
remains in all essentials the view of the Roman Catholic Church (an
explanation, perhaps, for the different way in which animals are
regarded by northern and southern Europeans). The Church's current
teaching states that animals are 'by nature destined for the common good
of past, present and future humanity'. Notwithstanding that 'men owe
them kindness', it is legitimate to use animals for food, clothing and –
'within reasonable limits' – for medical and scientific experimentation.[6]

Animals fared little better as society and intellectual thought were
transformed in the early modern period. The Renaissance saw the rise of
humanist (as distinct from humanitarian) thought, and the emphasis on
the potential, value and uniqueness of humans served only to distance
humans from other species, a rupture which culminated in the views of
the French philosopher and mathematician, René Descartes. He argued
that human consciousness resided in the soul ('I think, therefore I am');
animals had no soul, or language, and, therefore, he concluded, they
lacked consciousness. To Descartes, animals were nothing more than
machines, to be equated with the likes of clocks: however sophisticated
they might appear to be in their movements and reactions, they were
properly to be regarded as automata. They had no thoughts, no feelings,
and therefore they could not suffer. Consequently, humans owed them
no duty whatsoever: animals were mere things, and could be treated – or,
more appropriately from today's perspective, mistreated – as such.[7] The
cynic might observe that this was an extremely convenient conclusion at
a time when the increase in scientific inquiry was leading to a greater use
of live, conscious animals in vivisection, anaesthetics not yet having been
developed. The following eyewitness account of animal experimentation
in the late seventeenth century certainly suggests as much:

> They administered beatings to dogs with perfect indifference, and

made fun of those who pitied the creatures as if they felt pain. They said the animals were clocks; that the cries they emitted when struck were only the noise of a little spring that had been touched, but that the whole body was without feeling. They nailed poor animals up on boards by their four paws to vivisect them and see the circulation of the blood which was a great subject of conversation.[8]

CHALLENGING THE ACCEPTED ORTHODOXY

Notwithstanding the orthodoxy in European thought that humans do not owe other species any direct moral duty, there has long been an alternative tradition, which has sought to challenge the prevailing assumptions. It is important to emphasize that it was at all times a minority view, and in truth had very little practical impact until relatively recently, but it is a tradition one needs to be aware of, for it has played a major role in influencing the contemporary debate about the proper treatment of animals.

As early as at least the sixteenth century, there were lone voices questioning the prevailing human attitudes towards animals. For example, Michael de Montaigne, in his *Apology for Raymond de Sebonde*, published in the 1590s, observed that the vanity of man 'makes him equal himself to God', and thus 'pick himself out and set himself apart from the mass of other creatures', notwithstanding that they are 'his fellows and his brothers'. 'What comparison between us and them,' asked de Montaigne, 'leads him to conclude that they have the attributes of senseless brutes?'[9]

The seventeenth and eighteenth centuries witnessed a period of rapid development in a wide range of disciplines, culminating in the so-called 'Age of Enlightenment'. This intellectual fervour saw an outpouring of ideas – philosophical, scientific, economic, social and political – which inevitably challenged the *status quo*. Greater understanding across the scientific spectrum caused a fundamental reassessment of humanity's place in the universe. At the same time, there was a growing emphasis on the concept of 'Nature' and the natural world.[10] Spurred on by these developments, some thinkers, albeit a minority, began to question the assumption that there was an intractable gulf between humans and other animals. (One might note here the irony that while Descartes' apparently eccentric view of animals was used to justify vivisection of live creatures, the observations made during such procedures served to point towards similarities with humans rather than differences, for what was found were the same organs, apparently performing the same functions, as those in human bodies.) Most significantly, there was, at least in some quarters, a growing realization that humans might themselves be properly regarded as animals. In 1753, for example, Linnaeus published his *Systema Naturae*, in which he classified humans as part of the primate order, man being placed in the same genus as the orang-utang.

Moreover, it was at this time that, in considering humanity's relationship with other creatures, attention became focused on animals' capacity to suffer pain, rather than being confined to the traditional questions of language, immortality and reason. Largely because animal experiments had revealed the remarkable similarity between the physiology of humans and other animals, some writers openly questioned the manner in which animals were used, urging that they should be treated with 'kindness' and 'gentle usage'. Such attitudes represented a dramatic break with the past. Animals were now being recognized as sentient creatures, having the capacity to experience pleasure and pain, and once it was admitted that they could be harmed directly there was a logical argument for giving them at least some moral weight.

Running in parallel with these secular developments was a growing religious diversity: new sects with new ideas. Quakers, for example, were well known – as, indeed, they still are – for being concerned for animal life, and the Methodists rejected the traditional gulf between humans and the rest of creation. Their founder, John Wesley, expressed strong opposition to cruel sports, and argued that children should not be cruel to animals. Most significantly from a theological perspective, he went so far as to suggest the probability that animals had souls.

One of the consequences of this explosion of ideas was a challenge to the assumption that animals existed merely for the benefit of humans. It is during this period, the second half of the eighteenth century, that one begins to see the emergence of sustained arguments against meat eating, vivisection, the use of animals for sport, and the mistreatment of working animals. Crucially, these developments coincided with the emergence of the two most significant and influential moral theories of the modern world: the claim for universal rights, and utilitarianism.

The French Revolution, American independence, publication of Paine's *Rights of Man* and Wollstonecraft's *A Vindication of the Rights of Woman*, the debate over slavery; all these served to put the question of rights on the intellectual and political agenda. Even the concept of animal rights was raised, albeit as a satirical attack upon Paine and Wollstonecraft. In 1792 there was published in London a pamphlet entitled *A Vindication of the Rights of Brutes*, written by one Thomas Taylor. Intended as an attack on the proponents of *human* rights, it argued that such a notion was so absurd that one might as well argue for rights for animals, which Taylor proceeded to do. Ironically, although his intention was to mock, the case he presents comes across, two hundred years later, as a reasonably strong and coherent argument in favour of an idea which he certainly did not intend to be taken seriously, and which would have been totally incomprehensible to him and his peers.

It was, however, utilitarianism which provided the immediate theoretical stimulus for reassessing attitudes towards animals. As was observed above, concern was increasing about animal *suffering*. The relevance in this context of a moral theory which focuses on pleasure and pain will be readily appreciated. Jeremy Bentham himself made the connection, recognizing that it was not only humans who were 'susceptible to happiness', but that such an experience could also extend to 'other animals, which on account of their interests having been neglected by the insensibility of the ancient jurists, stand degraded into the class of things'. He continued:

> The day has been, I grieve to say in many places it is not yet past, in which the greater part of the species, under the denomination of slaves, have been treated by the law exactly on the same footing, as, in England for example, the inferior races of animals are still. The day may come, when the rest of animal creation may acquire those rights which never could have been witholden from them but by the hand of tyranny. The French have already discovered that the blackness of the skin is no reason why a human being should be abandoned without redress to the caprice of a tormentor. It may come one day to be recognised, that the number of legs, the villosity of the skin, or the termination of the sacrum, are reasons equally insufficient for abandoning a sensitive being to the same fate. What else is it that should trace the insuperable line? Is it the faculty of reason, or, perhaps, the faculty of discourse? But a full-grown horse or dog, is beyond comparison a more rational, as well as a more conversable animal, than an infant of a day, or a week, or even a month old. But suppose the case were otherwise, what would it avail? The question is not, Can they reason? nor, Can they talk? but, Can they suffer?[11]

It is generally the final sentence of this extract which is quoted, but the extent of Bentham's radicalism cannot be appreciated without including the preceding sentences. This view is significant for three reasons. First, there is a recognition that animals may have interests; second, there is a suggestion that humans may owe animals a direct moral duty; and third, it is clear that these views relating to animals grow directly out of the contemporary reassessment of the proper treatment of humans.

Here we have, then, at the end of the eighteenth century, a leading thinker making a clear connection between the treatment of humans and that of animals, and, drawing a conclusion which remains a matter of controversy as we approach the millennium. He was not alone. For example, a cleric named Humphry Primatt published in 1776 a *Dissertation on the Duty of Mercy and the Sin of Cruelty to Brute Animals*, in which he stated:

> As the differences among men . . . are no bars to their feelings, so neither does the difference of the shape of a brute from that of a man exempt the brute from feeling; at least, we have no ground to suppose it . . . . And if the difference of complexion or stature does not convey to one man the right to despise and abuse another man, the difference of shape between a man and a brute, cannot give to a man any right to abuse and torment a brute.[12]

A second example is taken from the writings of one Hermann Daggett, who published in 1791 a pamphlet entitled *The Rights of Animals: An Oration*. Having complained of the indifference shown for the cruelty and suffering inflicted on animals, Daggett went so far as to argue that the emerging notion of human rights should be extended to animals:

> If we judge impartially, we shall acknowledge that there are the rights of a beast, as well as the rights of a man. And because man is considered as the Lord of this lower creation, he is not thereby licensed to infringe on the rights of those below him, any more than a King, or Magistrate, is licensed to infringe on the rights of his subjects . . . . And I know of nothing in nature, in reason, or in revelation, which obliges us to suppose, that the unalienated rights of a beast, are not as sacred, and inviolable, as those of a man: or that the person, who wantonly commits an outrage upon the life, happiness, or security of a bird, is not as really amenable, at the tribunal of eternal justice, as he, who wantonly destroys the rights and privileges, or injuriously takes away the life of one of his fellow creatures of the human race.[13]

These extracts are striking in their immediacy and modernity, but they are also significant in the present context in emphasizing that the arguments in favour of animal interests and rights are firmly rooted in the same period, the same literature, and the same principles, from which the case for human rights originated. Moreover, notwithstanding that disquiet about humans' treatment of animals remained primarily the concern of a minority of radical thinkers, it was nevertheless becoming an issue of wider relevance. Slowly, but surely, the net of moral duties was being cast beyond humans, to include other species. As Thomas Paine observed: 'everything of persecution and revenge between man and man, and everything of cruelty to animals, is a violation of moral duty'.[14]

There was some practical significance in this changing attitude: the first attempt in Britain to enact legislation for the protection of animals was made in 1799, to the dismay of Parliament, which regarded such a matter to be below its dignity.[15] Between 1800 and 1835 Parliament debated no less than 11 anti-cruelty bills, and while all but one failed, this statistic indicates a surprising level of concern about the treatment of animals. The initial attack was on activities such as bull-baiting and cock-fighting, and it may well be that the impetus was more to do with maintaining public order than protecting the animals involved in such pastimes. It must be remembered that, in the absence of a regular police force, large gatherings which involved gambling and copious amounts of alcohol always threatened to get out of hand.[16]

When attention became focused specifically on protective legislation, it was a former Lord Chancellor who was the driving force. Lord Erskine unsuccessfully introduced bills to protect cattle in 1809 and 1810. However, it was not until more than a decade later, having joined forces with Richard Martin MP, that Erskine saw his efforts rewarded. On 22 July 1822, the Royal Assent was given to 'An Act to Prevent the Cruel and Improper Treatment of Cattle' (subsequently known as 'Martin's Act') which made it a criminal offence punishable by a fine of between ten shillings and five pounds to 'wantonly and cruelly beat, abuse, or ill-treat any horse, mare, gelding, mule, ass, ox, cow, heifer, steer, sheep, or other cattle'.

Martin's Act was extended and consolidated in 1835, and Parliament regularly legislated to further the protection of animals throughout the nineteenth century.[17] The transformation had been dramatic: a cause which was regarded in the 1790s as, at best, eccentric and, at worst, sub-versive and anti-religious had become, within just half a century, eminently respectable. The Society for the Prevention of Cruelty to Animals was formed in London in 1824 with the twin objectives of enforcing Martin's Act (there still being no organized police force) and educating those affected by its provisions. In 1835 Princess Victoria became a patron, two years before she acceded to the throne, and in 1840 the Queen granted the Society the 'Royal' prefix.

It is no coincidence that this growth of anti-cruelty legislation should arise during the same period that witnessed major advances in social legislation; many of the leading participants were involved in both campaigns. However, it would be wrong to suggest that these reforms reflected a wide acceptance that animals had a moral status. The momentum behind them was rather a combination of Victorian paternalism towards 'innocent' creatures, and a resurgence of the Thomist belief that violence towards animals would lead inevitably to violence towards people.

However, by the middle of the nineteenth century, the traditional belief that there was a biological distinction between humans and other species was being seriously questioned, and it was fatally undermined in 1859 by the publication of Darwin's *On the Origin of Species by Means of Natural Selection or the Preservation of Favoured Races in the Struggle for Life*. It is self-evident that a theory of evolution is inconsistent with a view of man as having been created by God in His own image, and set apart from other creatures. The inevitable conclusion was that we, ourselves, were indeed animals, realization of which was bound to be the basis for a fundamental reassessment of humans' relationship with other species and their proper moral status; the ramifications of this are still reverberating through society. Indeed, the implications of Darwin's theory went even further, for he suggested that humans were not unique in their capacity for moral actions. He argued that the basis of morality is our 'social instincts', by which he meant the presence of an instinctive urge to act not only for our individual benefit, but also for the benefit of others. Such behaviour, he said, could be witnessed in other species, although it was not so well developed as among humans. He was not suggesting that animals were moral agents, but rather that there was a continuity between humans and other species in matters of morality, in the same way that he described a continuity in respect of physical and mental attributes.[18]

THE CONTEMPORARY DEBATE

The contemporary debate regarding the moral status of animals has many facets,[19] but four principal views emerge. There is a fifth which occasionally surfaces, and that relates to the argument that humans do not owe animals *any* moral duty whatsoever, either direct or indirect. One might have thought that Cartesians were an endangered species, but life is full of surprises. For example, the late J. S. Kennedy, former Professor of Animal Behaviour at Imperial College London, expressed in a book published as recently as 1992 the view that 'it seems likely that consciousness, feelings, thoughts, purposes, etc. are unique to our species and it is unlikely that animals are conscious'.[20] I will not dwell on the controversy generated by such remarks; suffice it to say that they now represent a minority position.

Perhaps a more familiar approach which results in a similar conclusion is that of the legal positivists. Raymond Frey, for example, argues that sentiency is not an adequate basis on which to found animal interests. He distinguishes between something being in an individual's interest, and that individual having an interest in something. The former situation amounts to saying that the individual has a need, and self-evidently humans and animals both have physical needs which must be fulfilled if they are to survive. But, says Frey, only humans possess interests in the sense of being interested in something, on the basis that such an interest requires the individual to have desires, and thus beliefs, and he denies that it is possible for animals to have beliefs.[21] Notwithstanding this position, he accepts that they are sentient, and can therefore be wronged by pain being inflicted upon them. As Garner observes: 'It is surely churlish to deny that animals have an interest in not suffering pain whether or not they believe that a certain action will lead to the experience of pain.'[22]

Moreover, Frey goes further, claiming that if animals lack beliefs, then they cannot have reasons for their actions – a premise which he claims will be '*relatively* uncontroversial'.[23] One would have thought, on the basis of both common sense and observation, that such a view was not only controversial, but highly questionable. Frey's approach is surely Cartesianism in a different guise – a view of animals as little more than automata. However, it is little wonder that he denies animals moral status, for after 167 pages of detailed argument against such a view he reveals, in a postscript, that not only does he reject moral rights for animals, but he also denies them to humans,[24] a view he reiterates in a later work.[25] Although such an example of legal positivism has a perfectly respectable pedigree, it is somewhat atypical of the critical response that the proponents of animal interests and rights have excited. More usually, opponents of such ideas adopt a more orthodox position, seeking to endorse the moral status of humans, while denying it to animals.

The first such view, in the tradition of Aquinas, Locke and Kant, is that humans have only indirect duties towards animals. While early writers based this approach on the harm that may be done to humans through cruelty to animals, the modern proponents of indirect duties, such as Jan Narveson, John Rawls and Peter Carruthers, base their arguments on contractual principles. In short, their position is founded on a belief that those who are able to make moral judgments – moral agents – agree (or would agree) amongst themselves, on the basis of what is in their own interests, what the moral rules should be, and it is only parties to this 'contract' who can be directly wronged. As moral patients – unable to make moral choices themselves – animals fall outside this magic circle and thereby can only be wronged indirectly.[26]

Thus Rawls argues that an entitlement to 'equal justice' is restricted to those who are capable of having both a conception of their own good and a sense of justice; that is, 'a normally effective desire to apply and to act upon the principles of justice', which he does not consider applies to animals. However, while humans 'are not required to give strict justice to creatures lacking this capacity', Rawls recognizes that it does not necessarily follow that we can treat animals as we choose. He concedes that 'it is wrong to be cruel to animals and the destruction of a whole species can be a great evil'; and in respect of those animals which are sentient, the ability to experience pleasure and pain 'clearly imposes duties of compassion and humanity in their case'.[27] But this poses more questions than it answers: what behaviour constitutes cruelty? Why is the destruction of a whole species a great evil? What does a duty of compassion and humanity amount to in practice?

Similarly, Carruthers rejects the notion that animals are rational agents, and looks instead to contractual principles for guidance on how they should be treated. His starting point is what he terms 'common-sense belief', which he states in relation to animals as being acceptance of killing, but reluctance to endorse the infliction of unnecessary suffering.[28] From this position he argues that we may have an indirect duty not to be cruel to animals either because of the distress that such actions would cause to the many people who have concern for animals – 'causing animal suffering to an animal would violate the right of animal lovers to have their concerns respected and taken seriously'[29] – or, alternatively, because of what the infliction of cruelty says about the perpetrator's character, namely an indifference to suffering – 'animals thus get accorded indirect moral significance, by virtue of the qualities of character that they may, or may not evoke in us'.[30] It is unsurprising that Carruthers concludes 'that there is no basis for extending moral protection to animals beyond that which is already provided',[31] since what he takes as the basis – the 'common-sense belief' – is merely a way of describing the existing consensus; it seems inevitable that an argument founded upon it will result in support for the *status quo*.

The second position is the one which it is probably reasonable to regard as the present orthodox view, namely, that humans owe animals a *direct* duty not to cause them unnecessary suffering, and to prevent such suffering if possible, but the interests of other species may – and, indeed, in many circumstances, should – be overridden to give precedence to the interests of humankind. From this standpoint, activities such as raising and killing animals for food and using animals in at least some scientific procedures are morally acceptable, although involvement in blood sports or using animals for entertainment may be more questionable.

Robert Nozick comes close to this position in *Anarchy, State and Utopia*. Animals, he says, 'count for something', and the higher animals at least 'ought to be given some weight in people's deliberations about what to do'. Like Rawls, he considers that our treatment of them must be qualified because of their ability to experience pleasure and pain, arguing that it is only acceptable to inflict suffering on them if it can be shown to be justified. That is to say, it must be kept to a minimum; it gives rise to benefits which are greater than the suffering caused; and there is no practical alternative with which to reach a similar result.

While recognizing that the term is not altogether satisfactory, he suggests that an acceptable approach might be summarized as 'utilitarianism for animals, Kantianism for people': one should attempt to maximize the total happiness of all living beings, while recognizing that there are stringent constraints on what may properly be done to human beings. Thus, animals may be harmed for the gain of other animals and persons, but humans can never be harmed for the benefit of animals. But herein lies the deficiency, for as Nozick himself recognizes, taken literally this suggests that it is unacceptable to inflict penalties on humans for infringing laws which exist specifically to protect animals from cruelty. Moreover, might there not be situations in which it is right to inflict a small amount of discomfort on humans to prevent a large amount of suffering for animals? Accordingly, he concludes that, in the same way that the constraint on harming humans may be relaxed in circumstances where to do so can save people from 'excruciating suffering', so it might also be acceptable to relax it – 'though not as much' – when animal suffering is at stake.[32]

A view which falls within the same category is that of Michael Leahy. He argues that there is a significant difference between humans and animals, and this he identifies – as many have before him – to be the capacity of language. While acknowledging that animals' attributes may include intent, planning, choice, desire, fear, anger and some beliefs, and they can therefore be regarded as conscious, he denies that they are *self*-conscious. To be so, and to demonstrate emotions such as ambition, remorse and envy, can only come, he suggests, with the capability of speech. Without it, Leahy argues that we must regard other species as 'primitive creatures', and it is as such that we should assess their claims to proper treatment.[33] There should be recognition of 'their perceived needs', and animals should not be subjected to needless suffering, but that is the extent of our duty to them; and in deciding how they should be treated, it is legitimate to have regard to '*our* purposes for them'. Consequently, what constitutes proper treatment will vary, depending on the human use to which the individual animal is being put.[34]

It is the approach represented by the likes of Nozick and Leahy which is broadly represented by the law in the UK. Thus, in addition to prohibiting a number of specific practices such as baiting or abandoning an animal, the Protection of Animals Act 1911 makes it an offence wantonly or unreasonably to do or omit to do any act which causes unnecessary suffering to a domestic or captive animal (wildlife generally is not protected against cruelty). Similarly, the Agriculture (Miscellaneous Provisions) Act 1968 makes it an offence to cause, or knowingly allow, livestock to suffer unnecessary pain or unnecessary distress whilst on agricultural land. The significance is in the subjective qualification 'unnecessary' in each Act. Actions or omissions which might be deemed unnecessary in relation to a pet – and therefore unlawful – can be regarded by a court as necessary – and hence lawful – in the context of the commercial demands of agricultural production, notwithstanding that the detrimental effect on the animal in both circumstances is identical.

With regard to the use of animals in laboratories, procedures which would undoubtedly be regarded as unlawful if inflicted on a domestic or agricultural animal are not prohibited if carried out as part of a scientific procedure, provided those undertaking the work, the premises at which it is carried out, and the procedure itself, have all been licensed in accordance with the provisions of the Animals (Scientific Procedures) Act 1986.

In consequence, a rabbit, for example, will be subject to different degrees of protection depending on whether it is living in the wild, is a domestic pet, is being raised for meat or fur, or is being used in a laboratory for experimentation or testing; should it find itself in a pet shop, a zoo or a circus, it will be subject to one of a further three different legislative regimes. UK law, then, is not principally concerned with the needs of the individual animal, but rather seeks to qualify what might be regarded as proper treatment in the light of the needs, or the demands, or the convenience, of human interests.

It is this situation which the two remaining views of the moral status of animals seek, in their different ways, to challenge: namely, utilitarianism and the concept of animal rights. It is these positions which have been at the centre of recent debate about the proper treatment of animals. The argument in favour of a utilitarian approach is represented principally in the modern literature by the Australian philosopher, Peter Singer.[35] The thesis is straightforward, even if the consequences are not. Put simply, animals are properly regarded as sentient beings which experience pleasure and pain. Consequently, their interests should be taken into account in the utilitarian calculation to determine what is morally acceptable behaviour. Singer's is not a theory of animal rights as such, although, confusingly, he does on occasion use the term to refer to his own utilitarian views. Singer recognizes that there are significant differences between humans and other species, and that it would be inappropriate for all to be treated alike. Rather than arguing for equal treatment, he is a proponent of equal consideration: on the assumption that animals feel pain, he argues that there can be no moral justification for regarding the pain that animals feel as less important than the same amount of pain felt by humans.

To many, the practical attraction of a utilitarian approach is that there is recognition that we owe animals a *direct* moral duty, and this can be given full consideration in determining how they should be treated, while at the same time recognizing that there will be situations in which it might be appropriate to give human interests priority. The problem is, as with all utilitarian theories, how to measure and weigh the interests of animals against the competing interests of humans.

Finally, there is the contention which argues that at least some animals, by their very nature, should be regarded as having rights. All the exponents of animal rights proceed on the express or implied assumption that humans, all humans, have (generally unspecified) moral rights and, this being so, it is suggested that the concept must extend to at least some animals. The first modern writer to propose such an approach is generally regarded to be Henry Salt, whose *Animals' Rights* was published in 1892.[36] His starting point was that 'To live one's own life – to realize one's true self – is the highest moral purpose of man and animal alike.'[37] On the basis that animals have individuality, character and reason, Salt argued that they have the right to exercise such qualities. According to Salt, '[i]f "rights" exist at all – and both feeling and usage indubitably prove that they do exist – they cannot be consistently awarded to men and denied to animals, since the same sense of justice and compassion apply in both cases.'[38] It has to be conceded that Salt's underlying argument is somewhat superficial and, indeed, confused. However, his work has been significant in raising the banner of animal rights, and has acted as something of a beacon to modern adherents of the cause.

A much more intellectually rigorous argument is presented by the leading modern exponent of animal rights, the American philosopher Tom Regan, who has written widely on the subject, but whose thesis is most fully developed in his book, *The Case for Animal Rights*.[39] Again, the thesis proceeds on the assumption that humans have rights. Regan states that all the evidence points to the fact that mammals of at least a year old are conscious, and it is reasonable to view them as individuals, who, like humans, have beliefs and desires. On this basis, they can reasonably be regarded as acting intentionally in order to satisfy these desires. In other words, they do not simply react to external stimuli. Further, he contends that such animals must not only be able to perceive individual objects, but they must also be able to remember and, on the basis of past experience, form general concepts. Since many of the beliefs they have involve their having expectations about the future, they must also have a sense of that future – indeed, a sense of their own future. Thus they are reasonably viewed as being not only conscious, but self-conscious.

This mental life, which includes perception, memory, desire, belief, self-consciousness, intention, a sense of the future, emotion and sentience, means that they can be described as autonomous. Individuals with these attributes Regan describes as being subject-of-a-life in the sense that they have their own experiential welfare that is independent of their utility for, and the interests of, others. In other words, each individual animal has an inherent value, a value in itself, regardless of its value to anyone else, and irrespective of the fact that it is not a moral agent.

Regan is not suggesting that the mental powers of animals are akin to those of humans, but he can point to those of some animals being greater than those of some humans, thereby introducing the 'marginal cases' argument. Put simply, it relies on the fact that not all humans are moral agents; some, such as the very young, the very old and the mentally defective, are moral patients. That is to say, there are those within the human population who are not able to make moral choices and whose degree of autonomy is significantly less than that of the higher mammals. Yet they are still regarded as having an inherent value and are thereby accorded rights; indeed, some might argue that it is necessary to be more mindful of human moral patients' rights, as it provides a means for their protection. Unless it is argued that these individuals have inherent value merely because they are human – a contention which is overtly speciesist[40] and is rejected by Regan on moral and intellectual grounds – then it must follow that inherent value can extend to at least some moral patients, regardless of their species.

Much turns on the concept of inherent value, for, according to Regan, not only do all moral agents, that is all normal human beings, have inherent value, but they all enjoy an equal inherent value, which has to be taken into account in determining what treatment is morally acceptable. Moreover, because all moral agents have equal inherent value, just treatment for one must apply to all, regardless of sex, race or any other attribute. Hence, moral agents can be regarded as having rights. But if those rights flow from the fact that they have an inherent value, then any moral patient, including animals, that also has an inherent value must also be accorded rights:

> As a matter of strict justice we are required to give equal respect to those individuals who have equal inherent value, whether they be moral agents or moral patients, and, if the latter, whether they be humans or animals. That is something each is due. Injustice arises when we treat those who have such value in ways that fail to display proper respect (for example, by treating them as if their value was

reducible to their utility for others).[41]

These rights are said to be possessed independently of anyone's voluntary acts; they are universal, and all those who possess them possess them
equally. What, however, is their nature? Regan contends that the principal moral right possessed of all moral agents and patients is the right to
respectful treatment. This prohibits treating them as if their value is
reducible to their utility relative to the interests of others; in other words,
regarding them as lacking any value of their own. Moreover, it is said that
respectful treatment is incompatible with doing anything that harms the
individual.

This is significant, for, according to Regan, animals have a welfare, in
the sense that they fare well or ill according to their experiential life. The
degree of their welfare is determined by biological, sociological and psychological benefits (including the degree to which they can exercise their
autonomy). A harm is anything which detracts from an individual's welfare, regardless of whether or not it actually causes suffering, and
including death, again regardless of whether or not it is 'humane'.

Regan is claiming significantly more for animals than Singer. Singer's
utilitarianism demands that, as animals are sentient, their interests
should be given equal consideration with those of humans. Regan, however, goes as far as to claim that the capabilities of at least some animals
are such that they deserve the same moral consideration as humans. The
practical distinction between the two theories can best be seen with
regard to the question of killing animals. Singer is not comfortable with
the idea, but he is prepared to concede, albeit reluctantly, that it may be
morally acceptable to kill animals, as long as they do not suffer in the
process, while Regan claims for animals what amounts to a right to life.

If accepted, Regan's conclusions have profound implications for our
relationship with, and our treatment of, animals, for he regards our use
of animals in agriculture, hunting, education and scientific procedures as
prima facie morally wrong on the basis that it fails to treat them with the
respect they are due, but treat them instead as renewable resources having value only relative to human interests. This is only prima facie wrong,
because Regan does accept that there may be circumstances in which it is
morally permissible to override an individual's rights, provided that it
can be justified 'by appeal to valid moral principles'. Whatever that
means, it is clear that in Regan's mind such circumstances will be few and
far between for, as he concludes, on the basis of his theory, animals

> must never be treated as mere receptacles of intrinsic values (e.g.,
> pleasure, or preference-satisfaction), and any harm that is done to
> them must be consistent with the recognition of their equal

inherent value and their equal prima facie right not to be harmed.[42]

CONCLUSION

Clearly, a number of difficult but important questions arise from the preceding discussion. The concept of animal rights is used in common parlance in a confused and very general way. The media include a wide variety of views under the convenient umbrella of 'the animal rights movement'. Similarly, the term is often used to suggest that animals have absolute rights, which must be defended and enforced at all costs, up to and including endangering the lives of those deemed to be responsible for abusing animals. Those who hold such beliefs do not represent the mainstream view.

It is to be hoped that the foregoing makes clear that the debate about the moral status of animals is rather more subtle and intellectually demanding than much of the crude and simplistic sloganizing that surround the subject would suggest. Moreover, it is based on rational argument, not on mere emotion or sentiment.

The fundamental question, consideration of which has as much to tell us about our concept of the moral status of humans as it does about the moral status of animals, is this: when one talks of rights or, indeed, moral status, is it appropriate to restrict the ambit exclusively to humans? Of course other species are different from humans (as, indeed, they are different from each other), and it is a delusion to suggest otherwise. As Steve Jones has commented, 'A chimp may share ninety-eight per cent of its genes with a typical human being but it is certainly not ninety-eight per cent human: it is not human at all – it is a chimp.'[43] The issue is, however, whether the differences are such as to place other species in a completely different moral category from humans; it is well to remember in this context the observation of Charles Darwin: 'the difference in mind between man and the higher animals, great as it is, certainly is one of degree and not of kind'.[44]

Given the variety of living things, it is self-evident that different species experience life in different ways. While it might be reasonable to suggest that the behaviour of less complex life forms is the result of instinct and mechanical reaction to the environment, it is surely apparent that more developed species are sentient, conscious, and, at least to some extent, can be accurately described as autonomous. If one holds to a belief in man as the specific creation of God, formed in His own image, at the centre of the universe, and the rest of creation provided for human benefit, then attitudes to humans and animals can be reasonably easily defined. But once one moves away from such certainties, the position surely becomes much more difficult.

Acceptance of evolutionary theory involves accepting that humankind is part of a natural continuum; part of the overall whole, not separate from it. Moreover, as our understanding of the evolutionary process increases, so the moral questions become more complex. Coming to terms with the notion that we are related to other species was a major challenge to our forbears, and so it is for us; the implications are profound. Moreover, if evolution is not a single line of development, but a multitude of branches, then no species can be said to be at the top; more disconcerting, perhaps, no species – including humans – can be regarded as the ultimate, final example of what nature can achieve. In such a situation, can the human species be isolated morally from the rest of animal life?

Carruthers considers that concern with animal rights is 'a reflection of moral decadence': 'Just as Nero fiddled while Rome burned, many in the West agonise over the fate of seal pups and cormorants while human beings elsewhere starve or are enslaved.'[45] Of course, the relationship that those of us who are lucky enough to enjoy affluent lifestyles have with animals raises its own moral questions: is it acceptable that my dog is better fed than a significant proportion of the world's human population? Is it right that my cat should have access to better medical treatment than many people? But then, how do academic philosophers defend the nature of their existence in the face of that endured by their kin throughout the world? The argument for reassessing our attitudes to animals is not founded in preferring them to humans, or in ignoring human needs. Rather, it is about looking at life in the round, and making moral decisions on that basis.

We must always be careful not to fall into the trap of anthropomorphism, but as our understanding of animal behaviour increases, so the extent of their mental capacity becomes apparent. In such a situation, perhaps the burden of proof is changing: instead of those who believe that animals do have a moral status and should be treated accordingly having to justify their position, maybe the time has come when the onus should fall on those who contend that humans have rights to explain why a similar concept should not be accorded to at least the higher animals.

NOTES

1. Genesis 1:26–8.

2. Genesis 9:3.

3. Aristotle, *Politics*, Book I, Chapter 8; quoted in T. Regan and P. Singer (eds), *Animal Rights and Human Obligations* (Englewood Cliffs, New Jersey: Prentice-Hall, 1976), pp. 109–10.

4. Luke 12:7–8.

5. St Thomas Aquinas, *Summa Contra Gentiles*, Third Book, Part II, Chapter CXII; quoted in P. A. B. Clarke and A. Linzey (eds), *Political Theory and Animal Rights* (London: Pluto Press, 1990), p. 10. There are similar passages in Aquinas's other great work, *Summa Theologica*.

6. *Catechism of the Catholic Church* (London: Geoffrey Chapman, 1994), paras 2415–17.

7. R. Descartes, *A Discourse on Method – Discourse V* (1637); quoted in P. A. B. Clarke and A. Linzey, *op. cit.*, pp. 14–17.

8. N. Fontaine, *Memories pour servir a l'histoire de Port-Royal* (Cologne, 1738), 2: pp. 52–3; quoted in P. Singer, *Animal Liberation* 2nd edn (London: Thorsons, 1991), pp. 201–2.

9. Quoted in T. Regan and P. Singer, *op. cit.*, p. 82.

10. See generally K. Thomas, *Man and the Natural World. Changing Attitudes in England 1500–1800* (Harmondsworth: Penguin, 1984).

11. J. Bentham, *An Introduction to the Principles of Morals and Legislation* (1789) Chapter XVII, Section 1; quoted in P. A. B. Clarke and A. Linzey, *op. cit.*, pp. 135–6.

12. H. Primatt, *Dissertation on the Duty of Mercy and the Sin of Cruelty to Brute Animals* (1776); quoted in P. A. B. Clarke and A. Linzey, *op. cit.*, p. 125.

13. H. Daggett, *The Rights of Animals: an Oration* (1791); quoted in P. A. B. Clarke and A. Linzey, *op. cit.*, pp. 129–32.

14. T. Paine, *The Age of Reason, Part One* (1794); quoted in M. Foot and I. Kramnick (eds), *The Thomas Paine Reader* (Harmondsworth: Penguin, 1987), pp. 450–1.

15. See, for example, Cobbett's *Parliamentary History of England*, Vol. 36, cols 829–54 (May 24, 1802) (London: T. C. Hansard, 1820).

16. See B. Harrison, *Peaceable Kingdom. Stability and Change in Modern Britain* (Oxford: Oxford University Press, 1982), Chapter 2; I. Gilmour, *Riot, Risings and Revolution* (London: Hutchinson, 1992), Chapter 9.

17. For example: Prevention of Cruelty to Animals Act 1849; Cruelty to Animals Act 1854; Poisoned Flesh Prohibition Act 1864 (prohibiting the use of poisoned meat for the purpose of killing dogs and other animals); Drugging of Animals Act 1876; Cruelty to Animals Act 1876; Hare Preservation Act 1892; Injured Animals Act 1894; Cruelty to Wild Animals in Captivity Act 1900.

18. C. Darwin, *The Descent of Man and Selection in Relation to Sex* (London: John Murray, 1871); see also J. Rachels, *Created from Animals* (Oxford: Oxford University Press, 1990), pp. 147–64.

19. There is an enormous literature on this topic, of very variable quality. The following are amongst the most important texts: P. Carruthers, *The Animals Issue* (Cambridge: Cambridge University Press, 1992); S. Clark, *The Moral Status of Animals* (Oxford: Clarendon Press, 1977); M. Stamp Dawkins, *Animal Suffering* (London: Chapman and Hall, 1980); R. G. Frey, *Interests and Rights* (Oxford: Oxford University Press, 1980), *Rights, Killing and Suffering* (Oxford: Blackwell, 1983); R. Garner, *Animals, Politics and Morality* (Manchester: Manchester University Press, 1993); S. Godlovitch, R. Godlovitch and J. Harris (eds), *Animals, Men and Morals* (London: Gollancz, 1971); M. Leahy, *Against Liberation* (London: Routledge, 1991); A. Linzey, *Animal Rights* (London: SCM Press, 1976), *Christianity and the Rights of Animals* (London: SPCK, 1987), *Animal Theology* (London: SCM Press, 1994); M. Midgley, *Animals and Why They Matter* (Harmondsworth: Penguin, 1983); J. Rachels, *Created from Animals*, *op. cit.*; T. Regan, *The Case for Animal Rights* (London: Routledge, 1983); R. Rodd, *Biology, Ethics and Animals* (Oxford: Clarendon Press, 1990); B. Rollin, *Animal Rights and Human Morality* (New York: Prometheus Books, 1981), *The Unheeded Cry: Animal Consciousness, Animal Pain and Science* (Oxford: Oxford University

Press, 1990); S. Sapontzis, *Morals, Reason and Animals* (Philadelphia: Temple University Press, 1987); P. Singer, *Animal Liberation*, *op. cit.*

20. J. S. Kennedy, *The New Anthropomorphism* (Cambridge: Cambridge University Press, 1992).

21. R. G. Frey, *Interests and Rights*, *op. cit.*, Chapter VII.

22. R. Garner, *op. cit.*, pp. 16–17.

23. R. G. Frey, *Interests and Rights*, *op. cit.*, p. 127.

24. *Ibid.*, p. 169.

25. R. G. Frey, *Rights, Killing and Suffering*, *op. cit.*

26. J. Rawls, *A Theory of Justice* (Oxford: Oxford University Press, 1972); J. Narveson, On a case for animal rights (1987) 70 *Monist* 46; P. Carruthers, *op. cit.*

27. J. Rawls, *op. cit.*, pp. 504–12; quoted in P. A. B. Clarke and A. Linzey, *op. cit.*, pp. 154–6.

28. P. Carruthers, *op. cit.*, pp. 6–9.

29. *Ibid.*, pp. 106–7.

30. *Ibid.*, pp. 153–6.

31. *Ibid.*, p. 196.

32. R. Nozick, *Anarchy, State and Utopia* (Oxford: Blackwell, 1974), pp. 35–42; quoted in P. A. B. Clarke and A. Linzey, *op. cit.*, pp. 167–74.

33. M. Leahy, *op. cit.*, Chapter 6.

34. *Ibid.*, pp. 197–8.

35. P. Singer, *op. cit.*

36. H. Salt, *Animals' Rights* (1892) (London: Centaur Press, 1980).

37. *Ibid.*, p. 5.

38. *Ibid.*, p. 24.

39. T. Regan, *op. cit.* Note that Regan's argument is specifically restricted to mammalian animals of one year or more. While it is clear that a line has to be drawn somewhere, the one chosen does seem somewhat arbitrary, leaving as it does a significant proportion of the animal world outside its ambit. Regan does not make clear what he regards their moral status to be.

40. 'Speciesism' is a term coined by R. Ryder, *Victims of Science*, (London: Davis-Poynter, 1975), p. 16, to describe the practice of discriminating against an individual on the basis of its species.

41. T. Regan, *op. cit.*, p. 264.

42. *Ibid.*, pp. 327–9.

43. S. Jones, *The Language of Genes* (London: Flamingo, 1994), p. 38.

44. C. Darwin, *op. cit.*; quoted in D. M. Porter and P. W. Graham (eds), *The Portable Darwin* (Harmondsworth: Penguin, 1993), p. 330.

45. P. Carruthers, *op. cit.*, p. xi.

19

Environmental Rights: Taking the Environment Seriously?

Sionaidh Douglas-Scott

From space, we see a small and fragile ball dominated not by human activity and edifice but by a pattern of clouds, oceans, greenery and soils. Humanity's inability to fit its doings into that pattern is changing planetary systems, fundamentally. Many such changes are accompanied by life threatening hazards. This new reality, from which there is no escape, must be recognised – and managed.[1]

There is a great deal of controversy at present as to whether rights have any proper place in the management of this environmental reality. In particular, much of recent environmental ethics rejects the traditional human rights bias towards the individual, preferring to stress that nature has *intrinsic value*, which should be protected otherwise than by the enforcement of human rights. However, that it should be thought desirable to take a rights-based approach to the environment is, prima facie, intelligible. At least 50 national constitutions now contain human rights to the environment and there is a perception that some sort of right to the environment is forcing its way into international law.[2] Given the gravity and urgency of many of our environmental problems, which threaten human health and life, there is a need for an effective legal solution. Rights are supposedly strong things, not to be invoked lightly, or used when a weaker measure will do. They are superficially attractive ingredients in environmental regulation, which inevitably involves the balancing of very different interests. The insertion of rights into this balancing process introduces a feeling of safety, of strength, of (in Dworkin's famous metaphor) 'rights as trumps'. If we all have our environmental rights, then maybe the multinationals would not be able to buy their licence to pollute, and the dumping of toxic waste would have to stop. The promises held out by this admittedly overstated view are, of course, unfulfillable. The multinationals have their rights too, albeit different ones, so the trade-offs still have to be made. But, more importantly, rights are notoriously difficult to define, leading some to deny their existence and others to reject them as providing false comfort and misplaced ideology. However, in my mind, one of the most serious objections to rights, as they have so far found their way into the environmental context, is that they have done so in two radically different, contradictory forms, namely, in the form of a human right to the environment and in the form of rights inherent in the environment or in natural objects, themselves. To use the word this differently in the environmental context utterly debases its value.

TWO CONCEPTS OF RIGHTS

Traditional theory presents the notion of a right as protecting an interest that is of 'paramount importance' from political and legal abuse.[3] Although this analysis of rights does not tell us which interests will be considered sufficiently paramount to be protected in this way, the interests concerned are usually thought to be related to the vital needs and intrinsic dignity and worth of the individual.[4] It is certainly undeniable that many of the severest environmental problems, such as the Chernobyl disaster or global warming, do present a severe threat to fundamental human interests, such as life, health and well-being, not to mention those of the future generations who may inhabit the planet. But do we need to invoke some such thing as a right to a clean environment in order to address such a problem? There are particular disadvantages involved in introducing such a right,[5] particularly with regard to definition and enforcement, which lead one to believe that rights are no solution.

However, there is another view which holds that the *human* rights model is simply inadequate when it comes to protecting the biological world, because it is based on an anthropocentric view of the environment, with humans at centre stage, which (according to this view) is exactly where they should not be when it comes to environmental policy. Some environmentalists argue that humanity is only part of the total, interdependent planetary biosystem and that it is necessary for consistency to view *all* of the elements of that system as worthy of moral concern in themselves and not just as instrumentally valuable to us. This view may actually conflict with the human rights approach, in so far as it prioritizes environmental concern over human well-being. However, this holistic approach may also have a foundation in rights, albeit not human ones. In this case, the rights concerned are claims on behalf of the non-human world, which are based on the allegedly intrinsic value which these entities have. Not all who take the 'deep'[6] ecological view believe that actual rights can be claimed on behalf of the environment, although all believe that environmental regulation should be based on the intrinsic value of the natural world.

So, in the environmental context, there is a fundamental tension not only between those who believe that a rights model is the best way to advance environmental causes and those who do not, but also among those who accept rights as the correct basis of reasoning in this context. For it seems that if the notion of a right can be used by both those who believe in a human-centred right to the environment and also appropriated by those who believe in the rights of rocks and trees, they must mean something very different by the word 'right'. How significant is this for environmentalists? With the waters already this muddied, there might be something to be said for abandoning the use of rights altogether in the environmental debate as just too confusing.

This chapter will address some of the problems posed by the attempt to take a rights-based approach to environmental protection. First, I shall explore in greater depth the basis of the reasoning involved in the two approaches in an attempt to determine whether either of the views is coherent. This chapter will attempt to show that they are not, although I shall argue that there is some limited value in seeking to extend existing due process rights. Second, regardless of the internal contradictions associated with each of the views, I shall attempt to show that the two concepts of rights are in any case mutually irreconcilable and that it may be damaging to environmentalism to proceed on the basis of such radically different reasoning about rights. In brief, current thinking about rights does not take the environment seriously.

HUMAN RIGHTS TO THE ENVIRONMENT

There are certainly a number of reasons why it might be thought desirable to take a human rights approach to the environment. First, such an approach presents a strong claim which is theoretically immune from the lobbying and trade-offs which characterize bureaucratic decision-making. It also seems to give the applicant a different status. Joseph Sax, writing on the advantages of a rights-based regime for the environment, noted:

> The citizen who comes to an administrative agency comes essentially as a supplicant, requesting that somehow the public interest be interpreted to protect the environment values from which he benefits. The citizen who comes to court has quite a different status – he stands as a claimant of rights to which he is entitled.[7]

According rights is perceived as transforming the subject from, in Sax's words, a supplicant, to an individual who is treated with equal concern and respect to all others, even when it may be contrary to political expediency to do so. Second, the procedural dimensions of an environmental right, by ensuring participation in the democratic process, can provide access to justice in a way that standard domestic regulation or tort law cannot. Even if the introduction of environmental rights cannot dictate the desired result, it may have other legal effects, such as a liberalization of the standing rules, or a shifting of the burden of proof, transferring the burden on to those whose action may damage the environment. Third, a human rights approach may have some ripple-like effects, such as stimulating political action and debate on environmental issues. Fourth, rights need not become too static, unlike certain aspects of the common law. Some take the view that rights can be interpreted and reinterpreted creatively as issues and contexts change.[8] Finally, the introduction of rights into an arena can bring about changes in our language and action, even at a subconscious level. As Christopher Stone has pointed out:

> Part of the reason is that (rights) have meaning – vague but forceful – in the ordinary language, and the force of these meanings, inevitably infused in our thought, becomes part of a context against which the legal language of our contemporary 'legal rules' is interpreted . . . . There is, too, the fact that the vocabulary and expressions that are available to us influence and even steer our thought.[9]

However, there are also considerable disadvantages in taking the human rights approach. The most basic problem in this case is that of definition. Is the right substantive or procedural, individual or collective? If the right is to be a substantive one, then what should be its scope? Which aspects of the environment are to be protected and what degree of environmental change or degradation is to be permitted? And how are we to trade off certain factors against it such as the undesirable but commercially viable benefits of pollution? It is also not clear to what extent asserting a right may address the complex and often technical conditions of environmental regulation. There is a danger that rights, which by their very nature tend to the broad and abstract, will not dictate a concrete result. Thus our minds tend to be colonized by a misguided sense of the necessity of rights in this context, prompted perhaps by what A. N. Whitehead referred to as 'the fallacy of misplaced concreteness'. In sum, not all issues can be resolved in the 'simple' language of rights.

The Emergence of a Human Right to the Environment

To what extent is it legitimate to talk of an existing human right to the environment? It is undeniably emerging, both at international and national level. In 1974 Nobel Prize winner René Cassin[10] suggested that existing human rights protection be extended to the environment. However, the right to the environment, in whatever form, is still not to be found in most of the great post-War human rights conventions. Commentators usually point to the 1972 UN Stockholm Declaration on the Human Environment as being a source of such a right.[11] Principle 1 of the Declaration states: 'Man has the fundamental right to freedom, equality and adequate conditions of life, in an environment of quality that permits a life of dignity and well-being.' However, the Declaration is not legally binding, and, by itself, is insufficient to create such a right. However, the 1992 Rio Declaration reaffirms the Stockholm Declaration and builds upon it by a set of 27 principles which list environmental duties and emphasize the importance of sustainable development, although it does not actually contain an explicit right as such. Principle 1 of the Rio Declaration states that 'Human beings are at the centre of concerns for sustainable development. They are entitled to a healthy and productive life in harmony with nature.' Principle 4 states that 'environmental protection shall constitute an integral part of the development process'.[12]

Of the international human rights instruments, only the African Charter on Human and Peoples' Rights contains some sort of explicit environmental right. Article 24 of the Charter states: 'All peoples shall have the right to a general satisfactory environment favourable to their development'[13] (notably expressed as a peoples' right) although the Organization of American States has included a right to environment in Article 11 of its San Salvador Protocol ('Everyone shall have the right to live in a healthy environment and have access to basic public services').[14] Additionally, there is a reference made to environmental quality in Article 24 of the 1989 Convention on the Rights of the Child, which requires states to take appropriate measures to implement the child's right to health, 'taking into consideration the dangers and risks of environmental pollution'.[15] Further instruments which contain a right to the environment include the UNECE draft charter (adopted in October 1990) on environmental rights and obligations, which affirms the fundamental principle that everyone has a right to an environment adequate for their general health and well-being. The OECD has also suggested that a 'decent' environment should be recognized as one of the fundamental human rights, and UN GA Resolution 45/94 (1990) stated that 'all individuals are entitled to live in an environment adequate for their health and well-being' and called upon governments to enhance their efforts. At the European regional level, attempts to introduce human rights to the environment have not been so successful, with attempted additional protocols to the European Convention on Human Rights and attempts to amend the European Social Charter proving unsuccessful, partly through fears of watering down the European Convention. However, about ⅓ of all national constitutions contain rights to the environment, as do those of some states in the USA.

Just what does all of this amount to? Opinions vary at present as to whether there can be said to be any fundamental human right to the environment. Birnie and Boyle write that it is 'not yet possible to conclude that international law protects the right to a decent environment as such'[16] although they note that 'many states have recognised its importance in various forms, at national and international level'. Kiss and Shelton took the view that such a right is not yet in place,[17] although Gormley, writing in 1990[18] argues that it exists and that the Stockholm Declaration constitutes part of customary international law. As the Stockholm Declaration has recently been reconfirmed by the Rio Conference, there may be a stronger case for this argument. In any event, even if it can be said that such a right exists, there are still considerable problems regarding its actual nature and application which lead one to believe that it is not the panacea it may seem.

A New Substantive Right?

The growing number of instruments already mentioned seem to evidence the evolution of an autonomous right to live in a safe environment, even though the exact scope of such a right remains unclear. In 1989 the UN Sub-Commission on Prevention of Discrimination and Protection of Minorities of the Human Rights Commission resolved to study the relationship between the environment and human rights and appointed Fatma Ksentini as its Special Rapporteur. A preliminary report was delivered in 1991.[19] In part III of the report Ksentini considered whether a right to the environment could be said to exist and if so what its scope might be. Ksentini found that although many instruments have been adopted which could be used to strengthen environmental protection, the definition and content of these rights remains unclear. Ksentini suggested 'a new generation' of environmental rights because this 'would take up more completely the ecological challenges confronting mankind, while giving the beneficiaries of those rights the legal means of protection that any recognised right confers'. However, there would be considerable problems in accepting the preferred approach of the Rapporteur.

WHAT WOULD THE SCOPE OF SUCH A RIGHT BE?

There are many possible formulations of such a right. A variety of adjectives are used in national constitutional provisions. For example, the Constitution of Portugal declares the right to a 'healthy and ecologically balanced environment'. The Spanish Constitution goes further, requiring 'the right to enjoy an environment suitable for the development of the person'. Elsewhere, references are made to a 'clean', 'healthy', 'decent' or 'satisfactory' environment. The word 'sustainable' is sometimes added to the provisions. Nickel suggests that 'a narrow formulation focusing exclusively on human health and safety has the best chance of gaining acceptance as a genuine human right'[20] and proposes a 'right to a safe environment'. However, even this relatively focused form would provide difficulties for enforcement. What sort of standard would this require? Nickel proposes one which would be 'adequate for health and well being'. But such an approach has been criticized as overemphasizing human health and welfare at the expense of protecting the ecosystem itself. Additionally, all of the expressions of the right detailed above contain subjective terms and give very little idea of the sorts of measures that should be introduced to maintain them. How should observance of the right be ensured? By reacting to violations of it by the imposition of sanctions on those who breach it? Or by preventive action? Furthermore, to be effective, the right must be enforceable, not only against government agencies, but also against other parties (unlike the position under the European Convention on Human Rights, which has very little, if any, *Drittwirkung*). Therefore, the bare existence of such a right, even if entrenched in some constitution or human rights instrument, tells us little about how the right would be enforced in practice.

IS THE RIGHT TO BE EXPRESSED AS AN INDIVIDUAL OR AS A PEOPLES' SOLIDARITY RIGHT?

This is another major problem which has arisen in the context of a human right to the environment. UN Special Rapporteur Ksentini submitted in her preliminary report that the right to environment could not be reduced to the right of the individual to claim an environment of quality, and nor could it be separated from the problem of development. She therefore proposed a right of solidarity. So far, where the right has found expression it has taken the form of either an individual or peoples' right. As noted above, it is expressed as a peoples' right in the African Charter, although, for example, in Article II, section 2 of the Illinois Constitution it is expressed as an individual right: 'Each person shall have the right to a healthful environment'. What difference does this make? Solidarity or peoples' rights (sometimes called 'third-generation' rights) have been around for some time (the right to self-determination in the International Covenant on Civil and Political Rights is a good example) and their supposed distinctive feature is that, in order for them to be implemented, cooperation is required by all parts of society. The people possessing the right and those subjected to it are the same. Environmental harms are caused by thousands of actions, some of them relatively small, such as owning a car, and can be prevented by us all, and thus all must cooperate to ensure observance of the right. It seems therefore to make sense in this context to talk of a peoples' right rather than an individual right. Thus, this third generation of rights places rightholders solidly in their community or environment, displacing their importance as individuals, and there is thought to be something satisfactory about this, for such a right incorporates the commitments of the community into our rights discourse.

The *individualism* of human rights has been strongly criticized for some time. For example, Karl Marx wrote that the liberty rights vaunted by the revolutionaries in France and America represented a view of man as 'an isolated monad, withdrawn into himself' founded on 'the separation of man from man'.[21] More recently, classical theories of rights have been attacked as placing too much stress on the autonomy[22] of the individual, at the expense of the ties which the individual has with his or her community.[23] Theories of group or communal rights naturally can escape the charge of being too individualistic and isolating. But they are open to the challenge that such rights are not an intelligible concept. Why? Scepticism about peoples' rights is mainly premised on a view which sees rights as adhering only to individuals by virtue of the interests that those individuals have *qua* individuals. Neil MacCormick has written that 'rights concern the enjoyment of goods by individuals separately, not simply as a member of a collectivity enjoying a diffuse common benefit in which all participate in indistinguishable and unassignable shares.'[24] Kymlicka in turn has written that 'groups have no moral claim to wellbeing independently of their members – groups just aren't the right sort of beings to have moral status'.[25] The fundamental problem is that one of the main objectives of human rights is to place limits on the pursuit of community policies or goals. If we then create communal rights we run the danger of reclassifying as rights just the very thing which individual rights are supposed to have a power to override in certain circumstances. In this context Ronald Dworkin has written:

> If we now say that society has the right to preserve whatever sort of environment the majority wishes to live in, and we mean that these are the sorts of rights that provide justification for overruling any rights against the Government that may conflict, then we have anni-hilated the latter rights.[26]

Shelton, however, attacks the notion of third-generation rights on quite another basis. Her claim is that these so-called rights do not require the communal effort which is seen as their distinguishing feature. She claims that isolated violations of civil and political rights also affect society in a way going far beyond the individual rights-holder. Thus Shelton writes, 'a torture victim who achieves a remedy sets a precedent which could help to deter future violations, thus affecting all other actual and poten-tial torture victims'. In this regard, 'solidarity rights differ only in degree. While environmental harms more frequently occur with equal force over a wide area, non-"solidarity" rights violations also may have a general impact by producing a "chilling effect".'[27] She thus seems to see the alleged differentiation between third-generation and other types of rights as irrelevant, claiming that any human right will impose both affirmative and negative duties on the state and on its citizens.

What is the import of all of this? This discussion, of course, reflects a certain level of disagreement about what rights actually are. But in this context, discord over the exact nature of the right to the environment is an unfortunate indication of its questionable status and plays into the hands of those who wish to claim that it is not a 'real' right at all.[28]

THE ENFORCEMENT OF EXISTING RIGHTS TO THE ENVIRONMENT

Problems do not only exist at the definitional stage. A closer look at the application of existing rights to the environment indicates why such rights can provide a false hope. A couple of provisions in the USA pro-vide a good starting point. The Michigan Environmental Protection Act was originally enacted in 1971, and although it does not contain an actual right to environmental quality it has an extremely generous scope, pro-viding that an action may be brought against anyone who 'has or is likely to pollute, impair or destroy the air, water or other natural resources'. Section 1202(1) grants standing to any member of the public to sue government agencies and other members of the public: 'any person, part-nership, corporation, association, organisation or other legal entity may maintain an action'. Furthermore, the Act provides that the court may determine the reasonableness of any standards established by regulation and that, should the court find the standard unreasonable, it may adopt its own. The Act also reverses the burden of proof so that defendants must establish that their conduct was reasonable and 'consistent with the promotion of public health, safety and welfare in the light of the state's paramount concern for the protection of its natural resources from pol-lution, impairment or destruction' (section 1203(1)). However, although this statute significantly increases the opportunities for litigants to protect the environment, its effects have proved disappointing. Sax, the original drafter of the legislation, wrote that 'nothing that has occurred under the Act has approached the sort of big-time test litigation with which the legal literature is generally concerned'.[29] Elsewhere the comment has been made that 'Nowhere . . . is a connection between the Act and any large scale improvement in environmental quality demonstrated.'[30] And in the same article, the author, commenting pessimistically on this statute and its sister, The Minnesota Environmental Rights Act (a piece of legislation modelled on the Michigan Environmental Protection Act) wrote:

> The literature about environmental legislation has generally ignored the conservatism of many state court judges, as if they were somehow unable rather than unwilling to abolish the traditional doctrinal obstacles in environmental litigation . . . . So far . . . in both Michigan and Minnesota the role of Rights Act litigation has been essentially peripheral.

Nor have environmental rights fared any better under the state constitu-tions of the USA. Although quite a few of the states do have provisions dealing with environmental protection, in many cases these are aspira-tional only, or at least unenforceable in the absence of further legislation. However, Article I, s. 27 of the Pennsylvania constitution has been the basis of litigation. Section 27 provides:

> The people have a right to clean air, pure water, and to the preser-vation of the natural, scenic, historic and aesthetic values of the environment. Pennsylvania's public natural resources are the com-mon property of all the people, including generations yet to come. As trustees of these resources, the commonwealth shall conserve and maintain them for the benefit of all people.

This is a notably broad provision, incorporating the right as a peoples' right and also attempting to serve the interests of future generations.

Section 27 was considered in *Commonwealth of Pennsylvania* v. *National Gettysburg Battlefield Tower*.[31] In this case the state attorney general sought to enjoin the construction of a 307 foot tower in a private field next to the Gettysburg National Military Park. The developer planned to charge the public for admission to view the battlefield. At first instance the injunction was denied on the basis that the state had failed to provide 'clear and convincing' evidence that harm would result. The state's appeal also eventually failed in the Pennsylvania Supreme Court, but on a different basis. Two of the justices considered section 27 too vague 'to define the values which the amendment seeks to protect and to establish procedures by which the use of private property can be regulated to protect those values'. Another two justices were supportive of this reasoning. Thus there seemed to be some resistance to the recognition of a substantive right to environmental quality, even given the explicit language of section 27.[32]

In England, judicial interpretation has been no more promising. The senior judiciary here have been every bit as conservative as their North American brethren. There is no substantive right to a healthy environment under English law and interpretations of other provisions have not, until recently, held out much promise for what the judges would do with such a right. To name but one case, in *Ex parte Rose Theatre Company*,[33] Schiemann J had to consider an application by the Theatre Trust Company concerning the refusal of the secretary of state to schedule the site of the Rose Theatre as an ancient monument. He held that as the minister's power under the Ancient Monuments and Archaeological Areas Act 1979 was specifically to be exercised in the public interest, no individual or company had the right to challenge his decision.

These cases are of course just a few selected from a large corpus, not all of which are so environmentally unfriendly.[34] However, existing attempts to enforce or apply any sort of environmental rights have proved disappointing and do raise the question of whether environmental rights are the best way forward.

Two conclusions may be drawn from an examination of the right to the environment so far. First, the right itself is extremely indeterminate, proving very difficult to define and stalling on some tricky conceptual problems which beset rights theory generally. Second, even where it has been introduced it has fared none too well, suffering from the vagaries of judicial interpretation and conservatism.

RIGHTS OF FUTURE GENERATIONS

We have it in our power to make the world an extremely unpleasant place for our descendants by the actions we now take regarding the environment. The issue of environmental rights, unlike most other sorts of rights, has this difficult temporal factor. Do future generations also have rights to a healthy environment? Some commentators[35] argue that inter-generational equity already features in environmental law, and, indeed, references are made to future generations in various treaties and declarations. The 1946 International Convention for the Regulation of Whaling is concerned with the preservation of whale stocks for future generations. The policy underlying a number of pollution treaties is that of preventing irreversible harm. A generational perspective also underlies the Stockholm (especially Principle 6) and Rio Declarations. It clearly is not acceptable to follow Sir Francis Bacon's proposal, made in other times, that 'men must pursue the things that are just in present and leave the future to Divine Providence', given that the future seems to be less a matter of providence than of what we do now. But there is still a problem in determining what sort of consideration to give future generations in our management of the environment. It seems too much to give equal regard to the possible interests of future generations when the stringent environmental regulation this might require is bound to conflict with our obligations to existing persons, for whom rapid growth may be a greater priority than environmental protection. However, I am sure that the introduction of rights into this process only complicates things quite unnecessarily. There is a considerable conceptual problem in granting rights to remote and unidentifiable beings not yet in existence. Can a merely 'potential' person have rights or interests of any sort?[36] It seems that the most one can say is that they have rights contingent on their coming into existence. I think it is better to do without rights altogether in this context and to proceed, say, with the more flexible concept of sustainable development. Sustainable development, whereby global economic growth must be sufficient to meet current needs while allowing future generations to meet their needs, has become something of a buzz phrase recently, employed by the Brundtland Commission in its 1987 report, and finding its way into the EC Treaty as an overall Community objective in Articles 2 and 130U. This leaves room for debate about how intergenerational equity may be achieved, while avoiding the obscure metaphysics associated with the rights of future persons. In this context, the language of rights is more confusing than it is helpful to the environment.

Existing Human Rights

Given the difficulties involved in defining a right to the environment of some sort, it may be thought preferable to use existing human rights provisions to fight environmental wrongs. After all, a healthy environment is very often a prerequisite to the enjoyment of existing rights, such as the rights to life, health or privacy. Two cases give limited support to this sort of approach. In the *Yanomami*[37] case, the Inter-American Commission on Human Rights found that the Brazilian government had violated rights to life, health and well-being by not taking any measures to prevent environmental harm which had led to the loss of life, cultural property and identity among the Yanomami peoples. The importance of this case is that the Commission appeared to be affirming a *positive* duty of states to ensure the enjoyment of rights under the American Convention. Such duties may of course include steps to prevent environmental degradation. Likewise, in the *Velasquez Rodriguez*[38] case, the Inter-American Court held that the duty to prevent violations of existing rights 'includes all those means of a legal, political and cultural nature that promote the protection of human rights'.

In the *Port Hope*[39] case, residents claimed that 200,000 tons of radioactive waste left at a nearby nuclear waste disposal site in Port Hope, Canada, constituted a serious health risk in breach of Article 6(1) of the International Covenant on Civil and Political Rights. The UN Human Rights Committee dismissed the claim (because the residents had failed to exhaust local remedies) but commented that the case 'raised serious issues with regard to the obligations of States to protect human life'.

Attempts to assert environmental rights through the medium of the European Convention on Human Rights have been less successful. The *Powell and Rayner*[40] case concerned the noise pollution levels near Heathrow airport, which the applicants claimed infringed their right to privacy. Although the European Court held that noise pollution can interfere with one's right to privacy, because it can affect the quality of one's home and family life, the Court went on to find that privacy rights must be balanced against broader community interests.

Another case decided under the European Convention, *Fredin* v. *Sweden*,[41] although important on account of the extensive discussion by the European Court of the relation between environmental protection and the Convention, underlines another problem with environmental rights. They conflict with other sorts of rights. The applicant claimed that his property rights had been infringed by the unavailability of judicial remedies in Sweden following the Swedish government's revocation of his permit to extract gravel from his land. The Court stated that 'in today's society the protection of the environment is increasingly an important consideration' and that the state enjoyed 'a wide margin of appreciation with regard to choosing the means of enforcement and to ascertaining whether the consequences of enforcement are justified in the general interests for the purpose of achieving the object of the law in question'.

These cases raise the issue of limitations on the exercise of human rights. Few, if any, rights can be absolute ones. Environmental rights are no exception. Many of the rights under the European Convention contain substantial limitation clauses, and cases such as *Powell and Rayner* show that there is considerable scope for states to argue the 'broader community interest' limitation and an unwillingness on the part of the courts to interfere. Once again, one has the impression that a rights-based approach is not the best way forward.

A Procedural Environmental Right?

Faced with the problems involved in defining a substantive environmental right, some have preferred to abandon this notion altogether and concentrate only on procedural rights. This approach has certain distinct advantages. It avoids the pitfalls involved in attempting to set appropriate standards to be maintained through a substantive right, which invariably involve extremely subjective value judgments. The adoption of substantive rights also permits a great deal of variation from area to area, thus making it extremely difficult to arrive at a single, binding, international substantive right to a decent environment. With procedural rights this can be avoided. A procedural approach provides environmental protection by way of democracy. It ensures that those who have to live with the consequences of environmental degradation will be able to have their say in how, if and when it should occur. This is done by guaranteeing them certain rights to information, participation and review of environmental regulation.

Uninformed communities cannot adequately protect their livelihood and natural resources. A UN ESCOR document[42] on popular participation stated:

> Denied even basic information about the projects that affect them, the peoples of the Third World are cast into the role of passive recipients of aid, and more often than not become the victims of its arbitrary and ill-judged effects. In promoting this lack of accountability and excluding the public from any involvement in decision-making, these organisations are institutionalising undemocratic forces and reinforcing the very economic structures of

exploitation and repression that are responsible for the poverty and underdevelopment they are trying to alleviate.

The Rio Declaration, Principle 10, is a recent encapsulation of the view that procedural rights are an essential part of environmental regulation:

> [E]nvironmental issues are best handled with the participation of all concerned citizens, at the relevant level. At the national level, each individual shall have appropriate access to information concerning the environment that is held by public authorities, including information on hazardous materials and activities in their communities, and the opportunity to participate in the decision-making processes. States shall facilitate and encourage public awareness and participation by making information widely available. Effective access to judicial and administrative proceedings, including redress and remedy shall be provided.

RIGHTS TO INFORMATION AND PARTICIPATION

The right of freedom of expression and its corollary, the freedom to receive information, are fundamental rights recognized in most international human rights documents. Article 10 of the European Convention on Human Rights guarantees freedom to receive information. Until fairly recently, the exercise of these rights was not thought to entail a duty on the part of governments to provide information sought by the public. However, the European Court of Human Rights, in the *Sunday Times*[43] case, interpreted Article 10 as 'guaranteeing not only the freedom of the press to inform the public, but also the right of the public to be properly informed', especially where that information related to public health and safety.

There are many other international instruments which contain provisions concerning public access to information. For example, Article 6 of the EEC Council Directive 85/337 provides that states should make public all requests for authorization of a public or private project which might significantly affect the environment. Council Directive 90/313 provides that public authorities must make information relating to the environment available to any person on request (implemented in the UK by the Environmental Information Regulations (SI 1992 3240)). Additionally, Article 16 of the ASEAN Agreement on the Conservation of Nature and Natural Resources requires the widest possible circulation of information on the significance of conservation measures and their relationship with sustainable development objectives. The considerable amount of international documents which contain such rights are

evidence for an evolving customary international law right of the public
to information. (Whether there is a right to information about environmental disasters or accidents is less clear.[44])

There are fewer rights to participation, although, for example, Article
25 of the International Covenant on Civil and Political Rights provides
that 'every citizen shall have the right and opportunity . . . to take part in
the conduct of public affairs, directly or through freely chosen representatives'. However, there is an increasing recognition that states owe
informational duties to individuals within and *outside* of their borders. So,
for example, the 1991 UN Convention on Environmental Impact Assessment in a Transboundary Context requires states to provide an
opportunity for public participation in environmental impact assessment
procedures. The state must take account of the assessment and the views
of the individuals in the relevant area.

RIGHTS OF COMPLAINT/JUDICIAL REDRESS

Essential to give full effect to procedural environmental rights is the
ability to obtain review of decisions concerning the environment.
Principle 23 of the World Charter for Nature[45] states that

> all persons, in accordance with their national legislation, shall have
> the opportunity to participate, individually or with others, in the
> formulation of decisions of direct concern to their environment,
> and shall have access to means of redress when their environment
> has suffered damage or degradation.

Rights to prosecute and fairly liberal rights of standing exist in some
national legal systems (for example, under the Michigan Act already
mentioned anyone has standing) but there can be considerable problems
where individuals are affected outside of the boundaries of the state
where the damage was caused, and this tends to be a recurrent feature of
environmental problems. Extended procedural rights may conflict with
traditional notions of state sovereignty. However, under the 1974 Nordic
Convention on the Protection of the Environment, individuals of different nationalities are given full procedural rights and remedies before the
courts on an equal basis, and the UNECE draft charter on environmental
rights makes explicit provision for equal access. Some of the international
human rights charters contain provisions concerning equality (e.g.
Article 7 of the Universal Declaration, Article 26 of the Civil and Political
Rights Covenant) which might be of use in this context, but the
European Convention on Human Rights contains no *general* prohibition
on discrimination. Furthermore, equal access does not, of course, require

a member state to create new remedies, only to apply existing ones indiscriminately.

EC law is becoming an extremely important source of environmental rights and remedies and there are problems with individual redress here too. EC law is most likely to be relevant when a member state performs an act which conflicts with a provision of EC environmental law (e.g. as with the UK's failure to comply with certain aspects of the EEC Directive 76/160 on the quality of bathing water). However, it can prove difficult for individuals to obtain standing under EC law to challenge such unlawful member state action. Only the Commission may commence an action against a member state for violation of EC law in the European Court of Justice under Article 169 of the EC Treaty, although individuals may of course complain to the Commission (a cheap but lengthy process). It may also be difficult for individuals who wish to rely on EC law to obtain standing in the national courts, as there may be no relevant cause of action, or the relevant EC Directive may not be directly effective in the national courts. Individual rights to challenge EC acts in the European Court of Justice are even more limited.

However, individual procedural rights are expanding with the European Court of Justice's imaginative development of the doctrines of direct effect in cases such as *Von Colson* and *Marleasing*, and state liability for damages for breach of EC law in the *Francovich* case.[46] In principle, at least, EC law is *becoming* a promising future source of due process rights, which is significant, given the range of EC environmental law.

The due process approach to environmental rights will not solve all of our environmental problems, and nor will it prevent harm occurring in future. In particular, a right to information does not ensure that either the information or the procedures for obtaining it are intelligible. A right to participation, of course, also falls short of having a right to a particular decision, especially where the other party has substantive rights which would dictate a decision in his or her favour. However, this approach seeks to ensure observance of values which lie at the basis of our fundamental rights and arguably does so more effectively because it is not open to the challenges of vagueness, indeterminacy and unenforceability which beset a substantive right to the environment. It also seeks to ensure that participation in environmental decision-making is open to all and hopefully also ensures that all are treated with equal concern and respect in this process.

Regretfully, I would suggest that the traditional human rights approach is not the best means we can find of protecting the environment. Such a right to a good environment proves extremely difficult to define and to pin down in such a way that it can be anything other than aspirational, thus providing fuel for both those who are sceptical about the existence of such rights and those who do not wish to dilute the worth of existing rights. Additionally, it suffers from temporal and geographical problems not present in other rights, such as those arising from the needs of future generations and the territorial scope of state obligations. The differing needs of developing and developed states also raise issues as to whether there is a common approach to the sorts of measures needed to enforce such a right in any case. These factors, coupled with a further conceptual problem regarding the right's questionable status as both an individual and a people's right, make one deeply sceptical as to the possibility of ever reaching a concept coherent enough to be of any value. Add to this the disappointments carried over from failures with existing rights, such as, for example, the lack of, or contradictory inter-pretations of, the US Bill of Rights by the US Supreme Court, and there is a real issue as to whether abstract environmental rights are at all use-ful in bringing about social change. I think that, except on the very limited level of the procedural right suggested above, they are not, although they do have some value in heightening public perceptions.

All of this is not to deny that the protection of the environment is one of the most pressing concerns of our time and that serious legal measures are needed to effect it. It is simply to claim that a human rights-based approach is not the best way of going about this. The issue of other more effective means of protection of the environment is outside the scope of this chapter, but one relevant question remains to be considered. Does a biocentric approach, based on the legal rights of *natural objects*, fare any better?

LEGAL RIGHTS FOR NATURAL OBJECTS?

The typical (at least until recently) view among Western philosophers is that only human beings are the proper objects of moral concern and that only humans may have rights. However, in *A Sand Country Almanac*, pub-lished in 1949, the ecologist, Aldo Leopold, suggested that not only human beings but plants, animals and nature itself have moral rights. Leopold argued the need for a new ethic which would cover our relationships not only with other humans but also with non-humans and indeed with nature itself. Leopold proposed that his 'land ethic' would change 'the role of Homo Sapiens from conqueror of the land community to plain member and citizens of it'. It would judge our relationship with the non-human world as 'right when it tends to preserve the integrity, stability and beauty of the biotic community', and 'wrong when it tends otherwise'. For many, present environmental problems are in fact the result of what is per-ceived as orthodox Judaeo-Christian arrogance towards nature. Evidence for this attitude is adduced from a key passage in the book of Genesis, in which man is told to 'fill the earth and subdue it, and have dominion over the fish of the sea and over the birds of the air and over every living thing'.[47] (However, the 'dominion' view is not accepted by all. Some writers see in the Judaeo-Christian tradition a very different atti-tude towards Nature – that of stewardship, with humans being entrusted with the duty to preserve the earth's beauty. This view was expressed by Sir Matthew Hale, who wrote that, 'the end of Man's Creation was, that he should be God's Viceroy . . . Steward, Villicus, Bailiff or Farmer'.[48]) However, whatever the biblical roots, what is key is that Leopold's new 'land ethic', and those who followed him, focus on an attitude of respect for nature which is not based on its instrumental value to humans.

The concern of the 'deep'[49] ecologists has not spread very widely beyond the environmental ethics field, and although it has been embraced by quite a few philosophers and ecologists it is harder to find support among lawyers, and in particular to find much evidence of it in legislation. Most environmental legislation really does seem to be here to serve the interests of humans and not those of nature itself, should nature be thought capable of having them. The earliest examples of any-thing that could remotely be called environmental legislation in Britain were passed in response to public health problems caused by the Industrial Revolution and certainly, in Britain at least, until relatively recently, the focus has been on health and safety matters, with a shift only over the past 20 years towards the control of pollution. However, the Environmental Protection Act 1990 does introduce the notion of environmental harm, defining it as 'harm to health, or *ecological systems*'.[50] Under international law, the position is similar. Older treaties tend to stress that human life and benefit to mankind are the essential criteria (e.g. 1946 Whaling Convention) but there is more recent evidence that international law is beginning to recognize the intrinsic value of natural objects (e.g. 1959 Antarctic Treaty, 1991 Protocol to Antarctic Treaty on Environmental Protection). The World Charter for Nature, for example, states that 'every form of life is unique, warranting respect regardless of its worth to man'. The attitude of respect for nature also recently found support from a different source, when, in 1990, Pope John Paul stated that world peace was threatened not only by the arms race and war but also by 'a lack of respect for nature'. However, such references still remain the exception. The 1972 Stockholm Declaration on the Human Environment does not take this view: 'The natural resources of the earth, including the air, water, land, and fauna . . . must be safeguarded for the benefit of present and future generations.'

The Mineral King Lawsuit – Thinking the Unthinkable?

However, exceptionally perhaps, the view that natural objects should have legal rights found very strong support in the legal world in a series of articles[51] which appeared in the early 1970s, and in particular in Christopher Stone's 'Should trees have standing?' Stone was partly prompted to write his article by the infamous Mineral King lawsuit and the background to its publication is worth relaying. The US Forest Service had granted a permit to Walt Disney Enterprises Inc. to 'develop' Mineral King Valley, a wilderness in the California Sierra Nevada mountains, by the construction of motels, restaurants and leisure facilities. The Sierra Club applied for an injunction, claiming that the project would affect the area's aesthetic and ecological balance. The Ninth Circuit Court of Appeals rejected the suit on the basis that the Sierra Club had no standing to bring the case in question. The Sierra Club had been granted certiorari by the US Supreme Court and it was, in Stone's mind,

> the needed case, a ready-made vehicle to bring to the Court's attention the theory I was developing ... If I could get the courts thinking about the park itself as a jural person ... the notion of nature having rights would here make a significant operational difference.[52]

Although, in *Sierra Club* v. *Morton*,[53] the Supreme Court upheld the Ninth Circuit, Stone's theory was, in fact, reflected in the dissents of Justices Douglas, Blackmun and Brennan, Justice Douglas writing:

> Contemporary public concern for protecting nature's ecological equilibrium should lead to the conferral of standing upon environmental objects to sue for their own preservation ... This suit would therefore be more properly labelled as *Mineral King* v. *Morton*.[54]

One still has to ask whether Stone (and, for that matter, even the three dissenting Justices) is right. It is one thing to require that we respect nature. It is quite another to grant it rights. Stone suggests that 'it is not inevitable, nor is it wise, that natural objects should have no right to seek redress on their own behalf'.[55] But the basis of Stone's reasoning, and that of others who support such a rights thesis, is questionable. Stone submits that throughout legal history, the accordance of legal rights has involved what at the time is perceived to be the unthinkable. He writes: 'This is partly because until the rightless thing receives its rights, we cannot see it as anything but a *thing* for the use of us'.[56] We thus fail to see that natural objects have any moral worth, seeking only to manipulate them for our benefit. Stone's analysis captures something of the *evolving* nature of rights, which have certainly developed beyond the seventeenth- and eighteenth-century notion of individual liberties. However, Stone never reveals why the natural environment should have a moral claim. He argues that rights have been extended to women and ethnic minorities, which would have seemed unthinkable in the past. But this argument does not provide support for his claim, for people and plants are really not comparable. However, determining why people and plants are not comparable makes us think about what it is that makes an entity capable of having rights.

Autonomy-Based Theories of Rights

One view is that only human beings are capable of having rights because only human beings have the capacity for moral autonomy. Moral autonomy connotes the ability to act as a moral agent, to be capable of understanding moral principles. This view is partially derived from the Kantian position, which holds that only rational agents deserve moral consideration. H. J. McCloskey, a supporter of this view, wrote that 'it is the capacity for moral autonomy ... that is basic to the possibility of possessing a right'.[57] If moral autonomy *is* a necessary condition for possessing a right, then it would seem that only humans can qualify, for moral autonomy requires us to have certain critical capacities, such as self-awareness, or the ability to reason and accept responsibility for action. This view of what it is to possess rights stresses the individuality of the rights-holder – an autonomous person able to claim or waive his or her rights as he or she pleases but, in any case, able to calculate the impact of his or her own decision. The autonomy-based view is not, however, entirely satisfactory, and nor does it accord with all our intuitions about what it is to have rights. On the one hand, it posits the rights-holder as a rather isolated individual, apart from the rest of the community, a view which has been rejected by those such as Martha Minow, who suggest that rights are the product of an overlapping relationship between the individual and the community.[58] Furthermore, even if we only limit our consideration to humans, we may feel that those who are most in need of their rights are those who are not fully autonomous, liable to abuse and thus most in need of the protection that rights can give – typically the mentally retarded, children, and the very old. And yet if we regard moral autonomy as the *sine qua non* for the possession of rights, we must necessarily exclude them. We are thus faced with the choice between abandoning this basis of our reasoning for ascribing rights or denying rights to a whole sector. It might be said that persons within these groups are already denied the status of rights-holders – that children and the mentally ill or retarded are in any case not in possession of the full set of rights that most citizens should possess. They cannot vote, their rights of movement are limited, and indeed most of the civil and political rights are meaningless to them. However, I prefer to maintain that, in principle, at least, rights should adhere to all humans, regardless of whether they are capable of understanding what rights actually are, so an autonomy-based theory is not going to do the job I want.[59]

Rights as Protected Interests

How can we do better than an autonomy-based theory? We might try instead to claim that the sorts of beings which can have rights are not necessarily autonomous ones but are those which can possess interests. This theory holds that a right is an interest which is protected, usually by the imposition of a duty on another person or persons.[60] Joel Feinberg puts forward the following reasons for supporting this view of rights:

> (1) because a right holder must be capable of being represented and it is impossible to represent a being that has no interests, and (2) because a right holder must be capable of being a beneficiary in his own person, and a being without interests is a being that is incapable of being harmed or benefited, having no good or sake of its own.[61]

In this context, of course, this conception of rights simply raises a further issue – who or what can have interests and, in particular, can nature have interests?

Sentience seems to be a good place to start. Creatures that can feel pain clearly have an interest in avoiding it. This capacity to have conscious experiences is seen by some animal liberationists as a key reason for according rights to animals.[62] In Bentham's words: 'the question is not, Can they reason? nor Can they talk? but Can they suffer?'[63] This sentience might be a reason for according at least some animals some kinds of rights, such as the right to life, or the right not to suffer undue pain.[64] But does it get us to Stone's position of claiming rights for trees and other natural objects? I think not. To attribute rights to a being is to say something about the importance of protecting its interests. But do trees or rocks actually have any interests? Surely it does not make any sense to suppose that something could have interests of its own unless it has some form of consciousness, i.e. a mental life as well as a physical life.

Ronald Dworkin takes this view, commenting:

> Nor is it enough, for something to have interests that it be alive and in the process of developing into something more mature – it is not against the interests of a baby carrot that it be picked early and brought to the table as a delicacy.[65]

Similarly, Joel Feinberg comments:

> plants are not the sorts of beings that have their 'own sakes', despite the fact that they have biological propensities. Having no conscious wants or goals of their own, trees cannot know satisfaction or frustration, pleasure or pain. Hence there is no possibility of kind or cruel treatment of trees. In these morally crucial aspects, trees differ from the higher species of animals.[66]

Some commentators take issue with Feinberg for holding that plants cannot have a good of their own, maintaining that the latent tendencies, direction of growth and natural fulfilments which they display are quite sufficient to show that they do. Even if we accept this view, conceding that living organisms can have a good of their own, this does not help advance the cause of those who want to claim rights or interests on behalf of natural objects. If something is to have interests, there must surely be, as Dworkin and Feinberg maintain, some sort of awareness, however elementary, of those interests or some sort of consciousness. I think, all in all, these arguments are enough to dismiss Stone's legal rights for trees, and to show that, however much we respect Stone's intentions, according rights to trees is not the best way to fulfil them.

Intrinsic Value

Some writers have sought to avoid this vexed issue altogether and to advance a different but related claim, namely, that, regardless of whether plants and trees can have interests, they have *intrinsic (or inherent) value*[67] and this is a morally relevant fact. What does it mean to say that something has intrinsic value? I cannot put it better than Jeremy Waldron:

> If we assert that trees have intrinsic value we are saying that there are ultimate ends in the world beyond humans and their experiences: that it is objectively a bad thing if a tree is killed, not because anything is lost thereby, but because the universe is a poorer place on that account. Something that was alive and growing is so no longer.[68]

This notion of intrinsic value seems roughly to correspond with the attitude of respect for nature which is now finding its way into various bits
of environmental legislation cited earlier, although, unfortunately, the
concept is not always used in the same sense. Sometimes, this terminology just seems to be used when an attempt is made to introduce a
notion of environmental harm even in the absence of any harm to
humans. However, the concept of intrinsic value is sometimes used in a
more extreme sense to the effect that natural objects have this value quite
independently of whether any human beings are doing any valuing.
Does this latter, more extreme view make any sense? The deep ecologists
clearly think that it does and that we should recognize that humans are
not central in the scheme of the universe but only one small part of the
biotic community. There is one familiar argument which proponents of
this view use, which takes the form of a thought experiment. Imagine
you are the last person on earth and that there is absolutely no chance of
any further human life on the planet or of a visit from extra-terrestrials
who are capable of benefiting from any of the earth's natural beauties.
You are about to die from a deadly virus and you have it within your
power to destroy the earth. Would you destroy it? Attfield and Regan
claim that one would not in fact destroy the planet, in spite of the fact
that no sentient being will derive any further profit from it. Thus the
environment cannot be of instrumental value only. The philosopher,
Mary Anne Warren, using a variant of this hypothetical case writes:

> If we tend to think that it would . . . certainly be better to allow the
> plants to survive than to render the earth utterly lifeless . . . then we
> do not really believe that it is only sentient – let alone only human
> – beings that have inherent value.[69]

There is one problem with this view, which is that it is difficult to imagine
any system of value existing independently of the human beings who
value. The very notion of value seems to presuppose some rational
notion of the self as a valuing subject.[70] It really is impossible to escape
from an anthropocentric ethic, as the deep ecologists suggest we do,
because all ethics must be anthropocentric to the extent that it can only
be prescribed and consciously followed by humans.

CONCLUSION

If by the intrinsic value of the environment we simply mean that the environment should be respected because it is something of value in its own right, independently of any use it has for us, because nature can be majestic and beautiful, and because it really is a shame if we spoil vast areas of natural habitat, then surely this ethic is something which should be and already is being, as noted above, incorporated into environmental legislation. But this is a completely different matter from assigning the environment rights. To accord rights to trees and plants is simply an example of conceptually muddled thinking, by applying to natural objects the concepts which we use to regulate human life in communal society. Rights are the legal fictions we use to mould society together. It makes no sense to apply them to entities which are not only on the margins of that society but outside of it altogether. Using rights in this way only damages the strength and value they have in other contexts, and makes us wonder if the term can ever be used meaningfully. However, to take this view does *not* mean that we should not respect the environment or deny any duties regarding it.

However, there is one way in which Stone's theory can prove of benefit to the environment. Stone's intended practical effect of according legal rights to natural objects is that a guardianship approach be taken to nature, whereby concerned groups should be able to have standing to sue on behalf of the environment, to prevent its being harmed. Stone is right in saying that traditional litigation is not well placed to take account of harm to the environment as such. As he writes, 'the traditional way . . . has been to strike some sort of balance regarding the economic hardships on *human beings*'.[71] Stone goes on to illustrate his argument for personifying the environment using a welfare economics viewpoint, rightly stating that every legal economic system should be structured so as to confront us with the full cost of activities to society but that traditional legal institutions have a difficult time catching the full costs, particularly the environmental ones. He claims that natural objects should be able to prove the full cost of damage to them:

> By doing so, we in effect make the natural object, through its guardian, a jural entity competent to gather up these fragmented and otherwise unrepresented damage claims, and press them before the court even where, for legal or practical reasons, they are not going to be pressed by traditional class action plaintiffs.[72]

There is nothing that, as Stone writes, even 'the most unremittant human chauvinist' could quarrel with here.

A great deal of tortuous philosophical reasoning can be avoided if, instead of taking Stone's route to this result, we admit that while only human beings can effectively participate in legal systems, environmental harm should be taken account of both at the legislation stage and by assuring procedures whereby natural objects can be considered in the context of litigation. Stone's main policy thrust seems to be the extension of the Environmental Impact Assessment and of procedures to ensure the heavier weighting of environmental criteria. This can be done within the existing legal framework. For example, environmental impact should be a criterion to be considered by all legislators. To an extent, this already happens in the context of EC law. Article 130r(2) of the EC Treaty provides that 'Environmental protection requirements must be integrated into the Community's other policies'. The World Bank has recently promulgated proceedings to ensure that environmental impact is taken into account in its projects. Legislation can be passed to ameliorate the standing problem. As mentioned, the Michigan Environmental Protection Act of 1974 created a substantive right of any citizen to sue to prevent environmental harm. There thus seems little need to take seriously Stone's suggestion that 'we really have to put it that way' in creating legal rights for inanimate objects.

I would go further. We really *must not* put it that way. To argue for such environmental rights is to misuse totally the concept of a right. As rights have strength and value in other contexts, we should not endanger or dilute that value by using them inappropriately, however good our motives. Furthermore, if we really want to encourage respect for nature and to discourage its misuse by humans for their own purposes, it is better to be straightforward about it. We have a far better chance of protecting the environment and ensuring respect for nature if we legislate clear duties to avoid harming the environment and clearly enforceable standards with which public and private interests must comply, than if we insist on inserting rights into the appropriate legislation. The best way to take the environment seriously is not to accord it rights.

NOTES

1. *Our Common Future*, Brundtland Commission Report.
2. See, for example, D. Shelton, Human rights, environmental rights, and the right to environment (1991) 28 *Stanford Journal of International Law* 104, note 4 for references to those who take this view.
3. M. Cranston, *What are Human Rights?* (London: The Bodley Head, 1973), p. 67; J. Raz, *The Morality of Freedom* (Oxford: Clarendon Press, 1986), Chapter 7. The right is usually, but not always, protected by a correlative duty on the part of the state or other persons: see W. N. Hohfeld, *Fundamental Legal Conceptions* (New Haven: Yale University Press, 1919); H. L. A. Hart, *Essays on Bentham* (Oxford: Clarendon Press, 1982), essays 7 and 8; N. MacCormick, *Legal Right and Social Democracy* (Oxford: Clarendon Press, 1982), Chapter

8, for correlative theories of rights and duties.

4. For example, R. Dworkin, *Taking Rights Seriously* (Duckworth, 1978).

5. Some of these disadvantages are considered on pp.434–6.

6. The distinction between shallow and deep (i.e. biocentric) environmental ethics is made, *inter alia*, by A. Naess, The shallow and the deep, long-range ecology movement (1973) 16 *Inquiry* 95.

7. J. Sax, *Defending the Environment* (Consumers Union, 1970), pp. 58–61.

8. See, for an example of this view, M. Minow, Interpreting rights, (1987) 96 *Yale Law Journal* 1860.

9. C. Stone, Should trees have standing? (1972) 45 *Southern California Law Review* 10. See also note 51 for an expanded version of this article.

10. 1974 Hague Academy lecture, referred to in W. P. Gormley, *Human Rights and the Environment* (Leyden, 1976).

11. Declaration of the United Nations Conference on the Human Environment, UN Doc. A/Conf. 48/Rev. I (1972).

12. Rio Declaration on Environment and Development, UN Doc. A/Conf. 151/5/Rev. 1 (1992).

13. African Charter of Human and Peoples' Rights, OAU Doc. CAB/LEG/67/3/Rev. 5 (1982).

14. Additional Protocol to the American Convention on Human Rights in the Area of Economic, Social and Cultural Rights (1989).

15. UN Convention on the Rights of the Child, UN Doc. A/Res./44/25 (1989).

16. P. Birnie and A. E. Boyle, *International Law and the Environment* (Oxford: Clarendon Press, 1992), p. 196.

17. A. Kiss and D. Shelton, *International Environmental Law* (Cambridge: Grotius, 1991).

18. W. P. Gormley, The legal obligation of the international community to guarantee a pure and decent environment, (1990) 3 *Geo. International Review* 85. See also L. Sohn *The Stockholm Declaration on the Human Environment*, (1973) 14 *Harvard International Law Journal* 455.

19. Sub-Commission on Prevention of Discrimination and Protection of Minorities, UN Doc. E/CN 4/Sub. 2/1991/8.

20. J. Nickel, The human right to a safe environment (1993) 18 *Yale Journal of International Law*.

21. K. Marx, On the Jewish Question. In R. C. Tucker (ed.), *The Marx-Engels Reader* (New York: Norton, 1972), p. 40.

22. See below for an autonomy based view of rights. Perhaps the most classically isolated of rights is the right of privacy, which sets the individual apart from his or her community, often by marking out some spatial or decisional sphere with which the community may not interfere.

23. See, for examples of this view, C. Taylor, Atomism in *Philosophy and the Human Sciences* (Cambridge: Cambridge University Press, 1985); M. A. Glendon, *Rights Talk* (New York: The Free Press, 1991).

24. N. MacCormick, Rights in legislation. In P. M. S. Hacker and J. Raz (eds) *Law, Morality and Society* (Oxford: Clarendon Press, 1977).

25. W. Kymlicka, *Liberalism, Community and Culture* (Oxford: Clarendon Press, 1989).

26. R. Dworkin, *op. cit.*, p. 194.

27. D. Shelton, *op. cit.*, p. 124.

28. In the way that some officials in the Reagan administration claimed that economic, social and cultural rights were a 'myth' – discussed by P. Alston, US Ratification of the Covenant on Economic, Cultural and Social Rights (1990) 84 *American Journal of International Law*, 365.

29. J. Sax and J. Di Mento, Environmental citizens suits; three years' experience under the Michigan Environmental Protection Act [1974] *Ecology Law Quarterly*, cited in J. Swaigen and J. Woods, A substantive right to environmental quality. In J. Swaigen (ed.) *Environmental Rights* (Canadian Environmental Law Research Forum, 1981), pp. 37–52.

30. D. Bryden, Environmental rights in theory and practice (1978) 62 *Minnesota Law Review* 163.

31. 8 Pa. Commw. 231.

32. Although at first instance, Judge Rogers, for the majority, had declared section 27 self-executing, stating: 'Courts which have attacked with gusto such indistinct concepts as due process, equal protection . . . will surely not hesitate before such comparatively certain measures as clean air or pure water.'

33. [1990] 1 All ER 754.

34. In *R* v. *HMIP and MAFF ex parte Greenpeace* [1993] 5 ELM 183, however Otton J took a more expansive view of the rights of standing of environmental organizations.

35. For example E. Brown-Weiss. See *In Fairness to Future Generations* (Tokyo: UN, 1989).

36. See, for example, J. Feinberg, The rights of animals and unborn generations. In Blackstone (ed.), *Philosophy and Environmental Crisis* (University of Georgia Papers, 1974).

37. Case no. 7615, Inter-Am. CHR 24.

38. Inter-Am Ct HR 1988 App VI at 70–1.

39. *EHP* v. *Canada, No. 67*, (1980).

40. 172 Eur. Ct HR Ser. A at 18 (1990). Compare *Lopez Ostra* v. *Spain (*ECHR) Judgment of 9 December 1994 where a local authority's culpable inactivity in respect of a waste treatment plant violated the applicant's right to privacy.

41. 192 Eur. Ct HR Ser. A at 6 (1991).

42. Popular Participation in its Various Forms as an Important Factor in the Development and in the Full Realisation of Human Rights, UN ESCOR 47th Session, UN Doc. E/CN4/1991/1.

43. *Sunday Times* v. *UK* 1979, 2EHRR, at 245.

44. See L. Schwartz, International Legal Protection for victims of Environmental Abuse (1993) 18 *Yale Journal of International Law* 373, who takes the view that there is at least an obligation on states to provide information during *nuclear* emergencies.

45. World Charter for Nature, GA Res. 37/7 UN Doc. A/37/51 (1982).

46. Case 14/83 *Von Colson* [1984] ECR 1891; case C–106/89 *Marleasing* [1990] ECR I4135. For the implications for animal rights, see Chapter 18 above.

47. Genesis I:26.

48. Sir Matthew Hale, *The Primitive Origination of Mankind* (London, 1677); see also J. Passmore, *Man's Responsibility for Nature* (Duckworth, 1974) and R. Attfield, *The Ethics of Environmental Concern* (Oxford: Blackwell, 1991) for considerations of both the Dominion and Stewardship views.

49. Those who take a biocentric view of environmental ethics.

50. Sections 1(2)–(4) and 29.

51. See C. Stone, *Should trees have standing?* (Los Altos, CA: Kaufmann, 1974); L. Tribe, Ways not to think about plastic trees (1974) 84 *Yale Law Journal* 1315; M. Sagoff, On preserving the natural environment (1974) 84 *Yale Law Journal* 205.

52. C. Stone, *op. cit.*, Foreword.

53. 405 US 727, at 741 (1972).

54. Reprinted in C. Stone, *op. cit.*

55. C. Stone, *op. cit.*, p. iii.

56. *Ibid*.

57. H. J. McCloskey, Rights, (1965) *Philosophical Quarterly* 15, p. 121. Contrast the discussion in Chapter 18, above.

58. M. Minow, *op. cit.*

59. However, this theory captures something about the *circumstances* in which rights arise, which I think important. I really do not think it makes sense to talk of rights outside of human society. I would borrow an argument, which David Hume used in *A Treatise of Human Nature* (Clarendon, ed. L. A. Selby-Bigge, 1974) to describe the circumstances in which a need for justice arises – i.e. a society in which there are moderately scarce resources, individuals who are partially self-interested and thus a need for cooperation. Rights are tools which we use in order to regulate our society in a way which is morally acceptable. I just do not think that it makes sense to talk of rights outside of these circumstances, i.e. to talk about the rights of Neolithic people. For this reason, I also do not think that it makes sense to talk of animal rights (although I do think that we have strong moral obligations concerning their welfare), even although the interest-based analysis of rights which I outline below, taken on

its own, without this rider about the circumstances in which a need for rights-based protection arises, would certainly support the notion of there being at least some animal rights. See Chapter 18.

60. See, for example, N. MacCormick, Rights in legislation. In P. M. S. Hacker and J. Raz (eds), *Law, Morality and Society* (Oxford: Clarendon Press, 1977).

61. J. Feinberg, *op. cit.*

62. See, for example, T. Regan, The case for animal rights. In P. Singer (ed.), *In Defence of Animals* (Oxford: Blackwell, 1985).

63. J. Bentham, *The Principles of Morals and Legislation* (London: Methuen, 1982), Chapter 18, section 1.

64. Acceptance of this view might also result in some animal rights advocates opposing environmental rights, if the argument to follow is accepted.

65. R. Dworkin, *Life's Dominion* (London: Harper Collins, 1993), p. 16.

66. J. Feinberg, *op. cit.*, p. 588.

67. See R. Attfield, *op. cit.*, Chapter 8, for a distinction between these two concepts.

68. J. Waldron, Review of Ronald Dworkin, *Life's Dominion*, *London Review of Books* 12 May 1994.

69. M. A. Warren, The rights of the nonhuman world, in R. Elliot and A. Gare (eds), *Environmental Philosophy* (University of Georgia, 1983) pp. 133–4.

70. I. Kant, *Lectures on Ethics* (London: Methuen, 1930), translated by Louis Infield.

71. C. Stone, *op. cit.*

72. *Ibid.*

PART SIX

THE CLASH OF RIGHTS

20

Human Rights: The Solution to the Abortion Question?

James Kingston

INTRODUCTION

The title of this chapter is intended to provoke a further question – 'what is "The Abortion Question"?' – and possibly also the question: 'what are "human rights"?' Obviously (perhaps), abortion is a controversial topic and so we can see that the views of the person framing the question are relevant to what is meant by it. However, much rights rhetoric pre-supposes that the parameters of 'the question' are self-evident and, indeed, that the parameters of 'the answer' can be fairly readily identi-fied also. Despite the fact that it may seem self-evident to legal academics and the like that abortion is controversial and that, therefore, the mean-ing of phrases such as 'human rights' has to be further defined, much political debate is couched in language which suggests that there is only one possible view on abortion and, furthermore, that this point of view is reflected in a general system of human rights (assuming even further that such a system exists). Different 'sides' in the debate use rights rhetoric, but of course they reach rather different conclusions.

Having said this, I think that it is appropriate to state at the outset that I, personally, am pro-choice. Some may question the need for such a statement in what is supposed to be an academic book. However, in the light of what I have said already, I believe that it would be less than honest not to clarify my own position. This is not to say that this chapter sets out to present a pro-choice position: on the contrary, it will attempt to provide a balanced approach to the various issues dealt with, while recognizing that total objectivity cannot be achieved in so sensitive an area, and warning the reader of the inherent bias which (albeit un-consciously) may inform the arguments made herein.

This chapter first looks at the effect in the political arena of human rights rhetoric on abortion. Second, it explores whether or not international human rights law has any clear position on abortion. Third, it examines whether human rights law can actually deliver an end result which will satisfy either pro-choice or anti-abortion activists. Fourth, it looks more generally at whether or not human rights arguments comprise a useful tool for discussing abortion. Finally, it argues that there is an alternative means of looking at abortion, which places it in a broader political and social context.

THE HUMAN RIGHTS ARGUMENTS

I will outline some of the human rights arguments mooted by both pro-choice and anti-abortion activists in the political arena. I use these terms with a degree of reserve because neither expression is wholly clear. For the moment, I am using the term 'pro-choice' to describe people who argue that abortion should, as a general rule, be legally available, and the term 'anti-abortion' to describe people who argue that abortion should, as a general rule, be criminalized.

Anti-Abortion Rhetoric

The human rights argument used by anti-abortionists can, at its simplest, be stated quite briefly. Human life begins at the moment of conception (or implantation). At this moment a human being comes into existence. This human being has the same human rights as all other persons, including the right to life. Accordingly, society must ban termination of unborn life in exactly the same way as it bans the termination of the life of human beings who have already been born. Probably the clearest statement of this principle as a legally binding provision is to be found in Article 40.3.3 of the Constitution of Ireland, which provides that:

> The State acknowledges the right to life of the unborn and, with due regard to the equal right to life of the mother, guarantees in its laws to respect and, as far as practicable, by its law to defend and vindicate that right.[1]

As we shall see, international law does not provide such a clear statement.

I have used the term anti-abortion to describe people who wish to make abortion more difficult to obtain by means of criminal or constitutional prohibition. Of course, there are many people who are morally opposed to abortion but who do not believe that criminalization provides a solution and indeed believe that it may even lead to greater numbers of abortions.[2] Others may not believe that the unborn can be equated with people who have been born,[3] but nonetheless regard fetal life as having such great value that abortion cannot be permitted.[4] Some anti-choice activists may advocate criminalization of abortion but only for the person performing the operation and not for the pregnant woman herself. Some people who may fairly be described as subscribing to the anti-abortion school of thought may believe that abortion should be lawful in very limited circumstances: for example, where there is a major risk to the life of the pregnant woman which would be significantly reduced should her pregnancy be terminated. Some anti-abortionist activists advocate the use of contraception and comprehensive sex education programmes and endorse a wide range of economic and social measures which would improve the lot of pregnant women, children and their carers. Others, of course, oppose such moves.

Pro-Choice Rhetoric

The term 'pro-choice' may be used to describe people who argue that if a pregnant woman decides to have an abortion it should be legally available to her; however, as will be discussed below, the justifications put forward for this position vary. The purist line is that no restrictions should be placed on this decision, whether in terms of time limits, refusal of public funding or the grounds upon which abortion may be obtained. However, some people who fit within the broader 'pro-choice' camp would be prepared to accept such limits on the exercise of choice. A genuinely pro-choice position also calls for positive measures which would ensure that women can control their fertility and that a pregnant woman has a real choice about the future of her pregnancy. This may necessitate the need for measures, including the provision of contraception and other social and economic measures, such as those mentioned in the previous paragraph. However, some people labelling themselves 'pro-choice' advocate a more *laissez-faire* attitude and would not condone such measures. Some persons who may in the broadest sense of the term be labelled as pro-choice activists would also envisage a situation where the government encourages abortion as a means of population control.[5]

ABORTION IN INTERNATIONAL HUMAN RIGHTS LAW

Treaty Law

ANTI-ABORTION PERSPECTIVES

Some writers have attempted to show that international law protects the right to life of the unborn and that this protection requires states to prohibit abortion. The International Covenant on Civil and Political Rights (ICCPR) does not contain any clear guidelines on when life begins. Significantly, however, draft proposals which would have provided that life began at the moment of conception were not adopted in the final version of Article 6, the right to life provision, of the ICCPR.[6] Paragraph 1 of Article 6 states that 'Every human being has the inherent right to life. This right shall be protected by law. No one shall be arbitrarily deprived of his life.' To date, the Human Rights Committee has not dealt with the question of the conformity of any state's abortion laws with Article 6 in an individual application. The Committee as a whole has not made any statement on abortion in its general comments on Article 6. However, one draft of its first general comment on Article 6 'noted' that 'the extent of the protection of the right to life of the unborn is a controversial issue in many State parties and cannot be resolved by reference to this article'.[7] McGoldrick is of the opinion that this passage was not included in the final general comment because the Committee did not wish to provide a definitive answer on the question, rather than indicating that Article 6 can definitively be declared not to cover the unborn. However, there is little indication that this provision could become a significant factor in the prohibition of abortion at the international level. Indeed, in its consideration of Ireland's report,[8] those Committee members who raised the issue of abortion did not do so from the point of view of the right to life of the unborn, despite the fact that the Irish Attorney General had indicated that, in his opinion, Article 6 was relevant in this context. One Committee member, Mrs Evatt, indicated that in her view one area of conflict between the ICCPR and the Irish Constitution related to the right to life of the unborn 'which ... [is] not recognized by the Covenant'.[9] In other responses to state reports, individual members of the Committee have raised the issue of abortion. The general view seems to be that this is a difficult and controversial question and that the time is not yet ripe for the Committee to make a definitive comment on it.

Article 24 of the ICCPR, on the rights of the child, may also be of some relevance, but no definitive answer can be given on whether or not 'child' includes the unborn. However, the provisions of the Convention on the

Rights of the Child may possibly be regarded as covering the same category of 'children' as Article 24. There were moves during the drafting of the UN Convention on the Rights of the Child to give the fetus the right to life under the terms of the Convention.[10] However, these attempts failed and a compromise solution was reached. The ninth preambular paragraph to the Convention simply reiterates the provisions of the third preambular paragraph of the UN Declaration on the Rights of the Child: 'the child, by reason of his physical and mental immaturity, needs special safeguards and care, including appropriate legal protection, before as well as after birth'. In Article 1 of the Convention a child is defined as being a human being: 'human being' is not specifically defined. The entire Working Group on the Convention placed an interpretative provision in the *travaux préparatoires* to the effect that the ninth preambular paragraph was not intended to affect the interpretation of Article 1.[11]

Much discussion of the rights of the unborn centred around pre-natal health care and protection from fetal experimentation rather than abortion itself. Even a suggestion that the 'savings' provision of the Convention, Article 41, should include a statement that nothing in the Convention should affect any provisions more conducive to the realization of the rights of the child 'before as well as after birth' was rejected.[12] In any event, recognition that the unborn require certain protection does not in and of itself lead to a prohibition on abortion: appropriate legal protection may only extend to the provision of adequate pre-natal care for the pregnant woman or protection from fetal experimentation. So far as the author is aware, the Committee set up to ensure implementation of the Convention has not provided a definitive answer to this question.

A number of regional treaties also protect the right to life, and their enforcement bodies have considered whether this protection extends to the unborn. Article 2 of the European Convention on Human Rights (ECHR) guarantees the right to life in the following terms: 'Everyone's right to life shall be protected by law. No one shall be deprived of his life intentionally.' In the case of *Paton* v. *UK*,[13] the European Commission of Human Rights held that the provisions of Article 2 did not prohibit state parties from permitting abortion in a wide range of circumstances, such as those provided for in the Abortion Act 1967 (UK). The Commission was of the view that neither the term 'everyone', nor the term 'life', mentioned in that provision covered the unborn. It further noted that Article 2 did not contain an express statement as to the status of the unborn in the same way as did Article 4 of the Inter-American Convention on Human Rights (see further below). It rejected the possibility that the ECHR guaranteed to the unborn an absolute right to life, and held that if such a right were recognized this could lead to the denial of abortion to a pregnant woman whose life was at serious risk because of her pregnancy, which would constitute a denial of her right to life thereby requiring Article 2 to be interpreted in such a way that an additional restriction would be placed on the right to life of born persons.[14] It was influenced in this decision by the fact that at the time the ECHR was drafted all the members of the Council of Europe, 'with one possible exception', permitted abortion to save the life of pregnant women. The Commission declined to give a definitive opinion on whether the ECHR provided partial protection to the unborn or no protection at all, reiterating its view that the domestic legislation before it was in conformity with the ECHR. It did note, however, that the Austrian Constitutional Court, applying the ECHR as part of its constitutional law, had held that Article 2 did not provide any protection for the unborn.[15] A similar finding was made by the member of the Commission from the UK, James Fawcett, in the earlier case of *Brüggemann and Scheuten* v. *Germany*,[16] which was largely concerned with privacy (see further below), although the Commission as a whole declined to look at the question. To date, *Paton* is the only case in which an ECHR organ has considered the question of abortion from the standpoint of Article 2.[17] The Court has refused to consider whether or not Article 2 extends its protection to the unborn or whether the unborn are, in any way, directly protected by the ECHR.[18]

The ECHR has also been considered by a number of domestic courts when dealing with abortion. As already mentioned, the Austrian Constitutional Court referred to the ECHR in making its determination on the constitutionality of new abortion legislation. The Norwegian Constitutional Court has also considered Article 2 in the context of a law allowing abortion on request in the first 12 weeks of pregnancy. The Court held that the law was in conformity with the ECHR.[19] It refused to go as far as the Austrian court and declare that Article 2 had no application to the unborn; rather, it held that 'the provision must be regarded as not imposing any far-reaching restrictions on the legislator's right to set the conditions for abortion'.[20] It was influenced in its decision by the fact that many member states of the Council of Europe had legislation similar to that enacted by the Norwegian parliament.

The question of the right to life of the unborn has also been considered by the Inter-American Commission of Human Rights. Article 4 of the Inter-American Convention on Human Rights provides that every person has the right to have his or her life respected. It goes on to say that '[t]his right shall be protected by law, and, in general, from the moment of conception'. The Commission was asked to consider the meaning of this provision in a case brought by anti-abortion activists from the USA in what is known as the *Baby Boy* case.[21] The applicants claimed that US abortion law was contrary to the provisions of Article 4.

As the USA was not, and is not, actually a party to the Convention, the Court could not make a definitive finding in this regard. However, in *obiter* remarks it made it clear that it did not consider the USA's extremely liberal laws on abortion to be in conflict with Article 4.[22] The Court noted that an earlier draft of Article 4 did not include the words 'in general' and that they were introduced in order to avoid conflict with the domestic law of the members of the Organization of American States, which permitted abortion, *inter alia*, where pregnancy threatened the life of the pregnant woman or was the result of rape. Accordingly, it held that the parties to the treaty did not intend to modify the concept of the right to life enshrined in Article 1 of the American Declaration of Human Rights 1948, which contained no specific protection for the unborn.[23]

The African Charter on Human and Peoples' Rights also contains a right to life provision in Article 4, which provides that: 'Human beings are inviolable. Every human being shall be entitled to respect for his life and the integrity of his person. No one may be arbitrarily deprived of this right.' To date, as far as I am aware, this right has not been discussed in relation to abortion.

It would thus seem that international treaty law does not provide any basis upon which to ground a right to life for the unborn.

PRO-CHOICE PERSPECTIVES

The international human rights arguments raised by pro-choice activists cannot be stated so easily. Broadly speaking, the arguments can be divided into two schools of thought. The first line of argument is that the right to privacy or the right to liberty allows pregnant women to decide the fate of their pregnancy and, accordingly, the state cannot interfere with the decision to have an abortion without some justification. The second line of argument relies on the rights to health, equality and self-determination as grounding a right to abortion which may require the state not only to permit abortion, but also to enable pregnant women to carry out the decision to terminate a pregnancy.

The former arguments were the first to be utilized within the framework of rights discourse, and the latter have complemented, or perhaps replaced, them in recent times. This reflects a more general shift in emphasis as human rights arguments have been used ever more widely. The original concept of rights as largely civil and political, imposing negative obligations on states, has been replaced by a wider notion of rights which covers economic, social and cultural matters and which may impose positive obligations on states. Later in this chapter I will examine whether or not these changes have had any great impact on the international law of human rights so far as abortion is concerned.

The ICCPR contains a number of provisions in relation to privacy (Article 17), equality in respect of the rights guaranteed in the ICCPR (Articles 2 and 3) and a free-standing guarantee of equality before the law (Article 26), the rights of the family (Article 23) and the right of self-determination (Article 1), which may have some bearing on a possible right to abortion. However, to date, little consideration has been given to this issue. The right to self-determination is guaranteed by Article 1 (and by Article 1 of the International Covenant on Economic, Social and Cultural Rights (the ICESCR)); however, the Committee does not seem to have considered abortion in this context under the reporting system and it has indicated that it will not entertain arguments relating to self-determination in applications by individuals brought under the Optional Protocol.[24] The issue of abortion has not, to date, been considered under any of the other provisions of the ICCPR in individual cases under the Optional Protocol to the ICCPR. Nor has there been any clear statement by the Committee as a whole on the question of abortion under the general comment system (for example, abortion was not discussed in the Committee's general comment on Article 17, the ICCPR's privacy provision). However, there have been some indications in comments by individual members of the Committee on particular state reports.[25] In its consideration of Ireland's initial report under the ICCPR, a number of members of the Committee raised the issue of abortion. As already mentioned, Mrs Evatt was of the opinion that the right to life of the unborn as protected by the Irish Constitution conflicted with other, unspecified, provisions of the Covenant. The attitude of the Committee is, perhaps, best summed up by Mr Mavrommatis, who expressed the opinion that the question of the right to life of the unborn should be 'kept under constant consideration until such time as the Committee was in a position to pronounce on these issues'.[26] In extreme circumstances, the life of the pregnant woman may be threatened by the continuance of her pregnancy, and in such situations Article 6 of the ICCPR may come into play and entitle the woman to an abortion. Article 7, on the prevention of torture and cruel, inhuman or degrading treatment, may also be relevant in certain situations.

The question of abortion, in the context of privacy rights, has come up for discussion under the ECHR. As we have seen, the ECHR does not seem to prohibit abortion. However, it may require states to permit abortions in certain limited circumstances. In *Brüggemann and Scheuten* v. *Germany*,[27] the European Commission of Human Rights recognized that the decision whether or not to abort involves the private life of the pregnant woman, which states must respect by virtue of Article 8 of the ECHR. However, the Commission held that not every regulation of pregnancy could be regarded as an interference with the right to *respect* for private life guaranteed by Article 8 of the ECHR, as pregnancy 'cannot be said to pertain uniquely to the sphere of private life'.[28] It noted that all of the states parties to the ECHR regulated abortion to a certain extent. The Commission held that German law on abortion, which prohibited abortion except where the pregnancy would create a threat to the life or health of the pregnant woman, or where the pregnancy was the result of a crime, or on eugenic grounds, did not constitute an interference with respect for private life and, therefore, did not come within the ambit of Article 8. In this regard, the Commission noted that while abortion was a criminal offence if committed in circumstances other than these, the pregnant woman herself could not be punished.

The reluctance of the European Court of Human Rights, in the *Open Door* case,[29] to look at Ireland's extremely strict laws prohibiting abortion is an indication that the Strasbourg organs will not readily attempt to impose many limitations on states' freedom of action in this area. The case primarily involved a challenge to an injunction imposed on the first and second applicants by the Irish courts prohibiting them from providing information on the availability of abortion services abroad, including a ban on abortion referral and information as to the identity and location of abortion clinics in other states, on the basis that such information constituted an infringement of the right to life of the unborn enshrined in the Irish Constitution.

The Court looked solely at the freedom of expression aspects of the case. It held that Irish law constituted an interference with the applicants' right to freedom of expression, guaranteed by Article 10(1) of the ECHR. The Court then looked at whether the restrictions imposed by Irish law came within the permitted limitation set out in Article 10(2). It held that the interference was prescribed by law.[30] Furthermore, it had a legitimate aim for the purposes of that provision, namely the protection of morals. However, the Court declined to rule on whether the interference could be said to have the legitimate aim of 'protecting the rights of others', another ground on which states may interfere with the right to free expression under the terms of Article 10(2). The Court went on to hold that the interference could not be described as necessary in a democratic society. In this regard, it refused to consider the provisions of Article 2 and dealt with the matter on the sole basis of whether the correct balance had been struck between freedom of expression and the protection of morals. The Court accepted that the national authorities had a wide margin of appreciation in the field of morality, particularly in regard to abortion, and were in a better position than the Court to decide the exact content of morality and the necessity for restrictions and penalties intended for its protection.[31] However, states do not have an unfettered discretion in this area[32] and the Court has the ultimate say in such matters. It had to determine whether there was a 'pressing social need' for the measures in question and, in particular, whether they were proportionate to the legitimate aim being pursued.[33] The Court recalled the importance of freedom of expression under the ECHR, even in respect of information and ideas which were offensive, shocking and disturbing to society at large. The Court held that Irish law did not criminalize travel abroad for an abortion (although at the relevant time such travel was constitutionally prohibited). It was 'first struck' by the absolute prohibition imposed on the first and second applicants, who were not allowed to provide information on the availability of abortion services abroad, even in circumstances where the abortion could lawfully be carried out in Ireland, and held that on that ground alone the restriction was disproportionate.[34] It also noted that the ban extended to the provision of information in a non-directive fashion, that there was no direct link between the provision of the information and the termination of pregnancy, that the relevant information was available from other sources in Ireland, and that the restrictions imposed on the applicants led to later abortions, rather than a reduction in the number of abortions carried out on Irish women.

The Court refused to examine the compatibility of those laws with Article 8 of the ECHR, stating that 'having regard to its finding that there has been a breach of Article 10 ... the Court considers that it is not necessary to examine [the complaints in relation to Article 8]'.[35] This, coupled with the fact that the Court refused to consider the status of the fetus under Article 2, indicates that the Court will do all it can to avoid making a decision on abortion. Furthermore, the Court, in response to Ireland's argument that Article 10 should not be interpreted in such a way as to undermine other rights protected by either the ECHR or other legal instruments (see Articles 17 and 60 of the ECHR) even left open the possibility that Ireland could further tighten its restrictions on freedom of expression if it also ensured that women could not leave Ireland to obtain abortions abroad:

> Without calling into question under the Convention the regime of protection of unborn life that exists under Irish law, the Court recalls that the injunction did not prevent Irish women from having abortions abroad and that the information it sought to restrain was available from other sources .... Accordingly, it is not the interpretation of Article 10 but the position in Ireland as regards the implementation of the law that makes possible the continuation of the current level of abortions obtained by Irish women abroad.[36]

The thrust of the Court's judgment seems to be that, aside from the fact that the ban on abortion information seemed to extend to circumstances where abortion itself was permissible under Irish law, Ireland had unjustifiably restricted freedom of expression because the restrictions did not constitute an effective means of protecting unborn life.[37] The judgment did not, even implicitly, oblige Ireland to liberalize its law on abortion. The Court's reasoning in relation to Article 10 could be applied, in the same way, to interference with the rights guaranteed by Article 8, as paragraph 2 of the latter is in similar terms to paragraph 2 of the former. However, if it were to follow the reasoning of the Commission in *Brüggemann and Scheuten*, it could hold that quite extensive restrictions on a woman's choice to abort did not even fall within the scope of the right to respect for privacy guaranteed by Article 8(1) and accordingly did not need to be justified with reference to Article 8(2). The fact that judges from a relatively homogeneous region of the world do not seem to be able to find much common ground indicates that it is even more unlikely that any global body will be prepared to interpret the right to privacy so as to include a comprehensive right to abortion.

It would seem that only the most extreme cases would warrant intervention by the ECHR organs, possibly on the grounds that denial of abortion could constitute an infringement of the pregnant woman's right to life[38] or to freedom from inhuman and degrading treatment, rather than on privacy grounds.

The ICESCR also protects self-determination (Article 1), equality with respect to the rights guaranteed by the ICESCR (Articles 2 and 3) and health (Article 12). However, as far as I am aware, the committee set up under the ICESCR has not decided that these rights may ground an entitlement to abortion. The UN Convention on the Elimination of All Forms of Discrimination Against Women (CEDAW) expands upon and clarifies certain rights elucidated in earlier conventions, such as the ICCPR and ICESCR, in so far as they relate to women. In particular, Article 12, paragraph 1 of the CEDAW provides that:

> State Parties shall take all appropriate measures to eliminate discrimination against women in the field of health care in order to ensure, on a basis of equality of men and women, access to health care services, including those related to family planning.

Under paragraph 2, women are also entitled to 'appropriate services in connection with pregnancy'.

The right to health, while important in regard to reproductive freedom generally, cannot be said to provide a basis for a general right to abortion: World Health Organisation figures show that Ireland, with one of the strictest abortion laws in the world, also has one of the lowest rates of maternal mortality. Admittedly, Ireland is a developed country and can thus provide sophisticated health-care and alternative methods of birth control. However, this simply shows that any 'right' to abortion incorporated within the right to health is merely consequential or derivative. If the state can provide adequate health care by means other than providing abortion it may do so.

The right to equality and the right to personal self-determination may seem to provide a useful starting point from which to launch arguments for the protection of a right to abortion. On the other hand, disputes about the nature of equality abound even within feminist circles and so it is difficult to see what the substantive content of the right to equality in an international legal document might consist of. It should also be borne in mind that while principles of equality and self-determination (as variously defined) are a central concern for feminists, many feminists may reject the concept of 'human rights' itself. The Committee set up under the CEDAW has not decided that it provides a general right to abortion.

The Inter-American Convention has both liberty (Article 7) and privacy (Article 11) provisions, while the African Charter simply contains a right to liberty provision (Article 6). As far as I am aware, none of these provisions has been utilized in the context of abortion.

The argument for a general right to abortion based on international treaty law seems somewhat weak; however, in extreme circumstances, for example where a threat to the life of the pregnant woman exists, there may be a case for saying that a right to abortion exists.

TREATY INTERPRETATION

Finally, it must be remembered that if we wish to speak of rights as coming within the ambit of international law we must look at the rules of international law concerning treaty interpretation and, in particular, the Vienna Convention on the Law of Treaties. This chapter will not attempt to analyse such rules of construction, but it is possible to say that the intention of the parties to the treaty plays a significant part in the interpretation of any treaty. Conventions, such as the ICCPR, the Convention on the Rights of the Child and the CEDAW, will be interpreted in a manner that reflects the general consensus and state of domestic law amongst the states parties, as is evidenced by the jurisprudence emanating from both the European and UN conventions discussed above.

General International Law

Apart from treaty rules, we may look at general international law, made up of customary international law and general principles of law. Soft law provisions, such as those emanating from the UN conference on population and development held in Cairo in 1994, may also be of some use in ascertaining rules of international law.

Some writers have attempted to argue that a right to abortion can be found in customary international law or in the general principles of law.[39] Such arguments are based on surveys of national abortion laws throughout the world and on a synthesis of the provisions of the main international human rights documents (which are interpreted as including a right to abortion). Most states do seem to allow abortion in cases of risk to the life or even health of the pregnant woman (although many do not guarantee access to abortion in such circumstances),[40] but beyond this minimum threshold there seems to be little indication of any common principles.

Such laws may provide one element of a rule of customary international law, namely state practice. However, state practice in and of itself is not sufficient to ground a rule of customary international law. Evidence of *opinio juris* – i.e. that states recognize a legal obligation to follow a particular practice – must also be shown.[41] Given the widely varying laws on abortion throughout the world and the reasons why some states allow abortion (as a means of population control and/or gender selection and/or eugenics, rather than out of any concern for pregnant women), it is difficult to see how customary international law, at present, affords women a right to abortion in all but the most extreme of circumstances. As we have already seen, the treaties in this area do not seem to provide for a right to abortion, except, perhaps, in extreme circumstances. Similar considerations apply, *mutatis mutandis*, when looking at the question of whether customary international law protects the right to life of the unborn.

Furthermore, the diverse ways in which abortion has been dealt with in the framework of domestic human rights standards indicates that it is not possible to find any general principles of law which could provide the basis for either a right to abortion or a right to protection for the fetus in international law. Domestic constitutional provisions have been utilized by both pro-choice and anti-abortion forces. The former have been successful in the USA[42] and Canada,[43] while the latter have had more luck in Germany[44] and Ireland.[45] In countries such as Spain, France and Italy[46] constitutional provisions have been used to steer a middle course. This may show that either pro-choice or anti-abortion activists may usefully employ human rights arguments where (a) the elite from which the judiciary in the particular country is drawn is of roughly the same opinion as the pro-choice or anti-abortion activist, as the case may be, and (b) public opinion is not so radically opposed to this view as to cause political revolt. Human rights arguments, as such, do not appear intrinsically to favour any particular view of abortion.

Finally, the Cairo conference on population and development represented an opportunity for the international community of states to reach an agreed position on abortion. However, as anyone who followed the intense controversy before and during (and indeed after) the conference will have realized, this proved to be no easy task. The Cairo Document contains little discussion of abortion and most references are couched in deliberately vague language. The preamble 'affirms the application of universally recognized human rights standards to all aspects of population programmes',[47] but does not specifically state how these standards might be applied in the context of abortion, save to prohibit any coercion in the provision of reproductive health care.[48] Reference is made in the guiding principles[49] to the rights to life, liberty and health, again without explaining how these rights may be applied in the context of abortion. Chapters VII and VIII, dealing with reproductive rights and health and with health, morbidity and mortality respectively, mention abortion but not from a specifically 'rights' perspective. The document states that abortion should never be promoted as a method of family planning,[50] while saying that couples are entitled to regulate their fertility by methods other than family planning, so long as such methods are not against the law.[51] This somewhat agnostic approach is continued in the one paragraph in the document dealing specifically with abortion. Having stated that abortion should never be promoted as a method of family planning, it goes on to say that '[a]ny measures of change related to abortion within the health system can only be determined at national or local level, according to the national legislative process'.[52] The document says that all legal abortions should be safe and that states should take measures to reduce the need for abortion, *inter alia*, by providing contraceptives and education on fertility. All women who face unwanted pregnancies should be given information and counselling, and all women who have abortions, whether legal or not, are entitled to counselling, education and family planning services. The document stresses the fact that many abortions are carried out under unsafe conditions and urges improvements in the standards of care offered to women having abortions. Throughout the document, references are made constantly to reducing sexual inequality, the importance of sustainable development for the future of the planet and so on, but it never puts forward a right to abortion. On the other hand, the document cannot be said to provide any basis from which to construct a right to life for the unborn. The document reflects the lack of global consensus on whether abortion should or should not be legally prohibited, and this divergence of opinion means that international law does not lay down any clear rules on abortion.

WHAT CAN HUMAN RIGHTS LAW DO?

If international law, or indeed domestic law, did recognize either a right to life for the unborn which excluded the possibility of making abortion lawful, on the one hand, or a right to privacy, liberty or equality incorporating a negative obligation on states to refrain from criminalizing abortion on the other, this would not really address the concerns with which the anti-choice or pro-choice lobbies wish to deal. An acceptance, in the legal sphere, of the right to life of the unborn is worthless unless it is backed up by concrete measures to promote life: paid maternity (and paternity) leave; tax concessions for parents; provision of affordable crêche facilities; adequate housing; education; work opportunities; and the promotion of societal values in favour of children and their carers. It should also be noted that to draft a right to life clause which would outlaw all forms of abortion is no easy task: even the strongly worded anti-abortion clause in the Irish Constitution has not outlawed all abortions.

An acceptance, in the legal sphere, of a right to privacy or liberty – including a right to abort – is of little use to a pregnant woman unless she is guaranteed free (or at any rate affordable) abortion, freely available, and accompanied by comprehensive pre- and post-abortion counselling. Furthermore, the pro-choice philosophy is premised on the notion that while a woman should be free to abort, she should also be free not to abort: this may require adoption of an extremely wide range of measures, such as those mentioned in the last paragraph, which cannot easily be incorporated within the framework of the right to privacy. The right to liberty may provide a little more comfort, if we look at it in its positive sense, rather than in the purely negative sense, largely related to incarceration by the state, in which it was first formulated. Possibly, we could incorporate a right to abortion into a broadly framed right to equality, or a right to health, including psychological health. Another possibility would be to formulate a specific right to abortion, although it should be noted that pro-choice forces in Canada rejected the opportunity to push for the inclusion of such a right in the Charter on Fundamental Rights and Freedoms. More broadly conceived laws may provide greater assistance to these arguments but it is hard to see why, when we are addressing broader concerns, we have to classify such laws as coming within the rubric of human rights. The use of the term 'human rights' in the traditional Western liberal sense has little to offer in the context of abortion. The use of the term 'human rights' in a broader sense tends to deprive it of any real meaning.

WHAT CAN HUMAN RIGHTS RHETORIC DO?

One argument raised for using rights rhetoric is that the term has a certain resonance with the general public. Such rhetoric is often vague and internally inconsistent and is used simply to reflect those political goals which the speaker wishes to prioritize at a particular point in time, rather than in any theoretical way. One might even say that the phrase 'human rights' is used as a mantra rather than as a coherent concept in much political debate. As different individuals and groups have different priorities, the term is used more and more frequently to articulate an ever-broader range of concerns. If the aim of such rhetoric is to prioritize particular concerns, it should be remembered that to prioritize all issues is to prioritize none. Furthermore, the use of the term 'human rights' in such an indiscriminate fashion tends to weaken whatever resonance the term once had in the public and political arenas.

Rights rhetoric may strengthen a belief which is already widely held within a particular local, national, regional or global area or within a specific political grouping – it may even bring some people on the margins into the group. However, it is difficult to see how human rights arguments are going to have any effect on anyone who has firmly held beliefs on a particular subject, especially on a controversial issue; people who held homophobic views did not change their mind about homosexuality and the need to criminalize it because the European Court of Human Rights said that certain provisions of the Offences Against the Person Act 1861 were contrary to human rights, and specifically Article 8 of the ECHR, in the case of *Dudgeon* v. *UK*.[53] Similarly, the typical member of the anti-abortion group, the Society for the Protection of Unborn Children Limited, would not be convinced that abortion should be permitted if the Court were to hold that certain other provisions of the 1861 Act were also contrary to Article 8. If legally binding judgments of an international human rights court pronouncing on the oldest human rights treaty in the world have this little effect, the likelihood of rights rhetoric having any significant impact in shaping societal beliefs is somewhat slim.

More importantly, perhaps, there is the danger that the use of human rights arguments may actually be harmful. Despite what I have said about the increasing range of political concerns which are being drawn into the framework of 'human rights', the use of such rhetoric tends to encourage telescoped thinking and thus to set up false dichotomies between those who are 'for' or 'against' the particular right in question. Such arguments may well exaggerate the differences between pro-choice and anti-abortion activists, whilst imposing a false homogeneity on people within each camp. There are areas of agreement between anti-abortion and pro-choice groups and considerable differences within them, but these factors do not, and (as will be argued later) probably cannot, achieve recognition within rights-based arguments.

Some writers who wish to retain human rights discourse have sought, or at any rate claim to have sought, to square the circle of conflicting pro-choice and anti-abortion rights arguments. One of the most notable examples is Ronald Dworkin, who in *Life's Dominion* argues for some sort of *rapprochement* between anti-abortion and pro-choice points of view. The starting point of his thesis is his distinction between those people who believe that the fetus is a human being with the same rights as any other human being (the derivative ground) and those who believe in the intrinsic value of human life at any moment from conception but who do not regard the fetus as a human being with rights of its own (the detached ground).[54] He believes that most anti-abortion activists would, if they listened to him, realize that they belong to the latter school of thought and would therefore have to concede that abortion should be lawful: 'Almost everyone who opposes abortion really objects to it, as they might realize after reflection, on the detached rather than on the derivative ground.'[55]

Dworkin's analysis of the different ways of viewing a fetus is interesting and it may well be the case that many people do hold such a view. If this view was articulated, it might well lessen the tension surrounding much debate on abortion. His argument may well explain the views of several religious groupings, including some Jewish and Protestant churches.[56] It may even represent the views of many Roman Catholics and the official view of that church at a time when, relying on the writings of Augustine and Aquinas, it taught that a fetus did not become 'ensouled' (i.e. become a human being in the fullest sense of the word) until some point after conception, condemning abortion of a fetus pre-ensoulment as an offence against God's creation and condemning later abortions as murder. Dworkin argues that this view is based on the premise that pre-ensouled unborn life has a detached value. He also believes that it is 'historically firmer' than the present doctrine, as set out in more recent pronouncements (including the new catechism of the Roman Catholic Church) and argues that a return to its previous approach would have the advantage of diffusing the abortion controversy while allowing it to retain its condemnation of abortion in most circumstances. This argument is, to say the least, unconvincing. The Roman Catholic Church's view of abortion changed in accordance with advances in medical science which showed that fetal life develops along a continuum from the moment of conception. These advances also account for the fact that the common law distinction between quickened and non-quickened pregnancies (termination of the latter being regarded as outwith penal sanctions or, at any rate, punishable by milder penalties) was abolished in the Offences Against the Person Act 1861. Given that a continuum between conception and birth has now (arguably) been established and that the Roman Catholic Church has always regarded ensouled fetuses as being human beings, it would be illogical for it now to revert to its earlier position. There may well be theological arguments within the Roman Catholic Church as to the exact nature of fetal life, as Dworkin points out, but it is hardly likely that the church will change its views in order to facilitate more liberal abortion laws. At this stage in his argument Dworkin looks at theological arguments as though they are merely strategic (and, to an extent, they may well be), failing to appreciate, or give sufficient weight to, the depth of religious belief and its essentially non-negotiable nature. Whatever Dworkin may argue, there are, and there may always be, people who genuinely believe that the fetus, from the moment of conception, is a human being and has exactly the same value and entitlement to protection as anyone else.

Furthermore, many people may be perfectly aware of the distinction that Dworkin is making and still oppose the legalization of abortion, not on right to life grounds, but because they wish to reduce women's control over their fertility, and inhibit sexual freedom more generally, as a means of ensuring their own continued political, economic and social dominance. At the extreme end of the scale, one may look at Nazi Germany, which considerably restricted the availability of abortion, while permitting and mandating abortion on eugenic grounds.[57] One may also point to the example of Walter Grabher-Meyer of the Austrian Liberal Party, who advocated the offering of financial inducements to Austrian women who bore children and financial disincentives to immigrant women who gave birth.[58] This is not to suggest that most or many anti-abortionists can be classified as racists or fascists. Nonetheless, they may have a wider agenda of control which they are unlikely to admit to openly. It is certainly arguable that the views of at least some anti-abortion activists on issues such as social welfare, contraception and the treatment of unmarried women who give birth indicate more of a desire to increase or preserve their own power than a genuine concern for life.[59] If this is the case, then such people are unlikely to modify and weaken their arguments in order to facilitate more liberal laws on abortion.

Dworkin's conclusions are less than convincing even if one accepts his views on the detached value of fetal life. Many people may well find this model more in tune with their way of thinking, but still believe that abortion should be unlawful at least most of the time. Operating on the premise that all anti-abortionists take the detached view of the value of fetal life, Dworkin goes on to argue that a further diffusing of controversy about abortion may occur if anti-abortion and pro-choice activists recognize that they have a shared concern and respect for fetal life. Again, this may be the case, but it does not lead necessarily to the conclusion that Dworkin presents as inevitable. He argues that the difference between 'the' pro-choice viewpoint and 'the' anti-abortion viewpoint is, in essence, spiritual or religious.[60] From that starting point, he presents a detailed analysis of US constitutional law to support his position. It is unnecessary in this chapter to critique his arguments from within the framework of US constitutional law. Suffice it to say, he takes the classic liberal position that laws should not be based on religious belief and that everyone should have freedom to act in accordance with their own conscience. He regards the prospect of *Roe* v. *Wade* being overruled as a

> bleak day in American constitutional history, for it would mean that American citizens were no longer secure in their freedom to follow their own reflective convictions in the most personal, conscience-driven, and religious decisions many of them will ever make.[61]

Certainly, such a day would be a bleak one for Dworkinian liberals and indeed for the proponents of a liberal view of human rights. What Dworkin does not seem to realize is that such a prospect is not at all displeasing for the many people who reject liberalism. It does not seem to occur to him that an anti-abortion position may not be the result of an imperfect understanding of liberalism, but may be part of a comprehensive world view which is fundamentally opposed to the development of a liberal society, at least as envisaged by Dworkin. Many people do not believe that morality is not an acceptable basis from which to legislate and may want certain laws, such as those criminalizing abortion, to be enacted precisely *because* their moral, religious or philosophical beliefs tell them that abortion is wrong.

Dworkin also fails to realize that he is being as dogmatic as those who seek to have their religious, moral or philosophical beliefs enshrined in law. Many anti-abortionists seek to bring about a legal system which reflects their own position, i.e. abortion should be criminalized because it is wrong. Similarly, Dworkin seeks to bring about a situation which reflects *his* own moral or philosophical position, i.e. abortion should not be criminalized because people have differing views on its morality. His position involves the imposition of his values on people who do not share them, in much the same way as many anti-abortionists seek to impose theirs on people who do not agree with them.[62]

Lawrence Tribe, although not presenting identical arguments to those of Dworkin, also claims to seek a compromise between anti-abortion and pro-choice arguments along broadly similar lines. He points out that *Roe* itself represents a compromise and then goes on to suggest that this is the only possible compromise.[63] Both these writers, while claiming to seek compromise, stick firmly to their liberal guns, seemingly unaware of the fact that conflict about abortion may sometimes simply reflect a more general disagreement about the validity of liberalism. They also seek to present their arguments as somehow detached from their own personal views on abortion, which they fail to state,[64] but, by framing their arguments firmly within the liberal paradigm and their view of the proper relationship between law and morality, not surprisingly come to the conclusion that their own view on abortion should be reflected in the constitutional and legal order.

Other writers, such as Mary Ann Glendon[65] and Annette Clark,[66] argue for compromise, believing that this is what most people want. Glendon points out that the US experience is vastly different from that of most western European countries, and significantly different from that of Canada, because the judges have pre-empted more democratic ways of dealing with abortion. She places the blame for this at the feet of the US Constitution, with its overemphasis on individualism and corresponding lack of respect for the community and the principle of solidarity. She is of the opinion that an emphasis on rights can devalue solidarity and that rights discourse tends to locate the individual in isolation, rather than as a member of society. Glendon is talking specifically of 'rights talk' in the USA, which she contrasts with the less absolutist rhetoric in western Europe, but her arguments about the effect of rights rhetoric in the USA have considerable relevance for the way in which debates about rights are conducted on this side of the Atlantic. While I would disagree that compromise on the ultimate issue of who can decide whether, when and how a pregnancy can be terminated is possible (and her argument for compromise on this issue has, in my view rightly, been criticized as illogical),[67] her arguments about the lack of democracy and communitarianism in the US experience are of key importance in explaining the dangers of rights rhetoric.

Finally, Catherine MacKinnon shows that the concept of rights does not provide a useful framework within which to discuss abortion. She contends that arguments based on fetal rights are mainly directed against the pregnant woman (not against anyone else), as if there were automatically some sort of conflict between the two, rather than a recognition that it is generally the pregnant woman who is most concerned with and for the fetus.[68] She argues that one cannot regard the fetus as a wholly separate legal person, and nor can it be equated to a body part of the pregnant woman. Much rights discourse emanating from anti-choice activists tends to view abortion as a conflict between the rights of two separate individuals, one possessing the right to life and the other possessing conflicting rights, such as the right to privacy. On the other hand, pro-choice activists often speak of reproductive rights in the context of abortion without paying sufficient attention to the fetus. Both often fail to recognize the unique nature of pregnancy and the relationship between woman and fetus. MacKinnon is of the view that much debate on abortion ignores the broader social context within which pregnancy occurs and most notably fails to address the social phenomenon of sexual inequality (and other economic and social issues). Before moving on to the final section of the chapter, it is worth noting that, when looking at the admittedly small number of writers discussed herein, the women authors reject the somewhat sterile law and rights-based arguments favoured by the men.

CONCLUSION: AN ALTERNATIVE TO HUMAN RIGHTS STRATEGIES

By way of tentative conclusion, I would suggest that a move away from rights rhetoric may, in fact, have a better chance of ameliorating the conflict that exists between pro-choice and anti-abortion points of view. Most people who hold strong views about abortion are not prepared to compromise their principles. On the other hand, many people, perhaps the majority, occupy the middle ground. If we move away from human rights slogans and other labels we may see that the supposedly monolithic divide between those who favour free choice and those who are opposed to abortion does not exist in quite the same way as popular debate would have us suppose.

If we examine what people actually want, in concrete terms, we can see that *some* pro-choice activists and *some* anti-abortion activists have rather a lot in common, including respect for pregnant women and for fetal life. If improvements are agreed upon in areas where common ground exists, the amount of conflict may be reduced and the remaining differences could then be looked at in a calmer and more realistic light. Thus solutions may be envisaged which command genuine, popular support from most sectors of the community. In this regard, the means used to enshrine a particular view of abortion in law are as important as the end itself. As both the US and Irish examples show,[69] a legal situation which does not reflect widely held social beliefs and practices tends to be unstable. Unless laws are grounded in social realities they are unlikely to have any significant effect on societal behaviour.

In short, human rights arguments tend to oversimplify matters. In the context of abortion, the discourse provides us with a picture of two groups of people: each one composed of like-minded people, and each one in total opposition to the other. Rights arguments also tend to pit the 'rights' of the unborn against the 'rights' of the mother, rather than looking at the actual relationship between them.[70] Rather than looking at abortion in such a black and white way, perhaps a better view is that abortion is not only a controversial issue: it is also an extremely complicated matter. Abortion is not an isolated phenomenon; it occurs within a broader social context. Simplistic rights rhetoric cannot provide a solution to the multitudinous and interwoven factors which make up the abortion question.

NOTES

1. It should be noted that even this provision does not totally exclude the possibility of lawful abortion – where the continuance of pregnancy poses a real and substantial threat to the life, as opposed to the health, of the pregnant woman her right to life may mean that abortion is permissible: *per* the Supreme Court in *Attorney General* v. *X and Others* [1992] IR 1; see also J. Kingston and A. Whelan, The Protection of the unborn in three legal orders (1992) 10 *Irish Law Times* 93.

2. The German government argued along these lines when the Pregnant Women and Family Aid Act 1992, which would have liberalized Germany's strict anti-abortion laws, was impugned before the Federal Constitutional Court. The Court held that while the German Constitution did not require that women who seek abortions should always be criminalized, abortion had to be regarded as generally unlawful: see Cases 2 BvF 2/90, 2 BvF 4 and 5/92, judgment of the Federal Constitutional Court, 28 May 1992. For an English language précis of the decision, see P. Kriebel, Decisions of the German Federal Constitutional Court I, *ECANZ Newsletter*, September 1993, p. 20. See also the decision of the same court in 1975 in Cases 1–6/74, BVerfGE 39, discussed and translated in R. Jonas and J. Gorby, West German abortion decision: a contrast to *Roe* v. *Wade* (1976) 9 *John Marshall Journal of Practice and Procedure* 551.

3. See further the discussion on R. Dworkin, *Life's Dominion* (London, 1993) below.

4. This is a point raised by Ronald Dworkin and will be dealt with in more detail later in the chapter.

5. For a good example of this, see H. P. Kee, Abortion in Singapore: a legal perspective (1993) 42 *International and Comparative Law Quarterly* 382. Kee looks at the relationship between the Singaporian government's population policy and its policy on abortion, and argues that the latter should complement the former.

6. See M. J. Bossuyt, *Guide to the 'Travaux Préparatoires' of the International Covenant on Civil and Political Rights* (Dordrecht, 1987), pp. 113–26; D. McGoldrick, *The Human Rights Committee* (Oxford, 1991), p. 330 and n. 25 of Chapter 8.

7. D. McGoldrick, *op. cit.*, p. 350, n. 26.

8. See UN Doc. CCPR/C/SR. 1235, 16 July 1994.

9. *Ibid.*, para. 36.

10. See P. Alston, The unborn child and abortion under the Draft Convention on the Rights of the Child (1990) 12 *Human Rights Quarterly* 156; C. Cohen, Introductory Note [to the Convention] (1990) 12 *Human Rights Quarterly* 156; C. Cohen, Introductory Note [to the Convention] (1989) 28 *International Legal Materials* 1448.

11. P. Alston, *op. cit.*, p. 167.

12. *Ibid.*, p. 164.

13. Application No. 8416/79 (1980) 19 D and R 244.

14. This somewhat circular reasoning was avoided by the Irish Supreme Court in *Attorney General* v. *X and Others* [1992] IR 1, where the Court held that the equal rights to life of the pregnant woman and the unborn must be balanced in such a way as to permit abortion where it has been established as a matter of probability that it is necessary to prevent a real and substantial threat to the life of the woman.

15. Decision of 11 October 1974, Erk. Slg. No. 7400, EuGRZ 1975, p. 74.

16. Application No. 6959/75 (1978) 10 D and R 100, at p. 120: 'I am unable to attribute rights and freedoms under the Convention to an unborn child not yet capable of independent life.'

17. See generally G. van Dijk and P. van Hoof, *Theory and Practice of the European Convention on Human Rights* 2nd edn (Deventer, 1990), pp. 218 *et seq.*; W. Peukert, Human rights in international law and the protection of unborn human beings. In F. Matscher and H. Petzold (eds), *Protecting Human Rights: The European Dimension* 2nd edn (Berlin, 1990), p. 511.

18. See *Open Door and Dublin Well Woman* v. *Ireland* (1992) Series A, No. 246, discussed below.

19. N. Rt. 1983, p. 1004. The case concerned a clergyman who refused to carry out certain administrative duties he was required by law to perform in protest at the new law. His subsequent application to the European Commission of Human Rights was declared inadmissible on the ground, *inter alia*, that he could not claim to be a victim of any violation of Article 2 himself: Application 11045/84, *Knudsen* v. *Norway* (1985) 42 D and R 247. See also R. Ryssdal, Norwegian problems of compliance with the Convention and Norwegian perspectives on incorporation of the Convention. In J. Gardner (ed.), *Aspects of Incorporation of the European Convention of Human Rights into Domestic Law* (London, 1990), p. 31.

20. See the translation reproduced in the Commission's decision at p. 252.

21. Case No. 2141 (United States) (1981) 2 *Human Rights Law Journal* 110.

22. See W. Peukert, *op. cit.*, and D. Shelton, Abortion and the right to life in the Inter-American system (1981) 2 *Human Rights Law Journal* 309.

23. Article 1 provides that 'Every human being has the right to life, liberty and the security of his person.'

24. See *A.D.* v. *Canada* Doc. A/39/40, p. 200.

25. See D. McGoldrick, *op. cit.*

26. Para. 53 of the Committee's consideration of Ireland's first report under the ICCPR.

27. Application No. 6959/75, (1976) 5 D and R 103.

28. Para. 59 of the Commission's report in *Brüggemann*.

29. *Op. cit.*

30. Cf. the opinion of the plurality of the Commission, which have held that Irish law was insufficiently clear to be foreseeable by the applicants acting on legal advice, and thus violated Article 10.

31. See also the Court's earlier case-law in *Handyside* v. *UK* (1976) Series A, No. 24, and *Müller and Others* v. *Switzerland* (1988) Series A, No. 133, and its recent decision in *Otto-Preminger-Institut* v. *Austria* (1994) Series A, No. 295–A.

32. See *Norris* v. *Ireland* (1988) Series A, No. 142.

33. See para. 70 of the Court's judgment.

34. Paras 73 and 74.

35. Para 83.

36. Para 79.

37. Of course, any stricter measures would run the risk of infringing other rights guaranteed by the Convention system, such as the right to freedom of movement guaranteed in Article 2 of Protocol 4. Such measures could also restrict rights guaranteed under European Union law: see also J. Kingston and A. Whelan, *op. cit.*

38. See above for the comments of the Commission in *Paton* when refusing to interpret Article 2 in such a way as to give the unborn rights equal to those of the born under Article 2.

39. See B. Hernández, To bear or not to bear: reproductive freedom as an international human right (1991) 17 *Brooklyn Journal of International Law* 309.

40. Approximately 90 per cent of states, representing 96 per cent of the world's population, have policies which permit abortion to save the life of a woman: see *Programme of Action of the United Nations International Conference on Population and Development* (Cairo Document), p. 55. All references in this chapter to the Cairo Document are taken from the unofficial information version adopted by the conference in Cairo on 13 September 1994, the official version not being available at the time of writing. My thanks go to the United Nations Information Office for the United Kingdom and Ireland for supplying me with the document.

41. See, *inter alia*, I. Brownlie, *Principles of Public International Law* 4th edn, (Oxford, 1990), pp. 7 *et seq.*; I. A. Shearer, *Starke's International Law* 11th edn (London, 1994), pp. 34 *et seq.*

42. See, *inter alia*, R. Dworkin, *op. cit.*, Chapters 4 to 6; B. J. George, State Legislatures Versus the Supreme Court: abortion legislation in the 1990s. In J. D. Butler and D. F. Walbert, *Abortion, Medicine and the Law*, 4th edn (New York, 1992), p. 3.

43. See M. L. McConnell, Abortion and human rights: an important Canadian decision (1989) 38 *International and Comparative Law Quarterly* 905; M. L. McConnell and L. Clark, Abortion law in Canada: a matter for national concern (1991) 41 *Dalhousie Law Journal* 81; A. A. McLellan, Abortion law in Canada. In J. D. Butler and D. F. Walbert, *op. cit.*, p. 333; L. E. Weinrib, The *Morgentaler* judgment: constitutional rights, legislative intervention and institutional design (1992) 42 *University of Toronto Law Journal* 22.

44. See B. L. Hertburg, Resolving the abortion debate: compromise legislation, an analysis of the abortion policies of the United States, France and Germany (1993) 16 *Suffolk Transnational Law Review* 513; D. P. Kommers, Abortion in six countries. In J. D. Butler and D. F. Walbert, *op. cit.*, p. 303; T. E. Owens, The abortion question: Germany's dilemma delays unification (1993) 53 *Louisiana Law Review* 1315.

45. See M. Fox and T. Murphy, Irish abortion: seeking refuge in a jurisprudence of doubt and delegation (1992) 19 *Journal of Law and Society* 454; C. Gearty, The politics of abortion (1992) 19 *Journal of Law and Society* 441; J. Kingston and A. Whelan, *op. cit.*

46. See B. L. Hertburg, *op. cit.*; D. P. Kommers, *op. cit.*; R. Stith, New constitutional and penal theory in Spanish abortion law. In J. D. Butler and D. F. Walbert, *op. cit.*, p. 368.

47. Cairo Document, p. 5.

48. Nonetheless, the tension between the perceived need to promote macro population targets and the desire to promote freedom of choice for individuals remains.

49. Cairo Document, Chapter II.

50. *Ibid.*, pp. 44 and 57.

51. *Ibid.*, p. 39.

52. *Ibid.*, para. 8.25, p. 57.

53. (1981) Series A, No. 45. But see generally on this point of the effect of judicial decisions in human rights, Chapter 13, above.

54. *Op. cit.*, Chapter 1 and pp. 47, 48.

55. *Ibid.*, p. 13.

56. *Ibid.*, pp. 35 *et seq.*

57. For a history of German abortion law see the German constitutional cases on abortion and supporting literature referred to above.

58. For an account of this policy see *Oberschlick* v. *Austria* (1991) Series A, No. 204, pp. 3–6. I have personally seen leaflets distributed in Ireland by people associated with domestic anti-choice groups but purporting to originate in the USA which refer to 'white abortion' as 'racial suicide'.

59. For an interesting analysis of the links between anti-abortion organizations and other

groups campaigning on a wide variety of other issues which, arguably, do not promote a 'pro-life' society (e.g. opposition to state provision of crêche facilities for women working outside the home), see E. O'Reilly, *Masterminds of the Right* (Dublin, 1992).

60. *Op. cit.*, p. 101.

61. *Ibid.*, p. 172.

62. Cultural relativists, who argue that we all belong to cultural groups and that each group must be allowed to make up its own rules on human rights matters in order to avoid cultural imperialism, fall into a similar trap by failing to recognize: (a) that the groups they seek to protect may well fail to accord them the same freedom, such freedom being incompatible with their world view; (b) that many individuals and subgroups within each group do not agree with the dominant discourse and may well welcome help from those outside the group (e.g. cross-cultural feminist organizations); and (c) that any given individual may identify partially with any number of the groups identified by cultural relativists and may not identify totally with any of them. Compare Chapter 12, above.

63. Tribe, *Abortion: the Clash of Absolutes* 2nd edn (New York, 1992). For criticism of Tribe's work see, *inter alia*, A. E. Clark, Abortion and the Pied Piper of compromise (1993) 68 *New York University Law Review* 265, especially at pp. 274 *et seq.*; M. W. McConnell, How not to promote serious deliberation about abortion (1991) 58 *University of Chicago Law Review* 1181.

64. Tribe is chided for this failure by L. Clark, *op. cit.*, pp. 275–7.

65. See M. A. Glendon, *Abortion and Divorce in Western Law* (Cambridge, Mass., 1987), especially at Chapter 1 and at Chapter 3; *Rights Talk* (New York, 1991) *passim*.

66. *Op. cit.*

67. See R. A. Epstein, Rights and 'rights talk' (1992) 105 *Harvard Law Review* 1106, at pp. 1120 *et seq.* In fact, Glendon's view of Germany as a country which has achieved an equitable balance between pro-choice and anti-abortion points of view failed to anticipate the controversy which has arisen following the unification of Germany (see T. E. Owens, *op. cit*). She also does not place emphasis on the fact that the decision of the Federal Constitutional Court in 1975 overturned the compromise reached by the legislature, which is arguably in a better position to come up with a compromise than a court. Of course, the compromise reached by the legislature after unification was also overturned by the Constitutional Court, in 1992.

68. Reflections on sex equality under law (1991) 100 *Yale Law Journal* 1281, at pp. 1315–16. See also D. Johnsen, Shared interests: promoting healthy births without sacrificing women's liberty. In J. D. Butler and D. F. Walbert, *Abortion, Medicine and the Law* 4th edn (New York and Oxford, 1992), p. 254 (in the context of fetal protection laws in the USA).

69. See C. Gearty, *op. cit.*

70. See C. MacKinnon, *op. cit.*

21

Beliefs That Discriminate:
A Rights-based Solution?

Siobhán Mullally

Where religious doctrine entails beliefs or practices that might constitute discrimination on the basis of sex or in some way be perceived as violating women's human rights, a conflict can be seen to arise between the right to freedom of religion and the right to non-discrimination on the basis of sex. This chapter explores this unresolved normative conflict within the body of rules collectively labelled international human rights law. The division between public and private spheres, central to liberal theory, still persists within this body of rules and contributes in a number of ways to the difficulty that is experienced in resolving this conflict. Some responses to this problem have called for greater regulation of the 'private' sphere; others have pointed to the existence of such conflicts as evidence of the indeterminacy of rights' claims. This chapter examines Alan Gewirth's argument for a supreme moral principle that provides the justificatory basis for and determines the content of human rights. I will suggest that in providing us with a theory of rights that is directly applicable to interpersonal relations but seeks also to protect the freedom and autonomy of the individual, Gewirth enables us to resolve this conflict.

NORMATIVE CONFLICTS WITHIN
INTERNATIONAL HUMAN RIGHTS LAW

The right to freedom of religion protected by international human rights law embraces two distinct though related principles: first, the freedom to have a religion or belief, and second, the freedom to manifest one's religion or belief.[1] The first of these freedoms is generally broadly interpreted and free from any restriction. Article 18 of the International

Covenant on Civil and Political Rights (protecting the right to freedom of thought, conscience and religion), for example, is non-derogable, and no limitations upon the freedom of thought and the freedom to have a religion or belief are permissible.[2] By contrast, the freedom to manifest one's religion or belief may be subject to such constraints as are necessary to protect 'public safety, order, health or morals or the fundamental rights and freedoms of others'.[3] The precise meaning of this final phrase is, however, unclear and as such it has proved unhelpful in resolving conflicts that have arisen.[4]

The potential for conflict between freedom of religion and the right to non-discrimination on the basis of sex is exacerbated by the ambiguity of the content of the right to freedom of religion within international human rights law. As no definition of religion or belief is given, it is difficult to identify the 'objects' (in the Hohfeldian sense) of the right. Article 1 of the Declaration on the Elimination of All Forms of Intolerance and of Discrimination based on Religion or Belief (Declaration on Religious Intolerance) affirms the right to freedom of thought, conscience and belief, and the right to manifest one's religion or belief. Article 2 prohibits discrimination on the basis of religion or belief. Neither provision defines 'religion' or 'belief', and nor are these terms defined elsewhere. The *travaux préparatoires* reveal general agreement that 'theistic, non-theistic and atheistic beliefs' are all embraced within the phrase 'religion or belief'.[5] Some governments identified systems of thought that should be specifically excluded from the definition, such as racism, Nazism and apartheid.[6] This process seems, however, to have been a highly arbitrary one; no criteria were identified according to which such distinctions should be made. It was generally felt that it would be too difficult to formulate a definition of religion or belief that would be broad enough to be acceptable to a large number of states but sufficiently specific to expand the protections afforded.[7] Religion and belief therefore remain undefined.

Within the body of international human rights standards, conflicts arise both between co-existing pieces of legislation and within single instruments. The co-existence of the 1981 Declaration on the Elimination of all Forms of Religious Intolerance and Belief and the 1979 Convention on the Elimination of all Forms of Discrimination Against Women[8] (hereinafter the CEDAW) provides a striking example of bullish persistence in the face of an unresolved normative conflict. Article 1 of the Declaration provides that freedom of religion shall include freedom to manifest 'his' religion or belief in worship, observance, practice and teaching subject only to such limitations as are 'prescribed by law' and are 'necessary to protect public safety, order, health or morals or the fundamental rights and freedoms of others'. Fundamental rights and freedoms of others could include a woman's right to non-discrimination on the basis of sex. This is not clearly stated, however, and it is not certain that the intention to protect the 'fundamental rights and freedoms of others' extended to the elimination of gender-discriminatory practices. Meron alludes to this 'normative conflict' and questions whether the prohibition of discrimination against women would justify restrictions on the observance and practice of certain religious beliefs. This could only be the result if the particular right in question was accepted as constituting a fundamental right or freedom. However, Meron argues that the absence of any general agreement on the greater importance of some human rights *vis-à-vis* others suggests that there is no substantive or definable legal distinction between those human rights that are 'fundamental' and those that are not.[9] In the absence of any agreed criteria as to what constitutes a 'fundamental' right, normative conflicts between the CEDAW and the Declaration remain unresolved. Neither are such conflicts resolvable under the savings clauses of either instrument. The CEDAW provides that legislative provisions which are more conducive to the achievement of equality between women and men shall not be affected. However, it is unclear how the CEDAW purports to affect provisions in other international instruments which are less conducive to the achievement of equality. In any case, in the absence of any clear criteria, whether or not something is more or less conducive to equality is itself open to conflicting interpretations. The savings clause of the Declaration (Article 8) refers only to the primacy of the 1948 Universal Declaration of Human Rights and the 1966 International Covenants on Human Rights, leaving untouched the issue of conflicts with other international instruments.

The same unresolved normative conflict can be found between coexisting provisions of a single instrument. Both the Universal Declaration and the International Covenant on Civil and Political Rights (ICCPR) contain such conflicting provisions. Within the ICCPR the potential for conflict between Articles 23 and 26 (concerning equality of rights during marriage and at its dissolution and equality before the law) and Articles 18 and 27 (concerning freedom of religion and the protection of religious minorities) is great. Again, no criteria are provided to help resolve this conflict.

The effectiveness of the CEDAW has been severely curtailed by the failure to resolve this conflict. More reservations[10] and declarations of understanding have been entered by states parties to the CEDAW than to any other international human rights instrument.[11] Article 28(1) permits ratification subject to reservations, provided the reservations are not 'incompatible with the object and purpose of the present Convention' (Article 28(2)). However, no criteria are given for the determination of incompatibility. A number of states have ratified the CEDAW subject to reservations invoking the primacy of Sharia law. States have entered reservations to Article 2 of the CEDAW which outlines the basic obligation of means undertaken by states on becoming party to the CEDAW. States parties are required 'to pursue, by all appropriate means and without delay, a policy of eliminating discrimination against women'. The clearest instance of a general reservation is that entered by Bangladesh, stating that 'the Government of the Peoples' Republic of Bangladesh does not consider as binding upon itself the provisions of article 2 . . . as they conflict with Sharia law based on the Holy Quran and Sunna'. Egypt's reservation expresses willingness to comply with Article 2 'provided that such compliance does not run counter to the Islamic Sharia'. Libya has filed a 'general reservation' not referring to any specific provisions in the CEDAW but merely stating that there should be 'no conflict between accession and the laws of personal status derived from Islamic Sharia'. The presence of such general reservations renders it difficult to discern what obligations, if any, are being undertaken by states parties. The very general nature of the reservations ensures that a substantial degree of discretion is retained by states, with very little surrendering of state sovereignty being involved in ratification of the CEDAW. This is compounded by the fact that no single uniform interpretation of the requirements of the Sharia exists.

The main areas of conflict arise in matters relating to marriage and family relations, custody and guardianship of children and nationality and domicile of women. Bangladesh has entered reservations to Article 16(c) which requires states parties to accord women and men the same rights and responsibilities during marriage and at its dissolution, and to paragraph (f) which requires that women and men be accorded the same rights and responsibilities with regard to guardianship, wardship, trusteeship and adoption of children. In doing so, it has invoked the requirements of the Sharia as the motivating factor. Egypt has also entered reservations to Article 16, specifically referring to the wife's restricted right to divorce under the Sharia. (The wife's right to divorce is made contingent on a judge's ruling, whereas no such restriction is laid down in the case of the husband.) In place of the predominantly 'equal treatment' approach of Article 16 (the main requirement being that women be treated the same as men in all matters relating to marriage and family relations), Egypt argues that true equality between the spouses may only be achieved if women are accorded rights 'equivalent' to those of their spouses so as to ensure 'complementarity' and a just balance between them. Restrictions on the wife's right to divorce are justified, it is argued, because under the provisions of the Sharia a husband is required to pay bridal money to the wife and is required to maintain her fully throughout the marriage. He must also make a payment to her upon marriage (dower). The wife, however, retains full rights over her property and is not obliged to spend anything on her keep. Clearly, what is being invoked here is the concept of 'separate spheres'[12] for women and men – a woman's legal status is recognized but she is accorded a place different and distinct from that of her husband. That place is accorded to her on account of her different 'nature' and her distinct role within society and the family. This concept of 'separate spheres' is echoed in the reservation entered by Iraq to Article 16 which argues that because the Sharia requires that the wife maintain complete control over her own personal property, including her dower, and that she not be required to maintain herself or her family, the provisions of the Sharia are therefore more favourable to women than the provisions of the CEDAW and thus fall within the scope of Article 23 of the CEDAW, which provides that 'nothing in this Convention shall affect any provisions that are more conducive to the achievement of equality between men and women which may be contained: (a) In the legislation of a State Party.' However, the concept of separate spheres is clearly in conflict with the model of equality adopted by the CEDAW. The approach adopted by the CEDAW is essentially an equal treatment approach – that women be treated the same as men. Protective measures of a temporary nature only are permitted and are required to be kept at all times under review. Article 5 imposes an obligation on states to work towards the elimination of customary practices and prejudices based on stereotyped roles for women and men. Harking back to the doctrine of separate spheres is clearly at odds with this obligation.

Attempts to resolve the conflicts arising from the substantial reservations entered have not met with much success. In some instances this attempt has been greeted with open hostility, being perceived by Islamic nations as a threat to their freedom of religion. At its meeting in 1987 the Committee on the Elimination of All Forms of Discrimination Against Women adopted a decision requesting that the United Nations and the specialized agencies

> promote or undertake studies on the status of women under Islamic laws and customs and in particular on the status and equality of women in the family on issues such as marriage, divorce, custody and property rights and their participation in public life of the society, taking into consideration the principle of El Ijtihad in Islam.[13]

The Committee's recommendation was ultimately rejected. The General Assembly passed a resolution in which it decided that 'no action shall be taken on [the] decision . . . adopted by the Committee and request[ed that] the Committee . . . review that decision'.[14]

Other half-hearted attempts to resolve this normative conflict have been made by commentators on international human rights law. Theodor Meron, for example, detects efforts to establish a 'normative order in which higher rights could be invoked as both a moral and a legal barrier to derogations from and violations of human rights'. He admits, however, that so far there is 'no accepted system by which higher rights can be identified and their content determined. Nor are the consequences of the distinction between higher and ordinary rights clear'.[15]

In her discussion of the conflicts arising between rights stated in the Declaration and other rights protected by international human rights law, Donna Sullivan advocates adopting a 'balancing approach', taking into account the particular factors arising in conflict situations. In particular, she identifies the following: the significance of a particular religious practice to the underlying religion or belief; the importance of the countervailing, non-religious practice or interest to the right upon which it is premised; the duration of the restrictions imposed; and, finally, the degree to which each practice interferes with the other or with the underlying rights and interests – in other words, does the conflict result in only a slight degree of interference, or are either of the practices totally barred and the exercise of the underlying rights extensively restricted or foreclosed?[16] This approach is unhelpful, however, as conflicting interpretations of the significance of a particular practice to the underlying right may arise. Sullivan's approach leaves such clashes unresolved, as no criteria are provided for resolving such conflicts.

Similar difficulties have arisen within international human rights fora regarding the issue of female circumcision.[17] In 1990 the Committee on the Elimination of All Forms of Discrimination Against Women adopted a general recommendation on female circumcision.[18] The Committee 'expressed its concern' about the continuation of the practice of female circumcision and other traditional practices 'harmful to the health of women', and recommended that states parties take appropriate and effective measures with a view to eradicating the practice of female circumcision. Its practice was not condemned as a violation of women's human rights, but was rather identified as harmful to women's health. In 1992 the Committee adopted a comprehensive recommendation on violence against women.[19] In its general comments, the Committee stated that the definition of discrimination contained within the CEDAW included gender-based violence and defined such violence as 'violence that is directed against a woman because she is a woman or that affects women disproportionately'.

Further, it was stated that traditional attitudes by which women are regarded as subordinate to men perpetuate widespread practices involving violence, such as female circumcision; the effect of such practices on women's mental and physical integrity, the Committee stated, was to deprive them of the equal enjoyment, exercise and knowledge of human rights and fundamental freedoms. This was a significant move beyond the stance adopted in its previous recommendation on female circumcision.

The identification of gender-based violence as a violation of a woman's human rights was reiterated in the Vienna Declaration and the Declaration on the Elimination of Violence against Women.[20] Paragraph 30 of the Vienna Declaration identified discrimination against women as a gross and systematic violation of human rights. Paragraph 38 stressed the particular importance of working towards the elimination of violence against women in public and private life. Of particular interest is the reference to the need to eradicate any conflicts which may arise between the rights of women and the harmful effects of certain traditional or customary practices. The World Conference called upon the General Assembly to adopt the UN draft Declaration on the Elimination of Violence against Women;[21] this was duly adopted by the General Assembly without a vote on 20 December 1993. In this Declaration the General Assembly recognised 'the urgent need for the universal application to women of the rights and principles with regard to equality, security, liberty, integrity and dignity of all human persons'. Violence against women was defined as

> any act of gender-based violence that results in, or is likely to result in, physical, sexual or psychological harm or suffering to women, including threats of such acts, coercion or arbitrary deprivation of liberty, whether occurring in public or in private life.

As Christine Chinkin points out, the reference to violence as 'gender-based' emphasizes the specificity of the problem: 'In other words, the right is not an adaptation of a right built on male experience'. Rape (including marital rape), female genital mutilation and any form of violence within the family are all specifically identified as being prohibited.[22] Another step taken by the 1993 Declaration is its clarification in Article 4 that custom, tradition or religion cannot be used as a justification to avoid eliminating violence against women. The reference to 'female genital mutilation' and 'other traditional practices harmful to women' was included over the protest of some Islamic nations, particularly the Sudan.

While the symbolic importance of these recent developments should be recognized, it must also be remembered that the instruments within which these advances have been made do not in themselves give rise to any binding legal obligations.[23] At most they could be said to form part of the growing body of *lex ferenda* in the international sphere. This, coupled with the very weak enforcement mechanisms established under the CEDAW,[24] ensures that difficulties arising from such normative conflicts are continuously side-stepped by international human rights organs.

THE PUBLIC-PRIVATE DICHOTOMY OF INTERNATIONAL HUMAN RIGHTS LAW

The difficulties experienced in attempting to resolve this normative conflict have been intensified by the conceptual division between public and private spheres within international human rights law. The consequences of this normative commitment to a division between public and private spheres manifest themselves in a variety of ways.

Freedom of Religion

The priority accorded to the 'right' over the 'good' – the belief that individuals within 'civil society' should be left 'free' to pursue whatever ends they choose subject only to the proviso that they do not 'harm' others – provides the justificatory basis for a number of the protected freedoms, including, *inter alia*, freedom of religion. This justificatory basis is not always made explicit; the idea of public and private spheres is often hived off from the freedom-based argument for the limited state, and is applied in an apparently descriptive, yet ultimately question-begging, way to particular activities and institutions. Once a sphere is labelled 'private', normative conclusions that no intervention is appropriate are drawn, usually without the full argument for non-intervention being spelled out. The attribution of privacy, which should be the conclusion of the argument, is taken for the argument itself.[25] Contemporary liberalism expresses its commitment to liberty by sharply separating the public power of the state from the private relationships of civil society, and by setting strict limits on the state's ability to intervene in private life.[26] These limitations on the power of the state to intervene in the exercise of 'private liberty' provide 'escape from the surveillance and interference of public officials', thereby 'multiplying possibilities for private associations and combinations'.[27]

Individuals, therefore, are left free to form and participate in religious associations subject to limitations on the freedom to manifest religious beliefs. As noted earlier, it is unclear whether or not the limitation on interference with 'the fundamental rights and freedoms of others', found in a number of international human rights instruments, includes the right to non-discrimination on the basis of sex. Many of the conflicts between these norms arise with regard to activities within the domestic sphere or the family. The failure to resolve these conflicts may be attributable partly to the invisibility of the domestic sphere within either the public or the private sphere as conceptualized by liberal theory and practice.

The Public-Domestic Distinction

As Pateman notes, 'liberalism conceptualises civil society in abstraction from ascriptive domestic life', and so 'the latter remains "forgotten" in theoretical discussion. The separation between private and public is thus [presented] as a division _within_ ... the world of men.'[28] The public-domestic distinction has rendered invisible the 'harms' suffered by women within the domestic sphere as a result of the exercise of certain protected freedoms, including, _inter alia_, the right to freedom of religion; abuse of women's human rights has been perceived as a cultural, private or individual issue and not a political matter requiring state action.[29]

The public-domestic distinction is reinforced by the legal enforcement of the 'right to privacy'. MacKinnon notes

> the very things feminism regards as central to the subjection of women – the very place, the body; the very relations, heterosexual; the very activities, intercourse and reproduction; and the very feelings, intimate – form the core of what is covered by privacy doctrine. From this perspective, the legal concept of privacy can and has shielded the place of battery, marital rape, and women's exploited labour; has preserved the central institutions whereby women are _deprived_ of identity, autonomy, control and self-definition.[30]

The idea of the domestic sphere as constituting a separate sphere to which the concept of justice is not appropriate is accepted by Rawls. He suggests that the concept of an independent self distinct from its values and ends may not be appropriate when considering one's 'personal affairs' or family ties.[31] This leads one to Sandel's conclusion:

> As the independent self finds its limits in those aims and attachments from which it cannot stand apart, so justice finds its limits in those forms of community that engage the identity as well as the interests of the participants.[32]

For these reasons and others, the domestic sphere has not been subjected to the same tests of justice as the public sphere. Rights discourse has generally failed to transcend this notion of 'separate spheres of justice' and has instead concerned itself with problems arising within the 'public' rather than the domestic sphere. The discourse of privacy in areas such as sexuality and family life has, in fact, become a mechanism whereby women's oppression is not only constituted and maintained, but also, and most damagingly, rendered apolitical.

At another level, the traditional connection between women and the domestic sphere has led to an association between women's appropriate place and conduct, however defined, and notions of cultural authenticity; women have been perceived as 'the bearers of culture' and as the 'repository of traditions'. Consequently, attempts to agree on universally applicable rules prohibiting discrimination against women in general, and with regard to marriage and family relations in particular, have met with little success.[33]

Drittwirkung

The division between public and private spheres can also be seen in the failure to ascribe *Drittwirkung* (third party effect) to the rules of international human rights law. Traditionally, human rights have been regarded as protections or justified claims made by nationals against their states. The focus of rules relating to human rights has always been on the relation between the state and individuals, whereas the interpersonal relations within associations such as religious groups have been given less importance. Indeed, some commentators have suggested that the acceptance of *Drittwirkung* would lead to intolerable results: 'the principle of equal protection and the prohibition of discrimination can only be applied against the State, except by dissolving society and limiting unbearably the basic rights of the individual'.[34]

State Responsibility

This public-private dichotomy is reinforced by the traditional doctrine of state responsibility in international law. As Andrew Byrnes has argued:

> Despite the achievements of the international human rights movement in bringing about a situation in which it can be said that States owe duties to their own citizens, our present system of international law is still fundamentally a State-centred one of reciprocal rights

and obligations enjoyed and borne by States among themselves. International law has had difficulty in dealing with the question of the liability of States in relation to the acts of private individuals which cause damage to other individuals and States. It is still a relatively undeveloped subject in the area of international human rights.[35]

However, it has become increasingly accepted that the interests protected by human rights guarantees may in many cases be encroached on by private individuals as well as by government, and that this may have implications for the responsibility of the state under international law. The CEDAW imposes an obligation on the state not only to 'refrain from engaging in any act or practice of discrimination against women', but also to 'take all appropriate measures to eliminate discrimination against women by any person, organisation or enterprise' (Article 2(e)). Discrimination is defined by the CEDAW as

> any distinction, exclusion or restriction made on the basis of sex which has the effect or purpose of impairing or nullifying the recognition, enjoyment or exercise by women, irrespective of their marital status, on a basis of equality of men and women, of human rights and fundamental freedoms in the political, economic, social, cultural, civil or *any other field*. (Article 1) (emphasis added)

Again in Article 3, states parties are required to take *in all fields, in particular in the political, social, economic and cultural fields*, all appropriate measures, including legislation, to ensure the full development and advancement of women. The CEDAW has been welcomed by many feminist writers because of this attempt to transcend the public-private dichotomy and to move away from the very limited concept of state responsibility traditionally adopted within international fora. However, imposing duties on the state to prohibit discriminatory practices within civil society and within the domestic sphere is ineffective when that duty comes into conflict with rules requiring protection of a citizen's right to freedom of religion. Changes in traditional concepts of state responsibility are futile while this conflict remains unresolved by the rules of international human rights law. A state cannot be held responsible for permitting discriminatory practices to persist within civil society or the domestic sphere where that permissive stance is required by rules protecting the right to freedom of religion. It is essential, therefore, that an adequate and determinate justificatory basis is provided for rights claims so that such conflicting demands can be resolved in a non-arbitrary fashion.

THE BASIS AND CONTENT OF HUMAN RIGHTS: THE WORK OF ALAN GEWIRTH

In his outline of the basis and content of human rights, Alan Gewirth sets out a mechanism for resolving conflicting rights and duties.[36] Gewirth's main thesis is that every agent, by the fact of engaging in action, is logically committed to accept a supreme moral principle, specifying absolute human rights – the principle of generic consistency (PGC). Addressed to every actual or prospective agent, the PGC says: 'Act in accord with the generic rights of your recipients as well as of yourself'. In our postmodern world of conflicting value systems, arguments in favour of a supreme moral principle may appear to be forlorn anachronisms. According to MacIntyre, Nietzsche perceived most clearly that after the 'refutation' of Aristotelian teleology every attempt to base morality on a rational secular account has failed.[37] Gewirth attempts to prove Nietzsche wrong by providing us with a justificatory basis for a theory of rights. In doing so he claims to provide us also with the necessary and sufficient criteria for resolving conflicting duties.

Human rights, according to Gewirth, are 'claim rights' in the Hohfeldian sense, that is to say, 'they entail correlative duties of other persons or groups to act or to refrain from acting in ways required for the right-holders' having that to which they have rights'. The full structure of a claim right is given by the formula: A has a right to X against B by virtue of Y. A right, then, has five elements: first, the *subject* (A) of the right, the person or persons who have the right; second, the *nature* of the right; third, the *object* (X) of the right, what it is a right to; fourth, the *respondent* (B) of the right, the person or persons who have the correlative duty; fifth, the *justifying basis* or *ground* (Y) of the right. The subjects of the human rights are, says Gewirth, all human beings equally. The respondents of the human rights are also all human beings, although in certain respects governments have special duties to secure the rights.

In discussing the nature of human rights, Gewirth rejects the positivist claim that the existence or non-existence of human rights depends on whether or not they are guaranteed or enforced by legal codes or are socially recognized. This positivist interpretation of the existence of human rights is, he argues, posterior to a normative moral interpretation: 'to know or ascertain whether there are human rights requires not the scrutiny of legal codes or the empirical observation of social conditions but rather the ability, in principle, to construct . . . a moral argument.'[38]

The Justificatory Basis

The justificatory basis for human rights is a normative moral[39] principle, the PGC. The PGC is arrived at, according to Gewirth, by applying reason to the concept of action.[40] He uses reason in a 'strict sense as comprising only the canons of deductive and inductive logic' and argues that

> because they (deductive and inductive logic) respectively achieve logical necessity and reflect what is empirically ineluctable, deduction and induction are the only sure ways of avoiding arbitrariness and attaining objectivity and hence a correctness of truth that reflects not personal whims or prejudices but the requirements of the subject matter.[41]

He focuses on the concept of action because he argues that the necessary content of morality is to be found in action and its generic features; all moral precepts, regardless of their greatly varying contents, are concerned with how persons ought to *act* towards one another. The independent variable of all morality, then, he argues, is human action. The concept of action used by Gewirth is morally neutral. Because it comprises the generic features of all action, it fits all moralities rather than reflecting or deriving from any normative moral position as against any other. It is, therefore, the genuinely non-question-begging independent variable of all morality.

Action, in this sense, he argues, has two interrelated generic features:

> One is *voluntariness* or *freedom*, in that the agents control or can control their behaviour by their unforced choice while having knowledge of relevant circumstances. The other generic feature is *purposiveness* or *intentionality*, in that the agents aim to attain some end or goal which constitutes their reason for acting; this goal may consist either in the action itself or in something to be achieved by the action.[42]

How then can this 'morally neutral' concept of action serve to justify one supreme moral principle as against its rivals? The answer to this question lies in what Gewirth terms the 'normative structure' of action. Gewirth argues that

> logically implicit in action, there are certain evaluative and deontic judgements, certain judgements about goods and rights made by agents; and when these judgements are subjected to certain morally neutral rational requirements, they entail a certain supreme moral

principle. Hence, if any agent denies the principle, he can be shown to have contradicted himself, so that his denial, and the actions stemming from it, cannot be rationally justifiable.[43]

The argument undertakes to establish two main theses:

> The first is that every actual or prospective agent logically must accept that he or she has rights to freedom and well-being. The second is that the agent logically must also accept that all other actual or prospective agents have the same rights he claims for himself, so that he must act toward other persons with favourable consideration for their freedom and well-being as well as his own, even in circumstances where his own interests will be more effectively advanced by other sorts of actions.[44]

THESIS 1

Gewirth argues[45] that when any agent (defined as an actual or prospective performer of actions) performs an action, he or she can be described as saying or thinking: (a) 'I do X for end or purpose E'. Since E is something the agent unforcedly chooses to attain, the agent thinks E has sufficient value to merit him or her moving from quiescence to action in order to attain it. Hence *from the agent's standpoint*, (a) entails (b) 'E is good'. The kind of goodness here attributed to E need not be moral goodness; its criterion will vary with whatever purpose E the agent may have in doing X. But as Gewirth points out, the fact-value gap is here already bridged, for by the very *fact* of engaging in action, every agent must implicitly accept a certain *value*-judgment about the value or goodness of the purposes for which he or she acts.[46]

While doing X for E then, A must have a pro-attitude towards E. It follows from this that A must logically have a pro-attitude towards anything which is necessary to achieve E, that is 'the proximate necessary conditions of action'.[47] These are closely related to the generic features of action: voluntariness or freedom and purposiveness or intentionality. When purposiveness is extended to the general conditions required for success in achieving one's purposes, it becomes a more extensive condition which Gewirth calls well-being:

> Viewed from the standpoint of action, then, well-being consists in having the various substantive conditions and abilities . . . that are required if a person is to act either at all or with general chances of success in achieving the purposes for which he acts.[48]

Freedom and well-being then are the necessary conditions of action. From here Gewirth's argument proceeds as follows:

> Since every agent acts for the sake of achieving purposes which he regards as having some goodness or value, at least for himself, and since his having freedom and well-being is the proximate necessary condition of such achievement, every agent has to accept (1) 'My freedom and well-being are necessary goods'. Hence, he also has to accept (2) 'I must have freedom and well-being'. This 'must' judgement follows from (1) because of two interrelated aspects of the 'must'. On the one hand, it reflects the factual relation of means-end necessity that the having of freedom and well-being bears to all successful action. On the other hand, it reflects the practical pre-scriptiveness of the agent's conative attitude toward his purpose-fulfilment so that he advocates or endorses his having freedom and well-being.
>
> Now by virtue of accepting (2), every agent has to accept (3) 'I have rights to freedom and well-being'. For, if he rejects (3), then, because of the correlativity of claim-rights and strict 'oughts', he also has to reject (4) 'All other persons ought at least to refrain from removing or interfering with my freedom and well-being'. By rejecting (4), he has to accept (5) 'Other persons may (i.e. It is per-missible that other persons) remove or interfere with my freedom and well-being'. And by accepting (5), he has to accept (6) 'I may not (i.e. It is permissible that I not) have freedom and well-being'. But (6) contradicts (2). Since every agent has to accept (2), he must reject that denial, so that he logically must accept (3) 'I have rights to freedom and well-being'.[49]

A number of critics have questioned the transition from (2) 'I must have freedom and well-being' to (3) 'I have rights to freedom and well-being'. R. M. Hare, for example, while admitting that the agent must 'want' the necessary conditions of his action, asks: 'But does it follow that one must therefore think that other persons *ought* to supply these necessary conditions, by refraining from interfering?'[50] This point, however, misunderstands the nature of the objects being referred to by the 'must' in (2) and the rights claim in (3). As Gewirth points out, Hare's criticism suggests that the agent's desire for the necessary goods of action is on the same level as any of his or her contingent, dispensable desires. This is not, however, what Gewirth is suggesting. Rather, he says that it is only to *necessary goods* that his argument applies.[51] The 'must' used by Gewirth in his thesis signifies a *requirement*, recognized by the agent, as to him or her having what he or she needs in order to act – the necessary goods of freedom and well-being. Gewirth's thesis, as outlined above, is that by the very fact of engaging in action the agent is logically committed to claiming rights to freedom and well-being. To deny this, he argues, is to endure the pain of self-contradiction.

Another question pursued by critics is whether the agent may satisfy his or her own agency requirements without attributing any 'ought' requirement to other persons, and hence without claiming any rights against other persons. In answer to this question, Gewirth simply repeats steps 3 to 6 outlined above: if the agent denies the right claim (3) above, he or she is in the position of accepting that it is permissible that he or she does not have freedom and well-being; and this, as Gewirth points out, contradicts the unavoidable claim in (2) above, *viz.* that one must have freedom and well-being.

THESIS 2[52]

> Since the necessary and sufficient reason for which the agent claims these rights is that he is a prospective agent, he must accept (7) 'I have rights to freedom and well-being because I am a prospective agent'. Hence, by universalisation, he must also accept (8) 'All other prospective agents have rights to freedom and well-being'. Now this is a moral judgement, because it requires the agent to take favourable account of the interests of all other prospective agents. And (8), in turn, logically requires the agent to accept (9) 'I ought to act in accord with the generic rights of all other agents as well as of myself'. Since all other agents are the actual or potential recipients of the original agent's action, (9) is equivalent to the PGC.

Thus Gewirth argues, every agent, on pain of self-contradiction, must accept the PGC: 'Act in accord with the generic rights of your recipients as well as of yourself.'

The Content of Human Rights

An understanding of the specific contents of the rights to freedom and well-being is necessary if they are to be practically useful.[53] The right to freedom consists in controlling one's actions and participating in transactions by one's own unforced choice or consent and with knowledge of relevant circumstances.[54] Well-being, according to Gewirth, comprises three kinds of goods: basic, non-subtractive and additive. Basic goods are the essential preconditions of action. Non-subtractive goods are 'the abilities and conditions required for maintaining undiminished one's level of purpose-fulfilment and one's capabilities for particular actions', and, finally, additive goods are 'the abilities and conditions required for increasing one's level of purpose-fulfilment and one's capabilities for particular actions'.[55]

Gewirth distinguishes between dispositional and occurrent freedom and well-being. Thus, for example, the right to freedom consists both in the agent controlling each of his or her particular behaviours by unforced choice (occurrent freedom) and in his or her longer-range ability to exercise such control (dispositional). Occurrent well-being embraces 'the particular purposes any person may actually try to fulfil by his actions, including maintaining particular basic goods, retaining the particular goods he already has, and obtaining further particular goods'.[56] The dispositional well-being consists in the 'general conditions and abilities required for fulfilling any such particular purposes'.[57] Dispositional freedom and well-being are clearly more necessary for action; the loss of dispositional freedom by imprisonment or enslavement makes all or most purposive action impossible, while to lose some occurrent or particular freedom debars one from some particular action but not from all actions.

Application of the PGC

The PGC has two different sorts of applications according to Gewirth, direct and indirect. In the direct application, the PGC's requirements are imposed upon the interpersonal actions of individual persons. In the indirect applications, the PGC's requirements are imposed upon various social rules that govern the activities of large numbers of people and institutions, and include, therefore, the rules of religious associations and groups.

These indirect, institutional applications are of two kinds:

> The *procedural* applications derive from the *PGC*'s freedom component: they provide that social rules and institutions are morally right insofar as the persons subject to them have freely consented to accept them or have certain consensual procedures freely available to them. The *instrumental* applications derive from the *PGC*'s well-being component: they provide that social rules and institutions are morally right insofar as they operate to protect and support the well-being of all persons.[58]

The procedural applications may be either *optional* or *necessary*. They are optional insofar as persons consent to form or to participate in voluntary associations. They are necessary where the association or institution to which they apply is morally necessary in that it is not open to individuals' voluntary consent to determine whether or not such rules or institutions exist.[59] The justifications of these different types of rules similarly takes different forms. What Gewirth calls the necessary-procedural justification of social rules is an application of the freedom component of the PGC to the constitutional structure of the state: 'It provides that laws and state officials must be designated by procedures that use the *method of consent*. This method consists in the availability and use of the civil liberties in the political process.[60] The optional-procedural justification provides that if there are to be specific social rules and associations, then all their members must voluntarily consent to them. Gewirth refers to groups that are procedurally justified in this optional way as *voluntary associations*. He includes within this term religious associations and other groups such as the family.

Within this framework of voluntariness, conditions or constraints may be imposed on the members of the association that run counter to their particular desires or purposes at any given moment. This coerciveness is justified by the initial voluntary acceptance of the social rules so that persons may be legitimately required even involuntarily to obey particular applications of the rules. In such instances, Gewirth argues, the PGC is applied to the second-order level of the voluntary acceptance of the rules, not directly to the first-order level of the impact of the rules on the participants in a particular transaction. Rules which involve coercion of non-members are not justified even though accepted by the members of the association.

Of particular relevance to this chapter is Gewirth's argument that voluntary consent to the rules of such associations provides only a prima facie moral rightness or justification for those rules; to establish more than prima facie rightness, the relation between the consenting parties must fulfil the PGC's central requirement of the equality of generic rights, in its component of well-being as well as its component of freedom. Both the background and the contents of agreements and contracts must fulfil this requirement, according to Gewirth. Consequently, where the terms of an agreement or other arrangement reflect the adversely unequal positions of the parties to it, they are, he argues, to that extent not morally right. However, although the test of voluntary consent may be extremely difficult to satisfy, particularly where background historical and institutional factors are taken into account, as Gewirth insists they must, ultimately the possibility of consenting to the removal of one's dispositional freedom or well-being must be admitted.[61] This follows directly from the substantive neutrality of the PGC's moral premises; its rational justification is based on the objective necessary conditions for the pursuit of any and all interests.[62] Temporary interference with this pursuit may only be justified where a question legitimately arises as to whether the conditions of voluntariness have been met.[63]

Moral Conflicts

> An ethical theory should not only set forth a justified principle that grounds moral rights and duties; it should also show how the principle serves to resolve moral conflicts, including conflicts between the duties it grounds.[64]

Gewirth argues that the PGC, as well as providing the ultimate justificatory basis for human rights, also provides in general for the ordering of the rights in cases of conflict.

The question of conflicts, he says, has two interrelated aspects. One is extrasystemic; this concerns problems that arise where the duties and ordering required by the PGC conflict with other conceptions of comparative duties and values. The other question is intrasystemic; that is, it concerns the conflicts that arise within the whole system of the PGC itself.[65]

In discussing the issue of extrasystemic conflicts, Gewirth examines the contention that the PGC, with its focus on the necessary conditions of action, ignores the many kinds of values and the diverse orderings of goods that stem from concerns other than those of practical agency:

> There is a whole array of human situations and outlooks whose orientation is quite different from that of practical well-being, such as those of the aesthete and artist, the religionist, the intellectual, the libertine, and so forth. For such persons, the focus is not on action but on contemplation, worship, thought, or pleasure.[66]

In reply to this contention, Gewirth points out that the term 'action' in his thesis includes all the activities of the artist, the religionist, the intellectual and so forth. As all such pursuits are purposive actions themselves; they necessarily incur the 'right claims' and 'ought judgments' that follow from these. The rational justification for the PGC is, he says, invariant, 'because it is based on the objective necessary conditions for the pursuit of any and all interests'. 'The PGC, then does not remove the plurality of specific values or purposes that different agents pursue, but it requires that the necessary conditions of all such pursuits be provided for so far as possible.[67] With regard to intrasystemic conflicts, Gewirth makes a preliminary point regarding the nature of the PGC. It is, he says, both a material and a formal principle. Materially, it prohibits agents from 'harming' their recipients, that is, interfering with or depriving them of the necessary goods of action. As a formal principle, the PGC requires equal respect for the dignity of others as having rights equal to one's own. This 'equality of generic rights' is, Gewirth says, the standard or central requirement of the PGC and must be borne in mind amid the various conflicts.

The main criterion to be used in cases of intrasystemic conflict is degrees of necessity for action, that is to say, 'one duty takes precedence over another if the good that is the object of the former duty is more necessary for the possibility of action, and if the right to that good cannot be protected without violating the latter duty'.[68] In determining degrees of necessity for action, Gewirth distinguishes between dispositional and occurrent freedom and well-being and basic, non-subtractive and additive goods. Thus, for example, the duty to respect the right to particular occurrent freedoms is overridden by the duty to respect the right to basic well-being, where these conflict, 'the criminal law, with its prohibition of basic and other serious harms, takes precedence over and sets limits for the procedurally justified rules of voluntary associations, so that these rules may not require or permit basic or other serious harms'.[69] One important point that is stressed by Gewirth is that this criterion of degrees of necessity for action is concerned with preventing violations of rights, not with increasing amounts of goods;[70] it differs therefore from some versions of utilitarianism which would permit basic rights to be overridden if the consequence were a substantial increase in some other person's happiness.

DISCRIMINATORY BELIEFS AND THE PGC

In the direct applications, the PGC's requirements are imposed upon the interpersonal actions of individual persons. In the indirect applications, the PGC's requirements are imposed upon various social rules, including the rules of both 'necessary' and 'voluntary' associations. It is clearly, then, a theory of rights not concerned solely with the relations between the citizen and the state. Activities and practices within the domestic sphere as well as the rules and practices of voluntary associations such as religious groups are clearly subject to its requirements.

However, it is also clear that the recognition of an agent's right to freedom requires respect for a realm of privacy in which the agent is allowed to pursue his or her own purposes, including, presumably, participation in religious groups. Gewirth clearly states that the PGC does not remove the plurality of specific values or purposes that different agents pursue. Freedom to form and participate in religious associations as well as the freedom to manifest one's religious beliefs is, therefore, clearly included within the generic right to freedom. However, because the pursuit of religious beliefs is itself a purposive action, the activities of the religionist are subject to the rights claims and ought judgments that are necessarily incurred by all agents engaging in purposive action. The question relevant for us here is whether or not the duty not to discriminate on grounds of sex is a recognized limitation on the freedom to pursue one's religious beliefs.

In his discussion of moral conflicts, Gewirth frequently alludes to what he identifies as being the central moral requirement of the PGC – the equality of generic rights. Failure to respect this requirement would involve one, yet again, in the perils of self-contradiction, for it would be to deny what Gewirth calls the *argument from the sufficiency of agency* (ASA), that is that there is one, and only one, ground that every agent logically must accept as the sufficient justifying condition for having the generic rights, namely that he or she is a prospective purposive agent (PPA). To introduce a more restrictive necessary and sufficient reason R (such as one's sex) would entail a contradiction:

> it is necessarily true of every agent that he must hold or accept at least implicitly that he has rights to freedom and well-being. Hence, A would be in the position of both affirming and denying that he has the generic rights: affirming it because he is an agent, denying it because he lacks R.[71]

On pain of self-contradiction, every agent must accept the ASA and, by application of the logical principle of universalizability, the generalization that all PPAs have the generic rights, 'if some predicate P belongs to some subject S because S has the quality Q (where the "because" is that of sufficient reason or condition), then it logically follows that every subject that has Q has P.'[72]

To deny or refuse to accept this generalization in the case of any other PPA is to contradict oneself; rules introducing sex-specific conditions to the having of generic rights are, therefore, a violation of the PGC. The promulgation of such rules by the state is clearly prohibited. The state also has a duty to protect its citizens against discriminatory practices that constitute a violation of the requirement of an equality of rights, but what is the duty of the state with regard to voluntary associations or groups, such as religious associations whose members freely consent to being governed by discriminatory rules? And what happens where the state's duty to protect its citizens from discriminatory practices apparently conflicts with its duty to protect its citizens' rights to freedom of religion?

That no such conflict exists becomes abundantly clear, however, when we realize that the duty to protect freedom of religion is strictly limited. Any interference with the equality of generic rights required by the PGC is clearly prohibited, whether or not the pursuit of a religious belief requires it. The requirement of equality clearly takes precedence; to deny it involves one in self-contradiction, for it is to deny the logical consequences of agency.[73] With regard to voluntary associations, including religious groups, we saw earlier that the state has a duty to protect citizens' rights to form and participate in such associations. Such associations must, however, satisfy the tests laid down by the optional-procedural method of justification.[74] Any coercion of non-members by a religious group is thus clearly prohibited. Similarly, discriminatory practices are prohibited to the extent that they affect non-members who have not consented to be governed by them. It is clear, however, that one may voluntarily agree to be subjected to the application of rules which deny one's generic rights on grounds, *inter alia*, of sex. Under the optional-procedural test applied to voluntary associations, the test of voluntariness must be satisfied. As Gewirth points out, it may be difficult to satisfy this test, especially where an agreement is made against a background of historical and institutional inequality. Here, he echoes Catharine MacKinnon's scepticism of the possibility of a woman 'freely' consenting to exploitative sexual relationships where such consent is given against a background of systemic discrimination against women.[75] Ultimately, however, he concedes that where the test of voluntariness is satisfied, such associations must be allowed to exist. The state may only intervene, therefore, to ensure that the requirement of voluntariness is being met. Gewirth even goes so far as to suggest that one may be forcibly prevented from pursuing the activity in question until it is clearly ascertained that this requirement is met.[76] The exercise of the right to freedom of religion is therefore at all times subject to the constraints of the PGC. Discriminatory practices within voluntary associations such as religious groups are not immune from review; social rules are justified according to Gewirth in so far as they 'express or serve to protect or foster the equal freedom and well-being of the persons subject to them'.[77] The state has a duty to ensure that all associations within what may be labelled the public or private sphere satisfy the requirements of the PGC.

Conflicts between what have become known as 'group rights' (including, for example, the rights of religious minorities) and the rights of women within those groups may be resolved in a similar fashion.

Misgivings have been expressed, for example, with regard to provisions of the African Charter on Human and Peoples' Rights which emphasize the need to recognize communities and peoples as entities entitled to rights and further provide that individuals within the group owe duties and obligations to the group.[78] According to Gewirth, however, such duties can only arise where the rules of the group or association in question have themselves passed the test of validity laid down by the PGC. For voluntary associations like religious groups, this is the test of optional- procedural justification as outlined above. Similar requirements apply to another voluntary association, the family, often labelled as the 'natural and fundamental group unit of society'. As Charlesworth *et al.* have pointed out:

> These provisions ignore the fact that to many women the family is a unit for abuse and violence; hence, protection of the family also preserves the power structure within the family, which can lead to subjugation and dominance by men over women and children.[79]

Within Gewirth's theory of rights the family is a voluntary association and therefore subject to the requirements of the PGC in the same way as all others. Thus conflicts such as those arising from reservations entered to the CEDAW with regard to provisions covering marriage and family relations would be brought within the scope of the PGC and subjected to its tests. The limits imposed on the right to freedom of religion apply equally to the domestic sphere, thus providing a strong justificatory basis for the adoption of universal standards regulating relations within the family.

The direct relevance of Gewirth's theory to relations within the domestic sphere and within civil society enables it to overcome the difficulties raised by the public-private dichotomy of liberal theory. In doing so, it answers many of the criticisms put forward by feminists of international human rights theory and practice. A cursory glance at Alan Gewirth's theory of rights suggests that it, at the very least, merits further investigation from feminists concerned to rescue rights discourse from the onslaught of postmodern and other critiques.

NOTES

1. See: Article 18, Universal Declaration of Human Rights, GA Res. 217 A (III), UN Doc. A/810 (1948); Article 18(1), International Covenant on Civil and Political Rights (ICCPR), GA Res. 2200, 21 UN GAOR Supp. (No. 16), UN Doc. A/6316 (1966); Article 9(1), European Convention on Human Rights, 213 UNTS 221 (1950); Article 12(1), American Convention on Human Rights OEA/Ser. L/V/II. 65, Doc. 6 (1985); Article 8, African Charter of Human and Peoples' Rights, OAU Doc. CAB/LEG/67/3 Rev. 5 (1981); Article 1, Declaration on the Elimination of all Forms of Intolerance and Discrimination based on Religion or Belief (Declaration on Religious Intolerance), GA Res. 36/55, 36 UN GAOR Supp. (No. 51), UN Doc. A/36/51 (1981).

2. Article 18 of the International Covenant on Civil and Political Rights provides:

> 1. Everyone shall have the right to freedom of thought, conscience and religion. This right shall include freedom to have or to adopt a religion or belief of his choice, and freedom, either individually or in community with others and in public or private, to manifest his religion or belief in worship, observance, practice and teaching.
> 2. No one shall be subject to coercion which would impair his freedom to have or to adopt a religion or belief of his choice.

See generally: Partsch, Freedom of conscience and expression. In L. Henkin (ed.), *The International Bill of Rights: The Covenant on Civil and Political Rights* (New York: Columbia University Press, 1981) 208, pp. 213–14; A. Krishnaswami, *Study of Discrimination in the Matter of Religious Rights and Practices*, UN Doc. E/CN. 4/Sub. 2/200/Rev. 1. Similarly, the European Convention on Human Rights guarantees the right to freedom of thought, conscience and religion without qualification. Restrictions are possible only with respect to the *expression* of thought, conscience and religion. See generally P. van Dijk and G. J. H. van Hoof, *Theory and Practice of the European Convention on Human Rights*, 2nd edn (Deventer: Kluwer, 1990), p. 397.

3. Article 1(3) of the Declaration on Religious Intolerance and Article 18(3) of the ICCPR.

4. Conflicts have arisen both between co-existing instruments and within single instruments (see below). For a general discussion on normative conflicts in international human rights law see: T. Meron, *Human Rights Law Making in the UN* (Oxford: Clarendon Press, 1986), Chapter 4; On a hierarchy of international human rights (1986) 80 *American Journal of International Law* 1, at pp. 21–2. An analysis and discussion of the conflict between religious rights and women's rights in the context of India's *Shah Bano* case can be found in A. Rahman, Religious rights versus women's rights in India: a test case for international human rights law (1990) 28 *Columbia Journal of Transnational Law* 473.

5. See generally UN Doc. E/3925, Annex, at 1, 3–4 (1964); 1978 UN ESCOR Supp. (No. 4) at 62, UN Doc. E/1978/34.

6. UN Doc. A/C. 3/L. 2033.

7. See D. J. Sullivan, Advancing the freedom of religion or belief through the UN Declaration on the Elimination of Religious Intolerance and Discrimination (1988) 82 *American Journal of International Law* 487, at p. 491.

8. GA Res. 34/180, 34 UN GAOR Supp. (No. 46), UN Doc. A/34/46 (1979).

9. See T. Meron, On a hierachy of international human rights, *op.cit*.

10. For the full text of the reservations see United Nations, *Multilateral Treaties Deposited with the Secretary-General* (New York: United Nations, 1994).

11. See generally B. Clark, The Vienna Convention Reservations Regime and the Convention on Discrimination against Women (1991) 85 *American Journal of International Law* 281; R. Cook, Reservations to the Convention on the Elimination of All Forms of Discrimination Against Women (1990) 30 *Virginia Journal of International Law* 643.

12. The ideology of separate spheres recognizes a woman's legal personhood but assigns her a place different and distinct from that assigned to men. One of the best known expressions of the separate spheres ideology is Justice Bradley's concurring opinion in an 1873 US Supreme Court case, *Bradwell v. Illinois*, which begins with the observation that 'Civil law, as well as nature herself, has always recognized a wide difference in the respective

spheres and destinies of man and woman', and concludes that the 'paramount destiny and mission of woman are to fulfill the noble and benign offices of wife and mother' 83 US 130, 141 (1873).

13. UN Doc. E/1987/SR. 11, at 13, quoted in H. Charlesworth, C. Chinkin and S. Wright, Feminist approaches to international law (1991) 85 *American Journal of International Law* 613, at p. 636.

14. GA Res. 42/60, para. 9 (30 November 1987).

15. T. Meron, On a hierachy of international human rights, *op. cit.*, p. 21.

16. D. J. Sullivan, *op. cit.*, pp. 508 *et seq.*

17. See generally F. Beveridge and S. Mullally, International human rights law and body politics. In J. Bridgeman and S. Mills (eds), *Law and Body Politics* (Aldershot: Dartmouth, 1995).

18. General Recommendation No. 14 (ninth session, 1990), GAOR, 45th Session, Supp. No. 38 (A/45/38), 1990. See also the study of the Special Rapporteur on Traditional Practices Affecting the Health of Women and Children, E/CN. 4/SUB. 2/1989/42 of 21 August 1989 and the study of the Special Working Group on Traditional Practices, E/CN. 4/1986/42.

19. CEDAW General Recommendation No. 19, GAOR, 47th Session, Supp. No. 38 (A/47/38), 1992.

20. GA Res. 48/103, of 20 December 1993.

21. The initial draft of the declaration was prepared at an expert group meeting in November 1991, Report of the Expert Group Meeting on Violence Against Women, UN Doc. EGM/VAW/1991/1. The Commission on the Status of Women (CSW) revised the experts' draft at an intersessional meeting in August 1992, and adopted the revised draft at its regular session in March 1993, Report of the Commission on the Status of Women on its thirty-seventh session, UN Doc. E/1993/27–E/CN. 6/1993/18, at 11–16.

22. C. Chinkin, Women's rights as human rights under international law, paper presented at the W. G. Hart Legal Workshop (1994), p. 15. See further, Chapter 24, below.

23. The recognized sources of international law are listed in Article 38(2) of the Statute of the International Court of Justice. See generally J. Harris, *Cases and Materials in International Law*, 4th edn (London: Sweet and Maxwell, 1991), Chapter 2.

24. The only enforcement mechanism envisaged by the Convention is the reporting procedure. Unlike the 1966 Convention on the Elimination of All Forms of Racial Discrimination (GA Res. 2106 A (XX) of 21 December 1965) (CERD) on which the Women's Convention is closely modelled, no provision is made for individual complaints or inter-state complaints. The Vienna World Conference recommended that the Commission on the Status of Women and the CEDAW examine the possibility 'of introducing a right of petition through the preparation of an optional protocol', Vienna Declaration and Programme of Action, para. 40. The Convention is further considered in Chapter 24, below.

25. E. Fraser and N. Lacey, *The Politics of Community* (London: Harvester Wheatsheaf, 1993), p. 73.

26. W. Kymlicka, *Contemporary Political Philosophy* (Oxford: Clarendon Press, 1990), p. 251.

27. N. Rosenblum, *Another Liberalism: Romanticism and the Reconstruction of Liberal Thought* (Cambridge, Mass.: Harvard University Press, 1987). For a critique of the public/private divide based on Canadian law, see Chapter 23, below.

28. C. Pateman, Feminist critiques of the public/private dichotomy. In A. Phillips (ed.), *Feminism and Equality* (Oxford: Blackwell, 1987), p. 107.

29. C. Bunch, Women's rights as human rights: toward a re-vision of human rights (1990) 12 *Human Rights Quarterly* 486, at p. 489.

30. C. MacKinnon, *Feminism Unmodified* (Cambridge, Mass.: Harvard University Press, 1987), pp. 101–2.

31. J. Rawls, Kantian constructivism in moral theory (1980) 77/9 *Journal of Philosophy* 515, at pp. 544–5.

32. M. J. Sandel, Justice and the Good. In M. J. Sandel (ed.), *Liberalism and its Critics* (Oxford: Blackwell, 1984), p. 174.

33. The impasse over reservations entered to the CEDAW is just one example.

34. K. Doehring, Non-discrimination and equal treatment (1970) 18 *American Journal of Comparative Law* 305, at p. 319.

35. A. Byrnes, Women, feminism and international human rights law – methodological myopia, fundamental flaws or meaningful marginalisation? (1990) 12 *Australian Yearbook of International Law* 205, at pp. 226–7.

36. Gewirth's main thesis is set out in A. Gewirth, *Reason and Morality* (Chicago: University of Chicago Press, 1978). Other relevant writings by Gewirth include: *Human Rights: Essays on Justifications and Applications* (Chicago: University of Chicago Press, 1982); The justification of morality (1988) 53 *Philosophical Studies* 245; Human rights and conceptions of the self (1988) 18 *Philosophia* 129. A comprehensive and lucid analysis and defence of Gewirth's thesis can be found in D. Beyleveld, *The Dialectical Necessity of Morality* (London: University of Chicago Press, 1991). See also E. Regis Jr (ed.), *Gewirth's Ethical Rationalism: Critical Essays with a Reply by Alan Gewirth* (Chicago: University of Chicago Press, 1984) and S. Toddington, *Rationality, Social Action and Moral Judgment* (Edinburgh: Edinburgh University Press, 1993), especially Chapter 9.

37. A. MacIntyre, *After Virtue*, 2nd edn (London: Duckworth, 1985), p. 256.

38. A. Gewirth, The epistemology of human rights (1984) 1 *Social Philosophy and Policy* 1, reprinted in D. Lloyd and M. D. A. Freeman (eds), *Lloyd's Introduction to Jurisprudence*, 5th edn (London: Stevens and Sons, 1985), p. 229, at p. 231.

39. A moral position is defined by Gewirth as

> a set of categorically obligatory requirements for action that are addressed at least in part to every actual or prospective agent, and that are concerned with furthering the interests, especially the most important interests, of persons or recipients other than or in addition to the agent or the speaker. (A. Gewirth, *Reason and Morality*, *op. cit.*, p. 1).

40. In seeking to establish the justificatory basis of human rights, Gewirth proceeds by what he calls a 'dialectically necessary method':

> The method is dialectical in that it begins from statements presented as being made or accepted by an agent; it proceeds from within his first-person conative standpoint, and it examines what his statements logically imply within this standpoint. The method is *dialectically necessary* in that the statements logically must be made or accepted by every agent because they derive from the generic features of purposive action, including the conative standpoint common to all agents. (A. Gewirth, *Human Rights: Essays on Justifications and Applications*, *op. cit.*, pp. 20–1).

The statement 'logically must hold or accept' is not an empirically or phenomenologically descriptive one. Rather, Gewirth argues, it signifies what agents are logically committed to hold or accept insofar as they are rational, in the sense of being able to follow out the implications of the concepts of action and agent. This method stands in contrast to a *dialectically contingent method*, 'where the statements are presented as being made by and relative to an agent or other interlocutor, but there is no logical necessity that he make or accept those statements. (A. Gewirth, *Human Rights: Essays on Justifications and Applications*, *op. cit.*, p. 21).

41. A. Gewirth, *Reason and Morality*, *op. cit.*, p. 22.

42. A. Gewirth, The epistemology of human rights, *op. cit.*, p. 239.

43. *Ibid.*, p. 238.

44. A. Gewirth, The justification of morality, *op. cit.*, p. 246.

45. *Ibid.* See also A. Gewirth, *Human Rights: Essays on Justifications and Applications*, *op. cit.*, pp. 22–4; *Reason and Morality*, *op. cit.*, Chapter 3.

46. It is important to recognize at this point that (b) only follows from (a) within the first person perspective of the dialectically necessary method. As Beyleveld and Brownsword point out, it does not follow assertorically from (a) that E is good. It only follows that A must claim that E is good. It also does not follow from some agent other than A doing X for purpose E that A must claim that E is good. D. Beyleveld and R. Brownsword, *Law as a Moral Judgement* (London: Sweet and Maxwell, 1986), p. 130.

47. Beyleveld and Brownsword divide the conditions which are necessary for the achievement of E into two categories: those which are contingently necessary, and those which are generically necessary. 'Contingently necessary conditions are those which are purpose-specific. They vary according to E. If A wishes to play Bridge . . . then A needs to

obtain a pack of playing cards . . . Generically necessary conditions are those which are not purpose-specific. They are necessary conditions for the achievement of any purpose whatsoever' (D. Beyleveld and R. Brownsword, *op. cit.*).

48. A. Gewirth, The epistemology of human rights, *op. cit.*, p. 239.

49. A. Gewirth, The justification of morality, *op. cit.*, pp. 246–7.

50. R. M. Hare, 'Do Agents have to be Moralists?' in E. Regis *op. cit.* p. 53.

51. A. Gewirth, *Reason and Morality, op. cit.*, pp. 77–8, 81–2.

52. *Ibid.*, p. 247.

53. A. Gewirth, *Human Rights: Essays on Justifications and Applications, op. cit.*, p. 55.

54. *Ibid.*, p. 56.

55. *Ibid.*, p. 9.

56. A. Gewirth, *Reason and Morality, op. cit.*, p. 57.

57. *Ibid.*

58. A. Gewirth, *Human Rights: Essays on Justifications and Applications, op. cit.*, p. 61.

59. The PGC's instrumental applications may be either *static* or *dynamic*:
    The static applications serve to protect persons from occurrent violations of their rights to basic and other important goods and to punish such violations. The dynamic applications, embodied in the supportive state, serve to provide longer-range protections of basic and other rights where these cannot be obtained by persons through their own efforts (A. Gewirth, *Human Rights: Essays on Justifications and Applications, op. cit.*, p. 61).

60. *Ibid.*, p. 62.

61. A. Gewirth, *Reason and Morality, op. cit.*, p. 263.

62. *Ibid.*, p. 347.

63. *Ibid.*

64. A. Gewirth, Replies to my critics. In E. Regis Jr, *op. cit.*, p. 249.

65. A. Gewirth, *Reason and Morality, op. cit.*, p. 338.

66. *Ibid.*, p. 346.

67. *Ibid.*, p. 347.

68. *Ibid.*, p. 343.

69. *Ibid.*

70. *Ibid.*, p. 344.

71. A. Gewirth, *Human Rights: Essays on Justifications and Applications, op. cit.*, p. 51.

72. *Ibid.*, p. 52.

73. See the 'argument from the sufficiency of agency' outlined above.

74. See the outline and discussion of applications of the PGC above.

75. See generally, C. MacKinnon, Toward feminist jurisprudence (1983) 8 *Signs* 635.

76. A. Gewirth, *Reason and Morality, op. cit.*, p. 347.

77. A. Gewirth, *Human Rights: Essays on Justifications and Applications, op. cit.*, p. 241.

78. Within the African Charter there is clearly a potential for conflict between Articles 18 (prohibiting discrimination against women) and 29(1) (imposing a duty on all individuals to preserve the 'harmonious development of the family and to work for the cohesion and respect of the family'). See generally C. Welch, Human rights and African women: a comparison of protection under two major treaties (1993) 15/3 *Human Rights Quarterly* 549, and comments by H. Charlesworth *et al.*, *op. cit.* A similar potential for conflict may be found in the provisions on fundamental rights in the Constitution of Ireland. While on the one hand, Article 40.1 guarantees equality before the law, Article 41.2 speaks of the woman's life within and duties in the home, thereby perpetuating the ideology of 'separate spheres' for men and women.

79. H. Charlesworth *et al.*, *op. cit.*, p. 636.

22

Pornography and Rights – The Theory of the Practice of Control

Sheena N. McMurtrie

The aim of this chapter, as the title suggests, is to look at the theory behind the legal control of pornography; and also to consider how the theory influences the practical impact of the law within the UK legal system.

Recently, concern has focused on the operation (or non-operation) of the law relating to obscenity, and its perceived inability to deal effectively with pornography.[1] The object of this chapter is to review how a complete change in the theoretical basis of the law might remedy this problem. An alternative is to shift the basis of the legal test of obscenity from the harm caused to the individual consumer of the material, to the harm caused to society by the 'hate' speech contained in some forms of pornography.

This in itself poses another problem for civil rights lawyers, as many are not satisfied by the argument that pornography causes harm. As a result, there is a reluctance to allow this to be used as a justification for permitting a limitation on the right to freedom of speech. The debate has been inconclusive. Advocates of each side hold deeply entrenched positions. Little more can be said on this issue.[2]

What can be explored usefully is the *effect* of a change to a harm/hate speech approach in the UK. Therefore, this chapter is not concerned with the 'harm' debate, but seeks to move the debate beyond this one issue. It will focus on the impact of the adoption of such a scheme in relation to both rights theory (in particular the correlation to the current UK law on incitement to racial hatred) and the practical implications for the UK's obligations both to the European Union and to the European Convention on Human Rights.

THE PROBLEM

The solution to the problem of how to achieve effective legal controls over pornography has always been elusive. The recent problem has been how to control the use of computer technology to disseminate 'hard-core' pornography amongst the nation's schoolchildren.[3] This controversy has an air of *déjà vu*. In the 1950s the *bête noire* was the new genre of 'horror' comics, which led to the Children and Young Persons (Harmful Publications) Act 1955. At that time, it was felt by a number of commentators that the whole area of the law should be re-thought rather than addressed in a piecemeal fashion.[4] Eventually this view prevailed, and the result was the Obscene Publications Act 1959 in England and Wales. It is submitted that a similar solution be applied to the current legal problems – that is, that the legal basis itself should be changed.[5]

The proposed alternative model is that of the 'hate speech/harm-based' approach which has been adopted, perhaps most notably, in Canada. The British law, which is largely based on the provisions of the 1959 Act,[6] seeks to prevent moral harm to the consumer of pornography. Section 1(1) states:

> For the purposes of this Act an article shall be deemed obscene if its effect or (where the article comprises two or more distinct items) the effect of any one of its items is, if taken as a whole, such as to deprave and corrupt persons who are likely, having regard to all relevant circumstances, to read, see or hear the matter contained or embodied in it.[7]

The basis of moral principles can be seen as the cause of some of the perceived problems with the prosecutions under the 1959 Act.

Campaigners for the new law in the 1950s had envisaged an end to the prosecutions of literary works such as *The Well of Loneliness*[8] on the basis of the 'immoral' ideas that the writing contained.[9] Yet, in 1960 the publishers of *Lady Chatterley's Lover*[10] were prosecuted (unsuccessfully) under the new legislation.[11] There is little doubt that one of the main issues was whether it was 'obscene' to advocate adulterous (immoral) relationships with the lower orders.[12] Yet, it is clear that the intention of the campaigners had been to attack 'pornography' or 'smut for smut's sake' rather than literary works.[13] The desired focus had not been achieved. This was seen in the later prosecution of *Last Exit to Brooklyn*.[14] Whilst the law is based on moral principles, it will remain easy to target gay and lesbian material on the grounds of moral disapproval of the sexuality portrayed, rather than the nature of the actual representations or descriptions.[15] If there was to be a departure from the moral basis underpinning the regulation, fears about censorship might be allayed. The attraction of the alternative is that it need not be seen as a *negation* of the right of free speech, but as a *recognition* of the existing rights of other persons, individually or collectively, that is the right to equality, or protection from harm. It is similar to the basis for prohibition of speech inciting racial hatred.[16]

The basis for restriction would be the harm caused by the material to other individuals, or to society in general. This could be physical harm caused to the participants in pornography,[17] or the physical harm caused to victims of sex crimes inspired or embellished by the use of pornography. It can also be seen as the general harm caused to a group by the lowering of their equal status in society by their degrading and dehumanizing portrayal in pornography. This has been graphically described by a Canadian judge:

> The films . . . in my view, portray women in a most degrading way. They are exploited, portrayed as desiring pleasure from pain, by being humiliated and treated only as an object of male domination sexually, or in cruel or violent bondage. Women are portrayed in these films as pining away their lives waiting for a huge male penis to come along, on the person of a so-called sex therapist, or window washer, supposedly to transport them into complete sexual ecstasy. Or even more false and degrading one is led to believe their raison d'etre is to savour semen as a life elixir, or that they secretly desire to be forcefully taken by a male.[18]

It can also be seen as harm to society in allowing this propaganda or false image to affect collective standards of equal treatment.

With such a specific study, it is difficult to discuss the theory without greater reference to the proposed legal structure. The Canadian model is a good example of such a system. It is proposed to outline briefly the law in Canada, and then to evaluate what the adoption of a similar system would mean in the UK. As was stated above, for the purposes of this chapter, the approach of the Canadian Supreme Court as to whether pornography can be said to cause harm will be assumed:

> While the accuracy of this perception is not susceptible of exact proof, there is a substantial body of opinion that holds that the portrayal of persons being subjected to degrading and dehumanizing sexual treatment results in harm, particularly to women and therefore to society as a whole.[19]

It is accepted that many people will not agree with this view, but it is emphasized again that it is profitable to the debate to contemplate the effects if this model were to be adopted. After all, the Canadian Supreme Court has accepted the principle. Catherine Itzin, who has suggested a similar scheme for the UK, has likened the situation to that of tobacco consumption and cancer.[20] It is not possible to prove that a person has developed cancer solely because of smoking cigarettes – other factors may have been involved. There is, however, sufficient evidence of a strong correlation for most people to accept that smoking damages one's health.[21]

THE CANADIAN EXPERIENCE

The Canadian law controlling obscenity is found in the Criminal Code.[22] The concept of obscenity is defined as follows: 'any publication a dominant characteristic of which is the undue exploitation of sex, or of sex and any one or more of the following subjects, namely, crime, horror, cruelty and violence'.[23]

There was some confusion prior to 1992 as to what test should be adopted for the definition of 'undue'. The favoured test was the 'community standards' test, which was defined as

> a standard of tolerance, not taste. . . . What matters is not what Canadians think is right for themselves to see. What matters is what Canadians would not abide other Canadians seeing because it would be beyond the contemporary Canadian standard of tolerance to allow them to see it.[24]

In *R* v. *Butler* the following test for possible grounds for deeming material to be obscene within the terms of the Code was approved by the Supreme Court.[25] For this purpose pornography has been divided into three categories. The first is explicit sex with violence, which is specifically covered by s. 163(8). The second is explicit sex without violence, but which subjects people to treatment that is degrading and dehumanizing. It is envisaged that this may well be covered by s. 163(8). The third is explicit sex without violence that is neither degrading nor dehumanizing. This is less likely to be covered by s. 163(8), unless for example it involves children:

> In making this determination with respect to the three categories of pornography referred to above, the portrayal of sex coupled with violence will almost always constitute the undue exploitation of sex. Explicit sex which is degrading or dehumanizing may be undue if the risk of harm is substantial. Finally, explicit sex that is not violent

and neither degrading nor dehumanizing is generally tolerated in our society and will not qualify as the undue exploitation of sex unless it employs children in its production.[26]

There is protection for artistic work through the 'internal necessities' test derived from ss. 163(3) and (4) which deal with the public good defence. The 'internal necessities' test is decided on the basis of whether sex is the 'dominant characteristic of the work' or whether the portrayal of sex is an essential part of a wider artistic, literary or similar purpose:

> The court must determine whether the sexually explicit material when viewed in the context of the whole work would be tolerated by the community as a whole. Artistic expression rests at the heart of freedom of expression values and any doubt in this regard must be resolved in favour of freedom of expression.[27]

The majority of the Supreme Court in *R* v. *Butler* held that the content of the material was the basis of the test, and that the medium of representation should not influence whether the material was to be regarded as obscene or not. This means that whether an image appears within the covers of a magazine or appears in a shop window does not affect whether it is deemed obscene. It is the content of the image itself that matters. This is, of course, an important consideration, as it would have implications for the current UK law in relation to the Indecent Displays (Control) Act 1981. At present, images which are not 'obscene' in terms of the 1959 Act are nevertheless prohibited from being displayed in public places if they are deemed 'indecent'.[28] Therefore, there exists within the current British law a non-content-based element of regulation. It would be necessary for a decision to be taken as to whether the law would be content-based alone, or whether the mode of representation should also be considered in the decision as to whether an image was obscene.

This question has not been clearly resolved in Canadian law, as the minority in *Butler* felt that the third category of explicit sex could not be easily stated as being free from harm, and that the use of children was not the only objectionable ground. Gonthier J stated that an image of a couple making love (an example of the third category) would probably be unobjectionable in a book; more troublesome in a magazine or a film; and if on a billboard, then likely to be objectionable on the basis of its harmfulness:

> The harmfulness, in the billboard sign example, would come from the immediacy of the representation, inasmuch as the sign stands all by itself (as opposed to a passage in a book, a film or a magazine).

Its message is at once crude and inescapable. It distorts human sexuality by taking it out of any context whatsoever and projecting it to the public. This example goes to the extreme, of course, but it is meant to show that the element of representation may create a likelihood of harm that may lead to the application of s. 163 of the Code, even if the content of the representation as such is not objectionable.[29]

The Canadian law has not had a smooth passage since *R* v. *Butler*. There appears to be a division in the application of the judgment by the lower courts. Some judges have taken the view that material from the third category may well be beyond what Canadians will tolerate, a view in sympathy with the dissent in *Butler*. This view suggests that material falling into the second category will almost certainly be deemed obscene, and that material in the third category is more likely to be deemed obscene than was suggested in *Butler*.[30]

Other judges have taken the opinion of Sopinka J to mean that before material in the second category can be prohibited, particular material must be shown to cause social harm. This suggests that material in the second category will not be automatically deemed obscene, even if it is shown to be degrading and dehumanizing. This was the view expressed in *R* v. *Ronish*, which agreed:[31]

with the requirement that, in cases not involving depictions of explicit sex with violence, proof of social harm must be established and not assumed.

From this it may be seen that the necessity of proof of social harm generally applies, regardless of whether the impugned material can be classified in the second or third Butler category. Both Misener J. and Nosanchuk Prov. J. read the reasoning of Sopinka J. as indicating that only in the clearest of cases involving material in the second category can social harm be assumed. I agree.[32]

It is submitted that this is not in fact a correct interpretation of the relevant judgment. The *Butler* judgment listed the various reports which supported the view that material in the second category could be assumed to cause social harm as a class. If the *Ronish* decision is correct, it would mean that the debate about whether pornography which is degrading or dehumanizing causes social harm would have to be argued on every occasion. There is justification for this view only if the following passage from *Butler* is read alone: 'The stronger the inference of a risk of harm the lesser the likelihood of tolerance. The inference may be drawn from the material itself *or from the material and other evidence*' (emphasis added).[33] When the full judgment of Sopinka J is read, this interpretation does not seem to coincide with the sense of the *Butler* decision.

It is submitted that the *Butler* decision meant to establish that the contentious decision in such cases would be whether the material was classified in the second or third category. If it were degrading and dehumanizing, it would be in the second category, and given the evidence cited by the Court as to the social harm caused by such pornography, it would almost certainly therefore be deemed obscene. The slight qualification to any automatic classification of category 2 material as obscene would be that the internal necessities test may save some material in this category.

If the material were not degrading and dehumanizing, it would fall into the third category. It is submitted that if this is not the test, and the test is two-fold, that is, first, whether it is degrading and dehumanizing, and second, on this occasion, whether there is sufficient proof of social harm to warrant its classification as obscene, then there would be no need for a third category. It would only be necessary for two categories; explicit sex with violence, which would be obscene; and explicit sex in the absence of violence, which could be classified as obscene if there was, on each specific occasion, sufficient proof of social harm. Clearly, this was not what the *Butler* decision intended, as three distinct categories were defined. Therefore, the crucial test is whether the material is degrading and dehumanizing, and not whether there is sufficient proof of social harm on this occasion. It will be interesting to see how the case law develops in the future. It is worth noting that in the *Ronish* decision, the judge added his view that the matter was one for politicians and not the judiciary, and that the courts should not be left with such a vague test.[34]

IMPLICATIONS FOR LEGAL THEORY

One of the attractions of the harm-based approach is the removal of the overt use of 'morality' from this area of the criminal law. Thus it can be argued that the matter no longer falls into the parameters of the Hart-Devlin debate as to the acceptable limits to the legal enforcement of morality. This is, of course, using the term 'morality' in a narrow sense. It conveys the idea of a better form of conduct – a higher ideal – rather than protecting other individuals from detriment. It has already been noted that the current test of whether material has the tendency to deprave and corrupt the individual exposed to it has the potential to be used to target conduct that could be deemed to be only morally unsound, or of which it is possible to disapprove, rather than material which is actually harmful.

In adopting the 'hate speech/harm-based' approach, not all problems are solved. The question still remains as to who is being protected from harm. Certainly, the answer no longer seems to be the person consuming pornography. Therefore, it appears that there is a possible choice between the *harm* as the harm to society in general, or to specific individuals or groups within society.

The problem lies in whether there has to be a direct and immediate link between the speech and the harm. Must there be actual harm caused by the consumer/producer of pornography to another identifiable person? Or is it enough that it is likely that it will be caused at some point, or caused to society in general, merely through the existence of such hate speech? Some assistance might be gained from considering an already existing legal basis in the UK for protection from hate speech. This is the legislation prohibiting hate speech directed against racial groups.

Comparison with Incitement to Racial Hatred

Perhaps one of the more interesting aspects of such an approach to the regulation of pornography is the comparison with the UK's current laws in relation to the prevention of incitement to racial hatred. This has been noted by several writers – consider this evocative passage by Aminatta Forna:

> Imagine if you walked into your high street newsagent and saw that one of the shelves was taken up with magazines devoted to racist pictures. Each magazine showed black men and women being tied up, gagged, bound and humiliated. Inside, advertisements urged the reader to send off for violent videos, in which black people were shown being tortured by whites. People browsing in the shop select copies and flick through the photographs, deciding which to buy. Some of the magazines are specially tailored to the views of the readers – specifically anti-Semitic, or Oriental, or Asian for example. All advocate white supremacy. There are black people in the shop but, humiliated and intimidated, they merely avert their eyes. The black shop assistant rings up the total on the cash till without comment.[35]

Such material might well be prohibited by the provisions of the Public Order Act 1986 (Part III).[36] A two-part test governs whether such material/speech is prohibited under the Act. The words must be 'threatening, abusive or insulting'; and the person must 'intend to stir up racial hatred' or 'having regard to all the circumstances racial hatred is likely to be stirred up thereby'.[37] No prosecution under these provisions can be brought in England and Wales without the permission of the Attorney General.[38]

It can be argued that these provisions are based on a different theoretical basis, in that the intention is to preserve public order, to prevent actual violence, rather than making choices about harmful speech. This was specifically stated in the White Paper which preceded the 1986 Act:

> A variety of amendments to the section were suggested, many of which would alter the basis of the offence, so that the criminal law would be used against the production of material or the expression of views which are offensive in a multi-racial society. The Government believes that the reasonable exercise of freedom of expression should be protected, however unpleasant the views expressed, and has concluded that section 5A should continue to be based on considerations of public order.[39]

In an earlier White Paper it had been stated that these offences were

> similar to the offence under section 5 of the Public Order Act 1936 of using threatening, abusive or insulting words, in any public place or at any public meeting, with intent to provoke a breach of the peace or whereby a breach of the peace is likely to be occasioned. They are concerned to prevent the stirring up of racial hatred which may beget violence and public disorder.[40]

The offence referred to is now effectively contained in three offences in the Public Order Act 1986. Section 4 deals with the use of threatening, abusive or insulting words or behaviour with intent to cause the belief that immediate violence will be used against the person, or to provoke the person to immediate violence. Section 5 creates an offence when threatening, abusive or insulting words or behaviour are used which are likely to cause alarm, harassment or distress to a person in the vicinity. A third offence was added in 1994.[41] Section 4A creates an offence of causing intentional harassment, alarm or distress by using, or displaying threatening, abusive, or insulting words, or behaviour.

It may not be what was intended but it does seem that the provisions of Part III of the 1986 Act are capable of being more than just public order offences. The offences are wider than those in ss. 4 or 5. It is questionable whether separate offences dealing with racial hatred would have been necessary, if this was not the case.[42] The most obvious distinction is that Part III offences have more penalties than even a s. 4 offence.[43]

All the relevant offences are capable of being committed in public or private places, except where both parties are within a dwelling.[44] This is similar to the provisions of ss. 4, 4A and 5. The exception is contained in s. 23, which makes the possession of racially inflammatory material with a view to wider dissemination an offence. This, by definition, can be committed within a dwelling.[45]

Under the racial hatred offences there is no requirement that *actual* racial hatred is stirred up, if it is proved that it was the person's intention so to do. Whereas it is a requirement in ss. 4, 4A and 5 that someone is affected by the words or signs, this is not so under the Part III offences. Therefore, the justification of preventing public disorder is applicable only indirectly.[46]

Another interesting factor is that 'hatred' is not defined within the statute. It cannot mean, necessarily, actual violence, as otherwise that would be stated in the Act. Section 4 deals with 'immediate unlawful violence.' Presumably it is closer to the test in ss. 4A and 5 of being likely to cause harassment, alarm or distress, although 'hatred' might suggest a stronger meaning.[47] The fact that Part III of the 1986 Act does not just target situations where public disorder might occur, but also contains the pre-emptive measures in s. 23, clearly indicates that, intentionally or not, Part III of the Act does not confine its provisions to matters of public order.[48]

It might be argued that the prosecutions brought under Part III of the 1986 Act, and its predecessors, are more compatible with the justification of maintaining public order. Certainly, cases such as *R* v. *Malik*,[49] where the offending words were uttered at a public meeting, support this interpretation. Distribution of written material is not so directly linked to public order, particularly if not distributed at a public gathering. Unlike *Malik*, *R* v. *Hancock*[50] did not result in a successful prosecution. The publishers of *The Southern News* were found not guilty of incitement to racial hatred after they claimed that they had merely wished to educate the public about serious political issues of the day, and had printed a disclaimer to that effect.

It is debatable, however, whether such a prosecution would be successful under the new 1986 Act, given that a conviction can now be secured regardless of the intention of the publisher, if having regard to all the circumstances racial hatred is likely to be stirred up.[51] Again, there is no immediacy to the threat of public disorder in cases involving the prosecution of racist comic strips[52] and certainly not in the prosecution of the elderly Dowager Lady Birdwood for distributing anti-Semitic leaflets.[53] It is interesting to note that s. 4, in contrast, requires the threat of violence to be immediate.[54]

The overall impression is that the law relating to incitement to racial hatred is a practical, if not directly intentional, method of regulating hate speech on the basis of content as much as effect. If it was merely concerned with the effects of speech, and thus with public order, the offences contained in ss. 4 and 5 (and now s. 4A) would have sufficed. It is therefore submitted that the UK does already have a law which regulates hate speech, but which is theoretically vague in practice as to whom it protects from harm. Thus, the adoption of hate speech provisions relating to pornography would not be such a great theoretical leap, and nor does it appear to be a necessary pre-requisite for legislation that the precise harm to be prevented should be identified.

The retention of incitement to racial hatred legislation, its actual nature, and not its supposed theoretical base, must be justified by the theorists who would oppose a similar law in relation to pornography. It is not enough to say, as Geoffrey Robertson has done, that 'racism is a special case because of its particular propensity to cause public disorder'.[55]

Other Implications for Legal Theory

The other question which arises out of proposing to adopt this approach is whether the law should be gender-neutral. One feminist argument, from which the harm-based approach is derived, has frequently been attacked for simply focusing on the harm caused to women.[56] In fact, A. W. B. Simpson ponders whether feminists have ever seen any pornography, on the basis that it involves men, children and animals as well.[57] Catherine MacKinnon would reject this criticism on the basis that it is simply an example of the male 'me too' approach.[58] Subject to wishing to make a political point, that women are the main victims of pornography, a gender-neutral law would serve equally as well.

For example, the first Canadian category, explicit sex with violence or cruelty, would cover such acts as bestiality, whether or not women were involved, as there is little doubt that it is an act of cruelty to an animal to abuse it in such a way. The second category (of explicit sex which is degrading or dehumanizing) is again easily gender-neutral. The degrading or dehumanizing aspect comes from the objectification of the victim in pornography. This is most commonly a woman, but can also be a man or a child. Objectification means the conversion of the person from being a person with whom the consumer identifies, into an object through which the consumer, either directly or through the orchestrator in the picture (the person in control), obtains sexual gratification.[59] The third category (explicit sex) could involve men and women, without objectification, and thus would not be caught. It is submitted it could never include children or animals, as their presence would always amount to cruelty, and thus fall into the first category.

By adopting the three category classification, the objection that some feminists view pornography as 'one indivisible phenomenon' can be countered.[60] (Obviously not all feminists would agree with this approach.) Thus it is clear that should the hurdle of whether or not it can be accepted that pornography (or certain types) cause harm, there would be no strong theoretical objections to the adoption of such legislation.

COMPATIBILITY WITH INTERNATIONAL OBLIGATIONS

The second consideration is whether a law based on these principles would satisfy the UK's international obligations – for present purposes, the European Convention on Human Rights (ECHR), and membership of the European Union (EU). If such a theoretical basis were to be incompatible with these, it would be difficult (and possibly futile) to introduce it.

European Convention on Human Rights

Article 10 of the ECHR covers freedom of expression. Article 10(2) places limitations on these rights. At present, the UK law of obscenity would appear to be covered by the exceptions outlined in Article 10(2) which include 'such formalities, conditions, restrictions or penalties as are prescribed by law and are necessary in a democratic society . . . for the protection of health or morals'. The European Court of Human Rights has stated that Article 10 guarantees freedom 'not only for information . . . favourably received or regarded as inoffensive or as a matter of indifference, but also to those that offend, shock or disturb'.[61]

The Court, however, has ruled that national control over obscene material will not necessarily contravene the ECHR. In the *Müller* case, the Court considered the Swiss test of obscenity.[62] The test of the national courts had been 'whether the overall impression of the item or work causes moral offence to a person of ordinary sensitivity' – a test based on morality. The Court accepted that in the specific circumstances of the case, the law was compatible with the ECHR. This was because, first, the law was designed to protect morals – a legitimate aim under Article 10(2).

Second, in response to the argument that the law was too vague, the Court noted that obscenity fell within a category of offences which, as they had to keep pace with the prevailing views of society, were permissibly vague, although they must not be entirely lacking in predictability.[63] It would therefore seem that a new approach in the UK would not automatically breach the ECHR.

The harm-based approach would also be a legitimate restriction under Article 10(2), as it allows for restrictions necessary to 'public safety' and for 'the protection of the reputation or *rights* of others' (emphasis added). As the UK law in relation to racial hatred has been identified as comparable with this approach, the obvious question to ask is whether the Court has ruled on the compatibility of such legislation with the provisions of Article 10. There has been no challenge before the European Court as to the legitimacy of the UK's anti-racial hatred laws. The Court did consider similar legislation in *Glimmerveen and Hagenbeck* v. *The Netherlands*,[64] when it held that Dutch law did not breach Article 10. This would suggest that the UK law would also be acceptable. Thus, there are no obvious objections, in relation to the ECHR, to a change in the theoretical basis of the law.

The European Union

The UK's membership of the EU poses a potential clash of rights. To what extent can pornographers be said to have an economic right to sell their product? The jurisprudence of the EU provides interesting new questions as to the place of civil rights alongside economic 'rights' to free trade. At what point will civil rights defeat these 'economic' rights, if at all?

This assumes that there can be said to be such rights for the producers. The European Treaty does create enforceable rights in relation to trade, and therefore these could be seen as the economic rights of the producer. Certainly, the rights to free trade created under the European Treaty are not unlimited. If we consider tangible pornographic goods such as books, magazines and videos, as opposed to transmitted services such as satellite broadcasts, then the relevant provision is Article 30. Article 36 lists permissible grounds for restricting the rights created in Article 30. These include the 'grounds of public morality, public policy or public security; the protection of health and life of humans'.[65]

At present the European Court of Justice has ruled that if the member state imposes the same tests internally, then a restriction (or prohibition) on imports will be upheld under Article 36.[66] For example, in *R* v. *Henn & Darby*,[67] where pornographic goods were banned from import into the

UK, this prohibition[68] was challenged as being contrary to Articles 30 and 36. In answer to the point that the prohibition amounted to a restriction on trade, the Court stated:

> Whatever may be the differences between the laws on the subject in force in the different constitutional parts of the United Kingdom, and notwithstanding the fact that they contain certain exceptions of limited scope, these laws, taken as a whole, have as their purpose the prohibition, or at least, the restraining, of the manufacture and marketing of publications or articles of an indecent or obscene character. In these circumstances it is permissible to conclude, on a comprehensive view, that there is no lawful trade in such goods in the United Kingdom. A prohibition on imports which may in certain respects be more strict than some of the laws applied within the United Kingdom cannot therefore be regarded as amounting to a measure designed to give indirect protection to some national product or aimed at creating arbitrary discrimination between goods of this type depending on whether they are produced within the national territory or another Member State.[69]

In *Conegate* v. *Customs & Excise Commissioners*[70] the European Court of Justice (ECJ) held that goods could not be prohibited where there was no *ban* on manufacture in the member state, only restrictions on sales. This would apply to soft-core or indecent material.[71] Therefore, at present the UK's domestic laws do not appear openly to clash with the EU provisions.

If the basis of the law were changed to harm-based principles, this might pose a potential problem. It might well prove difficult to argue that they are laws in relation to public morality, in light of the reason for the change. It is quite possible that 'protection from harm' would fall into the 'public policy' exception, but this is not a clear point. Prima facie pornography controls stand a better change of being upheld under the morality test. The ECJ, however, has ruled that recourse to the public policy exception requires 'the existence . . . of a genuine and sufficiently serious threat to the requirements of public policy affecting one of the fundamental interests of society'.[72] The protection of members of society from harm, or even society itself (depending on the focus of the harm test) could be seen as a 'fundamental interest of society'. It is not impossible for a harm-based approach to be acceptable to European law. It would not necessarily be struck down on its theoretical base alone provided that it could be shown to be in the fundamental interests of society in the UK.[73]

CONCLUSIONS

If an approach similar to that adopted by Canadian law were to be adopted in the UK, it is clear that it would not obviously be in breach of the UK's international obligations in relation to civil rights. As regards the theoretical implications, this basis is attractive, but there are several issues which need to be resolved. The use of the term 'harm' is non-specific. If it is taken to mean harm to society in general, then it is open to the criticism that this is too vague a definition. Yet the present law in relation to incitement to racial hatred is non-specific as to the harm which is being prevented. In fact, prevention of public disorder (which is the nominal justification) could be seen as preventing harm to society in general. If it is to prevent harm to specific individuals in the violence that it is thought will ensue, then why was s. 4 of the Public Order Act 1986 not considered sufficient protection? Surely, it is the general disruption to society caused by public disorder that is targeted?

It is also difficult to suggest that specific individuals or groups from ethnic minorities are being protected, as the law has been used to 'protect' whites.[74] So clear identification of exactly who is being protected is not possible, apart from any group that comes under attack as a result of racial origins. This point is also important in deciding whether or not the reformed law should be gender-neutral. If an identifiable section of society has to be specifically protected, then women are an obvious choice. (This is assuming that children of both sexes and animals are protected.) This leaves the question of whether violent gay pornography would remain permissible. If a gender-neutral law is preferred, then it is not clear as to which class of society is protected – perhaps all those objectified by pornography. It becomes more attractive to say that it is society in general that is being protected from the harm caused by pornography as a result of the lowering in status within society suffered by group members portrayed in pornography. Another decision that should be reached before deciding on adoption of this scheme is whether the definition of pornography, and therefore the prohibitions placed on such material, are to be based on content alone, or whether the mode of representation will also be included. If it is based on content alone, then material in the third category discussed above could be freely displayed.

In the context of understanding human rights, this chapter has sought to take a current debate about the legal regulation of pornography beyond its current parameters to look at the practical implications of a change in its theoretical base. In doing so, it has highlighted a difficult area in rights theory. Is it possible to justify laws preventing the incitement to racial hatred, whilst rejecting a similar basis for the control of pornography? It seems to be taken on trust that race hate speech causes harm. Yet the law is vague on the definition of this harm. Rights theorists must guard against an approach which amounts to saying that inflammatory racism equals hate speech and therefore is harmful, but pornography equals free speech and therefore must be protected – at least until a clearer theoretical difference between the two forms of speech is identified.

ACKNOWLEDGMENTS

I wish to thank my colleagues, in particular Alistair Alcock, Michael Bools, Susan Edwards and Femi Elias, and also Francis Coleman, for their comments on ideas in this chapter. The views expressed, and any errors of fact contained in the article, remain my own.

NOTES

1. For the purposes of this chapter, pornography will be taken to mean sexually explicit material. Obscenity in terms of the current law has a wider meaning, including advocating the use of prohibited drugs – see *John Calder Publications Ltd* v. *Powell* [1965] 1 QB 509; *R* v. *Skirving* [1985] QB 819.

2. A useful summary of the debate can be found in E. Jackson, The problem with pornography: a critical survey of the current debate (1995) 3 *Feminist Legal Studies* 49.

3. As much of this material would be deemed obscene under the Obscene Publications Act 1959, it affects adults as well. See First Report of the Home Affairs Committee, 1993/94, *Computer Pornography*, HC 126 (London: HMSO, 1994); and now Part VII of the Criminal Justice and Public Order Act 1994.

4. See N. St John Stevas, *Obscenity and the Law* (London: Secker & Warburg, 1956), pp. 121–4 for discussion on this.

5. An alternative to the current law was proposed by the *Report of the Committee on Obscenity and Film Censorship* (Chairman: Professor Bernard Williams) (London: HMSO, 1979) Cmnd 7772, reprinted 1981, henceforth the Williams Committee. The recommendations were based on whether any harm was caused, but the Committee rejected the idea that pornography could objectively be shown to cause harm. The main recommendations were that all restrictions on the written word be removed. Images should only be prohibited if they involved the exploitation for sexual purposes of children, or if there was reason to believe that actual physical harm had been inflicted on the persons involved (content-based prohibition). However, 'live' sex shows were to be prohibited, although the same 'performance' would be permitted on film (an example of a representation-based restriction). Restrictions on sale and display of material (other than the written word) were permissible where unrestricted availability would be offensive to reasonable people by reason of the manner in which the material portrayed violence, cruelty or horror, or sexual, faecal or urinary functions or genital organs (representation-based restriction in that it restricts the display and ease of availability only – it does not prohibit on the basis of content).

6. In Scotland, the relevant statute is now the Civic Government (Scotland) Act 1982, s.

51. See K. D. Ewing and W. Finnie, *Civil Liberties in Scotland: Cases & Materials*, 2nd edn (Edinburgh: W. Green & Son, 1988), pp. 293–310.

7. Section 1(1) of the Obscene Publications Act 1959; this statutory test is based on the common law test found in *R* v. *Hicklin* (1868) LR 3 QB 360.

8. R. Hall, *The Well of Loneliness* (London: Jonathan Cape, 1928).

9. See N. St John Stevas, *op. cit.*, pp. 98–103.

10. D. H. Lawrence, *Lady Chatterley's Lover* (Harmondsworth: Penguin Books, 1960).

11. *R* v. *Penguin Books Ltd* [1961] *Criminal Law Review* 176.

12. See G. Robertson, Foreword to the thirtieth anniversary edition of C. H. Rolph, *The Trial of Lady Chatterley* (Harmondsworth: Penguin, 1990) at pp. xiii–iv.

13. Hence the defence of the public good in s. 4 of the 1959 Act, which in fact came to the rescue of Constance Chatterley.

14. *R* v. *Calder & Boyars Ltd* [1969] 1 QB 151; also see G. Robertson, *op. cit.*, pp. xiv–v.

15. See Liberty, Stonewall & Outrage, *Sexuality & the State* (London: National Council for Civil Liberties, 1994), pp. 31–2, concerning raids on gay and lesbian bookshops.

16. Public Order Act 1986, Part III.

17. It is too easy and convenient to assume that participants must be willing even in adult pornography.

18. Ferg J in *R* v. *Ramsingh* (1984) 14 CCC (3d) 230, at 239–41. Although women are specifically mentioned, the analysis can be applied to any objectified person in pornography.

19. *R* v. *Butler* (1992) 89 DLR 449 *per* Sopinka J at 467. The following reports were cited in support: Attorney General's Commission on Pornography (the Meese Commission), *Final Report* (Washington DC: US Department of Justice, 1986), vol. 1, pp. 938–1035; Metro Toronto Task Force on Public Violence Against Women and Children, *Final Report* (Toronto, 1984), p. 66; *Report of the Joint Select Committee on Video Material* (Canberra: Australia Government Publishing Services, 1988), pp. 185–230; *Pornography: Report of the Ministerial Committee of Inquiry into Pornography* (Wellington, New Zealand: Ministry of Justice, 1989), pp. 38–45.

20. See C. Itzin (ed.), *Pornography: Women, Violence and Civil Liberties* (Oxford: Oxford University Press, 1992), pp. 558–60.

21. Alternatively, whilst it is not yet certain how the HIV virus is transmitted, there is strong evidence to suggest that sexual behaviour plays an important part, and therefore it would be ridiculous not to modify sexual behaviour in the meantime – on the off-chance that it is not actually a means of transmission. The author is grateful to one of her colleagues, Alistair Alcock, for this comparison.

22. Criminal Code RSC 1985, c. C–46 s. 163.

23. *Ibid.*, s. 163(8) – this test has existed since the Criminal Code 1959 [s. 150(8)]. Prior to this, the test of obscenity was that of *R* v. *Hicklin*, *op. cit.* The test is not exclusive; see *Dechow* v. *The Queen* (1978) 1 SCR 951.

24. *Towne Cinema Theatres Ltd* v. *The Queen* [1985] 1 SCR 494 *per* Dickson CJ, at 508–9.

25. *R* v. *Butler*, *op. cit.*, p. 470. The three-part classification was put forward in *R* v. *Wagner* (1985) 43 CR (3d) 318. See also J. V. P. Check, The effects of violent pornography, nonviolent dehumanizing pornography, and erotica: some legal implications from a Canadian perspective. In C. Itzin (ed.), *op. cit.*, pp. 350–8.

26. *R* v. *Butler*, *op. cit.*, p. 471.

27. *Ibid.*, p. 471. S. Kappeler, *The Pornography of Representation* (Cambridge: Polity Press, 1986) discusses the dangers of allowing 'art' or 'literature' to be used to save what would otherwise be pornography. It is a matter of some sophistry or intellectual snobbery to distinguish 'porn' from 'art', although a representation test can be used for this purpose in that it can suggest that pornography can become art (and thus protected) under certain circumstances. A content-based approach would suggest recognition of pornography regardless of the medium.

28. See s. 1(1) of the 1981 Act.

29. *R* v. *Butler*, *op. cit.*, p. 494.

30. See *R* v. *Mawson* (unreported, 31 January 1992), where S. M. Harris Prov J stated: 'My sense . . . persuades me that Canadians *today* are no longer prepared to tolerate other

Canadians seeing specific depictions of casual, purely physically gratifying, unprotected sex bearing in mind (as only one cautionary factor) the present concern with AIDS and related dangers' (at 11; emphasis in original), quoted in *R* v. *Ronish* 18 CR (4th) 165, at 182; *Mawson* was decided before *Butler*, but is interesting for the judicial interpretation of current community standards. See also *R* v. *Jorgensen* (27 May 1992, unreported) and *Glad Day Bookshop Inc* v. *Deputy Minister of National Revenue (Customs and Excise)* (14 July 1992, unreported), both quoted in *Ronish* at 182–3.

31. See *R* v. *Hawkins* (10 April 1992, unreported) and *R* v. *Laliberte* (29 May 1992, unreported), both quoted in *R* v. *Ronish, op. cit.*, at 183.

32. *R* v. *Ronish, op. cit., per* Cole Prov J at pp. 183–4.

33. *R* v. *Butler, op. cit.*, p. 471; quoted in *R* v. *Ronish, op. cit.*, p. 183.

34. *R* v. *Ronish, op. cit.*, p. 184–5.

35. A. Forna, Pornography and racism: sexualizing oppression and inciting hatred. In C. Itzin (ed.), *op. cit.*, p. 106. See also S. Kappeler, *op. cit.*, pp. 5–10 for a comparison of an account of a racially motivated murder and pornographic images.

36. See ss. 17–23. Racial hatred is defined in s. 17 as 'hatred against a group of persons in Great Britain defined by reference to colour, race, nationality (including citizenship) or ethnic or national origins'. Groups defined by religion are not covered within Great Britain – see s. 8 of the Public Order (Northern Ireland) Act 1987 for the position in Northern Ireland.

37. The test is found in all the relevant sections: s. 18 (use of words or behaviour or display of written material); s. 19 (publishing or distributing written material); s. 20 (public performance of play); s. 21 (distributing, showing or playing a recording); s. 22 (broadcasting or including programme in cable programme service); s. 23 (possession of racially inflammatory material).

38. S. 27.

39. *Review of Public Order Law*, White Paper Cmnd. 9510 (1985), p. 39, para. 6.5.

40. *Racial Discrimination*, White Paper Cmnd. 6234 (1975), p. 30. The White Paper explained the need to move the offence from the mainly civil law based Race Relations Act 1965 to the criminal law of the Public Order Act 1936.

41. See s. 154 of the Criminal Justice and Public Order Act 1994.

42. Consider *Jordan* v. *Burgoyne* [1963] 2 QB 744, where Jordan was convicted under s. 5 of the Public Order Act 1936 for racist statements. Lord Parker CJ stated 'I cannot myself, having read the speech, imagine any reasonable citizen, certainly one who was a Jew, not being provoked beyond endurance, and not only a Jew but a coloured man, and quite a number of people of this country who were told that they were merely tools of the Jews, and that they had fought in the war on the wrong side, and matters of that sort.' (p. 748).

43. Section 4(4) states that the maximum sentence is six months imprisonment (summary trial), as does s. 4A(5), whereas s. 27 (Part III) provides for a maximum sentence of two years imprisonment on indictment.

44. See s. 4(2); s. 4A(2); s. 5(2); and s. 18(2). Dwelling is defined in s. 8 for Part I offences; it is to be assumed that it will have the same definition for Part III.

45. Section 24 of the 1986 Act grants powers of entry and search by warrant for possible contravention of s. 23.

46. The intention behind this provision was to close the loop-hole whereby material sent to persons unlikely to be affected (e.g. Members of Parliament) could escape prosecution, as racial hatred was not likely to be stirred up. Consideration was given to this point in *R* v. *Britton* [1967] 2 QB 51. See also *Review of Public Order Law, op. cit.*, p. 39, para. 6.6, where the justification was that material might fall subsequently into the hands of persons likely to be affected.

47. See A. T. H. Smith, *The Offences Against Public Order* (London: Sweet & Maxwell, 1987), p. 151, para. 9–06.

48. This point has been noted by a number of writers: D. Feldman, *Civil Liberties and Human Rights in England & Wales* (Oxford: Clarendon Press, 1993), pp. 811–2; W. J. Wolffe, 'Values in conflict: incitement to racial hatred & the Public Order Act 1986' [1987] *Public Law* 85, at pp. 86–7; P. M. Leopold, 'Incitement to hatred – the history of a controversial criminal offence' [1977] *Public Law* 389, at p. 403.

49. [1968] 1 All ER 582. The case involved 'Black Power' activist Michael X, who was imprisoned for 12 months.

50. *The Times*, 28, 29 March and 1 May, 1968.

51. The prosecution was brought under s. 6 of the Race Relations Act 1965. Under the 1986 Act a defence is available; see, for example, s. 19(2).

52. See *R* v. *Edwards* (1983) 5 Cr. App. R. (S) 145.

53. See G. Robertson and A. Nicol, *Media Law*, 3rd edn (Harmondsworth: Penguin, 1992), p. 170, for an account of this prosecution.

54. See *R* v. *Horseferry Road Justices, ex parte Siadatan* [1991] 1 All ER 324.

55. G. Robertson, *Freedom, the Individual and the Law*, 6th edn (Harmondsworth: Penguin, 1989), p. 90.

56. See D. Feldman, *op. cit.*, pp. 703–4.

57. A. W. B. Simpson, *Pornography & Politics: A Look Back to the Williams Committee* (London: Waterlow Publishers Ltd, 1983), p. 71. It is submitted that the real point is that they have seen all too much.

58. C. MacKinnon, *Feminism Unmodified. Discourses on Life and Law* (Cambridge, MA: Harvard University Press, 1987).

59. For a more lucid and detailed account, see S. Kappeler *op. cit.*

60. Suggestion quoted in D. Feldman, *op. cit.*, pp. 703–4, quoted from A. W. B. Simpson, *op. cit.*, p. 71.

61. *Observer and Guardian* v. *UK* (1991) Series A, Vol. 216, para. 59(a).

62. *Müller* v. *Switzerland* (1988) Series A, Vol. 133; (1991) 13 EHRR 212.

63. This is particularly interesting, as a similar charge had been laid against the Canadian approach, although this was rejected by the Supreme Court in *R* v. *Butler*, *op. cit.*

64. (1979) 4 EHHR 260.

65. Article 36 of the Treaty of Rome is subject to the provision that such restrictions do not 'constitute a means of arbitrary discrimination or a disguised restriction on trade between Member States'.

66. See *Adoui and Cornuaille* v. *Belgium*, Cases 115–116/81 [1982] ECR 1665.

67. Case 34/79 [1979] ECR 3795; [1980] 1 CMLR 246.

68. Under the Customs Consolidation Act 1876, s. 42, and the Customs and Excise Act 1952, s. 304.

69. [1980] 1 CMLR 246, at 247.

70. Case 121/85 [1986] ECR 1007; [1986] 1 CMLR 739.

71. In this case, the goods in question were life-like inflatable dolls.

72. *R* v. *Bouchereau*, Case 30/77 [1977] ECR 1999, para. 35.

73. It would not be necessary for other member states to adopt the same approach. In *R* v. *Boucherou*, at para. 34, the ECJ stated that 'the particular circumstances justifying recourse to public policy may vary from one country to another and from one period to another and it is therefore necessary in this matter to allow the competent national authorities an area of discretion within the limits imposed by the Treaty and the provisions adopted for its implementation'.

74. See *R* v. *Malik*, *op. cit.* However, it does not appear to protect Muslims, on the grounds that they are not a *racial* group, but defined as a religious group – see discussion in *Mandla* v. *Dowell Lee* [1983] 2 AC 548.

PART SEVEN:

REAPPRAISING ORTHODOXIES

23

The Limits of Constitutional Law: The Canadian Charter of Rights and Freedoms and the Public–Private Divide

Gavin W. Anderson

It is a commonplace nowadays to remark that we live in an ever-changing world; the proof of this is all too self-evident when we consider the dissolution of old hegemonies, and the transition to democracy in many former totalitarian states. Perhaps the most far-reaching change which is occurring is the globalization of the economy, resulting in the creation of new supra-national structures whose function is to police increasingly deregulated markets. In many ways, our traditional thinking about the state and government, and their relation to the individual, is being called into question. What challenges do these developments pose for the protection of human rights as the twenty-first century approaches? In particular, how adequate is present constitutional machinery, based as it is on the classical eighteenth-century conception of rights designed in the age of the nation state? One problem which has been highlighted is the trend towards separating economic power from governmental control,[1] and the consequent rise of the multinational corporation as a major centre of economic power whose influence can reach across whole continents and millions of people.

This chapter seeks to address this issue in the context of the public–private divide in the Canadian Charter of Rights and Freedoms.[2] In other words, do, and should, the Charter's guarantees apply as equally to the private sector as to government? One of the most controversial features of the Charter since its enactment in 1982 has been the granting of constitutional rights *to* corporations,[3] but to what extent can constitutional rights be enforced in private litigation *against* such corporations? The first section of this chapter critically examines the public–private divide which has been produced by the Supreme Court of Canada's jurisprudence on this point. The academic debate over whether this divide is 'not only technically correct, but sound as a matter of constitutional policy'[4] is then explored. It is argued that the Court's line of authority ignores the oppressive potential of private power. However, the solution is not necessarily the more widespread application of constitutional rights to the private sector, as there are doubts over whether constitutionalism is capable of acting as an effective safeguard against the abuse of private power.

THE PUBLIC–PRIVATE DIVIDE IN THE CANADIAN CONSTITUTION

Text

Section 32(1) of the Charter of Rights and Freedoms states as follows:

> This Charter applies
> (a) to the Parliament and government of Canada in respect of all matters within the authority of Parliament including all matters relating to the Yukon Territory and Northwest Territory; and
> (b) to the legislature and government of each province in respect of all matters within the authority of the legislature of each province.

This chapter explores what this section means in respect of the application of the rights and freedoms guaranteed by the Charter. What does the fact that the Charter applies to Parliament and the provincial legislatures 'in respect of all matters within [their] authority' mean? Is the consequence that the Charter applies to all laws, including the uncodified common law? How is 'government' to be defined? Does this refer to the act or the institution of government, and if it is the institution, does the Charter's reach extend to the courts? Might some ostensibly non-governmental bodies be subject to the Charter, and if so, on what grounds: because they are closely linked to government or because they are exercising a governmental function? Above all, does the Charter apply in private litigation between two apparently private persons where there is no evident involvement of governmental actors: for example, could the Charter apply in these circumstances in traditional 'private law' actions, such as a claim in tort or for breach of contract? In other words, does the wording of s. 32 result in a public–private divide in which only some breaches of the Charter's guarantees are punished?

Legislative History

Before considering how these issues have been dealt with by the courts, the question of why the drafters of the Charter seem to have left them open should be addressed. This does seem surprising in view of the undoubted influence on Canadian thinking of the literature and case law engendered by the US Bill of Rights, which should have alerted Canadians to the difficulties encountered by the US courts in determining the bounds of 'state action.'[5] Such has been the analytical confusion in this field that one leading commentator has described the situation there as being one of 'chaos'.[6] There are two views, one being that the question of the Charter's applicability was in fact dealt with, and in a manner designed to exclude private litigation. Here, it is important to bear in mind the three formative stages of the text of the Charter before its formal enactment: the federal government's Resolution of 2 October 1980 containing the initial draft, the Special Joint Committee of the Senate and House of Commons which considered this text in detail, and the 5 November 1981 agreement between Prime Minister Trudeau and the provincial premiers (with the exception of Quebec) which led to the signing of the Constitutional Accord requesting Westminster to legislate. At the first two stages, the wording of s. 32's precursor was markedly different because under its terms the Charter applied 'to the Parliament and government of Canada *and to* all matters within the authority of Parliament' (emphasis added). However, this was redrafted following the 5 November agreement, resulting in the current form of words. According to Professor John Whyte, it is 'historical fact' that the purpose of this alteration was 'to remove the ambiguity and to restrict the application of the Charter to legislative and governmental action'.[7] The evidence also is that the question of application was only raised three times in the Joint Committee, and each time a restrictive interpretation was advanced on behalf of the Justice Department.[8]

An alternative analysis of the Charter's legislative history is that the text is ambiguous on this point, and deliberately so. Professor Dale Gibson argues that the draft produced with the 2 October Resolution was clearly applicable to private litigation, and that while he concedes that the rewording reflects the wishes of many protagonists in the negotiations to restrict the Charter's effect to the public sector, the final text is best viewed as a compromise leaving the issue open to the courts. He suggests that it would have been possible for either view to have been conclusively enshrined in the constitutional text, and that 'the omission of the conclusive word "only" [before the reference to Parliament and government in the final draft] cannot be regarded as accidental'.[9] It has also been pointed out that apart from the three references in the Joint Committee, the issue of applicability was raised at neither the 5 November meeting nor in any session of either the Canadian or Westminster Parliament.[10] Even if the legislative intention can be determined, it is by no means self-evident that it should be determinative. Canada has perhaps been fortunate to have avoided the 'original intent' controversy which has plagued much of the US debate in recent years,[11] but even leaving the desirability of such an endeavour aside, the sheer practical problem of discerning who the framers were, and what they were thinking, should be clear from the foregoing discussion. In any case, Peter Russell reminds us that 'the constitution means what the judges say it means',[12] and so it is to the jurisprudence of the Supreme Court of Canada on the meaning of s. 32 that the focus now shifts.

Supreme Court Jurisprudence: *RWDSU* v. *Dolphin Delivery*

The judgment which has had the most decisive impact on this whole question was that of *RWDSU* v. *Dolphin Delivery*,[13] handed down in 1986. The appellant union, RWDSU, had initially been involved in a labour dispute with Purolator Courier Inc. in Ontario, but was now seeking to engage in secondary picketing with Dolphin Delivery, another courier based in British Columbia. This would have been permissible under the British Columbia (BC) Labour Code if the two companies were business allies, and so the union applied to the BC Labour Relations Board for the requisite declaration. This was refused because as Purolator was an inter-provincial undertaking, its dispute with RWDSU was governed by the federal Canadian Labour Code, and as the code was silent on this point, the legality of the secondary picketing depended on the common law. Dolphin Delivery then successfully applied for an injunction restraining the secondary picketing on the basis of the common law tort of inducing a breach of contract. The union appealed against the order to the BC Court of Appeal,[14] where the issue of the Charter's applicability was not directly raised. Instead, that court unanimously dismissed the union's appeal on the (majority) reasoning that neither freedom of association nor freedom of expression protected the activity of picketing (and that, in any case, the restriction on freedom of expression would be upheld as a reasonable limit in terms of s. 1 of the Charter[15]). The case ultimately came to the Supreme Court of Canada for decision, where the appeal focused solely on the union's right to freedom of expression.

The Supreme Court, *per* McIntyre J, cast the issue in terms of the Charter's applicability, and this came under two heads – whether it applied to the common law, or to private litigation – although the judgment also dealt with a third issue, namely whether the Charter applied to the courts.

Justice McIntyre first considered the question of the common law, holding, on the basis of the Charter's status as 'the supreme law of Canada',[16] that the Charter must apply, because otherwise it would be unrealistic to exclude 'the whole body of the common law which in great part governs the rights and obligations of individuals in society'.[17] However, the Charter did not apply here simply because the alleged restriction on the union's freedom of expression was a rule of the common law; something more than that would be required. McIntyre J clarified what this is by stating that the common law will be subjected to the Charter 'only in so far as [it] is the basis of some governmental action'.[18] Accordingly, although concerned not to exclude the 'whole body' of the common law, McIntyre J was content not to apply the Charter to that 'great part' of it which regulates private relationships.

The judgment accordingly turned on whether there was any 'governmental action' in this case sufficient to invoke the Charter. McIntyre J first dealt with the argument that this was supplied by virtue of the fact that the instrument by which the common law restrained the picketing was an order of the court, and therefore 'governmental action' on this account alone. Professor Hogg acknowledges that this argument could potentially render all private conduct subject to the Charter.[19] McIntyre J's view, however, was that as the actors specified by s. 32 were the 'legislative, executive and administrative branches of government',[20] the judicial branch was necessarily excluded from being directly answerable for all its decisions; the Charter applied to the courts only to the extent of their duty to apply the law 'as neutral arbiters'.[21] What would amount to an element of governmental intervention was found to be difficult to define, but there would have to be 'a more direct [and] precisely-defined connection'[21] than the granting of a court order. The crucial point, therefore, was whether there was anything present in this case which could amount to governmental action.

McIntyre J's use of terminology is confusing here, as on the one hand the textual reference to government is used in the specific sense of meaning the executive and administrative branches, and on the other it is also clear that legislation will amount to government action[22] (presumably used here in an expanded sense). It is the presence of legislation on which McIntyre J concentrates, quoting with approval Professor Peter Hogg's statement that 'all action taken in exercise of a statutory power is covered by virtue of the references to "Parliament" and "legislature" in s. 32'.[23] An example, therefore, of when the Charter would apply in private litigation would be if the (ostensibly private) violating party was acting on the authority of statute.[24] However, here there was 'no offending statute'[25] and so, as RWDSU's action was based on the common law with no element of government relied on to support it, this was an instance of purely private litigation to which the Charter did not apply. It should be noted, however, that if the tort had rested on statutory authority, the Charter would have applied not because of the nature of the law *per se*, but because of the presence of governmental action indicated thereby.[26] The Charter was not held to be wholly irrelevant to private litigation, and the courts were enjoined to apply the common law consistently with the Charter's principles, but this was held to be very different from the proposition that 'one private party owes a constitutional duty to another'.[27] Thus, the test which emerges is that the Charter will only apply in private litigation if one can point to the presence of either governmental or legislative action in the activities of an apparently private party, and the extent to which the Charter will apply to the common law and the courts is rendered contingent on this being established.

Later Cases

Supreme Court jurisprudence since *Dolphin Delivery* has elaborated on what constitutes a necessary element of governmental action, and in particular on when this test is satisfied by the existence of a relevant statutory provision. Although this point was not fully explored in *Dolphin Delivery* itself, subsequent cases have indicated that the Court will not conclude that the Charter applies purely by the existence of a statutory link alone; it has to be demonstrated that the statute in question compels a certain course of action. This approach was taken in *Lavigne* v. *OPSEU*,[28] in which there was a challenge by a faculty member of a community college to his payment of union dues. The payment was a term of his employment by virtue of an 'agency-shop' collective agreement entered into by the college's Council of Regents. Unlike in *Dolphin Delivery*, however, the legislature *had* directed its mind to this issue, and had passed a statute allowing such a term to be incorporated into a collective agreement. According to La Forest J (writing for the majority), the existence of an element of compulsion in the statute would be determinative of whether the Charter applied. Accordingly, the fact that the legislation did not compel the plaintiff to make contributions to the union, as the parties to the collective agreement could have agreed to such a term independently of any legislative permission,[29] meant (at least on this point) that there was no legislative involvement capable on this score of removing the action from the private sphere.

Recent cases have also clarified when government, as the executive branch, will be held to act *qua* government, and here the Court has developed an institutional test (hinted at in McIntyre J's reference to the need to find a sufficiently close link with government in *Dolphin Delivery*). Thus in *Lavigne*, the Charter was ultimately held to apply in the action between the faculty member and the union because the Council of Regents which had negotiated the agreement was held to be under the control of the provincial Minister of Education, and was therefore 'part of the fabric of government'.[30] However, a university and a hospital have been held not to be part of that same fabric in the cases of *McKinney* v. *University of Guelph*[31] and *Stoffman* v. *Vancouver General Hospital*[32] respectively. In both these cases, the institutions had been incorporated by statute, and were in receipt of sizeable government funds, but the crucial fact was that they enjoyed a considerable degree of autonomy in administering their own affairs, and this was sufficient to sever the institutional link with government and so exclude the Charter. Thus the mandatory retirement policies of the university and the hospital could not be challenged on the basis of their alleged violation of the equality rights of s. 15 of the Charter.

One further area where the operation of the Charter has been clarified since *Dolphin Delivery* is in its relationship with the courts. One reading of McIntyre J's exclusion of the judicial branch from the rubric of government could be that the courts are completely exempt from Charter scrutiny; however, his remarks in this regard should not be taken out of context, and, in any case, sit uncomfortably with some of the criminal procedure provisions in the Charter itself. In *R* v. *Rahey*,[33] the Court signalled that the more extreme conclusion was not the one that it favoured. In that case, the issue was whether s. 11(b) of the Charter, which guarantees to persons charged with an offence the right to be tried within a reasonable time, could be used to grant relief against a trial judge's excessive delay. As this section could only be meaningful if addressed to the courts, it was held that the Charter did apply, and the order was granted. In the later case of *BCGEU* v. *British Columbia*,[34] *Dolphin Delivery* was further distinguished. This case also involved the issuing of an injunction against secondary picketing, but here *ex proprio motu* of the Chief Justice of British Columbia, as he encountered picket lines on his way into the court building. This injunction was found to be subject to Charter scrutiny, the Court's reasoning being that it had been issued in the public interest rather than in the course of private litigation.

Nature of the Problem

The result of these decisions is that there are now two categories of Charter violations: those that are punished, and those that attract no official opprobrium. Is this problematic?

Some commentators point out that the violation of rights by private parties is not completely unregulated, and that legislatures have never

536 *Gavin W. Anderson*

believed in a public–private distinction,[35] and that in Canada the problem is further offset by the existence of provincial human rights codes which do reach into the private sector. However, these codes do not always contain as comprehensive a list of guarantees as the Charter, and in any case can themselves be violative of the Charter.[36] Is there not, though, a more fundamental problem in that Charter practice falls short of Charter rhetoric that it constitutes the 'Supreme law of Canada' and that its enumerated rights and freedoms extend to 'everyone' and 'every citizen'?[37] How can this be reconciled with removing a large area of conduct from the protection of the Charter, an area which is likely to increase given the current trends towards privatization of governmental services.[38] Academic opinion on the Court's approach has divided into two distinct camps: those who agree with the Court's line-drawing exercise, although they may disagree over where the line should be drawn, and those who doubt the validity of the line-drawing exercise itself. It is to this debate that attention now turns.

'NOT ONLY TECHNICALLY CORRECT, BUT ALSO SOUND AS A MATTER OF CONSTITUTIONAL POLICY'

One of Canada's most eminent constitutional lawyers, Professor Peter Hogg of Osgoode Hall Law School, broadly endorses the Court's stance in *Dolphin Delivery* and subsequent cases on the basis that these decisions were 'not only technically correct, but . . . also sound as a matter of constitutional policy'.[39] His support of the Court's jurisprudence rests on the idea that there *is* an area of private conduct into which the Charter is not authorized to intrude. This rests on two principal arguments which combine both descriptive and normative considerations. The first justification is that the Charter should not apply to private litigation because '[a] constitution establishes and regulates the institutions of government and it leaves to those institutions the task of ordering the private affairs of the people'.[40] Therefore the Court was correct to exclude the Charter in cases like *Dolphin Delivery* and *McKinney* because it lacked the constitutionally mandated presence of government. The second argument begins by stating that the reason why the Charter applies to governments and legislatures is that they enjoy 'the coercive power of governance'[40] which is not characteristic of private actors. Thus, the Charter should only apply to private litigation when one of the actors involved has been granted the ability to exercise a power of compulsion. How accurate is it, though, to depict the cases where the Charter has been held not to apply as both lacking any governmental action, and also as involving private relationships formed entirely by consent? Both propositions require careful scrutiny.

Does Government Act in Private Litigation?

Hogg's account of the purpose of constitutions is by no means uncontroversial, and can be doubted on a number of grounds. For one thing, a distinction can be drawn between constitutional law insofar as it regulates the institutions of government, and a principle of constitutionalism whereby rights and freedoms are entrenched as supreme law. It is certainly possible to construct an argument which sees the control of power, rather than the public nature of that power, as the *raison d'être* of this principle of constitutionalism. The origins of rights-based judicial review can be traced to the post-revolutionary constitutional settlement in late eighteenth-century America. The orthodox account is that the Bill of Rights sought to protect the now free ex-colonials from suffering the same oppression in their new state as they had at the hands of the Crown. Thus, an area of private freedom was constructed, immune from the intrusions of the state. The more critical account sees the US constitutional experiment as a deliberate attempt to protect the more affluent Americans who gathered in Philadelphia from losing their wealth and power.[41] Devices such as Article I, s. 10's prohibition on states printing their way out of the pre-War debt still due can be seen as indicative of this. In each case the enemy is viewed as the public power of the state, whether being used to assault individual freedom or private wealth.

Similarly, with the post-World War II explosion of charters of rights, especially in continental Europe, the received wisdom is that this was a reaction against the fascist tyranny which had gripped the continent in the 1930s and which had led to war. Again the enemy is seen to be the state, and the charters of rights (with the sole exception of Italy) sought to impose constraints solely on the untrammelled state power which had been so recently used in aid of the most appalling crimes against humanity. Thus, charters of rights have historically been used (whether as an antidote to tyranny or democracy) to curb the public power of the state. However, it can equally be argued that their main feature is the control of power which some group finds a threat to its political or economic freedom, and if so it follows that there are only political, not technical, obstacles to constitutional rights' more widespread application.[42] However, even accepting the *ex facie* validity of Hogg's account, and that the Charter should only apply in those cases where the government is acting, serious doubts arise over whether it is true to say that it is not acting in those cases where the Supreme Court says it is not.

ANALYTICAL COHERENCE OF THE COURT'S APPROACH

Accepting that the line between public and private action should be drawn does not necessarily mean that this will be easily achieved in practice, and some commentators doubt the analytical coherence of the lines drawn by the current jurisprudence.[43] One of the reasons advanced by Professor Gibson for eschewing the divide from the outset was the problem of agreeing when a sufficiently close link with government had been established. Writing shortly after the adoption of the Charter and somewhat presciently in view of the later *McKinney* and *Lavigne* decisions, he took the example of a university to show the extent of the predicament. He asked whether the Charter should apply by virtue of the fact that some students and academics receive government grants, or because some activities are supervised by a government-appointed grants commission, or because some professors have research contracts with the government.[44] The answer would depend on how direct or tangential a connection would be considered to amount to a governmental link.[45] As Professor Hogg himself states in another context, this is an area where it is easy for reasonable people to disagree,[46] so it is perhaps unreasonable to expect the task of classification to be readily accomplished on the principled basis that Hogg implies exists in this area. Brian Slattery takes the court's jurisprudence at its word, and queries its ability to compartmentalize the law so neatly into its statutory and common law sources. What he has in mind is the dependence of the common law in Canada on the *statutory* authority of the various Reception Acts, which leads him to argue that private law in common law Canada is in fact founded on legislation.[47] If the decision in *Dolphin Delivery* depended on the statutory or common law provenance of the tort of inducing a breach of contract, then Slattery argues that the decision should have gone the other way.

Professor John Whyte, although supportive of excluding some private conduct from the Charter, disagrees that the Court's methodology can produce determinative results. For him the inquiry is not the existence of a 'legislative mandate' or 'government support', but whether the private actor in question is fulfilling a public role.[48] This *functional* test would be administered by considering how the private body was seen to relate to government, and in the way it represented itself and its role to the public. Hogg, however, praises the Court's wisdom in rejecting a functional link with government as the test.[49] It is revealing, though, to discover that the basis of his opposition is that there is 'no principled way to classify the functions of public bodies into "governmental" (or "public") and "commercial" (or "private") categories'.[49] But as we have already seen, he has admitted difficulties of distinction with his own favoured approach. One further practical difficulty which is belied by the Court's discrete categories relates to the criteria which should apply in deciding if a statute is merely permissive or not, this being the test of applicability developed in *Lavigne*. It is instructive in this regard to observe that even someone in as broad agreement with the Court's approach as Professor Hogg has been critical over how its own test has been applied in practice. As was noted above, in the *Lavigne* case, La Forest J (for the majority) stated in the context of an agency-shop agreement that the fact that this was permitted by statute would not be enough to bring the Charter into play. Hogg concurs with this principle, but not with La Forest J's reading of the case. For Hogg, it was clear that an unwilling employee had to pay the union dues in this case 'as surely as if the statute had directly ordered him to pay'.[50] Might this not be another area in which it is easy for reasonable people to disagree?

DISTINCTION BETWEEN 'COMPELLING' AND 'PERMITTING' STATUTES

Accordingly, it is clear that even if one accepts the idea of a public–private division, it is possible on the Court's own tests to argue that government is acting in some of the situations where it is said not to be. However, could it be that government is in fact implicated in all private activity? The last point raised above reminds us of the distinction drawn in the Court's eyes between statutes which confer powers of compulsion on private actors, and those that are merely permissive. It is only in the former case that the Court has decided that there is sufficient governmental presence to make the Charter applicable (in other words, in this situation the private actor has been redefined to become 'government'). However, is it true to say that there is any less governmental action involved in the case of permissive statutes? When private actors are equated with government *qua* the executive branch because of some institutional link (e.g. ministerial control), it is not too strenuous, applying the principles of agency, to see why the private actor is equated with government. However, when one asks in what manner Parliament or a legislature contributed to or caused a hypothetical Charter abuse where the statute has granted a private actor a power of compulsion, the issue becomes more problematic. Although it granted the power to the private body to compel a certain result, the legislature itself did not commit the infringement of the right or freedom. This would only be true if the legislature had directed a particular course of action. Where the legislature only grants the capacity to a private party to compel a certain result, the direct legal cause of the breach, or *causa causans*, is the action of that private party.

The statutory authority is still a material part of the causative mechanism, but is properly seen as a necessary condition or *conditio sine qua non*. If the statute is not seen as the central cause, one wonders why the legislature should be implicated at all.

What is the difference of analysis arising in the case of so-called permissive statutes? It is here that the distinction begins to collapse. In both cases, the legislature is one step back in the chain of causation, acting as the facilitator. In both cases, the legislature could have procured a different result either by not granting the power of compulsion or by withdrawing its permission. Either the legislature is acting in both situations, or it is acting in neither. This contrast of compulsion with permission implies that the permissive statute is largely superfluous, as it merely confirms what was previously, and continues to be, authorized. If not, the statute would have conferred a power of compulsion. But the very terminology used to deny legislative involvement reveals the imprimatur of the legislature: the activity described in the statute can be engaged in *because the legislature permits it*, only in this case it chooses to advertise its continued permission in a public statute. It is not difficult to extend the logic of this position to those situations where the legislature has either not amended the common law or has refrained from legislating in those areas where it is silent; again, in both situations one can build into the causative mechanism the *conditio sine qua non* of inaction. Appreciating the precise manner in which governmental action is suggested to be present in 'compelling' statutes does seem to make the position that it is not acting in 'permissive' statutes somewhat tenuous.[51]

MEANING OF 'GOVERNMENT'

It should also be borne clearly in mind that the Court's distinction between those situations where government is acting, and those where it is not, is based on a particular conception of government, and one which should not go unchallenged. McIntyre J made it clear in *Dolphin Delivery* that the language of s. 32 refers to specific branches of government, and 'not to government in its generic sense – meaning the whole governmental apparatus of the State'.[52] The hermeneutical validity of this approach is itself open to doubt – it has been argued that the use of the lower case 'g' in the constitutional text should make for a more liberal construction[53] – but the more major problem is reconciling its limited conception of government and the state with modern understandings of the pluralism of power. One of Gibson's difficulties with such a narrow definition was that it looked more to the institution than to the act of government. Hence, it should not be surprising that the Court has not been able to accommodate within its jurisprudence what he sees as the rise of 'private government' (i.e. the carrying out of traditional governmental functions by private entrepreneurs, such as the provision of police services by a private security firm).[54]

If one looks more to the act than to the institution of government, one is likely to produce a more subtle and complex account of how we are governed. For example, one way is to characterize society as composed of various institutions, of which the government is just one among many, and some of which have more influence on daily lives than others. For the theorist Charles Sampford, there is a strong need to recognize that 'ours is a society in which organisations play a dominant role in every area of social life'.[55] Therefore, reliance on a public–private divide posits a false dichotomy between the state and weak individuals because it 'distracts our attention from the more critical distinction between institutions and individuals'.[56] Accordingly, law should take those non-governmental institutions much more seriously, and in particular it needs to curb the tendency evident in the 1980s 'to treat corporations as natural and be uncritical of their structure and operation'.[57] Recognition of the extent of power possessed by institutions such as corporations requires a restructuring of our thinking about government and the state.[58] As Allan Hutchinson points out, 'the state consists of much more than the government',[59] and a Court informed by this vision of society would have difficulty in not finding the Charter applicable in cases like *Dolphin Delivery* and *McKinney*.

Are Private Relations Wholly Consensual?

Even if it were accepted that government is implicated in all private relations, this of itself would not rebut the Court and Professor Hogg's argument. This is because private relations are divided by them into two-categories: those where one private actor enjoys a power of compulsion over the other, and those where the relationship between them has been constituted wholly by consent. It is only in the former situation that the Charter has been held to apply. But to what extent is consensus actually present in those cases where the Court has said it is? Again, a more rigorous examination reveals the problematic nature of this argument.

DE IURE *CONSENSUS?*

The lack of *de facto* consensus in those private relationships where the Charter has been excluded will be addressed shortly, but first the claim that at a technical level these embody *de iure* consensus merits closer attention. There is perhaps a strong case to attempt to rebut, as the argument is based on the absence of any legal compulsion in the constitution of the relationship. Taking the *McKinney* case as an example, the Court here had to decide whether the equality provisions in s. 15 of the Charter could be relied on by faculty members at the University of Guelph to overturn the university's policy of mandatory retirement at the age of 65. The Court held that the Charter could not apply as there was 'no statutory requirement imposing mandatory retirement on the universities',[60] and discounted the fact that the university was a creature of statute.[61] The fact that there was no power on the part of the university compelling McKinney to enter into a contract of employment with it, and on these terms, placed the relationship between them in the category of private relationships constituted by consent. However, it must be doubted whether this relationship can be described accurately in these terms.

It should be noted that the Court found the existence of consensus by a two-fold process of abstraction. First, it focused on the absence of legislative compulsion regarding the specific issue of mandatory retirement rather than on an examination of the overall nature of the relationship; and, second, it could only characterize the relationship as an unforced meeting of free wills by removing it out of time.[62] It is when the artificial nature of these abstractions is recognized that doubts over the existence of even *de iure* consensus begin to arise. First, when one considers the overall relationship, it is evident that this is not a freely entered consensus between equals: the university is in the much stronger position in terms of dictating the terms of employment, which are in effect presented to aspiring faculty members on a take-it-or-leave-it basis. It is interesting to observe that even in the law of contract (where the Court's line of reasoning has greatest resonance), it is accepted that whereas consensus is a formal requirement in the establishment of the contractual relationship, there are many situations where the lack of consensus is acknowledged by the creation of special remedies for the party in the weaker position.[63] Second, the legal history of the relationship *is* relevant: not so much because the university's statutory provenance indicates a possible institutional link with government, but rather because it reminds us that the current Canadian system of higher education is not some providential accident, but is rather the product of legislative enactment *and non-enactment*. Thus McKinney can be seen to be compelled to accept mandatory retirement as much by the lack of statutory prohibition as he would have been in the event of an express direction.

Two points emerge from the foregoing. First, in many 'private' legal relationships, although there is no law explicitly compelling one party towards a particular course of action, the existing state of the law is often such that by reversing the framework of analysis and asking what is not prohibited rather than what is expressly compelled, the unreality inherent in many so-called consensual relationships is exposed.[64] Second, the strict separation of cases into the two categories indicated above is revealed as an over-narrow approach, and not one that is sympathetic to the rich complexities of relationships in society. Between express compulsion and free consensus lies a broad continuum: the artificial categorization of cases like *McKinney* under the heading of consensus because of the (admitted) lack of a power of compulsion is all too evident.

CONSENSUAL ACTIVITIES OF GOVERNMENT

If consensus is not always an informing idea in those cases where the Charter does not apply, what does this say about the value of compulsion as an informing idea in those cases where it does? It is revealing here to consider the extent to which government *qua* government is subject to the Charter even where it is not exercising a formal power of compulsion. La Forest J in *Lavigne* provided the answer when he rejected the argument that the Charter did not apply to governmental activities which are 'private, commercial, contractual, or non-public [in] nature'.[65] Thus, decisions such as *Lavigne* should properly be seen as invoking the Charter not because of a governmental act of compulsion, but because of the contractual relationship between the (here college *qua*) government and its employees. Therefore, there must be some reason other than the presence of the formal power to compel which explains why the Charter *always* applies to the activities of government. Perhaps the answer lies somewhere in the recognition that despite the formal appearance of consensus, governments can in fact, by means of their power and status, compel results by more indirect and subtle means than by the use of the formal law. Is it not possible that the formal appearance of consensus in 'private' relationships also masks similar substantive coercion, and if this is the case, why (by analogy with the situation as pertains to government) should the Charter not equally apply there as well?

DE FACTO *CONSENSUS? THE OPPRESSIVE POTENTIAL OF PRIVATE POWER*

Even if one were to accept that the private relationships where the Charter has been excluded can be explained at a formal level in terms of consensus, at a substantive level the lack of consensus is all too apparent. A number of scholars have thus attacked the Court's position on the grounds that it is blind to the oppressive potential of private power. David Beatty believes the *Dolphin Delivery* case should be seen clearly in its political context as a contest between one group's right 'to make use of their property to do business free from heckling' against the rights of another group 'to communicate as effectively as they can with their fellow citizens'.[66] However, this is not a contest between equals; for Beatty the union is at a clear disadvantage given the background of the judicially created common law, which has consistently found in favour of the side of business in labour disputes. Accordingly, in part to redress the balance, he fails to see why a broader reading of s. 32 should not in fact be a 'preferred legal and social result'.[67] Implicit in Brian Slattery's conception of the Charter as laying down the fundamental values of Canadian society is the idea that 'actions threatening the basic values of a society are as likely to proceed from private persons as from governments'.[68] Accordingly, the appearance of consensus in private relationships may be as lacking in substance as in the so-called consensual activities of government alluded to above. For Slattery, then, only an examination of the text of each particular document can determine whether they affect relations between private persons.[69]

Allan Hutchinson and Andrew Petter present what is perhaps the most trenchant critique of the Supreme Court's jurisprudence.[70] Although aware of the potential danger to freedom posed by state power, they are more concerned about private power's capacity to oppress, particularly in the economic sphere. The restriction of the Charter's application to legislatures and governments excludes from its scrutiny what they regard as a major source of inequality, 'the maldistribution of property entitlements among individuals'.[71] Equating property with power, they take the example of access to the media as demonstrating how the ability of those with private wealth to control the airwaves restricts the freedom of expression of those without that wherewithal.[72] What really offends Hutchinson and Petter is the Court's attempt in *Dolphin Delivery* to ignore the extent of state complicity in the exercise of private power. They condemn the characterization of the public–private divide as some neutral approach to constitutional interpretation, because this denies the ideological direction of the Court's decision:

> The presumption underlying the public/private dichotomy is that existing distributions of wealth and power are a product of individual initiative, not state action. Conveniently overlooked is the fact that such distributions and accumulations of wealth generally depend for their very existence and legitimacy upon a panoply of state supported laws and institutions.[71]

The challenge, for them, is to replace the divide with a substantive vision of social justice which recognizes that society 'comprises a thick web of interdependent relations'.[73]

The Illusory Nature of the Public–Private Divide?

It is difficult to escape the persuasive conclusion of these critiques that the Court's interpretation of s. 32 attempts to mask the substantive operation of the public–private divide beneath the veneer of formal equality. While it has been argued that, even on *de iure* terms, it is analytically problematic to maintain that there is no element of compulsion in even the most ostensibly 'private' of relationships, the policy behind this approach is to mask the actual lack of consensus, or to put it another way, the main purpose of formal equality is to hide the *de facto* situation behind the formal facade. As has been made clear, implicit in the idea that only the state is endowed with, or may convey, the power to oppress is the inference that there is no cause to worry about the same potential in private power, and integral to this position is the concept of equality among private persons. This formal equality is transparent, though, and starts to dissipate on more thorough examination.

Formal equality is given meaning through the myth of free will. Derived from the classical liberal notion of a pre-societal state of nature from which the individual emerges imbued with rights which are to be protected against collectivities, it assumes that private persons interact as ahistorical beings, and so are blind to the advantages and hindrances which each brings to the bargaining table. Professor Sheldon Wolin, writing in the context of social contractarianism and the US Constitution, highlights the importance of realizing that any person's birthright is made up of 'ambiguous historical moments'.[74] Thus, the equality of individuals in any situation is entirely contingent on the ongoing historical process:

> We tend to assume that equality represents a quality that we are trying to recapture, that once we were equal, as in the moment before the contract, and so the task is to eliminate barriers, such as those stemming from segregation or sex discrimination. When this has been done, equality will have been restored, because equality has come to be identified with equal opportunity. But equal opportunity merely restarts the cycle of competition in the race, and races are designed to produce a single winner. Then it becomes obvious that social competition cannot be compared to a footrace between trained athletes; that the race for education, jobs, income and status is rarely between equals, but rather, between those with greater advantages and those with greater disadvantages.[75]

The Court's approach, however, is ahistorical and not only ignores, *inter alia*, the law's past sanctioning of the outlawing of combinations and its unfettered support of *laissez-faire* economics, but also the continuing effect of these very political decisions. The legacy of the common law for modern society comes from a time when there were few checks on the operation of private property, and, indeed, it can be argued with some force that the ideological purpose of the common law was to promote and preserve private property. To disregard the state's (using the term in its broader sense) historical endorsement of this body of doctrine is, at best, disingenuous.

From this perspective, it offends ordinary sensibilities to describe the situations in the cases discussed above as being disputes among equals. Thus, in *McKinney*, the classical liberal interpretation would be that the contract of employment between McKinney and the university was entered into without any element of force or coercion, and that if the terms of the contract were unacceptable to McKinney, he could have sought alternative employment. However, this approach is blind to the obvious imbalance between the university's bargaining power and that of the individual, who may have had little choice but to agree to the terms of employment in order to secure a livelihood. Indeed, in contracts of employment generally, it is fair to conclude that, apart from a minority of situations, the prospective employer has much less to lose from not hiring any particular individual than the individual if his or her application is unsuccessful. Similarly, a strong (although by no means uncontroversial) case can be made for comparing the relatively weak position of organized labour *vis-à-vis* the power of capital. Indeed, the special legal privileges which unions enjoy are themselves the past recognition of the need to protect workers against the unchecked power of their employers. As noted above, Beatty is particularly sensitive to the charge that historically the courts are perceived to be more sympathetic to the claims of employers. He worries that the decision in *Dolphin Delivery*, by paying homage to the transparent neutrality of the public–private divide, will support a claim that 'a strain of lawlessness and class bias on the bench continues'.[76] Given this historical advantage in favour of employers, it is not surprising that a form of adjudication which stresses formal equality more often than not finds in their favour.

Acknowledging the strength of the arguments that free will only exists in a historical vacuum leads to a very significant change of focus. The real nub of the issue should then be cast in terms of the basis on which persons can do some things, but not others. This makes one look more to the content of the positive law, rather than to the public or private nature of the actors involved. The issue of who should be liable for a Charter breach is then no longer seen as an inquiry into the identity of the protagonists, but is instead resolved by asking who is responsible for the state of the law. Thus, why McKinney could no longer enjoy the teaching career that he desired should not be seen as primarily related to whether there was a sufficiently close nexus between the university and government, but rather should be explained by reference to the fact that the ordinary law did not prevent his employers (whoever they were) from retiring him on what he saw as discriminatory grounds. Viewed from the perspective of who is responsible for the law enabling the university to retire McKinney in this way yields a very different result from an inquiry into the link between the university and government. If responsibility for the prevailing corpus of law does not lie at the door of Parliament and the legislatures, in whose hands rest the powers of enactment, repeal and amendment, then at whose door does it lie? What is clear is that the public–private divide which denies the existence of this responsibility is very much a judicial creation: it is not in any way required by the text of s. 32, and certainly not in the manner suggested by the Supreme Court in its various judgments.

FUTURE DIRECTIONS?

Care should be taken to avoid thinking that the debate is concluded by exposing the illusory nature of the public–private divide. Even if the ideological argument that public power alone merits constitutional restraint can be met by demonstrating the (at least) equal capacity for oppression in private power, it does not necessarily follow that the Charter should then have widespread application in the private sector. Two institutional concerns arise at this stage, one of which presents a much stronger objection than the other. The weaker objection looks to the practical effect that abolishing the public–private distinction would have on the workings of the judicial system. The worry here is that such a reform would result in a flood of litigation, which would overload the Court's docket and in turn lead to administrative chaos. This is not a particularly rigorous objection, and ignores the fact that courts always find ways of restricting their caseload through techniques such as mootness and *locus standi*. A Supreme Court which was minded to adjudicate on cases involving private actors would be perfectly capable of using these techniques to exclude other types of cases in order to find the time to develop this side of its jurisprudence. Evidence from other jurisdictions supports this contention. In the UK, for example, the Scottish Court of Session does not admit of a formal public–private divide in administrative law judicial review cases, but instead bases its jurisdiction on these matters on the establishment of a tripartite relationship in which two of the parties have assigned a jurisdiction to decide the issue to the third.[77] Thus, some 'private' actions will be held to be incompetent, but the basis of that decision is not (at least not overtly) the public or private nature of the litigants. It does not take a great deal of imagination to envisage a similar technique being adopted in constitutional law.

A second, and more demanding, objection looks not at the practical impact on the administration of justice, but rather at the adequacy of the judicial forum to deal with the kinds of cases which 'private' constitutional litigation would produce (and it is here that those who are alert to the need to offset the oppressive potential of private power disagree[78]). Robin Elliot and Robert Grant suggest that this, and not notions of when the state is actually disregarding Charter rights, is the true explanation of the Court's jurisprudence.[79] They start from the premise that entertaining private Charter litigation would fundamentally change the role of the courts, and that this would require the courts to balance competing claims on social resources. The courts would thus be transformed from mere reviewers into legislators, but they are unlikely to come up with either desirable or acceptable results, because

> [t]he judicial forum is far less conducive to consensus building amongst competing interest groups in the resolution of social and economic conflict than is the political forum; courts produce winners and losers, not compromises. The judicial forum also provides less opportunity for citizen participation in the resolution of social and economic conflict than does the political forum.[80]

Accordingly, reform should be left to the democratic processes precisely to protect us from what the judiciary may get up to if they assume competence in this area.

A stronger version of this argument is to acknowledge that the Court is already involved in decision-making of this nature, but then to assert that the record is not promising as far as a more progressive approach to the public–private divide is concerned. Most of the s. 32 cases discussed in this chapter arise in the context of labour disputes (perhaps the cutting edge of the public–private divide), but when one looks at the courts' jurisprudence, there is some cause for concern about trade unions using the Charter as a weapon against their employers. As was noted above, the Court has held that corporations are entitled to the Charter's guarantees, yet it has been unable to find anything in the constitutional text to protect that most basic of union rights, the right to strike. In *Reference re Public Service Employees Relations Act (Alberta)*,[81] the Supreme Court, *per* McIntyre J, held that the guarantee of freedom of association in s. 2(b) of the Charter was only exerciseable on an individual basis, and thus could not extend to activities of an inherently associational character, such as striking. It should also not be forgotten that in some cases where the Charter has been held not to apply, the Court has gone on to see how the cases would have been decided if it had. Thus, in *Dolphin Delivery*, the injunction was held to be a reasonable limit on freedom of expression in terms of s. 1,[15] as picketing should not be used to harm those parties not directly involved in a trade dispute.[82] Similarly, in *McKinney*, while the retirement policy was found to be discriminatory, this was again a reasonable limit on equality, as it permitted 'flexibility in resource allocation and faculty renewal'.[83] Accordingly, any move towards a more widespread application of the Charter should only be made after very careful consideration and with a clear expectation of the likely consequences.

CONCLUSION

This chapter has argued that the claim of those who argue that the public–private divide, as presently constituted, is both a technically correct interpretation of the Charter, and a sound statement of constitutional policy, does not pass muster. First, on closer scrutiny the divide fails to withstand the analysis of the self-same legal concepts, such as causation, which are deployed in favour of its continuation. Second, the alleged neutrality of the Supreme Court's current approach to constitutional adjudication is exposed as a shield for the substantive operation of the divide as a barrier to more progressive theories of constitutional entitlements. However, the strength of these critiques should not lead us to argue for the abolition of the divide altogether and for the application of the Charter in a widespread manner in the private sector. Such an argument exhibits a complacent faith in the ability of constitutions to deliver the utopian vision if only they were interpreted in the correct manner. The debate on how to control the exercise of private power consistent with the needs of the twenty-first century is a very complex one, which this chapter only touches on. However, that debate, which is essentially about the appropriate and possible extent of constitutional intervention necessary to achieve social justice in the modern age, is avoided when the question of the public–private divide is treated with the formal technicality exhibited by the Court. The issue is too important to allow this to happen.

NOTES

1. For example, the privatization programmes followed by Conservative governments in both Canada and the UK in the 1980s: see generally P. McAvoy *et al.*, *Privatisation of State-Owned Enterprises: Lessons from the United States, Great Britain and Canada* (Boston, MA, 1989).

2. Canadian Charter of Rights and Freedoms, Part I of the Constitution Act 1982, being Schedule B of The Canada Act 1982 (UK), c. 11.

3. See, for example, *Hunter* v. *Southam Inc.* (1984) 2 SCR 145.

4. P. W. Hogg, The Dolphin Delivery case: the application of the Charter to private action (1987) 51 *Saskatchewan Law Review* 273, at p. 279.

5. See, for example, *Shelley* v. *Kraemer* (1948) 334 US I; *Hudgens* v. *NLRB* (1976) 424 US 507; *Flagg Bros Inc.* v. *Brooks* (1978) 436 US 149; P. Brest, State action and liberal theory: a case-note on *Flagg Bros* v. *Brooks* (1982) 130 *University of Pennsylvania Law Review* 1296.

6. L. Tribe, *American Constitutional Law*, 2nd edn (Mineda, NY, 1988), p. 1691.

7. J. D. Whyte, Is the private sector affected by the Charter? In L. Smith (ed.), *Righting the Balance: Canada's New Equality Rights*, (Saskatoon, 1986), p. 153.

8. For example Deputy Justice Minister Roger Tassé's statement at the hearing on 15 January 1981 on behalf of the federal government: 'we do not see these rights or these prescriptions of the Charter to have application in terms of a relationship between individuals. We see them as applying in terms of a relationship between the state and individuals.' Quoted in R. Elliot and R. Grant, The Charter's application to private litigation (1989) 23 *UBC Law Review* 459, at p. 466.

9. D. Gibson, The Charter of Rights and the private sector (1982) 12 *Manitoba Law Journal* 213, at p. 213.

10. J. D. Whyte, *op. cit.*, p. 154.

11. See, for example, P. Brest, The misconceived quest for the original understanding (1980) 60 *Boston University Law Review* 204.

12. P. H. Russell, Foreword. In I. Greene, *The Charter of Rights* (Toronto, 1989), p. viii.

13. *RWDSU* v. *Dolphin Delivery* (1987) 33 DLR (4th) 174 (hereafter *Dolphin Delivery*).

14. (1984) 10 DLR (4th) 198.

15. The Constitution Act 1982, s. 1, states: 'The Canadian Charter of Rights and Freedoms guarantees the rights and freedoms in it subject only to such reasonable limits prescribed by law as can be demonstrably justified in a free and democratic society.'

16. The Constitution Act 1982, s. 52(1), states 'The Constitution of Canada is the supreme law of Canada, and any law that is inconsistent with the provisions of the Constitution is, to the extent of the inconsistency, of no force or effect.'

17. *RWDSU* v. *Dolphin Delivery*, *op. cit.*, p. 176.

18. *Ibid.*, p. 195.

19. P. W. Hogg, *Constitutional Law of Canada*, 3rd edn (Scarborough, Ontario, 1992), p. 846.

20. *RWDSU* v. *Dolphin Delivery*, *op. cit.*, p. 195.

21. *Ibid.*, p. 196.

22. *Ibid.*, p. 197.

23. *Ibid.*, p. 198, quoting P. W. Hogg, *Constitutional Law of Canada*, 2nd edn (1985), p. 677.

24. McIntyre J cited with approval the case of *Re Blainey and Ontario Hockey Association* (1986) 26 DLR (4th) 728, in which the Supreme Court of Ontario had held the Charter to be applicable to the activities of the association. This case involved a 12-year-old girl who had been refused permission by the Association to play in a boys' hockey team. Discrimination of this nature was permitted by the Ontario Human Rights Code 1981 (Ont.) c. 53. It was on the basis that this Code infringed the equality rights of s. 15 of the Charter that the necessary element of governmental action was found to exist: *RWDSU* v. *Dolphin Delivery*, *op. cit.*, pp. 196–7.

25. *RWDSU* v. *Dolphin Delivery*, *op. cit.*, p. 198.

26. This distinction between statute and common law created the potential anomaly that the Charter's writ might run more widely in the province of Quebec than in the rest of

Canada, as much of the subject matter covered by the uncodified common law applied there by virtue of the Code Civil. However, in *Tremblay* v. *Daigle* (1988) 2 SCR 530, the Supreme Court held that disputes between private parties brought under the Code Civil of Quebec would also be exempt from Charter scrutiny.

27. *RWDSU* v. *Dolphin Delivery, op. cit.*, p. 198.

28. (1991) 81 DLR (4th) 545.

29. *Ibid.*, p. 618.

30. *Ibid.*, p. 619; see also *Douglas/Kwantlen Faculty Assn* v. *Douglas College* (1991) 77 DLR (4th) 94.

31. (1990) 76 DLR (4th) 545 (hereafter *McKinney*).

32. (1990) 76 DLR (4th) 700 (hereafter *Stoffman*).

33. [1987] 1 SCR 588.

34. [1988] 2 SCR 214.

35. P. W. Hogg, *Constitutional Law of Canada*, 3rd edn, *op. cit.*, p. 850.

36. See *Re Blainey, op. cit.*

37. See s. 52(1) at note 16; also ss. 2, 3, 6, 7, 8, 9, 10, 11, 12, 15, 17, 20 and 24 of the Charter. See, for example, s. 24(1): 'Anyone whose rights or freedoms, as guaranteed by this charter, have been infringed or denied may apply to a court of competent jurisdiction to obtain such remedy as the court considers appropriate and just in the circumstances'.

38. See D. Gibson, The deferential Trojan Horse: a decade of Charter decisions (1993) 72 *Canadian Bar Review* 417, at pp. 425–6 (Gibson characterizes the Court's jurisprudence as creating 'private sector immunity' from Charter violations).

39. P. W. Hogg, The Dolphin Delivery case: the application of the Charter to private action, *op. cit.*, p. 279.

40. P. W. Hogg *Constitutional Law of Canada*, 3rd edn, *op. cit.*, p. 848.

41. See, for example, R. W. Galloway, *Justice for All? The Rich and Poor in Supreme Court History 1790–1990* (Durham, North Carolina, 1991), pp. 11–15.

42. See M. Mandel, Sovereignty and the new constitutionalism. In D. Drache and R. Perin (eds), *Negotiating with a Sovereign Quebec* (Toronto, 1992), p. 225.

43. See D. Gibson, Distinguishing the governors from the governed: the meaning of 'government' under Section 32(1) of the Charter (1983) 13 *Manitoba Law Journal* 505; B. Slattery, The Charter's relevance to private litigation: does *Dolphin* deliver? (1987) 2 *McGill Law Journal* 905; J. D. Whyte, Is the private sector affected by the Charter? *op. cit.*

44. D. Gibson, Distinguishing the governors from the governed: the meaning of 'government' under Section 32(1) of the Charter, *op. cit.*, p. 519.

45. Striking evidence of this difficulty with classification can be found in La Forest J's admission in *McKinney* that while the Charter did not apply to universities, they would be subject to judicial review in administrative law matters: *Stoffman* v. *Vancouver General Hospital, op. cit.*, p. 638f.

46. P. W. Hogg, The Dolphin Delivery Case: the application of the Charter to private action, *op. cit.*, p. 279.

47. B. Slattery, *op. cit.*, pp. 910–16.

48. J. D. Whyte, *op. cit.*, pp. 178–9.

49. P. W. Hogg, *Constitutional Law of Canada*, 3rd edn, *op. cit.*, p. 841.

50. *Ibid.*, p. 839.

51. A related point is how legislatures actually translate statutes into practice. This leads to the all too obvious conclusion that legislatures themselves do not act, but require some agency to implement their wishes. This is very often government (*qua* the executive branch), but, as the Court has pointed out, a private entity may sometimes be explicitly empowered to act on the legislature's behalf. Professor Hogg's rationalization of the Court's position is that while any statute *ultra vires* the Charter will be invalid, and that any public body exercising statutory power (such as ministers, civil servants and tribunals) must keep within its confines, an element of compulsion has to be established in the case of private actors (P. W. Hogg, *Constitutional Law of Canada*, 3rd edn, *op. cit.*, pp. 836–7). With respect, the former test does seem to imply that somehow statutes are violated in the abstract, when it is clear that they require the presence of some agency before the possibility of a Charter breach can become live. It is, therefore, incongruous to suggest that the nature of that agency should

determine whether the Charter applies. Again, it is hard to advance the conclusion that the public–private distinction arises because of an inherent distinction between 'compelling' and 'permissive' statutes; rather, the divide itself is only maintained by amending the test for invalidity of a statute when it arises in the course of private litigation.

52. *RWDSU* v. *Dolphin Delivery*, *op. cit.*, p. 194.

53. See D. Gibson, The Charter of Rights and the private sector, *op. cit.*, p. 217.

54. D. Gibson, Distinguishing the governors from the governed: the meaning of 'government' under Section 32(1) of the Charter, *op. cit.*, p. 520.

55. C. Sampford, Law, institutions and the public/private divide (1991) 20 *Federal Law Review* 185, at p. 201.

56. *Ibid.*, p. 208.

57. *Ibid.*, fn. 72, at p. 204.

58. *Ibid.*, pp. 217–18; Sampford advocates that 'law should be used to push institutions into fulfilling the purposes that justify them', although he warns against attempts to deal with institutions by law alone, which needs to be supported by ethical standards and institutional design.

59. A. C. Hutchinson, Mice under a chair: democracy, courts, and the administrative state (1990) 40 *University of Toronto Law Journal* 374, at p. 377.

60. *McKinney*, v. *University of Guelph*, *op. cit.*, p. 649b.

61. *Ibid.*, p. 637a.

62. This is reflected in the somewhat quaint characterization of the university as a 'community of scholars'. See *McKinney* v. *University of Guelph*, *op. cit.*, p. 642e.

63. See, for example, Sale of Goods Act 1979 (UK) c. 54, s. 14.

64. See also *Stoffman*, v. *Vancouver General Hospital*, *op. cit.*

65. *Lavigne* v. *OPSEU*, *op. cit.*, p. 621c.

66. D. Beatty, Constitutional conceits: the coercive authority of the courts (1987) 37 *University of Toronto Law Journal* 183, at p. 185.

67. *Ibid.*, p. 190.

68. He does not support, though, the blanket application of the Charter to private action; rather, the question of applicability 'can only be determined by a series of inquiries directed towards the Charter's individual provisions' (D. Beatty, *op. cit.*, p. 922).

69. B. Slattery, Charter of Rights and Freedoms – does it bind private persons? (1985) 63 *Canadian Bar Review* 149, at pp. 158–9.

70. A. C. Hutchinson and A. Petter, Private rights/public wrongs: the liberal lie of the Charter (1988) 38 *University of Toronto Law Journal* 278.

71. *Ibid.*, p. 292.

72. *Ibid.*, p. 293.

73. *Ibid.*, p. 296.

74. S. Wolin, Contract and birthright. In F. Krinsky (ed.), *Crisis and Innovation* (New York, 1988), p. 16.

75. *Ibid.*, pp. 18–19.

76. D. Beatty, *op. cit.*, p. 192.

77. See *West* v. *Secretary of State for Scotland* [1992] SLT 636; and also C. M. G. Himsworth, Public employment, the supervisory jurisdiction and points *west* [1992] SLT (News) 256.

78. A. C. Hutchinson and A. Petter, *op. cit.*, pp. 288–9.

79. R. Elliot and R. Grant, *op. cit.*

80. *Ibid.*, p. 495.

81. (1987) 38 DLR (4th) 161.

82. *RWDSU* v. *Dolphin Delivery*, *op. cit.*, p. 176.

83. *McKinney* v. *University of Guelph*, *op. cit.*, p. 546.

24

Women's Rights as Human Rights under International Law

C. M. Chinkin

INTRODUCTION

The Declaration and Programme of Action agreed at the World Conference on Human Rights held in Vienna in 1993 affirms the principles of universality, inalienability, indivisibility and interdependence of human rights.[1] The Conference asserted that the 'human rights of women and of the girl-child are an inalienable, integral and indivisible part of universal human rights' and that certain identified gender-specific abuses constitute violations of women's human rights. It also makes explicit that elimination of violence against women is a human rights obligation upon states. The Declaration and Programme of Action call for the integration of women's human rights throughout all United Nations human rights activities.

The Declaration and Programme of Action are not formal sources of international law.[2] They do, however, represent a political consensus on a forward-looking agenda for human rights within the framework of the United Nations.[3] This consensus has been carried forward by the adoption of the Conference statements by the General Assembly in December 1993. Further commitment towards the recognition and protection of the human rights of women have been made by the adoption by that same body of the Declaration on the Elimination of Violence against Women,[4] and by the Commission on Human Rights' approval of the appointment of a Special Rapporteur on Violence against Women in its resolution on violence against women.[5] These principles were reiterated by the Fourth United Nations Conference on Women held in Beijing in September 1995. These developments together represent significant progress in the struggle by women's rights activists, who have long been working at local, national, regional and international levels to have women's rights recognized as human rights under international law.[6] Indeed, this recognition has been identified as one of the successes of the Conference 'although it is regrettable that it is only after decades of omission that the subject of the worldwide occurrence of violence against women was seriously recognized by the UN'.[7] This chapter will examine the international instruments for the protection of women's rights, and discuss reasons for the long failure of international human rights doctrine and inter-governmental and non-governmental organizations to accommodate women's rights, despite formal assertions of women's equality.[8] It will focus throughout upon the issue of gender-specific violence as a human rights abuse.

INTERNATIONAL PROHIBITION OF DISCRIMINATION AGAINST WOMEN: FORMAL EQUALITY

The list of formal international legal instruments since 1945 for the protection of women's human rights is impressive. Article 1 (3) of the United Nations Charter states that one of the purposes of the United Nations is

> To achieve international co-operation in solving international problems of an economic, social, cultural or humanitarian character, and in promoting and encouraging respect for human rights and for fundamental freedoms for all without distinction as to race, sex, language or religion.

This basic principle of non-discrimination, including discrimination on the basis of sex, was followed up in Articles 1 and 2 of the United Nations Universal Declaration of Human Rights, 1948[9] and in both the 1966 United Nations International Covenants, which together constitute the so-called International Bill of Rights.[10] The rights recognized in each of the Covenants are to be respected without distinction of any kind, including sex.[11] The International Covenant on Civil and Political Rights also contains a general, free-standing non-discrimination provision, Article 26.[12] In addition to general human rights instruments, the particular needs of women have been recognized in specific human rights treaties both before the UN Charter and subsequently,[13] and in humanitarian law applicable in times of international and internal armed conflict, most notably in the Fourth Geneva Convention and the First Protocol.[14]

By far the most important step was the adoption by the General

Assembly on 18 December 1979 of the Convention on the Elimination of All Forms of Discrimination Against Women (the Women's Convention) as part of the United Nations Decade for Women which lasted from 1975 until 1985.[15] The explicit goal of the Women's Convention, which was drafted by the Commission on the Status of Women,[16] is to achieve equality for women based on the recognition that full global development, the welfare of the world, the establishment of a just new international economic order and the cause of international peace and security require the maximum participation of women on equal terms with men in all fields.[17] This goal explicitly links the protection and promotion of women's rights to other fundamental objectives of the international community.

The Women's Convention is more specific than the general assertions of sexual equality in other Conventions. It identifies areas where gender-based discrimination is most marked and includes provisions on such matters as suppression of prostitution and trafficking in women (Article 6), the participation of women in the public life of states (Articles 7 and 8), equality in nationality laws (Article 9), equality in access to, and in all other aspects of, education (Article 10), equality in employment (Article 11), equality in access to health services (Article 12), equality in other areas of economic and social life (Article 13), the specific needs of rural women (Article 14), equality before the law (Article 15), and equal rights within the family (Article 16).

These rights are amplified by the opening provisions of the Women's Convention. Article 1 defines discrimination against women.[18] Article 2 condemns such discrimination and imposes obligations upon parties to take positive steps to eliminate it in national laws and constitutions, and to take steps to ensure the practical realization of this principle. Article 5 recognizes that legislation and policy directives are not of themselves sufficient, and accordingly requires parties to take appropriate measures to change attitudes with respect to sexist stereotyping. Article 4 allows for positive discrimination during a transitional phase.

These initial Articles make it clear that ratification of the Women's Convention requires states to study their domestic laws and practices in order to identify those which are discriminatory, to determine appropriate means of modification and to ensure that such legal changes are implemented in practice. Ideally, states should take such steps as examining and adapting their policies in all fields, for example legislation, case law and policy directives within the public and private sectors, educational curricula, media representations, introducing gender awareness training programmes for members of the judiciary, the legislature, national and local policy makers and civil servants, and introducing legal literacy programmes. Such steps are time-consuming, expensive, require specialist expertise and are rarely priorities for governments.

The final Articles provide for implementation of the Women's Convention. The familiar pattern of UN human rights treaties is followed through the establishment of a monitoring committee (the Committee on the Elimination of Discrimination Against Women, CEDAW), comprising 23 independent experts (Article 17). The initial and periodic reports made by states in compliance with their obligations are scrutinized by the Committee in advance of the presentation of individual reports by a representative of the relevant state, who is questioned upon it in open session. However, unlike the position under the Convention on the Elimination of All Forms of Racial Discrimination and the Convention against Torture, there is no optional procedure for individual complaints to the CEDAW,[19] nor any right of inter-state complaint.[20] The CEDAW does not have the competence of the Committee Against Torture to examine 'reliable information' containing 'well-founded indications' of systematic violations of the Women's Convention.[21] The Vienna Conference recommended that the Commission on the Status of Women and the CEDAW examine the possibility 'of introducing a right of petition through the preparation of an optional protocol'.[22] In March 1994 an Expert Group Meeting organized by the Women in the Law Project of the International Human Rights Group and the Maastricht Centre for Human Rights adopted a Draft Optional Protocol to the Convention on the Elimination of All Forms of Discrimination Against Women.[23] This Draft Protocol includes procedures for individual complaints and an inquiry procedure. The Expert Meeting was sponsored by the Australian and Dutch governments and was attended by human rights experts, members of the CEDAW and members of the Human Rights Committee. The Draft Protocol has no legal authority but provides a negotiating text for improving the enforcement mechanisms available under the Women's Convention. The work and commitment which led to the drafting of this Protocol epitomize the combined efforts of academics and activists, who have worked through non-governmental organizations, while simultaneously seeking the necessary governmental support for initiatives to further women's rights.

In a number of ways the Women's Convention represents a significant advance for the legal guarantee of women's rights. It has been widely ratified by states from all regions of the world.[24] It includes both civil and political, and economic, social and cultural rights, which was a radical departure from previous UN instruments, which had maintained a sharp divide between the two.[25] This drawing together of rights recognizes that for women protection of civil and political rights can be meaningless without attention being paid to the economic, social and cultural context in which they are operating.[26]

The Women's Convention also attempts to break through the public–private divide which feminists have identified as especially detrimental to women.[27] It is argued that one of the reasons for women's lack of participation in public policy and decision-making is their traditional consignment to private life. Liberal political theory distinguishes between the public and private domains in that men are seen as properly functioning in the public arenas of governance and the workplace, where law, economics, politics, intellectual activities and power and authority are exercised, while women are seen as properly located in the private world of the family and the home. This distinction has a normative as well as a descriptive function: greater economic and political significance is attached to the public arena than the private, conferring primacy upon the male world and supporting the global exercise of power and control by men.[28] By asserting women's equal right to participation in public decision-making bodies at all levels, the Women's Convention locates women within the public arena.[29] Even more significantly, it explicitly affirms women's equality within the private arena of the family. The relegation of women to this private, invisible realm has obscured their domination and inequality there. Article 16 goes further than other human rights instruments, which have designated the family itself as the unit for protection, by affirming equality between the members of the family, before, during and after the marriage.[30]

THE REALITY FOR WOMEN

Global Violations of Women's Rights

Despite the proliferation of human rights instruments guaranteeing women's equality, and the particular advantages of the Women's Convention, women's rights have been marginalized and have remained outside the mainstream of international human rights protection. Failure to take seriously international commitments has had a negative influence on legal protection for women within domestic law.[31] The reality is that women's rights are routinely and universally disregarded, often in horrific ways. It is depressingly easy to catalogue such abuses, which range through violent physical and sexual abuse and terrorization, economic deprivation, lack of personal control over women's bodies and reproduction, harmful religious and traditional practices, less frequent and shorter periods of education than those made accessible to men and boys, restrictions in the holding of property, and the denial of access to forms of employment.[32]

These abuses occur globally and daily. They are neither random, nor happenstance. They occur because of gender. They do not receive wide-spread condemnation and are too often not even perceived of as constituting violations of international human rights law. This failure of the human rights movement to accommodate women's rights can be attributed both to defects within the Women's Convention itself and to wider understandings of international law.

The Women's Convention: A Serious Commitment?

A serious limitation of the Women's Convention is the large number of far-reaching reservations and restrictive declarations that have been made by states parties. As of September 1993, 45 parties had made reservations or declarations on ratification, accession or signature. While some of these are essentially procedural,[33] others raise fundamental questions about the seriousness with which the international community regards the objective of the Women's Convention.[34] Most notorious are reservations that give primacy to domestic law, and those made by a number of states, notably Iraq, Egypt, Tunisia, Bangladesh, Libya, Malaysia and the Maldives, which in different ways state that the Women's Convention is not binding in so far as its provisions conflict with domestic personal status law, or Sharia law, or that the country is willing to comply with the obligations of the Women's Convention provided that such compliance is not contrary to Sharia law.[35] Such reservations fail to satisfy legal requirements of determinacy and precision. Their intended scope is not explained and they subject the obligations incurred under the Women's Convention to change in accordance with evolving interpretations of the Sharia, and not in accordance with objective international standards.[36]

Reservations to the Women's Convention have not only been made by Islamic states.[37] The UK has entered the largest number of reservations, including one to Article 2 by which it postpones review and amendment of admittedly discriminatory legislation to such time as when to do so would be compatible with 'essential and over-riding considerations of economic policy'. The Women's Convention is amenable to progressive implementation, but this reservation makes implementation subject to external criteria without any commitment to a full analysis of the economic consequences of non-implementation.[38]

The Vienna Convention on the Law of Treaties provides a legal framework for reservations and objections to reservations on the grounds of incompatibility with the objects and purposes of the relevant Convention.[39] What is disturbing about the position under the Women's

Convention is that there has been little response to these reservations. Very few states have entered objections, and these objections have not included the option of declaring the Women's Convention to be inapplicable as between the objecting and the reserving states.[40] There is an ongoing tension in treaty law between the desire to ensure as wide participation as possible, especially in a standard-setting convention such as the Women's Convention and therefore to allow reservations on the one hand, and the need to preserve the integrity of the text by limiting reservations on the other.[41] Nevertheless, the apparent willingness of states to tolerate reservations which undermine commitment to the Women's Convention and to disregard principles of treaty law is unfortunate. This fosters an attitude that the obligations are not as serious as those in other treaties, and that their fulfilment can be waived under the guise of legal reservations.

In the absence of individual objections to the reservations it has been left to the CEDAW to express its concern to individual states, to all parties through its general recommendations,[42] and through other institutional mechanisms. Accordingly, when states' representatives present their initial and subsequent reports before the CEDAW, members have consistently questioned them on the continuing need for, and extent of, their reservations. The CEDAW proposed in 1987 within ECOSOC (Economic and Social Council of the United Nations) that a full investigation into the status of women under Islamic law and customs be carried out in order to be able to appraise more fully the effect of these reservations. Hostile reactions within ECOSOC and the General Assembly, instigated by a number of Islamic states which saw the initiative as an attack upon themselves, prevented this proposal from being adopted.[43] The Vienna World Conference on Human Rights encouraged states to seek ways and means of addressing the 'particularly large number of reservations to the Convention' and supported the work of the CEDAW in this respect. It also urged parties to withdraw reservations incompatible with the object and purposes of the Women's Convention 'or which are otherwise incompatible with international treaty law'.[44]

Underlying the issue of reservations, is of course, the controversial issue of the compatibility of women's rights with religious and cultural practices. Women are frequently presented as the guardians of a society's culture, and external interference on the grounds of upholding women's rights is resented and resisted as an intrusion upon a state's domestic jurisdiction and as a form of cultural imperialism. This ensures that other states are reluctant to challenge compliance on these grounds, and removes the question even from consideration by UN bodies, including the CEDAW. The Vienna Conference considered cultural and religious practices in the context of violence against women but failed to give clear direction. It called only for the eradication of conflict between women's rights and 'the harmful effects of certain traditional or religious practices, cultural prejudices and religious extremism' without stipulating that such eradication should be in favour of women's rights.[45] Further, even where ratification of the Women's Convention does indicate commitment at the governmental level to women's equality, deeply entrenched traditional, religious and cultural attitudes towards women are not displaced by adherence to legal instruments. 'Sex stereotyping ... is among the most firmly entrenched obstacles to the elimination of discrimination, and is largely responsible for the denigration of the role and potential of women in society.'[46] In many countries blatantly discriminatory laws continue to be passed, and even where they are repealed or amended governments frequently lack the political will or economic means to make effective the new laws or policies.

A further limitation of the Women's Convention is one that the CEDAW shares with the other human rights treaty bodies, but which is in many ways exacerbated within the CEDAW. The CEDAW's power to take up violations of women's rights is limited by the reporting system. If a state is not due to report under the terms of the Women's Convention (an initial report is required within a year after entry into force of the Women's Convention for the state concerned and thereafter at four-yearly intervals), there is no available mechanism for challenging a state's actions. This inadequacy was exposed at the 1993 meeting of the CEDAW by the obstacles to making an effective response to the atrocities committed against women in the territory of the former Yugoslavia. The only action that could be agreed was a letter from the CEDAW to the Special Rapporteur of the Commission on Human Rights, expressing its concern about the situation.[47]

States' reports are inevitably self-serving, and omissions and inaccuracies may be difficult to identify by a committee which sits for a limited period every year. The backlog of reports is enormous and weighs heavily on the CEDAW. There is the dual problem that on the one hand many states fail to report on time, but on the other that the CEDAW is unable to deal with them immediately. This situation undermines requests for the timely submission of reports. Unless the questions asked of government representatives are searching and the answers scrutinized, the reporting system cannot produce the desired effects. Preparation of probing questions takes time and requires expertise. Although there is no express reference to non-governmental organizations within the Women's Convention,[48] the CEDAW welcomes assistance from such bodies. This is necessarily limited by time, financial resources, and knowledge of the CEDAW's work. The Minnesota-based International Women's Rights Action Watch has made a tremendous input into monitoring reports, supplying the CEDAW in advance with information with which to question governments, and disseminating information about the CEDAW's activities.

It has been argued that the CEDAW is the poor relation of the human rights treaty bodies in terms of its resources and servicing.[43] It sits for a shorter period than the other human rights treaty bodies (two weeks each year under Article 20, although it was granted an extra week by the General Assembly for 1993 and 1994).[49] Its sittings have alternated between Vienna and New York, not Geneva, where the United Nations Centre for Human Rights is based. This is because of the historical location in Vienna of the Division for the Advancement of Women which supports the CEDAW. The other treaty bodies are serviced by the Centre, another indication that women's rights are not perceived of as being within the mainstream of human rights.[50] The Division was relocated in 1993 to New York, but the relationship between the Centre for Human Rights and the CEDAW remains uncertain.

International Human Rights Doctrine

The Women's Convention is not framed as a women's rights convention but as an international prohibition of gender-based discrimination.[51] Its standard is that of equality, whereby women are to be treated in the same way as men.[52] In general, it does not provide guarantees against harms suffered by women which are not shared by men.[53] Although its full implementation would improve enormously the position of women living under the jurisdiction of states parties, this would still not provide for women the same bodily security as effective implementation of other human rights guarantees would provide for men. In addition, the Women's Convention has had the detrimental effect of marginalizing women's rights and removing them from the mainstream as developed through the work of the other human rights treaties bodies. In turn, these other bodies have not given attention to gender-specific violations of their treaties, or interpreted them in ways that are especially meaningful for women. These lacunae can be illustrated by reference to the right to life, the prohibition of torture and acts of violence committed against women.

The Women's Convention does not explicitly prohibit violence against women, and nor does it assert such violence to constitute wrongful discrimination against women.[54] Other human rights instruments have gender-neutrally drafted provisions which uphold the right to life,[55] to bodily integrity, and to freedom from torture and other cruel, inhuman and degrading treatment.[56] However, a number of factors have combined to inhibit interpretation of these provisions being extended to include the violence routinely suffered by women.

First, the distinction between public and private arenas discussed above has had particular impact in international law.[57] Matters within the domestic jurisdiction of states are excluded from its ambit.[58] Human rights law has forced a considerable erosion of the area of exclusion, most significantly in the context of race discrimination and apartheid, but a state's treatment of its women is still widely regarded as falling within its domestic jurisdiction. Further, even when it is conceded that treatment of a state's own citizens is a matter of international obligation, that obligation is formulated by the doctrine of state responsibility, which has traditionally imputed liability to the state only for official acts performed by state officials and agents.

Definitions of human rights norms are made upon this assumption of imputability for public acts. Thus the right to life is primarily applicable to protect individuals from arbitrary deprivation of life by government officials through summary executions. Similarly, torture is defined as:

> Any act by which severe pain or suffering, whether physical or mental, is intentionally inflicted on a person for such purposes as obtaining from him or a third person information or a confession, punishing him for an act he or a third person has committed . . . when such pain or suffering is inflicted by or at the instigation of or with the consent or acquiesence of a public official or other person acting in an official capacity.[59]

The emphasis on official action in the doctrine of state responsibility, coupled with the primacy traditionally accorded to civil and political rights within Western political and legal philosophy, has located the understanding of what behaviour constitutes violations of human rights law in the public arena. This law is directed towards protecting men from the harms men commit against each other, not to those that are committed against women.[60] Violence against women does not fit within the definition of torture.[61] As Sharon Capeling-Alakiya, the Director of the United Nations Development Fund for Women (UNIFEM), has noted,

> the home is a metaphor of tremendous power. To debate a government's right or responsibility to intervene in a private home is to raise some of the most explosive issues of our day: What is a nation? What is sovereignty? Under what circumstances must outsiders act?[62]

In this sense the standard of equality enshrined within the human rights instruments is of little value to women: it is evidently important that where women suffer from abuse by public officials, for example in jails or other places of detention, in the same ways as men, they are entitled to the same human rights protection as men. However, this standard of equality fails to take account of the gender-specific ways in which women suffer death and violence through public agencies,[63] and of the many ways in which they are maimed and killed by private individuals. Freedom from private acts of racial violence was guaranteed in the Race Convention in acknowledgment of the harm that such acts cause to the objective of racial equality and the enjoyment of all other rights.[64] Fourteen years later the same connection was not made in the case of women.

The fact that violence against women occurs primarily in private has also meant that it has remained hidden from public view, with the consequence that the global incidence of such abuses has been obscured. Women themselves are often reluctant to report violence against them because of shame and the socio-economic pressure to remain in relationships. Within communities the incidence of violence against women has often been widely underplayed, one factor being the fear that acknowledgment will undermine the integrity of the family.[65] In many cases cultural and traditional attitudes and prejudices lead to tolerance of such levels of violence. These factors have combined to deflect international concern about the extent of violence against women. In order to bring it on to the international human rights agenda, women have had first to demonstrate its widespread incidence and second to urge acceptance of the view that this violence is structural, forms part of the subordination and oppression of women worldwide and is therefore a state responsibility.

Recognition of violence against women as a denial of human rights requires acceptance that a government can be made internationally accountable for the acts of private individuals within the home, the workplace and the community through the maintenance of a legal and social system in which violence against women is endemic and where such actions are trivialized or discounted. There is some support for such an approach in decisions of the European and the Inter-American Courts of Human Rights, which deal with the failure of states to provide adequate legal remedies for the protection of human rights. In *X and Y* v. *The Netherlands*, for example, the Netherlands was held to be in breach of the European Convention through the inadequacy of its criminal law.[66] A gap in the law meant that there was no action available to a 16-year-old mentally retarded child who had been sexually abused. The European Court of Human Rights held that respect for family life includes positive obligations upon states and may require the adoption of measures designed to secure respect for private life, even in the sphere of individual relations. In *Costello Roberts* v. *United Kingdom*, the same Court affirmed government responsibility for actions contrary to the European Convention committed within a private school.[67]

Similarly, in *Velasquez Rodriguez* v. *Honduras*, the Inter-American Court of Human Rights referred to 'the duty of the States Parties to organise the governmental apparatus and, in general, all the structures through which public power is exercised, so that they are capable of juridically ensuring the free and full enjoyment of human rights'.[68] It continued:

> An illegal act which violates human rights and which is initially not directly imputable to a State (for example, because it is the act of a private person. . .) can lead to international responsibility of the State . . . because of the lack of due diligence to prevent the violation or to respond to it . . .
>
> This duty to prevent includes all those means of a legal, political, administrative and cultural nature that promote the protection of human rights and ensure that any violations are considered and treated as illegal acts.

The extension of the guarantee to life to include situations where the government has failed to prevent killing has been continued by the Human Rights Committee. In its General Comments on the right to life (ICCPR, Article 6), the Committee has emphasized that the right should not be given a narrow interpretation and that states should adopt positive measures to preserve and protect life.[69] Further, in its General Comment 20 on torture (ICCPR, Article 7) it affirmed that states must ensure individuals' protection against acts of torture 'whether inflicted by people in their official capacity, outside their official capacity or in a private capacity'. While this formulation does not embrace private acts of violence against women, it does prevent such actions as rape and sexual abuse of women in detention being categorized as private acts of state agents rather than as acts of torture.

REDEFINING HUMAN RIGHTS WITHIN THE UNITED NATIONS?

Although none of the cases or comments discussed above directly concerned gender-specific violations of human rights, imputation of state liability for private actions can be applied by analogy to the failure of a state to apply its criminal law to prosecute private acts of violence against women, or to the upholding of a defence of honour which allows a man to kill a woman with impunity.[70] The Vienna Declaration and Programme of Action, and the Declaration on the Elimination of Violence against Women, together go some way towards redefining state responsibility to ensure accountability for private acts of violence against women.[71] Another important development is General Recommendation No. 19 adopted by the CEDAW at its eleventh session.[72] Recommendation No. 19 provides a substantive interpretation of the Women's Convention upon which the CEDAW will question states. It asserts that 'the definition of discrimination includes gender-based violence' and that 'gender-based violence is a form of discrimination that seriously inhibits women's ability to enjoy rights and freedoms on a basis of equality with men'. The preamble to the Declaration on Violence acknowledges the structural roots of violence against women by stating that violence against women 'is a manifestation of historically unequal power relations between men and women' and that it is a social mechanism whereby 'women are forced into a subordinate position compared with men'. This affirmation of the significance of power imbalance within society takes the analysis of women's rights out of the confines of anti-discrimination discourse. The fundamental problem women face worldwide is not discriminatory treatment compared with men, although this is a manifestation of the larger problem. Women are in an inferior position because they have no real social or economic power in either the public or private worlds.

Article 1 of the Declaration refers to violence as 'gender-based', thus emphasizing the specificity of the problem. The right to be free from violence is not an adaptation of a right built on male experience. The Declaration explicitly includes violence occurring within 'public or private life' and within the family. Article 4(c) requires states to punish acts of violence against women perpetrated by the state, or by private persons. Another advance for women is the clarification that 'custom, tradition or religion cannot be used as a justification to avoid eliminating violence against women'. The controversial areas of female genital mutiliation and 'other traditional practices harmful to women' are included in Article 2(a), despite opposition from some Islamic nations, particularly the Sudan.

The Declaration also gives prominence, and credibility, to women's groups. Non-governmental organizations perform many functions in the protection of human rights, including the collection and dissemination of information, the monitoring of government compliance, campaigning and lobbying for human rights, and providing input into standard-setting and norm creation. Women's non-governmental organizations have been especially assiduous in bringing women's rights on to the international human rights agenda. Thus the preamble to the Declaration welcomes 'the role that women's movements have played in drawing increasing attention to the nature, severity and magnitude of the problem of violence against women'. States are called upon to 'recognize the important role of the women's movement and non-governmental organisations worldwide in raising awareness and alleviating the problem of violence against women' and 'to facilitate and enhance' their work and to cooperate with them.[73] The important work of non-governmental organizations in raising public awareness about human rights issues was also recognized by the Vienna World Conference, which also emphasized the right of such organizations and their members to enjoyment of human rights guarantees.[74]

Supporters of women's rights have rightly seen these instruments as major advances in the reformulation of human rights doctrine and the incorporation of women's rights into the mainstream of human rights law. Nevertheless, there is still a long way to go. Neither the Declaration on Violence nor the Vienna Declaration and Programme of Action constitute binding legal obligations. 'Soft law' instruments of this sort create expectations as to future behaviour, but do not formally bind states.[75] Their language is more that of a programme of action and aspiration than of current obligation. Further, as has been seen, binding treaty obligations have been undermined by wide-ranging reservations. It is also unlikely that the principles of these instruments are currently accepted as customary international law.[76] Under the constitutional law of a number of states, treaties are incorporated into domestic law, and customary international law too may be relied upon. The soft law status of these Declarations lessens the likelihood of their domestic application. The strategy that must now be pursued is for these principles to be reiterated in treaty form and to generate sufficient state practice and *opinio juris* for them to become established customary international law.[77] Enforcement mechanisms such as the appointment of the Special Rapporteur on Violence Against Women and the questioning by the CEDAW of states on the implementation of its General Recommendation No. 19 are important aspects of ensuring that states are not allowed simply to ignore these principles.

Despite its textual strengths, the Declaration on Violence represents compromise. Its text was weakened in some respects during the drafting process. For example, an earlier draft included 'degrading representation of women in the media' as a form of violence against women but this was lost from the final version.[78] Significantly, the Declaration does not make explicit that violence against women is a human rights violation, and the linkage drawn between human rights and gender-based violence is unfortunately tenuous.[79] Although the Preamble reiterates the urgent need for the universal application to women of rights such as equality and security and affirms that violence against women affects women's enjoyment of their human rights, the numbered articles do not confirm this link. Violence against women is defined in Articles 2 and 3 without any reference to human rights, while Article 3 refers to human rights but not to violence against women. Strong opposition to describing violence against women as a violation of human rights was expressed, in particular by the USA and Sweden, during the 1992 intersessional Commission of the Status of Women meeting. It was argued that human rights provides protection from actions in which there was direct state involvement, and that extending the notion to cover 'private' behaviour would reduce the status of the whole human rights canon. This argument discounts the central problem for women in traditional human rights law: fundamental human rights are defined in categories that reflect typically male life experiences and offer protection from actions that men most fear. By excluding the 'private' realm from international human rights protection, human rights law becomes by and large irrelevant for most women. It is for this reason that the reaffirmation at Vienna of women's rights as human rights and, in particular, that violence against women constitutes a violation of human rights, is so important.

Significantly, in view of events in former Yugoslavia, the Vienna Conference reiterated that 'Violations of the human rights of women in situations of armed conflict are violations of fundamental principles of international human rights and humanitarian law.' Although this clarification is vital, the language of the Vienna Declaration is also weaker where it goes on to state that 'all violations of this kind, including murder, systematic rape, sexual slavery, and forced pregnancy, require a particularly effective response' without indicating what might constitute such a response and where responsibility lies for its enforcement.[80]

Finally, the Vienna Declaration itself undercuts its message that women's rights are human rights by its separate consideration of women. It is essential that the mainstream human rights treaty bodies examine ways in which they can incorporate gender-specific abuses and provide support to the CEDAW. Above all, what is needed is the genuine commitment of state governments to domestic compliance with the principles of these instruments.

ACKNOWLEDGMENTS

This chapter builds upon an ongoing research project with Hilary Charlesworth and Shelley Wright on Feminism and International Law. It draws especially upon H. Charlesworth and C. Chinkin, Violence against women: a global issue. In J. Stubbs (ed.), *Women, Male Violence and the Law* (Institute of Criminology Monograph Series, No. 6, 1994), pp. 13–34. The author thanks the Institute of Criminology, Sydney, Australia for permission to do this.

NOTES

1. United Nations World Conference on Human Rights: Vienna Declaration and Programme of Action, 25 June 1993, rep. 32 ILM 1661 (1993).
2. The Statute of the International Court of Justice, Article 38 (1), contains a widely accepted list of the sources of international law. Resolutions of the General Assembly are recommendatory: United Nations Charter, Article 10.
3. See D. Sullivan, Women's human rights and the 1993 World Conference on Human Rights' (1994) 88 *American Journal of International Law* 152.
4. GA Res. 48.104, adopted 20 December 1993.
5. The Commission on Human Rights, The Question of Integrating the Rights of Women into the Human Rights Mechanisms of the United Nations and the Elimination of Violence against Women, 4 March 1994; E/CN. 4/1994/L. 11/Add. 3. The Commission approved the appointment of the Special Rapporteur on violence against women in para. 6. Radhika Coomaraswamy from Sri Lanka has been appointed to the post.
6. There is a growing literature on women's human rights; see especially C. Bunch, Women's rights as human rights: towards a revision of human rights (1990) 12 *Human Rights Quarterly* 486; G. Ashworth, *Changing the Discourse: a Guide to Women and Human Rights* (Change Thinkbook IX, 1993); J. Kerr (ed.), *Ours by Right* (Zed Books, 1993); K. Tomasevski, *Women and Human Rights* (Zed Books, 1993); R. Cook (ed.) *Human Rights of Women. National and International Perspectives* (University of Pennsylvania Press, 1994); J. Peters and A. Wolpes (eds), *Women's Rights, Human Rights* (Routledge, 1995).
7. A. Dieng, Introduction, (1993) 50 *Review of the International Commission of Jurists* 4.
8. Cf. F. Butegwa, Women's human rights. A challenge to the international human rights community (1993) 50 *Review of the International Commission of Jurists* 71.
9. GA Res. 217 A (III), 10 December 1948.
10. International Covenant on Civil and Political Rights, 16 December 1966, 993 UNTS (United Nations Treaty Series) 3; International Covenant on Economic, Social and Cultural Rights, 16 December 1966, 999 UNTS 171.
11. International Covenant on Civil and Political Rights, Article 2 (1); International Covenant on Economic, Social and Cultural Rights, Article 3.
12. Article 26 provides: 'All persons are equal before the law and are entitled without any discrimination to the equal protection of the law. In this respect, the law shall prohibit any discrimination and guarantee to all persons equal and effective protection against discrimination on any ground such as race, colour, sex, language, religion, political or other opinion, national or social origin, property, birth or other status.'
13. For example Convention on the Nationality of Married Women, Montevideo, 26 December 1933 (1934) 28 *American Journal of International Law* Supp. 62; Convention on the Nationality of Married Women, 20 February 1957, 309 UNTS 65; Convention on the

Political Rights of Women, New York, 31 March 1953; Convention on Consent to Marriage, Minimum Age for Marriage and Registration of Marriages, adopted GA Res. 1763B (XVII), 1962. The Convention on the Rights of the Child, adopted GA Res. 44/736, 20 November 1989, prohibits discrimination, *inter alia*, on the grounds of the sex of the child or his or her parent's or guardian's sex. For all these instruments, and others, see *The United Nations and the Advancement of Women, 1945–1995* (United Nations, 1995).

14. Convention Relative to the Protection of Civilian Persons in Time of War, Geneva, 12 August 1949, 75 UNTS 287, Article 27: 'Women shall be especially protected against any attack on their honour, in particular against rape, enforced prostitution, or any form of indecent assault'; Protocol Additional to the Geneva Conventions of 12 August 1949 and Relating to the Protection of Victims of International Armed Conflicts (Protocol I), 8 June 1977, 1125 UNTS 17512, Article 76.

15. GA Res. 34/180 (XXXIV).

16. On the Commission, see L. Reanda, The Commission on the Status of Women. In P. Alston (ed.), *The United Nations and Human Rights. A Critical Appraisal* (Clarendon Press, 1992), pp. 265–303.

17. Convention on the Elimination of All Forms of Discrimination Against Women, Preambular Paragraphs.

18. The United Nations Human Rights Committee General Comment 18 on Non-discrimination (Article 26) (37th Session 1989) notes the definitions of discrimination within the Convention on the Elimination of All Forms of Racial Discrimination, 7 March 1966, 660 UNTS 195, and the Women's Convention for the purposes of defining discrimination under Article 26 of the International Covenant on Civil and Political Rights. This provides cohesion between the specific Conventions and the more general, mainstream human rights treaties.

19. Convention on the Elimination of All Forms of Racial Discrimination, Article 14; Convention Against Torture and Other Cruel, Inhuman or Degrading Treatment, 10 December 1984, GA Res. 39/46, Article 21. Individual petitions may be submitted to the Commission on the Status of Women.

20. Convention on the Elimination of All Forms of Racial Discrimination, Article 11; Convention Against Torture, Article 21.

21. Convention Against Torture, Article 20.

22. Vienna Declaration and Programme of Action, II, para. 40.

23. Text available with author. *Women using the Human Rights System* (British Council and European Commission, 1995).

24. As of 31 August 1995, 145 states had ratified the Women's Convention.

25. This is exemplified by the two United Nations Covenants of 1966. The Convention on the Elimination of All Forms of Racial Discrimination, Article 5 (e), lists economic, social and cultural rights, but does not expand upon their applicability in the same way as the Women's Convention and the subsequent Convention on the Rights of the Child.

26. S. Wright, Economic rights and social justice: a feminist analysis of some international human rights conventions (1992) 12 *Australian Yearbook of International Law* 242.

27. There is an enormous literature on the impact of the public–private divide. See especially J. Elshtain, *Public Man, Private Woman* 2nd edn (Princeton University Press, 1993); K. O'Donovan, *Sexual Divisions in Law* (Weidenfeld and Nicolson, 1985); C. Pateman, Feminist critiques of the public/private dichotomy. In S. Benn and G. Gaus (eds), *Public and Private in Social Life* (Croom Helm, 1983), p. 281. See also Chapters 21 and 23, above.

28. H. Charlesworth, C. Chinkin and S. Wright, Feminist approaches to international law (1991) 85 *American Journal of International Law* 613–45, at pp. 625–30.

29. Article 7 covers the rights of women to participate in the public life of the state, including non-governmental organizations and (in Article 8) international organizations. On the very unequal participation by women in international organizations, see H. Charlesworth, C. Chinkin and S. Wright, *op. cit.*

30. Cf. International Covenant on Civil and Political Rights, Article 23, which denotes the family as 'the natural and fundamental group unit of society which is entitled to protection by society and the state'.

31. F. Butegwa, *op. cit.*, p. 71.

32. There are numerous studies and reports which document the reality for women. See, for example, *Women: Challenges to the Year 2000* (United Nations, 1991); *The World's Women: 1970–1990 Trends and Statistics*, 2nd edn (United Nations, 1995); J. Connors, *Violence against Women in the Family* (United Nations, 1989). For personal accounts see D. Russell (ed.), *Crimes Against Women: The Proceedings of the International Tribunal* (Les Femmes Publishers, 1976) and the similar Tribunal held at the Vienna World Conference on Human Rights, 1993; for commentary see especially A. Sen, More than 100 million Women are Missing, *New York Review of Books*, 30 December 1990; M. Schuler (ed.), *Freedom from Violence: Women's Strategies From Around the World* (Unifem, 1992).

33. A number of reservations are to Article 29, which provides for the jurisdiction of the International Court of Justice for the settlement of disputes arising out of the Convention.

34. For a very full discussion of reservations to the Women's Convention, see R. Cook, Reservations to the Convention on the Elimination of All Forms of Discrimination Against Women (1990) 30 *Virginia Journal of International Law* 643; B. Clark, The Vienna Convention reservations regime and the Convention on Discrimination Against Women (1991) 85 *American Journal of International Law* 281.

35. For example, Egypt's general reservation on Article 2: 'The Arab Republic of Egypt is willing to comply with the content of this article provided that such compliance does not run counter to the Islamic Sharia.' The Bangladeshi reservation states: 'The Government of the Peoples Republic of Bangladesh does not consider as binding upon itself the provisions of articles 2, 13 (a) and 16 1 (c) and (f) as they conflict with Sharia law based on Holy Quran and Sunna.' For the full text of reservations see *Multilateral Treaties Deposited with the Secretary-General* (United Nations). For an attempt to reconcile freedom of religion with the right to non-discrimination on the basis of sex, see Chapter 21, above.

36. For a fuller critique of these reservations see B. Clark, *op. cit.*

37. Reservations have been made by states from varying geographic regions and of various political stances; for example, Australia, Austria, Belgium, Brazil, Cyprus, India, Jordan, New Zealand and Thailand have also made substantive reservations.

38. The UK has also made reservations to Articles 1, 9, 11, 13, 15 and 16. It has made a general understanding that 'none of its obligations under the Convention shall be treated as extending to the succession to... the Throne,... or as extending to the affairs of religious denominations or orders or to the admission into or service in the Armed Forces of the Crown.' At the World Conference on Women, Baroness Chalker, speaking on behalf of the UK government, made a commitment to withdrawing many of these reservations.

39. Vienna Convention on the Law of Treaties, 23 May 1969, 1155 UNTS 331, Articles 19–23. The Women's Convention, Article 28 (2), follows the Vienna Convention and permits reservations provided that they are compatible with the object and purpose of the Convention.

40. Germany, Mexico, Finland, Denmark, Norway and Sweden have entered formal objections to some of the reservations of some of these states.

41. See, for example, the Reservations to the Convention on the Prevention and Punishment of the Crime of Genocide Case, 1951 ICJ Rep. 15 (Adv. Op. 28 May).

42. CEDAW General Recommendation No. 4, 1987, and No. 20, 1992, both expressed the Committee's concern about 'the validity and legal effect of reservations to the Convention'. The latter recommendation suggested that states parties consider these questions in the preparations for the World Conference on Human Rights.

43. See A. Byrnes, The 'other' human rights treaty body: the work of the Committee on the Elimination of Discrimination Against Women (1989) 14 *Yale Journal of International Law* 1.

44. Vienna Declaration and Programme of Action, II, para. 39. Compare Beijing Declaration and Platform for Action, 15 September 1995, para. 218.

45. *Ibid.*, para. 38.

46. *Women: Challenges to the Year 2000* (United Nations, 1991), p. 9.

47. C. Chinkin and K. Werksman, CEDAW No. 12, *Report of the Twelfth Session of the Committee on the Elimination of All Forms of Discrimination Against Women* (International Women's Rights Action Watch, 1993).

48. In contrast, the Convention on the Rights of the Child, Article 45 (a), provides that the Committee on the Rights of the Child may seek expert advice from 'competent bodies.'

49. In a three-week sitting the CEDAW considered 12 reports in 1993.

50. In 1989 the General Assembly requested that an officer of the Centre for Human Rights attend the sessions of the CEDAW. It remains unusual for this to occur, at least for the whole session; A. Byrnes, CEDAW No. 10: *Building on a Decade of Achievement* (International Women's Rights Action Watch, 1991).

51. This is in contrast to the Convention on the Rights of the Child.

52. There are some exceptions; for example, Article 12 on health care provides for the specific health needs of pregnancy, and Article 14 identifies the particular position of rural women. For a European law perspective on equality, see Chapter 9, above.

53. The exception is Article 6, which requires states to suppress trafficking in women and exploitation through prostitution.

54. Another omission from the Convention is the related issue of pornography.

55. For example, International Covenant on Civil and Political Rights, Article 6; European Convention for the Protection of Fundamental Rights and Freedoms, 4 November 1950, ETS No. 5, Article 2; American Convention on Human Rights, 22 November 1969, OAS TS No. 36, Article 4.

56. For example, Convention against Torture and other Cruel, Inhuman or Degrading Treatment or Punishment, Article 1; International Covenant on Civil and Political Rights, Article 7; European Convention on Human Rights, Article 3; American Convention on Human Rights, Article 5 (2).

57. H. Charlesworth, C. Chinkin and S. Wright, *op. cit.*, pp. 625–30; H. Charlesworth, The public/private distinction and the right to development in international law (1992) 12 *Australian Yearbook of International Law* 190; R. Cook, Accountability in international law for violations of women's rights by non-state actors. In D. Dallmeyer (ed.), *Reconceiving Reality: Women and International Law* (American Society of International Law, 1993); S. Wright, Economic rights, social justice and the state: a feminist appraisal. In D. Dallmeyer, *op. cit.*, p. 117; F. Olsen, International law: feminist critiques of the public/private distinction. In D. Dallmeyer, *op. cit.*, p. 157.

58. United Nations Charter, Article 2 (7).

59. Convention Against Torture, Article 1 (1).

60. H. Charlesworth and C. Chinkin, The gender of jus cogens (1993) 15 *Human Rights Quarterly* 63.

61. C. MacKinnon, On torture: a feminist perspective on human rights. In K. Mahoney and P. Mahoney (eds), *Human Rights in the 21st Century* (Kluwer Academic, 1993), pp. 405–18.

62. UNIFEM, Calling for Change: International Strategies to End Violence against Women; Conference held at The Hague, The Netherlands, 6–9 June 1993.

63. Gender-specific methods of torture are beginning to be recognized; see Amnesty International, *Women in the Front Line* (1991).

64. Convention on the Elimination of All Forms of Racial Discrimination, Article 5 (b), guarantees the right to 'security of the person . . . against violence . . . whether inflicted by government officials or by any individual, group or institution.'

65. J. Connors, *Violence against Women in the Family* (United Nations, 1989), p. 17.

66. (1985) 91 European Court of Human Rights (Ser. A).

67. (1993) European Court of Human Rights (Ser. A). No. 247–C. See also *Airey* v. *Ireland* (1979) 32 European Court of Human Rights (Ser. A).

68. 28 ILM 294 (1989).

69. On the General Comments on the right to life, see D. McGoldrick, *The Human Rights Committee* (Clarendon Press, 1991), pp. 328–36. Positive measures include health, environmental and safety matters, as well as the investigation of 'disappeared' persons. For the relevance of the right to life in the context of abortion, see Chapter 20, above.

70. See the argument developed on this point in Americas Watch, *Criminal Injustice: Violence against Women in Brazil* (1991).

71. However, on the dangers for women of extending government responsibility, and therefore intervention, into the private arena, see K. Engle, After the collapse of the public/private distinction: strategizing women's rights. In D. Dallmeyer, *op. cit.*, p. 143.

72. CEDAW, General Recommendation No. 19, GAOR, 47th Session, Supp. No. 38

(A/47/38), 1992.

73. Declaration on the Elimination of Violence Against Women, Article 4 (o) and (p). Article 5 (h) calls on the organs and specialized agencies of the United Nations to do likewise.

74. Vienna Declaration and Programme of Action, I, para. 38.

75. C. Chinkin, The challenge of soft law: development and change in international law (1989) 38 *International and Comparative Law Quarterly* 850–66. The Platform for Action adopted at Beijing in September 1995 is also a non-binding instrument, although its re-affirmation of these principles on violence in paras. 113–124 strengthens the political consensus.

76. See C. Chinkin, Sources of international law: entrenching the gender bias. In R. Lefeber (ed.) *Contemporary International Law Issues: Opportunities at a Time of Momentous Change*, 1993 Conference, American Society of International Law and Nederlandse Vereiniging vor International Recht, pp. 418–21.

77. The Inter-American Convention on the Prevention, Punishment and Eradication of Violence against Women was adopted by the General Assembly of the Organization of American States, 9 June 1994, Belem do Para, Brazil. The Committee of Ministers of the Council of Europe has discussed the possible adoption of a Protocol to the European Convention on Human Rights on the fundamental right of women and men to equality and the adoption of a plan of action to combat violence.

78. The initial draft of the Declaration Against Violence was prepared by an expert group in 1991. It was revised by an intersessional meeting of the Commission on the Status of Women in August 1992. The Commission adopted the revised text in March 1993 which then went to ECOSOC and the General Assembly; see D. Sullivan, *op. cit.*, p. 164.

79. The French text of this provision is considerably stronger than that of the English.

80. See further, C. Chinkin, Rape and sexual abuse of women in international law (1994) 5 *European Journal of International Law* 326–41.

25

'Rights' and International Humanitarian Law

Elizabeth Chadwick

INTRODUCTION

Armed conflicts are frequently fought to achieve human rights, and with the emergence from colonialism of many new states in the post-1945 era, the distinction between human rights law and the International Humanitarian Law of Armed Conflict (IHL) has become blurred in the minds of many.[1] Moreover, IHL is increasingly perceived as part of, and dominated by, post-1945 human rights law.[2]

This 'blurring' is caused in part by the incorporation of limited human rights provisions in new IHL documents. An integrationist focus appears appropriate for situations in which force is utilized to achieve human rights, for instance, during wars of self-determination or against aggression. Yet an impression that IHL forms part of human rights law is misleading. The two legal régimes evolved separately, and reflect different philosophies. To focus in particular on the growing content of human rights law in IHL documents is thus to be deceived as to the influence exerted by the prior codifications of IHL over the more recent development of human rights law.

It is the purpose of this chapter to develop the premise that human rights law arguably forms part of IHL or, at the least, is guided by IHL frameworks of state cooperation. Several factors support this premise. First, IHL has traditionally been a minimalist inter-state agreement,[3] in that protection is provided at the most basic level of international cooperation – during times of war – to combatants, non-combatants, and those finding themselves in occupied territory. The modern IHL was first codified in the nineteenth century in the separate forms of war law, or Hague law, and humanitarian law, or Geneva law. In light of the wars fought in this century, additional protections, many termed 'human rights law', have been developed in IHL.[4] The four 1949 Geneva

Conventions and Geneva Protocols 1 and 2 of 1977[1] reflect a growing spirit of integration of all three areas – war law, humanitarian law, and human rights law – in order to achieve protection for the individual in all circumstances against the actions of states.

Moreover, the many humanitarian documents which pre-date human rights law reflect an inter-state contract of self-restraint. Developed despite the many conflicting interests implicit in power politics and economic competition, the early IHL agreements for governmental restraint in wartime in turn provided an indication of the post-1945 cooperation to be expected in maintaining peace and developing a law of human rights. In that war has not ceased to occur, it is also relevant that the many developed IHL protections help form the basis from which to negotiate the end of a conflict, and to re-build peace.[5]

A further shift in perspective allows the 'habit of restraint' found in IHL to be viewed as helping to create the conditions necessary for, and to guide the content of, human rights law today, particularly the civil and political rights (see later). Should the patterns of cooperation initially developed in IHL, and carried forward into human rights law, be recognized, much of the abuse of each legal system might be better clarified, and the need to alter those political mechanisms which allow abuse would be identified.

In order to illustrate these many points, this chapter will be structured as follows. The nineteenth and early twentieth century codification of IHL is first reviewed – a period in which 'war' waged to pursue economic interests was not prohibited. The use of force by governments – the regulation of which forms the purpose of IHL documents – and the ways in which such uses of force have conditioned the emergence of the three generations of human rights law are then considered in order to compare the development of human rights law with that of IHL. The shift from war to peace in the post-1945 era, and the crucial importance of the UN prohibition on the aggressive use or threat of inter-state armed force, are then discussed. It is concluded that, until the use of armed force to achieve political change ceases, human rights law will remain confined by the scope of state cooperation found in IHL, and that any insistence that human rights law dominates IHL could reduce the ability of either legal régime to constrain governments in their uses of force.

THE DEVELOPMENT OF IHL

The Historical Context

A nineteenth-century imperialist era of economic competition for new markets and resources among capitalist states was the early context of IHL. Perhaps of greater importance, the international community at the time did not forbid recourse to war. Wars were fought largely by professional armies, and power élites controlled the law, the means of production and the use of armed force.

In earlier times, the 'just' war of the Christian prince required at least a 'just' cause.[6] In turn, a 'just' cause required little or no restraint over the means and methods utilized to punish the wicked. By the nineteenth century, war tended to be viewed in a more neutral light, and the laws of war gained in importance. The rules and customs of war were developed and used to regulate wars in relation to the scale and intensity of the fighting.[7] These customs of war thus applied to civil wars of high intensity, as well as to war waged between sovereign entities.[8]

While many wars in the nineteenth century were fought for political reasons or territorial acquisition,[9] the industrialist's war was one means by which to ensure ready access to resources and the continued exchange of goods.[10] The struggle was intense for the division of the world and for world hegemony.[11] Wars were frequent and the military–industrial complex, developing since the 1850s, made its appearance in the UK in the mid-1880s.[12] However that term is understood, its appearance transformed the ways in which questions of war and peace were approached and settled. Yet, as long as Western nations targeted each other's economic bases, efforts to 'humanize' war were made, and it was only exceptionally that their own civilian populations were made the express targets of attack.[13]

Duties imposed by the laws and customs of war, and subsequently codified in IHL, fell on governments, which mutually accepted the obligation to protect and care for the sick, the wounded, the shipwrecked and the prisoners of their wars. The US Lieber Code of 1863[14] first recorded the proper confines of military necessity, the protection of non-combatants in occupied territory, and the European notion of respect between professional armies.[15] A perceived need to harness new military technology, in part fuelled by the increased participation of the masses in public life, led in turn to numerous international efforts to regulate and control the usages of war. Trainin[16] notes that between 1815 and 1910, 148 international meetings were held for this purpose, 90 of which were convened in the first decade of the twentieth century. This need to harness new military technology led in time to the Hague Conventions and Regulations of 1899 and 1907,[17] in which contractual restraint in the use of various means and methods of warfare was negotiated.[18] Government concern for humanitarian restraint was further in evidence with the founding of the Red Cross in 1863, whose Conventions of 1864 and 1906[19] were designed to ensure better protection for the victims of these wars. Given the attractiveness of the new theory of *Kriegsräson*,[20] and the bare fact of international life at the time – state sovereignty – it was a remarkable development that these many conventions ever succeeded in entering into force.

The late nineteenth-century was also famous for efforts to achieve disarmament and arbitration accords, as the laws of war were increasingly overshadowed by peaceful developments such as the international regulation of maritime law, intellectual property, and the carriage of mail. Best notes that 'humanitarianism was all the rage from the sixties; the "peace movement" was noisy and prestigious'.[21] Disarmament proposals of one sort or another were put forward by Russia in 1816, 1859 and 1899, France in 1863 and 1877, the UK in 1866, 1870 and 1890 and Denmark in 1893. Moreover, while Germany opposed the creation of an agency of international arbitration at the Hague Conference in 1899, it gave its formal consent to an optional tribunal.[22]

Efforts to restrain aggressive state behaviour after 1918 concentrated on arbitration, and the redistribution of former German and Turkish dependencies in the League of Nations mandate system. New standards to govern the integration of minorities in the new states created after 1919 served a peace-making function by potentially preventing transboundary alliances. Economic prosperity was thought to ensure the conditions of independence, and thus it became a condition precedent for statehood. When faced with a choice between justice or security, the League favoured security interests.[23]

The neglect of war law resulted in its development being regarded as unnecessary.[24] Hague law could not regulate methods of warfare which were unknown in 1899 and 1907, and further developments in this area were stymied by opposition to the coming into force of any further document other than an agreed prohibition in 1925 on the use of 'Asphyxiating, Poisonous or Other Gases and of Bacteriological Methods of Warfare'.[25] The 1928 Pact of Paris condemned recourse to war.[26] Ten years after the Pact of Paris, racist and nationalist ideologies provoked war, transforming World War II into a 'moral' conflict more in keeping with an ancient 'just' war, as opposing systems of public order fought to prove the 'rightness' of their respective value systems in a trial by arms which saw decreasing restraint in the means and methods utilized to achieve victory.

This 'moral' characterization of World War II supported the insertion of a natural rights philosophy into the Nuremberg and Tokyo Tribunals[27] the assessment of individual responsibility in times of armed conflict,[28] and into the content of the 1949 Geneva revisions.[29] Inter-state wars of aggression were condemned as international crimes. The importance of the relationship between the government and the individual for building a 'just' society was recognized, and 'significant movements took place towards strengthening the institutional safeguards against abuse of authority'.[30] However, post-War ideological differences were apparent between the two power blocs and the laws of war, which had arisen initially to require standards of humanity between Western cultures during a time in which war was legal, were transformed in 1949 into a code of action to protect, *inter alia*, human rights and documents yet to be developed and utilized.[31]

The Growth of 'Rights' in IHL

Given the neutrality of nineteenth-century European attitudes to war, it is of interest that a codified IHL was in many respects the result of public pressure to make war usages more humane. The codification of the laws and customs of war was also felt to be appropriate for use by 'civilized' nations,[32] and efforts to 'normalize' and make predictable the methods of conducting wars reflected a state-state contractual approach.[18]

The government's troops alone were enemies under the law. In view of the soldier's importance, his status was improved in 1929 in a new Red Cross Convention to protect prisoners of war.[33] The 1929 Red Cross Conference also recommended the drafting of a convention for the protection of civilians, to be discussed at the next conference in Geneva, scheduled for 1940. World War II intervened, but disagreement with the premise of this convention was also expressed, as actions taken against enemy territory and in territory occupied by a hostile army could be justified by military necessity.

When in doubt, humanitarian 'civilized' nations preferred instead to refer to the Martens Clause in the Preamble to Hague Convention IV:

> [U]ntil a more complete code of the laws of war has been issued, the High Contracting Parties deem it expedient to declare that, in cases not included in the Regulations adopted by them, the inhabitants and the belligerents remain under the protection and the rule of the principles of the law of nations, as they result from the usages established among civilized peoples, from the laws of humanity, and the dictates of the public conscience.

Thus, military damage to persons and property was allowed in war, but only to the extent required to force the enemy to put down its arms with a minimum of human destruction. Military action could be taken for these ends, but only if legally permitted by the rules in force. These early efforts to regulate war concentrated attention on the task of bringing a war to its speediest and least destructive conclusion for the three categories of a population: the regular army, irregular military units or armed forces, and non-combatant civilians.[34] There is thus an in-built compromise in IHL between the dictates of military necessity, proportionality and the principles of humanity.

Nevertheless, technological advances achieved during the industrial revolutions of Europe produced changes in the means for waging war, and in societal structures. As workers began to live in the vicinity of their factories, the worker became an active participant in the war effort. Being thus 'mobilized', an entire civilian population could become the legitimate target of attack. Tanks, artillery, submarine and air power made an organized debut in World War I, as did the theory of 'total war'. It no longer appeared practical to distinguish between military and non-military, or civilian, objectives, or to avoid collateral damage.

Common Article 3

In view of the public horror at the atrocities perpetrated against civilians during World War II, the need to protect civilians was finally fulfilled in 1949.[35] The Geneva Convention revisions of 1949 further provided an improved Prisoners of War Convention,[36] and a 'mini-treaty' for non-international armed conflicts in Common Article 3 to the four 1949 Geneva Conventions.[37] Common Article 3 provides minimal humanitarian protections for individuals 'in all circumstances'.[38] The standards contained in Common Article 3 have as their source the Martens Clause, and in so far as the 1949 Geneva Conventions have been applicable in internal conflicts, it has been on the basis of this Article.[39]

Common Article 3 is of particular importance because UN prohibitions against the threat or use of force[40] do not prohibit internal or civil wars, which remain 'legal'. By codifying international standards for non-international wars, states parties to the 1949 Geneva Conventions agreed in effect that their own domestic 'armed conflicts' should be controlled and assessed within internationally agreed limits on the use of force – limits which would apply to future rebel forces as well as to threatened governments.[37] The inter-state agreement to include Common Article 3 in the 1949 Geneva Conventions, and to regulate domestic uses of force within international limits, thus appears to be a voluntary extension of the spirit of the prohibition against the use or threat of force in inter-state relations.

Common Article 3 also reinforced existing assumptions and values already contained in traditional war law, for example the individual protections in war which had resulted from public pressure to 'humanize' its occurrence. Furthermore, humanitarian treatment in all circumstances requires respect for humanitarian law by all persons, regardless of their status, and clearly implies that there is a minimum standard below which governments may not go in their uses of force.[41]

Common Article 3 in 1949 was thus an attempt to protect individuals at the very moment when the future human rights documents would prove to be at their weakest – during a domestic armed uprising. In turn, whenever governments use armed force to restore domestic order, Common Article 3 should become applicable, if only for purposes of guidance, from the commencement of armed hostilities.[42] To posit otherwise would be to imply that states have intentionally carved for themselves a gap in their uses of force from a post-1945 framework designed to ensure international peace and security.[43]

THE CONDITIONING EFFECT OF THE USE OF FORCE ON HUMAN RIGHTS LAW

'I Burned with Rage to Pursue the Murderer of My Peace'

IHL is designed to protect and ensure respect for persons involved in an armed conflict – whether enemy soldiers, medical personnel, or civilians – and thus to restrain the actions of states. Governments are primarily responsible for the implementation, observance and respect of this treaty régime, but individuals are also internationally responsible for breaches of the law.[28,29]

Human rights, too, restrain governments, but in their dealings with those under state jurisdiction.[44] Governments are responsible for the implementation, observance and respect of those human rights treaties which have been ratified,[45] as well as a growing number of *jus cogens* rights.[46] In that human rights arguably are designed to make accessible to individuals those goods or conditions which can ensure freedom and well-being,[47] human rights law helps to restrain revolution – the counterpart of international war.

Nevertheless, the maximization of human rights is conditioned by many discretionary boundaries, the one in issue for purposes of the present discussion being the use of force by governments.[48] Only the 'core' rights remain non-derogable during times of armed conflict – domestic or international.[49] In view of the use of armed force to confine the maximization of human rights, and, in particular, the use of the state domestic monopoly over force in the UN era, the progression of human rights into three generations will now be considered.

The Three Generations of Human Rights Law

The three 'generations' of human rights are civil and political rights, economic and social (and cultural) rights, and collective group rights. These will each be discussed briefly in order to illustrate the conditioning effect of the state use of force, and, by way of corollary, the role played by the state-reserved domains of rights derogation and margins of appreciation on their separate development. The purpose of this discussion is to assess whether the development of the three generations of human rights has been affected by a pre-existing IHL treaty régime. In particular, the strength of each generation of human rights law will be assessed at its weakest point – during times of armed conflict – and thus may be compared and contrasted with the protections afforded by an integrated IHL.

DEROGATION AND 'MARGINS OF APPRECIATION'

While it is not contended that human rights are neither valid nor worthwhile, their true strength may most quickly be assessed at their weakest point – situations of national emergency which may threaten domestic security and stability. In such a case, states retain sufficient flexibility to exercise a margin of discretion, or 'appreciation', when interpreting a domestic emergency.[50] In order to take authoritative action to restore order, the derogation of human rights obligations may also result.

As a preliminary point, emergency rights derogations should be officially declared, and should not last any longer than is necessary. They should be subject to periodic review by relevant state mechanisms, preferably a law-making body.[51] A basic safeguard remains in that derogation is not allowed regarding 'core' rights, including the right to life.[49] Thus, the temporary derogation of rights, for the purpose of restoring public order, constitutes one situation in which a state may disregard many individual protections against state power, a prime example of which is the suspension of criminal procedure safeguards, or of the writ of habeas corpus.[52]

Margins of appreciation involve a pre-existing, rebuttable

presumption in favour of a state when a domestic situation endangers the public interest.[53] This presumption permits states to take action to exclude aliens,[54] or to curtail the freedom of the press,[55] for example. Margins of appreciation can affect the observance of human rights obligations by permitting a state to declare a rights derogation. The use of margins of appreciation thus may precede, or operate concurrently with, an emergency derogation, and may be applied to individuals, to classes of individuals, or to an entire population.

An interesting point about margins of appreciation and rights derogations is that a state may suspend the freedoms of its population almost to vanishing point. While the public may support draconian action to slow immigration, or to maintain the secrecy required by an external war, the discretion afforded by human rights law to governments is not exhausted when extended to situations of domestic unrest. Of further interest, post-1945 practice has shown that state governments utilize margins of appreciation during domestic armed conflicts to derogate from individual human rights below the levels provided by IHL obligations.[56]

The relevance of derogation and margins of appreciation to this chapter is the resulting confinement of the observance of human rights law within non-absolutist frameworks of interpretation. While this should not necessarily imply a weak point in human rights law, it is of particular interest when placed alongside the restraint required by IHL, should a state authoritatively interpret armed domestic unrest as a situation to which IHL applies.[57] In particular, there is no concept of derogation in IHL, as its rules already represent a realistic compromise between military necessity and humanity. As for margins of appreciation, a similar concept is in evidence with regard to the rules constraining the means and methods of warfare, the breach of which are subject to penal prosecution.[58] Given the early emergence of a human rights content in IHL, this 'weak point' in human rights law is in evidence when viewed through the post-1945 Cold War recognition of three generations of human rights, and the numerous armed conflicts which have occurred to secure their respective advantages.[59]

CIVIL AND POLITICAL RIGHTS

The civil and political rights favoured by the West have their origin in the notion of human equality so violently stated at and since the French Revolution,[60] and in the development of constitutional law, generally. Grounded in the importance of methods of consent, the value of being human is emphasized.

Civil and political rights promote both the freedom and the autonomy of the individual. Free from the constraints of restrictive government to the extent allowed by the requirements of security and stability, the autonomous individual can devolve to himself or herself maximized levels of personal initiative and responsibility, in order to secure for himself or herself access to the conditions of freedom and well-being.

Another aim of civil and political rights is a share of power with government. Civil and political rights thus encourage governmental non-interference with the private lives of citizens so long as security is maintained, and, should public order break down, the individual remains under the protection of his or her autonomy through procedural and due process rights, such as the right not to be arbitrarily interfered with.

It was realized at the end of World War II that the development of civil and political rights could not be left to states, which were also in a position to violate them. The UN Charter thus imposed obligations on states to develop and protect human rights, and the Universal Declaration of Human Rights was approved.[61] The latter was a non-binding document, yet enumerated both civil and political and economic and social rights.

As for the 'worth', or the distributive function, of civil and political rights, their exercise requires the use of individual resources, and it is at this point that the politicization of civil and political rights by capitalist ideology becomes clear. Property and the inequality of its distribution are explained by the inequalities in the distribution of human talents, 'for which possessions are the reward'.[62] Effective access to, *inter alia*, education, the suffrage and justice systems remains a function of the devolved and autonomous individual ability to amass sufficient personal resources with which to gain the extra political weight directly attributable to the possession of wealth. The distributive function of civil and political rights thus seeks the identity of those persons who can and should have their most important interests furthered or favourably considered.[63] Thus, wealth acquisition becomes a primary goal in a civil/political system.

The power structure which in turn emerges reinforces the value of wealth accumulation in the economic and social structures of society. The economically dominant force can maximize its utilization of civil and political rights, and the illusion of universal participation in government through democratic representation effectively hides the methods of coercion by which the wealthy, through ready access to government, may maintain power.[64] Should social order break down, civil and political rights may be derogated by governments, and force may be used to restore the pre-existing public order. The military may then perform a function far removed from its traditional role of meeting an external threat. The use of the military at such times is aimed at controlling political life, and frequently without any consideration of the 'rights' counterbalance provided by IHL.[65]

As for the existence of civil and political rights within IHL, rules requiring minimal due process wartime guarantees, and governing the lawful occupation of enemy territory, have existed in codified form since the Lieber Code of 1863, and the 1899 and 1907 Hague Conventions.[66] Nevertheless, IHL has always reflected a level of disregard for provisions which apply to a belligerent's own populations,[67] and it would appear that this 'weakness' in IHL is in turn reflected in the scope contained in human rights law to derogate from civil and political rights, particularly the protective rights.[68] An additional implication is that those states which were involved in formulating UN Charter principles knew well the utility of the methods of consent underlying civil and political rights, and their corollary – the use of force, for the maintenance of domestic order – from their experiences with IHL.

SOCIAL AND ECONOMIC RIGHTS

Social and economic rights attained recognition in the nineteenth century with the advent of socialism and the increased participation in public life of the masses. Recognition of these rights grew in large part because of the prosperity provided societally by the industrial revolution, and they appeared initially in state monopolies – one form of state intervention which was adopted in response to political perceptions of societal need. Social and economic rights are viewed largely as aspirational by Western capitalist states, with minimal levels of implementation, intended primarily to avert civil disturbance.[69] After widespread support was heard for the eight-point Atlantic Charter of 1941, social and economic rights made a concrete appearance in the post-1945 era in the Universal Declaration of Human Rights. Given the duty resting on states to ensure international peace and security, it is of interest that the UN views social and economic (and cultural) rights as equal in status to civil and political rights, and the two 1966 Covenants are evidence of this.[70]

Such rights require the positive use by governments of economic resources, including the right to be given food and other necessities when they are not otherwise obtainable. Social and economic rights aim for a more equitable share in the goods of society. Whether such rights meet the test of 'practicability', however, remains a contentious issue in the UN era, as many states do not have the necessary resources to provide them.[71] Social and economic rights are frequently not viewed as human rights at all, in that a right–duty correlation may be difficult to rationalize jurisprudentially.[72]

Capitalist democracies prefer citizens to exercise their multitude of freedoms to provide the necessities of life for themselves. In contrast to civil and political rights, economic and social rights require that resources be managed for the use of all, thereby implying intense governmental control over individual wealth accumulation. At the same time, until economic and social rights such as to subsistence, housing and employment are made operable, the distributive worth of civil and political rights is reduced, and the possibility of revolution increased.[73]

Social and economic rights are incorporated into IHL through numerous provisions regarding the care and protection of the sick and wounded, prisoners of war, and civilian populations during times of armed conflict.[74] The effective implementation of these provisions, however, can be financially burdensome. Given even the minimal protections provided by IHL for domestic armed conflicts, it is rarely in a threatened state's interests to refer to the laws of war or to afford recognition to insurgents through humanitarian treatment.[75] Nevertheless, should deprivations of social and economic rights provoke civil armed unrest and human rights derogation, implementation of at least minimal levels of IHL should be considered, if only to ensure internationally agreed standards of protection to individuals.

Should a gap in international protection emerge between the protections found in human rights law and IHL, such as during domestic labour strikes,[76] it is closely connected with the jealously guarded state monopoly over the use of force. Where social and economic conditions deprive citizens of the worth of civil and political rights, the mobilization of the army to maintain and restore public order reflects the interests of those whose 'rights' are felt to be more important. Thus, where an effective use of civil and political liberties is interfered with by economic inequalities, as manifested through a lack of education, poll tax/literacy tests, and little 'effective' access to judicial systems, an economically dominant faction is less subject to the full force of the political process of consent. There is to that extent less assurance that the public order will be maintained within internationally agreed limits regarding the use of force, or that the international rights of all individuals will be respected.

COLLECTIVE GROUP RIGHTS

The modern content of collective group rights has been developed in part by the success of many armed uprisings by 'peoples', particularly during the 1950s and 1960s, which were provoked by a stalled UN decolonization programme.[77] In turn, any applicability that IHL has had in such armed uprisings has been minimal, as people whose rights have little or no worth are frequently hardened against humanitarianism,[78] and governments rarely afford recognition to a people's struggle by virtue of humanitarian treatment.[79]

The Western emphasis on an eighteenth-century European model of natural rights has in turn meant the denial of the meaning of human rights to the vast majority of the world's population. Largely ignored until the UN era, collective group rights include the self-determination of 'peoples', and development. What support may be found in the UN Charter regarding group rights can be derived from the 1941 Atlantic Charter, even though the binding nature of the Atlantic Charter is a matter of dispute.[80] Subsequently, numerous UN Resolutions and Declarations supported the rights sought,[81] and helped to inject content into the notion of 'peoples' left undefined in the UN Charter. Resolution 2625, in particular, supports the conclusion that states which abide by the principles of equal rights and self-determination are alone protected against a new-found right to rebel.[82]

It is in the area of third-generation or collective group rights that IHL has been most influential over the content and development of post-1945 human rights. Recognition of the means and methods of warfare utilized by and against groups struggling for collective group rights occurred in 1977, when IHL was updated and modernized. However, the laws and customs of war mandated in the nineteenth century applied in relation to the scale of armed force utilized.[83] The post-1977 application of IHL in relation to the 'cause' of a particular armed conflict is new.[84] Further, an enlarged content of peacetime human rights law within IHL has made IHL both cumbersome and controversial to utilize. As a result, some influential Western states refuse to ratify either Protocol, and, in particular, Protocol 1.[85]

Further, the recognition of an armed conflict in any situation other than the full invasion of one state by another is so politically charged that states have refrained from recognizing their own insurrections as either international or civil wars to which IHL should apply.[86] It has thus become more convenient to view IHL as part of a larger, derogable system of human rights. As IHL only applies during an 'armed conflict', domestic (para)military and police units are instead mobilized to restore public order through 'peacetime' shows of strength which more resemble war.

THE SHIFT FROM WAR TO PEACE

The Departure from Geneva

The UN clearly prohibited the use of aggressive armed force in inter-state relations in Article 2(4), which was set down simultaneously with the appearance of a human rights content in the UN Charter.[87] Sovereign states, protected by the territorial integrity of existing boundaries and

political independence, were thus made the guardians of the maintenance of international peace and security.[88] Should this peace break
down, the new UN organization was imbued with sufficient authority to
intervene to restore international order.[89] Thus, it was hoped that the
UN would prove to be the missing super-authority in a previously state-
centric world.[90]

The need remained to ensure the necessary conditions for the restoration of national prosperity. Economic prosperity had been a precondition
to independence for new states under the League system,[91] and the UN
also viewed it as essential, if only in order to fulfil the conditions of peace,
equal rights and self-determination of 'peoples'.[92] Thus, instead of a
policy of armed expansionism to ensure equitable access to the world's
resources, peace, independence and equal rights and self-determination
became the new standards.

An early indication of the new thinking may be found in the 1941
Atlantic Charter,[93] which was later to form an appendix to the January
1942 Declaration by the UN. The Atlantic Charter stated in pertinent
part as follows:

> First, their countries seek no aggrandizement, territorial or other; . . .
> Third, they respect the right of all peoples to choose the form of
> government under which they will live; and they wish to see sover-
> eign rights and self-government restored to those who have been
> forcibly deprived of them;
> Fourth, they will endeavor, with due respect for their existing oblig-
> ations, to further the enjoyment by all states, great or small, victor
> or vanquished, of access, on equal terms, to the trade and to the raw
> materials of the world which are needed for their economic
> prosperity;
> Fifth, they desire to bring about the fullest collaboration between all
> nations in the economic field with the object of securing for all,
> improved labor standards, economic advancement and social
> security; . . .
> Eighth, they believe that all the nations of the world, for realistic as
> well as spiritual reasons must come to the abandonment of the use
> of force . . . They will likewise aid and encourage all other practica-
> ble measures which will lighten for peace-loving peoples the
> crushing burden of armaments.

The Atlantic Charter was subsequently to have a profound influence on
the development of both the UN Charter and Organization, but the
pursuit of the stated aims of the Atlantic Charter was to lead to conflict.[94]
The new focus on economic stability and *equal* access to trade implied a

certain level of reciprocity, and given the balance of power which emerged after World War II, this reciprocity would be difficult to achieve without a degree of coercion. While depriving themselves of the 'right' to use aggressive force to achieve political or economic ends, it is perhaps understandable that the Allies felt the need for a new mechanism of influence and/or control by states over states.

The Need for New Mechanisms of Control

In that the generic rights of individuals are 'absolute' only in so far as a system to protect those rights exists, a primary object of human rights law must be stability and security.[95] Thus, a peaceful and stable world order – one which can safeguard individual human rights – is the responsibility of states.

Despite the importance afforded to the maintenance of peace and security, the use of armed force continues, and military capabilities have expanded in a post-1945 era in which the aggressive use or threat of force by states in their mutual relations, even when utilized for the furtherance of human rights, is prohibited.[96] Attention then is focused on the state monopoly over the use or threat of force, and, in particular, on the use of force to preserve domestic order.

The use of force domestically by governments is rarely assessed by threatened states beyond human rights law confines,[83] and the post-1945 human rights régimes contain considerable scope for derogation in times of national emergency,[97] and to maintain and make secure 'public order', whatever form that should take. For example, UN Charter Article 2(4) can be easily violated, while the degree of armed force utilized domestically against a populace (or a government) can remain outside the ambit of international regulation should a threatened state prefer not to regard a domestic conflict as one to which IHL applies.[98] A slight shift in perception permits this practice to be viewed as a mutation of the pre-1945 right to use force aggressively in international relations, particularly as armies are used against internal insurrection as easily as against external threats.

The result is a heavily armed, ideologically divided world. Economic reprisals and coercion remain legal,[99] and Western states in particular have frequently used human rights records to deny overseas economic aid. The anti-colonial thrust of the UN system has afforded sufficient scope to some liberation groups to inject meaning into the rights sought, through successful uses of rebellious armed force.[59] The apparently limited scope of the UN principle of the equal rights and self-determination of 'peoples'[100] has left aggrieved minorities with little or no international support for their armed conflicts.[101]

It could have been foreseen that a logical consequence of the prohibition on the threat or use of force in inter-state relations was the simultaneous appearance of a human rights content in the UN Charter. Human rights would provide a peaceful means with which the victorious Allied nations could work to encourage the emergence of new states and new spheres of influence.[102] In so doing, they could also pursue their 'fair share' of political and economic influence.

The Uneasy 'Mix' of IHL and Human Rights Law

Although IHL is viewed in some government quarters as an unwieldy body of complicated provisions which encroach unrealistically into military decision-making, states parties to IHL were accustomed to a basic regulation of war. In view of the future potential of human rights law as a new method by which citizens could assess government action, IHL became the first area of international law to enter into binding force in the post-1945 era[103] and thus contained the 'first edition' of the new human rights law. The Protocols of 1977 were to expand this human rights content.

The 1949 Geneva revisions provide an insight into the extent to which states are prepared to promote a degree of power-sharing. When the Geneva Conventions were supplemented by Common Article 3, and the two 1977 Protocols, objection was voiced in many quarters to this 'new' mix of war law, humanitarian law, and human rights. It was felt that the integration of these three areas, each separately implemented by different state mechanisms, could cause confusion at the point of application. Several advanced capitalist governments, which found themselves in the minority at the Geneva Diplomatic Conference 1974–1977, expressed dismay at new categories of prohibited military targets, and means and methods of warfare, including environmental and cultural targets and reprisals. This is despite the 'spirit' of UN Charter Article 2(4) having found expression in Common Article 3, and the Martens Clause having received codified rather than preambular form in the text of Protocol 1.[104]

Whether these new prohibitions were disliked by those countries which feared an excessive admission of the democraticized principle that there are limits to the use of force that governments may legally utilize against opposing armed forces is beyond the scope of this chapter. What is relevant is the rapid development of post-1945 derogable human rights documents after the 1949 Geneva revisions, in the transition from world war to world peace. Implicit in this transition are new political frameworks, designed to ensure strategic defence and national prosperity, albeit 'by other means' than the waging of war and the oppression of domestic society. Nevertheless, the tools with which states maintain order are largely as before – by utilizing force, within certain internationally agreed limits – and there is a widespread apprehension that the new 'human rights' content in IHL makes the modern IHL appear to be additional, derogable human rights documents, and therefore less likely to be invoked readily in times of armed conflict.

CONCLUSION

After World War II, the laws of war were strengthened to protect individuals more comprehensively from the actions of states. In particular, IHL contained the earliest form of the new human rights régimes to enter into force. What then becomes an issue is whether IHL will be applied by states which derogate from their human rights obligations when they resort to the use of armed force to impose and maintain particular forms of public order. If not, then the risk of recognizing an 'armed conflict' through humanitarian treatment forms a weak point of IHL.

This latter point should not negate the textual guidance afforded to human rights law by IHL, however, as the limits of the 'possible' in state cooperation to ensure the rights and duties of individuals were first formulated by and through the laws of war. States then retained in their subsequent human rights documents the flexibility to derogate from rights obligations, and to use force domestically. Further, in that the scope of rights derogations reserved to states allows human rights protections to fall below those standards contained in the minimal levels of IHL, it appears that human rights law should be viewed as a part of IHL, and not the reverse.

There is a grave danger that to the extent that IHL has acquired a human rights law content, its obligations are viewed as non-binding,[105] and if there is any evidence of IHL forming part of human rights, it is in the lack of political will to make IHL applicable, in the sense that any 'armed conflict' should be viewed as such. It is only to be hoped that individuals continue to disobey orders,[106] and to rebel against unjust government. Victor Frankenstein created a monster which outlived him, despite the many hardships which were no fault of its own. States risk their own destruction should the laws of war be disregarded.

Farewell, Frankenstein! If thou wert yet alive, and yet cherished a desire of revenge against me, it would be better satiated in my life than in my destruction. But it was not so; thou didst seek my extinction, that I might not cause greater wretchedness. . .[107]

NOTES

1. Modern IHL documents include the following: 12 August 1949 – Geneva Convention for the Amelioration of the Condition of the Wounded and Sick in the Field ('First Convention'), the Geneva Convention for the Amelioration of the Condition of Wounded, Sick and Shipwrecked Members of Armed Forces at Sea ('Second Convention'), the Geneva Convention Relative to the Treatment of Prisoners of War ('Third Convention'), the Geneva Convention Relative to the Protection of Civilian Persons in Time of War ('Fourth Convention'); 8 June 1977 – the Protocol Additional to the four Geneva Conventions of 1949 and Relating to the Protection of Victims of International Armed Conflicts of 1977 ('Protocol 1'), and the Protocol Additional to the four Geneva Conventions of 1949 and Relating to the Protection of Victims of Non-International Armed Conflicts of 1977 ('Protocol 2'). Protocol 1 Article 1(4) extends Geneva obligations in full to wars 'in which peoples are fighting against colonial domination and alien occupation and against racist régimes in the exercise of their right of self-determination'.

2. See, for example, P. Nobel, The role of the International Red Cross and Red Crescent Movement in promoting respect for human rights, *International Review of the Red Cross*, No. 293, March-April 1993, p. 139; L. Doswald-Beck and S. Vité, International humanitarian law and human rights law, *International Review of the Red Cross*, No. 293, March-April 1993, p. 94.

3. G. Willemin and R. Heacock, *International Committee of the Red Cross*, Vol. 2 (Boston, 1984), p. 167.

4. See the Third Convention, the Fourth Convention, Common Article 3 to the four 1949 Geneva Conventions, Protocol 1, and Protocol 2. The four 1949 Geneva Conventions entered into force on 21 October 1950.

5. For example, IHL conditions the impact of war through, *inter alia*, provisions for humanitarian assistance, and for the prosecution of war crimes, generally.

6. See J. von Elbe, The evolution of the concept of the just war in international law (1939) 33 *American Journal of International Law* 665; Comment, J. L Kunz, Bellum Justum and Bellum Légale (1951) 45 *American Journal of International Law* 528; P. Haggenmacher, Just war and regular war in sixteenth century Spanish doctrine, *International Review of the Red Cross*, No. 290, September-October 1992, p. 434.

7. Observance of the customary rules of warfare was a precondition to a recognition of belligerency. H. Lauterpacht (ed.), *Oppenheim's International Law*, Vol. II, 7th edn (London, 1952), p. 209.

8. As during the American war between the states, 1861–65.

9. For example, the Crimean War (1854), the Austro-Prussian War (1866) and the Franco-Prussian War (1870).

10. For example, after the Franco-Prussian War, 35 Bremen and three Berlin commercial firms requested that the French surrender of Cochin-China be made part of the peace terms. This was only one of many such proposals made by traders.

11. For a brief but comprehensive review of European colonial strategies, see G. A. Craig, *Germany 1866–1945* (Oxford, 1981), pp. 116–24.

12. G. Best, The restraint of war in historical and philosophical perspective. In A. J. M. Delissen and G. J. Tanja (eds), *Humanitarian Law of Armed Conflict – Challenges Ahead* (London, 1991), pp. 3, 22.

13. See, for example, Capt. E. Colby, How to fight savage tribes (1927), 21 *American*

Journal of International Law 279; J.-P. Sartre, *On Genocide* (Boston, 1968).

14. *Instructions for the Government of Armies in the Field*, 24 April 1863, prepared by Francis Lieber, a German by birth, and promulgated by President Lincoln as General Order No. 100 for use by the Northern troops during the American war between the states. The Lieber Code was regarded as generally reflecting customary law at the time. See also the Paris Declaration respecting Maritime Law of 16 April 1856 and the St Petersburg Declaration Renouncing the Use, in Time of War, of Explosive Projectiles Under 400 Grammes Weight, of 29 November/11 December 1868.

15. Article 15 of the Lieber Code states that 'men who take up arms against one another in public war do not cease on this account to be moral beings, responsible to one another and to God'.

16. I. P. Trainin, Questions of guerrilla warfare in the law of war (1946) 40 *American Journal of International Law* 534, 536 n. 2.

17. In particular, the following instruments are referred to: the 1899 Convention regarding the laws and customs of war on land; the 1907 Convention respecting the laws and customs of war on land (IV) and annexed Regulations respecting the laws and customs of war on land.

18. These early instruments applied only 'between Contracting Parties, and then only if all the belligerents (were) parties to the Convention(s)'. The two Geneva Conventions of 1929 bound contracting parties whether or not the war was joined by a non-party belligerent.

19. Geneva Convention for the Amelioration of the Condition of the Wounded in Armies in the Field, 22 August 1864; Geneva Convention for the Amelioration of the Condition of the Wounded and Sick in Armies in the Field, 6 July 1906.

20. Kriegsräson geht vor Kriegsmanier (necessity in war controls the manner of warfare).

21. G. Best, *op. cit.*, p. 10.

22. I. P. Trainin, *op. cit.*, p. 546.

23. H. Lauterpacht defined 'security' as 'a system of obligations to enforce by common international action the existing limitations upon the right to go to war': H. Lauterpacht, *op. cit.*, p. 93, n. 1. The League of Nations and the Pact of Paris (see note 26) were attempts to limit the right to go to war.

24. See J. L. Kunz, The chaotic status of the laws of war and the urgent necessity for their revision (1951) 45 *American Journal of International Law* 37, who termed this the 'policy of the ostrich'.

25. In force on 8 February 1928. The treaty operates on a no-first-use basis, and does not prohibit the use against civilians of, *inter alia*, tear gas.

26. General Treaty for the Renunciation of War 1928.

27. The International Military Tribunal at Nuremberg began on 20 November 1945. Judgment was rendered on 30 September and 1 October 1946. The International Military Tribunal for the Far East (Tokyo) (3 May 1946 to 4–12 November 1948) was based on the same legal principles.

28. Hague Convention (IV) Article 3 called for each contracting party to accept responsibility 'for all acts committed by persons forming part of its armed forces' and 'if the case demand(ed) . . . to pay compensation'.

29. First Convention Article 49, Second Convention Article 50, Third Convention Article 129, Fourth Convention Article 146.

30. J. M. Kelly, *A Short History of Western Legal Theory* (Oxford, 1992), p. 353.

31. L. Doswald-Beck and S. Vité, *op. cit.*, p. 107.

32. For example, the St Petersburg Declaration applied 'between civilized nations'; see also the 1899 Hague Convention (see note 17).

33. Geneva Convention Relative to the Treatment of Prisoners of War, 27 July 1929. This development reinforced the 'career' aspect of military service as another domestic trade.

34. See L. Doswald-Beck and S. Vité, *op. cit.*, pp. 95–6.

35. Fourth Convention.

36. In particular, the categories of those entitled to prisoner of war protections were expanded.

37. Common Article 3 provides as follows:
In the case of armed conflict not of an international character each Party to the conflict shall be bound to apply, as a minimum, the following provisions:
1. Persons taking no active part in the hostilities, including members of armed forces who have laid down their arms and those placed *hors de combat* by sickness, wounds, detention or any other cause, shall in all circumstances be treated humanely, without any adverse distinction founded on race, colour, religion or faith sex, birth or wealth, or any other similar criteria.
To this end, the following acts are and shall remain prohibited . . . with respect to the above-mentioned persons:
    a. violence to life and person, in particular murder of all kinds, mutilation, cruel treatment and torture;
    b. taking of hostages;
    c. outrages upon personal dignity, in particular, humiliating and degrading treatment;
    d. the passing of sentences and the carrying out of executions without previous judgment pronounced by a regularly constituted court affording all the judicial guarantees which are recognized as indispensable by civilized peoples.
See further L. C. Green, *The Contemporary Law of Armed Conflict* (Manchester, 1993), p. 305.
38. Common Article 3. See also *Military and Paramilitary Activities in and against Nicaragua (Nicaragua* v. *United States of America), Merits,* ICJ Reports 1986, pp. 14, 114, 218. The rights of active combatants are reduced, obviously.
39. Common Article 3 was most likely invoked for the first time in a major post-1945 conflict during the Algerian War, 1954–1962. The problem lies in the definition of the term 'armed conflict', as in such a situation Common Article 3 must by implication be declared applicable.
40. UN Charter Article 2(4) provides as follows: 'All Members shall refrain in their international relations from the threat or use of force against the territorial integrity or political independence of any state, or in any other manner inconsistent with the Purposes of the United Nations.'
41. See, for example, the Declaration of Minimum Humanitarian Standards, *International Review of the Red Cross,* No. 282, May-June 1991, pp. 330–6.
42. See P. H. Koojimans, In the shadowland between civil war and civil strife: some reflections on the standard-setting process. In A. J. M. Delissen and G. J. Tanja, *op. cit.,* p. 225.
43. See L. Doswald-Beck and S. Vité, *op. cit.,* p. 116.
44. The jurisdictional confines, however, may vary. Compare the European Human Rights Convention (1950) and the European Social Charter (1961).
45. Human rights law further differs from IHL, as human rights law includes both universal and regional treaties.
46. States cannot derogate in their treaty agreements from *jus cogens,* or peremptory norms, such as the prohibitions of slavery or genocide.
47. A. Gewirth, The basis and content of human rights. In A. Gewirth, *Human Rights – Essays on Justifications and Applications* (Chicago, 1982), pp. 41, 47.
48. For example, that allowed in derogation and limitation clauses. See note 97. IHL contains no concept of derogation.
49. The 'core' rights are the right to life, the prohibition of torture or of cruel, inhuman or degrading treatment, of slavery, and of retroactive criminal legislation or punishment. Humanitarian law goes yet further with an extensive inclusion of 'non-derogable' judicial guarantees.
50. See P. H. Koojimans, *op. cit.* See, for example, *Ireland* v. *UK,* ECHR, Series A (18 January 1978).
51. See S. R. Chowdhury, *Rule of Law in a State of Emergency* (London, 1984); W. Finnie, Old wine in new bottles? The evolution of anti-terrorist legislation (1990) Pt. 1 *The Juridical Review* 1.
52. See, for example, *Brogan* v. *UK,* ECHR, Series A (29 November 1988). Compare *Fox,*

Campbell and Hartley v. *UK*, No. 18/1989/178/234–6 (16 October 1990).

53. See D. J. Harris (ed.), *Cases and Materials on International Law*, 3rd edn (London, 1983), p. 516.

54. See, for example, *Judgment in Cases concerning Deportation Orders*, 10 April 1988, reprinted in (1990) 29 *International Legal Materials* 140.

55. For example during the Falklands 'crisis' of 1982. See also J. Smyth, Stretching the boundaries: the control of dissent in Northern Ireland (1988) 11 *Terrorism: An International Journal* 289.

56. The extensive inclusion of judicial guarantees in IHL are too numerous to list individually.

57. Usually a precondition. See note 39. Not to be forgotten are the many compromises found in IHL which allow an army to win a war.

58. See note 29. Protocol 1 Article 85(1).

59. For example, the Algerian War, see note 39; the PLO; the ANC; the emergence of new states in the former territory of Yugoslavia.

60. J. M. Kelly, *op. cit.*, p. 352.

61. UNGA Resolution 217A (III) of 1948.

62. J. M. Kelly, *op. cit.*, p. 293, quoting E. Burke (citations omitted).

63. A. Gewirth, *op. cit.*, pp. 62–6.

64. See Note, Constructing the state extraterritorially (1990) 103 *Harvard Law Review* 1273. See, for example, *Holtsman* v. *Schlesinger*, No. 73–C–537 (EDNY 1973), discussed in S. J. Wenner, The Indochina War cases in the United States Court of Appeals for the Second Circuit. In R. A. Falk (ed.), *The Vietnam War and International Law*, Vol. 4 (Princeton, 1976), pp. 720, 731.

65. For example the Algerian War (France observed IHL provisions after heavy reprisals); East Pakistan, 25 March 1971 (West Pakistan army struck Dacca without warning to 'pacify' the East); the Northern Ireland Emergency Provisions Act of July 1973 (see *Doherty* v. *MOD*, Unreported, House of Lords; J. R. Rowe, Liability in tort for the use of lethal weapons (1981) 44 *Modern Law Review* 466; *McGuigan* v. *MOD (1982)*, 19 NIJB).

66. See Hague Regulations (see note 17), Article 10 (parole), 18 (religion), 48 (rights of occupied territories).

67. Fourth Convention Article 23; Protocol 1 Article 70. See also Common Article 3 (note 37); Protocol 2 (see notes 1 and 83).

68. 'Protective rights' include the personal security rights of habeas corpus, and the non-infliction of torture, cruel punishment, and genocide. Tesón terms this an 'agency relationship' between a government and the public. F. R. Tesón, International abductions, low-intensity conflicts and state sovereignty: a moral inquiry (1994) 31 *Colombia Journal of Transnational Law* 551, 560.

69. In other words, a supportive state can provide for the supply of basic goods (A. Gewirth, *op. cit.*, p. 62). Civil and political rights are not viewed as requiring any particular level of economic development. Thus, the 1966 International Covenant on Civil and Political Rights (ICCPR) came into immediate effect, while the 1966 International Covenant on Economic, Social and Cultural Rights (ICESCR) required that steps be undertaken to the maximum of a state's available resources.

70. See D. J. Harris, *Cases and Materials on International Law*, 4th edn (London: 1991), p. 601.

71. See, for example, A. H. Amankwah, Constitutions and bills of rights in third world nations: issues of form and content (1989) 12 *Adelaide Law Review* 1, 6; K. P. Saksena, *Reforming the United Nations: the Challenge of Relevance* (New Delhi, 1993).

72. A. Gewirth, *op. cit.*, p. 64.

73. See note 69. While the expression 'food first, freedom after' has validity, revolutions may occur when there is no food, for example the Ethiopian civil war and famine that lasted throughout the 1980s.

74. The Geneva Conventions and Protocols specify in detail the physical conditions required to sustain life in as reasonable a condition as possible in an armed conflict.

75. This has 'routinized' emergency situations. R. A. Falk, The terrorist foundations of recent US foreign policy. In A. George (ed.), *Western State Terrorism* (Cambridge, 1991), pp.

102, 106.

76. While not usually falling within the terms of applicability of Protocol 2, it is conceivable that labour strikes in which armed force is used are covered by Common Article 3 (see note 83).

77. For example, UNGA Resolution 1514 (XV) of 14 December 1960 was applicable to about 100 territories in existence between 1945 and 1978; Resolution 2936 (XXVII) of 1972 reaffirms UN recognition 'of the legitimacy of the struggle of colonial peoples for their freedom by all appropriate means at their disposal'; Resolution 3103 (XXVIII) of 1973 recognizes the applicability of the Third and Fourth Geneva Conventions to liberation wars. See also ICCPR Article 47 and ICESCR Article 25.

78. See note 39. The Vietnam War was considered both a Common Article 3 situation, and an international war by the US. The atrocities of that war led to the Diplomatic Conference of 1974–1977.

79. See E. D. Fryer, Applicability of international law to internal armed conflicts: old problems, current endeavours (1977) 11 *International Lawyer* 567. Note that special prisoner category status (not grouping Irish Loyalists and Republicans together) in Northern Ireland was withdrawn in March 1976, during the Geneva Diplomatic Conference of 1974–1977.

80. See notes 93 and 94, and accompanying text; E. A. Laing, The norm of self-determination, 1941-1991 (1993) 22 *California Western International Law Journal* 209, 294.

81. See for example, note 77.

82. Resolution 2625 (XXV) of 24 October 1970 states the following:

Nothing ... shall be construed as authorizing or encouraging any action which would dismember or impair ... the territorial integrity or political unity of sovereign and independent states conducting themselves in compliance with the principle of equal rights and self-determination of peoples ... and ... possessed of a government representing the whole people belonging to the territory without distinction as to race, creed or colour.

83. Before 1949, the scale and intensity of the hostilities made the laws of war applicable (see note 7). This has continued to be the case with Common Article 3 (see note 39). Compare Protocol 2, which applies to:

1(2). ... all armed conflicts which are not covered by [Protocol 1] and which take place in the territory of a High Contracting Party between its armed forces and dissident armed forces or other organized armed groups which ... exercise such control over a part of its territory as to enable them to carry out sustained and concerted military operations and to implement this Protocol.
2. This Protocol shall not apply to situations of internal disturbances and tensions, such as riots, isolated and sporadic acts of violence and other acts of a similar nature, as not being armed conflicts.

84. Protocol 1 Article 1(4). See note 1.

85. In particular, the US and the UK. US opposition to the extension of IHL to liberation wars in Protocol 1 resulted in part from the use of internal armed 'workers struggles' by Communist-led insurgents to overthrow capitalist forms of government. G. Best, *Humanity in Warfare* (London, 1983), p. 321. On 19 July 1995 the UK Geneva Conventions (Amendments) Act (1995, c. 27) received the Royal Assent. This Act implements Protocol 1 and 2 domestically.

86. See P. Rowe, *Defence: the Legal Implications* (London, 1987).

87. See note 40; UN Charter Articles 1, 55, 62.

88. UN Charter Article 2(4) (see note 40) and Articles 2(6), 73, and 84. See also UNGA Resolution 3314 (XXIX) of 14 December 1974, and UNGA Resolution 2625 (see note 82).

89. UN Charter Chapters VI, VII and VIII.

90. UN Charter Article 24(1).

91. P. M. Brown, 'Self-determination in central Europe (1920) 14 *American Journal of International Law* 235; Q. Wright, Status of the inhabitants of mandated territory (1924) 18 *American Journal of International Law* 306.

92. UN Charter Chapters IX, X, XI, XII, XIII.

93. Text reprinted in (Suppl. vol. 1941) 35 *American Journal of International Law* 191.

94. See E. A. Laing, *op. cit.*; K. P. Saksena, *op. cit.*

95. A. Gewirth, Can utilitarianism justify any moral rights? In A. Gewirth, *Essays, op. cit.*, pp. 143, 156.

96. See UN Charter Article 2(7); UNGA Resolution 2131 (XX) of 21 December 1965; Resolutions 2625 and 3314 (see notes 82 and 88, respectively). In light of recent initiatives taken in Somalia, Bosnia-Herzegovina, and Haiti to provide humanitarian assistance, this may be changing. The problem remains the cost of such operations.

97. See, for example, the ICCPR Article 4(1); the European Convention on Human Rights Article 15(1); the American Convention on Human Rights Article 27(1).

98. See notes 39 and 42. As regards the December 1994 invasion of the breakaway republic of Chechenia by Russian troops, should an armed conflict be recognized? Is it a Common Article 3, a Protocol 2, or a Protocol 1 situation? Conversely, IHL in full should apply to a full-scale civil war, or after an act of international aggression, as in the Gulf War.

99. See, for example, Resolution 2625 (see, note 82), in which the legality of economic coercion was purposely not clarified.

100. Protocol 1 Article 1(4) arguably only covers South Africa and Palestine. I. Detter de Lupis, *The Law of War* (Cambridge, 1987), p. 161.

101. See, for example, the Conference on Yugoslavia, Arbitration Commission [11 January and 4 July, 1992], Opinions 2 and 3, reprinted in 31 *International Legal Materials* 1488, 1497–8 and 1499–1500 respectively (*uti posseditis* denies the entitlement of self-determination to the Bosnian and Croatian Serbs).

102. See F. Jhabvala, The Soviet-Bloc's view of the implementation of human rights accords (1985) 7 *Human Rights Quarterly*, 461; F. R. Tesón, *op. cit.*

103. See note 4. The UN Charter imposed obligations on member states to realize and protect as yet unspecified human rights. The Convention on the Prevention and Punishment of the Crime of Genocide of 1948 entered into force on 12 January 1951.

104. Protocol 1 Article 1(2) provides as follows:

> In cases not covered by this Protocol or by other international agreements, civilians and combatants remain under the protection and authority of the principles of international law derived from established custom, from the principles of humanity and from the dictates of public conscience.

105. For example, Protocol 1, Article 75 and Protocol 2 Article 6 are derived directly from the ICCPR. See C. Greenwood, Customary law status of the 1977 Additional Protocols. In A. J. M. Delissen and G. J. Tanja, *op. cit.*

106. First Convention Article 49(1); Second Convention Article 50(1); Third Convention Article 129(1); Fourth Convention Article 146(1); Protocol 1 Articles 16(2), 40, 85(1); Protocol 2 Article 4(1).

107. M. Shelley, *Frankenstein* (1818 ed.), (P. Lyons, ed.) (London, 1992), p. 191. Lyons indicates that by the mid-nineteenth century, Shelley's monster had become a symbol for the dread felt by the Victorian bourgeoisie at the increased participation of the masses in political life (Introduction, pp. viii–x).

26

Deconstructing the Mythologies of International Human Rights Law

Geraldine Van Bueren

Despite the development of international law which historically has focused on the relationship between nation states, it is the individual who is the ultimate beneficiary of the international legal system. However, for most of the period in which the foundations of international law were being laid, the international legal system was not concerned with limiting states' powers over individuals. Hence the transformation of the status of the individual in international law is, as Oda observes, one of the most remarkable developments in international law.[1]

As the twenty-first century approaches, international human rights law is facing a number of challenges. These include the protection of human rights in the traditionally described private sphere; the artificial distinctions between specific classes of rights; the attempted removal from international scrutiny by some states of cultural and religious issues; and the need for improved procedural devices to accompany the progress made in the creation of substantive rights. As Abi-Saab observes, law does not emerge 'out of social nothingness – nor does it come into being with a big-bang. In most cases it is a progressive and imperceptible growth over a large grey zone separating emerging social values from the well-established legal rule'.[2] Because of the fundamental importance to individuals' lives of ensuring that their human rights are protected, it is timely to deconstruct some of the mythologies surrounding international human rights law.

THE MYTH OF HUMAN RIGHTS INACTION IN THE PRIVATE SPHERE

As society grows more complex and the privatization of institutions and personnel is continuing, the division between the public and private spheres is growing more blurred. The nub of the issue for international human rights law is that 'international law operates in the most public of all public worlds, that of nation states',[3] and although international law has challenged in one sense the private in moving the boundaries of domestic jurisdiction, it is only beginning to probe the much deeper public–private dichotomy. To be able to protect human rights in private spheres effectively, including in the family, international law must be sufficiently flexible to accommodate a wide range of different private structures and values whilst simultaneously enshrining universally agreed minimum standards. Such a role has been impeded by traditional assumptions in international law that set the public areas apart from the private and reinforce domestic legislative approaches which treat what occurs in private as comparatively unimportant and based in any event on consent not affecting society at large.[4] This erroneous assumption persists despite the clarion calls of several treaties that one private group, the family, is the basic unit of society.[5]

International human rights law protects the individual against the state but the limits of state responsibility have been drawn narrowly,[6] thereby offering an illusion of fairness to those who spend much of their time in traditional private spheres – women and children. Such a blinkered perspective of the potency of international human rights law, although rooted in history, is not inherent in it, as the potential of the comparatively recent jurisprudence of Inter-American and European regional human rights fora illustrate. *X and Y* v. *Netherlands* arose because of an unintended gap in Dutch law whereby a 16-year-old mentally disabled victim of rape was unable to initiate criminal proceedings because Dutch law required the filing of rape proceedings by victims over the age of 12.[7] Dutch law lacked any provision whereby a parent could file proceedings on child victims over the age of 12 who were regarded as mentally incompetent. The Dutch government argued, *inter alia*, that Article 8 of the European Convention on Human Rights could not be interpreted to require a state to create criminal procedures where civil remedies were available.

Although the rape was in a private institution, *X and Y* v. *Netherlands* has major implications for the protection of individuals within other private institutions, including the family, where a state's legislation only provides for civil remedies against sexual attacks within the family. The European Court of Human Rights found that Article 8 obligations 'may involve the adoption of measures designed to secure respect for private life even in the sphere of relations of individuals between themselves'.[8]

In *Velasquez-Rodriguez* v. *Honduras* the Inter-American Court specifically commented on state tolerance of human rights violations and stressed that:

What is decisive is whether a violation of rights recognised by the Convention has occurred with the support or the acquiesence of the government or whether the state has allowed the act to take place without measures to prevent it or to punish those responsible.[9]

Thus the Court's task is to determine whether the violation is the result of a state's failure to fulfil its duty to respect and guarantee those rights as required by Article 1(1) of the American Convention on Human Rights.[10] Importantly, the Court determined that an illegal act which breaches human rights and which is not directly imputable to the state, because it is an act of a private person or because the person responsible has not been identified, can lead to international responsibility of the state not because of the act itself but because of the failure 'to prevent the violation or to respond to it as required by the Convention'.[11] Further, the Court elaborated on the prevention obligation on states, explaining that it included all means of a 'legal, political, administrative and cultural nature'.[12] The Court also concluded that where human rights violations by private parties are not seriously investigated, the parties are in a sense aided by the government making the state responsible on the international plane. These parts of the decision were unanimous.[13]

Although reliance on the state nexus, which is the basis of responsibility in international human rights law, can be criticized as being defined in relation to people's experience of being subjected to power, such a basis is not necessarily exclusionary provided that the jurisprudence of *X and Y* v. *Netherlands* and of *Velasquez* is built upon to reflect a more contemporary and relevant concept of state responsibility.

THE GENERATIONAL MYTH

Although human rights have been proclaimed as indivisible and universal, traditionally international law has adopted different approaches to the standards of implementation of civil and political rights than it has with regard to economic, social and cultural rights.[14] The International Covenant on Civil and Political Rights calls on states parties to 'respect and ensure' its rights, while the International Covenant on Economic, Social and Cultural Rights provides that states parties should 'take steps individually and through international assistance and cooperation . . . to the maximum of its available resources with a view to achieving progressively the full realisation of the rights'.[15] Hence international law has developed in such a way that civil and political rights are regarded as being of immediate implementation, in contrast to economic, social and cultural rights which are only regarded as aspirational goals to be achieved progressively. In relation to the latter, this has had a major influence on the relatively weak forms of implementation and the low priority which such rights attract in state expenditure.

This primacy of civil and political rights is reinforced by the historically inaccurate notion that civil and political rights are first-generation rights whereas economic, social and cultural rights tag along behind as second generation. The first human rights instrument embracing a broad range of 'rights' was the Declaration of the Rights of the Child 1924, predating the Universal Declaration of Human Rights 1948 by almost a quarter of a century, and this focused mainly on economic and social rights.[16] The same can be said for the oldest specialized agency, the International Labour Organization.

The maintenance of such a distinction between the two groups of rights is questionable.[17] First, the division between the rights may have owed its origins not to the intrinsic nature of the rights but to reasons of diplomatic and political compromise arising from the Cold War. Such reasons, if ever justified, can no longer be sustained since the demise of socialist states in eastern Europe. Furthermore, there is not any authoritative definition of the distinction between civil and political rights and economic, social and cultural rights, although reference to the classification adopted by the two Covenants or the relevant regional instrument may assist. The right to education, for example, embraces both civil and cultural aspects concerning rights of access to education and economic and social facets in the provision of the different levels of education.[18]

Admittedly there are a number of differences which are commonly held to distinguish the two sets of rights. Civil and political rights are frequently characterized as negative, as states are only under a duty to refrain immediately from actions which would be in breach, whereas economic, social and cultural rights oblige states to intervene actively and produce basic goods and services. The Human Rights Committee has, however, pointed to the positive duties involved in protecting the right to life[19] and the European Court of Human Rights has emphasized the same in relation to the respect for family life and privacy.[20] Similarly, civil and political rights, because they require abstention from specific activities, are assumed to be cost-free, whereas economic, social and cultural rights entail significant government expenditure. However, the provision of a juvenile justice system in conformity with the Beijing Rules and the Convention on the Rights of the Child[21] requires both action and substantial expenditure, whereas the provision of oral rehydration therapy (ORT) to prevent dehydration caused by diarrhoea, which in the 1980s claimed 10,000 lives a day, is a simple and cheap solution.[22]

Although the demise of the distinction is hardly imminent, there is a small but growing number of treaties which combine both sets of rights in one treaty, thus underscoring even further the artificiality of the distinction. The inclusion of both civil and political rights and economic, social and cultural rights in the Convention on the Rights of the Child, the Convention on the Elimination of All Forms of Discrimination against Women, and the African Charter on the Rights and Welfare of the Child in single treaties to be monitored by single bodies highlights the artificiality of such distinctions.

The traditional relationship is also being called into question by the use of indicators which traditionally have been used to measure the extent of the implementation of economic, social and cultural rights but which are now also being used in the collection of data on civil and political rights, albeit with some criticism. In its second annual report on human development, the United Nations Development Fund ranked states according to a Human Freedom Index.[23] This was shortly followed by the World Development Report 1991 and 1992. UNDP devised their own series of indicators and released Human Development 1992 with a new Political Freedom Index. The underlying problem of indicators is that they raise questions of feasibility which in turn introduce the issue of priorities. In reality, a developing state may have to choose for lack of resources between free compulsory universal primary education, an effective juvenile justice system and the highest attainable standard of health. These are not choices upon which human rights bodies are able to give guidance. By retaining a division between the civil and political rights on the one hand and economic, social and cultural rights on the other, this choice of priorities can be more easily postponed.

It is also widely believed in industrialized states that civil and political rights are concepts untainted by ideology, whereas economic, social and cultural rights are infused with political doctrine. Both sets of rights have a strong ideological basis but this ought not to prevent effective judicial implementation. The real problem, as the prohibition on female circumcision demonstrates, is not the labelling but the artificial distinctions in implementation. There are minimal resource implications attached to prohibiting female circumcision through the drafting and adoption of national legislation. The resource implications are only engaged when educative programmes which would accompany such legislation are implemented. Hence it is difficult to defend the approach of international human rights law that states parties are only under a progressive as opposed to an immediate duty to prohibit the practice.

Despite repeated assertions of the universality of all human rights, the reality is, as Dias correctly observes, that civil and political rights have become justiciable and the focus of international human rights advocacy, whilst economic, social and cultural rights remain mostly in the sphere of international development assistance.[24] However, there is nothing inherent in the rights which makes this situation permanent. A report on the implementation of economic, social or cultural rights may reveal an underlying disparity of access which is based on gender or religious grounds, thus transforming an apparently economic, social or cultural issue into a civil right.

All reforms depend upon resources, which are not a matter of international law but of international political will. However, even in treaties which enshrine resource limitation clauses such as the 'maximum extent of their available resources',[25] these refer to resources which are unconstrained by concepts such as the financial and economic. As Himes notes, resources also include human resources, although this ought not to be used to justify placing a greater burden on heads of households, frequently female.[26] The true nature of the differences between the various substantive human rights ought to be re-examined to provide states with a practical rather than a tainted ideological approach to their implementation.

THE MYTH OF REMOVAL FROM INTERNATIONAL SCRUTINY

Neither the full extension of international human rights law into the private nor the reconceptualization of civil, political, economic, social or cultural rights will be able to have a significant impact in improving the protection of human rights, if states are permitted to attach either a large number of reservations or a single wide-ranging reservation to human rights treaties. Although this is not the place to consider whether human rights treaties are or ought to be governed by a separate treaty law regime, it has to be realized that the issue of reservations to human rights treaties goes beyond the ambit of any specific human rights treaty and raises the question of whether there is too great an emphasis placed on participation at the cost of maintaining standards, and whether the implementation of human rights treaties ought to depend upon the political strategies of states. It also raises fundamental questions about the nature of rights in the private sphere. Although the concepts of religious rights or cultural rights must not be manipulated in such a way that they reinforce the inequalities of the most vulnerable of family members (women and children), how can universal human rights be recognized and protected in fundamentally different communities without either

Mcdonaldizing the globe or being paralysed by extreme stances of cultural relativism?

In effect, reservations, as the name implies, reserve to that state's domestic jurisdiction the implementation of a particular right or group of rights. Reservations do not necessarily signify a lowering of standards. The reservations by Scandinavian states to the International Covenant on Civil and Political Rights contributed to the raising of standards on the separation of juveniles in Article 37(c) of the Convention on the Rights of the Child.[27] There are also reservations which seek to harmonize a state's obligation under other human rights treaties, and reservations which may be 'useful guides' to interpretation, although any such reservation which provokes objection has a lesser influence.[28] However, there are other types of reservations which are of a qualitatively different type and which invoke either religious or national laws as reasons for not considering themselves bound by provisions of human rights treaties.

The Human Rights Committee has recently expressed its growing concern over reservations. As of 1 November 1994, 46 of the 127 states parties to the International Covenant on Civil and Political Rights had entered 150 reservations of varying significance. The number and the scope of reservations undermine the effective implementation of the Covenant and tend to weaken respect for the duties of states parties.[29] This has been reinforced by the Commission of Human Rights stressing of the importance of strict compliance with states parties' obligations under the Convention on the Rights of the Child. The Commission has appealed to states which have made reservations to examine their compatibility.[30]

The concern of the Human Rights Committee is shared by other human rights treaty monitoring bodies. Egypt's reservation to Article 16 of the Convention for the Elimination of All Forms of Discrimination Against Women is a case in point. Article 16 concerns the equality of men and women in all matters relating to family relationships and marriage, which in Egypt, in common with a number of states, is governed by Sharia.[31] Sharia family law evolves around the principle of qawama (male guardianship) and undermines international standards of equality. The Committee on the Rights of the Child has also expressed concern at the number of wide-ranging reservations attached to the Convention on the Rights of the Child.

The problem of reservations is not unique to human rights treaties which incorporate protection of the right to family life, but this is the area which has attracted most reservations. States which have attached such reservations to the Convention on the Rights of the Child which have been objected to by other states parties include Bangladesh, Djibouti, Indonesia, Jordan, Tunisia, Thailand and Turkey.[32] Kuwait and

Myanmar have withdrawn and redrafted their original reservations in light of such objections but the majority of states have not.

The formulation and subsequent acceptance and objections to reservations are governed by general rules of international law[33] and by the specific treaty itself.[34] The Convention on the Rights of the Child echoes Article 19(c) of the Vienna Convention on the Law of Treaties in that reservations are permissible provided they are not 'incompatible with the object and purpose of the treaty'. The object and purpose test is very difficult to apply to general multilateral human rights treaties such as the Convention on the Rights of the Child, because of the complex range of issues involved.[35] However, under the Vienna Convention, failure to lodge an objection within one year after notification of the reservation implies acceptance of the reservation *inter partes*.[36]

Not all states object to reservations, as some may believe that it is better to accept a reservation than to keep a state outside of the regime of the human rights treaty. Hence the rejection by the International Court of Justice in *Reservations to the Genocide Convention* of a system where reservations would require unanimous consent.[37] Specifically in relation to human rights treaties, states may also be nervous about the dynamic approaches to interpretation adopted by human rights bodies.[38] The Committee on the Rights of the Child appears to be developing such an approach in relation to corporal punishment.

The problem arises from the fact that although human rights treaties are a part of the public international legal regime, human rights treaties have distinguishing features. They do not establish relationships between the states parties *inter se* because human rights are of an absolute nature. Reciprocity does not have a place in the human rights system[39] except in relation to procedural matters.[40] Yet reciprocity is one of the cornerstones of the Vienna Convention on the Law of Treaties 1969.[41] Reservations and objections are perceived as having only a bipartite relationship affecting only the relationships between states. Hence if one state objects to a reservation, that reservation is not in force in relation to that state.[42] The issue of consent is appropriate for many areas of international law but not necessarily for human rights obligations, whose very nature, it could be argued, transcends the inter-state relationship.[43] If a state makes a reservation, there is in reality very little that the other states parties can do. Despite the arguably incompatible reservations by the USA to the juvenile death penalty provisions of the International Covenant on Civil and Political Rights, by November 1993 only nine states had objected to the reservation.[44]

Even the objecting states to the US reservation did not go so far as to state that the reservation would constitute an obstacle to the entry into force of the covenant as between themselves and the USA. Such a consequence is hardly effective to protect the rights of individuals living within the jurisdiction of a reserving state if the only effect of an objection is to render non-recognition of the reservation by another state party.

Nevertheless, Schmidt observes, in relation to the two Covenants, that in the final analysis it is for each state party to decide whether specific reservations meet that test.[45] His view appears to be supported by the Committee on the Elimination of Racial Discrimination.[46] The UN Subcommission on the Prevention of Discrimination and Protection of Minorities resolved to consult the Committee on the Elimination of Discrimination against Women and the Commission on the Status of Women on the desirability of requesting an Advisory Opinion from the International Court of Justice on the validity and legal effect of reservations.[47] However, it is unlikely that treaty bodies at present have the competence to seek an advisory opinion from the International Court of Justice. The Human Rights Committee has recently taken a more vigorous approach. As the Human Rights Committee comments, the absence of protests by states cannot imply that a reservation is either compatible or incompatible with the object and purpose of the Covenant. In relation to the International Covenant on Civil and Political Rights, the Human Rights Committee concluded that the pattern is so unclear that it is not possible to assume that 'a non-objecting State thinks that a particular reservation is acceptable'.[48]

Even where a reservation is accepted without objection either by the states parties or by the Secretary General of the United Nations, in his capacity as depository for UN human rights treaties, this does not necessarily deprive a human rights treaty monitoring body of all judgment. There is some authority that the 'silence of the depository and the Contracting States does not deprive the Convention organs of the power to make their own assessment',[49] although this was stated in relation to the European Convention on Human Rights, which was adopted prior to the Vienna Convention on the Law of Treaties. The same is true of the International Covenant on Civil and Political Rights, where the Human Rights Committee recently concluded that it falls to the Human Rights Committee to determine if a specific reservation is compatible with the object and purpose of the Covenant.[48] The Committee appears to be accepting that this is an inappropriate task for the states parties to human rights treaties. If it is an inappropriate task for states parties to human rights treaties, this must be because of the nature of the treaty and not be dependent upon whether a human rights treaty was concluded prior to or since the Vienna Convention on the Law of Treaties. Thus the same line of reasoning would apply to the Committee on the Rights of the Child, which would be able to determine if specific reservations are compatible with the Convention.

The Human Rights Committee has concluded that the consequence of an unacceptable reservation is that such a reservation will be severable. Thus the International Covenant on Civil and Political Rights will be operative for the reserving party without the state being able to benefit from the purported reservation.[48] The approach of the UN Human Rights Committee is a welcome one which hopefully will be adopted by other human rights treaty monitoring bodies. It is, however, an approach which is likely to be criticized by the more traditionalist international lawyers, who may also warn of the dangers of states parties withdrawing from specific human rights treaty regimes. Nevertheless, when considering protecting the human rights of individuals in daily life there is very little point in having a large number of states parties to a human rights treaty if the treaty becomes only a shell with the meat of substantive rights removed.

REFORMING INTERNATIONAL PROCEDURES TO PROTECT HUMAN RIGHTS

At its strongest, the implementation of international human rights law can lead to a significant improvement in the quality of human life. At its weakest, the recognition that specific interests and basic needs have been recognized by the international community as legal entitlements may add strength to the arguments of those in the political process seeking to improve the daily life of individuals. However, the legal authority of international human rights law risks being seriously undermined unless there is effective implementation. Of particular concern is the lack of a regional human rights system within Asia.[50]

There is a lack of balance under international law between the entitlements of individuals to specific rights and the limited procedural capacity they have to protect those rights. In general terms, international law has developed five different methods of both promoting and protecting human rights: complaints procedures by individuals and groups alleging violations of their rights; inter-state complaint procedures; reports of impartial experts, including fact-finding on alleged violations; the establishment of report-receiving bodies on measures which states have taken to comply with international human rights law; and the provision of technical advice and assistance to help states bring their domestic protection and promotion of human rights up to international standards.

The rationale behind the majority of these forms of implementation has been the belief that if the facts are clearly established and criticized during or after the violation, such criticism will reduce the possibilities of further violations occurring. However, human rights law is beginning to take a broader preventative focus and seeking to avoid the initial abuses ever arising through the provision of technical advice and assistance which aims at preventing or at least ameliorating such situations.

With the exception of established individual communications procedures, the method of protection directly depends upon the willingness of states. The principal advantage of petitioning mechanisms is that they provide a more direct, effective and speedier remedy than the submission of state reports. Yet neither the Convention on the Rights of the Child nor the Convention on the Elimination of All Forms of Discrimination Against Women incorporates a petitioning system, either inter-state or individual. However, the Vienna Declaration and Programme of Action has mandated the Commission on the Status of Women to draft an optional protocol for complaints under the Convention on the Elimination of All Forms of Discrimination Against Women.[51] In relation to children, the right to petition has already proven to be effective under the European Convention on Human Rights. However, during the drafting of the Convention on the Rights of the Child, where the possibility of an individual petitioning system was informally raised by Amnesty International, the idea was not taken forward, as many believed it would transform an implementation mechanism based on cooperation into one fraught with confrontation. This has not proven to be the case within the Council of Europe, where states parties generally abide by the judgments of the European Court of Human Rights.

The individual petitioning system represents one of the most direct and progressive methods of remedying human rights violations. It is not, however, without its weaknesses. Petitioning can be used as a sword with which governments can cut down rights, and not exclusively as a shield to protect rights. In *Abdulaziz* v. *United Kingdom*, the UK, in putting into effect the judgment of the European Court of Human Rights, did not extend to women the right to bring in their spouses but rather restricted the categories of men who previously had been so entitled.[52] Furthermore, the right of petition has developed as a measure to remedy violations once they have occurred and has generally been ineffective in preventing violations. It is only rarely that the petitioning system prevents violations happening to a future victim.[53] Another principal weakness is the length of time which is taken to reach a final decision. This can be even more harsh where it is a child who is the petitioner, as a child's perception of time is different from an adult's.[54] Although delay is common with municipal systems, because regional and international human rights petitioning systems only have jurisdiction after a petitioner has first exhausted all effective domestic remedies, the period of time awaiting a decision of an international or regional human rights tribunal is in addition to that of the domestic legal system.

Those opposed to individual petitioning systems being attached to other existing human rights treaties argue that it is only appropriate for civil and political rights and is not suited to treaties which also protect economic, social and cultural rights. However, the incorporation of a right of individual petition into the African Charter on the Rights and Welfare of the Child is evidence that it may be in the best interests of the child if such assumptions are challenged. The recent drafting of a communications procedure by the Committee on Economic, Social and Cultural Rights[55] also seems to imply that it is time to challenge the assertion that economic, social and cultural rights are non-justiciable.

Hence it would be possible to have reporting, technical advice and assistance together with an optional petitioning system. For the right of petition to be included in human rights treaties it would mean that either the treaties themselves would have to be amended or an additional optional protocol attached. The latter is more realistic, although it would not automatically follow that states which are party to the principal treaty would become party to the Protocol.

Extending the right of petition would be both egalitarian and evolutionary. However, many of the contributing causes of the violations of children and women's human rights are structural, and although class actions exist in a number of national jurisdictions, international law has not developed a similar procedure. This is in part because of the excessive individualization which characterizes many aspects of international human rights law. The underlying purpose of a class action is that it binds all the parties represented and in effect implements rights which are of concern to the public interest. At first sight the creation of an international legal class action would appear to be unnecessary. A judgment from a regional human rights body, for example, will on occasion prompt a state party to amend its legislation, hence removing the necessity for future actions. However, an international legal class action would have particular implications for the enforcement of group rights, particularly in the economic, social and cultural sphere.

Many of children's and women's concerns are in the economic, social and cultural areas, and the lack of an international legal class action has had a significant negative impact on the protection of their economic, social and cultural rights. One of the reasons behind the mistaken assumption that economic, social and cultural rights are not justiciable is that they raise complex economic, social and cultural questions which human rights fora have demonstrated a reluctance to consider within the confines of one case. Hence the argument becomes circular. There is not a suitable implementation mechanism for economic and social rights and therefore they are not justiciable. The creation of an international legal class action would assist states in the goal of reassessing the potential justiciability of these rights in both the public and the traditionally private spheres.

CONCLUSION

Although international substantive law is developing rapidly to encompass a greater number of internationally recognized human rights, progress is being artificially restrained by the limpet-like clinging to traditional public-private boundaries and to outdated concepts of implementation. More is required than simply mobilizing shame, which is the aim of the reporting procedures.[56] Progress is resisted for fear of opening what are perceived as floodgates. However, the floodgates argument is not a reason for resisting reform. On the contrary, it is a reason for providing sufficient resources so that effective human rights machinery can function efficiently into the twenty-first century. As Popper observed in relation to science, international human rights law 'must begin with myths and with the criticism of myths'.[57] The beginnings of international human rights law has long passed and the redundant myths of international human rights ought to be discarded and reclassified under history.[58]

NOTES

1. S. Oda, The individual in international law. In M. Sorenson (ed.), *Manual of Public International Law* (London: Macmillan, 1968), p. 471.
2. R. J. Cooke (ed.), *Human Rights of Women – National and International Perspectives* (Philadelphia: University of Pennsylvania Press, 1994), p. 89.
3. *Ibid.*, p. 70.
4. (1989) 130 UPLR 1289.
5. See C. MacKinnon, *Towards a Feminist Theory of the State* (Cambridge, MA: Harvard University Press, 1989), p. 190.
6. See in general A. Clapham, *Human Rights in the Private Sphere* (Oxford: Clarendon Press, 1993). See further G. Anderson, above, Chapter 23, and C. Chinkin, above, Chapter 24.
7. *X and Y v. Netherlands*, judgment of European Court of Human Rights 26 March, 1985, Series A, No. 91.
8. *Ibid.*, para. 23. See also *Costello–Roberts v. UK* (1993) 19 EHRR 112.
9. Inter-American Court of Human Rights (Ser. C) No. 4, 1988.
10. *Ibid.*, para. 173.
11. *Ibid.*, para. 172.

12. *Ibid.*, para. 175. See also D. Shelton, Private violence, public wrongs and the responsibility of states (1990) 13 *Fordham Journal of International Law* 1, at p. 21.

13. There was a partial dissenting opinion of Judge Piza Escalante on the legal standing of the victims with regard to compensation.

14. Article 13, Proclamation of Tehran, proclaimed by the International Conference on Human Rights at Tehran, 13 May 1968.

15. Article 2(1), International Covenant on Economic, Social and Cultural Rights.

16. G. Van Bueren, *The International Law on the Rights of the Child* (Dordrecht: Nijhoff/Kluwer, 1995), p. 6.

17. See G. Van Bueren, The international system of human rights: an overview. In *Manual on Human Rights Reporting* (New York: United Nations, 1991).

18. G. Van Bueren, Education: whose right is it anyway? In L. Heffernan and J. Kingston (eds), *Human Rights: A European Perspective* (Dublin: Roundhall Press, 1994).

19. See the discussion in Van Bueren, *op. cit.*

20. See, for example, *Marckx* v. *Belgium*, judgment of the European Court of Human Rights, 13 June 1979, Series A, No. 31.

21. In G. Van Bueren, *International Documents on Children* (Dordrecht: Nijhoff/Kluwer, 1993).

22. G. Van Bueren, *The International Law on the Rights of the Child, op. cit.*, note 16, p. 304.

23. Human Development Report 1991, based on *World Human Rights Guide* (Humana, 1991); also see R. L. Barsh, Measuring human rights: problems of methodology and purpose (1993) 15 *Human Rights Quarterly* 87.

24. C. Dias, Rural development, grassroots education and human rights. In K. Mahoney and P. Mahoney (eds), *Human Rights in the Twenty-First Century: A Global Challenge* (Dordrecht: Nijhoff/Kluwer, 1992).

25. Article 4, Convention on the Rights of the Child 1989.

26. J. Himes, The UN Convention on the Rights of the Child: more than a new utopia? In J. Himes, *Three Essays on the Challenge of Implementation* (UNICEF, 1993). However, there are resource limitation clauses in a number of instruments, including those focusing on health and education. The repetition, and arguably unnecessary repetition in light of Article 4, has caused some doubt that this will operate as a stagnating justification amongst both developing and industrialized states.

27. As distinct from the reservation of the UK in relation to Article 37.

28. See the observations of the European Commission of Human Rights, *Kjeldsen, Busk Madsen and Pedersen* v. *Denmark* European Court of Human Rights Series A, No. 21, para. 154.

29. UN Doc CCPR/C/21/Rev. 1/Add. 6. General Comment No. 24.

30. UN Doc CRC/C/SR.

31. See Jenefsky, Permissibility of Egypt's Reservations to the Convention on the Elimination of All Forms of Discrimination Against Women (1991) 15 *Maryland Journal of International Law and Trade* 208.

32. See B. Clarke, The Vienna Convention Reservations Regime and the Convention on Discrimination Against Women (1991) 85 *American Journal of International Law* 281.

33. See Articles 19, 20, 21, 22, and 23, Vienna Convention on the Law of Treaties 1969, Cmnd 7964.

34. See the Convention on the Rights of the Child. See also Article 64, European Convention on Human Rights; Article 75, American Convention on Human Rights and Effect of Reservation on the Entry into Force of the American Convention (1982) 22 ILM 37.

35. This is not an issue exclusive to human rights treaties; see B. Oxman, The Third United Nations Conference on the Law of the Sea: The Eighth Session (1979) 74 *American Journal of International Law* 35.

36. Article 20(5), Vienna Convention on the Law of Treaties.

37. *Reservations to the Genocide Convention*, Advisory Opinion, ICJ Reports, 1951. 'The complete exclusion from the Convention of one or more States would not only restrict the scope of its application but would detract from the authority of the moral and humanitarian principles which are its basis' (p. 24). See, however, for criticisms of this approach,

G. Fitzmaurice, The law and procedure of the International Court of Justice 1951–4: treaty interpretation and other treaty points (1957) 33 *British Yearbook of International Law* 203; I. Sinclair, *The Vienna Convention on the Law of Treaties* (Manchester: Manchester University Press, 1984), pp. 55–8.

38. A. Drzemczewski, The sui generis nature of the European Convention on Human Rights (1980) 29 *International and Comparative Law Quarterly* 54.

39. An approach taken by the European Court of Human Rights, *Ireland* v. *United Kingdom* Series A, No. 25, para. 239.

40. In relation, for example, to inter-state complaints under the European Convention on Human Rights.

41. Another is compatibility, and there is much debate over whether incompatible reservations may be accepted. Ruda argues in the affirmative: Reservations to treaties (1975) 146 *Recueil des Cours D'Académie De Droit International* 95, at p. 190.

42. Article 20(4)(c), 'an act expressing a State's consent to be bound by the treaty and containing a reservation is effective as soon as at least one other Contracting State has accepted the reservation'.

43. Advisory Opinion on the Effect of Reservations on the Entry into Force of the American Convention. Reprinted in (1983) 22 ILM 37, at p. 47.

44. Netherlands, Finland, Germany, Denmark, Norway, Belgium, Portugal, Italy and Spain. UN Doc. ST/LEG/Ser. E/Add. 1993.

45. Schmidt, Reservations to United Nations Rights Treaties – The Case of the Two Covenants. Paper delivered at the British Institute of International and Comparative Law 1994.

46. UN Doc. A/33/18. The Committee observed that even a unanimous decision that a specific reservation was unacceptable did not have any legal effect.

47. UN Doc. CRC/C/SR. 50.

48. UN Doc. CCPr/C/21/ Rev. 1/Add. 6.

49. Statement made in relation to the European Convention on Human Rights in *Belilos* v. *Switzerland*. Judgment of European Court of Human Rights, 29 April 1988, para. 47. See also note 48.

50. Although for children this is somewhat ameliorated by a significant number of Asian states that have become party to the Convention on the Rights of the Child.

51. UN Doc. A/CONF. 157/23, 1993.

52. European Court of Human Rights Series A, No. 94, 1985.

53. See *Soering* v. *United Kingdom* (1989) 11 EHRR 439. Soering successfully resisted being extradited to Virginia, USA, on the basis that the period of time he would spend on death row would give rise to breach of Article 3 of the European Convention on Human Rights.

54. See generally G. Van Bueren, *The International Law on the Rights of the Child, op. cit.*

55. Although its chances of coming into effect are slim.

56. Paraphrasing Frank Newman expanding the phrase used by Ernest Landy, the then Chief of the Application Standards Branch of the International Labour Organization.

57. K. Popper, The philosophy of science. In C. A. Mace (ed.), *British Philosophy in the Mid-Century* (London: Allen and Unwin, 1957).

58. An expanded version of this chapter has been published in *Human Rights Quarterly* in 1995.

27

The Governance of Special Powers: A Case Study of Exclusion and the Treatment of Individual Rights under the Prevention of Terrorism Acts

Clive Walker

INTRODUCTION

It may appear gratuitously offensive to associate the Prevention of Terrorism Acts 1974-1989 (PTA) with the word 'rights'. There are certainly some who take the view that the two are entirely antithetical. A recent book by Hillyard contained the following extract:

> The use of successive Prevention of Terrorism Acts has often constituted the terror of prevention. Law is thus an integral part of the repression and organisation of state violence, whether it takes place in a person's home or in police custody.[1]

That I had not envisioned the PTA solely in this way probably should come as no surprise. After all, passages in the same book comment that Walker 'does not . . . produce any evidence to support his view', or even, as the ultimate insult to a notorious liberal, that he 'is too charitable to the police'.[2] This ability to incur the wrath of fellow academics has a venerable history. The first substantial review of my first ever book stated uncompromisingly that I suffered from 'glaring inconsistencies' and 'a lack of realism'.[3]

Such criticism is painful but nonetheless carries an important lesson – that the expression of any viewpoint about the PTA is more likely to raise the hackles than expositions, on, say, the law on frustration in contract or perpetuities in land law. This rage seems to be a predictable reaction. After all, political violence in Ireland is in part fascinating and worthy of research because of the very passion and the fundamental nature of the conflict, which is so important to some of the participants that it is worth the price of a life. So depth of feeling and partisanship could also be described as endemic, a failing which, as shall be noted later, affects judges, legislators and politicians as well as academics.

A second set of criticisms, by Professor Wilkinson, reflects a school of thought which contends that the PTA is needed more to protect rights than to pose a threat to them. Certainly, it is arguable that the activities of paramilitaries involve violence and destruction which even the laws of war, assuming we accord the IRA combatant status in the first place, would not excuse.[4] On reflection, it should be accepted within the context of the UK that terrorism properly so-called is inimical to rights and democratic development. So, the dilemma posed by Chowdhury of an obligation to protect the integrity of the state versus the obligation to protect rights[5] is not entirely accurate – the suppression of terrorism may protect individual rights as well as collective interests. Measures against crimes need not necessarily be uniform. Just as variations have been adopted against serious fraudsters, drug traffickers and child molesters, so terrorists may warrant different approaches because of their atypical threat, motivations and methods. Consequently, the possibility of special powers is in principle acceptable, provided that the agenda of the power elite in charge of national security is not, say, the maintenance of their power but the maintenance of individual rights and other acceptable values.

Let us then assume that special powers will justifiably endure for ever. On the face of it, this seems to be a singularly ill-timed assumption. Surely a transformation is taking place as a result of the Downing Street Declaration of 1993 and the paramilitary cease-fires of 1994?[6] However, there are several reasons to suppose that special powers will persist and that their governance will remain a live issue. One problem is the reluctance to cede such powers even at a time of relative calm. At the time of writing, the peace process is far from secure, and a heavy political price might be payable if the official guard is lowered too soon. In addition, there are vested interests, as police and security services vie for the maintenance of budgets and personnel.[7] Finally, emergency powers are not solely associated with Irish Republicanism, so the possible decoupling of that movement from political violence may not wholly destroy the *raison d'être* of special powers. Indeed, the most venerable set of special powers currently available are those in the Emergency Powers Act 1920 against industrial disruption, and even the focus of the PTA has in part been aimed towards 'foreign' terrorism.[8] Furthermore, the activities of animal rights protesters are increasingly labelled as 'terroristic', and police resources are being redirected accordingly. If peaceful times are not a sufficient antidote to the existence of special powers, it remains vital to design mechanisms which ensure that legislation like the PTA is subject to constitutional governance through a proper rights audit, democratic accountability and constitutionalism.

These principles must be both explained and justified. A 'rights audit' means that the rights of individuals are respected according to traditions of the domestic jurisdictions and the demands of international law. The latter will include the review of the very existence of the emergency under Article 15 of the European Convention on Human Rights, but the focus of this chapter will be on the individual rights affected by exclusion. Another collective right which will not be considered here is self-determination, which brings into question the authority, rather than the governance, of legislation and powers. Next, 'democratic accountability' includes attributes such as information, open debate and an ability to participate in decision-making. Thirdly, constitutionalism might be defined as encompassing in general the subjection of government to legal norms. More specific requirements in the field of special powers include 'the public articulation of reasons in support of particular actions taken for the public welfare',[9] concern for human dignity, assurances that the crisis cannot be ended by normal means and that powers will not be used arbitrarily, and adherence to the overall purpose of the restoration of fundamental features of constitutional life. As for the justification of all these principles, it is assumed that these are liberal values which, in the context of that tradition, can be considered as universal moral goods and not simply autopoietic features. They are not especially British values nor dependent upon British sovereignty but are of course recognized and cherished by the Republic of Ireland's Constitution[10] and are values which proponents of joint sovereignty or even of a united Ireland would surely wish to secure. On a deeper level, the credibility of the 'grand narrative' of liberalism must also not be taken for granted, but to take issue with the currently fashionable outbreak of value-scepticism would take us beyond the scope of this chapter.

Taking these principles as given, it is planned to focus on just one special power, namely exclusion under the PTA. This area of law is selected for three main reasons. First, exclusion has been the subject of scrutiny by means of judicial, political, administrative and legislative mechanisms, both at national and international level. Second, exclusion excites some of the most profound disagreement between the main political parties in their debates over special powers in that the disharmony concerns retention rather than redesign.[11] Third, more wide-ranging surveys have already been published concerning the compliance of other aspects of the UK's emergency laws with international rights norms.[12]

EXCLUSION – THE POWERS
AND THE PRACTICE

Powers

The design and operation of exclusion orders under Part II of the PTA has been fully explicated elsewhere.[13] By way of brief recap, under s. 5(1), the Home Secretary may prohibit a person from being in, or entering Great Britain, if satisfied that he or she

> (a) is or has been concerned in the commission, preparation or instigation of acts of terrorism to which this Part of this Act applies; or
> (b) is attempting or may attempt to enter Great Britain with a view to being concerned in the commission, preparation or instigation of such acts of terrorism . . .

Exclusion from Northern Ireland to Britain or, more likely, from the whole of the UK is permitted in turn by s. 6 and 7. Orders are subject to various limits, including a three years' residence exemption for British citizens.

The first step towards obtaining an exclusion order in Britain is the referral of a potential case by the relevant police force to the National Joint Unit (consisting of Special Branch officers) at New Scotland Yard. Its report will be forwarded to the Home Office. The Northern Ireland Secretary deals with cases in the Province, but applications from Scottish police forces are routed through the Home Office. Three categories of information will be scrutinized. First, there will be personal particulars. Second, there will be relevant background information about views, associations and movements. Third, and most important of all, there must be evidence of 'active personal involvement',[14] such as the planning of terrorism by carrying out reconnaissance or preparing plans, or by providing money, materials or facilities. Aside from personal particulars, most of the information will be hearsay and low-grade information which will derive from intelligence sources. Another source of information will be the transcript of any police interrogation of the suspect.

An exclusion order may be revoked at any time by order of the Secretary of State.[15] In addition, a periodic review must be conducted after three years.[16] It will be noted that there is no power to suspend an order, a lacuna which caused problems in the case of *R* v. *Secretary of State for the Home Department, ex parte McQuillan*,[17] an excludee from Northern Ireland whose presence was demanded in the Old Bailey for the purpose of giving evidence in the trial of two acquaintances for conspiracy to cause explosions.

Once an exclusion order has been made or renewed, schedule 2, paragraph 3(1) states that the person against whom [the exclusion order] is made may

> (a) . . . make representations in writing to the Secretary of State setting out the grounds of his objections; and
> (b) include in those representations a request for a personal interview with the person or persons nominated by the Secretary of State . . .

When an interview is arranged,[18] a single adviser is delegated to form an independent view of the merits of the case, based on information provided by the person and on the papers which are forwarded by the Secretary of State. The Secretary of State is then enjoined to 'reconsider the matter as soon as is reasonably practicable'.[19] In practice, the Home Secretary has, with one exception, always followed a recommendation to revoke and has even cancelled some orders contrary to an adviser's wishes. After reconsideration, the Secretary of State must give written notice of the final decision 'if it is reasonably practicable to do so . . .'.[20] The notice specifies the relevant statutory authority and terms of the order, but there is no statement of the evidence relied upon. Finally, schedule 2 grants powers physically to remove the person. A variety of offences under section 8 deals with breaches of exclusion orders.

Practice and Impact

The following tables indicate how exclusion has actually been implemented.[21] Overwhelmingly, exclusion is from Britain to Northern Ireland, but there has been a substantial decline in both the issuance and maintenance of orders over the past decade, with none now in force in Northern Ireland.

Some see exclusion as 'of proven value',[22] and both the Shackleton and Jellicoe Reports concluded that it has successfully attained its objective.[23] The basic objective of, and justification for, each exclusion order is that it prevents terrorism:[24]

> First . . . exclusion has rid Great Britain of dangerous terrorists. Second . . . terrorists have found their effectiveness in general substantially impaired by the fact that they were no longer able to travel legally between Northern Ireland and the mainland or between the Republic of Ireland and the United Kingdom as a whole.

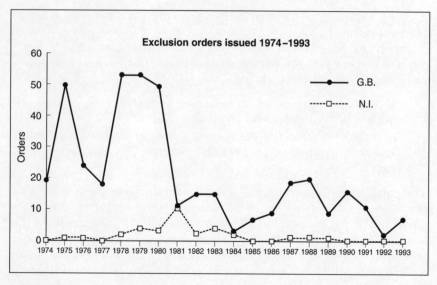

Figure 27.1

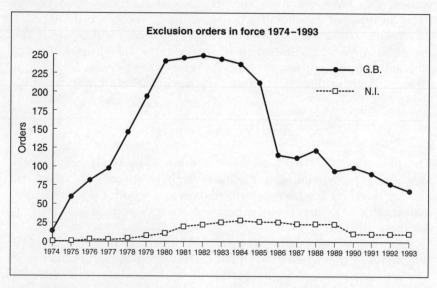

Figure 27.2

The system may be unfair to the suspect compared to a criminal trial, but this is felt to be more than outweighed by the likely reduction in terrorism.[25] As is conceded by the Home Office Circular on the PTA,[26] criminal charges are preferable if sufficient evidence is available to sustain them, for imprisonment is a more effective method of prevention. However, exclusion does possess some countervailing attractions. First, it allows disruptive intervention at an earlier stage, since an order may be based on inadmissible evidence and may be granted even when the level of proof does not reach the criminal standard. Second, the police may prefer to resort to exclusion in order to avoid disclosing in open court the names of informers or methods of investigation.

Critics of exclusion cast doubt on the claim that it has, or is ever likely to, prevent terrorism. Evidence that the person is likely to engage in terrorism in the future is of dubious quality, and the enforced change of abode does nothing to hinder any potential involvement in terrorism by putting suspects out of harm's way. The only convincing counter-argument is perhaps that exclusion saves police time, since there is no need to build up a painstaking forensic case against the suspect.[27] However, this reasoning would only be acceptable if terrorism were overwhelming police resources in the territory benefiting from exclusion, which has never been the circumstance in Britain.

Further criticisms may be levelled at the 'inherently arbitrary and oppressive'[28] procedures prevailing under Part II, which derogate still further from the civil rights of suspects. A further consequence is that exclusion is a propaganda liability, and there is no convincing day in court to answer the complaints of its victims. A related point concerns the effects of exclusion on human rights which not only excite political 'criticism and turmoil'[29] but may also seriously damage employment prospects and the physical security of persons returned to Northern Ireland.[30] Finally, hard evidence that terrorism has been reduced by exclusion is difficult to adduce, and this evidential doubt leads to the suspicion that it is the appearance, rather than the reality, of prevention that has most impressed Parliament and the executive. Thus, the reasons for the continuance of exclusion may more clearly be located in the political desire to be seen to be taking overt action against, and to 'Ulsterize', Republican terrorism. It is also further evidence of the political difficulty of resisting the demands of the security forces.

Having described exclusion as a system, it is now intended to examine the governance of the mechanism by the various constitutional means which are available.

GOVERNANCE BY JUDGES

Governance by the UK Legal System

An initial difficulty to be faced by litigants is justiciability – whether the courts will entertain at all complaints about exclusion. The issue arose in *R* v. *Secretary of State for Home Affairs, ex parte Stitt*,[31] when Sean Stitt, a community worker from Belfast, sought to overturn an order. In the leading judgment of Watkins LJ, three grounds advanced by the respondent were examined: the 'package' argument, a claim that national security and confidentiality made review inappropriate, and concern about delay in bringing the application. The first argument was that the statutory adviser system under s. 7 provides 'a comprehensive package of rights' which renders common law judicial review impliedly unnecessary. The courts are often reluctant to accept this argument 'particularly when the statutory remedy is in the hands of an administrative body',[32] and no comment on it was offered by Watkins LJ. The second ground, national security, prevailed as 'powerfully persuasive' and 'the central issue'. Delay was said to be unimportant. The judgment of MacPherson J was more forthright on the package argument: 'I agree that Parliament prescribed in the [Prevention of Terrorism Acts] a defined package of rights for those who might be or have been excluded from this country.' Yet delay and confidentiality are also cited by him as reasons for the rejection of review. Thus, the issue of sensitive information is the common basis for the decision, but this consideration, though relevant to many orders, need not arise in all challenges or prevent review without consideration of the evidence. However, the balance of *obiter* remarks also points towards acceptance of the 'package' argument, which is a more fundamental obstacle and was ominously echoed in the deportation case of *ex parte Cheblak*,[33] in which the further point was floated that the Home Secretary was accountable to Parliament and so judicial review was superfluous.

In summary, any decision by a Secretary of State to exclude may be treated as non-justiciable, and this rather bleak interpretation of Stitt's case has support from influential sources, such as Viscount Colville.[34] Nevertheless, it is arguable that the reluctance of the courts to intervene extends only to the substance of the decision by the Minister and not to other matters (such as procedures). This approach was effectively adopted by the Divisional Court in *R* v. *Secretary of State for the Home Department, ex parte O'Neill*,[35] and was expressly conceded by the Home Secretary in *R* v. *Secretary of State for the Home Department, ex parte Gallagher*.[36] O'Neill was born in Northern Ireland but also held Irish citizenship. He had lived intermittently in London since 1985 but was excluded in 1990. Following *ex parte Stitt*, Rose J felt that the substantive basis of the order could not be challenged, so reasons did not have to be provided. However, there was scrutiny of the procedures by which it had been made and whether representations from O'Neill had been properly considered, the judge being fully satisfied in all respects. Gallagher was an Irish citizen who had lived in Britain in periods between 1987 and 1991 in order to work. He had been arrested under the PTA in September 1991; no charges were brought, but he was then excluded. The important concession was that 'the decisions [of the Home Secretary] are susceptible to review by this court, and that the jurisdiction of this court is in no sense barred by any consideration of public security or claim relating to the interests of national security'.

Assuming that some review remains possible, it will now be determined how far it might bite. There are various forms of error affecting jurisdiction which may trigger judicial intervention, such as where the competent authority has misdirected itself by applying the wrong legal test or by misunderstanding a matter in respect of which it must be satisfied. This form of review is relevant to exclusion, but, as shall be described later, will be constrained by judicial unwillingness to seek out sensitive information. Thus, as in *Stitt*, there will be no effective inquiry into whether the suspect can properly be labelled a 'terrorist'. However, four other issues affecting jurisdiction may be examinable. The first two – whether the person is 'ordinarily resident' and whether residence has endured for three years or more – are relevant to ss. 5 and 6. A third area where intervention may arise is whether the person qualifies as a 'British citizen' under the British Nationality Act 1981. Finally, the 'appropriateness' of an order may be challenged but it will be difficult to show that the interpretation of such a vague term is wholly mistaken in law.

As well as jurisdictional errors of substance, certain procedural errors may be reviewable. Thus, the courts might ensure that an order has actually been made and has been approved by the proper authority. Next, the formal requirements under schedule 2 such as the giving of the relevant notices, allowing representations, requiring reference to an adviser and conferring a right to a personal interview, must all be considered mandatory. Questions may also be raised when the Secretary of State reconsiders the case, though proof that he did not genuinely apply his mind will be difficult to find. Finally, the right of non-removal pending reconsideration is also enforceable.

Judicial review may next be triggered by abuses of discretion. By and large, evidential difficulties will ensure that challenges on the basis of irrationality have little impact or are non-justiciable, subject to three exceptions. First, if, contrary to its common practice, the executive reveals the information on which it acted, these reasons can be scrutinized. A second area where reasonableness is relevant concerns the duration of exclusion orders. A third possible line of attack concerns the time which elapses before any final decision to exclude, especially as the person may in the meantime be incarcerated. The next forms of abuse of discretion are disregarding legally relevant, or taking into account legally irrelevant, considerations. For example, it would be improper for the Home Secretary to deploy his powers against Arab terrorists whose activities are unrelated to Northern Ireland. A further abuse would occur if the Home Secretary signed an order without reflection of any kind. However, the processing of a large number of applications in a short time does not raise such an inference. Failure to specify any substantive reasons for exclusion (that is beyond the civil servant-drafted affidavits, which are decidedly economical with the truth) will certainly not be deemed to be evidence of abuse in view of the sensitive nature of the evidence involved. Problems of proof are also the main hindrance to the last form of abuse of discretion, namely bad faith on the part of the decision-maker.

The final basis for judicial review is procedural impropriety. It is unlikely that the initial making of an order by the Secretary of State is at all affected. One reason is that the statutory adviser system rather than natural justice is available to remedy any errors at the earlier stage. A second reason is that such prior notification of a suspect could defeat the preventive aim of the Act. By contrast, natural justice may be applicable to the adviser system. Personal impartiality is certainly demanded, both in reality and in appearance. For example, it was suggested by Farquharson LJ, somewhat impertinently, in *ex parte Gallagher*, that the appointment of a Unionist politician would be tainted. Refusal to reveal the identity of the adviser diminishes the chances of detection of such faults but was not seen as legally objectionable by the Court of Appeal. Amongst the implied procedural requirements could be the giving of adequate notice of the interview with the adviser, so that the suspect may prepare a case. Similarly, reasonable requests for adjournments should be granted, for example if a person wishes to obtain the statement of a material witness. However, the recurrent problem of sensitive information makes it unlikely that the present practice of suppressing the adverse allegations or reasons for the Secretary of State's decision could be impugned, though the courts have regrettably also elided factual reasons with legal grounds and placed them equally behind the veil. Natural justice will also have a restricted impact on the procedures followed at the interview itself. For example, the suspect will probably be denied a right to call or cross-examine witnesses. Aside from the risks to security, the Act grants only a 'personal' interview,[37] which seems to debar third parties. Equally, legal representation is not required in most cases, since the procedure is meant to be inquisitorial and informal, though it is in fact allowed. A similar view was taken in Northern Ireland concerning representations before the Advisory Committee reviewing internment orders. In *re Mackey* in 1972,[38] it was held that only in complex or special cases would it be unfair to forbid full legal representation. The Court reserved its judgment on how far lawyers could act as mere 'agents', but their use was subsequently allowed in practice. In *ex parte Cheblak*, the court emphasized that the Advisory Panel was to be viewed as inquisitorial in nature, and so it, rather than the subject, should take the lead in amassing information.

An obstacle to most forms of judicial review mentioned hitherto is the sensitive nature of the information involved:

> It is intelligence information, whose disclosure may involve unacceptable risks. Information which is specific about a person's participation in an act of terrorism may be known to only two or three people. It could, without difficulty, be traced back to its source if it became known to the subject of the exclusion order or to a wider circle of his associates and friends. From this might follow the death of the informant. The flow of information which can lead, and in many cases has led to convictions in the courts would be endangered.[39]

Judicial aversion to security matters was the rock on which review in *Stitt* foundered. He complained that he had not been given 'the gist or the substance of the objection which [was] made to his presence' in Britain, so it was impossible to make cogent representations to the adviser. However, Watkins LJ held that reasons could not be imparted since '[n]ational security is very much at stake in matters of this kind, especially the need to protect confidential sources.' Similarly, once Gallagher began voicing complaints about lack of reasons for the decision, the official defences were raised again by McCullough J:

> It is plain beyond argument that the whole reason for the Act was the consideration of public security, and it is clear that Parliament intended to leave to the Secretary of State the widest discretion in deciding what the public interest did and did not require.

Likewise, Farquharson LJ in the Court of Appeal seemed close to asserting non-justiciability when he concluded that 'only the Home Secretary could form a judgment and appraise the risk.'

There was a more expansive inquisition into these issues in *R* v. *Secretary of State for the Home Department, ex parte McQuillan*.[40] No reasons were, as usual, forthcoming for the exclusion which was first imposed in 1987. McQuillan had no convictions for terrorist offences, but he had been a prominent official in the Irish Republican Socialist Party, which is allied to the proscribed Irish National Liberation Army. However, he claimed to have severed his connections in 1992. Sedley J was sympathetic to the administrative law challenge based on the lack of reasons:

> If the matter were free of authority, I would hold with little hesitation that the reasons of the [Home Secretary] do not necessarily amount to reasons of national security at all. They are, on the contrary, the straightforward and familiar reasons for the invocation of public interest immunity to protect sources of police information. If so, it would fall within the obligation of the court to scrutinise material, subject to proper safeguards, in order to decide whether the interests of justice called for its disclosure, notwithstanding its possible effects on informants.

This reasoning appears seriously confused in two respects. One is that the claim of the Home Office was based on national security as a factor to be weighed against the applicant's rights. Whether the jejune statement in support was sufficiently weighty is raised in the next point. However, it was not in any event a direct demand that the court should not investigate further. Had further and better particulars or discovery been demanded by the applicant in interlocutory proceedings, then a Public Interest Immunity Certificate (PIIC) might have been issued,[41] but here the Court was asked to weigh the evidence as it stood and not as it might stand if all were revealed. Sedley J was confusing the concept of national security as a substantive legal argument with national security as a procedural defence. The other confusion arises from the implication in the quoted passage that the courts must inquire into the assertion of national security in the context of a PIIC but not in the context of a supporting affidavit. As already described, it has not been universally accepted by the judiciary that supporting affidavits are wholly non-justiciable, nor is it certain that the grounds for a PIIC will be explored exhaustively.[42]

Similar judicial reactions have been observed in response to challenges to analogous security measures, such as internment in Northern Ireland[43] and refusal of entry or deportation on grounds of national security.[44] From this experience, it may be predicted that judicial review of Part II of the Prevention of Terrorism Act will be largely sacrificed to the totem of security interests. So long as the Home Office answers any complaints with an affidavit rehearsing satisfaction of the statutory grounds and setting out any reasons which can be disclosed without endangering security sources, the courts will not require more.

It must be concluded that judicial review in the English courts to date has not entailed searching scrutiny of exclusion orders, so that the criticisms that exclusion is inherently arbitrary and oppressive remains unanswered by UK administrative law. Indeed, the cases have exemplified several fundamental problems common to this type of civil liberties litigation. These include the fact that litigants are forced to pitch their cases around inappropriately hostile, narrowly technical and irrelevant sites, rather than being able to confront the rights issues head on. Stitt could not claim a right to pursue a private and family life,[45] a right to movement within the UK or a right to due process. Next, no special weight is accorded as such to the right which is under threat. It may or may not be part of English common law, but it certainly does not gain any sanctity by being domesticated in this way and often will be outweighed by more specific and quantifiable interests in national security.[46] Next, the courts can only speak about rights reactively and in response to litigation which is 'largely a matter of chance'.[47] Another problem is that the procedures and remedies in domestic litigation are more geared towards property claims than autonomy claims. In regard to procedures, parties have difficulties in handling evidence which verges on national security, an obstacle which is likely to increase as the role of MI5 grows in relation to counter-terrorism. As for remedies, 'treat me with respect' involves much more imagination on the part of courts than 'return my goods' or 'compensate me for my injury'. Finally, the special passion and sensitivity of terrorist cases brings extra problems and a disinclination on the part of the judges to challenge the executive. Not only are they dealing with national security, but it is national security in a time of perceived crisis. So, the tendency is towards terse, assertive judgments which are deferential to security concerns.[48]

Clearly, domestic judicial review is unlikely to pick up anything other than disastrously and blatantly ill-founded cases. The cases are manageable in that they involve an individual and inquiry about that individual, but the judges have not been effective rights auditors. In any event, no matter how adventurous the judges may wish to become, courtrooms have very limited possibilities in English law as the venue for democratic accountability or even for reflecting broader aspects of constitutionalism.

Governance by the European Union Legal System

Though grounded in narratives of trade and employment, European Union (EU) law has had a deepening and widening impact on the treatment of rights within the UK, as enforced by the UK judiciary themselves or by the Court of Justice. Likewise, EU law and has been called in aid by an increasing number of excludees. Initially, this litigation centred upon economic rights under Article 48 of the Treaty of Rome, but in substance these do little to prevent the banning or removal of Irish suspects designated as terrorists, for three reasons. First, Article 48 rights benefit only 'workers' or those genuinely seeking work and not persons whose purpose of entry is to perpetrate political violence. Of course, an entrant's intentions may be far from obvious, and a terrorist may also enter as the spouse or dependant of a genuine worker. Therefore, removal will usually occur after entry pursuant to Article 48(3), by which the movement and residence of EU nationals is 'subject to the limitations justified on grounds of public policy, public security or public health'.[49] Most suspected terrorists will readily fall under the 'public security' exception.[50] Thus, exclusion cannot readily be impugned because of its substantive effects.[51]

The third substantive limitation is that Article 48 is probably applicable only to non-British citizens,[52] and therefore not to the majority of wholly 'internal' exclusions, from Britain to Northern Ireland. This point has sparked some interesting submissions in *O'Neill, McQuillan* and *ex parte Adams*[53] concerning persons holding dual British and Irish citizenship. Although the internal nature of the exclusion was considered to be 'a knockout blow' to claims under Article 48 in *O'Neill*, the better view seems to be that EU law is prepared to treat dual citizens as 'foreigners' so that they can avail themselves of the protection of EU law.[54]

More important are the arguments of due process which have arisen in connection with Article 48. These have been mainly centred upon its detailed implementation by Directive 64/221, which was raised in the cases of *O'Neill* and *Gallagher*. Article 6 of the Directive requires that a person being removed on grounds of public policy, public security or public health be informed of those grounds, 'unless this is contrary to the interests of the security of the State involved'. One imagines that neither British nor European judges will take much persuasion that the proviso applies to terrorist suspects.[55] However, there was more weight in Gallagher's complaints concerning Article 9(1): that the expulsion must not be carried out until considered by a 'competent authority' which must be distinct and independent from the original decision-taker, and which must allow for rights of defence, assistance and representation. Though McCullough J was of the view that Article 9(1) was satisfied by the adviser system, the Court of Appeal was troubled on both counts. The doubts concerning the independence of the adviser were not strong; the Court of Justice has ruled in other contexts that independence is not compromised by anonymity, by absence of security of tenure, or by payment by the administrative authority.[56] But whether the same logic extended to the feature of appointment by the administrative authority was a matter for referral. More worrying was the further procedural

safeguard in Article 9 which requires delay in execution until consideration by the independent authority. Under the PTA, an exclusion order is
made before an adviser is even selected, and the assignment will only happen in any event if requested by the excludee. There may be some excuses
for these PTA features. Article 9 does not demand these procedural
decencies 'in cases of urgency'; given that the suspect is often suffering
custody pending the outcome of the case and that advisers act on a
leisurely, part-time basis, there may be arguments that it is not practical to
delay the making of an order. A second response, adopted by Hirst LJ,
dissenting in *ex parte Gallagher*, is to interpret the exclusion order as in
reality provisional until confirmed by the Home Secretary after consideration by the adviser; in this way, it is the removal order which is final.

Whatever the resolution of these uncertainties, it is notable how
narrow has been the scope of attack under Article 48. Indeed,
Farquharson LJ viewed it as 'technical', while Hirst LJ thought it was so
'highly technical' as to be unworthy of inconveniencing the Court of
Justice. These views underestimate the potential benefits of due process
to a suspect. Nevertheless, it would not take much imagination to solve
any shortcomings. At worst, the Court of Justice may require the Home
Secretary's order to be expressly provisional and to be confirmed by an
adviser in every case. However, advisers almost always agree with the
Home Secretary and do not in any event elicit the explanations which
Stitt, O'Neill and Gallagher had sought.

Moving on from Article 48, the (Maastricht) Treaty on European
Union[57] may have transformed the legal battlefield between the Home
Office and excludees. The first challenger was Gerry Adams. Adams, a
resident of Northern Ireland, a dual citizen and the President of Sinn
Féin, was first excluded from Britain in 1982 but the order was lifted in
1983 when he was elected to the House of Commons. He visited Britain
several times between 1983 and 1992, when he lost his parliamentary
seat. In 1993, he accepted an invitation to speak at a conference in the
Parliament buildings. His host, Tony Benn, informed the Home
Secretary, and an exclusion order was issued the following day.
Representations to an adviser were to no avail, so legal action for judicial
review was undertaken. Rather than the limited economic rights under
the Treaty of Rome, Adams based his complaint on the more expansive
rights of all EU citizens to move and reside within member states, as
granted by Article 8a of the Treaty. Reliance upon Article 8a brought two
potential advantages.

First, its ringing declaration of a new citizenship seems to bypass limits
in relation to 'workers' or 'foreigners'. In the Divisional Court, Steyn LJ
was certainly sympathetic to such a broad purposive interpretation which
is also in line with views expressed by the Commission,[58] but the question

of whether Article 8a is more than declaratory of existing economic rights has been referred to the Court of Justice. In the later case of *ex parte Vitale*,[59] a differently constituted Divisional Court gave a clear signal to Portuguese and Italian income support claimants that Article 8a gave no open-ended right to enter and reside freely but had to be understood in the context of Article 48.

The second point is that the new basis of claim allows Adams to reopen the issue of limits to the rights under Article 8a, which vaguely mentions that it is 'subject to the limitations and conditions laid down in this Treaty and by measures adopted to give it effect'. In these changed circumstances, Adams raised two points. One was to attack the exclusion order as illegally based. No reasons for it had been expressed, and the circumstances could give rise to an inference that it was a politically motivated attempt to avoid embarrassment to the government arising from the disclosure of secret contacts prior to the Downing Street Declaration and to pay back Ulster Unionists, ironically, for their support in the House of Commons on the bill which implemented the Maastricht Treaty. In response, the Home Office affidavit asserted that security concerns alone were relevant and that Adams' planned visit had affected the timing but not the rationale. The Home Office could not call in aid any terrorist convictions and would not reveal any further evidence, but even Steyn LJ offered the hostile comment that 'It would be naive not to infer that [Adams] has at least substantial connections with the IRA.' Furthermore, Steyn LJ viewed Article 8a as potentially limited by Article 223(1)(a) of the Treaty of Rome: 'no Member State shall be obliged to supply information the disclosure of which it considers as contrary to the essential interests of its security'. In this light, the assertion of potential damage in the Home Office affidavit was sufficient reply to the duty to give reasons. However, it was felt that the evidence provided was a less convincing reply to allegations of disproportionality – that in the context of a short, well-publicized open visit, a three-year blanket ban seemed excessive. That issue was also referred to the Court of Justice, though the sensitivity of the information may have some bearing even at that stage.[60] Whether that Court ever responds to these issues remains to be seen. In the light of the revocation of the order against Adams, the High Court withdrew its references in April 1995, and so, subject to possible appeal, the case has ground to an unresolved halt.[61]

Taking stock at this point, the capacity of European laws and mechanisms as regulators of state powers has clearly increased substantially post-Maastricht and has done so in a way potentially less hidebound by technicality. Even so, as argued elsewhere,[62] the very role of the European Communities in the area of security and terrorism remains contentious. Amongst the arguments in favour of such a presence are:

the enforceability of necessary measures by the Luxembourg Court; the possibilities of consultation with, and greater accountability to, the European Parliament; and greater acceptability of pan-European laws by the public. Yet the implication that European judges would be more adventurous in handling security matters than English or Irish judges must be doubted. Further, the lack of strong commitment to European unity displayed during 1992 in countries such as Denmark, France and the UK must cast a shadow over the transfer of any new responsibility to a rather distant and distrusted polity, the writ of which would be fiercely resisted.[63]

European Convention Mechanisms

On the face of it, the Council of Europe appears to be a more promising vehicle for the governance of special powers. Its actual impact on the subject of terrorism is certainly more impressive than that of the European Communities. Thus, at a domestic level, there have been dozens of relevant applications under the European Convention on Human Rights (ECHR). Their influence in the UK has been both specific, in terms of modifying the design or operation of given measures,[64] and general in that the threat of adverse judgments has rendered politically unacceptable the more militaristic solutions to terrorism advocated by Unionists and so tempting to their Conservative sympathizers. The Council of Europe has also attained successes at a legislative and executive level, especially through the Convention on the Suppression of Terrorism of 1977 and the Convention for the Prevention of Torture.

Has this pan-European model of judicial rights review performed any better in relation to the governance of exclusion than the municipal judges so far considered? ECHR mechanisms certainly can overcome the most fundamental of the difficulties of English civil liberties jurisprudence – they dare to speak openly of rights and to base case law around them. But it is desirable to examine carefully the actual performance on this basis before being carried away by the rhetoric. Several articles of the ECHR relevant to exclusion have been cited before Strasbourg fora.

There are various ways in which rights to life and humane treatment, as required under Articles 2 and 3, could be jeopardized in connection with exclusion. One is the danger of excluded persons becoming targets for terrorists and potentially also victims of security force harassment. This complaint was raised in *ex parte McQuillan*. Following his exclusion in 1987, McQuillan had been the target of two assassination attempts by paramilitary groups, so he perceived that the effect of the exclusion had been 'to trap him . . . inhumanely'. The threats were accepted as 'real and continuing' by the Divisional Court, and the possible breach of the ECHR is probably a relevant consideration in assessing compliance with EU law. A response may be that the threats to life which prevail in Northern Ireland are not sufficiently serious and are not the responsibility of the state, and that, in any event, McQuillan is excluded from Britain rather than confined to Northern Ireland. These arguments await the decision of the Court of Justice and possibly later an application to the Commission on Human Rights. Aside from dangers to the excludee, one should also have regard to the dangers to the Northern Ireland populace from the potential activities of the excludee. If we take at face value the assertion by the Home Secretary that excludees are terrorists, why confine them to the area of the UK where the terrorists are most active and where they have the least chance of being prevented or detected in their dastardly acts? The answer is, of course, a political one – that the origins of the PTA lie in the protection of the British public and in the Ulsterization of the conflict.

The right to personal liberty under Article 5 seems to be less compromised by exclusion. Though no case from Northern Ireland has been decided on this basis, it is a conclusion which seems to flow from the Italian case of *Guzzardi*,[65] who was subjected to a special supervision order under Italian laws dealing with Mafiosi. For the first year of the period, the terms of the order required him to reside apart from his family within a small area of the island of Asinara, off the north-west of Sardinia, and there to report to the police and to observe a curfew. The applicant described the island as a 'concentration camp'. The European Court of Human Rights concluded that these conditions could amount to a deprivation of liberty and could not find any element of Article 5(1) to justify the detention. However, it is unlikely that a similar result could flow from exclusion to Northern Ireland or the Republic. The essential differences concern, first, the degree of confinement in terms of geographical area. Northern Ireland is a much larger territory, and it should also be noted that there is no objection to excludees leaving Northern Ireland for any destination in the world except Britain. The second difference concerns supervision of excludees within Northern Ireland. They are not required to report to the police, live in a specific place or observe other restrictions. In summary, it is most unlikely that exclusion can amount to a deprivation of liberty in the sense of Article 5. However, it is strongly arguable that any detention pending the making of an order violates Article 5 (unless for a very short time).[66]

Obviously, exclusion orders have an adverse effect on family relations and friendships and chances of employment, all of which are relevant to Article 8. Two cases have arisen on this basis. In *Richard Daniel Ryan* v. *UK*,[67] the applicant was an Irish citizen who had been excluded in 1975 from the whole of the UK after some decades' worth of residence in Britain. During his British sojourn, his family had expanded by the birth of seven children, at least four of whom continued to reside in Britain plus one in Northern Ireland. One was out of contact altogether, and another two resided in Dublin (the youngest, aged 17 in 1980, with the applicant), which is where the applicant himself had relocated. The applicant complained of disruption to his family life. It became impossible for him to visit the children remaining in Britain, two of whom had married and produced grandchildren who the applicant had never seen. Assuming that mature and independent children could be said to be part of the applicant's family life, which the Commission doubted, his complaint was answered by the observation that 'it has not been established that any substantial obstacle exists to prevent them [the children] from maintaining that relationship by visiting the applicant in Ireland'.[68] This seems to follow logically from the refusal to recognize a right to reside in a foreign country.[69]

The second case concerning Article 8 involved Michael Joseph Mooney.[70] Mooney, a citizen of the UK, was released from prison in 1984, having served 9 years of a 12-year sentence for conspiracy to cause explosions in Birmingham. He was excluded from Britain but seems to have elected to be removed to Dublin, where his parents resided. One effect of the exclusion was that contact with family members in Britain, with whom he had forged close links whilst in prison, was broken. The Commission was rather less convinced of the strength of this complaint as compared with *Ryan*. There was little evidence of the strength of the links in Britain, and it was equally clear that his family links with Dublin were substantial. Thus, it will be difficult to establish a case under Article 8(1). Only if family contacts are made practically impossible will exclusion breach Article 8. Even then, the exceptions under Article 8(2) come into play, and public security and the prevention of crime might well be invoked successfully in those circumstances.

Moving on to Article 6, it must be accepted that the system of advisers is farcical as a process of independent justice. Many excludees are put off applying in the first place by the nature of the mechanism, and those who do apply are usually bemused by the focus of the inquiry (often in terms of friends and contacts rather than activities) and the refusal to divulge details against them. Hunt and Dickson believe there may be a breach of Article 6,[71] but they rightly cast doubt on the applicability of Article 6 to a process which may not be interpreted as affecting 'civil rights and obligations' or as determining a criminal charge.

Article 6 was pleaded in *Guzzardi* and *Mooney*. In *Guzzardi*, the Court determined that the proceedings did not involve the 'determination . . . of a criminal charge',[72] nor did they directly affect civil rights and obligations. In any event, there was oversight by judicial procedures sufficient to satisfy Article 6. Mooney's complaints of procedural injustice were again met with the response that no criminal proceeding or penalty was at stake. The reasoning was that exclusion was essentially a preventive security measure rather than a condemnatory judgment. However, given that for the purposes of Article 5 security actions against 'terrorism' have been presented as akin to actions against suspected crimes,[73] one has the feeling that the usual indulgence of the Commission and Court in respect of counter-terrorism measures is at work here.[74]

One of the more common occasions in recent years for the imposition of a wholly new exclusion order (as opposed to the renewal of an existing one) is the release from prison of a person who has served a sentence for a serious terrorist-type offence. There are also instances of orders being applied against those acquitted of such offences – the *Winchester 3*,[75] John Matthews[76] and Kevin O'Donnell[77] are such instances. Mooney likewise fell into the first category, and one of his complaints was that he was thereby the victim of a retrospective penalty, contrary to Article 7. The answer of the European Commission was identical to that under Article 6 – exclusion is about the prevention of terrorism, not the punishment of crime. Mooney lodged further complaints that the exclusion restricted his freedom of conscience or religion contrary to Article 9 in that he had been excluded because of his Republican beliefs. This argument was also rejected. It is not a legitimate belief to concur with terrorism, which was the official justification for his exclusion. The case of *Adams* may also raise issues about freedom of expression under Article 10. But given the nature of the organization for which he speaks and given the antipathy shown toward it in *Purcell* v. *Ireland*[78] and *Brind* v. *UK*,[79] that argument will probably also fail to impress.

In conclusion, intervention by the Council of Europe remains an attractive form of rights audit, as might be expected from a system based explicitly upon the prime value of individual rights, both procedural and substantive.[80] In addition, the system arguably raises fewer hackles in connection with national sovereignty. Yet this tolerance can only be secured because the ECHR enforces only a lowest common denominator rather than an intrusive standard. For instance, it does not itself include freedom of movement, which is relegated to Article 4 of Protocol 4 and is still awaiting signature by the UK. It is often assumed that ratification of that Protocol by the UK would be fatal to exclusion orders (and a great deal of immigration legislation to boot). However, a system of police supervision was recently found by the European Court of Human Rights not to breach Article 4 of Protocol 4 in *Raimondo* v. *Italy*.[81] If Mafia-type activities justified proportionate restrictions on grounds of maintenance of *ordre public* and the prevention of crime, then less intrusive exclusion orders might likewise escape condemnation. Thus, it is as well to remember that even within Articles of the ECHR which have been ratified, there are 'gaping exceptions', [82] especially in Articles 8 and 10.

Another factor which limits the influence of the ECHR is that there is, as already mentioned, a special indulgence conferred by the Court, in terms redolent of the British passion for security, on contracting states assailed by terrorism. The 'margin of appreciation' allowed to states may well widen in the coming years in the context of the knocks at the Strasbourg door from eastern Europe, where a less interventionist Court may wish to encourage attainable standards rather than risk disenchantment. Furthermore, there is always the safety valve of derogation under Article 15, which currently moderates the impact of Article 5 in the UK. The readiness of the UK government to resort to derogation is apparent.[83] Equally apparent is the readiness of the European Court to accept the need for every derogation, especially if questioned by a private individual rather than another state.[84] For example, in *Brannigan and McBride* v. *UK*[85] the notion of margin of appreciation seemingly answered all questions about the nature and timing of the UK response to the emergency, the existence of which was not seriously in doubt. The result was the thinnest judgment in recent times on the existence of an emergency. The treatment of emergencies has always been problematical in international law,[86] and, incidentally, it is far from evident why domestic review, which is closer to the feelings of crisis, would fare any better. Most proponents of a domestic bill of rights concede the notion of a derogation in given circumstances. But whether directly in the hands of judges or not, derogation or a claim of emergency will very much shape the outlook and parameters of any judgment in the security field. In any event, as pointed out by Gearty,[87] judicial review, whether international or domestic, tends to be most sure-footed, firm and convincing when it is confined to due process concerns for procedural fairness and participation rather than questions of a substantive nature, such as whether an emergency exists or not.

There are also procedural deficiencies to contemplate. Both the process and the outcome of ECHR litigation are often most unsatisfactory for the individual applicant who is seeking to vindicate rights claims. There are obvious problems with the time delay and possible expense. There is the fact that they may be treated unsympathetically even if they win – McVeigh, Fox and Brogan were all denied compensation. And there is the fundamental problem of trying to pour into the singular facts of an individual application the concerns of a wider audience. This may be too heavy a burden for an individual to bear and may also adversely affect those aspirants whose cases are yet to be decided. The impact of adverse judgments, which can set in stone a repressive measure and be used as a source of state intransigence, should not be forgotten by pressure groups sometimes too ready to seek the limelight with hopeless causes.

The judicial mechanisms of the ECHR cannot hope alone to transform the scenery of the application of special powers, whether exclusion or otherwise, under the PTA. The realistic role of the ECHR is not, then, to provide dramatic breakthroughs in individual cases, leading to major legal revisions. Its more effective constitutional role in terrorist issues is ideological – providing standards and reminders when rights are wholly ignored or expressly breached and mobilizing the rights agenda not just through courts but through all the corridors of power. In the light of this assessment, it might be asked whether the incorporation of the ECHR into English law would have made much difference to cases like *Adams* and *McQuillan*. Aside from the inherent limitations and deficiencies already adduced, the prospects for major revisions in English judicial thinking prompted by such a change alone do not seem bright. One reason for pessimism is the emerging line of judicial thought that this unavailing document called the ECHR was dreamed up by British civil servants to reflect English common law. There is some historical truth in this assertion,[88] and the House of Lords in particular has seized upon it as an excuse, *inter alia*, to reject the line of thinking first noticeable in Australia and New Zealand[89] and now espoused by some academics[90] and even some judges[91] that true believers in common law rights and the rule of law ought to take rights much more seriously as a matter of domestic law. Therefore, one should not assume that the jurisprudence and judicial attitudes prevalent under the US Constitution would be replicated solely as a result of incorporation of the ECHR and without regard for other constitutional features of the USA, such as the separation of powers, federalism and the general distrust of government and belief in law as an impartial arbiter. Finally, and to come back to the start of this chapter, the persistent concern about terrorism and the emotions it arouses will mean that the executive will not be as readily taken to task as it might be in other areas of rights litigation. The evidence from the cases discussed is that this observation applies as much in the context of the European Court of Human Rights as it does in the English High Court.

EXECUTIVE AND LEGISLATIVE GOVERNANCE OF SPECIAL POWERS

Lawyerly and judicial interventions do not exhaust even the repertoire of rights auditors and address far less comprehensively the principles of democratic accountability and constitutionalism. Consequently, one should look to other checks, particularly internal and external executive review, scrutiny by Parliament, and the voicing of public opinion. In this way 'We have the responsibility to ensure that our executive, legislative and judicial branches function responsibly.'[92]

Executive Governance

Though internal government scrutiny would be timely and least disruptive, it is unlikely that the government will internally keep an effective check on its own security apparatus or that the public will trust it to do so.[93] Turning, then, to externally sited reviews, the mechanism which immediately hoves into view is the system of representations to advisers under the PTA itself. There are a number of reasons why this system has not inspired confidence, some of which have been outlined already. These include the method of appointment and choice of personnel. Though most have been lawyers and though they are paid as if Crown Court Recorders,[94] no holders of high judicial office have been selected and their appointment by the Home Office lacks any form of security. An even greater obstacle to the inspiration of confidence in the system is that there can be no effective investigation of the case against the excludee. The advisers themselves have no investigative facilities and, aside from a possible live interview with an excludee who is given no idea of the incriminating evidence to be explained away, usually attempt no more than to second-guess papers prepared by the security services, police and Home Office. Despite all these constraints, it must be conceded that the advisers are having an increasing impact on the issuance of orders. Thus, their recommendations have accounted for revocations in about a third of cases referred to them, but the main reason for the growing impact is not increased stringency on their part but the fact that many more (up to 50 per cent) excludees now choose to avail themselves of the opportunity to make representations because of more generous time limits enacted in 1984.[95]

Arguably, the most important of all the outside review mechanisms, including judicial varieties, are the periodical reviews which have been performed to date by Lord Shackleton, Viscount Jellicoe and Lord Colville. Doubts may again be raised concerning the remit of these reviews[96] and even the personal competencies of the reviewers. Few have given any deep thought to issues of principle or structural reform, but have instead proceeded with vague notions of balancing both effectiveness and rights. In addition, they almost always are handicapped by the assumption that special powers are necessary and thereby that normal laws are inadequate or cannot be adapted. Their evidence-gathering is far from perfect. When it is available, the most influential information arrives in secret from security forces – there is no open debate or exchange, even as to what legislative changes they are urging. And the manner of publication of the reviews is hardly calculated to capture public attention. But whatever their shortcomings, they have occasionally produced some radical reforms and suggestions, including the abolition of exclusion.

The tide began to flow against exclusion with Sir Cyril Philips' Annual Report for 1985, wherein he noted that the use of exclusion was declining, that coordination between British and Irish police forces had improved, and that English forces had increased powers under the Police and Criminal Evidence Act 1984 to deal with suspects *in situ*. Thus, he cautiously suggested a moratorium on new orders against British citizens.[97] Viscount Colville adopted the even more radical stance in his Report on the Operation of the PTA for 1986 that exclusion be dropped in the light of the intelligence capabilities of the police in proportion to the more moderate level of political violence then prevalent.[98] An even bolder tone was evident in his principal report on the PTA in 1987, in which he refuted the Home Secretary's announcement earlier that year not to discontinue exclusion: 'the alternative is a hard decision, but I express the view that it would be the correct one both in terms of civil rights in the United Kingdom and this country's reputation in that respect among the International Community'.[99] In response, the government agreed that exclusion should be the first part of the Act to lapse,[100] but this is not likely to happen until the declining level of extant orders renders police surveillance of suspects a viable option. Whilst not 'remotely realistic' in early 1994,[101] there now is a growing prospect of the demise of exclusion in the light of further withdrawals of orders and the political difficulties which would be entailed by the issuance of new orders.

In summary, the tailored review mechanisms connected with the PTA have delivered useful, though often rather technical, alterations, which should be credited in terms of an audit of the protection of rights. For example, changes to the residence exemption period in respect of exclusion is certainly a worthy achievement. However, this ability to ameliorate falls short of fundamental change. It is also noticeable that the focus of the reviews has mostly been in the direction of the treatment of rights, so the broader issues of democratic accountability and constitutionalism remain unattended.

As to what would be in outline an effective executive internal review system, some of the following features should be included. The first concerns the personnel conducting the review. There is a periodic need for an infusion of new blood into the process. Those who stay seem to become complacent or discouraged. Officially presented versions of reality tend eventually to become persuasive or at least immutable. This feature might best be achieved by the appointment of a panel so that difficulties caused by the inexperience of new members can be minimized. Second, the review must be principled. If the reviewers themselves show no inclination to devise clear principles on which to proceed, then the legislature should set the necessary standards. Third, the review must be adequately resourced. The PTA is now a multi-faceted piece of legislation whose complexity and range have grown enormously over two decades. Effective review can only be achieved by individuals working full-time and continuously. Resourcing also entails express statutory powers, akin to those of the Parliamentary Commissioner for Administration, to be able to look behind the presented papers into filing cabinets and desks and to be able to interrogate members of the police and security services and not just hapless excludees. Fourth, reviews must be more firmly linked with the legislature so as to encourage democratic accountability. This feature requires the clearer dissemination of information by the reviewers so as to facilitate reasoned debate and to engage its attention in a constructive manner. There is also a gap in structural linkage. This relationship has been neglected by the PTA reviewers and is not even a feature of the more independent and permanent Standing Advisory Commission on Human Rights in Northern Ireland, despite its firmer statutory existence.

Governance by Parliament

The last point brings us to the role and performance of the legislature itself in regard to the PTA. It would be wrong to suppose that exclusion has escaped review from all non-judicial sources. Indeed, it is difficult to disagree with the *cri de coeur* uttered by the Home Secretary Michael Howard during the 1994 renewal of the PTA that it is 'just about the most reviewed legislation on the statute book'.[102] This sustained and repeated exposure to scrutiny is important. Almost any system, whether based on a judicially reviewable constitution or on British parliamentary sovereignty, can temporarily lose its nerves and its principles, no matter what safeguards exist on paper. After all, it has happened in the USA, for example in dealing with Japanese–Americans during World War II. This experience led retired Supreme Court Justice Brennan recently to comment that:

> Prolonged and sustained exposure to the asserted security claims may be the only way in which a country may gain both the

discipline necessary to examine asserted security risks critically and the expertise necessary to distinguish the bona fide from the bogus.[103]

Yet, despite a considerable investment of time, Parliament has been somewhat ineffectual in tackling emergency laws. This may be symptomatic of a wider malaise, but it seems particularly marked and serious in the case of emergency legislation. It is also in a sense a surprising failure. There is a widespread and not unfair view that the PTA is in significant part political legislation for political show as much as a matter of reform of police powers or criminal procedure. But if critics and commentators analyse the PTA as serving political purposes, then one cannot hope to mould it without political discourse or strategies. This observation points to the judiciary, either in London, Luxembourg or Strasbourg, as being rather peripheral players and further suggests that we should be focusing our attention on review and control mechanisms within the political process rather than outside it. This does not imply that the judges are apolitical, but only that there exist more obvious and powerful lions on the throne than under it. So, the quiescence of the legislature is perhaps of more pressing concern than the unfulfilled but limited role of the judiciary.[104]

In fact there is a great deal of opposition to the PTA within Parliament on both sides of the political divide. The problem at present is that our political mechanisms only allow that opposition to be expressed within a very partisan and confrontational context, in other words mainly within the Commons chamber. We need to be more inventive about the circumstances of public debate and about the monolithic structure of the Act. It would then be politically more feasible to express reasoned opposition to the Act and to allow lapses of it in part.[105] What sort of reforms might achieve such democratic accountability?

The first goal is to make the debate more principled and informed and less emotional. This process could be developed by stating more explicitly some of the desirable limiting principles adduced earlier. For each part of the special powers Act there should be expressed criteria by which to judge its value or dispensability. It follows that each part of the Act should be considered and voted on distinctly, a feature which was vaguely promised in 1984 but was then never delivered.[106]

Second, there should be a permanent investigative standing committee to replace the annual reviews by Colville *et al*. Such a body would be able to keep the legislation under constant scrutiny, would be more accessible to outside representations than moonlighting reviewers and would be less politically oriented than a parliamentary committee. However, the pronouncements of this body must not simply gather dust or be overridden by diktat, which is arguably the fate of the existing reviewers and the Standing Advisory Commission on Human Rights. So, its reports should be referred not only to the Home Secretary but also to a select committee, such as the Home Affairs Committee (or perhaps a security-vetted subcommittee attached to it) which could give further prominence and support to any proposals and in this way internalize them within the parliamentary system. Next is the issue of how to engage the attention of the Commons Chamber. After all, most select committee reports are ignored. It is equally vital to avoid an arid exchange of partisan insults on the renewal debate. The suggestion here is to adopt the precedent of the Boundary Commission procedure, by which the Home Secretary is obliged to lay the committee's report together with a draft renewal order.[107] Indeed, one could strengthen this model by requiring an Order which reflects the Committee's desires as well as any alternative, Home Office-designed Order.

A final, more controversial point, is to make the Act as comprehensive as possible, in order that all provisions are fully examined and debated *ab initio*. This avoids the danger that if existing political violence changes its form or intensity, the present legislation will be viewed as irrelevant, so new measures will be rushed through Parliament on the basis of 'the politics of the last atrocity', thereby repeating all the mistakes made in 1974. Models of this type include the Emergencies Act 1988 in Canada and New Zealand's International Terrorism (Emergency Powers) Act 1987 and Defence Act 1990. Other proposed mechanisms should guard against the common criticism of such an approach, which is that it normalizes the extraordinary.

The model of a permanent legislative code reflects the philosophy of constitutionalism – the legislature can secure an important input if it can speak in advance in a way which cannot be drowned by the screams of a crisis. This observation has relevance to the current peace process. In the light of the Downing Street Declaration of 1993,[108] the configuration of the emergency laws will eventually become part of the negotiation process. An immediate response might be that special emergency regimes are inevitably nasty, brutish and rather uncertain in effect, so the opportunity of peace should be the occasion for the wholesale dismantling of such laws, especially if they are practically redundant. However, this first reaction may well turn out to be facile. There is ample evidence to suggest that governments of wholly different complexions will, in a tight corner, wish to resort to much the same measures and react in much the same ways.[109] Thus, if the legal field is left unattended, the power elite will very soon fill it with architecture which, in the circumstances of an emergency, will be rather ugly. As argued elsewhere,[110] one cannot coherently complain about 'panic' legislation but at the same time deny to the state the refined means to defend itself and allay its genuine fears (and often those of the majority of the general public). Is it foolish not to plan for contingencies in this way, especially as the planning process can allow the legislature to have its say? Questions will then properly arise as to the dangers inherent in such a code of special laws. It might be said that it will become moribund, since 'the exact powers thought to be needed to deal with subversion will therefore always be highly particular'.[111] Yet studies of emergency measures in history or across jurisdictions tend to reveal the repetition of constant themes, suggesting that the tailoring of countermeasures is more a matter of degree than of design. In any event, even if all emergencies are historically and politically unique, the demand of this chapter is for the response of the state always to be tempered by adherence to universal, transcendental principles. Another danger to be considered is that the special code will seep dangerously into 'normal' laws. This is a real possibility which has happened in reality,[112] but seepage is arguably more tempting with an emergency model which may not always be available in any circumstances. Whether a code of special powers would be in force in whole or part after a cease-fire or peace settlement would be doubtful, but the availability of such powers might paradoxically make the slippage into disuse less traumatic.

Pressure Groups

It is an uphill struggle for civil liberties groups who espouse the cause of those subjected to the PTA. Public pressures and sympathies are firmly in the opposite direction. As a result, it cannot be claimed that they have achieved any significant impact on the shaping or administration of the legislation. Relevant activities by groups such as Amnesty International, the Committee on the Administration of Justice and Liberty mainly cover three aspects. First, litigation has been sponsored, especially by Liberty, which is involved in the *Adams* case. Second, there have been occasional reports and reviews.[113] Third, there has been the lobbying and briefing of MPs, especially at times of review or renewal of the PTA. No doubt all this work is valuable in its own way, but the indication from this chapter is that the emphasis should be on the political and legislative connections, especially in the context of a reformed scrutiny system. This reform might in turn empower a participatory public to a much greater degree than at present.

CONCLUSION

The message in this chapter in response to concerns about the incursions

of special powers on rights, democratic accountability and constitutionalism is that all branches of the state have a role to play in the governance
of special powers. Miscarriages of justice in narrow and broad senses[114]
can arise when one branch of the state, whether police, Home Secretary
or judges, becomes unchecked, as the separation of powers doctrine constantly warns us. This combination of ideological pressure, executive and
legislative review and the occasional court decision can have an impact.
After all, deep interrogation and brutality and perhaps also the supergrass system, to take two examples, were moderated not because of army
or police doubts about their worth but because of concern expressed in
Parliament, by pressure groups and, later, by national and international
courts about the erosion of principles such as the rule of law. Looking at
the PTA, one may count amongst successes of this multi-pronged attack
the stronger safeguards as to treatment under s. 14, including tape-
recording, greater access to solicitors in Northern Ireland and outside
inspection in the holding centres. A lesson may also be learnt from the
pressure on the Irish broadcasting ban, which lapsed in 1994, while the
UK broadcasting ban stumbled on aimlessly for a few months longer.
Perhaps an important difference was the requirement to defend it not
only in the national[115] and international courts[116] (none of which proved
burdensome for the Dublin government) but also in the Oireachtas. It is
true that the order was never specifically debated, but the pending acri-
mony planned for the 1994 debate must have added to the pressure to
take free speech seriously. In short, special powers arise in part for political reasons and operate within a political milieu. The overriding impact
of politics apply as much to exclusion as to any other power, the treatment of Gerry Adams being a paradigm case. An order which the Prime
Minister said could not be lifted in September 1994 was duly lifted in
October 1994, and Adams entered one of the citadels of the state, the
Palace of Westminster, in November 1994.[117] What had changed was not
Gerry Adams, his views, or his alleged links with the IRA. Indeed, it is
those links with the IRA that made his presence desirable, as the political
process of unravelling the mystification and demonization of Republican
politics begins to be contemplated.

There is receptivity to the agenda of liberal rights, accountability and
constitutionalism, whether through sympathy with it or fear of its clout.
Its voice should be loud, but lawyers and campaigners must not expect
judges and the legal system to do all the shouting. Special powers arise
from political circumstances, and it is the political system which will
ultimately decide their fate.[118]

NOTES

1. P. Hillyard, *Suspect Community* (London: Pluto Press, 1993), p. 262.

2. *Ibid.*, pp. 67, 88, 290.

3. P. Wilkinson, Review of the prevention of terrorism in British law (1987) 7 *Legal Studies* 236.

4. See C. Walker, Irish Republican prisoners: political detainees, prisoners of war or common criminals? (1984) 19 *Irish Jurist* 189.

5. J. R. Chowdhury, *Rule of Law in a State of Emergency* (London: Pinter, 1989), p. 9.

6. See C. Walker and R. L. Weaver, A peace deal for Northern Ireland? The Downing Street Declaration (1994) 8(2) *Emory International Law Review* 817.

7. MI5 has won a major battle to take the lead in intelligence-gathering: HC Debs, Vol. 207, cols. 297–298, 8 May 1992.

8. See C. Walker, *The Prevention of Terrorism in British Law*, 2nd edn (Manchester: Manchester University Press, 1992), pp. 24–5.

9. See J. E. Finn, *Constitutions in Crisis* (Oxford: Oxford University Press, 1991), p. 30.

10. G. Hogan and G. Whyte, *Kelly's The Irish Constitution*, 3rd edn (London: Butterworths, 1994).

11. HC Debs, Vol. 239, col. 301, 9 March 1994, Mr T. Blair.

12. See C. Warbrick, The ECHR and the prevention of terrorism (1983) 32 *International and Comparative Law Quarterly* 82; The PTA 1976 and the ECHR (1983) 32 *International and Comparative Law Quarterly*, 757; P. Hunt and B. Dickson, Northern Ireland's emergency laws and international human rights (1993) 2 *Neths Quarterly on Human Rights* 173.

13. See C. Walker, *op. cit.*, note 8, Chapter 6; G. Hogan and C. P. Walker, *Political Violence and the Law in Ireland* (Manchester: Manchester University Press, 1989), p. 96.

14. HC Debs, Vol. 110, col. 267, 10 February 1987, Mr Hurd.

15. Sched. 2, para. 2(1).

16. Sched. 2, para. 2.

17. (1994) *Independent*, 23 September.

18. Sched. 2, para. 3(6).

19. Sched. 2, para. 4.

20. Sched. 2, para. 4(3).

21. Sources: Statistical bulletins from the Home Office and the Northern Ireland Office, 1979–1994.

22. P. Wilkinson, British policy on terrorism. In J. Lodge, *The Threat of Terrorism* (Brighton: Wheatsheaf Books, 1988), p. 45.

23. *Review of the Operation of the PTA 1976* (the Jellicoe Report) (Cmnd. 8803, 1983), para. 176; *Review of the Operation of the PTA 1974 and 1976* (the Shackleton Report) (Cmnd. 7324, 1978), para. 130.

24. Jellicoe Report, para. 176.

25. Shackleton Report, para. 115.

26. Home Office Circular 27/1989, para. 2.8.

27. HC Debs, Standing Committee D col. 143, 15 November 1983, Mr L. Brittan.

28. Shackleton Report, para. 50.

29. *Review of the Operation of the PTA 1984* (the Colville Report) (Cmnd. 264, 1978), para. 11.4.1.

30. HC Debs. Standing Committee B col. 100, 15 December 1988, Mr Mallon.

31. *The Times* 3 February 1987 (QBD), reported fully on LEXIS from which all quotes are taken.

32. H. W. R. Wade and C. F. Forsyth, *Administrative Law* 7th edn, (Oxford: Clarendon Press, 1994), p. 726.

33. [1991] 2 All ER 319.

34. See his Annual Report for 1992 (1993), para. 2.1.7..

35. (1992) LEXIS.

36. (1992) QBD, *The Times* 16 February 1994, CA, LEXIS.

37. Sched. 2, para. 3.

38. (1972) 23 *Northern Ireland Legal Quarterly* 173.

39. Shackleton Report, para. 52, quoted with approval in *ex horte Stitt, op. cit.*

40. *Independent* 23 September 1994, LEXIS.

41. See A. Bradley, *Public Interest Certificates* (British Irish Rights Watch, 1993).

42. See A. Tomkins, Public interest immunity certificates after Matrix Churchill [1993] *Public Law* 650.

43. *Re Mackay, op cit.*

44. *R* v. *Secretary of State for the Home Department, ex parte NSH, The Times* 24 March 1988.

45. *Malone* v. *MPC (no. 2)* [1979] Chapter 344.

46. *R* v. *Secretary of State for the Home Department ex p. Brind* [1991] 1 AC 696.

47. Lord McCluskey, *Law, Justice and Democracy* (London: Sweet and Maxwell, 1986), p. 5.

48. See S. Livingstone, The House of Lords and the Northern Ireland conflict (1994) 57 *Modern Law Review* 333.

49. This is further explained by Directive 64/221.

50. T. C. Hartley, *EEC Immigration Law* (Amsterdam: North-Holland, 1978), p. 232.

51. The application of ss. 5 and 6 to Irish citizens could be discriminatory, since the three-year residence exception does not apply: T. C. Hartley, *op. cit.*, pp. 232–3. In practice, s. 7 is always invoked.

52. *R* v. *Saunders* [1979] 3 WLR 359; *Re the Habeas Corpus Application of Narinder Singh Virdee* [1980] 1 CMLR 709; *R* v. *Governor of Pentonville Prison, ex p. Healy* [1984] 3 CMLR 575; *Moser* v. *Land Baden-Wurttenburg* [1984] ECR 2539; *R* v. *IAT, ex p. Aradi* [1987] Imm. AR 359.

53. *The Times* 10 August 1994, Div. Ct., LEXIS. A further argument based on the interference with Adams' right to deliver or receive inter-state services could involve a similar response but was actually peremptorily dismissed on the more dubious ground that Adams' political visit was not the delivery of services nor was his hotel booking any more than incidental to it.

54. *Gullung* v. *Conseil des Avocats du Barreau de Colmar* [1988] ECR 111; *Micheletti* v. *Government of Cantabria*, C369/90.

55. The point was firmly dismissed in *ex p. Gallagher, op. cit.*

56. *Adoui* v. *Belgian State and City of Liege* [1982] 2 ECR 1661.

57. See Cm. 1934, 1992; European Communities (Amendment) Act 1993.

58. *Report on the Citizenship of the Union* (COM(93)702).

59. *The Times* 18 April 1995.

60. Compare *Johnston* v. *Chief Constable of the RUC* [1986] ECR 1651.

61. *Irish Times* 13 April 1995, p. 7.

62. Review of A. Vercher, *Terrorism in Europe: An International and Comparative Legal Analysis*, (Oxford: Clarendon Press, 1992), (1993) 13 *Legal Studies* 415.

63. See *Fire Safety and Policing of the Channel Tunnel* (Cm. 1853, 1992); C. Walker, *op. cit.* note 8, Chapter 9; Sir L. Brittan, 1992 and the common man (1992) 86 (34) *Law Society Gazette* 39.

64. Examples include the judgement in *McVeigh, O'Neill and Evans* v. *UK*, Appl. nos. 8022, 8023, 8027/77, DR 25, p. 15 (which affected practices in relation to notification to relatives of detainees) and support in the Baker Report (Review of the Operation of the Northern Ireland (Emergency Provisions) Act 1978, Cmnd. 9222, 1984) for the introduction of a reasonable suspicion criterion into the exercise of most special powers.

65. Appl. no. 7367/76, Ser. A, no. 39.

66. *X and Y* v. *Sweden*, Appl. no. 7376/76, DR 7, p. 123.

67. Appl. no. 9202/80.

68. *Ibid.*, p. 4.

69. *De Becker* v. *Belgium*, Appl. no. 214/56, Ser. A 4; *X* v. *UK*, Appl. no. 3325/67, 10 YBEC 528. But see *Bonzano* v. *France*, Appl. no. 9990/82, Ser. A, no. 111.

70. Appl. no. 11517/85.

71. P. Hunt and B. Dickson, *op. cit.*, p. 182.

72. *Op. cit.*, note 65, para. 108.

73. *Ireland* v. *UK*, Appl. no. 5310/71, Ser. A, no. 25, para. 196; *Brogan* v. *UK*, Appl. nos. 11209, 11234, 11266/84, 11386/85, Ser. A, 145–B, para. 50.

74. See especially *Brogan* v. *UK* (1989) 11 European Human Rights Reports 117; *Fox,*

Campbell and Hartley v. *UK*, Application nos. 12244, 12245, 12383/86, Ser. A 182, para. 28; *Murray* v. *UK*, Application no. 14310/88, Ser. A 300, para. 47.

75. See *R* v. *Shanahan, McCann and Cullen*, *The Times* 1 May 1990.

76. F. Russell, Keeping terrorists out (1993) 137 *Solicitors' Journal* 732.

77. *The Times* 7 March 1991, p. 3.

78. Appl. no. 15404/89.

79. Application no. 18714/91.

80. Compare J. Bengoetxea and H. Jung, Towards a European criminal jurisprudence? (1991) 11 *Legal Studies* 293; C. Gearty, The European Court of Human Rights and the protection of civil liberties (1992) 52 *Cambridge Law Journal* 89. Specific substantive standards were set in *Brogan* and *Brind*.

81. Appl. no. 12954/87, Ser. A 281–A, 1994. The Protocol had not been ratified by Italy at the time of *Guzzardi*.

82. R. L. Weaver and G. Bennett, The Northern Ireland broadcasting ban (1989) 22 *Vanderbilt Journal of Transnational Law* 1119, at p. 1132.

83. Since 1968 in connection with terrorism in Northern Ireland, see: 12 YBEC 72 (1969), 14 YBEC 32 (1971), 16 YBEC 24 (1973), 18 YBEC 18 (1975), 21 YBEC 22 (1978). Derogation was lifted in 1984 but was reimposed in December 1988: DH (89) 1 (Def) 10. The other country with a comparable history is Turkey, which currently derogates under Article 5: DH (92) 5.

84. The existence of an emergency was not disputed in *Ireland* v. *UK*, *op. cit.*

85. Appl. nos. 14553–4/89, Vol. 258–B, 1993.

86. S. Oraa, *Human Rights in States of Emergency in International Law* (Oxford: Clarendon Press, 1992).

87. *Op. cit.*

88. A. Lester, Fundamental rights [1984] *Public Law* 46.

89. See K. Ewing, New constitutional constraints in Australia [1993] *Public Law* 250.

90. T. R. S. Allan, *Law, Liberty and Justice* (Oxford: Clarendon Press, 1993). See also J. W. Harris, Privy Council and common law (1990) 106 *Law Quarterly Review* 574.

91. Compare N. Browne-Wilkinson, The infiltration of a Bill of Rights [1992] *Public Law* 397; J. Laws, Is the High Court the guardian of fundamental constitutional rights? [1993] *Public Law* 59; Judicial remedies and the constitution (1993) 57 *Modern Law Review* 213; T. Bingham, The ECHR: time to incorporate (1993) 109 *Law Quarterly Review* 390.

92. C. Blakesley, Terrorism, law and our constitutional order (1989) 60 *University of Colorado Law Review* 471 at p. 501.

93. O. Lomas, The executive and anti-terrorist legislation of 1939 [1980] *Public Law* 16.

94. HC Debs. Vol. 143 cols 281–282, 6 December 1988.

95. C. Walker, *op. cit.*, note 8, p. 76.

96. *Ibid.*, p. 37.

97. Para. 21. The idea derived from the phasing out of expulsion orders under the Prevention of Violence (TP) Act 1939.

98. Para. 2.3.6.

99. Cm. 264, 1987, para. 11.6.1.

100. HC Debs, Vol. 92, col. 434, 19 February 1986, Mr D. Waddington.

101. HC Debs, Vol. 239, col. 299, 9 March 1994, Mr M. Howard.

102. HC Debs, Vol. 239, col. 293, 9 March 1994.

103. J. Brennan, The American experience. In S. Shetreet, *Free Speech and National Security* (Dordrecht: Nijhoff, 1991).

104. See N. Stammers, *Civil Liberties in Britain during the Second World War* (London: Croom Helm, 1983); P. Hillyard, The normalisation of special powers. In P. Scraton (ed.), *Law, Order and the Authoritarian State* (Milton Keynes: Open University Press, 1987), p. 307.

105. C. Walker, *op. cit.*, note 8.

106. *Ibid.*, p. 36.

107. Constituencies Act 1986, ss. 3, 4.

108. C. P. Walker and R. L. Weaver, A peace deal for Northern Ireland? (1994) 8 *Emory International Law Review* 817.

109. C. Walker, *op. cit.*, note 8, Chapter 13.

110. *Ibid.*

111. C. A. Gearty and J. A. Kimbell, *Terrorism and the Rule of Law* (London: King's College, 1995), p. 65.

112. Perhaps the most startling example is the application in Ireland of the Offences against the State Act 1939: see G. Hogan and C. P. Walker, *op. cit.*

113. See, for example, Amnesty International, *Northern Ireland: Killings by Security Forces and Supergrass Trials* (London, 1988); Committee for the Administration of Justice, *Civil Liberties in Northern Ireland* (Belfast, 1993). Other significant groups in the field are British Irish Rights Watch, The Haldane Society of Socialist Lawyers and JUSTICE.

114. See C. Walker and K. Starmer, *Justice in Error* (London: Blackstone, 1993), Chapter 1; S. Greer, Miscarriages of justice reconsidered (1993) 57 *Modern Law Review* 58.

115. *State (Lynch) v. Cooney* [1982] IR 337; *O'Toole v. RTE (no. 2)* (1993) 13 ILRM 458; *Brandon Books Publishers v. RTE* (1993) 13 ILRM 806.

116. *Purcell v. Ireland, op. cit.*

117. *The Times*, 5 September 1994, p. 2, 22 October 1994, p. 1, 18 November 1994, p. 1.

118. The text of this chapter is updated to the end of April 1995.

Index

in the United States 11, 257
see also positive discrimination
affirmative rights, and the US bill of
  rights 13–14, 15
African Charter on Human and People's
  Rights (Banjul Charter) 139, 151, 427,
  430, 502
  and the right to life 461
agency, freedom of 182
AIDS/HIV 336–53
  detention and isolation 345–8
  disclosure of HIV status 342–5
  and employment 348–50
  and homosexuality 336–7, 347, 351
  and the media 337–8
  public health campaign 336, 337
  testing for 338, 339–42
animal rights 403–20, 444
  animal experimentation 405–6
  and indirect duties 412–13
  protective legislation 410–11,
    414–15
  traditional attitudes 403–6
  and utilitarianism 407, 414, 415–16,
    418
anti–discrimination legislation 239,
  240–2, 249–57, 261
  direct discrimination 250–2
  indirect discrimination 252–3, 259,
    261
  positive discrimination 247, 248,
    253–7
  United Kingdom 250, 267
  United States 250
Aquinas, St Thomas 404–5
Aristotle 404
armed conflict *see* IHL (International
  Humanitarian Law of Armed Conflict)
ASA (argument from the sufficiency of
  agency) 500
assembly, freedom of
  and communal goods 147
  in South Africa 82
  in Sweden 54
association, need for 185–6
association, freedom of
  and employees' rights 361, 380, 381
  and the European Convention on
    Human Rights 51–3
  in the Republic of Ireland 53
  in South Africa 72–3

in Sweden 54
Atlantic Charter (1941) 583, 585,
  586–7
Australia
  Australian Capital Television case
    99–100
  charter/bill of rights 36, 44, 102, 105
  common law 91, 92–4, 102, 103, 107
  fundamental rights 97–102
  ICCRP (International Covenant on
    Civil and Political Rights) 102–5,
    106, 107
  political equality 57
  and UK law 91
autonomy 182
  moral 443–4
  and the right to meritorious
    treatment 242–3, 249, 258
  and self–determination 279

Bacon, Sir Francis 434
Bailey, P.H. 97–8
Banjul Charter *see* African Charter on
  Human and People's Rights
basic human needs (BHN) 171–86,
  187, 190
  object of 176–9
  self–realization needs 178–9, 180,
    182–4
  social participation needs 178–9,
    180, 184–6
  subject of 172–6
  survival needs 180–2
basic human propensities 177–9, 180
Beatty, David 543–4, 546
Benn, Tony 42
Bentham, Jeremy 408–9, 444
Bernstein, Eduard 45
bill of rights
  Australia 36, 44, 102, 105
  Canadian Charter of Rights and
    Freedoms 20–37, 529–49
  courts enforcing 15
  and employees' rights 359, 360, 361,
    371, 375
  formalist interpretation of 16, 17
  and free speech principles 7–10, 14
  instrumental interpretation of 16, 17
  and private litigation 537
  and sexual orientation 308–9
  South Africa 60–87